LIVING ABOARD

THE SAILBOAT

ROBIN LEE

By

Donald G. Rose

Based on the Journal Written

By

Robin Lee Rose

ABOUT THE AUTHORS

Robin Lee Rose was born and raised in Urbana, Ohio. During the ten-year period following her graduation from high school, she was devoted to raising her daughter by her first marriage, Shelly, and worked at various part-time jobs. Robin was employed as a Licensed Nursing Home Administrator in the early 1970s. In 1976, she enrolled as a full-time student in the Registered Nursing Program at Clark State Community College in Springfield, Ohio. Robin graduated in 1978 with an Associate's Degree of Applied Science and became a registered nurse. She worked full-time in that capacity from 1978 until 1985 for the Central Ohio Medical Group in Columbus, Ohio in that organization's Department of Obstetrics and Gynecology.

Donald G. Rose was born and raised in Dublin, Ohio, where he attended school from the first grade through graduation from Dublin High School in 1956. He attended Ohio State University and graduated with a Bachelor of Science degree in mathematics in 1963. During the period from 1960-1962, Don served 27 months in the U.S. Army.

After his graduation in 1963 from undergraduate school at Ohio State, he was admitted to The Ohio State University College of Law, from which he graduated in 1966, and later that year, after passing the bar examination, was admitted to the practice of law in the State of Ohio. From 1969 until 1971, Don was a partner in the law firm of Chester, Rose and Bolon and from 1971 until 1981, was a partner in the firm of Chester, Hoffman, Park, Willcox and Rose, which was subsequently renamed Chester, Saxbe and Willcox. He left that firm in 1981 and formed a partnership with his law school classmate, Erick Alden.

He has held various positions in the community, including the following: Attorney for the Village of Dublin, 1967-1974; member of the Mid-Ohio Regional Planning Commission, 1969-1972; member of the State Underground Parking Commission, 1969-1985. He was chairman of the commission for four years.

Don has a son, Chip Rose, by his first marriage.

Robin and Don began dating in April 1978 and were married in 1980. In 1986, they temporarily left their professions to go on the sailing adventure, the subject of this book. After their sailing adventure, they traveled extensively in foreign countries on two trips. The first trip was for 10 ½ months in Mexico, Central America, and South America. The second trip was for 6 ½ months and took them around-the-world.

When they returned from their travels in 1992, Don resumed the practice of law as a sole practitioner, and Robin returned to her nursing career. She went to work for The Ohio State University Medical Center as office manager at the Stoneridge OB/GYN Facility in Dublin. A year later she transferred to the Department of Maternal-Fetal Medicine where she was employed from 1993 until she quit in 1998 so she and Don could do more traveling. She returned to the Ohio State University Medical Center in 2003 as a part time employee with the High-Risk Pregnancy Project and continued at that job until her retirement.

Robin retired at the end of 2007 and Don retired at the end of 2010.

They are members of the Indian Lake Yacht Club and the Dublin Historical Society. They have continued to travel since 1992. They have a ten-year-old grandson, Mitchell Olson, with whom they enjoy spending as much time as possible.

Don's hobbies include playing duplicate bridge with his brother, Clayton Rose, his regular partner; cooking; and doing special projects such as writing this book. Since her retirement, Robin has stayed busy doing volunteer work with the following organizations: Dublin Methodist Hospital; Honor Flight of Columbus; and The Daughters of the American Revolution, in which she is currently serving a three-year term as the State Chaplain of the Ohio Society. She participates regularly in activities and worship at the Dublin Baptist Church. She occasionally serves as a travel aide for the seniors at the Dublin Recreation Center, taking them on various day trips.

ACKNOWLEDGEMENTS

We owe a huge "thank you" to Mimi Mullin for transcribing the damaged journals into digital format. It was a difficult job. They were not easy to read. In several of the journal books, because of dampness, the writing had bled through the paper and was mixed with the writing on the other side of the paper. She also proofread and edited the manuscript. Her contribution to the book was done out of kindness and she did a terrific job. This book would never have been completed without her assistance.

We would like to thank Tim Sells for allowing us to work with him on the production of his recent book, *When Dublin Wasn't Doublin'*. We learned from that experience how to publish a book in the computer age. Without that knowledge we would not have undertaken this project, although we have wanted to tell the story since returning from our sailing adventure. We would also like to thank him for his encouragement, suggestions, and friendship.

Phyllis Hill and Mike Epp also proofread the manuscript and made many helpful suggestions, for which we are very grateful.

We also thank Mary Biscuso for her professional guidance.

The maps used in the book were generated by Microsoft's "Streets & Trips 2001" computer program.

TABLE OF CONTENTS

LIVING ABOARD

THE SAILBOAT

ROBIN LEE

FORWARD
By Tim Sells

A couple of years ago I was afforded the opportunity to read to the Dublin Historical Society, excerpts from a book that I was writing, *When Dublin Wasn't Doublin.'* The book was still in rough manuscript form (my fourth version). The excerpts were well-received, and immediately after I read them, an Ernest Hemingway figure approached me and extended his hand, "Tim, my name is Don Rose, and you have to get that published!" The Roses have lived in Dublin, Ohio, for many years. In my younger years, I did my best to avoid sitting across the bench from Don's dad, Judge Rose, who was Juvenile Judge and was in charge of the Franklin County Juvenile Detention Center for many years. "I really mean it, Tim," Don persisted, "Your manuscript needs to be published for the people of Dublin." "Don, thank you for your kindness. In fact, since I am a disabled veteran, I may be able to secure funding for publishing it under their Vocational Rehabilitation Program." "I'll help you edit, compile, and format the manuscript just for the fun of it. It won't cost you a penny," Don said. Now, I did know that Don is a retired attorney, and when a lawyer offers his time, his "stock in trade," for free, one should not let that opportunity pass.

Lo and behold, I received backing from the Department of Veterans Affairs for publishing costs. Immediately thereafter, Don and I began putting the book together for CreateSpace and Amazon.com. I had written down all the stories I had heard about Dublin: its being founded by my great, great, great grandfather, John Sells in 1810, the establishment of the Sells Brothers Circus in 1870, and, most important, what life was like for me growing up in Dublin in the 1950s, 1960s, and early 1970s—before Dublin started "doubling" in size, in what seemed like every day. Don Rose did the rest of the work. Without him, my book would never have materialized. Don's wife, Robin, also helped by researching genealogical records for information concerning my family's history. The book was a success and continues to sell at various locations in Dublin and at Amazon.com.

However, a strange thing happened along the way. Through the process of osmosis, through the times of us sitting shoulder to shoulder, elbow to elbow, and yes, even hip to hip for seven consecutive months, my editor and his wife caught the bug of storytelling.

On September 25th, 1986, Don and his beautiful wife, Robin, having disposed of—or stored—their worldly possessions and having purchased a thirty-foot Catalina sailboat, set out from Port Clinton, Ohio, for parts unknown. Their two and one-half year's journey was recorded in a journal written by Robin. Don and Robin have at last decided to publish Robin's journal and thereby chronicle their adventures and "lay it all down" for the rest of us: the great times he and Robin had together, the perilous times when they wondered whether they would make it back home, and being a complete chronicle, even the occasional spats in those cramped quarters—if you can imagine that.

I recommend the book, *Living Aboard the Sailboat Robin Lee*, to anyone who wants to learn the do's and don'ts about cruising the open waters, to anyone interested in adventure in strange and wonderful places, and to the young-at-heart and romantics out there—no matter your age.

LIFE ABOARD THE SAILBOAT ROBIN LEE is not a mystery book, but it does contain mysteries, and by reading it, you will find the answers to the following mysterious and puzzling questions: Did the man on the boat anchored next to *Robin Lee* accidentally drown or was he murdered? How is it possible that both Robin and Don were struck by lightning multiple times and lived to tell about it? Why did one of the people Robin and Don entertained on their boat end up being shot? And who shot him? Where were they on their scariest night? Which aspect of cruising did they have the most trouble mastering? Why did one of their cruising companions get put in jail in the Bahamas? Can sailboats fly? Their mechanic's boat did.

If you are anywhere between nine to ninety years old, get this book. You won't be sorry you did. But a note of warning: do not read it late at night—it's a page turner. And do not read it if you are on a diet—Captain Don is a gourmet chef, and he whipped up a lot of exotic meals in their galley. I was hungry the entire time I was reading the book.

So, ahoy mates, get aboard the *Robin Lee* for a sailing education and adventure.

Tim Sells, Author
When Dublin Wasn't Doublin'

INTRODUCTION
By Donald G. Rose

Early in our relationship, Robin and I talked about living aboard a boat. During a conversation, I made the remark that I thought it would be fun to take a boat down the Mississippi. I was reading *The Adventures of Huckleberry Finn* at the time. That led to my telling her that when I was a boy, I had a toy sailboat with a cabin on it, and I remembered looking at the boat and wondering what it would be like on the inside. Sometime later, when I was still a boy, I got to go aboard a boat. When I went below, I found that the cabin was very homey. It was then that I decided it would be fun to live and travel in a sailboat, at least for a while. I was surprised at Robin's response. She said that she also thought it would be fun to live on a sailboat. At the time, I doubted that she was sincere. I thought she was probably just saying what she thought I would like to hear.

Robin and I started dating in April 1978 and were married in August 1980. Not long after we were married, out of the blue, Robin said, "If we are going to have a sailing adventure, we need to do it soon. We can't wait until we get old because we need strength and agility to deal with bad weather." She had to remind me of our conversation about living aboard a boat and going down the Mississippi because I had forgotten it. Then she said that she thought we should be prepared to leave during the summer or fall of 1986, soon after Shelly, Robin's daughter, graduated from high school. After the shock of her statements passed, I began to consider seriously whether it was something I really wanted to do. I questioned whether I would be able to make much of a living at the practice of law after being away for an extended time. Robin said that she was confident that the financial matters would work out. After a lot of thinking about the various considerations, I concluded that finances were the only reason for possibly not going and decided that, if Robin was willing to suffer from any financial consequences involved, I should be willing also. I've never had the desire to live "high on the hog."

I don't recall discussing it after that until the winter of 1983 - '84, when Robin said: "We need to start looking for a boat. That should be our project for next summer, and we should spend the following summer sailing on the Great Lakes to see whether we enjoy it enough to make the drastic decision to leave our careers and sell our house." As usual, what she said made sense. Neither of us had much sailing experience. I didn't learn to sail until I was in my early 30s when I bought an 11-foot plastic-coated styrofoam boat called a Sunflower made by the Snark Boat Company. In 1979, I bought a 24-foot Windrose weekend cruising sailboat, which I sailed at the Delaware Reservoir in central Ohio during the first half of the summer, and sailed on Lake Erie during the last half of the summer. The following year, in July 1980, my son, Chip, and I spent a month sailing it from Sandusky, Ohio, to Beaverstone Bay on the north side of Lake Huron's Georgian Bay and back to Sandusky, a total distance of 750 miles, getting home just a few days before Robin's and my wedding on August 9th. I sold that boat shortly after Robin and I were married. That was the extent of my sailing experience. Robin's experience was limited to being out with me a couple of times on my sailboats.

Finding the right sailboat was our project during the summer and fall of 1984. We went from Port Huron, Michigan to Buffalo, New York along the Saint Clair River, Lake Sinclair, the Detroit River and the south shore of Lake Erie, stopping at nearly every marina and sailboat dealer we came to, looking for the right boat. The Toronto area on Lake Ontario was also included in our shopping area. After considering and reconsidering the size of the boat to buy, the manufacturer, and the age of the boat (if we decided to buy a used boat) we finally decided on a 30-foot sloop in Toledo, for sale by owner. It was a 1980 Catalina, standard rig, with a fin keel. Its auxiliary power was furnished by an 11 horse power (hp) diesel engine. The boat was named *Sheila.* The owner was not a sailor; he liked to fish and had bought it for his girlfriend who liked to sail. Sadly, she was diagnosed with cancer and died not long after he bought the boat. The sailboat proved not to be a good fishing boat, and so he decided to sell it.

THE MAIN CABIN OF THE CATALINA 30

THE GALLEY

During the winter, we negotiated with the owner through the Toledo Beach Marina, which had the boat listed for sale. We eventually made a deal to buy it for $32,500.00. We hired a professional boat surveyor to inspect it to be sure it had no structural problems, and after getting a satisfactory report, we closed the deal in Toledo in early April 1985. After the closing, the seller, John Hubay, showed us how to operate the various equipment and systems on the boat. I videotaped it, so we could refer to it later.

At the time of the closing, the boat was docked at the Toledo Yacht Club on the Maumee River, where Hubay had kept it during the winter. The yacht club had a "bubbling" system that kept their marina from freezing, thereby making it possible to leave boats in the water for the winter. Robin and I decided to celebrate our purchase by spending the night on the boat. That night there was a major storm with high winds from the southwest. In the morning when we tried to get off the boat, we couldn't. The winds blew so much water out

AGROUND AT THE TOLEDO YACHT CLUB (NOTICE THE WATER LINE ON THE PILINGS)

of the western side of Lake Erie, and out of the river, that the water level in the marina dropped 4 1/2 feet. Our keel was stuck in the muddy bottom. The boat was too far from the dock to jump off. We hailed a member of the club and asked him to bring a wooden plank and lay it from the dock to the boat so Robin and I could get ashore. That was our first misadventure on the boat.

Our first trip on the boat was moving it to the Harrison Marina, also on the Maumee River, near the yacht club. While it was there, we renamed the boat, *Robin Lee,* and had the name painted on the transom. We also familiarized ourselves with the water, sewage, electrical, and refrigeration systems, and with the engine and other equipment on board.

We also made an inventory of items on board and bought additional items we felt we should have. The boat already had all the required safety equipment and a ship-to-shore radio with a 25-mile range. It was well equipped with nautical gear and had a 21-gallon fuel tank for its 11 hp diesel engine. It had a main sail and a roller furling jib, but no spare sails. It also had a knot meter, a depth sounder, an autopilot, an electric bilge pump, two batteries, a marine battery charger, and two anchors. We bought a man-overboard-flag, a sea anchor, two safety harnesses, a five gallon container for additional diesel fuel, and two more batteries.

Following is a list of some of the items used for everyday living that came

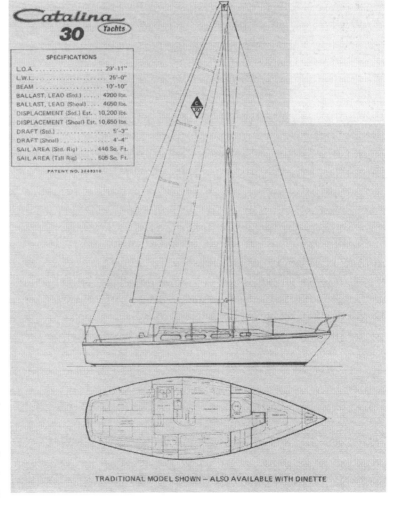

Catalina **30** (Yachts)

SPECIFICATIONS	
L.O.A.	29'-11"
L.W.L.	25'-0"
BEAM	10'-10"
BALLAST, LEAD (Std.)	4200 lbs.
BALLAST, LEAD (Shoal)	4650 lbs.
DISPLACEMENT (Std.) Est.	10,200 lbs.
DISPLACEMENT (Shoal) Est.	10,650 lbs.
DRAFT (Std.)	5'-3"
DRAFT (Shoal)	4'-4"
SAIL AREA (Std. Rig)	446 Sq. Ft.
SAIL AREA (Tall Rig)	605 Sq. Ft.

PATENT NO. 3649316

TRADITIONAL MODEL SHOWN – ALSO AVAILABLE WITH DINETTE

with the boat: A three burner alcohol stove with an oven; a 10" deep sink for dishwashing; and a refrigerator with a small (3" by 6" by 10") freezer compartment powered by either 110v while at a marina or by 12v battery power. We had water tanks holding 46 gallons of fresh water; a water pressure pump; a hot-water heater that used 110v while at a marina and heat from the engine while the engine was running; a dockside garden hose pressurized water hookup for using the water available at a marina; a shower; and a marine head with a holding tank. We also had screens for all of our hatches, and a wind scoop to increase the flow of air through the boat. We purchased a 110v two burner electric hotplate, a 110v toaster oven, a pressure cooker, a 12v fan, a 110v fan, a 110v heater, two small hand-held Dust Buster vacuum cleaners—one for 12v and one for 110v, a sun shower, and a five gallon container for additional water. We also purchased a five inch TV and a camcorder.

Eventually, it was time to go for a sail. As I said earlier, neither of us had much sailing experience, and we had never even been guests on a boat as big as *Robin Lee,* let alone sail one that size ourselves. Unfortunately, we picked a day when the wind was again blowing hard from the southwest, down the Maumee River. With the wind behind us, we made it quickly down the river and into Lake Erie. We sailed awhile, making some mistakes along the way, such as failing to tie stopper knots at the end of our jib sheets to keep them from flying out of the fairleads. One of the sheets did get loose and flapped violently in the wind until I could start the engine and turn the boat into the wind to retrieve it. After an hour or so of fighting heavy winds, we headed for the marina. That is when we discovered that we had made at least one important mistake in choosing our boat: It was underpowered. We lost our headway as we were going up the river directly into the wind. The wind and the waves created by the wind took the speed out of the boat down to where it was registering zero on the knot meter, and that caused us not to have steering. The boat drifted backward, but while drifting, the boat was turned by the wind, and when it was at about a 45° angle to the wind, we started moving slowly forward again and gradually built up some speed. We had to zigzag up the river, barely making headway. It was a long ride back to the marina.

Later, we got the following advice which I think is good advice: A cruising sailboat should have an auxiliary engine that produces about two hp for every 1,000 pounds of weight of the boat. The *Robin Lee's* displacement (weight) was about 10,000 pounds, so we should have had a 20 hp engine, and ours was 11 hp. Putting in a new engine was not economically feasible, so we had to make do with an underpowered boat for our adventure. We think of our first sail on our boat as our second misadventure. We were off to a bad start!

After three weeks at Harrison Marina, Robin and I, along with my brother Clayton, sailed the boat to Port Clinton and docked it at Brand's Marina where we continued to get ready for our summer's Great Lakes cruise. We purchased a "Loran C" navigation system and had it installed. We also got some sailing experience on the boat by taking short trips to Put-In-Bay and other Lake Erie island destinations.

We left Brand's Marina on June 7, 1985, for our Great Lakes cruise, learning as we went. Studying books about seamanship and navigation was a major activity on the trip. We had quite a cruise: up the Detroit River, across Lake Saint Clair, up the Saint Clair River, along the Canadian side of Lake Huron, across the Georgian Bay from Tobermory to Beaverstone Bay, down the eastern shore of the Georgian Bay on the small craft route, and back to Tobermory. We crossed the Georgian Bay again, this time to Killarney, and went through the North Channel to Detour, MI, up the Saint Mary's River to Sault Saint Marie. We spent an afternoon sailing in Lake Superior and then went back down the Saint Mary's River to the Straits of Mackinac, and Mackinac Island. From there we went to Beaver Island and after that down the Michigan shore of Lake Michigan, across Lake Michigan to Chicago, up the western shore of Lake Michigan to Milwaukee, and next entered Green Bay through Sturgeon Bay. We went north in Green Bay to Washington Island and after that crossed Lake Michigan, went through the Straits of Mackinac, and down the Michigan shore of Lake Huron, back to the Saint Clair River, Lake Saint Clair, the Detroit River, and finally crossed Lake Erie to Brand's Marina. We returned to Brand's on August 19th, after living 74 days and traveling 2,600 miles on water.

The cruise on the Great Lakes was a success. We decided our choice of boats was a good one, except for being underpowered, and that we could be happy "living aboard" and cruising for an extended period, even in such limited space. So, we made the decision to sell our house, temporarily give up our careers, and cruise for as long as we enjoyed the "live-aboard life" and our money held out.

OUTLINE OF THE GREAT LAKES CRUISE

When people heard about our plans, the general reaction, including that of our families, friends, neighbors, and casual acquaintances, was that we were being very foolish. People seemed to think we were crazy to walk away from our careers to go on an adventure, and a dangerous one at that. Our elderly friends were an exception. They said that they thought it was a great idea. "Go for it!" they said, and when I expressed doubt as to whether we would be able to make a decent living when we returned, their answer was, "Don't worry about that. Just do it!"

In 1981, I left the firm with which, in 1966, I had begun my law practice. I joined my friend and law school classmate, Erick Alden, and formed a partnership with him. The partnership was made with the understanding that Robin and I planned to leave and go sailing in 1986 for an indefinite period of time, and that the partnership would have to end at that time.

We sailed during the fall of 1985, and then took the boat out of the water and put it on its cradle for the winter. That fall, we joined the Columbus Power Squadron and took courses in seamanship and navigation. During the winter, the following spring, and the summer of 1986, we worked at our jobs and spent the rest of our time doing what needed to be done to be ready to go. We were told by other sailors that we should leave by September 15th. There was a lot to do in addition to working, and time flew by.

Robin began keeping a journal while we were making preparations to leave and continued keeping the journal until the end of our sailing adventure. Our trip began on September 25, 1986, without any definite plans as to where we were going, or when we would return. I was 47 and Robin was 36 when we left. The trip ended two and a half years later, on April 1, 1989. On April 1st, we packed our gear in two old cars that we purchased, one for $250 and the other for $500, and returned to central Ohio. We left the *Robin Lee* in Fort Walton Beach, Florida, with a boat broker to be sold.

By the end of our voyage, Robin had ten full journal books. We returned from our sailing adventure in the spring of 1989, but continued our travels for three more years by public transportation, and didn't buy a home until 1992. During the last couple of years of our travels, we stored some of our possessions, including the journals, at an old farm house we owned. It was occupied by a tenant, but the tenant wasn't required to pay rent; we just asked him to look after the place. There was a spare room, so we used it for our things. A plumbing leak developed above that room while we were traveling, and water dripping on our possessions ruined most of what we had stored. Robin's Journals were badly damaged.

After we bought our house in Dublin in July 1992, we moved our possessions from the farm house to our garage. That gave us the chance to sort through them at our leisure and save what we could, even though they were mostly ruined and black with mold. During the process, lots of stuff went to the trash. One Saturday, while we were going through the sorting and disposing process and being helped by friends, the journals were mistakenly thrown into the trash. We didn't discover the mistake until after Dublin had picked up our trash the following Monday and transferred it to a big city dumpster. On Wednesday morning, Robin went to Dublin's location for storing trash until it was taken to the landfill, and was able, with the help of Dublin city employees, to identify the exact dumpster our trash was in. Although she wasn't allowed to try to recover the journals from it; she was told that it would be hauled to the landfill at four o'clock that afternoon. I hurried home from the office, and she and I followed the truck hauling the dumpster containing her journals to the landfill in Amanda, Ohio, about a two-hour drive from Dublin. We lost sight of the truck a couple of times along the way but had it in sight when it reached the dump.

At the landfill, she was told she shouldn't attempt to recover the journals because she wouldn't be able to find them; if she did find them, they wouldn't be usable; and she could be hurt tramping through the trash. She told the landfill operator, "There's no way I'm not going to try; they are the manuscript of my book!" We followed the truck in, and after they dumped the trash, she started looking while the man with the backhoe waited to cover it up with dirt. Robin found every one of the ten books, and their condition was about the same as when they went into the trash, except they were a little damp and muddy.

For the next 20 years, the journals sat in a box in our basement. Last year (2012), our friend Mimi Mullin, a retired secretary who worked with Robin at The Ohio State University Medical Center, converted the journals to a digital format on Robin's computer.

After so much effort in keeping the journals and in view of the difficult life that they have had, and Robin's determination to preserve them, they deserve to be published. I am going to see to that, and I hereby dedicate my efforts to my wife, Robin, who was wise enough to know that we needed to have our "big adventure" before we got too old, and who planned the voyage and wrote the journals, and whose persistence saved them from being buried in the landfill.

What follows are Robin's long suffering and long neglected journals of our adventures while living aboard the sailboat *Robin Lee*, as augmented by a few details that she didn't include, but that were recalled to me by reading her journal and the log I kept for the purposes of engine maintenance and navigation. I also watched the videos we took on the trip and reviewed our navigational charts.

If you are looking for a book about high adventure and daring, this is not the book for you. However, if you have dreamed of boat cruising and have wondered what it would really be like, this book will give you a good idea, on a day-by-day basis, of what the cruising life is like, including the good and the bad. And, if you plan to take such a trip, pay close attention to what you read, and you will learn some things you should do and some things to avoid. You will also get some tips on what characteristics a cruising sailboat should have for a trip like ours. And finally, you will learn about some places you may want to visit on your boat.

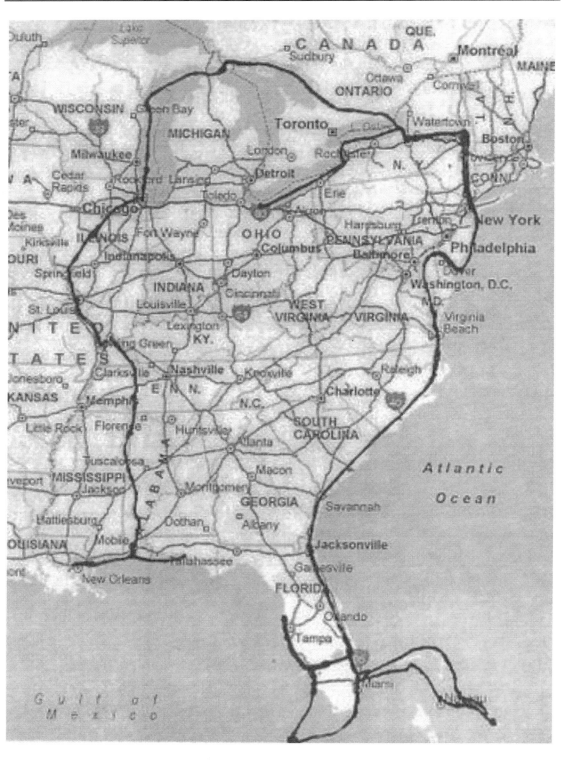

**OUTLINE OF THE CRUISE WHICH STARTED IN PORT CLINTON, OHIO, SEPT 25, 1986
AND ENDED AT FORT WALTON BEACH, FLORIDA, ON APR 1, 1989.**

CHAPTER ONE
FINAL PREPARATIONS

[NOTE: The information that follows, concerning our preparations and the cruise was taken from Robin's journals. She wrote them in the first person, so from here on Robin will be telling the story. Her first entry was made on August 15, 1986. In it she recounts earlier events.]

August 15, 1986, Friday

Today I will begin keeping a journal, because Don and I are about to embark on a new way of life. We are going to sail off into the sunset, so to speak. We are selling our house and will be selling our cars, some of our furniture, household goods, and other belongings. What we don't sell, we will loan to family members and friends, or put in storage until we return.

I didn't start the journal until now, because it didn't look like we were going to get our house sold in time to leave this year. We need to leave soon in order to get south before winter sets in. Our voyage will begin at Port Clinton, Ohio, on Lake Erie, where our boat has been in storage since last fall, and so we have a long way to go, and a sailboat of our size has a top speed of only about six miles per hour. We've been told by experienced cruising sailors that we should leave by September fifteenth at the latest, or we will have a very cold trip south. We thought we were going to have to wait until next year to leave because we hadn't had any luck in selling our house on Sandown Lane in Old Sawmill, northwest of Dublin, Ohio, primarily because it backs up to Smoky Row Road, and the traffic is noisy.

We listed our house for sale in March 1985, shortly after we made our contract to buy our boat, and have had it listed ever since with various brokers, without success, but now we have a contract! We accepted an offer on the very last day of the latest listing agreement, July 30th. The offer was for $103,500, which was about $4,000 less than we expected. We were very disappointed at not getting more. However, we were desperate and we accepted it because it gives us the opportunity to leave on the boat this year. A few days after accepting the deal, we overcame our disappointment about the price. Now, we are just happy we have the deal and are going to be able to begin our extended cruise, something many dream of, but never have the opportunity to do. So it looks as though we will be moving from our 2000 square foot, four-bedroom house and moving into our boat, which has, at most, 150 square feet of living space.

I've dreamed of having a sailing adventure and experiencing that way of life. Now, we are doing what is necessary to prepare for it. We actually began preparing for it a couple of years ago when we spent the summer shopping for "our" boat. We spent last summer on our shake-down cruise on the Great Lakes, seeing whether we and the boat were "up to it." In order to have the summer off, I had to quit my job as a registered nurse at Central Ohio Medical Clinic because they would not allow me a leave of absence. Don made arrangements with his law partner, Erick Alden, for a leave of absence for the summer.

When we returned from last summer's cruise, I first worked at Central Ohio Medical Group in an eight week temporary position. Then I went to work for Med-First Humana Corporation doing urgent care nursing. I quit that job to go to work for Dalt's restaurant as a waitress. When I was a teenager, I worked as a "tray girl" for Ewing's Restaurant in Urbana,

Ohio. I made good tips, and for a long time I had thought about "trying my hand" at being a waitress. My job at Dalt's only lasted two months. I found the job difficult, and since I worked during the lunch hours and not the dinner hours, I wasn't getting much in tips–not enough to suit me.

Since then, I have been working as a nurse in urgent care, in obstetrics, and in other positions as a contingent employee at the Blue Cross health maintenance organization called Health One, and I have also done a variety of registered nursing assignments for the Medical Personnel Pool. It has been rewarding, both for the experience and monetarily. One month I made more money than I had ever made in a month. My schedule has been very hard to keep straight. Some days I work double-shifts, sometimes I work weekends, sometimes nights, and sometimes on holidays. Occasionally, I work for two organizations on the same day. I have done private duty nursing for two very nice gentlemen: One was a retired Chief Executive Officer (CEO) of Nationwide Insurance, and the other was a former advertising executive. I have even done industrial nursing assignments at the United States Post Office. Needless to say, Don was very much on his own the past year. We have both hated not being able to spend more time together.

Shelly, my daughter by my first marriage, was very busy most of the time this past year. She was really caught up in the excitement of her senior year at Worthington High School and her graduation. I didn't see much of her. Sometimes I wish she was still a little girl, but I know I must accept the fact that she is now a grown up. I feel I have given her the best parenting, support, lifestyle, etc. that I could. Don and I realize that we will have to stand back and be observers for the most part, from this point on. Our children are both adults and will be making their own decisions. Don has a son by his first marriage, Chip, who is a junior at Kent State University. While we are away, they will have the supervision and guidance of their other biological parents. We can do little more than "trust the Lord." Hopefully, God will watch over them and guide them in all that they do. Being in another place won't make us any less concerned about their welfare, their happiness, and their future. We are hopeful that our being away will help them learn to be more independent and self-sufficient young adults.

Getting back to our preparations, today we started packing things for storage. Tomorrow we are going to Port Clinton to work on our boat. Our buyers have closed on the sale of their home, and we were notified that their loan for purchasing our place has been approved. It would be highly unlikely now that our deal would fall through. We have a lot to do and very little time to get ready for our cruising adventure.

Shelly has spent the past eight weeks at Bowling Green State University going to summer school, and now she's home for ten days. After that, I need to help her get settled in at Bowling Green for the fall term. Don needs to wind up his law practice, his law partnership, and our personal business matters. Chip is going to live off campus this year and needs to find an apartment, and he and his dad need to move the furniture we are giving him into his place. We need to put things in the storage unit we have rented and move things to various family members' homes for storage.

We also need to get the boat ready. It has been sitting on its cradle at Brand's Marina since we took it out of the water last fall. We have been too busy here to go sailing this summer, so we need to paint the bottom with antifouling paint, put the boat in the water, make some modifications to the boat, and move aboard, along with doing what is needed down here. All of this needs to be accomplished within the next 30 days! This is going to be a very busy and hectic period of our lives. It's actually overwhelming when I think about it, but we'll take one day at a time, try to stay focused, and think positive. I am an optimistic person who always believes that things will work out–a "Pollyanna" at heart.

August 21, 1986, Thursday

Last Saturday was rainy and dreary, so we stayed home and packed instead of going to Port Clinton. Shelly and I took a load of things to Mom's condo. Most of the items were Shelly's, and will be stored there while we are gone so she will have access to them. Don fixed a nice dinner of spinach lasagna and cheesecake, which were requested by Shelly. Dad and Martha, Dad's friend, stopped for a visit.

On Sunday, Don and I got up early and drove to Port Clinton to work on the boat. I don't know why, but I wasn't feeling up to my usual self. I was very tired and unable to put in a full day's work. Don, bless his heart, worked hard washing the hull, and after that did part of my job, which was cleaning and waxing. We ate dinner at our favorite fresh perch restaurant in Port Clinton, Jolly Rogers, and stopped for a dessert at the Dairy Queen at Attica on the way home. We arrived home at nine thirty, both of us very tired!

Monday and Tuesday were both typical work days at one of my private duty jobs. On Tuesday, I stopped by to visit briefly with my sister, Randy. Her daughter, Danielle, decided to go to our house to have dinner with Don and me. After dinner, I took her shopping for a birthday gift; she wanted a "back to school" outfit. She will be eight on October 20th, and we will not be home to celebrate with her. I ended up buying her four pairs of slacks and three shirts. She was very excited to take her things home to show her mom. She put everything on and then took off, one item at a time. It was cute. I hope she hasn't forgotten that Don and I got her some things when her birthday comes around.

On Wednesday, we did some more packing, and I did the laundry.

There is a full moon tonight and cool temperatures. It should be a great night to sleep. I'm tired. I think both of us are weary and anxious about all the things we need to accomplish in such a short time. The closing on the house is set for next Tuesday, August 26.

September 12, 1986, Friday

It has been a long time since I've written, and a lot has happened. I've not had time to journal, even with my "cushy private duty job."

Both kids are settled now for the school year. On Sunday, August 24th, I took Shelly to Bowling Green. On the same day, Don took Chip to Kent with his furniture, and got him situated in his small apartment near the University. Both of our cars made the trips without incident. Don was driving his 1978 Buick LeSabre, and I was driving my 1974 Lincoln Mark Four; both have lots of miles on them.

The house closing was on August 26th. I worked that day, but Don was there. All parties were pleased to get the deal closed. Noreen, our realtor, was happy she was finally paid a commission after having our house listed for nearly a year. The previous owners, who had sold the house to us on land contract, were happy to be completely out from under their mortgage obligation that we had been paying under the terms of our land contract. The new owners were excited about the good purchase price. Under the terms of our sale contract, we have the right to be in the house until September 25th.

Don sold his car on August 27th, and on Friday, August 31st, he officially terminated his law partnership with Eric Alden.

We spent the entire Labor Day weekend, August 30th and August 31st, at Brand's Marina in Port Clinton, Ohio, sanding the bottom of the boat and getting it ready to paint with an anti-fouling paint for tropical waters. I worked on Monday, Labor Day, and got paid time and a half. Don spent the day packing and making a peach cobbler, with peaches from our big backyard crop. He also made a black raspberry pie from berries that were in our freezer; both were delicious.

After Don sold his car, we both used mine until September 3rd, when I sold mine. Don then borrowed his brother, Clayton's, pickup truck, Old Blue. I use the public bus system to get to and from my private duty job in Bexley. To get home, I go from Bexley to Town and High Streets and transfer either to the Worthington or to the Smoky Road express bus. Don picks me up at the bus stop. Obviously, getting to my job is the reverse process. It is approximately a two-hour ride each way, but it isn't a bad experience, and it is cheap.

On September 4, we went out to dinner at Mark Pi's Chinese restaurant with our dear old friends, Joe and Lois Dixon. Joe is 82 and Lois is 79. They are very excited about our plans.

On September 5th, I received my first letter ever from Shelly. It was the highlight of my day! It was very well written, and she was complementary to Don and me. I will miss her. I'm confident she will do OK; she is very mature in many ways. She is also very thoughtful!

This past weekend (the 6th and 7th of September), Dad, Don and I went up to the boat. We launched it for the first time in 1986. It was exciting. Dad put up shelves in the hanging locker and laid carpet in the cabin. Hopefully, we will enjoy both changes. I did a lot of cleaning in the cabin and the cockpit and oiled the teak. Don kept busy by doing several chores. He came up on Wednesday prior to the weekend just to put the second coat of anti-fouling paint on the bottom. We were all very tired from working, and after driving back on Sunday evening, it was nice of Martha, Dad's friend, to have a lovely meal awaiting us at her place in Columbus. We had used Don's sister, Carol, and her husband, David Scott's, van for the weekend, so after dinner we exchanged it for Old Blue, and finally got home and to bed at twelve thirty. It was a late night, but what else is new!

Our evenings have been busy with packing, arranging, storing things, and saying our good-byes to family and friends. We have had very little time to enjoy each other. Things have been so hectic that it's even been hard to remember to say, "Sleep well." and "Good morning." We've only been married six years. This part of the living-aboard experience neither Don nor I will miss.

Wednesday, September 10th, Don's office staff had a dinner party for us. It was a very pleasant evening with farewells, etc. Eric & Nancy Alden, Don's partner and his wife; Gale King, who rented an office from Don and Erick, and Gale's wife, Janine; along with Jane, Don and Erick's secretary, were there.

September 22, 1986, Monday

Believe it or not, it's only nine thirty, and we're both lying here in the newly redecorated, as of today, V-berth[1] of the *Robin Lee*, our 30' Catalina Sailboat, and our new home. So much has taken place since I last wrote. I'll recap the past ten days as briefly as possible.

September 12: This was my last day of employment.

September 13: Movers came to Sandown Lane to move our things into our storage unit. Don and I helped them, and then we went to Newark to Don's niece, Linda, and her husband, Jeff Dayhuff's home, for dinner with all of Don's family. They had a going-away party for us

---

[1] The V-berth is in the forward area of the boat. It is V-shaped like the bow. The berth is spacious and out of the way, and therefore is the ideal place to sleep. It was our place to sleep for the entire trip.

with cake, cards, etc. All Don's nieces and nephews were there with their children except Phyllis & Mark, who live in Arizona. We ended up spending the night with Carol and David at their home, getting to bed at one in the morning.

September 14: We woke up late, had breakfast with Carol and David, and then drove to Sandusky for the 1986 Cedar Point boat show. We bought a two hp Honda motor for our new Achilles dinghy. The total cost of boat and motor was $1,100, exactly what we got for my Lincoln Continental, so we are going to call the dinghy *The Lincoln*. I bought a foul weather outfit. We spent the night on the boat.

September 15: We worked on the boat most of the day, and then went to Bowling Green to see Shelly. We left her about six and headed for Columbus. Martha had a good-bye dinner for us. She invited my Grandma Boydston too. We left about ten thirty to go to Clayton and Betty's, home to spend the night.

September 16: After breakfast with Clayton and Betty, Don went to his office. I went to Cub Foods to buy canned goods for the boat and then came home for more packing. In the afternoon, our neighbors, Marilyn Neiss and her daughter, Heather, came over to our house and helped me sort and package canned goods. We took the paper labels off and then wrote the name of the contents and the date of purchase on the cans. We've been told that sometimes labels come off due to wetness and should be removed before stowing. I finished my sewing projects for the boat and also mowed the grass.

At five, Don and I went to Dean and Paula Brown's home in Bexley for dinner. They have just returned from a two-year cruise aboard their sailboat and wanted to hear about our plans and share their experience. They showed us their charts and gave us some insight into living aboard, and also showed us on the charts places they had anchored. Dean is a friend of Al Wing, our insurance man. Al suggested the get-together, and he and his wife were there also. Coincidentally, Don bought the sailboat he and Chip sailed to Beaverstone Bay from Dean. Dean's work was as a home remodeler, working with his brother in a business they simply called Brown Brothers. Don remembers hearing their ads on the radio. Dean also does woodcarving and draws. He gave us a carved sandpiper and also a drawing of a ship. We returned home at nine.

I then took a load of things, including my sewing machine, to our friends Pam and Bob Bertha's home to be stored, and I picked up the sheets for the V-berth that Pam sewed for me and a picture frame for the "Robin Lee Compact" that she bought for us. The "Robin Lee Compact" is an agreement between Don and me that I wrote.

Don's niece Connie's husband, Henry Montgomery, came over to learn how to run the videocassette recorder (VCR), my wedding present to Don, since he and Connie are going to use it while we are away.

Our final task of the day was to take our last load of items down to my mom's condo for storage. We got there at one thirty and finally went to bed at two fifteen, at Mom's.

What a busy day!

September 17: We had breakfast with Mom at Paul's Pantry, went to say good-bye to Aunt Maude at the nursing home in Hilliard, and then back to our house to pack more clothes to take with us and storage items. Around two thirty we left in Old Blue, to go to Cleveland to pick up some charts we needed, a part for the wind vane, the sails we had repaired, and the new dinghy. All were in the Rocky River area. From there we went to Port

Clinton but stopped at Harbor North in Huron where we talked with the owner about spare parts for our jib's roller furling gear. We worked on organizing the boat until twelve thirty and finally went to bed at one, on the boat.

September 18: We got up at five to return to Columbus because Don had a nine o'clock hearing to handle at the courthouse in Columbus. The drive back was awful because of pouring rain. This was our day to move the remaining items into the storage unit, say good-bye to my sister Randy and her children, Danielle and Nick, and then bring the remaining items, like the boat cushions, back to Port Clinton. Don got home from the office at five, and after feeling rushed all day, we made it out of Columbus at midnight. Fortunately, we could borrow Don's sister, Barbara, and her husband, Lee Headlee's van to protect our things from the rain. We returned Old Blue to Clayton's place. Don and I were amazed that we got moved out of the house, cleaned it up, and put everything in storage, exactly according to our plan. We arrived at the boat at three in the morning exhausted from another hectic day. Hopefully, we will look back and laugh about all of this someday.

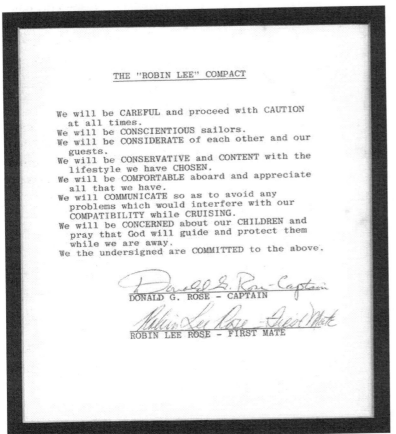

THE "ROBIN LEE" COMPACT

We will be CAREFUL and proceed with CAUTION at all times.
We will be CONSCIENTIOUS sailors.
We will be CONSIDERATE of each other and our guests.
We will be CONSERVATIVE and CONTENT with the lifestyle we have CHOSEN.
We will be COMFORTABLE aboard and appreciate all that we have.
We will COMMUNICATE so as to avoid any problems which would interfere with our COMPATIBILITY while CRUISING.
We will be CONCERNED about our CHILDREN and pray that God will guide and protect them while we are away.
We the undersigned are COMMITTED to the above.

DONALD G. ROSE - CAPTAIN

ROBIN LEE ROSE - FIRST MATE

September 19: We finally became "live-aboards!" We both were very excited, but these next few days will be hectic because of all the work yet to be done on the boat and the moving in and organizing process. We worked until seven, at which time Pam and Bob Bartha came and took us out to dinner. They bought us a nice meal and gave us $25 cash, a pie and a couple of cards. They wanted to get us a going-away gift but didn't because they knew we didn't want anything extra on the boat to take up space. So they gave us money and told us to use it someday for a nice meal at a restaurant. We enjoyed the break from steady work and also enjoyed their company. After they left at nine thirty, we continued to work on getting the boat organized, and around eleven o'clock our friends, the Edwards, stopped over to say good-bye. Barbara Edwards works at the courthouse with Clayton. They are sailors and are excited about our adventure. They own a 26 ft. sailboat which is docked near Port Clinton and were on their way home after spending the day on their boat. They bought us a 12v search light to carry on the boat as a going away present, which was very nice of them.

September 20: We worked on the boat nonstop until ten thirty. I called Dad to wish him a happy birthday, and then we had a good night's rest.

September 21: We slept in until eight thirty, and then worked on the boat until four. I fixed enchiladas for dinner; they weren't bad, considering I made the dinner. We had Pam's chocolate pecan pie for dessert. Shelly came over to see us, which was a surprise, so we went for ice cream at Toft's Dairy. Earlier in the day, Don and I had assembled the dinghy, attached the motor to it, and launched it; Shelly and I went for a ride in it. She left about eight to go back to Bowling Green.

September 22: We spent another day working on the boat. I showered, washed my hair, and spent my time leisurely until noon. Then Stewart Brand worked on our battery system. I made leftovers from Friday night's dinner, and also made a blueberry crisp for dessert; it was pretty good. The blueberries were from the freezer at home. Then I wrote in this journal until bedtime at ten thirty.

September 23, 1986, Tuesday
Another workday, totally! The Bimini and Dodger were installed, and they look beautiful. The man who made them and put them on does excellent work. We hope his bill is not any higher than quoted at $1,300. We also hope all the extra hardware doesn't present a problem while we are sailing. I gave the head a good cleaning and did laundry. Stuart was on board again working on the wiring and batteries. We ate the last of Don's homemade summer spaghetti sauce tonight.

September 24, 1986, Wednesday
I didn't get out of my nightgown until five when I went up to shower and clean up because David and Carol were coming to pick up Barbara and Lee's van to take it back to them. The four of us went to Jolly Rogers for dinner and then to the drive-through for Toff's hand dipped ice cream. We got a lot accomplished on the boat today, but Stewart didn't finish his projects, so Don and I were disappointed. We want to pull out of here tomorrow.

At three in the morning, I woke up due to storm activity. I stayed up to check for leaks and while doing so, I recorded the current selling prices of my stocks on a chart that I keep. It's nice to know I can go back to sleep and sleep in.

CHAPTER TWO
PORT CLINTON, OH to SANDY HOOK, NJ
Sept. 25, 1986 – Oct. 18, 1986

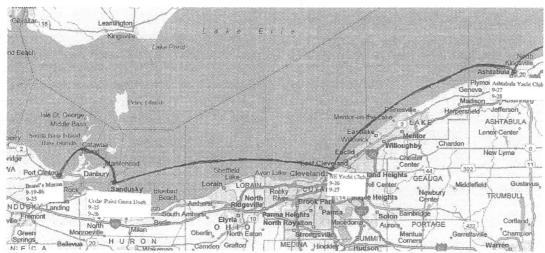

September 25, 1986, Thursday

Today was a big day; we got under way! However, a couple of unfortunate incidents slightly tarnished it.[2]

We were at Brand's Marina until almost four taking care of all the last minute projects. Because of our late start, we decided to make Cedar Point Marina our destination for the night. That's not much of a start, only 24 miles, but at least we would be underway. As we were going through the drawbridge in Port Clinton during its four o'clock opening, much to our surprise, Shelly drove up. We met her at the Fish Dock on the other side of the bridge and visited there for about 15 minutes. She gave me a Bowling Green State University sweatshirt with "MOM" and a big heart on it. It was great and made our departure even more special. Her timing was amazing. If she had been one minute later, we would have been down the river and wouldn't have seen her. I loved her gift and love her for thinking of me. I am so thankful we didn't miss her! I didn't call to tell her we were leaving because I figured she would be busy during the day. I planned to call her after we docked at Cedar Point.

Shortly after we got into open water, Don let out the jib sheet, and the line burned off the vinyl on a two-inch area of the dodger. We both were upset over that. I was mostly upset because I hadn't asked for any scrap fabric to use as repair pieces. I will write to the man and ask him for some, and he can mail it to us in case we need it.

The trip to Cedar Point was otherwise uneventful. We motored the entire way because the wind was "on our nose" from the northeast. It was hot, in the 80s, and very muggy. Don

---

[2] We have included maps which show the entire trip. The lines show the approximate track we followed, and the dots show the places we stayed overnight. We have also included small labels that show the name of the place we stayed and our arrival and departure dates.

wore shorts and no shirt. I put shorts on too. I listened to my radio with the headset and loved it. It got exceptionally good reception, which brings me to the other unfortunate incident. I jumped from the boat to the dock at Cedar Point, and the radio/tape player came unhooked from my waistband and dropped into the water. No way could I find it in ten foot deep murky water, and it would have been ruined anyway. I was just sick over losing it. I bought it a couple of months ago for about $25. Fortunately, it didn't have any tapes in it.

It was about eight thirty when we arrived at Cedar Point, and the sun was setting quickly. I killed some flies while Don finished his navigation chores. I prepared a dinner of macaroni and cheese, hotdogs, and warmed up blueberry cobbler.

At eleven thirty, we walked to the marina facilities, took showers, and then returned to the boat to sit in the cockpit and enjoy the beautiful dry, clear night, happy that we were underway at last, although we have only gone a short way. We didn't go to bed until one thirty.

Yes, we are underway on a trip for which we don't have definite plans of where we are going or for how long we will be gone. We want to spend time in Florida, and we want to see the Bahamas. We have decided to get to Florida by traveling along the south side of Lake Erie to the eastern end, and then crossing to Port Colborne, Ontario, on the north side, where we will go through the Welland Canal into Lake Ontario. After that, we will follow the south shore of Lake Ontario to Oswego, New York. From Oswego, we will go through the Oswego Canal and follow the Oswego River south, to the Erie Canal, and then take the Erie Canal east to the Hudson River. We'll go down the Hudson River to New York City and the Atlantic Ocean. From there, we will follow the coast, mostly in the Intracoastal Waterway, to Florida. We will decide what we do next after we get to Florida.

We realize we are novices and that we will need to learn as we go how to deal with problems that go along with this new and very different way of life.

Cedar Point, OH - Distance Traveled: 24 miles[3]

September 26, 1986, Friday

Today began rather early. Don awoke at seven and prepared to leave. We were under sail from eight until noon. We had nice conditions, although there was a lot of storm activity north of us. We took two-hour shifts at the helm, and that worked out fine. We put in at North East Yacht Club near Cleveland at six o'clock, after making approximately 66 miles for the day.[4] We went aground when we tried to enter the club area. It wasn't marked with buoys, and the charts didn't give details about depth. We saw other sailboat masts ahead of us, so we thought we were OK. We simply backed up to get off the bottom and felt our way in from there. It was about seven when we docked; I cooked dinner. We changed docks at the suggestion of a club member who had heard a severe storm warning for the area. One of the members invited us to the club for a beer, so about nine, after securing the boat for the storm, we went into the club house. While we were in the club house, the storm hit. Two

---

[3] At the beginning of each day's entry, we show the date, and if it is a special day we so indicate. At the end of each entry we show our location at the end of the day and, if we traveled that day, how many miles we went. There was a knot meter and log (equivalent to a speedometer and odometer) on the boat that gave us the distance traveled, measured in nautical miles. That was converted to statute miles for the entries.

[4] We chose the various marinas, yacht clubs, town docks and anchorages that we stayed at during the trip from chart books and guide books we carried with us and from recommendations of other cruising sailors. We chose to put in at the Northeast Yacht Club based on information in the *Richardson's Chartbook & Cruising Guide* for Lake Erie.

boats that were out of the water for winter storage were blown off their chocks (supports that keep a boat upright when it is resting on its keel out of the water). One man said his boat's anemometer showed 50 mph winds, and another said he was heeling 15° at his dock. We escaped without any problems. Don went out to check our boat during the storm, and was soaked when he came back. The storm passed in about 20 minutes. When we left to go back to our boat, the docks were covered with water. This was apparently due to water being blown to the south side of the lake by the north wind, and perhaps partly due to a drop in the barometric pressure. Whatever the cause, some electrical cords were underwater. That's scary!

North East Yacht Club, Euclid, OH - Distance traveled: 66 miles

September 27, 1986, Saturday

It was very calm when we woke up at seven thirty. We left around eight and steered clear of the shallow area, so we wouldn't go aground again. It was pretty out for a while, and then the swells started and the clouds came rolling our way. It became a very foul day. I did manage to write to Shelly during my watch from noon until two. Don was slightly nauseated most of the day. It rained off and on, and the wind was on our nose. The waves were three to four feet; this wasn't a fun day. We finally made it to Ashtabula at six thirty, and then it started to clear up. The humidity was very high. After going aground again this evening, we found an empty guest slip, docked, secured the boat, and then walked to town. We bought a few groceries, and on the way back stopped for pizza. It was tasty and not expensive. A local store owner gave us a ride back to the boat. We sure appreciated the ride, especially since we were carrying the groceries. While in town, we found a pay phone and made some calls to family to let them know we were underway and where we were. Upon returning to the boat, Don made some entries in the boat's log concerning our day's run. We went to bed around eleven thirty.

Ashtabula Yacht Club, Ashtabula, OH - Distance traveled: 56 miles

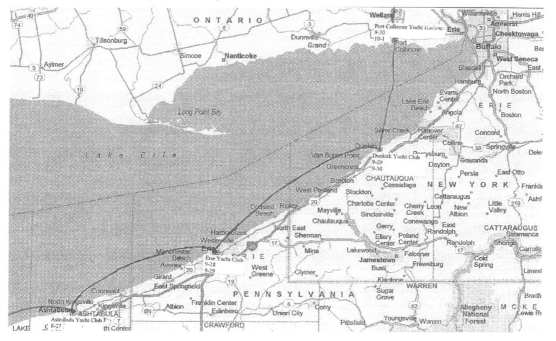

September 28, 1986, Sunday

We sailed half the day and motored the rest of the day. It was calm enough today to lie on the deck and do some sunbathing while we were underway. We arrived at Erie, Pennsylvania about five, bought fuel at a marina and then dodged weekend boaters in the busy Presque Isle Bay on our way to the Erie Yacht Club. By the time we were tied up, it was almost seven. It's a plush yacht club. The only other one we've seen that is this luxurious is Catawba Island Yacht Club, near Port Clinton. Don and I worked hard scrubbing down the deck after we ate dinner. We didn't go into town at Erie; we just walked around the club and took hot showers. It felt like the Hilton—first class décor. We watched TV until approximately ten on our five inch TV, and I wrote a few letters before bedtime.

Erie Yacht Club, Erie, PA - Distance traveled: 54 miles

September 29, 1986. Monday

We were awakened at six by heavy thunderstorms to the north of us. I called my sister, Randy. She has a 1-800 toll-free number that we will use for keeping in touch. Don tried Jane, his secretary, but she wasn't available. We sailed away from the dock at nine. Note: We did **sail** away from the dock.

There were very few boats in the bay this morning since it is Monday. We were able to sail three-quarters of the day with southwest winds at ten to 15 knots. It was sunny most of the day, but we also had a storm. The sky around us got terribly dark, and there was a lot of thunder and lightning. It only rained a little. Naturally, the storm came during my watch.

Don and I have felt a bit nauseated the past couple of days. It must be due to us not yet getting our "sea legs." We made it to Dunkirk, New York, a little after six thirty and docked at the yacht club. Most yacht clubs offer a free space for transients who are members of other yacht clubs. We should have joined a yacht club before leaving on the trip, and then we could always have a free space. A friend gave us her card from the Put-In-Bay Yacht Club to enable us to stay free, but Don and I didn't want to be dishonest, so we chose not to use it. However, we have lucked out and not been charged any docking fees so far. It is late in the year, and most boats have been taken out for the winter, so there is no shortage of docks.

After dinner, we walked into town; it is pretty run down. We stopped for dessert at a steakhouse that two people had recommended. We wasted our money on a lousy piece of pie and a sundae. After that, we walked to a convenience store for milk and bread. We should have skipped the steakhouse and bought a Pepperidge Farm dessert at the convenience store; it would have been better.

Don is half asleep trying to read. I'm writing letters, and we are listening to a tape of George Shearing; the flip side is Andy Williams. I need to do the dishes, and then I'm going to bed because I'm sleepy.

Dunkirk Yacht Club, Dunkirk, NY - Distance traveled: 52 miles

September 30, 1986, Tuesday

Well, Don felt guilty, so he left eight dollars for the Dunkirk Yacht Club dockmaster since we didn't see him before leaving. We left for Port Colborne, which is on the north side of the lake. Our seven-hour trip across the lake was less than pleasant, with waves four to six feet the entire way and rain. The only positive things were that there wasn't any boat traffic to worry about; there was no fog; and best of all, "Vern," our autopilot,[5] worked the entire day.

---

[5] Vern is the nickname we gave to our autopilot. It was powered by our 12 volt battery system. We attached it to the wheel and set it to stay on a certain compass heading. It was not a good autopilot; it

That saved us a lot of time at the helm and enabled us to stay out of the elements by standing under the Bimini top rather than behind the wheel. We arrived at five fifteen and went through Canadian Customs. They didn't take the two handguns we brought with us; we were afraid they might. The customs man just told us to keep them stowed. We plan on going through the Welland Ship Canal to Lake Ontario in the morning. We rented a couple of bags filled with straw for $3.50 each. They will serve as fenders, protecting our boat from the slimy cement lock walls. We also got $40 in Canadian money.

I wrote a lot of thank-you letters tonight and did the dishes before making tuna salad sandwiches for tomorrow. We have been told that we'll both be very busy during the nine-hour Welland Canal passage, during which we will be locking down, in eight locks, to the level of Lake Ontario, which is approximately 325 feet lower than here in Lake Erie.

We've not slept much lately, and I feel a bit cantankerous; Don does also. Oh well, the severe wind will let up eventually. "Tomorrow is another day." We're safe and feel blessed for all we have, and someday we'll be south enjoying warm, pleasant weather.

Port Colborne Yacht Harbor, Port Colborne, Ontario - Distance traveled: 31 miles

October 1, 1986, Wednesday

We left early this morning, at a little past six thirty, for the Welland Canal. We pulled up to the dock so Don could call the lockmaster on a phone there to get permission to start through the canal, and when he stepped from the boat, he slipped on the slimy, wet cement platform. He fell and hit his head. Fortunately, he wasn't hurt. When he recovered, he went to the phone, and the lockmaster told him we could start through the locks. Locking through was fairly simple. In each of the eight locks, we were the only boat being taken down. It took us about 8 ½ hours to complete the canal and cost us $48 Canadian. It would have been 35 % less in American money. We're glad we did it. A lot of people advised us against going this

---

did a poor job of staying on course and was prone to breakdowns. When it did break down we had to ship it to its manufacturer in Florida and arrange for it to be sent back to a place we knew we were going to. A good autopilot is a valuable asset on a cruising sailboat but Vern was an off-brand and was more trouble than it was worth. We eventually stowed it.

way and told us that we should go directly to the Erie Canal at Buffalo, but we wanted to go by way of Lake Ontario since we sailed in all the other Great Lakes last year.

After transiting the canal, we followed the south shore of Lake Ontario to the Niagara River. Fort Niagara was on our port side as we started up the river. We went up the river to a very popular town for sightseeing, Niagara-on-the-Lake. We docked at the town's yacht club. We met a fellow there by the name of Doug Wood who is on the club's board of directors and also has a small sailboat at the club. He came aboard, and we talked quite some time; he gave us the combination to the lock at the clubhouse so we could take showers. He's done a lot of sailing in the Caribbean. We went to bed early, as we were very tired, and it was rather chilly.

Niagara on the Lake Sailing Club, Niagara on the Lake, Ontario - Distance traveled: 41 miles

October 2, 1986, Thursday

We woke up at eight thirty, went to the clubhouse, showered, and then went into town to sightsee. Niagara-on-the-Lake is clean and picturesque; we enjoyed walking around.

About noon, we crossed the river in our boat to Youngstown, New York. We will be in New York from here to the mouth of the Hudson River. In Youngstown, we went to Pierce Marine and talked with the people working there about Catalina products because they are dealers. Later, we went into town, did laundry and ran some other errands. We had to climb a steep hill with the laundry on our backs. We called Don's Secretary, Jane, and asked her to send our mail to us at Oswego. This town is old and is a typical small American town which probably hasn't changed much over the years; the people here have been friendly. We treated ourselves to ice cream after dinner and called Sister Carol to give her an update. By Sister Carol, I mean Don's sister. She is not a nun—far from it. Don and Carol have a niece named Carol. When she was little, she came to be called little Carol and Don's sister became known as Sister Carol. I wrote some letters this evening.

We met a fellow living aboard a Non-Such sailboat who, last year, made the same trip we're going on. He and his wife left in September and came back in April. He said that wasn't enough time. He works for a local yacht dealer during the summer months. We also met a couple who go south every winter, Barbara and husband, Bob Finn, owners of Yachting World Store in Youngstown. They live on *Nellie Bly*, a 36-foot Alban Trawler. They stay in the Saint Petersburg area during the winter.

I made mashed potatoes in the new pressure cooker, but it didn't work right. I don't know why; I'll try it again soon.

I have been in a bad mood over the fact that our Y-valve for direct pump-out that Brand's put in isn't working properly. We spent nearly $300, and it still needs more work in order to function correctly. This was a really pleasant day except for my bad mood—poor Don. He went to bed early, but I stayed up and wrote to Pam and Bob; I sent them some tourist information on Niagara-on-the-Lake and their annual George Bernard Shaw Festival when some of Shaw's plays are performed.

Youngstown Yacht Club, Youngstown, NY - Distance traveled: 1 mile

October 3, 1986, Friday

We didn't have any dockage fees last night. We got up at eight and left Youngstown at eight thirty in the pouring rain. I didn't want to go. It was 60°, but Don felt conditions could worsen and wanted to move on.

We didn't make it to our planned destination, Point Breeze at Oak Island. It rained all morning, and I talked Don into putting in at Olcott shortly after noon. We took a short walk into the grocery store and bought milk and bread. We warmed up, but were still wet. On our walk to the grocery store, Don was excited to spot an old Scott-Atwater, Bail-a-matic outboard motor like the one he used to own with his brother-in-law, Lee Headlee, back in the '50s.

We are using an empty slip. Quite a few of the slips are empty because it is the end of the season and some of the boats have been taken out of the water for the winter. However, there is no electric hookup, so we are pretty cold and damp.

Olcott, NY - Distance traveled: 25 miles

October 4, 1986, Saturday

We started at eight thirty for Rochester, but the wind was on our nose, and conditions worsened. It got very windy and cold, only 55°, and, of course it rained. We put in at Oak Orchard around two in the afternoon. I noticed today that I lost a small diamond out of my emerald ring. I must've caught the ring on one of the dock lines and loosened a prong; I put the ring away. I'm writing in this book while lying on the starboard berth trying to get warm; the electric heater is on. Our wet clothes are hanging over the grab rails. Don made us sandwiches for lunch, and he's reading the book, *Living Aboard*. We are fair-weather sailors, and these conditions are beginning to get us down. Vern, our autopilot, quit working, so it's a real pain because one of us has to be at the helm at all times to keep us on course. We spent the night here, and I never left the boat. The scenery was pretty, and Don said the yacht club was nice. It started to rain when we were getting ready to take a walk. We gave that idea up and stayed in for the evening. I wrote several letters tonight.

Oak Orchard Marine, Point Breeze, NY - Distance traveled: 32 miles

October 5, 1986, Sunday

We started out at seven forty-five this morning and encountered six-foot waves. It was cloudy, and the temperature was between 50° and 60°. Much to our surprise, conditions improved, and we made 69 miles. We sailed all but the last two hours and were docked by seven at Sodus Bay. I made Hawaiian Sausage Stir-Fry, and then we took a walk to mail my letters and see the town. Sodus Bay is a small village and actually not a bad place to visit. The Sodus Bay Yacht Club is classy, and the bay has a picturesque entrance as you come through the channel from the lake. As we entered, the sun was setting, and it was calm. It was a long hard day, and the showers at the yacht club felt terrific. We looked for a pay phone to call Shelly, but there wasn't any close by, so I will have to wait until tomorrow. Tonight I plotted the course for our trip tomorrow to Oswego. The destination is 31 miles away; our heading will be 60° for the first 4.6 miles, then 70° for 23 miles, and finally 75° for 2.3 miles. That should get us to the light at the head of the channel. Don did all the dishes while I did the navigation, and I thought that was great. We went to bed about ten thirty. Bad storms are predicted for the next 24 hours. We are affected considerably more by the weather than when we were living on land, and therefore are much more interested in weather forecasts.

Sodus Bay Yacht Club, Sodus Bay, NY - Distance traveled: 69 miles

October 6, 1986, Monday

We stayed docked all day and walked to town to get a few groceries. We stopped by a local restaurant; I drank a Coke, and Don drank a cup of coffee. We used their pay phone, and I talked to Shelly for about ten minutes. That was the first time I had talked with her since leaving Ohio. It was great. Don called a bank about some business matter, and because of the cost, he was frustrated with being placed on hold for a long time.

We tried using the pressure cooker again, but it wasn't very successful; the clam chowder burned. We are bound to get better at it. In the evening, we listened to the radio, and I did some cross-stitch. Don read the first chapter of *Tender is the Night* to me. The wind speed peaked at 39 mph at eleven thirty today. It was cold as well as windy. The outside temperature was 45°, but we were content in a warm environment thanks to our electric heater.

Sodus Bay Yacht Club, Sodus Bay, NY

THE SAILBOAT ROBIN LEE

October 7, 1986, Tuesday

We went to bed at nine last night and slept until seven at which time we listened to the weather forecast, ate, and then prepared to leave. It's amazing how much the weather and lake conditions can change in one day. Today we have a gentle breeze, and the lake is smooth. The dockmaster at the yacht club locked the shower house since we only paid for one night's dockage. That was disappointing.

We learned on our Great Lakes cruise that finding a marina with good showers is very important. Although we have a shower on the boat in the cabin where the head is, we don't like to use it. Everything gets wet (including the wood-paneled walls), and that makes everything susceptible to mildew. It is also cramped. Furthermore, the water supply on the boat is limited to 46 gallons, and since the shower head is about 15 feet away from the hot-water tank, a lot of cold water is wasted in getting hot water to the shower head and getting it set to a suitable temperature. We have also learned that good showers at marinas are the exception, not the rule. Most of the customers at a marina are weekend or day sailors who are close to home and don't need to use the showers at their marina. Transients are a very small part of a marina's business, so the owners aren't too concerned about the showers. Unclean conditions, bugs, low water pressure, and a lack of hot water are all common problems in marina showers, and so are damaged plumbing, bad lighting, an absence of a place to put your clothes while you are showering, and a place to sit while you are getting undressed. Finding a good place to take a shower makes the day a pleasant one for a cruising sailor.

We enjoyed a nice sail to Oswego, arriving about two thirty, and tied up at the Oswego Marina. We walked to the post office and shipped Vern to Florida for repairs. We also picked up our mail which Don asked Jane to send here. When we moved out of our house, we asked the post office to forward our mail to Don's office. Don called Jane a few days ago and asked her to send the accumulated mail. We asked her to address it to us, care of the postmaster here in Oswego and to write on the package, the following: "General Delivery – the addressee will pick this up at the post office." The post office will hold mail addressed that way for 30 days. We will ask Jane to send mail to us from time to time in that manner.

We will be un-stepping our mast at this marina and securing it to the deck. This is necessary because we will be going under fixed bridges from here to the Hudson River. We spent the evening getting the sails and boom down and constructing wooden supports to use for securing the mast on the deck. Don has been uptight about the process of un-stepping and securing the mast. He thought the people at the boatyard where we are would do the carpentry work, and Don isn't confident in his abilities to engineer and build a proper support. We will be crossing Lake Oneida, which is about 23 miles across, and it can get rough. It will take us about four hours to cross. We sure don't want our mast going to the bottom of the lake. We opened mail, paid bills, and then went to bed at twelve thirty.

Oswego Marine, Oswego, NY - Distance traveled: 31 miles

October 8, 1986, Wednesday

We got up very early so we could make the final preparations for un-stepping the mast before the man at the marina got there to do it. The mast is too heavy to be taken down by hand. The man will use a hoist to hold it, move it into position, and then lower it onto the supports. Don did most of the work in designing and building the supports. He doesn't think my "good" ideas and suggestions of ways to do things are helpful, so I've done little. It is better to stay out of his way since he's up-tight.

This marina is the only place for un-stepping masts prior to entering the Oswego River and Canal, but their charge didn't seem out of line. The cost was $40. Dock fees are a little high at $17.40 for the night, but the showers are very clean and well-equipped and have private dressing rooms with plenty of shelves and hooks. We had some other expenses here. We bought diesel fuel, pumped out our holding tank, and paid for postage to mail Vern to Florida. We also bought some materials to construct supports for the mast, but we used mostly scrap lumber, which is plentiful here because the marina also steps masts on boats that are coming out of the canal and going into Lake Ontario. The boat owners generally leave their supports.

The Oswego Canal follows the Oswego River and has seven locks that will raise us 120'. It is 24 miles long and terminates at Three Rivers where it connects with the Erie Canal. It is the only direct connection between Lake Ontario and the Erie Canal.

We left Oswego around noon. At six thirty, we were tied up along the river bank at Phoenix, which is beyond the last lock on the canal. We went ashore to mail letters. I think the most important thing for me to do for Shelly at this point is to write letters frequently and send postcards, so I'm going to try very hard to send at least three letters or cards per week. She loves mail.

Later, we went to a local restaurant where we met a most interesting couple and sat with them for dinner. Their names are Don and Louise Rasmussin. She reminded us of Edith Bunker from the TV show, *All in the Family;* she even has a Brooklyn accent. We told them

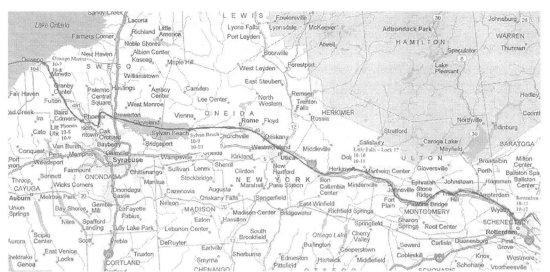

why we happened to be in town, and they were excited to see our boat. So after dinner, they walked with us to the boat and got on board. Imagine Edith Bunker in her dress, hose and heels climbing down a two-foot wall to get into our boat–what a sight! She was determined and made it safely aboard even though it was pitch dark and all the mast and boom rigging was lying on the deck. The rigging is a jungle of attached spars, cables and lines. The Rasmussins are retired folks with a family of five kids. He built and flew his own airplane; she knits hats, polishes stones, and once owned a business in Arizona. Our conversation was enjoyable; they were a delight to meet. Twenty minutes after they left, they returned with pictures of their family and a picture of their airplane. They also brought a warm knitted hat, a strawberry cake, and two bags of apples for Don and me. What a treat. I'll keep in touch with them. Tonight was cold, and we had no electricity at the town dock. We needed two extra covers in the V-berth.

Tomorrow we will leave the Oswego Canal and enter the Erie Canal. The Erie Canal will take us to the Hudson River. The Erie Canal connects Lake Erie, at Buffalo, New York, to the Hudson River, at Troy, New York, just north of Albany. It is 363 miles long and has 36 locks. It was opened in 1825 and has played an important role in the history of the United States. It opened up trade between the mid-west and the rest of the world. Moving goods on the Erie Canal was much easier, faster, and cheaper than across mountainous terrain on the primitive roads that existed in the early to mid-1800s. States, such as Ohio, constructed canals to connect their cities and villages to the Erie Canal. Ohio built two such canals shortly after the opening of the Erie Canal. They too emptied into Lake Erie, and therefore were connected, through Lake Erie, to the Erie Canal because it also empties into Lake Erie. The Erie Canal is still used by some commercial traffic, but most traffic on the canal is now pleasure craft. Unlike Canada's Welland Canal, the Erie Canal is free. We will be coming into the canal at a place called Three Rivers, which is roughly the halfway point of the canal, so we will just see the eastern half of it and will go through only some of its locks.

City dock along river, Phoenix, NY - Distance traveled: 21 miles

October 9, 1986, Thursday

We woke up at seven thirty, left Phoenix, and headed to the Erie Canal. We met up with a family we had previously met while going through locks in the Oswego Canal. They are in a homemade orange boat named *Completion*. The family consists of a husband and wife and their two small sons, ages four and two. We motored to Brewerton and tied up after deciding it was too windy to make the 23-mile crossing of Lake Oneida.

Finally, at two thirty, we left Brewerton for Sylvan Beach across Lake Oneida. As the boat pitched and rolled during the crossing, Don worried about his engineering and carpentry work and whether it was good enough to keep the mast from going into the lake. We made it safely with the mast and all of our gear still on board. It only took about four hours to cross the lake.

After docking we went into a restaurant to warm up. The temperature today was 45°, with winds out of the north–Brrr! We are glad to be docked with electric tonight.

From here to the Hudson River, the Erie Canal follows the course of the beautiful Mohawk River.

At a marina, Sylvan Beach, NY - Distance traveled: 46 miles

October 10, 1986, Friday
We got up early, and it was very cold–22°! There was a coating of ice on the dock. The people who told us that we should leave Port Clinton no later

MAST UNSTEPPED AND STOWED ON DECK ON THE ERIE CANAL

than September 15th were right. The dockmaster came by at seven thirty as we were leaving and asked us for $15. It ticked us off a little because we didn't even get to use the showers to clean up. They are locked up for the winter. We were out of cash, so we used our Visa card. It was a beautiful day, cold but with blue skies and sunshine the entire day. The high was 50°. We took lots of video at the 1st lock we came to on the Erie Canal, Lock 21. The foliage was pretty, and I took a couple of pictures of Don with my camera. At Lock 18, we were delayed because the lockmaster wasn't there when we arrived, and he didn't show up until a half-hour later. We didn't get to Lock 17 at Little Falls until dark. Locking through at Little Falls was an eerie experience with lots of strange sounds as the lock gate was closing. It dropped us 40 feet. It was very dark, and the lower gate is a lift gate, a big metal door that goes up to open and down to close. When it was raised to let us out, it reminded us of a guillotine getting set for the next victim, which added to the spookiness. When we went out of the lock, we started looking for a place to tie up for the night. The area was creepy, and we were under a four-lane highway bridge and close to railroad tracks. There was a carload of teenagers who were drinking, parked under the bridge near where we wanted to tie up. They asked Don a lot of questions. Fortunately, they didn't want to hang around since we were using our spotlight. We waited until they left before we tied up. We had no heat, and it was very cold, so Don and I slept fully clothed. Even with hats, mittens and jackets on, I never warmed up; so I couldn't sleep. Don slept OK and snored the entire night. No one bothered us, but one of our loaded guns was beside Don's pillow all night. This is the most concerned we have ever been about the possibility of someone bothering us.

Tied up below Lock 17 E, Little Falls, NY - Distance traveled: 57 miles

October 11, 1986, Saturday

We shoved off in the welcome sunlight. Frost was everywhere. Don took the helm from seven thirty until nine thirty, while I lay in bed with covers and an extra sleeping bag over me trying to get warm. We made the first two locks without incident. As we were approaching the third one, I turned my ankle and fell! I hurt my shoulder, and my right leg went into the water between the lock wall and boat. No damage was done to my leg, but it scared me. I even forgot about being cold. I wrote Shelly a note while Don was at the helm. After ten hours traveling on the water, we stopped for the night at Lock Nine near Rotterdam. We tied to the wall above the dam, and there was no barrier between us and the dam. It would have been awful had the boat gotten loose, but thank goodness Don knows how to tie up securely. After eating our dinner of a shrimp, tuna, and rice casserole, we walked to a nearby convenience store. We purchased bread, milk, a pound of baloney, and one candy bar. It was cold, but not as cold as last night. We both slept with coats and hats on to keep warm for the second night in a row.

Tied up above Lock 9, Rotterdam, NY – Distance Traveled: 52 miles

October 12, 1986, Sunday

We didn't wake up until eight. My shoulder hurts when I move it to certain positions. The fog was so thick we couldn't leave, so I lay in bed for a while. The condensation was terrible; there were drops everywhere above us in the V-berth dripping on our heads. Don fixed me cereal and Café Vienna so I could eat in bed and have a quick bit of fuel to burn for body heat and energy. Actually, he was hoping the energy would help me get up because he wanted to leave. We left at nine.

While we were waiting for the fog to lift, we had a strange experience. There were about 30-40 bass boats milling around above the lock waiting for it to open. They were apparently going to a bass fishing tournament somewhere. As they maneuvered around in the fog, they sounded like a bunch of bees and looked like water bugs.

It has been a while since we last bought fuel. Don keeps track in the boat log of how many hours we have run the engine since the most-recent fill up and calculates how much fuel we have because we don't have a fuel gauge. According to his calculations, we are getting low on fuel, so we will try to stop for the night at a place where we can buy it. Hopefully, they will have showers and also electric for our heater.

We just came through Lock eight. Both locks this morning had smooth walls, and each only dropped us 15 feet. We are finally handling the boat better in the locks. Maybe by the time we are finished with our trip, we'll feel confident about going through them.

We stopped to get fuel at the Schenectady Yacht Club. Fuel was available there, and we decided we should get it while we could. It was too early to stop for the day, so we went on.

The "Flight of Locks" is a series of five locks. They are close together and very near the end of the canal. They dropped us 165' to the level of the Hudson River at Troy, New York, just north of Albany. After coming out of the last lock, we made a right turn and headed south toward New York City and the Atlantic Ocean on the Hudson River. In a short distance, we went through a lock on the Hudson, known as the Federal Lock. There are no locks on the Hudson between the Federal Lock and the Atlantic Ocean. We have gone through 38 locks so far; eight on the Welland Canal, seven on the Oswego Canal, twenty-two on the Erie Canal, plus the Federal Lock. We went down in the Welland, up in the Oswego, up in the first three locks of the Erie and down in the rest of the Erie and in the Federal Lock.

By the time we cleared the Federal Lock, it was very late; it got dark while we were going down the Flight of Locks. We went through the last few locks with a boat named *Renegade* from Harbor North in Huron, Ohio. The skipper, Randy Frances, suggested that the Albany Yacht Club would be a convenient place to tie up for the night. We followed *Renegade* to the yacht club, but they were full. Then Randy suggested that we go on to the Castleton Boat Club in Castleton, New York, about ten miles down the river. We didn't have a chart for the river; we didn't know exactly where Castleton was; and it was dark, so we followed *Renegade*. We arrived at the Castleton Boat Club at eleven fifteen. *Renegade* is a charter boat owned by Harbor North. Its home is Huron, Ohio, in the summer, and Marathon, Florida, in the winter. Captain Randy Frances and his crewman, Paul Weckner, are taking *Renegade* to Florida for the winter, where it will be made available for chartering.

We tied up and were glad to get off the boat and go into the bar at the Boat Club. Don drank a beer, and I drank a ginger ale and ate a bag of pretzels. We also bought beers for the two guys on *Renegade*. We spent all of our cash except $0.75. Hopefully, tomorrow we will find a bank and get some money after we get our mast stepped (put up). The Castleton Club has a hoist for stepping and un-stepping masts. Therefore, we have our choice of doing it ourselves, or going on down the river to Catskill and paying $75 at a marina to have them do it. Captain Randy and Paul on *Renegade* are experienced at stepping masts and so we have decided to help them and have them help us. Both of us will save $75. We took showers. After five days without one, it felt absolutely terrific. Life is GOOD, once again!

Castleton Boat Club, Castleton, NY - Distance traveled: 51 miles

October 13, 1986, Monday

We worked on the boat the entire day. We put the masts up on both boats without difficulty, and the guys from the Harbor North boat, Captain Randy and Paul, helped Don with the rest of the rigging. I gave the teak a good scrubbing. At about seven o'clock, some new boaters docked in front of us. They are Hope and Harry Eilers from Edena, Minnesota, near Minneapolis, on a boat named *Passages.* We invited them out to eat at Albert's Bar. We enjoyed the evening; it was great to socialize with such a friendly couple. Harry is Don's age, and Hope is about the same. Harry worked for IBM for over 20 years in sales, but developed a health problem and took a disability retirement. They are doing about the same thing we are except they plan to settle in Sarasota. I think Harry will attempt to get work there. Harry is a very likeable guy, and Don says that if he and Harry had grown up together, he is sure they would have been good friends.

We used a check to pay our bill at Albert's Bar since we were out of cash. No banks were open because it is a holiday—Columbus Day. Castleton is a nice small town. We went to bed at ten thirty, exhausted, but happy about getting so much work done today.

Castleton Boat Club, Castleton, NY

October 14, 1986, Tuesday

Our boat is clean and everything inside is well organized and it feels great. Today we didn't wake up until nine. It was raining, and we were happy to be docked and able to sleep in. I wrote a letter to Shelly, and Don put the mainsail on. I did the dishes, and then we went to town.

In town, while I did laundry, Don went to the bank to get money from our checking account at Bank One in Columbus, using our debit card, which is how we always get our money. Before we left home, we gave Don's sister, Carol, power-of-attorney, so she can move money from our savings account to our checking account when necessary. Jane, Don's secretary, deposits money into our savings account that Don is entitled to for work done before the law partnership was dissolved, but collected after we left.

Don also went to the hardware store and grocery. We both went to the post office, and then we ate lunch at Albert's Bar. I called my sister, Randy, from their pay phone to bring her up to date, and Don called the bank again to discuss business. After all our errands were done, we went back to the boat, topped off the water tanks, and showered. Then we pulled out of the boat club and tied the boat to a nearby mooring buoy for the night. [Mooring buoy: a buoy attached by chain to a heavy object on the bottom of the body of water which is used to moor a boat]

The Hudson River is affected by the tide from where it empties into the ocean all the way up the river to the Federal Lock at Albany. The tidal current is evident here in Castleton and is surprisingly strong. We had to consider the current in deciding how to get away from the dock. We watched a little TV after dinner and then went to bed at ten.

On a mooring buoy, Castleton, NY

October 15, 1986, Wednesday

We are in the Hudson Valley, which was the setting for Washington Irving's short stories "Rip Van Winkle" and the "The Legend of Sleepy Hollow." The Catskill Mountains are on our starboard side as we are going down the river. However, we haven't seen any characters like Rip Van Winkle or Ichabod Crane, nor have we seen a headless horseman or heard the sounds of people playing at "ninepins."

We left our "mooring can" at around eight this morning for Catskill, New York, and arrived about noon. Hope & Harry on the boat *Passages* were there and so were Randy and Paul on *Renegade*. They told us about the *Clearwater,* which is a 106-foot sloop that sails on the Hudson and conducts science-based environmental education to make people aware of the pollution of the Hudson. The singer, Pete Seeger, lives along the river and is a co-founder of the organization that owns the boat. The *Clearwater* was tied up very close to us. They also told us that Pete was in town and was going to give a benefit concert at eight in the church to raise money for the Clearwater Project.

Hope and I shared a taxi fare to the grocery store. I bought quite a few groceries—good prices. I spent about all of our cash, and when we went to the concert later we barely had enough to pay the $3.00 "admission donation" for "the cleanup of the Hudson." (We obviously need to get bigger cash withdrawals.) We enjoyed the performance and took a lot of video.

Randy picked up another crew member for *Renegade* at Catskill, Martin Gilbert. Martin paid to make the trip from here to Florida and is doing it for the experience. He is older, probably in his mid-sixties.

City dock, Catskill, NY - Distance traveled: 27 miles

October 16, 1986, Thursday

We got up early and left our dock at six forty-five. We didn't have to pay dock fees because we were at a free city dock. I blew a fuse because the hot-water heater and portable heater were on at the same time. We motored the entire day and put in at West Point. Along the way, we passed President Franklin Roosevelt's home at Hyde Park, and a little further down, at Poughkeepsie, we passed Vassar College; both were on our port side. We reached West Point about five and tied up at the floating public dock consisting of several small metal floating docks lashed together. They made a lot of noise and rocked back and forth from each passing boat's wake. Don made fried chicken in the pressure cooker. We also had mashed potatoes and corn.

We walked to town, the village connected with West Point. I ate ice cream, and then we went to McDonald's and Don drank a cup of coffee. The walk was strenuous, a mile or two with a steep incline.

We got back late and called Randy and Paul on the marine radio to see what their plans are. I also wrote to Shelly.

At the City Dock, West Point, NY - Distance traveled: 62 miles

October 17, 1986, Friday

We awoke at eight, got dressed, and went to town. We went to the bank first since we were out of cash again. (This time we got more cash.) Then we ate breakfast at McDonald's, and after that went to the visitors' building at West Point Military Academy to buy tickets for a tour. The tour included a 15-minute video presentation and a one-hour bus tour of the military academy. It was interesting and we took lots of video. We walked back to the boat and left West Point about one thirty. We went about 18 miles south and tied to a mooring buoy for the night at Grassy Point in Haverstraw Bay. The rate for docking was $1.25 per foot; that's too high for our budget, so we had another cold night for sleeping. Oh well, Don promises me warm weather is around the next bend.

We conversed on the marine radio briefly with *Passages*. They are a little way behind us at Newburgh, New York. We didn't see or hear from *Renegade.* I fixed beef stroganoff in the pressure cooker and it was delicious. We are finally getting the "hang" of using it. We didn't have hot water to wash our dishes. Our hot-water tank is heated by 110 volt shore power, and when our engine is running it is heated by the hot water coming out of our engine's cooling system. The hot water from that system is run through a radiator inside the hot water tank. The engine's cooling water is maintained by a thermostat at a temperature of 180°, and it heats the water in the tank very well, but it takes quite a while to get the water hot. We didn't have power at West Point, so the water was cold this morning, and we only used the engine for about three hours today. The water was barely warm.

On a mooring buoy at Grassy Point, in Haverstraw Bay, NY - Distance traveled: 18 miles

ROBIN AT THE HELM PASSING THE STATUE OF LIBERTY

October 18, 1986, Saturday

Today was a beautiful day, but I got sick in the morning after our delicious melon and muffin breakfast! I was making brownies at the time.

We woke up early and headed downriver at seven thirty. We passed a couple more points of interest. The first was the New York prison known as Sing Sing, and the second was "The Big Apple" itself, New York City. *Passages* caught up with us, but we didn't see *Renegade*. We sailed past New York City, running before the wind. The city was fascinating to see from the water, and we heard lots of unusual marine radio traffic on Channel 16. One boat reported that there was a boat off Coney Island using a shotgun, and a sailing vessel called in to request an ambulance to pick up a crew member. A motor boat was transporting the injured person from the sailboat to a local yacht club. They wanted an ambulance to be at the yacht club waiting! Another boat was aground due to the tide being low.

Passages and *Robin Lee* were side by side and taking lots of video of all the scenery as we passed Ellis Island and the Statue of Liberty. Around five, we ended our day at Sandy Hook, New Jersey, on the south side of New York's Lower Bay. We picked up a mooring buoy at Atlantic Highlands Yacht Club because they charge $1.00 per foot for dockage, and we aren't interested in tying up for a dollar a foot. We will just have to go another day without showers and electric. *Passages* felt the same. We tied to mooring buoys close by each other and used their dinghy for transportation between the boats. We spent the evening visiting them on their boat. Their boat is big and very expensive. It probably would cost more than

$100,000 new. It has a center cockpit and a nice layout below with a big main cabin, a stereo system, and two sleeping quarters—one fore and one aft. It has two heads, plenty of storage, and it carries 200 gallons of water. We enjoyed our evening visiting and having chicken wings and veggies, with tea, amaretto, and honey. We went back to our boat at ten thirty, tired and wanting to stay warm, so we went to bed right away. The warmest place in the boat is in bed, inside of a sleeping bag wearing long underwear. We discovered right before going to bed that the refrigerator wasn't working. There's always something to do. We'll take care of that tomorrow.

On mooring buoy, Atlantic Highlands Yacht Club, Atlantic Highlands, Sandy Hook, NJ - Distance traveled: 67 miles

ROBIN AND I IN OUR DINGHY WE CALLED *THE LINCOLN*

CHAPTER THREE
SANDY HOOK, NJ to THE NC/SC BORDER
Oct. 19, 1986 – Dec. 1, 1986

October 19, 1986, Sunday

We slept well and didn't wake up until eight, and then decided to lie in bed awhile longer. When I finally got up, I served melon and pancakes for breakfast. We ate, and then I made enchiladas for the evening meal. We had ground beef I didn't want to spoil, so I cooked it and made the enchiladas. Now, all we need to do is heat them up. Don worked on the refrigerator problem while I sat in the sun on deck, keeping warm and writing. Hope, Harry and I went ashore to look over the yacht club and check into the possibility of showers, then go into town to shop a bit. I returned to the boat at five o'clock and fixed the enchilada dinner. Don fixed the stove, oven, and refrigerator while we were away; he was very busy. We spent a pleasant evening watching TV, happy to be able just to relax. We haven't seen *Renegade* lately. It's cool this evening on the boat. I can hardly wait to get a hot shower in the morning.

Sandy Hook, On mooring buoy, Atlantic Highlands Yacht Club, Atlantic Highlands, NJ

October 20, 1986, Monday

We woke up early and moved the boat to a dock at the yacht club. Don called Clayton, and I talked with Randy. We like to let our families know, from time to time, that we are all right and where we are. Then I cut Don's hair. We talked to the repair shop in Florida about Vern. They were to repair it and ship it here, but the repairman didn't get Vern shipped out until today, so the post office here is going to send him on to Annapolis for us. We left Sandy Hook about three thirty in the afternoon after we cleaned the boat and I did laundry. We inflated the dinghy and towed it behind the boat. We traveled together with *Passages,* staying in contact with them all the way. It was dark during the last three hours of the trip. Our first adventure in the Atlantic was easy. However, we lost our wind-indicator from our masthead. I don't know why it fell off, but it did. Fortunately, it didn't hit us. We went into Point Pleasant, New Jersey, at the Manasquan Inlet at ten that night, after a 41-mile trip, mostly in the Atlantic Ocean. I didn't get to bed until one. There was no dock fee here because we tied up at a courtesy dock for a restaurant called The Shrimp Box, which is now out of business.

Guest dock, The Shrimp Box Restaurant, Point Pleasant, NJ – Distance traveled: 41 miles

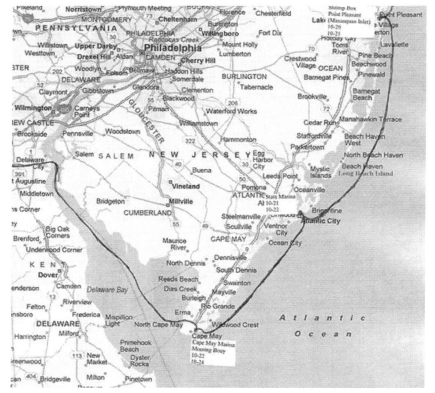

October 21, 1986, Tuesday

It was sunny and in the high 60s today. We were en route to Atlantic City all day. The distance was 63 miles, and it took us about 11 hours.

We left early. Rollers were about four feet, and the wind was on our nose the entire way. Yuk! We took lots of water over the bow of the boat, but none got into the cabin. We found a dinghy while on the way. It was just bobbing around. Then we realized it was *Passages'* dinghy, and it came untied from their stern. We rescued it for them, tied it to our stern alongside our dinghy, and took it to them in Atlantic City. They were surprised. I don't think they had missed it yet. We arrived at Farley's Marina at seven. We have an electric hook-up, and that means we have heat for the night.

For our evening's entertainment, we took the mini bus to about a half-dozen gambling casinos after dinner with Hope and Harry. We also walked along the boardwalk. This place is a disappointment when compared to Las Vegas, but we all still enjoyed a fun evening doing something different from our normal activities. The marina facilities are good. The journey today was crummy, but the evening was fun, and Hope and Harry were very happy that we rescued their expensive dinghy. We didn't get to bed until two in the morning.

Farley's Marina, Atlantic City – Distance traveled: 63 miles

October 22, 1986, Wednesday

Gosh, it was nice to be able to sleep in today. We ate a leisurely breakfast of eggs and bacon with English muffins, and spent time looking over the charts. At twelve thirty, we left for Cape May, New Jersey, along with *Passages*. We made the 47 mile trip in seven hours, arriving at seven thirty. The conditions in the Atlantic, both weather and seas, were pleasant. I was even comfortable enough to write a letter. We ran aground a couple of times trying to get into the marina at Cape May because of its shallow depth, but finally found a way in, docked safely, and secured for the night. *Passages* also made it in. The four of us went into town and ate pizza at a tavern, and then went to the grocery store. We didn't get back until midnight. Don and I watched a little of the World Series game on TV. I didn't even pay attention to what teams were playing.

Cape May is the country's oldest seaside resort. It began hosting vacationers in the mid seventeen hundreds and is now best known for its large number of well-maintained Victorian houses. Its year-round population is about 4,000, but in the summer, its population expands to about 40,000. We like the town so much that we would like to come back here someday.

Marina, Cape May, NJ – Distance traveled: 47 miles

October 23, 1986, Thursday

We woke up about eight thirty, but stayed in bed until nine. After breakfast, I ran the sweeper, emptied the trash, and did a few other chores. Later, we saw Randy, Paul, and Martin from *Renegade* at the Dockside Restaurant and spent some time catching up on their activities. I talked with my sister Randy; all is fine in Columbus. Don and I took the boat out and tied up to a mooring buoy for the night; the marina charges $22 per night, and the mooring buoy is free. We took our dinghy back to the marina to go sightseeing with Hope and Harry. We walked three or four miles around town, sightseeing and shopping. We enjoyed seeing the Victorian homes. I bought postcards and a couple of throw rugs for the boat. After we returned to the marina, we went to *Passages* for a glass of wine, and then the four of us went out to dinner.

We enjoyed a relaxing day and evening. Our dinghy and motor are working out very well as transportation to and from our boat/home. Today's weather was great. It was the fifth day in a row of blue skies and sunshine with warm temperatures. We went to bed at eleven.

Mooring buoy, Cape May, NJ

October 24, 1986, Friday

We got up early, left our mooring buoy, and headed for the Chesapeake Bay. In order to get to the Chesapeake Bay you have to go up the Delaware Bay. There are two ways to get into the Delaware Bay from the town of Cape May. One is to go out into the Atlantic and go around the Cape, and that will take you into the bay. That is the long and potentially treacherous way. The other way is to go through the Cape May Canal which goes directly into the Delaware Bay from the town of Cape May, and that is the way we went. There is a fixed bridge over the Cape May Canal with an overhead clearance of 55 feet. Fortunately, our mast is only 46 feet tall. From there we headed northwest to the Chesapeake and Delaware Canal. The C & D Canal, as it is commonly referred to, is 14 miles long and connects the Delaware Bay to the Chesapeake Bay.

The C & D Canal has been in operation since 1829, but the idea of building it was proposed much earlier, in the mid-1600s. Benjamin Franklin advocated for it in the late 1700s, but, because of lack of financial resources, it wasn't built until the 1820s. Pennsylvania, Maryland, Delaware, and the federal government jointly financed its construction.

We are now at Chesapeake City, Maryland, most of the way through the C & D Canal. After a few more miles, we will be in the Chesapeake Bay. We are spending the night here. This was a long day, 63 miles in eleven hours. Don hasn't been at ease today. We have developed a slight leak. We have a small amount of water coming into the bilge from outside the boat, but we aren't sure where it is coming in. We think it's around the strut which holds the propeller shaft in place. There is always some minor concern...if you are lucky, and it's not a major one. *Passages* has a big leak; they take on about 200 gallons of water every day. After dinner tonight, I rowed the dinghy over to see them while Don stayed on the boat to do some navigation work. We were having tea and amaretto, and their bilge pump came on. It was so noisy, I nearly jumped out of my seat!

Later, the three of us walked into town to mail letters. The town is so quaint I rowed out to get Don so he could see it. Chesapeake City reminds us of "Old Dublin" except it has water surrounding it—a really neat place. At a restaurant in town, we ate a piece of Peanut Butter Pie, and liked it so well we asked for the recipe. We went to bed very late.

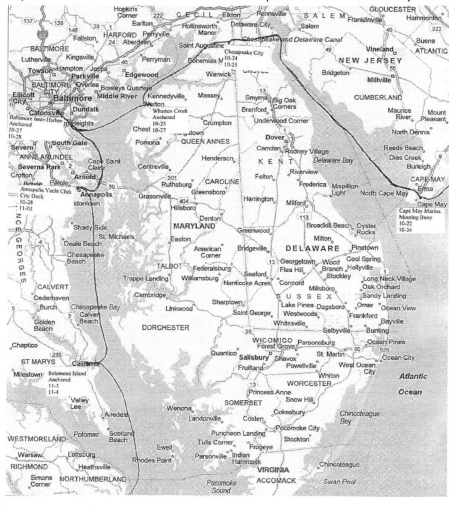

Anchored at Chesapeake City, MD – Distance traveled: 63 miles

October 25, 1986, Saturday

It turned cooler today, and we didn't see the sun at all. We bought fuel this morning, and because we started late, only sailed about 36 miles. We passed some gorgeous farms and homes along the way and anchored at a lovely spot on Worton Creek.

Worton Creek is in Maryland, on the eastern shore, about 30 miles east of Baltimore and flows into the Chesapeake. It sprinkled lightly, but we did get to sail, which was the second day in a row. We stopped at a marina here and pumped out our holding tank. The people were friendly, and the place is beautiful. The leaves are probably at their peak fall colors now. After anchoring the boat for the night, I made dinner. We worked on our itinerary for the next seven days, and will call Clayton tomorrow and give it to him because we plan to try to get together with Clayton and Betty in about ten days. We like this place so much; we have decided to stay here tomorrow and sightsee.

Anchored in Worton Creek, MD – Distance traveled: 36 miles

October 26, 1986, Sunday

We stayed over at Worton Creek to sightsee, rest and relax. It rained most of the day, but we dinghied to the closest marina and paid $3.00 for showers. The people were wonderful, but their showers were terrible. They had bugs and there were no hooks for our clothes; at least the water was hot. We bought milk and butane lighter fuel, and then looked around on shore. After that we went exploring in the dinghy. Here in the Chesapeake, that's called "gunk holing." The scenery was pretty, even in the rain. We also went back to the marina that we went to yesterday and bought one quart of gas for the dinghy. (It doesn't hold much more). They were just as friendly today as yesterday. They wouldn't let us pay for it. We visited with them a bit and then came back to the boat. For the rest of the day we just lay around the boat; I did some cross-stitch while Don read his books. It was nice to have free time.

We enjoyed listening to the radio in the evening prior to going to bed. The "gnats" are bad at this spot; other than that, it is a very pleasant place to anchor. There isn't any town but lots of God's beautiful nature. We tried to call Clayton while ashore, but no answer.

Anchored in Worton Creek, MD

October 27, 1986, Monday
We were underway at seven thirty this morning. The fog was thick, but it lightened up and was only hazy after a couple of hours. We motored the whole way to Baltimore, which was about 30 miles. We docked in Baltimore's Inner Harbor, in downtown Baltimore, around noon. On our way into the Inner Harbor, we passed the place where, in 1814 during the Battle of Baltimore, a prison ship was anchored with Francis Scott Key aboard. That's when he wrote the words for "The Star-Spangled Banner."

I made potato soup, and we ate lunch while we were under way. It was convenient to have the mess cleaned up before we arrived at the Inner Harbor to go sightseeing. The price for docking was $1.00 per foot. We decided to anchor and save $30. Money saved here means money to spend elsewhere. Shortly after anchoring, we took the dinghy to shore. The shops and Harbor Mall buildings are great. We pigged out on all the different kinds of foods that were available: ice cream, cookies, cheese toasts, etc. We bought a few groceries, and went back to the boat about five. We went ashore a second time in the evening for a walk and more food. It rained hard that time. After eating, we rowed the dinghy to a 360 ft. coast guard ship which was in the harbor for decommissioning and talked with some sailors on board.

Anchored in Inner Harbor, Baltimore, MD – Distance traveled: 30 miles

October 28, 1986, Tuesday
We ate breakfast on deck today while watching people going to work in downtown Baltimore, and we loved every minute of it. Baltimore's Inner Harbor was interesting, and because it was in the middle of a big city, a very different type of anchorage. The Inner Harbor reminded me of an enlarged version of Portside in Toledo, Ohio. We left around ten from our anchoring spot and sailed the entire way to Annapolis, about 34 miles, getting there a few minutes after three thirty. I did another quick oiling of the teak while Don fixed chicken paprika in the pressure cooker. It made a good meal with noodles and freshly steamed broccoli.

We docked tonight at the Annapolis Yacht Club. After dinner, we topped off the water tanks, and I ran the sweeper and cleaned up a mess from a leak under one of the windows. I wrote Shelly before going to bed.

At Annapolis Yacht Club, Annapolis, MD – Distance traveled: 34 miles

October 29, 1986, Wednesday

We woke up very early and moved the boat to the Hilton Hotel guest dock. We saw Hope and Harry on *Passages.* Harry came over to visit and to watch the video tapes we have taken during the trip. We also saw *Renegade* early in the day. Late this evening, Randy came over to visit and watch the video tapes. *Renegade* is leaving tomorrow to go south again. We spent most of the day running around doing errands and buying things needed for boat maintenance and improvements. We purchased some twelve volt fluorescent lights, which I am delighted about. We also went to the post office and picked up Vern. I tried raw oysters for the first time at a local fish market. They weren't as gross as I thought they would be.

Annapolis is a charming city. In addition to its historic colonial buildings, it has thousands of sailboats and scads of shops catering to sailors—a sailor's paradise. One of the sailors we met told us that Annapolis is known as the city with 40,000 people and 65,000 boats. It is located on the Severn River, just off the Chesapeake, and has several sizable creeks in the downtown area, including Spa Creek, Back Creek, and College Creek. The creeks flow into the Severn or directly into the Chesapeake. It was the capital of the United States for a short time, and is the location of the U. S. Naval Academy. We will probably stay for a few days; there's a lot to do and see here.

Guest dock, Hilton Hotel, Annapolis, MD

October 30, 1986, Thursday

Today started off "crappy" and I mean it, literally. As Don was fixing the joker valve on the head, dirty water and "crap" spilled all over the floor—what a mess to clean up. Later in the morning, we visited Hope and Harry, and made plans for dinner on our boat at six tonight. We came back to the boat and ate a sandwich for lunch and then carried our laundry about a mile and a half, so I could do it. Don ran errands while I did the laundry. When we returned to the boat, I put away all the laundry while Don fixed crab thermidor for dinner. At just about dinnertime, the manager of the Hilton came out and asked us to move from the guest docking area, so we moved over to the city marina next to *Passages*. Hope and Harry came to the *Robin Lee,* and we ate and socialized until ten thirty. Then, to avoid dockage fees, we moved the boat back to the yacht club where we stayed our first night in Annapolis.

Annapolis Yacht Club, Annapolis, MD

October 31, 1986, Friday

Today we enjoyed a walking tour of the Naval Academy at Annapolis. Hope and Harry were with us. Afterwards, we went back to the boat and moved it to a boat yard on Back Creek where some boat repairmen looked for our leak. They think the leak is coming from the engine cooling system, rather than from the strut. We ended up spending the night there, but we were rafted off another boat. It was very windy for a time. Don fixed chili con carne and cornbread.

Boatyard, Annapolis, MD

November 1, 1986, Saturday

We began the day by adding up our expenses during October. We spent way too much-- $825. We will have to do better in November. Then we moved over to the Spa Creek city dock for the day. Don worked on putting in wiring for the fluorescent lights. I took a walk to the post office to mail cards and ended up finding a painting job for the day. The people who hired me were Francis and Bill Edwards. They have a little pottery shop in the colonial part of Annapolis. Bill bought my lunch and paid me $40 for helping to paint the fence for four hours, from eleven to three. Francis gave me a little ceramic tumbler; it is now our pen and pencil holder. I finished there and then went window shopping through town. When I returned to the boat at five, Don and I went shopping and bought a lantern for anchoring with the money I made. We also bought a ship's clock, an early Christmas gift for each other.

Don let the lantern burn while we were out for dinner, and when we got home it was covered in black soot—what a mess. I couldn't believe it. Now we want to take it back, but the people we bought it from weren't friendly, so that should be interesting.

City dock, Spa Creek, Annapolis, MD

November 2, 1986, Sunday

This morning, Harry brought over our light. He trimmed the wick and Hope and he cleaned off all the soot. They say it works fine, so I guess we will keep it. Don and I filled the

ROBIN THE FENCE PAINTER AND HER BOSS

water tanks and I cleaned up the boat. Later, we finished wiring the new lights and scrubbed the deck. Then we decided to take a break and go out for a milkshake. We went to an ice cream parlor named Chick and Ruth's for our milk shakes, a place that Bill Edwards, my employer yesterday, suggested. They were great. We stopped at the market on the way home and bought a freshly baked, big, chocolate-chip cookie. The milkshake and the cookie was our dinner. Actually, we were stuffed.

We left around five, and went to the yacht club again to tie up. Hope and Harry aboard *Passages* stayed at the city dock. I made a peanut butter and cream cheese pie, with a graham cracker crust, using the recipe from the restaurant in Chesapeake City. Don watched Masterpiece Theater. Later, we walked up to the Hilton to use the phone and mail a letter to Shelly. Don couldn't reach Chip, but I did talk to Shelly. She sounded as though she is feeling more content with Bowling Green.

We went back to the boat at eleven. Don took down my mobile of sailboats, and hung up the new kerosene lamp. I hung the mobile over the table. The adhesive didn't stick, and it fell and broke. I was upset because it was a gift from Shelly. I got out of bed when I heard the crash and re-glued it. I hope it holds together. I had trouble getting back to sleep. Don slept well…until I flushed the head.

Annapolis Yacht Club, Annapolis, MD

November 3, 1986, Monday

We got up at six thirty today and left Annapolis about seven. I sure hate those early hours. I would much rather sleep until eight thirty or nine, but we can't because the days are getting shorter. We needed to go about 52 miles to get to Solomons Island.

It was a beautiful sunny day, on the cool side, but pleasant. We hoisted our sails, but we still had to motor the entire day. *Passages* was behind us. I made tuna salad for lunch.

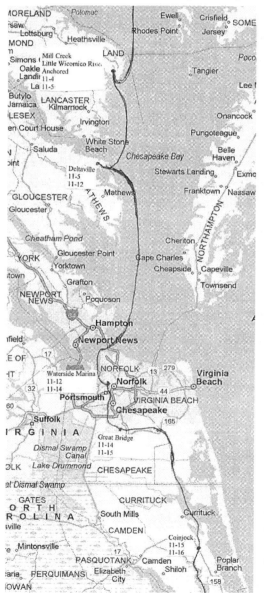

After we were anchored for the night at Solomons, I heated up leftovers, we ate, and I washed dishes and cleaned up while Don did tomorrow's navigation plotting. Later we changed the engine oil and filter, and then read a little before going to shore in the dinghy.

We ran into Hope and Harry at a restaurant, where we visited with them for a while, and then Don and I took a walk. Hope and Harry went with some girl they met to a local craft shop the girl owned. About ten thirty they followed us to our boat, and we all drank tea and ate some of my peanut butter pie. Everyone wanted seconds. Hope and Harry stayed to visit until one in the morning; I was very tired when they left. Even though it was cold, Don and I managed to get warmed up and slept fine.

Anchored at Solomons Island, MD – Distance traveled: 52 miles

November 4, 1986, Tuesday

Today is voting day, but we didn't vote because we didn't fill out absentee ballots.

Don disposed of the old engine oil from last night's oil change at the gas dock, we quickly washed off the boat from where the anchor made a mess, and then we pulled out.

So far, it has been a relatively calm day. Weather conditions are pleasant; the sun is out, and it is not too cold. We've been motoring, and at present we are close to the mouth of the Potomac River. A little while ago we heard a Coast Guard call on the marine radio telling boaters to be on the lookout for a sailor lost overboard from a naval vessel. It happened in the ocean east of Norfolk, a long way from us.

In the late afternoon, we listened on the marine radio to the rescue of a sinking boat. We had left the Chesapeake Bay and were in Mill Creek looking for a place to anchor. Mill

Creek flows into the Great Wicomico River near where it empties into the Chesapeake just south of the Potomac. We were only three or four miles away, as the crow flies, from the sinking boat, *Bola Bola,* a 36' sport fishing boat with one man on board, when it called: "Mayday, Mayday, Mayday." It was very interesting. Even a Navy helicopter helped in the rescue by lowering a pump to the vessel. We finally anchored, and Don fixed our dinner. We ate while we listened to the marine radio. We recorded some of the radio transmissions on our tape recorder. It was comical at times because some of the people involved in the rescue were local folks and obviously amateurs at what they were doing. However, there was a happy ending; the vessel was saved and towed up the Great Wicomico River to a boatyard. After the rescue, we enjoyed a quiet evening. We talked to Hope on the radio; they listened to the rescue also. They are anchored for the night, but I don't know exactly where. I went to bed at ten. Don was up off and on during the night due to heavy wind and rain. I slept soundly.

Anchored, Mill Creek, VA – Distance traveled: 51 miles

November 5, 1986, Wednesday

We got up at nine, and Don fixed breakfast of oatmeal, soft-boiled eggs, crackers, and bread. I did the dishes, and then we left for Deltaville. It had been raining for hours, but it seemed to be subsiding. The waters were rough and choppy. The wind was on the nose a lot during the day, but we sailed some.

We heard a Coast Guard message concerning another vessel, *Katrina,* a 38' pleasure craft that was overdue and might have sunk. The Coast Guard told boaters to be on the lookout for her and to report any sightings to them. We had some anxiety of our own. We developed a leak. Water was spraying around in the engine compartment. It wasn't a lot of water, but we were afraid it might get worse before we arrived at Deltaville, but we made it. Then we set out to find someone who could help us with the problem. A mechanic looked at it and determined that the freeze-out plugs in the engine cooling system had corroded and were leaking. He told us that it wasn't an immediate threat, but that the plugs should be replaced because the leaking would get worse in time. The manufacturer of our diesel engine was Kubota, a Japanese company that makes diesel-powered tractors. Our motor is the same as one that is used on one of their small tractors. The motor is marketed for use in boats under the name of "Universal Atomic Engines." When the engine is to be used in a boat, the steel freeze-out plugs are supposed to be replaced with bronze ones. It wasn't done on our engine. This is probably where the water was coming from when we were in Annapolis.

John and Sally, on a 65' fishing and sailing boat that had been converted to a live-aboard boat, invited us over tonight for tea. They are tied up nearby us at the town dock. They've lived aboard for over five years. The boat is spacious and well laid out. It's also nicely decorated and well maintained. They are an interesting couple, and have a four-year-old son named John Lee who has lived on the boat his entire life. He's a cute kid and proudly showed us the cabin where he sleeps and plays. We visited with them, drank a cup of tea, warmed up, and then came back home and ate a sandwich for dinner. All in all, it was a difficult, rainy, cold, miserable day, but with a nice ending.

We talked to *Passages* and told them about our problem, and that we would be delayed for a while. They will continue south. Maybe we will see them again someday, but probably not. That's sad because we really enjoyed hanging out with them. Don went to the town pharmacy and used a pay phone to call Jane at the office to tell her to send our next batch of mail to Beaufort, North Carolina, and he also called Clayton to let him know where we are, and that we will be here for a few days. Clayton and Betty plan to visit us on Sunday and stay overnight. We were soaked most of the day, and I feel good lying here in bed with warm covers over me. We came 30 miles today in about five hours.

The town dock, Deltaville, VA – Distance traveled: 30 miles

November 6, 1986, Thursday

We moved our boat to the Deltaville Marina early this morning. The people at the marina said they would help us with our problem. Before we left the town dock, we entertained John and Sally Lee on our boat, so they could see our little home. I talked to Randy, and she reported that Celeste won the Ohio Governor's race over Rhodes, the Republican candidate.

The mechanic at the Deltaville Marina contacted the company that markets our engine about the problem. Proper freeze-out plugs were ordered. They will be coming from Wisconsin, so we will be here a few more days. We rode into town with the grocery store owner. He was kind enough to stop by the seafood market, post office and hardware store for us–an obliging fellow. Everybody has been hospitable here, but there isn't much to do at night. Deltaville is quite different from Annapolis. Don worked very hard on *The Lincoln*, our name for the dinghy, cleaning and treating it with ArmorAll. I tried to fix a few leaks around the windows, but we will have to wait to see if I succeeded. I may have bought the wrong kind of caulking.

Don fixed chop suey tonight in the pressure cooker; I am glad he enjoys his new toy. I hoped he would.

Deltaville Marina, Deltaville, VA

November 7, 1986, Friday

It was cloudy and sprinkled on and off all day. I did laundry, visited with the girl who works in the marina office, and called Randy. Don worked on *The Lincoln* some more, and then we launched it. It looks brand new. He fixed dinner again tonight: baked scallops; marinated artichokes; and bread, butter, and jelly. The parts for the boat won't be in until Monday, so I think we will have a boring weekend in Deltaville. We listened to the tape of songs having to do with sailing that Bob and Pam made for us. Some of the songs are familiar and some we had never heard, but we like them all. It's eleven thirty, and I am just now finishing writing in this journal. For some reason, the flies are bad tonight. I am running the fan, hoping to chase them all away. I hate flies!

Deltaville Marina, Deltaville, VA

November 8, 1986, Saturday

Today, we spent some time in the dinghy exploring the area. It was a pretty day, and it was mild. No one worked on the boat because the parts haven't come in. We expect to be here until mid-week–what a drag. There is very little to do here, and everything is far away. We walked to another local restaurant tonight, a 3.5 mile trek, and played darts. I beat Don; that was a surprise. After a long and tiring walk home, we went to bed. It was a good day, except when Don took my bread and jelly away from me at dinner and ate it. I didn't think that was mannerly at all. He was just kidding around, but I didn't laugh.

Deltaville Marina, Deltaville, VA

November 9, 1986, Sunday

I cleaned the boat and did a load of laundry this morning, so we would have a clean house and clean sheets for Betty and Clayton, who are coming today for an overnight visit.

They are on their way home from seeing Betty's brother in Charlotte, North Carolina. It was a relaxing day, but a little boring until they arrived. It was good to see them. We served veggies and dip on board and then went out for pizza. We stopped by the grocery after eating pizza, and after that, drove back to the boat. Don showed them some of the videos we have taken with our camcorder. After watching the videos, we ate brownies and ice cream. We all went to bed around eleven thirty. It was good to hear about what was going on back in Dublin. The building boom hasn't stopped yet.

Deltaville Marina, Deltaville, VA

November 10, 1986, Monday

Today we had a very interesting day with Betty and Clayton. They slept in their camper van and said that they slept well. We were up early and enjoyed a breakfast of juice, scrambled eggs, and coffeecake. Then we left in their van and drove to Yorktown, Virginia, to see where the last major battle of the Revolutionary War was fought. We stopped at Wendy's for lunch, and it hit the spot. It was the first Wendy's we had eaten at since we left home. About two thirty, we came back to Deltaville. We stopped by the grocery, and then Betty and Clayton dropped us off at the marina and left. I sent my ring with the missing diamond back with them to be repaired. We said our good-byes and took a few pictures. Their visit gave us a break in our routine, and we very much appreciate them coming to see us.

In the evening, we read and wrote letters. The engine still isn't repaired, but will be tomorrow...we hope.

Deltaville Marina, Deltaville, VA

November 11, 1986, Tuesday

I slept in this morning while the guys from the marina worked on the engine. The engine compartment is right in the middle of the boat, so that kept me out of their way. They changed the freeze out plugs in about 15 minutes and then left. Around ten thirty, Don served me cereal with bananas in bed. I showered and then went to the office to say good-bye to Betty, the secretary. I called collect to Pam, my closest friend, and I think we talked for 45 minutes to an hour, but she insisted on continuing. Hopefully, they will be down in January to see us. Shortly thereafter, I came back to the boat and did the dishes. Around two thirty, Don paid our bill and bought fuel, and then we moved out to the town dock. We spent five nights at Deltaville Marina. Our total bill was $256: $13 for fuel and $243 for repairs, but nothing for dockage. The good news is that the engine company is going to reimburse us $100, since they made a mistake by not changing the freeze-out plugs to begin with. In addition, the new freeze-out plugs were free.

After tying up at the town dock, we visited with an older couple, Charles (Mack) and Betty McComas, on their trawler named *Mafoogie*, which was tied up next to us. They invited us on-board to get warm. It rained the entire day; we were pretty wet. Don reviewed charts with Mack while I visited with Betty. Mack was an airline pilot and Betty was a Latin teacher, but they gave up their careers 41 years ago, in 1946, when Mack was 31. At that time, they moved onto a sailboat to go cruising, and have lived on various boats they have owned —mostly sailboats—from then until recently. They raised their only child, a son, while living aboard. He is now 36, my age. Mack is now 71 and they have a home near Baltimore, in Bel Air, Maryland, near the Middle River, where they live in the summers. Every fall they take Mafoogie to Daytona, Florida, and spend the winter on the boat.

I walked into town about seven thirty to mail letters while Don fixed sweet and sour pork for dinner. We didn't eat until eight. It is still raining, but at least we have the electric heater hooked up, so it isn't cold in here. There is, however, a lot of condensation due to the difference in the temperature, inside and out.

Deltaville Marina, Deltaville, VA

November 12, 1986, Wednesday

What a crummy, cold, wet, rainy, dismal sail we had from Deltaville to Norfolk. It was a rolling, following sea and the rain was also following, overtaking us actually, so that it blew into the cabin. We left Deltaville at six forty-five and traveled 57 miles in 9 ½ hours. We tied up at Waterside Marina, and boy, were we glad to get docked! It stopped raining just as we arrived, so at least we were able to do our work without getting soaked, (i.e., fill the water tanks, hook up the electric, etc.) I called Amy, my cousin, and she came to the marina and picked us up. We went to her home for dinner Amy's mother, my Aunt Marjorie, and Amy's little boy, Andrew, were there. We had a warm evening's visit with them. The heat felt great. Amy brought us back to the boat at eleven. Her husband, Jack, is a career naval officer, and is stationed here. Amy dropped us off at the marina and Don and I walked around in the Omni Hotel near the marina prior to coming back to board the boat. Don tried to call Chip again, but didn't get an answer.

Waterside Marina, Norfolk, VA – Distance traveled: 57 miles

November 13, 1986, Thursday

Norfolk's greatest assets are its location near the mouth of the Chesapeake Bay and its deep water channels. In Norfolk, there is one thing you can't avoid seeing, the United States Navy. The naval base here is the largest in the world. There are ships everywhere having repairs and maintenance work done. The military is the largest and most important industry here, and the

AMY AND ANDREW IN NORFOLK

second largest is commercial cargo shipping.

We relaxed today. I fixed muffins and grapefruit for breakfast, and we watched some TV. I ran the sweeper while Don checked on tours of Norfolk. Amy, Andrew, and Aunt Margie came over to the boat to visit. I served veggies for lunch, and we visited and watched the videotape Don made last night. After that, we all walked over to Waterside for lunch and shopping. They finally left around four, and Don and I continued to look around for a couple of hours. We bought a couple of atlas reference guides for our kids for Christmas gifts. This was the first of our Christmas shopping this year. Oh well, it's only mid-November; we have plenty of time.

It was so cold in the boat, even with the heater running, that it was hard to enjoy the dinner Don fixed. We watched a little TV and a movie, and looked over the charts. It's now eleven o'clock, and we are going to go to bed. The wind is blowing hard, and it is in the 30s outside.

Waterside Marina, Norfolk, VA

November 14, 1986, Friday

We got up early and pulled out of Waterside. We went only as far as Great Bridge at Mile 12 on the Intracoastal Waterway.

The Intracoastal Waterway is a more comfortable and safer way to travel by boat along the coast, and we will be using it as much as we can. It's partly protected from rough ocean conditions and is made up of several segments. The segment we are now on is called the Atlantic Intracoastal Waterway, and it extends from Norfolk to Key West. There is also a Gulf Intracoastal Waterway which has two sections: one between Fort Myers and Tarpon Springs and the other between Carrabelle, Florida (20 miles east of Apalachicola) and Brownsville, Texas. In North Carolina, the waterway goes through some large bodies of water, Albemarle Sound and Pamlico Sound. Although these bodies of water are protected from ocean waves by the outer banks, they can become treacherous. There is no protected waterway between Key West and Ft Myers, or between Tarpon Springs and Carrabelle, Florida. There is some commercial traffic on the Intracoastal Waterway, and it is used extensively by recreational boaters. Many "snowbirds" use the waterway to move their boats to the South for the winter and to the North for the summer. The waterway intersects with several navigable rivers, including the Mississippi and Mobile, which, in turn, connect to numerous other navigable inland rivers and lakes, including the Great Lakes.

It is possible to circumnavigate the eastern continental United States in mostly protected waters. The route used is called the Great Loop. We intend to do most of it, if not all, on this trip. The Intracoastal Waterway provides the southern and eastern route. North of Norfolk you have some protected waterways that are not officially part of the Intracoastal Waterway. The Chesapeake Bay, the C & D Canal, and the Cape May Canal are protected. The Delaware Bay and the New Jersey coast from Cape May to the Hudson River are not protected. Once on the Hudson River one can travel on protected waters all the way to the Gulf of Mexico by way of the Erie Canal, the Great Lakes and the Illinois and Mississippi Rivers. As an alternative to taking the Mississippi River all the way to the gulf, one can take the Mississippi River to the Ohio River, the Ohio River to the Tennessee River, the Tennessee River to the "Ten-Tom Waterway," the "Ten-Tom Waterway" to the Tombigbee River, and continue on the Alabama & Mobile rivers to Mobile, Alabama, and the gulf where it intersects the western section of the Gulf Intracoastal Waterway.

Twelve miles from Norfolk, Mile 12 on the Atlantic Intracoastal Waterway, there is a lock at a town called, Great Bridge and it was so cold going through the lock that we decided to quit for the day, although it was only ten thirty. We docked at the government wharf and walked to the local shopping area for breakfast. I dropped off my jacket to be dry cleaned, and stopped at the post office to drop off mail and buy stamps. I also called Randy around noon. All is well at home. It was very cold, in the 30s, so we went to bed early. We saw the "family" aboard *Completion* at the wharf. We hadn't seen them or their boat since Castleton, New York.

Great Bridge, Chesapeake, VA – Distance traveled: 12 miles

November 15, 1986, Saturday

Well, it's still very cold. The dew and condensation are terrible. I do not enjoy all the wetness and cold. It is miserable. We left the government wharf at seven, and it started raining again about a half-hour after we left the dock. How depressing! It continued all the way to Pungo Ferry, where we rafted off some other boats and waited 2.5 hours for the drawbridge to open. It apparently broke down in the middle of opening. While waiting, we put up the Bimini top and ate lunch. The Bimini kept some of the rain from pouring down on us and Vern. What a dreary day to be going into North Carolina. We docked at Coinjock shortly before five, just before dark. We traveled about 41 miles today. While Don registered at the marina, I called Sister Carol, and we talked for 15 minutes. My ring is going to cost $80 to be fixed; Carol received another letter from Shelly; Carol is having Thanksgiving dinner at her place; and she has invited both our kids. Don called Chip and talked awhile. When he finished, we visited a little with the clerk at the marina and looked through the groceries at the marina store, debating whether to buy or not to buy ice cream. We decided that it was too expensive, so we didn't. We learned that the Fairfield Bridge, at "Mile 114," is closing for repairs for two days on Monday morning after its eight o'clock opening. So, we will try to get to it tomorrow afternoon and go through when it opens in the morning. We will need to get an early start and make good time because the bridge is over 69 miles from here. It will be a long day. We went back to the boat, ate leftover sweet and sour pork, and enjoyed the warmth from the electric heater. I still have a slightly sore throat, so I took some aspirin. Don did the dishes and even though it was early, we hit the sack to keep warm. It feels great to be in a warm cozy bed.

Marina, Coinjock, NC – Distance traveled: 41 miles

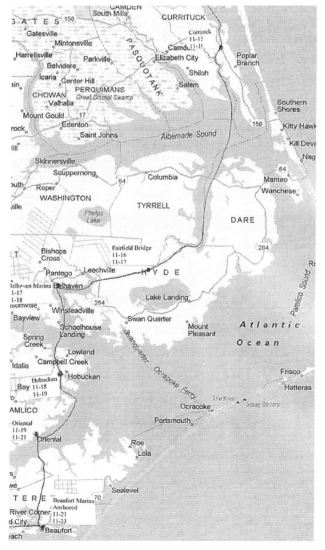

November 16, 1986, Sunday

We woke up early and left promptly at six fifteen, before daylight. The others at the marina who are heading south left in good time also, including a couple we talked who are aboard a boat from Alaska. That made for plenty of boats to follow. I fixed cream of wheat and a pot of tea while underway, and then about nine fifteen we ate a snack of graham crackers. Don fixed our lunch of peanut butter and jelly (PB&J) sandwiches at noon. We had a following wind and therefore could sail with the jib. With motor and sail, we made a better than average speed of about six knots. It was still cold today, and I only saw the sun once, for less than one minute, but at least there was no rain. That made it a little more bearable. The canal leading to the bridge on the last leg of our day's journey was swampy and not very pretty. We arrived at the Fairfield Drawbridge at dusk and got permission to tie to a towboat for the night from Harold, the crane operator who was aboard the boat and was there to work on the bridge starting tomorrow. He was good enough to let us plug into his electric generator; so we had heat. We made a total of 70 miles and now won't have to sit and wait for two days for the bridge to get repaired, so long as we don't sleep through the eight o'clock opening. The boat from Alaska didn't get all the way to the bridge. They anchored at Pongo Point and will come to the bridge early in the morning.

I made pizza for the first time on the boat, and it turned out all right. We invited Harold aboard to share our pizza and visit. Tonight was the first time in a long time that I didn't sleep with all my clothes on. The heater kept us warm. I wrote Shelly a letter in the evening and made some blueberry cookies out of a Jiffy muffin mix.

Fairfield Drawbridge, NC – Distance traveled: 70 miles

November 17, 1986, Monday

We made the seven o'clock bridge opening. Boy, are we glad we came all the way last night. The fog was thick early this morning. We talked to the Alaskan couple later, and they told us that they made it in time for the eight o'clock opening, but they left their anchorage at five in the morning and, because of the fog, needed to be guided into the channel by a powerboat with radar. At eight o'clock, the bridge opened for the last time for two days.

As we were motoring on our way to Belhaven, our next stop, we ran aground right in the middle of the channel. No damage was done, and we got off the bottom quickly. The trip to Belhaven was only 27 miles; we arrived there at noon. It started pouring down about the time we arrived. We decided to stay at River Forest. It's an old mansion, now converted into a hotel and restaurant. It cost us $22.50 for the night. We took the River Forest golf cart into town to see the area and stopped by the post office to mail letters. We also bought groceries, and of course it began to rain again. We were wet, but decided to go to the library. It was warm and cozy. I sat by the heater in a rocking chair and read magazines. When it was time to leave, it was still raining. We went back to the boat, but were soaked. Don made a meat loaf with potatoes in the pressure cooker for dinner. We watched a movie on cable TV, and then walked to the restaurant at the marina for dessert and to pay for dockage. The people were cordial, and their smorgasbord boasts of serving distinguished people. The desserts weren't that great, but Don tried to cheer me up by treating me to one. I was in a foul mood, primarily because of the lousy weather.

River Forest Marina, Belhaven, NC – Distance traveled: 27 miles

November 18, 1986, Tuesday

This morning we slept in for a change. I showered and then came back to the boat and ran the sweeper. I always feel better when I do those things. I will feel still better today if it doesn't start raining again until we get situated tonight. I phoned Randy before we left Belhaven. We were underway about noon, and shortly afterward I fixed PB&J sandwiches for lunch. Poor Don, he has been so nice to me, and for some reason I just feel mean. I hope my attitude improves soon or I will drive him crazy. He keeps telling me: "Remember the saying,

'Tough-times don't last, but tough-people do'." And it is true, but I have a hard time smiling when it is so dreary and rainy and there's been no sunshine for days and days.

We motored the entire four hours to the Hoboken Bridge, and arrived just in time for the four o'clock opening. Thankfully, there was no rain today. We tied up at a commercial fishing company just on the other side of the bridge. We got dockage with electric for only $0.20 a foot which was a great price, $6.00 for us, so we were happy. Mosquitos began pestering us, but we burned a coil called a "pic" which makes a smoke that repels mosquitos, and that took care of them. I worked on cross-stitch, and Don plotted our navigation for the next few days in our chart book. We ate leftovers for dinner. We went to bed around ten, and only one time, about six o'clock in the morning, did it rain–what a surprise.

Fish Company, Hobucken Bridge, NC – Distance traveled: 24 miles

November 19, 1986, Wednesday

This day began with beautiful sunshine and no clouds. It was a welcome change. The weather forecast was for 30 mph winds from the northeast, but they would be following winds, (blowing in the direction we were traveling), and since we were going to be on a river, we thought that if they became that strong, we would sail with a partially furled jib only, and that we would be OK. We left early with either Oriental or Beaufort as our destination, whichever seemed to be best after a few hours.

Conditions turned very bad after a couple of hours. After we had gone only a short way on the Neuse River, it became even more windy than predicted. Winds were 40 mph with gusts of 50 mph. We had eight-foot waves, and it was cold. Still, we were doing alright until the wind flipped our dinghy up in the air, and it came down upside down, and then its painter snapped. The dinghy's dodger and its inflatable seat came off when it flipped. We reversed our course, retrieved the seat, and then went after the dinghy. It took us a while to get it within reach. We patiently turned circles, getting upwind of the dinghy, then downwind, and repeating that until Don was eventually able to grab hold of it. Unfortunately, when the dinghy flipped and came down upside down, it formed a partial vacuum inside the dinghy between the river surface and the bottom of the dinghy, and when Don finally got hold of it, he couldn't overcome the suction. He almost went overboard and did cut two of his fingers on something and bruised his chest badly. He tried to use the boat hook to break the vacuum by pulling on the lines that go around the dinghy, but that didn't work and the boat hook was pulled out of his wet hands and went to the bottom. Finally, he managed to get the vacuum broken and the dinghy turned upright. Then he was able to re-tie it to the stern. By then the dinghy's bow dodger was out of sight, and we didn't try to find it. Don's cuts aren't too bad, and I am very thankful for the way things turned out; it could have been disastrous. Oriental was the closest of our two possible destinations and that's where we went. We were too exhausted to continue, and the winds weren't getting any better. We were out for five hours, from eight until one, and traveled 28 miles. Adding to our day's woes, we noticed a small leak in one of the hoses attached to our engine, after we docked. What a day!

We realize that leaving Hobucken with that weather forecast was a bad decision. However, at the time we didn't know how treacherous the Neuse River can be with a strong northeast wind. Looking at a map after this incident, we saw that the Neuse River is over five miles wide and is a continuation of Pamlico Sound which is about 20 miles wide, and that, with a northeast wind, the fetch (the distance traversed by waves without obstruction) to where we were located was over 80 miles. That's a long distance for waves to build up. The chart book we are using doesn't show that

We tied up at the town dock and walked all over the small town of Oriental. We went to the post office and stopped by a local restaurant to eat a sandwich and split an ice cream sundae. We also went to the grocery for a few items. While there, the manager, Jerry, offered to give me a ride to the laundry. I took him up on it. Don stayed on the boat and fixed a nice dinner of pork chops and stuffing. We were both hungry and shaken up by the day's events. We went to bed early because it was so cold.

Town dock, Oriental, NC – Distance traveled: 28 miles

November 20, 1986, Thursday

Today was OK. We stayed in one spot. Don found a mechanic who came over and replaced the hose on the motor while I browsed in some of the shops. After that, we went to a restaurant at the local marina and drank a cup of hot tea, and then, between rain showers, we walked around. For dinner, we ate leftover chop suey and stuffing, which actually tasted good together. I bought a Pepperidge Farms chocolate cake for dessert. It cost a lot less than our other desserts have cost, but the biggest reason for buying it was that we knew we would like it. Because we were both tired, and it was so cold, we went to bed at nine o'clock. The cost to repair the hose was only $20; we lucked out.

Town dock, Oriental, NC

November 21, Friday

This morning we were up and ready to leave early. It was a beautiful day of clear skies, and we were anxious to move on. When we tried to back out of our slip, we found that we

were stuck in the mud and couldn't move. It was low tide. In about an hour, around nine, the water level had risen enough that we were off the bottom, so we headed for Beaufort, North Carolina (pronounced Bo-fort). It was a relatively calm day, and we were in fairly protected water, so it was an easy trip until I steered the boat slightly out of the channel to make a little more room for a shrimp boat that was coming the other way. We suddenly hit bottom, and I mean hard! It shook me up. My captain took over, without lecturing me...much. At one thirty, without further problems, we docked at a marina in Beaufort.

I washed off the boat while Don went to the post office to get the mail Jane had forwarded to us. It was great getting the mail. I received several statements from the Ohio Company where my stocks are held and a letter from Shelly. All the rest were bills and business correspondence for Don. We looked it over and then went to a marine store where we bought a new boat hook. When we returned to the marina, we ran into a 67 year old guy named Dennis, from Grenada, and New York City. He is on a boat called *Wind Dancer*. We first met him in Norfolk. The three of us went to a local pub to visit. Afterwards, he came over to our boat to visit some more.

After Dennis left, we ate Sloppy-Joes, and stayed aboard for the evening, enjoying the warmth. Don wrote checks to pay our bills and got them ready to mail in the morning. He also wrote Chip a letter. He hit the sack at ten. I wrote letters and finally went to bed at one. I enjoy my late night, quiet time.

Dockage was $0.70/foot x30ft ($21); we sure hate to pay that much.

Marina, Beaufort, NC – Distance traveled: 29 miles

November 22, Saturday

Don was up at four doing paperwork again. He woke me up at seven thirty, and I got up, fixed rolls and coffee, put away the laundry, and ran the sweeper. Dennis came over to say good-bye. The marina loaned us their van, so we went shopping for groceries and to buy a heater. Yes, Don gave up telling me that since we are heading south there is no need for a heater because it will be warm. We have been cold most of the way from Port Clinton to here. The heater we bought uses kerosene. Its brand name is "Kero-Sun." It's new, but is a two-year-old model and only cost $100. When we returned to the boat we saw that *Completion* was anchored nearby us. What do you know? They caught up with us again. We filled our water tanks and then pulled out of the docking area, and spent the night "on the hook" [anchored]. We had a juicy pot roast dinner and spent the evening enjoying our warm, heated boat. The Kero-Sun heater works well. Hopefully, we will pay for our heater with savings on dock fees by anchoring more often, and we will be a lot more comfortable to boot. Don says that his resistance to buying a kerosene heater wasn't because of the cost. It was because it would take up a lot of space. I think it will be worth the money and the space. We went to bed at eleven.

Anchored, Beaufort, NC

November 23, Sunday

Today sure doesn't seem like a Sunday. We have discovered that when you do the same sort of things seven days a week, a day on the weekend is no different than any other day. When we were leaving Beaufort around seven thirty this morning, we saw wild horses grazing on an island on our port side. The island is called Shackleford Banks and is about nine miles long. The horses are called Shackleford ponies, although they are actually small horses. The island is a sand dune with grass. Beaufort is known for the wild horses. They have been there since the 17th century.

Today, we only went as far as Swansboro, approximately 30 miles. We first went to the town dock and tied up for a couple of hours. I walked into town to mail my letter to Shelly and also call Uncle Bob to tell him where we are. He is going to come and pick us up on Thanksgiving, wherever we are, and take us to his house for dinner.

Don worked on the boat, tightening the stuffing box. The propeller shaft goes through the stuffing box as it passes through the hull from the motor to the propeller The stuffing box, which contains packing, is supposed to be loose enough for a little water to seep through, which lubricates the shaft, but tight enough that it doesn't let more than a little water into the boat. We are still trying to figure out why we are getting a bit of water in the bilge.

Finally, we moved out to anchor for the night. Don made chicken a la king with rice, and I made no bake cookies. We are eating well. The temperature was warmer today, and we had some sunshine in the morning. I didn't have to wear six layers of clothes. We didn't turn on the heater until nine, shortly before we went to bed, and then only for a few minutes to get the boat warm before we went to bed. We won't leave the heater on when we go to bed for fear of fire or asphyxiation.

Anchored, Swansboro NC – Distance traveled: 30 miles

November 24, Monday

It is a beautiful, warm, and sunny day—one of the first "perfect" days since we left Port Clinton. We left the anchorage around eight this morning, and made it to Camp Lejeune Marine Corps Base at nine. However, they were conducting firing drills, and we were required to drop anchor and wait for an hour for them to finish before we could go on. While waiting, we saw two porpoises swimming close to the boat. About 20 minutes after we were under way again, at mile marker 250, we saw a large school of porpoises. Don thought there were approximately 20 swimming together. The weather was good until two, and then it started raining. When it was Don's turn at the helm, it stopped raining—not fair. Military helicopters flew over us most of the day. It seems to me; they waste a lot of money on fuel.

The current is swift and changes direction and speed as we travel down the waterway. It's with us, then it's against us and then it's with us again, now slow and then fast. We haven't been able to predict the changes. Tidal books aren't much use when one travels along the Intracoastal Waterway, moving from a channel to a creek to a lake and then along a river with big and small inlets from the ocean. The tidal range has been between three and five feet. The tidal current concerns the captain every day when we tie up or anchor. The tidal current changes direction four times a day, every six hours. When we anchor we set the anchor so that the current will dig the anchor in deeper, but the direction will change by 180° when the tide reverses. Then the current will tend to release the anchor, so we usually use two anchors and set one in each direction. But, whether it will hold is a worry to my novice captain. Last night, he woke up at three to check things over and then stayed up the rest of the night.

Around four, after traveling 39 miles, we arrived at an anchoring spot for the night. We were glad to get anchored, because it was getting hazy, and we couldn't see very far. Good anchoring places are scarce on this part of the waterway. This spot was recommended to us as the best place available around here. We positioned the boat as far out of the navigation channel as we could, but we were in a narrow stretch of the waterway, and were not very far out of it.

We were behind Topsail Island. It was named that because pirates, including Blackbeard, hid near where we were anchored waiting for merchant ships loaded with goods to pass. When the pirate in the lookout spotted a merchant ship, the pirates would attack it and claim the cargo as their own. Eventually, the merchants became aware of the hiding place and began looking for the "topsail," the only part of the pirate ship that could be seen by the passing victim.

One of us was awake all night. My watch was from ten to three, five hours. We wanted to alert any boats coming by us that we were very close to the edge of the channel. We put two anchors out. It was a long night, but I read articles and did cross-stitch. I also used the heater, so I was content. I finally woke Don up at three and went to bed.

Anchored, Topsail Island, NC – Distance traveled: 39 miles

November 25, Tuesday

We got underway at seven fifteen, and motored to Wrightsville Beach. At ten fifteen, we put in at a marina and bought fuel. The attendant said it would be OK for us to tie up at their guest dock for a few hours. We walked to a nearby shopping area, and Don bought a badly needed pair of shoes. We also bought a few groceries. I tried to call Randy, but she was out, so I called Lois Dixon to let her know where we were and asked her to call Randy and let her know. At one fifteen, we left Wrightsville Beach and motored down the waterway to Carolina Beach, arriving at three thirty, having made 32 miles for the day. The wind was getting worse, so we found an empty dock at a condo complex and tied up. No other boats were there because it was off season. In the evening, we walked to a local shopping area for ice cream.

The weather was pleasant enough, windy and cool, with some sunshine.

At condo complex, Carolina Beach, NC – Distance traveled: 32 miles

November 26, 1986, Wednesday

We got up at eight thirty and moved our boat to the nearby municipal marina, so we could leave it until Friday. We will go to Uncle Bob's, at Southern Pines, for Thanksgiving. There was a McDonald's close by, and we ate a little breakfast there after tying up the boat. The weather was pretty good. I even took a girl, Kathy, for a ride in the dinghy. She said she was thinking about buying one. I think she was the dockmaster's wife. After Don hooked up the electric, I made cookies and brownies for Shelly and Chip's Christmas packages. Around four o'clock, I finished, and then we took a walk along the beach and went Christmas shopping. Just as we finished and were leaving the store, about a mile and a half away from the boat, it started pouring again. There we were with all of our gifts, getting soaked. If that wasn't bad enough, cars were coming by, splashing us with water from puddles. There were no sidewalks, it was dark, and there were no street lights—what a bummer. When we returned to the boat at seven, we ate leftover chicken and noodles. Later, we called Uncle Bob to tell him where we were. The phones were messed up, and it wasn't until eleven that we reached him. I tried to get my Christmas packages straightened around and separated: Chip's, Shelly's, Randy's, and the kids'. I also packaged the cookies and brownies for Shelly and Chip, and finally turned in at one thirty.

At marina, Carolina Beach, NC

November 27 & 28, 1986, Thursday & Friday, Thanksgiving

It was in the 60s and partly sunny today. Uncle Bob and my mom (she surprised us) came to the boat to pick us up. We served coffee and donuts on board and then headed to Southern Pines. Mom and my cousin, Scott, Uncle Bob's son, drove all night to get to Southern Pines. It was a wonderful day, and Uncle Bob made a tasty traditional Thanksgiving dinner. He served turkey, stuffing, etc. Everybody fell asleep after eating except Uncle Bob and me. I called Shelly in Urbana, made a fire in the fireplace, and fixed popcorn. I spent most of the evening wrapping Christmas gifts, so I could send them home with Mom.

The next morning, after breakfast, Don, Scott and Uncle Bob played golf. After the golf game, Uncle Bob drove Don around the area and showed him the Southern Pines and Pinehurst resort areas. Mom and I went shopping. She bought me three pairs of slacks and some tennis shoes as Christmas gifts–fantastic. She also bought some things for herself, and I bought a gift for my nephew, Nick's, birthday, which is on December 7. We lunched at a local place in Southern Pines, and didn't finish with our shopping until four-thirty. It was a treat to have a pleasant day with my mom. When we returned to the house, we all ate a dinner of steak and leftovers. I did laundry, and then Uncle Bob and Mom took us back to the boat. It was a two-hour drive. Don and I both enjoyed our time away, but were happy to get back to our boat. The boat has definitely become our home, and it was good to get home. We were both exhausted, but I stayed up late to put everything away. I am sure Mom and Uncle Bob had a tiring trip back to Southern Pines. Scott stayed by himself at Uncle Bob's for the evening.

At Uncle Bob's in Southern Pines, NC & *Robin Lee* at Marina, Carolina Beach, NC

November 29, 1986, Saturday

The day dawned with blue skies, and it was in the sixties. After paying our dockage and talking with the dockmaster about our dinghy, we left Carolina Beach a little after eight thirty.

We were having a pleasant day and enjoying the scenery when, around noon, I ran aground right in the middle of the channel. It was low tide and apparently the area needs dredging. The captain didn't get upset, because we were in the middle of the channel and the same thing could have happened to him.

We are "finding the bottom" too often. Our boat has a fin keel and draws 5'3" according to the specifications, and it probably draws closer to 5'6" with all the gear we have on board. The 30' Catalina is also made with a shoal draft keel and that version only draws 4'4". The shoal draft version is slightly less maneuverable, but that would be a small price to pay for 11" more clearance from the bottom.

We saw baby sea gulls standing next to their mom and people digging for clams today. Shortly before four thirty, having come about 45 miles, we docked at Inlet View Marina, near Tubbs Inlet, close to Calabash, North Carolina, and only about three miles north of the South Carolina border. The price of $0.50/foot isn't bad, except there aren't any showers, and it is in the middle of nowhere. We washed the deck and sail cover where the sea gulls had pooped. After a dinner of chicken paprikash and rice, we sat around and relaxed. I did cross-stitch while Don napped, and at nine o'clock we walked to a local gas station and made a call to Sister Carol. We mostly talked about Chip and his plans to go to Italy to study for one term. It was a long walk, and we didn't get back to the boat until midnight. The tidal range here is between five and seven feet, which is greater than further up the coast, and it was low tide when we returned to the boat. Don held me as I lowered myself down from the dock to the level of the boat deck. Our keel was stuck in the mud. It is weird to be below the dock and sitting in the mud. Floating docks in areas with a big tidal range are better. We went to bed shortly after returning from the walk.

Inlet View Marina, Home of the Turtles, Calabash, NC – Distance traveled: 44 miles

November 30, 1986, Sunday

We stayed put and slept late today because of weather conditions. It was raining, cold, and very windy. We added the monthly expenses, which again were too much: $1,125. Don made pancakes for brunch, and ham and scalloped potatoes for supper. We read and listened to the radio all day. I also wrote to Pam, Shelly, and Mom and did some cross-stitch. Don mostly read articles, which I cut out of *Cruising World* magazines. The tide came or went every six hours. We would be at dock level, and six hours later down in the mud, and then we would be raised up again. The weather forecast for tomorrow is for conditions similar to today. Maybe we will stay put again. We played crazy eights in the evening after the dishes were done. Don won all three games. That isn't unusual, he always wins. With the electric and kerosene heaters running, we were cozy all day.

Inlet View Marina, Home of the Turtles, Calabash, NC

December 1, 1986, Monday

We had heavy rain and lots of wind all night. The tide was two feet above the normal level due to the wind. We got off the boat about nine thirty in the morning and paid the dockmaster, who is also the owner. He let us use his car to go to Ocean Isle Shopping Center, which is about five miles away. We bought basic groceries, mailed letters, and then returned to the boat. It didn't rain much during the day, but the wind was very bad, approximately 30-40 mph all day. I sewed our wind sock, which needed repairing, and also did some cross-stitching. Don read most of the day.

We enjoyed a comfortable and lazy day, and around five we went to the marina and visited with the owner. He initiated us into the "Turtle Club." To gain admission, we needed to answer four questions. Each question suggests a vulgar answer, but the right answer isn't vulgar, and we needed to figure out the socially correct response. For example, one question was, "what does a man do standing up, that a woman does sitting down?" and the proper answer is, "Shake hands." We finally got all four correct, and he gave us a card saying we were "Turtles." It was silly, but the dockmaster/owner had fun with it, and so did we. It was originated by pilots during World War II as a drinking club. When a pilot, applying for membership, gave a wrong answer, he had to buy drinks for the members present.

I fixed linguini with white clam sauce and broccoli for dinner. Don did the dishes afterwards, and we watched a movie on a videotape. Later, we watched a little TV, and then went to bed at nine thirty.

Inlet View Marina, Home of the Turtles, Calabash, NC

CHAPTER FOUR

NC/SC BORDER to FORT MYERS, FL
Dec. 2, 1986 – Jan. 11, 1987

December 2, 1986, Tuesday

The forecast was for more windy and rainy weather, but we didn't want to sit for another day at the "home of the turtle" in the middle of nowhere. We left around seven and motored through the Myrtle Beach, South Carolina, area. It rained very hard, and the wind didn't let up.

Near Myrtle Beach, we passed under a huge cable car that was crossing over the waterway. It looked like a gondola for skiers, but was carrying golfers from the parking lot, on the ocean side of the waterway, to the 1st hole, on the mainland side. A huge power boat called *Seadozer Five* passed us, and I noticed it was from Toledo, Ohio. We called it on the marine radio and chatted with the skipper on channel 68 for a few minutes. His name is Gale Fisher. He is not the owner, but is moving the boat to Florida for the owner. He told us about his trip thus far and gave us a tip on an inexpensive marina in the Bahamas that he likes. The entire trip was scenic, with mossy cypress trees and lots of mistletoe growing in the treetops.

We anchored at Butler Island on the Waccamaw River at four thirty, ate sausage paprikash for supper, and spent the evening relaxing. The tidal current is strong here and changes direction by 180° every six hours, so we put out two anchors, one about 100' upstream (according to the current), and the other, about 100' downstream (according to the current). We backed down on both anchors. Of course, when the tidal current changed direction, the upstream anchor would become the downstream anchor, and vice versa.

We went to bed thinking everything was under control for the night, but around one o'clock we were awakened by an unusual sound that turned out to be one of our anchor lines slapping the side of the boat every few seconds. The captain got up and investigated. The boat was sideways to the current, and one anchor line was around the rudder and extending upstream, and the other anchor line was extending upstream from the bow. The anchor lines were so tight they didn't feel like lines at all. They felt like rigid steel reinforcing rods. Apparently, in the middle of the night, when the current was changing direction, (at which time neither anchor would have been holding the boat in place) the wind blew the boat around, and in the process, an anchor line became lodged in a narrow opening on top of the rudder, between the rudder and the hull of the boat.

Using the boat hook and all his strength, the captain was able to loop the anchor line that was running upstream from the rudder, around the winch for the starboard jib sheet. Then he attached a spare

A CATALINA 30 RUDDER

line as far out as he could reach, using a timber hitch, and hauled that line in with the winch for the port jib sheet up to where the timber hitch was tied. That created enough slack in the line that he could wrap the anchor line around the starboard jib winch a couple of times. Using that winch, he shortened the anchor line until the anchor broke out of the bottom, and the boat swung back, and was held by the anchor from the bow. Then he brought the other anchor on board. The whole process of figuring out the problem and getting the boat properly anchored took about three hours. There was still an anchor line wedged between the rudder and the hull, but the boat, the rudder, and the anchor lines were no longer under the extreme strain caused by the boat being sideways to the current. Remember, this was a dark and stormy night, and we were in the middle of nowhere, in alligator infested waters! The captain and I were so stirred up by the experience that we didn't get any more sleep. When the sun came up, the captain went to work on the line that was around the rudder. He even went down the swim-ladder to see if he could get it unhooked, but he couldn't. However, he succeeded in pulling all of it through the place where it was wedged, except the eye-splice, which he had to cut off. What a night! This is certainly not stress free living. [6]

Anchored off Butler Island, SC – Distance traveled: 54 miles

December 3, 1986, Wednesday

Boy, oh boy, last night was our worst experience yet! How bad can it get?

When things were finally straightened around, we sat down, ate some cereal, drank a cup of coffee, and had a heart-to-heart talk. We aired our thoughts and made the following observations: that we are learning an entirely new way of life; that the problems we must now deal with are so different from the problems we dealt with living on land, they are not even comparable; that last night was potentially dangerous, like the day on the Neuse River when the dinghy overturned; and that last night was stressful and not at all fun. The captain concluded that in time, if we use our heads and carefully think things through, we should get better at avoiding difficult situations, and that, if we don't, then we should give up the live-aboard life.

We then weighed anchor and headed for Georgetown, South Carolina. We motored all the way. It only took us 2 ¼ hours, and it would have been less if the wind and current hadn't been against us. We docked at the town dock, and ate lunch of broccoli and cheese soup and cheese croissant rolls. Then we set out to see Georgetown. Don mailed our Christmas box to Chip. We purchased, for each of the kids, 25 small, inexpensive presents, one for each day of December until Christmas; and marked the days on which they were to be opened. I had already sent Shelly's box home with Mom.

I found a material shop that would let me use their sewing machine to make a man overboard flag. We walked back to the boat and picked up the material with which to make it, and returned to the shop. I finished the flag in about an hour and a half. Don went to the grocery store during the time I was sewing. He walked back uptown and met me to walk back to the boat.

Georgetown has a shopping area near the waterfront with restaurants and other public places, and it also has a library near the waterfront. We like the town and have decided to

---

[6] Recently, at Lake Erie, I stopped at a marina and took this picture of an old, poorly maintained 1980 Catalina sitting on its cradle. At Butler Island our anchor line became lodged in the gap between the rudder and the hull which, along with some dragging of the anchors, caused the boat to get sideways to the current. The current pushed on the side of the boat and created so much tension on the anchor line that it was compressed and the line's diameter was reduced and it became wedged in that gap all the way to the axle (pintle).on which the rudder rotates.

stay an extra day, "to lick our wounds" and relax. We stopped at a restaurant we passed earlier in the day and ate a meal as part of the wound licking process. Pam and Bob Bartha gave us money for that kind of thing. The restaurant is called Daniel's and sits at the water's edge. It was clean and decorated for Christmas. We enjoyed the view of the evening sky, with its bright moon and silhouetted trees, and we liked the food. It was a treat, compliments of our friends.

We returned to the boat around six thirty, lit the heater, and while Don did dishes, I made up our bed in the dining area. The table can be lowered and made into a bed, and that's what we have done. We slept there, because we had moved lots of gear forward to the V-berth, so we could look for leaks in our continuing effort to find the source of a small amount of water that is going into our bilge. After that, we took long overdue showers at the marina. It felt great to be clean. The shower house was heated, and the showers had plenty of hot water. Needless to say, after showering, we went directly to bed and fell promptly asleep because we were so tired from being up all night the night before.

Marina, Georgetown, SC - Distance traveled: 12 miles

December 4, 1986, Thursday

We spent the entire day doing chores on the boat. Don tied a temporary loop in the anchor line to replace the eye splice he cut off; he checked for damage to the rudder, but found none; he checked the water system for leaks, and found none; and he did sundry other things. I ran the sweeper, washed down the boat, wrote to Shelly, and did a few other chores.

We are tied up next to a single-handed sailor. [A single-handed sailor is one who sails by himself.] He is originally from Port Clinton, Ohio. He graduated in electrical engineering from the U. S. Naval Academy at Annapolis. He spent four years in the navy and then worked as an electrical engineer in civilian life, but decided to become a live-aboard. He has been living aboard and cruising for five years. For the past two years he's been working as an electrical engineer here in Georgetown at the paper mill while living on his boat.

The water in the Georgetown area is brackish, and because of that, the guy tied up next to us has seen a large variety of fish and sea animals here. He says he has seen porpoises and crappies, to name a couple of very different critters.

About four, we moved to the municipal docks, which are free. The weather was clear, cool, and sunny. The town has one drawback. There is a bad odor given off by the paper mill that can be smelled throughout the town. We went to a local pool hall, and Don played a fellow two games of pool; he won one and lost one. Then we went window shopping on the street from the pool hall to the Grab Bag, the shop where I made the man-overboard flag. We stopped at another restaurant, and each of us drank a glass of wine. When we went back home, I worked on making Christmas decorations from fresh holly that I picked in a park close to the town's clock tower and ribbon I purchased. Don made chop suey and rice for dinner.

Town dock, Georgetown, SC

December 5, 1986, Friday

We got underway to McClennanville at seven o'clock in the morning, but I went back to bed and slept until eight thirty. I didn't sleep well during the night. The trip to McClellanville was pleasant and very scenic. I was only at the helm for an hour and a half, and that made it better yet. We arrived at noon, and the first thing we did was to take a walk. McClellanville is enchanting, with big old houses and huge live oak trees covered with Spanish moss. It reminded us of scenes of plantation life in *Gone with the Wind* and other pictures about the Old South. We got a lift to the grocery store and back to the boat. Then we walked to the Fish House to buy seafood for our dinner. We bought a half-pound of shrimp and a pound of flounder which Don cooked. Both were excellent. After dinner, we went aboard a 50' Taiwanese sailboat that was tied up near-by us and visited with the two guys on board, Bill and John. We looked at their charts of the Caribbean islands. The day was beautiful and sunny, but it got very cold in the evening. We had a snack of hot chocolate and cookies and then went to bed. It was "toasty-warm" inside the boat with our wonderful, new kerosene heater!

Marina, McClellanville, SC - Distance traveled: 33 miles

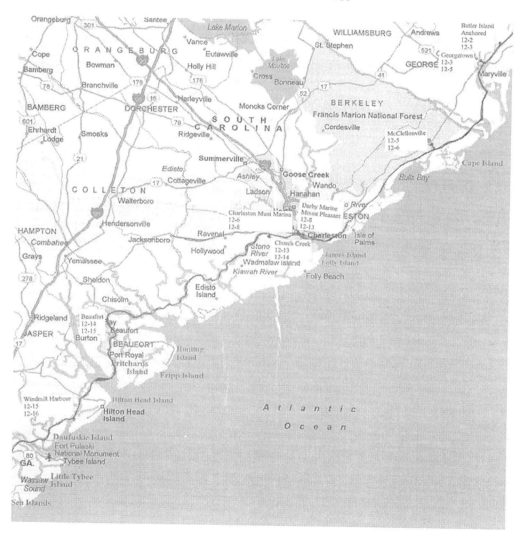

December 6, 1986, Saturday

We slept in until seven thirty; then I got up and made muffins. After eating a couple of muffins, I went to the shower house while Don finished off the muffins. This shower house was warm and had plenty of hot water. We were underway at eight thirty. We lucked out again with the weather. It was a beautiful day, although it was cold in the morning. I just love warm weather! I guess we will have more of it when we get farther south. Then, I will probably be complaining that it is too hot.

We have seen a lot of new housing and houses under construction along the ocean in North Carolina and South Carolina. That seems foolish to us. It is only a matter of time before a lot of those houses get blown or washed away by hurricanes. I hope we aren't expected to pay for the losses out of our insurance pool.

We arrived in Charleston around four in the afternoon and decided to put in at the Charleston Municipal Marina. We were held up at the entrance because the presidential yacht, *Sequoia,* was just coming out. The *Sequoia* was used by several presidents, starting with Herbert Hoover and ending with Jimmy Carter. It is 104 feet long and, of course, luxurious. It is no longer in service as the presidential yacht; it was sold by President Carter.

We had a difficult time docking at the marina because there was a strong current inside the marina. The marina is in the Ashley River, and the reason there is a current in the marina is that the marina walls don't go all the way to the bottom of the river, and therefore, the river's current flows through the marina. The Ashley is a tidal river, so its current is affected by the tide as well as the natural current created by the flow of rainwater toward the ocean. When we were docking, the tide was ebbing. The tidal current, combined with the natural current, produced a current of a couple of miles per hour through the marina. The slip we were assigned to by the dockmaster was at the downriver end of the marina and was in line (parallel) with the current. This meant that the captain had to go along the narrow row of slips where our slip was located, crabbing our way to our slip with the bow pointing a little upriver in order to keep the current from pushing us into the boats docked on the downriver side. When we reached our slip, he had to turn the boat quickly downstream, get in the slip, and stop the boat before hitting the concrete wall at the back of the dock. A sailboat isn't very maneuverable in close quarters compared to a boat with twin engines or even a boat with a single outboard engine, and a sailboat does poorly in reverse. *Robin Lee is* underpowered, and that added to the problem. It wasn't pretty, but we succeeded in docking without doing any damage to our boat, other boats, or the dock, although we did "make contact" with a 60-foot Chris Craft and with the back wall.

We are docked next to a young man by the name of Brian, originally from Cleveland Ohio, who is here for his fourth winter doing free-lance sign painting. He is living at the marina on his 26' wooden sailboat. We visited with him briefly and then went back to our boat and ate dinner. Dinner consisted of leftover sausage paprikash again. After dinner, we met a man by the name of Martin Pritchard who, along with his wife, delivers boats. Owners hire them to take their boats south for the winter and then hire them to take the boats back north for the summer. They live in Saint Petersburg. He gave us a lift to the Market Street area. Don and I then walked around town. We must have walked four miles; it's a great city to visit. We stopped at Swenson's and ate the best banana split ever, with real whipped cream. It was exceptionally good, but was very expensive. After we finished the ice cream, we called Clayton and gave him a progress report. We walked back to the boat, which took forever, and watched Saturday Night Live and went to bed.

Charleston Municipal Marina, Charleston, SC - Distance traveled: 45 miles

December 7, 1986, Sunday

It was sunny and in the high 50s, a lovely day. We slept late, and then; at around eleven thirty, we went out to see more of the city. We took a self-guided walking and sightseeing tour and also watched the annual Christmas parade. After that, we continued walking around the historic part of town, and didn't get home until four. Don fixed dinner while I washed *The Lincoln.*

Each day we were at the municipal marina, the dockmaster came by to ask us if we were "staying and paying." He's the first dockmaster we've encountered who was "on the ball." He is a friendly fellow who apparently likes his job.

We are both very tired, so, after eating dinner and washing the dishes, we will relax, watch a little TV, and go to bed. We are staying another day, so we can have someone from the Catalina Boat Company fix the leak, which we finally located as being near the diesel fuel tank.

Charleston Municipal Marina, Charleston, SC

December 8, 1986, Monday

It was another day of great weather. I can't believe we've had so many in a row. We woke up around eight thirty, and I did laundry since a laundromat was close by. Don called the Catalina Company, and they recommended that we take the boat to Darby Marine, in Mt. Pleasant, which is nearby, and have them deal with the leak. We spent the afternoon trying to determine, with the help the workmen at Darby Marine, where the water was coming from.

Don has been very concerned about the leak. It's not a bad leak; the bilge pump only runs a couple of times a day. We are following advice given to us back in Oswego, New York, from a sailor who has cruised extensively. Don told him that we were planning to cruise for a couple of years and asked him if he had any advice for us. His advice was that if we developed a small problem, we should fix it before it becomes a big problem. He said that often "cruisers" don't grasp the difference between living on land, where help is readily available, and living on the water, where it isn't. He said: "You can't just pull off the road, stop, and call AAA when you have a problem, and trying to fix the problem at sea in bad weather, with the boat rolling and pitching, is not an easy thing to do, and is impossible if you don't have the parts or the right tools. Furthermore, you are in an inhospitable environment that can kill you. So, if you have a concern, don't put off checking it out—do it right away! If you find that you have a problem, fix it! 'Murphy's Law' rules the seas and says: 'whatever can go wrong, will go wrong, and it will go wrong at the worst possible time.' You need to live by that law, which means that you need to find and correct anything that could go wrong." I'm sure the guy's advice was sound, and I'm glad my captain is following it.

We finally took a walk at about five thirty through the business district close to the marina, and then came home and ate cornbread and a bacon and butter bean casserole that Don made yesterday. This place has a clean, well equipped shower house, which was a surprise since the marina doesn't cater to transients. We lucked out.

Darby Marine, Mt. Pleasant, SC - Distance traveled: 8 miles

December 9, 1986, Tuesday

The Darby Marine repairmen have determined that the water is coming in around the strut that holds the propeller shaft in place. This is what my captain has suspected since we first realized there was a leak, back in Cape May. To fix it will require fiberglass work. We have bagged all of our shelved items in preparation for sanding and fiberglass repairs to the hull. Our sleeping arrangements have become lousy. Last night, we slept in the dining area. It's kind of cramped, but it's the way it has to be until the leak is fixed. We have a bunch of our gear stored in the V-berth, and the quarter berth has the fuel tank sitting on it—what a pain. We were hauled out today and are up on chocks. *Robin Lee is* high and dry like a fish out of water.

I took a long walk to the grocery and returned carrying two heavy bags—not fun. I shouldn't have done it. In addition, I took the dinghy out for a ride and decided to row it instead of using the motor. It was fun exploring, but my arms and shoulders are sore from rowing in the wind and current; next time I'll use the motor. Cooking would be a pain with things the way they are, so we ate at Pizza Hut tonight. It's comfortable on the boat when everything is in its proper place, but not now; so we walked until time for bed. I hope the repairs don't take long.

Darby Marine, Mt. Pleasant, SC

December 10, 1986, Wednesday

What a mess this place is! We will surely be glad to have this experience behind us and be back on our way again. We left the boat at ten to go sightseeing while the repair people did the fiber glass work. We walked to the Mt Pleasant Pharmacy and ate breakfast at their soda fountain. Then we caught a bus and went to downtown Charleston and looked around at the slave market again. We returned to the boat at three and started cleaning up the mess since the sanding and fiber glass work was done. I continued to straighten things up while Don fixed the meal and did the dishes.

While we were gone today, there was a murder-suicide here in Mt. Pleasant. It was a husband and wife with domestic problems—a big news event for this small town. All the locals were talking about it. It happened at a store close by us, one we had passed on the bus just a few minutes before it happened.

Darby Marine, Mt. Pleasant, SC

December 11, 1986, Thursday

It rained a lot today, off and on. The workmen put the boat back in the water. I stayed aboard while the lift picked us up off the chocks and lowered us into the water. After doing some straightening up on the boat, we made another visit to the Mt Pleasant Pharmacy's soda counter for a chocolate milk shake, and then enjoyed a leisurely walk looking at lots of neatly restored homes. We ate leftover chop suey and watched some TV in the evening. We went to bed early, as usual. We are rafted off another boat this evening. The workmen think they should have the boat completely finished tomorrow.

Darby Marine, Mt. Pleasant, SC

December 12, 1986, Friday

This should be our last night in Mt Pleasant. Boy, did it rain today; there were almost two inches of water in the dinghy when we emptied it. I didn't get off the boat all day. I worked the entire day finishing the job of cleaning up and getting everything put back in its place. What a job. When I was done, I sat down and celebrated by drinking a Coke. After my break, I copied recipes onto cards for the recipe box. I have many to copy from newspapers and magazines. Tonight, we ate leftover spaghetti and peas for dinner. We watched a little TV, and I wrote letters to Cousin Amy and Uncle Bob, thanking them for the good times we enjoyed at their places. I also wrote Shirley at the Grab Bag Store in Georgetown, thanking her for the use of the sewing machine. The bill for the repair of our boat was $509.50. We thought it would be a lot higher. We stayed up late tonight and watched Johnny Carson.

Darby Marine, Mt. Pleasant, SC

December 13, 1986, Saturday

This morning we walked to a local place for breakfast. We couldn't leave Darby Marine until the tidal current was favorable, and that didn't happen until about eleven thirty. It was a beautiful day with sunny, clear blue skies, but cool—only in the 50s. We arrived at a place to anchor in Church Creek, at mile maker # 487, around four thirty. The place is in the middle of nowhere. It is just a little tributary to the main channel on the waterway in a marsh with lots of water-grass and no trees, but it was recommended as a suitable place for overnight anchoring by Mac, whom we met in Deltaville aboard *Mafoogie*.

When we went from Charleston to Mt. Pleasant, we traveled north. Mt. Pleasant is on the north side of Charleston Bay. Today we went south again, and are about 15 miles south of Charleston.

Tonight, we are relaxing and reading. Earlier, I did some cross-stitch. I am reading the book, *Chesapeake* by James Michener. Don is reading *The Life and Story of Abe Lincoln*. Don fixed tostados for dinner, and I made tapioca pudding for dessert. It is cool, but we have the heater running and are very comfortable.

Anchored in Church Creek, SC (mile marker # 487) - Distance traveled: 28 miles

December 14, 1986, Sunday

We left our anchorage at eight, after getting the anchors untangled. Yes, our anchoring

system again failed to work properly. This time we attached one anchor at the bow and another at the stern. When the tidal current changed direction during the night, a line managed to get around the keel. How discouraging! However, it wasn't nearly as hard to undo as it was when we were at Butler Island. The captain thinks we need to use more chain and less line in order to solve the problem. We only have five feet of chain on each anchor. He also thinks that if we had a shoal draft keel, instead of our long, narrow fin keel, we wouldn't have had this problem.

It was very cold last night, but today it is clear and in the high 40s. We went to Beaufort, South Carolina, (pronounced "Bewe-fort") and tied up at the Downtown Marina at about three thirty. Then we went for a walk to see the town. It's a charming place, with beautiful old homes on streets lined with moss-covered live oak trees. We hope to come here again.

At the marina, we met a likeable couple, Donna and Bill Jordon, from Richmond, Virginia. Like us, they are cruising for an indefinite time aboard their boat, a 37 foot Taiwanese boat named *Orchid Boat*. We visited on their boat for an hour or so and then came home, ate dinner, and did laundry. I gave Don a beard trim and haircut and also cut my hair a little. I was up until one o'clock trying to get the laundry done. The dryer didn't work, so I had to take all the wet clothes back to the boat. I wrote Shelly while I was doing the laundry.

Downtown Marina, Beaufort, SC - Distance traveled: 53 miles

December 15, 1986, Monday

Our spirits are high today. We feel as though we've been refreshed by beautiful Beaufort. We enjoyed home-baked cinnamon rolls at a local place this morning, and then shopped for groceries. Don called Jane and asked her to send our mail to Daytona and also called Chip. I called an Achilles dealer about replacing the dinghy dodger that we lost in the Neuse River. I also talked to Randy. Everyone is OK at home. We called Sister Carol yesterday; they leave for Florida on Friday and we plan to get together with them. We met another couple while trying once more to dry the laundry, Paul and Nell, who live aboard a 27-foot sailboat, *Double Fantasy*. I hope we see them, as well as Donna and Bill Jordan from *Orchid Boat* again, somewhere along our way.

We motored in the rain to Hilton Head Island, about 20 miles from Beaufort. We put in at Windmill Harbor Marina, an exclusive place that has its own lock, and offers docking to boaters in the pool behind the lock, free from worry about the water level rising and falling because of the tide. Docks cost $1,800/year for a boat our size. That's expensive, but the place offers a lot of amenities, including a pool, Jacuzzi, and sauna for all guests. It rained most of the night. We took showers but were too late for the pool and the other amenities; they were closed. We read and spent a quiet evening aboard the *Robin Lee*.

Windmill Harbor, Hilton Head, SC - Distance traveled: 20 miles

December 16, 1986, Tuesday

It was cloudy and in the 50s most of the day. We walked around the Windmill Harbor resort and visited with Kyle, the dockmaster, before leaving. We didn't go sightseeing on Hilton Head Island because the cost of renting a car would have been too much for our budget We headed for Savannah at eleven thirty and arrived at Thunderbolt Marina, at about four fifteen, after an easy trip. We did run aground once, even though we were in the channel. It was at low tide, and apparently some dredging is needed. At the marina, we met and briefly visited with a couple from Fish Creek, Wisconsin. They were surprised that we had sailed up there from Ohio last summer. We ate barbequed spareribs and salad and, after cleaning up the mess, took a walk. I called Mom and Shelly tonight. I sure miss Shelly, and I hope she is doing all right.

Thunderbolt Marina, Savannah, GA - Distance traveled: 26 miles

December 17, 1986, Wednesday

Today was sunny, off and on, in the low 60s. We awoke at six in the morning, left the boat at six thirty, and took a bus into Savannah to sightsee. We ate breakfast, boarding house style, at Mrs. Wilkes' Boarding House. It was featured on *The Today Show* last year. We happened to be watching it at the time, and decided it would be fun to go there someday. We were required to carry our dirty dishes to the kitchen after we were finished with our meal—a boarding house rule. It was fun, and we had a big meal for only $3.00 per person.

Before breakfast, we were able to spend some time sightseeing on our own. After breakfast, we went into the visitor center, saw a slide show, and took a tour in a van with a guide. It is a charming historic city with a variety of architectural styles.

We returned to the marina at one o'clock and then left. The marina was very clean and well maintained. It was nicely decorated and even had wallpapered and carpeted showers. Dockage included a morning paper and a box of donuts, which is most unusual. The dockmaster, however, was very unfriendly. Approximately 15 miles south of Savannah, we found a spot to anchor in the Vernon River. At about four fifteen, we anchored and got the boat prepared for the night. Don fixed *coq au vin* for dinner. While we were on the tour in Savannah, a local news show filmed us going into one of the churches that we visited. Our evening's entertainment was videotaping us on Channel Three's, six o'clock news, getting off our tour bus earlier in the day. The evening was quiet and peaceful, and we didn't have any problems with the anchors. Don went to bed early. I stayed up and watched Hotel Dynasty, the news, and Johnny Carson. The reception was decent. Our TV reception is not always good, especially when the boat swings around while we are at anchor. I also addressed Christmas cards I purchased at the marina.

Anchored in the Vernon River, a few miles south of Savannah, GA - Distance traveled: 16 miles

December 18, 1986, Thursday

We were underway from our anchoring spot in the Vernon River at seven forty-five and anchored in Cattle Pen Creek on Saint Catherine's Island at one fifteen in the afternoon. It was a pleasant day with a little sun in the late afternoon, and we had a relaxing evening. We listened to Christmas music on the radio.

I wanted to call my brother, Roger, on his 38th birthday. I also wanted to call Sister Carol to find out if Don's niece, Connie Montgomery, had her baby. She was supposed to have it today. I haven't gotten the baby's cross-stitch project done yet. Because we are anchored in the boondocks, no phone is available. We ate leftovers for dinner, and chocolate-chip cookies that I made for dessert. We mostly read and wrote Christmas cards in the evening. It rained a little and the wind blew, but not hard enough to be worrisome.

Anchored in Cattle Pen Creek, Saint Catherine's Island, GA - Distance traveled: 32 miles

December 19, 1986, Friday

We weighed anchor at seven forty-five and headed south. Vern worked well part of the day. I wrote cards, did a little cross-stitching, and continued to read *Chesapeake*.

It was a nice day, with blue skies and lots of sunshine. We were concerned whether we would be able to make it to our destination, Golden Isle Marina at Saint Simon's Island, before dark. However, we arrived at four forty-five, having completed the 57-mile trip in nine hours. I hosed down the boat, and then we drank a glass of wine. We ate at Emmeline and Hessie's, a restaurant Joe and Lois Dixon recommended. We could only afford soup and salad, but we won't tell them.

I called my brother, Roger, and belatedly wished him a happy birthday. I also found out from Sister Carol that yesterday Connie Montgomery had a new baby girl, Mallory. I went to bed after writing a few postcards. I'm getting a sore throat.

Golden Isle Marina, Saint Simon's Island, GA - Distance traveled: 57 miles

December 20, Saturday

It was drizzling when we left Golden Isle Marina at nine this morning. My throat was very sore by this time. I felt miserable and, to make matters worse; it was dark and dreary. We only went nine miles and put in at Jekyll Island. Boy, was I glad. I am happy to have a day off, especially since I don't feel good. Dockage is only $0.40 per foot per night, $12.00 for us— cheap for a resort area. After we were situated at the dock, we walked to the post office in town, bought stamps, and mailed some of our Christmas cards. We also got a map, and walked around on the island and along the beach. I collected some shells for a Christmas wreath I am making. Don took a picture of me with summer flowers and Christmas decorations in the background. It seems strange to me that people decorate for Christmas here just as we do up north, even though it's a warm climate.

We rented a tandem bike for two hours and rode around on the island. The area is just

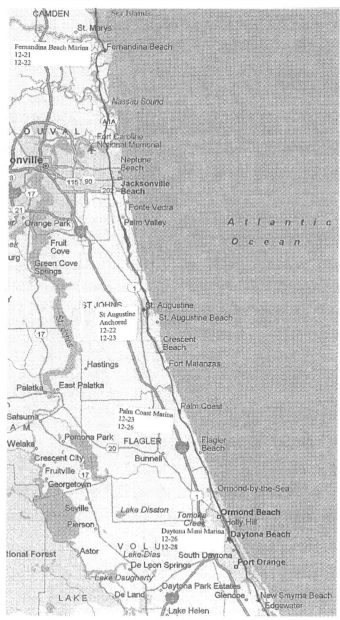

beautiful. In the 1920s, many of the famous and wealthy people built summer homes here. Some of them are now being restored, including Rockefeller's. Some of the homes are referred to as cottages, but even those look like they have about 20 rooms.

On the way back to the boat, we bought fresh shrimp and fish. I washed the black soot from our diesel exhaust off the boat's transom while Don fixed dinner. Later, we read and wrote more Christmas cards and then walked to the marina office and called Betty and Clayton. We also took video of the shrimpers with their day's catch. We enjoyed our day off at Jekyll Island.

Jekyll Island Marina, Jekyll Island, GA - Distance traveled: 9 miles

December 21, 1986, Sunday, The first day of winter

We left Jekyll Island at about seven forty-five heading for Fernandina Beach, Florida. Our route took us through King's Bay, which was a confusing area, but we made it through without straying off the waterway. We arrived at Fernandina Beach at about one o'clock. The marina there charges $0.65/foot plus

$3.00 for electric, which is more than we like to pay. However, the marina is well protected from wave action and has floating docks, and so we didn't have to worry about the tide and enjoyed a comfortable night. Fernandina Beach is also a nice little town. I guess those are the reasons why the marina can charge that much.

At the marina, we talked with a couple, Dave and Marian, on a Cape Dory 30-foot motor sailor, called *Meibs Too*.

We walked through town, and then returned to fix fish stew with carrots. Don made it in the pressure cooker. I sure am lucky to have a husband who likes to cook and does it so well. About everything he fixes is great. After dinner, we took a walk to get ice cream. We did the usual things in the evening, but tonight we included an oil and filter change to our routine. We didn't settle down for bed until eleven.

Today was the first day of winter. The sun was only out for a short time, and it was a very cool day. It was also our first day in Florida. Here we are in Florida, and it's still cold. The captain now definitely agrees that the kerosene heater was a smart purchase.

At marina, Fernandina Beach, FL – Distance traveled: 34 miles

December 22, 1986, Monday

Well, there was a nor'easter blowing 20-30 knots the entire day. This type of situation always puts the captain on edge. We started this morning at about seven thirty and traveled all the way to Saint Augustine, but had a difficult time after getting there. The "Bridge of Lions," a drawbridge in Saint Augustine that crosses the Intracoastal Waterway, opens every hour on the half-hour and stays open for about five minutes. We tried to make the four thirty opening, but didn't get to the bridge until four thirty-five. We talked to the bridge operator on the radio and asked him, practically begged him, to keep it open for us, pleading that the high winds and darkness would make it difficult for us to maneuver for an hour until he opened it again at five thirty. Our pleading didn't move him, and he closed the bridge as we were approaching it and were only about 100 yards away. Consequently, we made circles in a small area just north of the bridge for an hour, in 20-30 knot winds, in the dark, and then went through the bridge at five thirty; that was a stressful hour. I think I noticed the captain motioning to the bridge operator with one of his fingers as we passed through it, but I'm not sure. We went to a marina just south of the bridge and tied up, but the location was terrible so far as protection was concerned. The waves threatened to push our boat onto the floating dock. The wind was incredible, and the boat seemed to try to rear up onto the dock like a bucking bronco trying to get out of its stall. The dockmaster, who had worked there for eight years, told us that his location just wasn't safe in a strong nor'easter. He said we should go out and anchor in the basin, which we did. We took turns standing an all-night anchor-watch because the anchorage was crowded, and the wind was strong. During the night, our anchor line managed to get around the rudder again. It was a lousy night.

Anchored in Yacht Basin, Saint Augustine, FL- Distance traveled: 59 miles

December 23, 1986, Tuesday

After being up half of the night on anchor watch, I finally went to sleep about three and slept until five thirty. We left the anchorage at seven thirty this morning. The conditions were improved, but we couldn't find a suitable dock, so we didn't stay to sightsee. We headed for Daytona. We will see Saint Augustine on the way back, or by car, someday. Saint Augustine was not a pleasant experience, from the time we got there to when we left.

Don's sister, Carol, and her husband, David, are vacationing near Sarasota, on Florida's West Coast. They are staying at Aloha Kai, a condominium resort on Siesta Key that is managed by Don's cousin, Norbert Chase and his wife, Barbara. Our plan was to go to Daytona, rent a car, and drive to Siesta Key to spend Christmas with them. It started to rain hard at about eleven, when we were near Palm Coast, about 30 miles north of Daytona, and we decided to stop there instead of going on to Daytona. We will rent a car at Palm Coast to drive to Siesta Key instead of at Daytona. Dockage was a bit high again, at $0.65/foot/day, but we took a dock for a three-day stay over Christmas. So, for the time being, we are living at Palm Coast, Florida.

At the marina office, I made arrangements to rent a car for Christmas day, so we could drive to Siesta Key. We stayed on board for the rest of the day and night due to excessive wind and continuous rain. We ate leftovers for dinner, and I made brownies for dessert. We used up everything in the refrigerator.

Palm Coast Marina, Palm Coast, FL- Distance traveled: 26 miles

December 24, Wednesday

We got up at nine and spent a little time watching Dolly Parton on the *Phil Donahue Show,* and then I did laundry. Afterwards, I took some canned goods out of the locker under the V-berth to restock the galley and put our winter clothes in bags, and stowed them under the quarter berth. I made tuna & macaroni salad for lunch. Don did a few things on the boat, and we both visited with people on the docks.

At about four, we took the water taxi to the Sheridan Hotel. We each had a drink and talked to the employees at the Sheridan and then walked along the beach and looked around. Palm Coast is just developing; what has been done so far is luxurious. We think it will become a popular destination.

We came back to the boat and relaxed. While we were watching a Christmas special, *The Messiah,* we heard loud Christmas music and went above to find out what was happening. A boat decorated for Christmas and playing Christmas music was going by

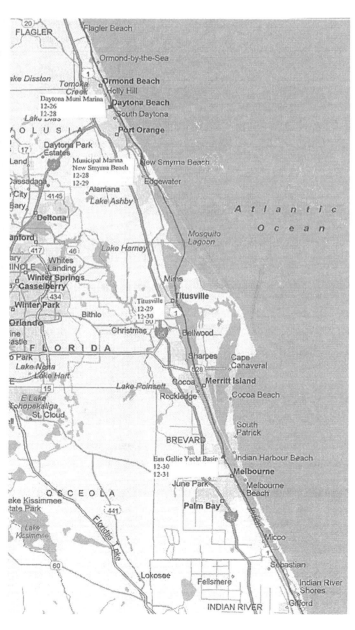

the marina. In the evening, I fixed popcorn, and we went to bed early. It was a very relaxing, easy day. We needed one after our ordeal in Saint Augustine.

Palm Coast Marina, Palm Coast, FL

December 25, 1986, Thursday, Christmas

We left early and drove to Sarasota. It's a three-hour drive, and it went quickly. Traffic wasn't bad, but was fast. We needed to drive about 70 mph just to keep up. We enjoyed a good visit with Carol and David and their son, Craig, as well as with Norbert and Barbara and some of Don's distant relatives. We called Shelly and Chip and wished them a Merry Christmas. We spent about two hours having a big meal, and then took a walk on the beautiful Siesta Key beach. After that, we drove up to see the condominium on Longboat Key that Don's parents' formerly owned. They bought it in 1968, shortly before Don's dad, Judge Clayton Rose, Sr., retired from the Franklin County Common Pleas Court, Division of Domestic Relations and Juvenile Delinquency. They sold it soon after his dad suffered a stroke in 1975. On the way back we stopped at Harborside Moorings, on Longboat Key, and visited with Hope and Harry Eilers aboard *Passages*. We last saw them in the Chesapeake Bay. They are staying on their boat at the marina for the winter. It was fun to see them again; they are an enjoyable couple. In the evening, we ate at the condo at Aloha Kai that Carol and David rented. It is right on Siesta Key beach, one of the most beautiful beaches in the world. We spent the night there. It was the first time in three months we slept in a real bed. (At Uncle Bob's house, during our Thanksgiving getaway, we slept on the floor.)

It was sunny and in the 60s in Sarasota. We had a great Christmas.

At Carol and David's, Aloha Kai, Siesta Key, FL, *Robin Lee* at Palm Coast Marina, Palm Coast, FL

December 26, 1986, Friday

We left Siesta Key at five in order to get the rental car back on time. Before we returned the car, we did have time to go to Daytona to buy groceries and pick up the mail, which Jane sent. Then we drove to Palm Coast and turned in the car. A man at the car rental agency drove us to the Palm Coast Marina.

We left our dock at Palm Coast at eleven forty-five and headed for Daytona. We arrived at the Daytona Municipal Marina at four thirty. After we got settled in at the dock (the boat properly tied up, the water hose connected and the electric plugged in), we ate dinner and then went for a walk. On the way back to our boat, we found *Mafoogie* in the marina; Mac and Betty were on board. They are the older couple who have been live-aboards for most of their lives whom we met in Deltaville. They are a super couple, and both obviously know a lot about boating. It was fun to be able to visit with them again and thank them for the helpful tips they gave us in Deltaville, such as places to anchor on the way down here. They told us in Deltaville that they spend their winters in this marina, and that was why we picked it as our destination.

When we returned to our place, I did the dishes, and at ten, we went to bed. We were both tired, but happy to be in Daytona.

Daytona Municipal Marina, Daytona, FL - Distance traveled: 32 miles

December 27, 1986, Saturday

We started the day by walking to the Saturday morning Farmer's Market where we bought some fresh fruit and vegetables, a sweet roll, and miscellaneous items. I phoned Shelly, who is on vacation in California with her friend, Kiki. It sounded as though they are having a busy ten-day vacation with Kiki's family. We ate breakfast out and then browsed in a used-book store.

Carol and David invited us to come back to Siesta Key, and we said we would see if we could. I tried to arrange it, but couldn't work it out, so I phoned Carol and told her we would not be coming. I was disappointed, but Don was lukewarm on the whole idea because of the car rental expense and because he thinks we need to keep moving along.

I rowed over to *Mafoogie* in the *The Lincoln* and visited with them awhile. Don spent the afternoon opening mail. I did that yesterday while traveling. I received a letter from Shelly; Christmas cards; and a new tape and tape player, which were gifts from Pam and Bob. We listened to the tape at dinner last night. Today was a cloudy and cold day, so it was nice just to relax, safely docked. Mac and Betty gave us a coupon for eating at a local buffet for dinner, so we did that. I told Don that it was in lieu of my fixing him a birthday dinner. Tomorrow is his birthday. The food wasn't terrific, but we both pigged out. On the walk home to the boat we stopped at *Mafoogie* to return the coupon book and say good-bye to them.

Don finished paying the bills and dealing with the rest of the mail, and I fiddled around with the wreath of shells that I have made; then we went to bed.
Daytona Municipal Marina, Daytona, FL

December 28, 1986, Sunday, Don's 48th birthday
The day was cool, with no rain. We awakened early, but the wind sounded strong, so we took our time getting up and then ate the sweet roll that we bought at the farmer's market. Today is Don's birthday; he is 48. We left the marina at about nine forty-five, after buying fuel. We motored to New Smyrna Beach, only 16 miles south. After tying up at a little past noon and getting situated, we walked to a local fish restaurant for lunch and split a grouper dinner. Grouper is a mild-tasting fish. We then walked on to the grocery store, purchased a few things, and came home. I read and took a nap. We ate leftovers heated on the Kero-Sun heater; it works well for a one pot-dinner and is convenient if it's on anyway.

We met some live-aboards today from Hicksville, Ohio. They owned a trailer park there in 1975 and knew Uncle Bob Craig, who practiced veterinary medicine in Hicksville for many years. We went to bed at nine thirty.

We have heard favorable things about Florida's West Coast from other cruising sailors. Several have told us that the west coast is better than the east coast for cruising, so we have decided to see for ourselves. There are two ways to get there from here. We could continue down the east coast to the Keys, follow the Keys to Key West, and then head north to Naples. The other way is to go across the Okeechobee Waterway, which goes from Stuart, Florida, on the east coast to Fort Myers, on the west coast. The Okeechobee Waterway follows the Saint Lucie River on the east side, crosses Lake Okeechobee and then follows the Caloosahatchee River to the west coast. It is the much shorter way, and we hear it's an enjoyable trip, so we have decided to go that way. We will continue on the Intracoastal Waterway until we get to Stuart, about 25 miles south of Fort Pierce, and then make our way over to where the Okeechobee Waterway begins.
At marina, New Smyrna Beach, FL - Distance traveled: 16 miles

December 29, Monday, Marina
Starting at eight, we motored to Titusville and tied up for the night. *Kracken* from Fish Creek, Wisconsin, and *New Morning* were there also. We have seen them several times since leaving Thunderbolt where we first met. The showers were very small and buggy; we used

them anyway. I added up our December expenses. So far, we have spent $270 on dock fees, $130 eating out, (snacks and desserts, mostly), $175 on groceries, $500 on repairs, $60 on car rental. That totals $1,135–way too much. I surely hope we can do better in the months to come.

Titusville, FL - Distance traveled: 31 miles

December 30, Tuesday

One of the things that has made our cruise interesting is that each place we've been has been very different from the others. Each section of the waterway has its own

characteristics. For example, Georgia has marshes; North Carolina has swamps; Florida has palm trees; and Georgia has live oak trees covered with Spanish moss. The types of buildings we have been gazing at are also different. Sailing past old homes with verandas in South Carolina and Georgia is a very different experience from passing by the skyscrapers of New York City. Watching a pelican diving for fish along the waterway in Florida is quite different than gazing at thousands of masts sticking up from sailboats in Annapolis. Even the tides are different in the different areas. Some of the areas we have been in have very little tide, a foot or two, and on the other hand, we encountered nine foot-tides in Georgia. At Jekyll Island, Georgia, we were sitting in mud at low tide. The water surrounding the boat was completely gone, and the nearest water was about 20 feet away. Each area we've been in is unique, and that adds a lot to our enjoyment.

We started today at nine and stopped at Cocoa Beach for a short time thinking we would sightsee, but the docking conditions were less than desirable, so we gave up on the idea. We went on to the Melbourne area and tied up at a marina called Eau Gallie Yacht Basin. It is one of the best marinas we've seen. It's quiet; the people are friendly; and it's in a pretty area. They let us use their car, which they call the Blue Bomb, and we drove to the E&B Marine Store in Melbourne. We bought two 30' sections of chain for our anchors. When we came back, Don fixed dinner. After dinner, the people in the boat next to us, Betty and John, invited us over for champagne and ice cream, a weird combination. She reminded both Don and me of a nursing friend back home, including her looks, speech and mannerisms. Later in the evening, she came aboard to see the layout of our boat. They are on a 34-foot Cal sailboat. We had eaten a big dinner prior to going over to visit: marinated steaks; fresh steamed cauliflower with cheese sauce; and a salad. We squeezed in the ice cream and champagne. Boy, did we consume the calories tonight.

Eau Gallie Yacht Basin, Melbourne, FL - Distance traveled: 41 miles

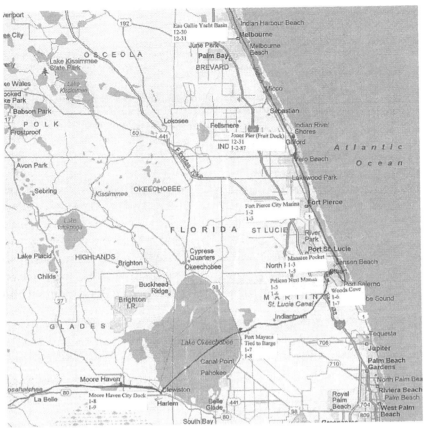

December 31, 1986, Wednesday, New Year's Eve

It was cloudy and cool, on the last day of the year and lightly sprinkled early in the day. Don went to the hardware store this morning and found chain there which was considerably cheaper than we paid at E&B Marine. Such is life.

The weather worsened as the day went on. It was nice of Don to stay at the helm all day in the rain. We would have enjoyed the area more without the wind and rain. Along the way, we passed Pelican Island, and true to its name, there were plenty of pelicans there (they were white pelicans) and many other birds such as egrets and herons. It was named by President Theodore Roosevelt, and he made it a bird sanctuary.

We docked a few miles north of Vero Beach, at Jones Fruit dock, for $5.00/night. It was a very quiet New Year's Eve, and we went to bed at nine thirty. It stormed and rained all night; there was even a tornado warning issued for our area.

Jones' Fruit Dock, Indian River, FL - Distance traveled: 36 miles

January 1, 1987, Thursday, New Year's Day

It was still very windy today, with winds recorded at 25-35 mph in our area, but the sky was clear, so thankfully it didn't rain. We slept late since we weren't going any place. Mr. Jones, who owns the dock where we are tied up, raises grapefruit and brought some down to us. His are sold under the name Indian River Orchard Grapefruit. We ate one for breakfast, and it was the best grapefruit we had ever eaten. He said that his entire crop is now shipped to Japan. We are on the Indian River, and have been since we left New Smyrna Beach on Monday; we will continue on it until we get to Stuart.

After breakfast, we took a walk to the beach, and on the way, stopped to look at some new homes under construction in an exclusive development called The Shores. They are huge, and no doubt will be very expensive and quite beautiful when finished.

At one o'clock, we watched the Cotton Bowl game on TV: OSU vs. Texas A&M. OSU won 28-12. I fixed some popcorn to snack on. Later, Don made a meatball and rice dish for dinner in the pressure cooker. The evening was quiet and relaxing, and we went to bed early.

Jones' Fruit Dock, Indian River, FL

January 2, 1987, Friday

The weather this morning was beautiful. It was on the cool side, but with blue skies. What a difference a day makes. Starting at eight fifteen, we "motor sailed" (used both the motor and the sails for power) to Fort Pierce. We passed Vero Beach without stopping. Oh well, we'll catch it on the return trip. It was a short travel day; we put in at noon. That gave us a chance to run some errands. We bought groceries and went to the post office because I was out of stamps. It was another pleasant and easy day, and we are safely docked. The current coming past the dock is strong. I made chicken enchiladas tonight while Don showered, and then he did the dishes while I showered. I called Mom and Pam this evening and visited a short time with each. I tried to call Sister Carol and David at the condo on Siesta Key, but the phones weren't working properly. I wish all days were as relaxing and pleasant as today.

The towns and villages we saw during the earlier part of the trip such as Georgetown, McClellanville, Beaufort, Solomons Island, Chesapeake City, Catskill and Youngstown, New York have been replaced by what appears from the waterway to be one continuous Florida city, stretching for hundreds of miles. We've left a lot of charming places behind us. It will be fun to visit them again when we head north on the boat.

Fort Pierce City Marina, Fort Pierce, FL - Distance traveled: 22 miles

January 3, 1987, Saturday

What a pleasant day, again. I got up about eight, ran the sweeper, and then fixed muffins and grapefruit for breakfast. We went to J. C. Penney's at about nine thirty and bought Don his birthday gifts from me: jeans, socks, and underwear.

We shoved off from Fort Pierce at about noon. There was a terribly strong current at the drawbridge, flowing toward the bridge, but we made it safely through. A strong current in the direction of a closed drawbridge is dangerous, because if you get close to the bridge before you recognize the danger you might not be able to get turned around and get away from it. Current has carried many sailboats into closed bridges, tearing up the boat's mast and rigging. Remember, a sailboat doesn't back up worth a darn and turning 180° takes time. The current will carry the boat quite a distance toward the bridge while the boat is turning.

We anchored for the night, a few miles south of Fort Pierce, in Manatee Pocket, at Stuart. Manatee Pocket is a beautiful and very well protected anchorage. The sunset was very pretty tonight, but I didn't take any pictures because there is no way I could have captured the beauty I saw through my eyes. We have seen lots of beauty on our trip.

I fixed Taco's and tortillas tonight, and we liked them fairly well. The corn tacos weren't very fresh, but everything else was. We both read this evening, and I also worked on my Spanish moss and sea shell wreath. I am trying to make bows for it. It was cold enough for the Kero-sun heater to be on, but we were very comfortable with it. We are having temperatures in the 60s, much higher than up north, but both of us now realize that a kerosene heater is an important piece of equipment for cruising in Florida during the winter.

Anchored in Manatee Pocket, Stuart, FL - Distance traveled: 24 miles

January 4, 1987, Sunday

We didn't get up until nine this morning. We planned to take *The Lincoln* out for a day of exploration, but during breakfast, we heard a forecast for bad weather, so we didn't go. In fact, a tornado warning was in effect, from nine until three. That altered our day's plans. We sat on the boat and read. The storm hit at noon. We had lightning, thunder, rain, and lots of wind.

At one o'clock Don fixed us popcorn, and a little later I fixed coffee. About two thirty, the sky cleared, and I tried to catch some fish but failed. Around four, we put the motor on the dinghy, bailed it out, and left to cruise around the area. While in the dinghy, we talked with a couple aboard a boat named *Fre-Mar*. They are a very interesting couple and truly self-sufficient live-aboards from the area of Goderich, Ontario, Canada. We returned to our boat just before a second storm hit. Tonight we ate left-overs, and I made Don a birthday cake. He went to bed early. I stayed up to read and watched a movie made for TV. I enjoyed it, but it was continued, so I don't know if I will see the ending. It is called, *At Mother's Request*.

Anchored in Manatee Pocket, Stuart, FL

January 5, 1987, Monday
We raised our anchors at eight; they were extremely muddy. The new chain seemed to work well at keeping the anchor line from getting around the keel or rudder, and Captain Don slept soundly both nights we were anchored in Manatee Pocket. We only came about seven miles today to the Pelican Nest Marina, on the Saint Lucie River, near Stuart. We wanted to be at a dock, so we could use their water to clean the dinghy because we are going to have some repairs done to it. We also arranged for the First Mate Company to come over and pick up Vern for repair. Vern has a tendency to drift off course. I did laundry. The people who own the marina offer free oranges and grapefruit to transients. They also have an electric juice squeezing machine, so I squeezed enough oranges for us to have about a gallon of fresh juice.

The weather was terrible—windy and cold all day. This isn't the weather we expected in Florida, but it didn't matter much today because we were docked and working on projects. Don made Eight Bean Soup, and homemade corn bread for dinner. We bought the beans at the Daytona Farmers' Market. Later, we watched some TV and were planning to take a walk until it started to rain; we stayed in and went to bed early.

Tonight, while looking out at some Christmas decorations, it occurred to me that I haven't talked about the many boats we have seen that have been beautifully decorated with Christmas trees and lights, except for the one I mentioned we saw while we were at Palm Coast. We have seen many fancy Christmas boats during the holidays. Some people go to a lot of trouble to decorate their boats at Christmas time. I'm sure it requires big expenditures of money and much labor.

Pelican Nest Marina, Saint Lucie River, Stuart, FL - Distance traveled: 7 miles

January 6, 1987, Tuesday
Today was certainly pleasant. We awoke to beautiful sunny weather, and it lasted all day. We spent most of the day doing chores and errands. While we were still at Pelican's Nest Marina, we changed the fuel filter and air filter on the engine, and also changed the transmission fluid. I did a load of laundry.

We pulled out of Pelican Nest Marina at about one thirty and spent the next hour motoring to Wood's Cove Marina, which is also in the Stuart area. After arriving, I walked into town to buy kerosene and some small light bulbs. Don stayed on the boat to wait for Vern and *The Lincoln* to be returned. I also bought a new chart kit for the West Coast of Florida for $75—not cheap! I surely hope we enjoy the areas that it covers. Vern's repair only cost $10 and *The Lincoln* was under warranty and therefore there was no charge for its repair.

At five thirty, after Vern and *The Lincoln* had been returned to us, Don and I left the boat and walked to a Kentucky Fried Chicken (KFC) restaurant for dinner; our meal was disappointing. On the return walk, we picked up a few groceries, and I phoned Randy to make sure Shelly made it home safely from California. She did, and has already left to go to her dad's.

We made it home in time for me to see the end of the movie *At Mother's Request*. I liked it; it was based on fact.

We are now ready to head for Florida's West Coast on the Okeechobee Waterway.

Wood's Cove Marina, Stuart, FL - Distance traveled: 5 miles

January 7, 1987, Wednesday

It was another beautiful day. We wore shorts and got a little sun. We went through the Saint Lucie Lock at noon and began our trip through the Okeechobee Waterway. We locked through with a fellow by the name of Newt Becker aboard *My Time,* a small cruising sailboat. We traveled alongside him most of the afternoon. Newt and we are now at Port Mayaca, on the edge of Lake Okeechobee, tied to a barge for the night. Don made chicken noodle soup, and Newt joined us for dinner. He is a single-handed sailor, and says he gets lonely. He is from Grand Rapids, Michigan, and recently retired after teaching school in Michigan for 30 years. He left in August on this trip. He is also a canvas maker and is going to work at that here in Florida. He's about 55 years old, and seems to be a nice guy. We chatted, and then, at

about eight, he returned to his boat for the night.

On the way to Port Mayaca we had to pass under a railroad lift bridge. When not in use, it is lifted so boats can pass under it. When it is lifted, it is 49' above the water. The mast head on our standard rig Catalina 30 is 46' above the water

SAINT LUCIE LOCK WITH NEWT ON MY TIME AHEAD OF US

and we have an antenna attached at the mast head which makes our overall height about 48'–very close. (The tall rig Catalina 30 is two feet taller.)

The mosquitos are bad tonight. We spent the rest of the evening reading and relaxing, and I wrote to Shelly. It's now ten o'clock, and we are going to bed.

Tied to barge at Port Mayaca, FL - Distance traveled: 32 miles

January 8, 1987, Thursday

It was sunny with mild temperatures. I wore shorts part of the day. We traveled with Newt all day. We went through the lock at Port Mayaca and then crossed Lake Okeechobee, which is about 25 miles across. We were able to sail all the way across the lake. We both put in at Clewiston for fuel after crossing the lake. We also walked to a convenience store and bought milk and ice cream. A local fisherman at the docking area caught a nine pound large-mouth bass while we were there, and it was fun watching him land it. Nice fish! The next part of the day was really different because, as we traveled along the canal, we passed several alligators and wild turkeys. We put in at the town of Moore Haven at five o'clock for the night, after going through the Moore Haven Lock. We tied up at the city dock which was reasonably priced for dockage, at $10 per night, including electric and showers. Don made an excellent Hungarian Beef Stew tonight for dinner, and I baked brownies. We invited Newt to join us for the second night in a row.

At the city dock, we met a boater by the name of Lloyd Wilder, on *Ty One On*, a power boat. He and his girlfriend, Betty, invited Newt and us aboard his boat for drinks. They also invited two guys on *Lydia Rose*, a 25 ft. sailboat, from Duluth, Minnesota to join them. Lloyd is a psychiatrist who trained at OSU. As he shared his life story with us, we learned that he was divorced in Columbus and Don's father, Clayton Rose, Sr., was the judge who heard the case. It was a cordial visit, notwithstanding. At ten, Don and I went home and went to bed.

City dock, Moore Haven, FL - Distance traveled: 41miles

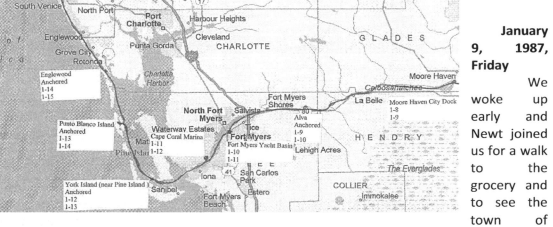

January 9, 1987, Friday

We woke up early and Newt joined us for a walk to the grocery and to see the town of Moore Haven. When we got back, we left the city dock at nine and continued toward Fort Myers.

Today was the most beautiful day of all. Temperatures were in the mid-70s, with a light breeze keeping us cool when the sun was beating down on us. The sun was out the entire day, and I did a lot of sunbathing on deck. We went through one lock today, at Ortona, where we went down eight feet; locking through went smoothly. We didn't see any unusual wildlife, but we did see a lot of pretty vegetation near the town of La Belle. Prior to that, we saw a lot of farmland and cows. We could see and smell smoke from sugar cane fields being burned off. As the old crop stubble is burned off, the "dustings," so called by the locals, float out and drop onto everything, including boats, leaving a mess of ashes.

We anchored tonight by the Alva Bridge. Newt came over again for dinner of Welsh rarebit, made with Muenster cheese. I made it from a recipe out of a cookbook one of my private duty patients gave me, and served it on toast. We all liked it. Newt brought over vodka for screwdrivers (orange juice and vodka) and ice cream bars for dessert.

We visited and looked over the charts, and then took his dinghy ashore for a walk. After returning to the boat, I finished a letter to Shelly and went to bed.

Anchored at the Alva Bridge, Alva, FL - Distance traveled: 38 miles

January 10, 1987, Saturday

We left the Alva Bridge at about eight thirty in the morning, and motored about four hours to Ft Myers. On the way, we went through the W.P. Franklin Lock, the final lock on the waterway. Ft Myers marks the west end, for practical purposes, of the Okeechobee Waterway. To reach the west coast and the Gulf Intracoastal Waterway from Fort Myers you just continue down the Caloosahatchee River.

The Waterway, from east to west, goes up the Saint Lucie River, through the Saint Lucie Canal, across Lake Okeechobee, through the Caloosahatchee Canal and down the Caloosahatchee River. There are five locks on the waterway, which you go through in the following order when you are traveling in that direction: Saint Lucie; Port Mayaca; Moore Haven; Ortona; and W.P. Franklin. The locks operate on demand from seven in the morning until seven in the evening. There are several bridges to pass under, and they also open on demand. We communicated with the lock and bridge operators on our marine radio. There is no charge for using the waterway or going through the locks. The waterway is very peaceful and an easy way to get from one coast to the other. It is also scenic, with some charming little towns along the way; we enjoyed it a lot. As I mentioned before, there is a railroad bridge that limits the use of the waterway to boats with a height of less than 49 feet, including antennas, etc. We like the waterway so much that we would want the mast height of any boat we bought for sailing in Florida waters to have a mast height under the limit for the Okeechobee Waterway.

I was ticked when we found out at the Yacht Basin in Fort Myers that we would have to pay $25 for the night, which amounts to more than $0.80/foot. We have been paying, on average, about $0.50/foot. The reason given by the dockmaster was that they didn't have the depth we need in a 30' slip, and the only available slip that would accommodate us was a 45' slip and if we wanted it, we would have to pay as though *Robin Lee* were 45 feet long. Newt had to pay the same, so we decided to use an inside wall—no slip. We only took up 60' between the two of us, but they still made each of us pay $25.00. What a rip-off! We will never go back there.

Later, we went walking and took a bus to Edison Mall. Newt bought dinner and drinks for us. We spent a nice evening, and when we got back Newt found a friend, Cliff, who was to meet him there that day. His name is Cliff. He is on a boat called *Wax Wings* and is from New York. We all visited on our boat and looked over the charts. I did a load of laundry and called Shelly. She and I talked for a half hour.

The boat rocked all night. I didn't get to sleep until four because of the rocking; it was horrible. We should have taken the slip where we could have tied off four ways.

Fort Myers Yacht Basin, Fort Myers, FL - Distance traveled: 20miles

January 11, 1987, Sunday

The winds were uncomfortably high, so we only came two hours today to the Cape Coral Marina. Don called the marina on the radio to check the price and make reservations. It's a good marina, and it's well protected from the north wind.

Don, Newt, and I took a bike ride on the marina's loaner bikes to the grocery store and then came back to the boat and ate a German dinner. Don made hot potato salad and sausage with kraut and sour cream. Newt brought ice, vodka for screwdrivers, and cookies for dessert. He left at seven thirty. We did the dishes and watched TV. It was sunny today, but cool.

Cape Coral Marina, Cape Coral, FL - Distance traveled: 10miles

CHAPTER FIVE

FORT MYERS, FL to KEY BISCAYNE, FL
Jan. 12, 1987 – Mar. 16, 1987

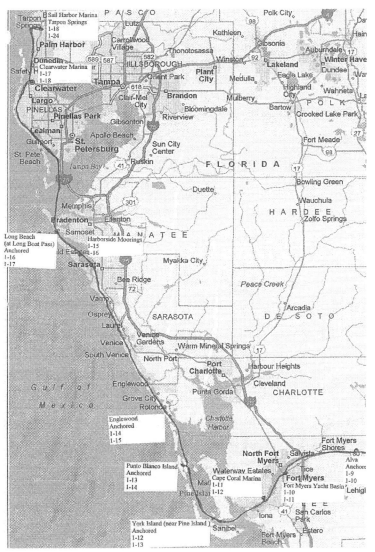

January 12, 1987, Monday

Newt went into town and re-registered his boat as a Florida boat because he intends to stay here, so Don and I had a pretty relaxing day. I made cookies and afterwards, we changed the engine oil.

We met an interesting sailor, a converted Buddhist, originally from Ohio, but now living in Nebraska. We call him the "Buddhist from Nebraska," because we never did get his name! He was out in the Gulf in the big nor'easter we had while we were anchored in Manatee Pocket. He was having trouble and called for help on his marine radio. The Coast Guard flew over his boat to fix his position and stayed in touch with him until he was safely in port–I'm glad it wasn't us.

When Newt got back we pulled out and headed for nearby Pine Island to anchor for the night. The trip was OK, even across the notorious "miserable mile," called that because of a strong current which tends to push you out of the channel. However, just when we thought we were done with the "miserable mile," we went aground and realized we were out of the channel. The captain was at the helm and admits that the grounding wasn't because of the current; it was his fault. He saw a red marker about a mile ahead, 15° to starboard, and knew he needed to keep it on his starboard side, so he turned 15° to starboard and headed toward it, keeping it a little to starboard. But, he looked too far ahead.

Nearer to the boat, about ½ mile dead ahead, was another red marker which he should have kept on our starboard side. By turning 15° to starboard he was "cutting the corner" which took us out of the channel and grounded us. He would have seen that the channel continued straight for another ½ mile, and passed that next red buoy before turning to starboard if he had looked at the chart, but he hadn't. He apologized to his first mate (me) for his mistake. He felt he needed to apologize since he had been very critical of his first mate on those occasions when she had gotten out of the channel and gone aground because of lack of attention. Fortunately, Newt was behind us and pulled us off the ground.

We anchored off York Island, near Pine Island. After anchoring, Newt came over for dinner. We had leftover bean soup, biscuits and salad. After dinner, we looked over the charts and made plans for the next couple of days. The night was pleasantly uneventful.

Anchored off York Island, near Pine Island, a few miles west of Cape Coral, FL - Distance traveled: 12 miles

January 13, 1987, Tuesday

The past two days have been cool but sunny. Today was warmer with lots of sunshine. Our days are getting noticeably longer. We anchored again today, shortly after noon, early enough to do some exploring. We are at Punta Blanco Island, near Cayo Costa Island. We took a picnic lunch ashore and walked around. The island is about 1.5 miles long and a little less than a half mile wide at its widest. We met Norma Jane and Ralph, who are cruising on the boat, *Norma Jane,* from Massachusetts. They are anchored near us. Ralph showed us an artesian well on the island. It smelled

ROBIN AND NEWT

like sulfa water, but was very clear. The island is beautiful, uninhabited, serene, and has small white sandy beaches all the way around it. It also has mango trees and tall Australian pines, with long, soft needles. The anchorage is totally isolated from people, except boaters, and sure is a lot nicer than the Florida you see when you are on the streets and highways in the bumper-to-bumper traffic.

Later in the afternoon, we decided to take the dinghy to a place known to the boaters as the "Tunnel of Love," a tunnel of overhanging mangrove trees, which winds along a half-mile channel across Cayo Costa Island and empties into a small pool near the beach on the Gulf side. It is shallow, and at one place, we had to get out of the dinghy and pull it through the water. Although I am sure thousands of boaters have explored it over many years, to us it was a wonderful discovery. We were the only people there at the time, and it was enchanting. The roots of the mangrove trees make an entwined vine-like network just above the surface of the water, and the trees themselves extend over the water, with leaves that block the sun. The water in the channel is crystal clear. I wish I could describe it adequately, but words can't do it justice. It was wonderful! On the gulf, we walked along the white, sandy beach. I found several shells of a type I had never seen, and while we were there, we saw osprey, wild turkeys, a raccoon, and three wild pigs. Boy, was I shocked to look up and see wild pigs staring at me. We decided to leave shortly after that, because we were a little intimidated by the wild pigs and also due to the late hour and the long trip back in the dinghy. We didn't see another person during the entire adventure. If that wasn't enough to make this a very special day, in a very special place, when we got back to the anchorage, we had fish jumping all around us. I dinghied over and thanked Norma Jane and Ralph for suggesting that we should go through the "Tunnel of Love."

Later, we had leftovers for dinner, and Newt joined us for the seventh night in a row. We have gotton to know him well. He's very nice, and we have enjoyed his company. We all watched a little TV, and I did some cross-stitch. We didn't go to bed until after watching a documentary on AIDS, the newly diagnosed disease that people are talking about. I wrote to Shelly and went to bed around ten thirty, having had a terrific day.

Anchored off Punto Blanco Island, FL – Distance traveled: 22 miles

January 14, 1987, Wednesday

At about eight fifteen, we left our anchorage at Punta Blanca Island. Ralph, on *Norma Jane,* led us out of the narrow, unmarked channel leading to the anchorage, but we still touched bottom. At around ten o'clock, we stopped for fuel at Miller's Marine on Boca Grande Island, about five miles north of Punta Blanca Island. The attendant at Miller's Marine said it would be OK to leave the boat tied up there for a little while, and so we took a walk and looked around. Boca Grande impressed us as being a delightful place to spend time.

IN THE TUNNEL OF LOVE

It's a quaint little, out-of-the-way village and is supposedly a favorite place for some wealthy people. It has a very well protected natural harbor where boats can anchor for a few days. We would like to go back and spend a few days there just relaxing and getting to know the place. We bought groceries and take-out food for a picnic. Newt also bought groceries for Don to use to make a Swiss steak dinner.

It was a beautiful day, warm and sunny. We had our swimming suits on from the time we left Boca Grande. We arrived at our next anchorage, near the town of Englewood Beach, around four. I took the dinghy ashore and mailed a letter to Shelly. We also walked on the gulf side of the town. After getting back at five thirty, the three of us had Fuzzy Navels (orange juice and peach schnapps) and the Swiss steak dinner provided by Newt, but cooked by Don, which included sweet potatoes. Don and I read and did chart work before going to bed at ten thirty.

Anchored at Englewood Beach, FL - Distance traveled: 17 miles

January 15, 1987, Thursday

We got underway at about seven this morning and saw a pretty sunrise. I took snapshots of Newt, aboard *My Time,* coming under a bridge with the sun rising behind him. We motored through very shallow water while I was at the helm on our way to Venice. We had to wait quite a while there to go through a bridge that only opens every half-hour. We stopped briefly at the Crow's Nest in Venice for Newt to get gas. We didn't leave the boat because the dockmaster said it would be $7.50/hour to tie up.

We made it to Longboat Key, north of Sarasota, at about three, and put in for the night at Harborside Moorings where Hope and Harry, aboard *Passages,* are docked. It is the nicest marina we have been in on the entire trip. You get a marina with four-star rating and service with a smile for $0.60/foot/day, plus $3.00 for electric. The amenities available include: grocery shopping at the Publix supermarket, a short walk away; great showers; a clean, well equipped laundry; and free transportation to and from a hotel on the beach, about a mile from the marina, which is owned by the same company that owns the marina. At seven, after we were finished with dinner, we called the marina office on our marine radio and asked for the van to pick us up and drive us to the hotel. The fellow driving was just like a chauffeur, opening and closing doors for us, etc. We enjoyed using the Jacuzzi; swimming in the pool under the starlit sky with the palms swaying in the breeze; and walking on the beach. It was gorgeous. Hope and Harry picked us up at the hotel, and we visited with them until midnight at the "Buttery" on Saint Armand's Circle. It felt strange introducing them to Newt as our cruising buddies from Castleton, New York, to Solomons Island, Maryland, because it seemed so long ago. It was great to share with each other our experiences since going our separate ways.

They took us back to our boat at midnight. They are living on their boat at Harborside Moorings and are looking for a place to live in Sarasota.

Harborside Moorings, Long Boat Key, FL - Distance traveled: 24 miles

January 16, 1987, Friday

I got up early, did laundry, ran the sweeper and then went to visit Hope. Don went to the Publix supermarket. Harbor Side Moorings is so nice and clean we may want to dock here on a monthly basis next winter. The monthly charge is $7.00/foot, which would only be $210 per month ($7.00 per night) for us.

We had a pleasant afternoon motoring to our anchorage at Moore's Seafood Restaurant, but the wind was picking up and the temperature was only in the 60s. We got settled by three, and while Don worked on our dinner of lentil soup and cornbread, I put the laundry away and made up the beds with clean sheets. Newt came over at five, and we had our usual—Fuzzy Navel cocktails and dinner.

After dinner, we took the dinghy to the restaurant, had a dessert, and watched their captive porpoise. Later, we reviewed the charts, and went to bed at ten thirty.

Anchored at Moore's Seafood Restaurant, Longboat Pass, Longboat Key, FL - Distance traveled: 9 miles

January 17, 1987, Saturday

We had a long day. We "upped" the anchor at Moore's in a light fog, at about eight, and anchored at Clearwater at six thirty. We passed up Saint Petersburg because getting into and out of it would have taken us a couple of extra hours.

We first anchored at Clearwater in front of the city marina, but the dockmaster said we would have to move. I was disappointed because it was near the downtown area of Clearwater Beach. After we got re-situated, we ate leftover Swiss steak for dinner, and then Newt and I went ashore in our dinghy. Newt got a few groceries, and I called Betty and Clayton to tell them where we are. Don "boat sat" and watched some TV. When we got back from the store, we fixed popcorn, watched a little TV, and went to bed at the usual time of ten thirty. The weather today was sunny but cooler.

Anchored at Clearwater, FL - Distance traveled: 58 miles

January 18, 1987, Sunday

Newt, Don and I had coffee and rolls for breakfast, and we pulled up the anchors at about nine o'clock and left for Tarpon Springs, Newt's home for the rest of the winter and maybe longer. Newt went to Tarpon Springs some time ago to check it out. He liked it and decided he would live on his boat there and work in the canvas business awhile—for as long as he likes it. He left his car there and traveled north to get his boat and bring it down. At about twelve forty-five we arrived at Sail Harbor Marina in Tarpon Springs where Newt plans to stay. The wind was starting to pick up, so I'm glad we got docked when we did. However, we are on the main channel leading from the waterway to the town and are on the outside

of the pier, getting lots of rocking motion from the Sunday boat traffic. This marina is nice, but very different, with a laid-back attitude. I don't think we would want to spend a long time here. I hope Newt likes it.

I cleaned some of the teak in the afternoon, and then the three of us had chicken Marengo for dinner. In the evening, at about eight, we went in Newt's car to buy groceries. I also called Mom. There was no earth-shaking news from Columbus. It sure was windy and rainy today and this evening.

Sail Harbor Marina, Tarpon Springs, FL - Distance traveled: 21 miles

January 19, 1987, Monday

Today was a day to run around in Newt's car to various places. We spent the entire day shopping. We left early to go to a plumbing supply place for a new faucet for our galley sink. Then we went to Boat US and bought a new anchor and anchor line. We had decided that, before going to the Bahamas, we would replace the homemade wishbone anchor that John Hubay had, and which came with the boat, with one of the more popular designs. We bought a Bruce anchor and a 300' anchor line. We also purchased a three inch thick, closed-cell foam pad to use as a new mattress in the V-berth. In addition, we bought a small 12 volt fan for the cabin. The day's shopping cost us about $600.

Newt insisted on taking us out to eat at a local buffet because he knew we could get all we wanted for a great price. The food was not bad for that type of place, and we did eat more than enough to get our money's worth. We got back at a little after eight and worked on some minor projects, like the hatch opening and the clothes hammocks in the V-berth. Then we watched some TV and went to bed.

It rained and was windy most of the day, but finally in the evening the wind shifted and became less of a problem.

Sail Harbor Marina, Tarpon Springs, FL

January 20, 1987, Tuesday, Sail Harbor Marina, Tarpon Springs, FL

The weather was still cloudy and rainy. Don was able to borrow a VHS recorder from Don Andrews, the skipper of a boat named *Bonnie Doone,* Don Andrews, and spent most of the day transferring our video from the 20-minute tapes used in the camcorder to two-hour tapes, thereby freeing up the 20-minute tapes for using again. He put in wiring for our new 12 volt fan. Afterward, he made stuffed peppers for our evening meal. Newt and I cut the foam mattress and put it in the V-berth, and I did a bit of cleaning. Later in the day, Newt and I went to the mall and returned the sink faucet for the galley; it wasn't suitable. We got something else, and I don't know if it will work either. The man in the store assured me it would.

At five thirty, we were invited to *Bonnie Doone* for snacks and drinks by Don and Alice Andrews. Don is a professional boat surveyor and has also worked in the boat-building industry. He recently spent several months living in Taiwan, overseeing the construction of a large, very expensive yacht for a wealthy buyer and has been hired by another buyer to do the same for an even bigger yacht; he will be going back to Taiwan soon. They have also done a lot of cruising, and we discussed the Bahamas and the fun we expect to have there in the coming summer. Don (Andrews) fixed us a Bahamian drink called a "Yellowbird," which we both liked, so he gave us the recipe.

Don (Andrews) also told us of a scary experience he had, which I will relate: Sometime in the past, he and Alice were anchored on a small river, close to an inlet on the Florida coast. It was after dark and Don and Alice were below relaxing when Don decided to go above and check to be sure everything was as it should be. He got a flashlight and went on deck. He immediately heard a scream for help, and using his flashlight, he spotted a man in the water being swept downstream by the tidal current. Don jumped in his dinghy and set out to try to rescue him. With the help of his flashlight and the man's yelling, he was able to get to him and pull him into his dinghy. The guy was a single-handed sailor and had anchored his boat for the night somewhere upstream from *Bonnie Doone.* He went in the water to check his prop. He had attached a line to his boat and was holding it, but it got away from him, and he was swept down the river. He tried to swim against the current to get back to his boat, but couldn't. The average swimmer can only swim about two miles per hour (mph) and competition swimmers only about four mph. Tidal currents can be much faster than that, and this one was. He was being taken out to sea and there was nothing he could do about it. Don took him back to his boat, gave him a cup of coffee, got him settled down, and then took him to his own boat.

We visited on *Bonnie Doone* until seven and then came home to eat. Later, Don and I looked at the charts and read *Cruising World* articles before going to bed. Don was still a bit

down in the dumps about all the money we have spent, and that's understandable. We don't have much money, and no income, and would like to continue our adventure for a long time.
Sail Harbor Marina, Tarpon Springs, FL

January 21, 1987, Wednesday

We are still at Tarpon Springs. It rained most of the day. Don worked outside as much as possible. Newt and I worked on the new galley faucet. Alice, from *Bonnie Doone,* took me to the grocery store, and at five thirty, we had drinks and then dinner on the *Robin Lee.* Newt, Don and Alice joined us for beef stroganoff and marinated asparagus and an evening of entertainment, provided by Newt. He knows a lot of jokes and magic tricks.

Don has taken over the cooking except for times where he has a pressing need to do something else. I'm happy about that, because I don't like to cook. He always did our cooking at home, but our plan was for me to do the cooking on board because he has so many other things to attend to. Nevertheless, now he is agreeable to doing most of the cooking (which probably says something about the quality of my cooking, or the amount of complaining I have done about having to do it). He has been fixing all of our favorite recipes, just like he would at home. We sure aren't living on Dinty Moore Stew and Spaghettios like some of the people back home probably think.

Furthermore, he is preparing more food on board the boat than he did at home. There are two reasons for that. There are no restaurants or fast-food places available while we are moving from one place to another or are at anchor in some remote place, so if you want something, you have to fix it on board. We are also on such a tight budget, we can't afford to eat out. In addition, we wash more dishes and cooking utensils on board than we did at home. We now know that if one is going to go cruising, one needs to get a boat with a good galley. A good galley should be high on the list of important characteristics when shopping for a cruising sailboat.

We are happy with our galley, but it's not perfect. We have a three burner alcohol stove with an oven. It works pretty well, and an alcohol fire can be extinguished with water. However, it requires maintenance from time to time, and it takes a while for it to "get going" and doesn't get as hot as other stoves. Furthermore, the oven doesn't heat evenly. The alternatives are propane or bottled natural gas. The problem with propane is that it's heavier than air, and if you develop a leak your boat could fill with propane gas and explode. Many boats have been blown up because of that problem, and we wouldn't risk it. Natural gas is lighter than air and if a leak developed, the gas would escape out of the hatches, so it is safer. However, there is a scarcity of places where you can refill your natural-gas bottles, but I think that bottled natural gas would be our choice if we were starting over. Electric is not an alternative because it would require a big generator to power it and there is no room for such a generator on a boat our size.

We are happy with our water system, except we wish we had a greater water storage capacity. Our water tanks only hold 46 gallons. Our hot-water system, which I have already described, is good. And we don't have to use a pump to get hot or cold water. We have pressurized water from a little compressor in our system that comes on when we open a water spigot and goes off when we shut it.

Our refrigerator has a freezer and is adequate in size. It can use 110 volt shore power to operate or 12 volt battery power if shore power isn't available. We have a separate set of two automobile size batteries which are only for the refrigerator. However, the refrigerator uses a lot of battery power, and it will run its two batteries down in a day or so when we are at anchor or on a mooring buoy. We have tried running the engine to have the alternator on the engine keep the batteries charged, but that doesn't work very well. We have found that you have to run the engine a lot to do that. I'm afraid we are going to have to learn to do without refrigeration when we don't have shore power. We have heard of a different type of system, called a cold plate system, that may work better away from shore power than ours, but we will probably stick with what we have and get used to only having refrigeration when we are at a dock with electricity.

Sail Harbor Marina, Tarpon Springs, FL

January 22, 1987, Thursday, Sail Harbor Marina, Tarpon Springs, FL

It got extremely windy during the night. The wind was pushing *Robin Lee* into the pier. Don fended our five ton boat off as well as he could and put on additional fenders to help. The pressure was so strong it ruined one of our fenders. It was a difficult night, and today, Don's back is hurting him. The wind was so strong it blew a big sailboat off its chocks, onto the parking lot. Don has lain around most of the day on a heating pad because of his sore back. In the afternoon, Newt drove us to downtown Tarpon Springs to buy some spices and get an ice cream sundae. It is the first time in over two weeks that he didn't have dinner with us, but later in the evening he came over for a fuzzy navel. He loves to make them.

Sail Harbor Marina, Tarpon Springs, FL

January 23, 1987, Friday

I got up around nine. It was sunny, but cool. Newt took me into town this morning to go to the bank, the laundry, and the grocery. We had lunch at Wendy's. Don stayed on the boat to work on some projects. After I got home, I worked on the teak. What a backbreaking job that is! It does look nice, however. Because we plan to leave Tarpon Springs tomorrow, Newt joined us for a last supper and Fuzzy Navels. We had pork chops and stuffing along with cottage cheese and of course, bread and jelly, which is a must at every meal. Afterwards, we sat around and talked. We were using the electric heater and bragging about how great it was, when it shorted out causing sparks and burning the towel it was resting on. Fortunately, no damage was done except for the burnt electrical cord and the scorched towel, which can be replaced. However, it made me shudder to think of what might have happened, if we hadn't been on board. Newt left immediately to go back to his boat and check his heater.

Sail Harbor Marina, Tarpon Springs, FL

January 24, 1987, Saturday

Since the weather was nice this morning, we stuck with our plan to leave Tarpon Springs, and busied ourselves with getting ready. I finished the teak, with Newt's help. Don spoke with Capt. Don Andrews of *Bonnie Doone* about some concerns my captain has with stripped threads on one of our shrouds and its turnbuckles and the backstay and turnbuckle. Captain Andrews, the surveyor, confirmed that they were potential problems and suggested that we replace them. That depressed me—more headaches and more dollars. However, in accordance with the advice we got in Oswego and Don Andrews assessment, my captain made the decision to fix them in Clearwater. We got underway at one fifteen and motored south to Clearwater. I cleaned the brass lamp while Don was at the helm. When we got to Clearwater, we tied up at Island Yacht Club in Island Estates.

A friendly sailor, Robin Linker, on a boat tied up near where we docked, helped us get settled into our slip. We invited him for a dinner of tuna and macaroni. Dinner was made by me. It wasn't bad. Robin stayed to visit until nine thirty. When he left we went to bed.

Island Yacht Club, Clearwater, FL - Distance traveled: 22 miles

January 25, 1987, Sunday

We moved our boat to another slip close to where we had spent the night and tied up with additional lines for better protection from a severe storm that had been predicted. We stayed on board during the storm, but it really wasn't as severe as expected.

The wiring for our new 12 volt fan shorted out and caused the wires to smoke and melt. Don burned his hand dealing with the problem. It scared me! We have had two completely unrelated electrical problems in three days. The heater problem was caused by the heater going bad, but the captain took responsibility for the fan problem. He made two mistakes when he made a new circuit for the 12 volt fluorescent lights, which now has the fan on it also. He used some old wire, the insulation was faulty, and he didn't put a fuse in the circuit. And to think he spent 3 ½ years in electrical engineering at Ohio State! Scary! He has taken out his wiring and will redo it properly when he can get the materials.

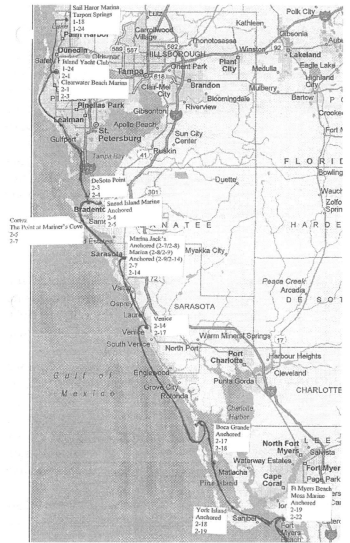

About three thirty we left for a walk to the grocery store. I called Sister Carol, and I made a birthday card to send to a friend. We had a good dinner of Cornish game hens and carrots, and after the dishes were done we took showers, and read until bedtime.

Island Yacht Club, Clearwater, FL

January 26, 1987, Monday

It was still very windy and cold, and "roly-poly" on the boat last night. I slept in and then, because we didn't want to take down the backstay and shroud in the wind, Don and I walked over to the Marine Science Museum. It was only $1.00 each for admission and was pretty interesting.

Around noon, we came back and called the Catalina Boat Co. They are going to give us a discount on the new parts we need for the rigging. Furthermore, their Morgan plant here in Clearwater will do the repair work. We will take the damaged rigging to them and they will replace or repair the parts.

The damaged rigging consists of one shroud and its turnbuckle, and the backstay and its turnbuckle. The shrouds, the headstay and the backstay are stainless steel cables, attached to the mast, and hold the mast up. On our boat, there are six shrouds, two lower on each side and one upper on each side. They are attached near the sides of the boat beside the mast. They keep the mast from falling sideways, the backstay is attached at the stern and keeps the mast from falling forward, and the headstay is attached at the bow and keeps the mast from falling backwards. Each of these cables is attached to the boat with a turnbuckle. Turnbuckles are threaded devices that are used to apply tension to the cables to "tune" the rigging, and by that I mean, to make the cables as tight as the captain wants. The threading in two of our turnbuckles, the one on our backstay and the one on our aft starboard lower shroud, are nearly stripped and could give way and cause a dismasting. To prevent that, we need to take the backstay and the damaged shroud off the boat and take them and their turnbuckles to the Catalina facility for repair or replacement. We will use lines as substitutes for the cables to hold the mast up while the repair work is being done. The lines will suffice so long as we are not sailing. We have hired a man by the name of Alan to remove the shroud and backstay along with their turnbuckles and replace them with lines, and to do the reverse when the repairs are done. We are hiring him because he is experienced at this type of work (and because, we don't want to be hoisted four stories in the air on a rocking boat to try to do the job ourselves).

I watched a TV soap opera, *All My Children*. I first watched it in 1974. Some of the same people are still on it. I had a relaxing afternoon; I even took a nap. We talked to a few live-boards and then Don made veal scallopini for dinner. We watched some TV and read during the evening.

Island Yacht Club, Clearwater, FL

January 27, 1987, Tuesday

We are still at Clearwater. It is cold and continues to be very windy, but at least the sun is out most of the day. I got up at seven thirty, and we ate muffins (Jiffy Banana Nut) and grapefruit for breakfast. After that, we watched Phil Donahue and a program about sleep abnormalities. (I think Don has an abnormality—he snores a lot.) Then we took a walk. Alan could not take down the rigging today because of the wind.

We walked to the beach in Clearwater and visited the Welcome Center. I called the man I used to take care of in Bexley. I am sure he was happy to know I was thinking of him. He owns property in Clearwater, so I knew he would enjoy knowing I had made it to his territory. His main activity, while I was caring for him, was to watch a television show that has a continuous report of the most-recent stock trades running across the bottom of the screen. He always muted the sound and just watched the trades. He watched this all day long, which got me interested in the stock market. It was during that time I quit my job at Central Ohio Medical Clinic and withdrew the money from my retirement account. I decided to invest my retirement money in the stock market. The Dow Jones Industrial Average is now up to 2,150, and I heard on TV that Worlds of Wonder, Inc., one of the stocks I invested in, did well last year, so we decided to spend $0.50 on a Wall Street Journal to check my stocks. It is the first paper we have purchased on the trip. Unfortunately, nothing that I own is doing great, alright, but not great. Oh well, too bad!

We took a bus to the Clearwater Mall and rode it back to our area without getting off, just so we could look around. It's a cheap way to sightsee. We walked back to the boat and then took down the jib. We got some grease on it while taking it off and spent about an hour cleaning up the mess.

Don fixed dinner at five thirty. We had a pork roast, mashed potatoes and gravy, and sauerkraut, with bread, butter, and jelly for dessert. We are eating well and I sure am glad the captain is doing the cooking! The winds finally started to subside about dinner time, and it has become a lot more comfortable without the rolling and pitching. The current conditions are probably the best we have had since Friday night in Tarpon Springs. However, we still needed to use the kerosene heater most of the evening. We watched the news, and after dinner I did the dishes while we watched *Wheel of Fortune*. Don and I both read before going to bed. We didn't watch President Reagan's State of the Union Address on TV. We figured it would be about the same as it was last year. He probably mentioned the Space Shuttle Challenger disaster, which occurred one year-ago tomorrow.

Island Yacht Club, Clearwater, FL

January 28, 1987, Wednesday

We finally got the damaged rigging off. Alan went up the mast and took down the bad rigging, and replacing it with lines that were tightened enough to hold up the mast. He then drove us to Catalina's Morgan plant where we left the rigging to be repaired.

Since we knew that we were going to have extra time on our hands, we checked to see if there were any duplicate bridge games close by in which Don could participate. We found a couple and so getting Don into a bridge game became the goal for the rest of the day. There was a game scheduled for one thirty at a facility near the beach close to where we are docked. We got back from the Morgan plant at one fifteen. Don and I went directly to where the bridge game was to be played, but by the time we got there, the game had already started. Don kibitzed. I went to the beach to lie out in the sun. It was sunny and in the mid-60s. It did get cooler around four in the afternoon, but by that time, Don was finished kibitzing at the bridge center, and we went home. We rushed dinner, so we could go to a different area of Clearwater where another bridge game was to begin at seven. In order not to be locked out of our marina for the night, we dinghied over to another marina and left our dinghy there. We took a bus to near where the game was to be played and then walked the remaining mile and a half. Don made it in time for the game. I shopped while he played bridge. I got a card for Shelly's birthday and Valentines for everyone at home. Some of the bridge people (Marge and Shorty) gave us a ride back to our dinghy. Don placed second and enjoyed the evening.

Island Yacht Club, Clearwater, FL

January 29, 1987, Thursday

We left the marina at about ten thirty, and headed for the bus-stop to get a bus to Saint Petersburg. We just wanted to do some sightseeing. On the way to the bus-stop, we stopped at a convenience store and bought a bag of donuts. When we got to the bus-stop, there were six or eight people waiting for the bus. There were no conversations going on; everybody was keeping to themselves—not being friendly at all. I decided to try to do something about that. I passed out donuts to everybody, and that worked like magic. Everybody got friendly. It was a fun experiment that worked. The friendliness continued after we were on board the bus.

After some sightseeing, we stopped at a bank and got cash with which to pay Catalina and then went to their place to pick up the rigging which was supposed to be ready, but it wasn't. We then caught another bus back to Island Estates where the boat is.

We didn't get back until six thirty. We ate leftovers because it was so late. I also fixed popcorn while we watched TV. We were both pretty tired, so we went to bed early.

Island Yacht Club, Clearwater, FL

January 30, 1987, Friday

I got up, confident that we would get to re-rig the boat and leave today, but the rigging won't be delivered to us early enough in the day for my plan to work; so, "Plan B" is to do laundry, clean, and work on the teak. Don did a few chores and, at about three thirty, went to the office to wait for the man from Catalina to bring the rigging. Catalina did bring the rigging, so hopefully we will get underway tomorrow.

We had Robin Linker over for sausage and kraut and fried potatoes, and then he invited us aboard his boat, *Promise*. It is a 44' Lafitte, a well-made Taiwanese boat, with lots of teak. The boat would cost about $160,000, new. It would be a great cruising boat for two couples. Robin has been a live-aboard for 17 years. He is 39 years old and has been living aboard a boat since he was 22. He intends to make it his way of life for his remaining years.

The weather was nice today, but began getting windy towards midnight.

Island Yacht Club, Clearwater, FL

January 31, 1987, Saturday

I have come to hate strong winds! They cause us problems in lots of ways. Today the wind is too high for Alan to climb to the top of the mast and re-rig our shroud and backstay. Don and I were both disappointed because we would like to get under way. My day consisted of very little work. I did walk to the grocery store to get a few things in preparation for leaving. Don rested and read most of the day. We rocked and rolled a lot.

One thing that we have learned is that Florida has a lot of bad weather during the winter. When we started we had the idea that about everyday would be sunny and warm in Florida during the winter. It seems like we have had more windy, rainy, cold days, than nice ones. Next year, we might find a place we like especially well and sit out the winter there.

We ate early (meatballs and rice with tomatoes) and then, at about six, we took a walk on the beach. We explored the strip of shops and hotels north of where we are and also went into one of the hotels along the strip, the Holiday Inn, and listened to a lady playing the piano. After that we sat out and swung for a time on a porch swing along the beach. It was a pleasant evening. We got back to the boat around nine thirty, showered, watched a little TV, and went to bed at midnight.

Island Yacht Club, Clearwater, FL

February 1, 1987, Sunday

The wind died down, and today was beautiful. Alan came over, climbed the mast, and re-rigged the shroud and backstay. We hope that now everything is as it should be. It cost us $100 for Catalina and $40 for Alan's services! However, dockage for the eight days we were here was free, which would normally have cost us $120 or so! They didn't charge us because this is a yacht club and we were disabled and getting repairs.

I talked to Shelly Friday night about her coming to Florida over spring break and about how we should pay for the plane ticket. She gave me the address where to send the check, so I got that in the mail along with a card to Mom before we left.

We pulled out of the dock at Island Estates at three thirty. We went to the drawbridge which crosses the Intracoastal Waterway at Clearwater. It was closed and not scheduled to open for twenty minutes or so. Rather than circling in very limited space, in the strong current and strong wind, we decided to drop anchor and wait. Don was at the helm, and I was at the anchor. We went against the current quite a way so that we would have room for the anchor to bite while the boat was still a safe distance from the bridge. I lowered the anchor and the 30 feet of chain and some line, unfortunately enough line that the current took it "downstream" to the stern of the boat and around the rudder, and it wedged itself into that narrow place between the rudder and the hull! Don was ticked off, and I felt bad. After spending nearly an hour trying to get the anchor line out of where it was wedged, we gave up and motored into the Clearwater Marina and tied up for the night.

We walked on the beach and swung on the swings again and just tried to recover our composure from our setback. We certainly didn't expect to be here tonight! It just goes to show; you take one step at a time. Each day is a new beginning. Don says it seems like we take about three steps forward and two back. I fixed pizza and even it was a disaster. What a day!

Clearwater Beach Marina, Clearwater, FL - Distance traveled: 6 miles

February 2, 1987, Monday

When I awoke, Don was already up and was making a lead line. A lead line is used to determine the depth of the water around the boat and where the deeper water is. When you are aground, it is helpful in figuring out which way you need to go to get ungrounded.

**THE BOTTOM OF A CATALINA 30 WITH A FIN KEEL
THE PROPELLER, THE SHAFT, THE STRUT,
AND THE ZINC, MOUNTED ON THE SHAFT, ARE VISIBLE**

I slept until nine thirty, and it felt great. After I had breakfast of Trix and hot chocolate, I got to work on the teak doors and drink holder. Don worked on the rudder and anchor line problem from the dinghy and even got in the water. I helped a little, but it still took almost 2.5 hours to get it free. I had a late lunch and then worked some more on the teak. Don showered and rested. He is bruised and cut up from his battle with the rudder and line. Around three thirty we took a nice long walk to the laundry. I only had a small load, but it was made up of clothes that Don had worn while working in the dinghy, and they had salt water on them. While the laundry was in the machines, we went over to the beach and pier. Don made supper of fried chicken, mashed potatoes and gravy, and we ate at seven. After that we had a relaxing evening watching TV. Reception is pretty good here, not like in the marshes of Georgia.

Clearwater Beach Marina, Clearwater, FL

February 3, 1987, Tuesday

The Florida State Fair will start tomorrow. A fair in the middle of winter seems strange to me. We got up early, bought fuel and paid the dock fees, and then took off for DeSoto Point at the mouth of the Manatee River, near Bradenton. It was sunny and a lot less windy than yesterday. Temperatures were in the 60°-70° range most of the day. Just as I put on my swim suit, the clouds came out to stay. Oh well, there will be plenty of sunbathing ahead.

We got to our anchoring spot at about four thirty. I heated leftover pizza, meatballs and rice, and mashed potatoes; I also baked a chocolate cake. We ate, and then I went out to the deck to sand some teak. Everything was peaceful until about nine thirty when Don realized the anchor line was around the keel. For an hour, we worked getting the line free–what a problem! Will we ever be able to anchor without problems? That is the $64,000.00 question! We stayed up until midnight watching TV and reading. Don made a diagram of the boat and the anchor lines, hoping he could figure out what is going on under water. Well, we'll see how that goes.

After studying the problem, Don believes that there are several things that are combining to cause our problems with anchoring: 1) the current; 2) the wind; 3) the fact that nylon anchor line is light enough for the current to lift the line off the bottom and sometimes lift it to near the surface of the water; 4) the wind can be strong enough to overpower the current and move the boat against the current so that the boat passes over the anchor, at which time the anchor line is not under any tension and is moving around like a water snake in the vicinity of the keel and rudder and can get around the keel, and/or caught on the rudder; 5) our long thin fin keel is a good anchor line catcher and so is our rudder; 6) on the Catalina 30, where the rudder is attached to the hull, there is a place where the anchor line can become wedged; and 7) with two anchors down, the potential for trouble is doubled.

An anchor line became wedged in the opening between the rudder and the hull at Butler Island on December 2, 1986 and at Clearwater last Sunday. The opening between the rudder and the hull becomes narrower near the pintle (the axle around which the rudder turns). When the anchor line is under tension and stretched, the line's diameter can become small enough that the line can get wedged all the way to the pintle, and then when it is no longer under tension and goes back to its normal diameter it is very difficult to get it out of the narrow opening.

A CATALINA 30 (NOT OUR BOAT) SHOWING GAP WHERE THE RUDDER CONNECTS TO THE BOAT

Chapman's book on piloting and seamanship, which is widely used by sailors, recommends that when you anchor you should have a scope of about seven to one, meaning that your rode (the length of your anchor line plus your chain) should be about seven times the distance from the bottom to the place on your boat where the anchor line is connected. Our boat draws about 5'6" when loaded with us and our gear, so we need to anchor where the chart shows a minimum depth at low tide of at least six feet. We normally anchor in deeper water. If the tidal range is four feet, then at high tide, the water will be 10' deep. The cleat where we connect the anchor line on the bow of our boat is four feet above the water level.

To have a scope of seven to one at high tide, we need a rode which is seven times longer than 14', or 98'. That means 30' of chain and about 70' of line. It's the 70' of line that's giving us trouble. Asking other boaters for advice hasn't been helpful, because every make of boat has its own bottom characteristics, and the boaters we have talked to don't have a fin keel and probably don't have the narrow opening above the rudder to contend with. We will try using less scope when we are anchored where there is a current. Don thinks a shorter line will help.

If we were starting over, we would get 50 feet of chain for each anchor, we would have a shoal draft keel, we would devise some way to keep the anchor line out of that notch on top of the rudder, and we think we would have a lot less trouble. We love our Catalina 30; it is great, but the fin keel is designed with racing rather than cruising in mind.

Anchored at Desoto Point on the Manatee River, near Bradenton, FL - Distance traveled: 43 miles

February 4, 1987, Wednesday

We both slept well and didn't get up until nine thirty. It was a beautiful day. We took the dinghy ashore to DeSoto National Park and saw a 20-minute film and a live performance by the park rangers. It was all about DeSoto's exploration in the southeastern part of America during the years of 1538-1541. He was looking for gold; he found the Mississippi River, but no gold. DeSoto Point is on the trail his expedition followed. We got back to the boat at one, had a quick lunch of leftovers, weighed anchor, and headed for Bradenton.

We got to Bradenton at three thirty, tied up at a marina, and walked around. It was pretty, but rather disappointing from a live-aboard's standpoint. A live-aboard likes a place with electric and water hook-ups, good clean showers and the following facilities nearby: laundromat; post office; hardware store; supermarket; bank, a pay phone, and a trash receptacle. This marina doesn't have much to offer. We motored over to another marina, but it wasn't anything special either. We were underway again by five thirty to find a place to anchor for the night. We anchored near Snead Island Boat Works between Bradenton and the mouth of the Manatee River.

I worked on the teak, oiling a few pieces while Don fixed dinner. We had cauliflower soup with cheddar cheese and grilled cheese sandwiches. For dessert, we had leftover chocolate cake. After the dishes were done, we watched a little TV, and I wrote some postcards. We had a relaxing evening. All in all, it was a very good day. It's now ten, and the wind has picked up; it's hard to say what kind of night this one will be.

PS - Don bought us a great book on Florida's water birds. It has lots of beautiful pictures.

Anchored at Snead Island Boat Works on the Manatee River, near Bradenton, FL - Distance traveled: 8 miles

February 5, 1987, Thursday

Today started off badly; Don was wearing my watch and lost it overboard when the watchband broke while he was raising the anchor. It was a Timex I had bought while I was working at Central Ohio Medical Group. It wasn't expensive—maybe $30.00.

We "upped" the anchor and motored into the wind for approximately ten miles in the direction of Sarasota, and then decided to put in because the wind had picked up and was blowing about 25 knots. We tied up for the night at The Point at Mariner's Cove, which is a new condominium complex near Cortez. The condos are about $300,000. It has a floor plan Don and I would like when we settle down again.

We paid our dockage fees ($14.50) and then took a walk. We stopped at a local fish market, where we bought some smoked mullet for dinner. We also looked for a place that sells kerosene because we are getting low. We got back to the boat and fixed our dinner of smoked mullet, cottage cheese, fruit, and blueberry muffins. In the evening, we walked to the shower at the marina next door (Seafood Shack) and paid for showers, and then took a walk and a dinghy ride in the harbor. Back on the boat we read until midnight. The moon has a halo around it tonight. It is cool and has sprinkled a couple of times; the waves are about two feet.

The Pointe at Mariner's Cover, Cortez, FL - Distance traveled: 12 miles

February 6, 1987, Friday

It was calm throughout the night. We slept well. After breakfast, Dave the dockmaster came over and said he was going to Snead Island Boat Works and offered to take us. Of course we accepted. It was a pleasant 15-mile trip for us. So, we got to see Bradenton by car, having seen it on the previous day by boat and walking. When we got back, around noon, Don worked on the rigging, and I worked on the teak. The teak now has one full coat of oil on all pieces. At about four, we walked to the firehouse for a dinner put on as a money-raising project by the firemen—a fried mullet dinner—all you could eat @ $3.00/head. It was very good, and we had a nice time talking with people. We went to bed at eight and read for a couple of hours before falling asleep. It started to rain around midnight.

The Pointe at Mariner's Cover, Cortez, FL

February 7, 1987, Saturday

We left Cortez in mid-morning and had a pleasant trip to Sarasota. We sailed most of the way. It was cloudy, but pretty warm, and the wind was just right (on the beam), so we made six knots most of the way.

We got to Marina Jack's at about one thirty and anchored. I worked a little on wrapping the steering wheel with cord and I also started the second coat of oil on the teak. Don read until time to fix dinner. The wind picked up at about dinner time and blew hard all evening. We had pork chops, potatoes, gravy and carrots. It tasted great, but I was nauseated from all the motion, so I lay around all night. We watched a program on whales, and I fell asleep early. The motion was excessive all night.

Anchored on the south side of Marina Jack's, Sarasota, FL - Distance traveled: 16 miles

February 8, 1987, Sunday

By morning, the winds had subsided and the conditions were finally calm. We decided to tie up at Marina Jack's for the day in order to get some things done and then spend the night there. When we started to move the boat, I accidentally fouled the anchor trip-line around the prop by running over the trip-line buoy. Oh, No! What a start! Don had to go diving. Fortunately, it was sunny and in the 60s; the water temp is about 65. It took an hour for him to cut the line away. He used his mask and snorkel and came up very often. After all that, we got safely docked.

We met an interesting older couple, and they drove us to the grocery which was great because I had invited Norbert and Barbara Chase, Don's cousin and his wife, to join us for dinner. In the afternoon, we washed the boat deck, and I did laundry.

While I was walking from the laundry room to the boat, I saw a familiar face. Martin Gilbert was standing on the dock. We first met Martin in Catskill, New York, where he joined Captain Randy and Paul as an additional crew member of *Renegade*. I was certainly surprised to see him. *Renegade's* destination was Marathon, and we had no idea Martin's destination was Sarasota. He and his wife, Mary, rented a condo across a small bay just north of Marina Jack's. We hadn't met Mary because only Martin had flown to Catskill to join *Renegade*. He went to the condo and got her and brought her back to Marina Jack's to meet us. We visited aboard *Robin Lee*.

We barely had time to get dinner prepared for Norbert and Barbara, but we did, and it turned out great. We had beef Stroganoff, noodles, broccoli and bread, and served fresh cut up fruit as dessert. After dinner, we took a walk on the docks to show them the marina. I think they had a good time and were favorably impressed with our live-aboard lifestyle. It was a great day (other than the bad beginning), and we had a much more comfortable night at dockside, even though it was still blowing about 30 mph.

Docked at Marina Jack's, Sarasota, FL

February 9, 1987, Monday

Martin came by about ten to see if he and Mary could take us around town and show us the highlights of Sarasota. We accepted his invitation and had a great day. We saw various points of interest, including the Ringling Museum. We also stopped at a bank because we were low on cash again. We had lunch with them at a little place on Main Street in the old part of Sarasota, near the marina, and then had an ice cream cone.

Around six, after moving our boat out of the marina and anchoring it in the little bay between the marina and Martin and Mary's condo, we dinghied over to their place for a spaghetti dinner. It was very good, and we really enjoyed their company. Martin is 67, but doesn't look his age and the same is true for Mary. She is 47 and looks like she is my age (36), except she is totally grey. They are a fun couple to be with. We dinghied back home to *Robin Lee* at eleven thirty.

The weather was nice during the day, but it is really cold tonight.

Anchored on the north side of Marina Jack's, Sarasota, FL

February 10, 1987, Tuesday

Today was so fun! We took Mary and Martin out for a day-sail, leaving about ten, and arriving at Harborside Moorings, on Longboat Key, around twelve thirty to visit Hope and Harry. They had company when we got there, so we went to the nearby shopping center for refreshments. I had served lunch onboard, so Mary and I just had an Italian ice drink. It tasted super. We returned to Hope and Harry's boat around two and visited until four thirty. We made the six o'clock bridge opening on our way back into Sarasota. The sail over was great, but we did have to motor back in the evening.

At seven, the four of us drove back to Harborside Moorings and picked up the Eilers, and the six of us went out to eat at a Chinese place. The food was so-so, but we had fun visiting. We got home very late. The weather again was pretty, but it was a very cold night.

Anchored on the north side of Marina Jack's, Sarasota, FL

February 11, 1987, Wednesday

I left our boat at about eight thirty and dinghied to Mary and Martin's condo. I showered and then ate breakfast with Mary. Harry came over at ten and we all sat around and talked until twelve thirty. Then Harry took Don and me to Venice to get our mail, and I mailed all our Valentine cards.

Tonight we stayed on board, went through our mail, and read Christmas cards that had been sitting around for a couple of months waiting for us to catch up to them and also looked at pictures sent by Connie Montgomery (pictures of Connie's new baby, Mallory, and her other children, Maggie and Matt). I loved them! We also had our neighbors in the anchorage, Judy and Richard, who are living aboard a 1928 wooden power boat, *Aldene Arnold*, over to visit. They are an interesting couple who have lived aboard for several years. At one time, they shipped *Aldene Arnold* across the Atlantic on a container ship and traveled the waterways of Europe, and then shipped it back to the U.S. They left at about eleven. It has been great staying here in Sarasota because we have had so much fun making friends and just "playing."

Don says he feels that this trip has been his first real opportunity to make friends and enjoy people since graduating from school. He says that when he was in school and when he was in the Army he spent a lot of time just "messing around" with people and sharing experiences, and that is how friendships are made. After finishing school he got too busy with work, home and family to have time to play with people, and therefore, didn't develop any close relationships. He says that to him, the most enjoyable thing about this trip is having the chance to do so. I agree.

Anchored on the north side of Marina Jack's, Sarasota, FL

FROM LEFT TO RIGHT: MARTIN, HOPE, DON, MARY, AND HARRY

February 12, 1987, Thursday

Mary and I had another fun day. I went over and picked her up in the dinghy, and we motored to O'Learys to have lunch and visit Martin. O'Learys is a cute little restaurant near the beach next to Marina Jack's. Martin is retired, but works part-time at O'Learys as a busboy, just for the fun of it. On the way back, after getting gas for the dinghy, we motored over to see the 1928 *Aldene Arnold*. It wasn't quite as impressive inside as I had expected from the outside appearance, but Judy and Richard, the owners, were very pleasant to talk with.

Afterwards, we motored back to Mary's condo and went to the condo's pool. We lay out in the sun until four. I used the shower at Mary's apartment and then went to *Robin Lee* to get Don. We had a Mexican meal with Mary and Martin at their condo. It was tasty, but quite unusual, since they are vegetarians and put yogurt, nuts, and raisins in with the vegetables. It didn't taste very Mexican. At seven Norbert and Barb came by to pick us up, and the four of us went to the Sarasota airport to pick up Betty and Clayton. We were glad to see them and had coffee and dessert at Norbert and Barb's place while visiting. We got back to the boat around eleven thirty. The dew on the dinghy was as much as if it had rained.

Anchored on the north side of Marina Jack's, Sarasota, FL

February 13, 1987, Friday

We did some minor clean-up chores this morning and got the laundry ready to take with us. Betty and Clayton picked us up at noon. We did some grocery shopping and then went to Aloha Kai, which is the Condo Complex Norbert and Barb manage and where Betty and Clayton are staying. While there, I used their laundry facilities and lay out at the pool while Don visited with Betty and Clayton at their condo. In the evening, we had a huge dinner party with 25 people—friends and family that happened to be wintering in the area. The food was great, and everyone was interested in hearing about our trip so far and our plans for the rest of the trip.

Anchored on the north side of Marina Jack's, Sarasota, FL

February 14, 1987, Saturday, Valentine's Day

Don gave me a Valentine card, but I didn't have one for him. I don't know why—I guess I was too cheap. I hated to spend any more money than I had already spent for all of those cards I sent to Randy, Nick, Danielle, Dad, Mom, Grandma, Shelly, and Chip. I figured Don wouldn't mind. I hope it didn't hurt his feelings. I would never want him to feel bad or think I didn't care. He's a jewel, a real gem, whom I treasure. I feel so lucky to have him and his love!

We weighed anchor early and moved the boat over to Marina Jack's. Don's Aunt Gladys and Glennis and Yvonne wanted to see our boat. They also brought Betty and Clayton over so they could join us for a sail down to Venice, about 17 miles south, along the Intracoastal Waterway. We gave our guests a tour of the boat; it didn't take long. Aunt Gladys (Don's father's 85-year-old sister) was especially interested and asked a lot of questions. After we showed them the boat, Aunt Gladys, Glennis and Yvonne left.

We had a pleasant trip to Venice. The weather was good, but we didn't have wind, so we motored. Clayton was at the helm most of the time and Betty sat in the sun in the cockpit. We ate lunch on board, having leftovers from Friday night's dinner at Aloha Kai. Everything tasted good, especially the honey baked ham and homemade bread and cookies. Barb came to Venice to pick up Betty and Clayton around two thirty. We barely had time to unwind and clean up before Hope and Harry came to see us and return our video cassette tapes. They had borrowed them to copy the tapes that included video of them. In the evening, Hope, Harry, Mary, Martin, Don and I went to the Crow's Nest restaurant to eat and to celebrate Valentine's Day. We spent the entire evening visiting, and saying our good-byes, since we plan on heading south from Venice tomorrow or the next day. On the way back to the boat, we stopped at a grocery store. It was after midnight before we went to bed.

Tied up at Town Dock, Venice, FL - Distance traveled: 20 miles

February 15, 1987, Sunday

Boy, it's really true: "Time flies when you are having fun." We are six weeks into 1987; winter is half over. The weather has been just beautiful for the past week, sunny every day, with no clouds. It is so wonderful here in the winter compared to Ohio; it seems like paradise.

The Coast Guard did an inspection of our boat today and found a couple of wires that should be replaced. Don will fix them, but not today. Since there was a bridge game close by, he left me to write and do some sunbathing while he played duplicate bridge. I visited with a few people walking by on the docks while sunning myself at a small park near the docks. It is always fun to talk with people about cruising life. I also explored in the dinghy.

Don got home around four thirty. I had already taken my shower on deck, using the "sun shower." A sun shower consists of a strong plastic bag with a hose attached. It has a shower head and an "on and off" valve attached at the end of the hose. It is filled with water and laid where the sun will shine on it. The bag is designed to absorb the solar heat, and it is surprising how warm the water gets after a few hours in the sun. It is then hung from the boom and the person taking the shower sits, or squats, in the cockpit. It works well. In order to have privacy, we use our cockpit cushions to make a screen and wear our bathing suits.

When Don got home, he fixed our first vegetarian meal: Brussels sprouts with cheese and water chestnuts. Both of us liked it. Later, we took a walk along the beach on the gulf. It was just beautiful, and the stars were very bright. We have seen many beautiful beaches, and I don't think we will ever tire of them.

Tied at Higel Park, Venice, FL

February 16, 1987, Monday

The winds were strong today, so we stayed put. It turned out to be quite an unusual day. First, around noon, we left to walk to the community center where a duplicate bridge game was to be played, and some locals gave us a ride. They are environmental employees and were in a pick-up truck. They dropped us off for lunch at a local restaurant that is run by former circus performers. The restaurant had an interesting group of circus people there for lunch. The Ringling Brothers' Circus winters in Venice. We left there in plenty of time for the bridge game, but it poured down, and we stopped frequently at buildings with awnings or other protection from the rain to avoid getting soaked clear through. However, by the time we got to the community center four blocks away, we were completely wet. I had planned to spend my time doing cross-stitch while Don played bridge, but they didn't have anyone available to be his partner for this game, so he had to play with me or not play. He chose me, unfortunately. I managed to play, albeit poorly, for three hours.

On the way home, we stopped for ice cream, and as we were sitting and looking out the window, we saw Hope and Harry pass by. We were excited to see them. They had gotten my message off the recorder and knew we had stayed an extra day in Venice. It was nice of them to come down to visit one more time, and they insisted on taking us out to eat at Captain's Table restaurant in Englewood Beach.

We visited, taking a long time to eat, and didn't get back to our boat until ten thirty. On the boat, Don and Harry talked about business matters concerning a job Harry is considering. They talked until two in the morning. We were sorry it was time to part again. It sure would be nice if they could cruise with us some more. They really are a fun couple. When we got up this morning, we never would have dreamed we would be going to Englewood Beach tonight for dinner. We never know what the day may bring.

Tied at Higel Park, Venice, FL

February 17, 1987, Tuesday, Shelly's 19th birthday

I got up at seven, just so I could call my darling daughter on her 19th birthday before she left for her first class. This is the first birthday I have not spent with her in her whole life. I feel bad about it, but it was unavoidable. No doubt there will be other such days in the years ahead. We left Higel Park at eight thirty and went out the Venice Inlet into the Gulf of Mexico. We motored 35 miles south from the inlet and then left the gulf through the Boca Grande Pass into Charlotte Harbor. In the gulf, we had four-foot swells all day long. Don and I both felt nauseated, and were glad to get into protected waters and away from the swell. We went into Boca Grande, which we had explored on our way north. We anchored and tied off mangrove trees in the quiet anchorage by the Pink Elephant restaurant. We "dropped the hook" at about three thirty.

After dinner of stuffed green peppers, Don and I rowed across the bayou and walked to the gulf. As usual, the gulf was beautiful from shore, and we watched the sun set. We then

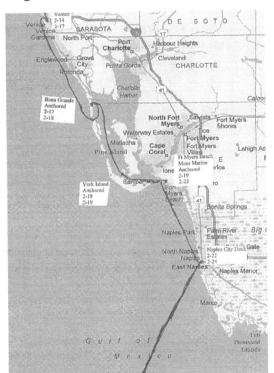

continued our walk, stopped at an ice cream parlor, and over-indulged. We sure are living the good life. After getting back to the boat, I wrote letters and Don read. This is a great anchorage. There are six other boats here.

It was a pretty day and evening.

Anchored at Boca Grande, FL - Distance traveled: 37 miles

February 18, 1987, Wednesday

We got up to a thick cloud cover and no wind. We didn't leave the anchorage until ten thirty. It was a lazy kind of day, so we took it easy. We spoke by radio with *Aldene Arnold* (Judy and Dick). They are at Punta Gorda. We motored south ten miles to Cabbage Key and had lunch there. Cabbage Key is very small, and the only way to get to the island and restaurant is by boat. The restaurant is famous for its decor. It is known for the dollar bills that are pinned up on the walls and every other place you can stick one. They are signed and dated by the customers who pinned them up. That tradition has been going on for a long time. The walls are completely covered. Dick Solove's son, Jerry, was there. Don recognized him as he was coming into the dock in his boat. He was with his fiancée and her family and had come from Captiva Island to have lunch.

Being conservative (tight), as we are, we didn't pin up a dollar. We just ate lunch, paid up, and left. Lunch came to $7.00 with tip. After leaving there at two, we sailed 16 miles southeast to York Island and anchored for the night. We got settled in by five and ate scalloped potatoes and ham at six. I wrote letters in the evening. We watched a little TV, and went to bed at ten thirty.

Anchored off York Island, FL - Distance traveled: 25 miles

February 19, 1987, Thursday

We had breakfast at eight and then watched the Today show. After that, we pulled up the anchor and went, by motor, 12 miles to Moss Marine at Fort Myers Beach. After tying up, we worked the rest of the day cleaning and doing odd jobs. Don fixed the bilge switch, and we changed the oil. Towards evening, we walked to the beach and bought pizza for dinner.

Then we walked over to the Lani Key Motel where Shelly stayed last year during spring break. On the way back home, we stopped at a dive shop and bought snorkeling gear. We spent $120 today on docking fees, fuel, snorkeling gear and other items. We do try to make our money stretch as far as we can, but it's tough.

When we got home, we took it easy. We watched Sherlock Holmes and 20/20 and then went to bed. I lifted up the anchor today and am sore from using muscles that aren't normally used. Don is having trouble with his back. Hopefully, it will get better, if I continue to raise the anchor.

Moss Marine, Fort Myers Beach, FL - Distance traveled: 12 miles

February 20, 1987, Friday

Today was a very warm day with the temperature in the low 80s. We walked three miles in the morning to a bank, a grocery store, the post office, a hardware store, a shop where I bought a two piece-bathing suit, and a Dairy Queen. After that, Don continued with errands, while I did the laundry.

I talked with Randy today, and she told me that Janine King had died. She was the wife of Gale King, one of the lawyers in Don's office. We ate dinner with Gale and Janine along with the rest of the people at Don's office shortly before we left for this trip. She was diagnosed as having brain cancer only six weeks ago. We were shocked by the news.

After we got back to the boat, we cleaned the stainless steel topside with Soft Scrub and then hosed the deck. Soft Scrub really cleans things up. About five thirty, just as we were getting ready to leave the dock to go anchor, it started raining. So, instead of anchoring, we stayed and spent another $22. Don fixed leftovers for dinner, and then, after the rain showers passed, we took a long walk, and I mailed a letter to Shelly. We stopped at the Dairy Queen again. I only got a small cone this time, because I had a nice big one in the afternoon while doing laundry. Don had a hot fudge sundae. We then walked about two miles to the Winn Dixie Super Market, bought five bags of groceries, and started home. About halfway home, we stopped to rest and get some water to drink. A taxi cab driver on his meal break saw us and must have felt sorry for us, because he brought us the rest of the way home, right to our dock, and didn't charge us one cent—our lucky day. Maybe he has done some cruising on a boat and understands how much walking live-aboards must do.

Moss Marine, Fort Myers Beach, FL

February 21, 1987, Saturday

I got up late this morning, sunbathed briefly in my new suit, and then worked for about ½ hour wrapping cord around the wheel to give it more grip.

A single-handed, live-aboard lady asked me to tail for her as she was hoisted to the top of her mast to take care of a problem. She got on her boson's chair, a simple canvas and wood seat with a line that is attached to the mainsail halyard, and some guy, using the halyard winch, hoisted her up in the same way a sail is hoisted. My job was to manage the tail (the end part of the halyard that has already passed around the wench), making sure it didn't get tangled. I spent about a half hour helping her.

Afterwards, Don and I put our anchors, anchor chain, and line away. He worked most of the day getting the anchors ready for anchoring at the Dry Tortugas, where we will be anchoring in water 40' to 50' deep. I showered, and then we left the marina and anchored for the night in Matanzas Pass on the east side of Estero Island, just south of the bridge in Fort Myers Beach. The pass has a swift current, and so we put down two anchors. We stayed aboard for about an hour and then took the dinghy ashore. A kind couple gave us a lift to the hardware store. They happened to be in the area boat shopping. They even gave us a ride back. We have found that most people are very nice to the live-aboard boating community. We bought a cable and a lock at the hardware store to use to secure the dinghy when we are ashore. Hopefully, it will do the trick. The traffic along the highway was terrible, and we were glad to be going back to the boat. We like traveling on the water, where there aren't any traffic jams. Before going back to the boat, we stopped at the Charlotte and Bob Wallace Residence, where we had left our dinghy, to 'chat' and sign their guest registry. The Wallaces are an older couple who are interested in making the cruising boaters' lives easier by providing a 'dinghy landing'. All they ask is that you go up to the porch, say "Hi," and sign the guest book. They enjoy meeting people and hearing the stories cruisers tell. Ralph and Norma on *Norma Jane,* from Massachusetts told us about them. After signing the guest book, we took the dinghy to a nearby store and bought some beer, because we had heard that professional fishermen anchor at the Tortugas, and that you can use beer to barter for fish and lobsters.

Don fixed Beef Stew for dinner; we stayed on board to read and relax in the evening. The mosquitoes are really bad tonight. I just smashed one in this 'log book'—yuck, how gross!

Anchored in Matanzas Pass, just south of the bridge, Fort Myers Beach, FL

February 22, 1987, Sunday

We weighed anchor at nine forty and left for Naples. The weather was sunny and warm, but at about two the winds increased. We had a long day motoring in the Gulf of Mexico with the wind on our nose the entire trip. I did get to wear my two-piece bathing suit for a couple of hours. We tied up at about four thirty at the city dock in Naples. I telephoned Pam Parramore at her hotel late in the evening; we are the same age and were middle & high school friends back in Urbana, Ohio in the mid-1960s. She and her husband, Doug, are in Naples.

Don made stir-fried chicken tonight, and after dinner, I did the dishes. We took a walk later and found a ship's store selling flags, among other things. We bought a Bahamas Courtesy Flag, talked with the store owners briefly, then came home, and watched a little TV before turning in for the night. This tiny five inch TV works pretty well. We only bought it for reviewing our video taken with our camcorder, but have used it more than we ever thought we would for watching programs. Dock fees are cheap considering the area ($0.50/foot/night). Naples is a beautiful city, for sure!

City Dock, Naples, FL - Distance traveled: 35 miles

February 23, 1987, Monday

We slept well and late as usual, except we were awakened at four in the morning due to an unusual feeling. We were listing 20 degrees to the Port Side. Rolling to the side of our berth was a strange feeling. This alarmed us because it had never happened before. We wondered if we were sinking. We found no water in the boat, not even in the bilge. We finally figured out that we were, once again, aground at a dock, but this was the first time it caused the boat to list. At Jekyll Island in Georgia, our entire fin keel was in the mud; our bottom was sitting flat on the bottom and there was no water within several feet of the boat. There the boat didn't list, because the mud was soft and deep, enough so that the keel just sunk strait down without hitting anything hard, until the bottom of the boat came to rest in the mud. Neither did the boat list at the Toledo Yacht Club nor in Oriental, North Carolina. At those places probably only the tip of the keel was in soft mud; just enough to keep us from moving. However, here the keel apparently came down on a hard surface, either at the bottom or a little under it, and since the boat wasn't perfectly balanced on it, it leaned. Once we had this all figured out, we went back to sleep. By the time we got up, the boat was floating upright again; the listing apparently happened at low tide. The tide and a strong wind from the east combined to push the water out of the bay where the marina is located. This was the fourth time the wind and/or tide had taken the water out from under our keel while we were asleep. We now realize that this is a common occurrence. We also realize that it doesn't damage the boat. Keels are designed to support the entire weight of the boat. In fact, a very common way of storing a sailboat on shore is to set its keel down on a hard surface, such as asphalt or concrete, and to use chocks (props) just to keep the boat from falling over on its side.

I spent an hour oiling the teak, and visiting with the couple on the boat next to us. They are from Chicago and are visiting the wife's brother who has a home here in Naples. This week, the boat, a 41 ft. Hans Christian, which belongs to her brother, is serving as a guest house. Don and I also talked to some other boaters about listing last night. Some of the boats listed and some of them didn't, depending on how much their boats draw.

Don and I watched a little TV and waited for Pam and Doug Parramore to stop by for a visit. After they got to the boat, the four of us and two other couples (their friends) went to The Dock restaurant to eat lunch. It was fun and Pam and I had a little time to ourselves to chat. She is pregnant, due in May. I was glad we could get together.

Around four, they all left and Don and I went for a walk around Naples to see the city. First we went to the 3rd Street shopping area, and I was finally able to buy the book, *Where Was Mom When I Needed Her!* which I had wanted to buy for Shelly's Birthday. It's called an aid to survival, and contains various instructive articles, such as recipes, how to sew on a button, how to do laundry, how to remove stains, etc. I will send it to her as a late gift. I think it's something she will always be able to use and can keep to remember this time in our lives.

After that we went out to the fishing pier and then down Fifth Avenue. We stopped at 'Ad Miller's Real Estate Company'. He is deceased but his wife, Casey (Mary Jo), now in her 80s and their son Tex, in his 40s, were there. The Millers moved from Dublin, Ohio to Naples in the mid-1940s. They played a significant role in Naples' development and are partly responsible for so many central Ohioans having winter homes there. Don's parents and the Millers were good friends when they lived in Dublin, and Don and Tex were childhood friends. The Millers were also good friends of Johnny and Dortha May Moffitt. I am sure that Casey appreciated our visit. She is now quite feeble, and Tex runs the business. We left there at six and walked back to the boat. The weather looks good for a sail to the Dry Tortugas tomorrow.

City dock, Naples, FL

February 24 & 25, 1987, Tuesday & Wednesday

The Dry Tortugas are 130 miles south-west of Naples and 70 miles west of Key West, in the Gulf of Mexico, and are part of Florida. Ponce de León was the first European to discover them, and he gave them the name "Las Tortugas," meaning "The Turtles." The word "Dry" was added because there is no fresh water on the islands. The Dry Tortugas are a small group of low lying islands, the biggest of which, Loggerhead Key, is ¾ of a mile long and less than 1/5 of a mile wide. Loggerhead's highest elevation is only ten feet above sea level, and that is the highest elevation of all the islands in the group. Garden Key is the second largest island. Fort Jefferson is located on Garden Key. It was built during the period from 1835 to 1865 by the U.S. Government for protection from an attack from the Gulf of Mexico. It was never fired upon. The fort was converted to a prison, and its most famous inmate was Dr. Samuel Mudd, the doctor who treated the leg of John Wilkes Booth that was broken when he assassinated President Abraham Lincoln. Dr. Mudd was convicted of being one of the persons who conspired to kill President Lincoln and was imprisoned at Fort Jefferson. He was recently cleared from having taken part in the conspiracy. The entire group of islands and the waters surrounding them are now a national park–The Dry Tortugas National Park. We have been told by several cruising sailors that they are worth the long trip, so we are going to go see them.

I got up at eight and set out to get some bread and ice, and to mail some postcards. We filled our water tanks and extra water containers, and checked to be sure our fuel tank was full. We will have to use our supply of water sparingly because there isn't any fresh water available. Don tested the radio, the Loran, the navigation lights, the anchor light and the spreader lights, to be sure they were working. He checked the bilge to be sure it was dry, the oil level, the glass bowl in the fuel filter system, and about everything else on the boat to be certain that everything was ship-shape. Don called his office, and I called Randy to let her know we were leaving on a 130-mile voyage across open water. We had considered going to Marco Island, which is 15 miles south of Naples, before going to the Tortugas, because we have heard it's nice. This would be our only opportunity to go there on this trip, but that would have delayed the trip to the Tortugas for a least a day, and since the weather forecast for today and tomorrow is good and the forecast for the next couple of days is not, we decided we should take advantage of the favorable weather and go directly to the Tortugas. We will have to go to Marco Island some other time.

As we went out the channel into the gulf, at 10:30 a.m., Don checked the compass, the knot meter and log, and the depth sounder to be sure they were working properly. Because The Tortugas are a very small, low lying group of islands, in the middle of the gulf, with nothing around them, we will have to rely on our Loran system and dead reckoning to find them. If we are more than a couple of miles to one side of them, we won't see them and will go right on by. We have been disappointed in our Loran System because its readings are sometimes unreliable. The captain has been quite anxious about our 130-mile voyage. To boost his confidence, I have tried not to show any concern.

At noon, we started a two-hour watch routine. He took the 12-2 p.m. watch while I rested and fixed tuna salad. I couldn't eat. I was nauseated because of the large following swell. We had easterly winds the entire 24-hour trip, averaging 10-15 knots. My watch began at 2 p.m., and I steered until 4 p.m. because Vern can't handle a following sea. A following sea is one where the waves are moving in the same direction as the boat or at a slight angle and therefore are striking the stern, which tends to turn the boat. Vern isn't able to correct for that and keep us on our course. I was really exhausted when Don came on duty for the 4-6 p.m. watch. I still didn't feel like eating, but he had made me a PB&J sandwich, and I ate it.

It didn't settle, my queasy stomach, but it didn't come up…right away. I rested on my time off. I didn't feel like doing anything. Things in our home were starting to move around a little, shifting from here to there. I did the best I could to secure things, but knew it would be somewhat messy, by the time we arrived. Sunset was at six forty and was pretty; Don took some video of it. By this time, we were about 50 miles out of Naples. My watch, from 6-8 p.m., was uneventful except for the sun setting and the seas calming enough for Vern to go back on duty. Darkness quickly set in. I was glad to be relieved when Don came on duty at 8 p.m. Along with the darkness fell the heavy dew, and soon everything, including me, was wet. I slept from 8-10 p.m. and when I got up to go back on duty at 10 p.m., I was still nauseated. The wind was increasing, and I asked Don to take down the main. He had already furled the jib. I didn't want to sail in the middle of the Gulf, at night, with no autopilot, and high winds. The motion of the boat pitching and rolling finally did bring up what little food was in my stomach. I started my watch at 10 p.m., after cleaning myself up. I was feeling a little better. Don doesn't get as nauseated as I do. He hasn't come close to up-chucking on the whole trip. Don took down the mainsail after I took the helm at 10 p.m. I didn't feel too good during my 2-4 a.m. shift either, but I managed to complete it. I just kept thinking of all the good things to look forward to, including that when we got to the Tortugas the longest leg of our voyage would be behind us. I don't think we will have any more trips this long. I saw the lights of many fishing boats on the horizon during my 2-4 a.m. watch, but we never came close to any. During my break from 4-6 a.m., I slept the entire time and I felt a little better, although I still had some nausea. By the end of Don's watch, I was rested. From 6-8 a.m., I watched and steered. Sunrise came at about 7 a.m.

After eight o'clock, Don and I both stayed on duty. We shut Vern off and put him below, because we knew we would be coming into shallow water and wanted to be in complete control. During the trip, the Loran intermittently gave us warnings that its readings were unreliable, and that did not boost the captain's confidence. However, because Don is conscientious about his dead reckoning navigation, I remained confident. At nine, we saw the light from the Loggerhead Lighthouse. Shortly after that we saw Buoy Number One marking the entrance into the channel leading to Garden Key. According to the chart, Garden Key was just a couple of miles away from that buoy, but we still couldn't see any land. What we did see when the sun came out was beautiful, clear, clean, aqua-colored water. Don and I both started feeling very good at that point. We arrived safely and anchored near Garden Key at ten thirty, exactly 24 hours after we had left Naples. We were both very tired, so we stayed on board until 2:30 p.m. In the early afternoon, we had a little something to eat. I put my two-piece suit on and did some sunbathing. It was pretty warm, probably in the low 80s. We listened to the radio but the FM stations were out of range, and the AM stations were Cuban or Mexican. I found one AM station from Key West, and although it wasn't very clear, at least they spoke English. We were surprised to find 16 pleasure boats at the anchorage here at Garden Key and several large commercial fishing boats.

At 2:30 p.m., we put the motor on the dinghy and went ashore to do some sightseeing and picture taking at the fort. All day long, sea planes came and went, and after a while, we figured out that they were bringing tourists to see Fort Jefferson. Later, we learned that each person pays $95 to come out for a few hours and then fly back. By plane, it is only 35-40 minutes. It took us 24 hours, but only cost five gallons of diesel fuel, which would cost about $7.00—not a bad price for moving two people and their home 130 miles.

The fort was a big undertaking when it was built. It was never completely finished although it was under construction for 30 years. It was finally turned over to the park service by President Roosevelt in 1935 and became a national historic landmark.

On the way back to the boat, at about 4 p.m., we swung by a commercial fishing boat, *Daddy's Boy* to ask the captain if he wanted to trade some lobsters for a six-pack of beer. Luckily, he had a few lobsters left, and he gave us four really big meaty fresh ones for our six-pack of Carling Black Label. Don and I were glad we had bought the beer and brought it along, and wished we had bought more.

The meal was excellent–fresh lobster and melted butter with a couple of pieces of bread and jelly; we were happy cruisers! The fishing boat *Daddy's Boy* became a party boat in the evening. There were about 15 people on board partying. We sat out in the cockpit and watched until sundown, and then the moisture from the dew drove us inside. We read, relaxed, and now I'm writing in this book before retiring. The wind is blowing pretty hard. I hope we can get through the night without the anchor dragging or the line getting fouled up.

First night at sea & second night anchored off Garden Key, The Dry Tortugas, FL - Distance traveled: 130 miles

February 26, 1987, Thursday

The wind is blowing hard. Don is concerned about the anchor holding, so he decided not to leave the boat unattended today. I took the dinghy ashore and met two boys, Kelly and Keith, ages 18 and 11, who live aboard a narrow beamed 28-foot sailboat from Mississippi, with their parents, Anita and Brian. The parents are about my age. That is a small boat for four people to live on. The boys told me that they can't stand up in the cabin. It must be terribly crowded. The four of them have been living on it for seven years. Kelly and I walked along the moat around the fort and looked at the sea creatures, including starfish, barracuda, conch, urchins and unknown varieties of fish.

The Dry Tortugas are home to a large seabird colony which includes Sooty Terns, Brown Noddies, Masked Boobies and Magnificent Frigate Birds. The terns are now nesting and mating over on Bush Key, so it is closed to the public. They sure make a lot of noise. There are thousands of them.

I also saw the owner of the fishing boat, *Daddy's Boy*, the man we bartered with yesterday for some lobsters. His nickname is Pelican. Ross is his first mate. Pelican invited Don and me to come aboard *Daddy's Boy* for dinner. We accepted and had a very interesting evening. First, we toured *Daddy's Boy*. It is a 53' commercial fishing vessel and is only six months old. Pelican and Ross both speak Spanish and were originally from Cuba. They immigrated to Key West many years ago. After our tour, we enjoyed our meal of kidney bean, potato, and cabbage stew, and another dish of hamburger, olives and tomatoes, both of which were served over rice. There were several other people on board who had also been invited for dinner, including the young boys I met earlier today and their parents. A farming couple from Iowa and their two small kids, ages three and one, were also there. They farm during the summers and cruise on their sailboat in the winters. Their boat's name is *Whisper*; it's anchored close to us. So tonight we were part of the party on *Daddy's Boy*.

About six thirty another fishing boat, *Mary D II*, ran over our anchor line and snagged it and dragged our boat part way across the anchorage. We and the other people aboard *Daddy's Boy* did a lot of hollering and hand waiving and eventually got their attention, and they saw what they were doing. They stopped and got the line unsnagged. Don and a crewman from *Daddy's Boy* went to *Robin Lee* and made sure it was secure and not damaged. We left the party a short time later and went back to our boat.

Anchored off Garden Key, The Dry Tortugas, FL

February 27, 1987, Friday

The wind is a lot stronger today. We checked our anchor line because of last night's incident and found that a 10' section is chaffed, which really ticks us off because it is a brand new 300' line we just bought for this anchorage. The park ranger suggested that we report the incident to the Coast Guard at Key West. We put out a second anchor as a backup.

DADDY'S BOY WITH PELICAN WAVING

Don and I took a picnic bag ashore in the dinghy and spent the day at the Fort and on the beaches, talking with people. This place is gorgeous. The beaches are pristine, and the water is the most beautiful we have ever seen. The water is crystal clear, and the underwater vegetation gives it color. I just wish the wind would stop blowing so hard. Don read a little, and I did some cross-stitch. We asked one of the tourists we met, who had come out by plane, to please call Randy and tell her we made it here safely.

Last night, a fisherman who was on the boat next to us, drowned. He was an older man, in his 60s. The people on the boat with him said that he got drunk and fell overboard. Everyone was talking about it, and the Coast Guard's big boat came to investigate and take the body to Key West. It's still here investigating.

After we got home, a man on his way to *Daddy's*

GARDEN KEY ANCHORAGE FROM INSIDE FORT JEFFERSON

Boy for lobster, Paul Blackburn, stopped and visited with us. At five, we again went to *Daddy's Boy,* at Pelican's invitation, for lobster stew and rice. The same crowd was there again; we had a good time. However, shortly after we arrived, the Coast Guard boarded the boat and did a search. That was concerning to Don and me, but they found nothing amiss and left; Pelican said it was routine. We got home at nine thirty and went to bed. The boat was rocking and rolling all night.

Anchored off Garden Key, The Dry Tortugas, FL

February 28, 1987, Saturday

We got up late and took it easy. I lay on the deck until after one and then went out in the dinghy, even though it was still quite windy. I went by *Daddy's Boy* and Pelican treated me to a dish of ice cream; I stopped at three other boats and visited with the people on board, *Tabby's Boat*, *Blue Wind*, and *Whisper*. *Whisper* served me some fish snacks and other goodies. Next, I picked Don up and we went to the fort and took some snapshots. On the way home, we stopped and visited with Paul and Gwenna, a couple, on board another boat.

Don made crab meat stuffed avocados for us, and later we went to *Daddy's Boy* for a fish dinner, our third night in a row to have dinner there. It was another fun evening; we got home about nine thirty. I didn't sleep well, and so I got up and wrote to Pam.

The sky and temperature were fine, but the wind was strong again today.

The Coast Guard is still here investigating the drowning. Do they suspect foul play?[7]

Anchored off Garden Key, The Dry Tortugas, FL

March 1, 1987, Sunday

I got up late since I didn't sleep well. It is so nice to know I don't have to work and there is really no hurry in the morning. Don made blueberry pancakes for breakfast. We decided to go snorkeling today since the wind isn't so strong. We had fun, and the water and air temperatures were both about 80°. We are happy with the snorkeling gear we bought at Fort Myers Beach; I'm sure we'll enjoy using it in the Bahamas.

We visited a little with the other boaters and the park ranger's wife, Laurie. They and a few coast guard personnel who maintain the lighthouse and other aids to navigation in the area are the only people living at the Dry Tortugas. The total population is less than 15. The boaters only anchor temporarily. They come; they see; and they leave. The greatest number of boats that we have seen here at one time has been about 20. There would be about 50 people aboard them. There are no stores or gift shops. You can buy a postcard from the park ranger, but that is the only thing available for purchase anywhere on the islands.

Don fixed linguini and white clam sauce for dinner. In the evening, he fixed popcorn. We went to bed early, but I did manage to write a few cards and letters. This is our last night at the Dry Tortugas. We would have left earlier, but the winds have been strong and the forecasts have not been good. Our next destination is Key West, and the trip will be about 75 miles. The route to Key West will take us close to some shallow areas, including the place where the Spanish Galleon, *Atocha* hit a reef and sank. A couple of years ago, the *Atocha* was found by Mel Fisher, a treasure hunter. He has brought up a lot of silver and gold from the ship and has it in a museum in Key West. We hope to visit the museum while we are there. We will have to navigate carefully, and would like to do our navigating in fair weather. We have waited for a decent forecast to leave. The forecast for tomorrow is good, so we are going. Since it is a long and treacherous trip, we are going to leave at daybreak in order to do as much of it as possible in daylight.

---

[7] While writing this book I contacted the Coast Guard and obtained information concerning the investigation. They concluded that the man, "fell over side of vessel and drowned. There is no evidence of foul play. Autopsy revealed a blood alcohol level of .26 mg/l."

There's no dinner-party tonight on *Daddy's Boy*; they pulled out today. Apparently, they decided to go fishing. We didn't talk to them about fishing and don't know how they go about it. Perhaps they use nets and check them every few days. That could explain why they were here for four days. We did figure out that they didn't need that six-pack of Old Milwaukee for which they gave us four nice lobsters. They had plenty of beer on board. When he invited us to dinner on our second night here, we told Pelican that we didn't have any more beer. He laughed and said it didn't matter and to come to the boat for dinner. He gave us those lobsters and the three dinners, just to be nice to us. We never did find out why he wanted to be nice to us and the other people he fed, and we will never know why. Maybe he is just nice.

Anchored off Garden Key, The Dry Tortugas, FL

March 2, 1987, Monday

We got up at five and prepared to leave at daybreak. We raised our anchor and got underway at six thirty, heading for Key West.

There is a saying that "the well-made plans of mice and men sometimes don't work out," and that certainly applies to our carefully waiting for good weather to make the trip to Key West, across treacherous waters. The good weather forecast we had gotten for today was wrong—very wrong. It was the worst day ever! Beginning at about seven thirty, we had severe thunderstorms, and whereas a thunderstorm is normally over in a half-hour or so, these lasted for several hours, in fact, most of the day. Apparently, we were in the path of a long band of severe storms, and we got to experience all of the storms in the band. We had severe lightning close by, high winds with heavy gusts, at least eight-foot waves and lots of rain. We didn't see the sun all day. It took us 14 hours to get to Key West, and the last couple hours were after dark. Fortunately, we spotted the buoys marking the shoal areas and safely navigated through those areas.

I didn't get sick, but I didn't have anything to eat all day except for a few vanilla wafers and at one point, some candy corn just to give me some energy. Both Don and I were relieved to make it safely to Key West. The only loss was Don's Greek captain's hat that blew off his head and went overboard as we were nearing Key West. We tied up at the Galleon Marina at eight thirty in the evening. When we got off the boat, we both got down and kissed the ground. Even though I was soaking wet, I lay flat on the dock for five minutes just to be able to lie still. The boat managed the bad conditions very well, but was a mess. We took a lot of saltwater spray on board, and the rain hit the boat from every possible angle. We didn't have any accumulation of water in our bilge, but our bedding and practically everything else onboard was wet. We were so miserable we didn't even take a walk into town.

Galleon Marina, Key West, FL - Distance traveled: 78 miles

March 3, 1987, Tuesday

I spent the whole day cleaning up the boat, not only the salt from the spray, but also mildew and mold on the teak inside the boat. My hands burned from using Clorox and Lysol. Don spent the day doing the laundry.

In the evening, after dinner of tuna stroganoff, we took a walk uptown. There's a lot of night life here. What a contrast to Naples. Everything in Naples closes up at five thirty. We had some ice cream and then walked some more, finishing on Duval Street. It was midnight when we finished our walk.

The weather wasn't too bad today, but it did cloud up and rain about four thirty, and it's still blowing from the northeast. We are both tired and sore from yesterday's long ordeal, but are thankful that no harm came to the boat or to us.

Galleon Marina, Key West, FL

March 4, 1987, Wednesday

Again, I spent the day cleaning the boat, from bow to stern, and from the overhead to the cabin sole. Don went back to the laundry. I guess we shouldn't complain; this is our spring housecleaning. It was needed anyway after living in the boat for six months. I did have time to go into the pool and the whirlpool here at the marina for about a half hour, just to freshen up.

After a dinner of leftovers, we took a walk on the dock and met a couple, Phil and Wendy, who have been living aboard here in Key West for the past eight months "on the hook" (anchored) in an anchorage near our marina. Now they have come in and docked to clean up the boat and prepare for their next cruise. They haven't decided yet, where they will cruise to next.

In the evening, we had a heck of a storm, with thunder, lightning, and lots of rain. We didn't leave the boat after our short walk. I wrote letters and read the paper in the evening.

Galleon Marina, Key West, FL

March 5, 1987, Thursday

Don slept on the starboard berth last night. It is a lot better for his aching back than sleeping in the V-berth. I didn't get up until nine. Don made muffins for breakfast, and later he went to the grocery while I stayed home and finished cleaning. I am glad that today will be the last day of "spring" cleaning. After a lunch of barbequed butter-beans, we went out sightseeing. It was our first day of entertaining ourselves in Key West since we arrived. We hit all the hot spots—Mel Fisher's Treasure from Shipwrecks Museum, Sloppy Joe's (the bar where Ernest Hemingway hung out), and Mallory Square, where people go to celebrate the sunset with various types of entertainment and other activity—a Key West tradition. We visited some shops and also went to a couple of night spots, some of which had really good live entertainment. Don and I both think that this is the place to come to in Florida if you enjoy night life and entertainment. We had some nachos at a Mexican place, and had coffee later at another spot. We are glad we found the time to see and enjoy Key West; we like it a lot. We wouldn't have left anyway because the winds are out of the east at 20-30 mph with higher gusts, and we are heading east. Don called a lawyer from Columbus, George Gross, who spends his winters here. George invited us to his place for breakfast in the morning, and to swim. I hope he offers to let us shower after swimming. The Galleon where we are staying is nice, but they are re-doing the boaters' showers and at present have none for us transient cruisers to use.

MALLORY SQUARE

I talked with Randy today, and all is OK at home. Don called Clayton Tuesday night and filled him in on our whereabouts. The wind is howling and whistling through the rigging at this time.

Here is a poem I wrote some time ago, and Don wanted me to save it. I think I wrote it after a bad day.

ODE TO THE *ROBIN LEE*:

Here I lie in my salty bunk, early in the morning.
Listening to howling wind, the sound of a gale's warning.
What a life we live, in our boat, the *Robin Lee*!
Others think our life serene, peaceful and stress free.
How wrong they are, but we are happy and content,
And home, the boat will be, until our funds are spent.

Galleon Marina, Key West, FL

March 6, 1987, Friday

Still the winds blow. We had gale-force winds from the east again today. Since we want to go east, we have to wait. Waves are predicted to be 10-15 feet in the Gulf. No way do we want to deal with that.

We left at nine with George Gross, the attorney from Columbus, and his friend Ed Kahn, an Ob/Gyn doctor in Medina OH. They took us over to George's condo for brunch. Rae, George's wife, and Holly, Ed's wife, were there and breakfast was ready. We had Bloody Marys, eggs, sausage, sweet rolls, and fruit. It was great. As we were visiting, it began to rain, and it ended up pouring down the entire day. We had a good day of socializing. About seven, Rae and Ed went out and bought steaks, so we ended up having steak dinners with them also. No one wanted to leave in the rain to take us home. Finally, about nine thirty, the rain stopped and Ed and Holly drove us through all the flooded streets back to the marina. We enjoyed our day with them very much.

Galleon Marina, Key West, FL

March 7, 1987, Saturday

Here we are, still in Key West. A week has passed, and we are still in the same spot. It is nice to be in a clean, dry home and feel the security of being safely docked, but we would like to move on. The dock fees in Key West will be our highest so far—over $120.

Don went uptown and wrote down three popular Key West recipes he had seen in a store printed on tee-shirts. One is for *Arroz con Pollo*; another is for *Picadillo*, and the third one is for Key Lime Pie. The first two are Cuban recipes. We had *Picadillo* the first night we had dinner on *Daddy's Boy* at the Dry Tortugas. Don didn't want the tee-shirts, just the recipes, so he wrote them down on blank recipe cards we had on the boat. While he was gone, I had some free time to clean up and write.

The sun is shining, the blue skies are pretty, and we have a good forecast for tomorrow, so we plan to leave. After an early evening meal of chicken curry, we walked uptown for a last visit to Mallory Square, had some ice cream and brownies at the Haagen Das store, looked around, and then came back to the boat. Mallory Square was filled with entertainers at sunset as usual. I did the dishes, while Don worked on the charts for tomorrow. I also called Sister Carol, and Dad and Martha. Not much happened in the Columbus area today. The most exciting thing was that the temperature was 70°; all three of them talked about it.

Galleon Marina, Key West, FL

March 8, 1987, Sunday

Today we finally had a nice day to sail. We left Key West at ten minutes past seven. The waves were bad in the morning, and we considered turning back, but we didn't, and we're glad we went on. It could be worse tomorrow, rather than better. The sun was out, and it was about 80 degrees most of the day. We took two-hour watches and at three forty made it into Sombrero Marina at Marathon. I called Dortha May Moffitt after we got settled. She and Johnny, her husband, have invited us to stay with them for a couple of days at their winter home on Tavernier, Key.

There are a lot of live-aboards in the Boot Key Harbor anchorage, which is normal for Marathon at this time of the year. Marathon is a very popular place for live-aboards to spend the winter. It's warm, the Boot Key Harbor anchorage is good, and the town has everything a live-aboard needs. There are so many sailboats here, it reminds us of Annapolis. After we ate leftovers for dinner, Don studied the charts again.

Sombrero Marina, Marathon, FL - Distance traveled: 47 miles

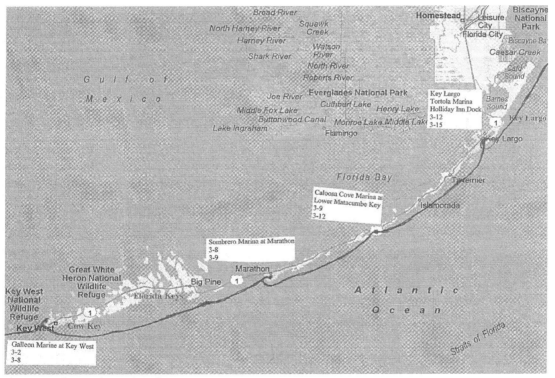

March 9, 1987, Monday

Don fixed a big breakfast of eggs, bacon, toast and grits. After I got the dishes done, we pulled out of our dock in Marathon. It was a beautiful morning. We sailed until noon. At twelve thirty, while I was on duty, we had a severe thunder and lightning storm; it surrounded us. The storm lasted 40 minutes; the visibility was almost zero. Don relieved me early so I could go below and get dry and warm. At two thirty, we arrived and docked at Caloosa Cove on Lower Matecumbe Key. I phoned Johnny and Dortha May to let them know that we had arrived.

The Moffitts came to the boat and picked us up and took us to their home for a visit. We

JOHN AND DORTHA MAY MOFFITT

had a great meal and spent the evening getting caught up on the Dublin area news. The Moffitts are from Dublin, and Don has known them all his life. They were close friends of his parents, and have also been close friends of Don's brother, Clayton, and his older sister, Barbara, and us. I went to bed around midnight after doing a couple loads of laundry.

At about three in the morning, we were awakened by gunshots. We were sleeping on the second floor, and our bedroom had big sliding glass doors with screens. The doors were open, and we had enjoyed listening to the sounds of nature as we were going to sleep. It was very quiet except for the sounds of nature and now, these very loud gunshots. We were scared because whoever was doing the shooting was nearby. We heard several very loud shots, and between the shots, we could hear the spent casings, ejected after each shot, hitting a concrete surface and that sound was even very loud. It was eerie. After several shots had been fired there was a pause, and we could actually make out the sounds of the shooter, reloading. Then there were more shots and more reloading. We rolled out of bed and crawled to the window and looked out, but saw nothing. The house is located on a canal and the sliding glass door we looked out of faced the canal. It sounded to me like the shots were coming from the house next door, but we saw nobody. Then we crawled out of our bedroom and across the hall and looked out the window facing the street. There were several Sheriff's patrol cars parked in the area, and we noticed several Deputy Sheriffs behind bushes and trees with drawn weapons. We could hear voices, but couldn't make out what was being said. The shooting stopped when about 20 rounds had been fired. They were fired over a period of perhaps 20 minutes. About a half-hour after the shooting stopped the patrol cars left. Then we and our hosts, who had done their own crawling around to find out what was going on, decided that whatever it was, it was over, and we could go back to sleep. The next day we got the rest of the story. The next door neighbor, perhaps under the influence of liquor or something else, had decided to do some target shooting across the canal at three in the morning. That was a relief to us, because we were convinced that "he had done his wife in" at the very least. No harm came to us, but it is the scariest and most bizarre situation, we have ever been in.

Caloosa Cove Marina, Lower Matecumbe Key, FL - Distance traveled: 32 miles - We stayed at the winter home of Johnny and Dortha May Moffitt at Tavernier, Key

March 10, 1987, Tuesday

We spent the day with the Moffitts. They showed us the area around their home and took us to some places we needed to go, the grocery store, the post office, the bank, and the hardware store, four of the most common stops for a live-aboard. They also fed us well.

Dortha May is a great cook, and we had three big meals a day, plus snacks in the afternoons and desserts in the evenings. Don had made a key lime pie on the boat, using one of the recipes he had copied off a tee-shirt in Key West, and had taken it to their place, so we ate that also. We had an abundance of food while we were there. In the evening, we sat around visiting. It was a good break for us from the live-aboard life.

At the Moffitts' home on Tavernier Key, FL, *The Robin Lee at* Caloosa Cove Marina, Lower Matecumbe Key

March 11, 1987, Wednesday

I did another load of laundry at Dortha May and Johnny's. Don and I both showered and got haircuts. We had heard that there are very few places on the "out-islands" in the Bahamas to buy meat and had been advised to take canned meat with us. We were able to buy canned ham and even canned bacon, but we hadn't found any canned ground beef for spaghetti, chili, etc., so Don and Dortha May canned ground beef which we had bought at the grocery store yesterday. They used Dortha May's big pot for sterilizing the jars, which we had gotten yesterday at the hardware store. They canned eight pint jars full of ground beef.

CANNING GROUND BEEF

In the evening, we went to the home of one of their friends to have drinks and watch the sunset. Then after a dinner of fried chicken, we got our belongings together, and they drove us back to our boat.

We had an enjoyable visit with them, but as usual, we were glad to get home. We felt terribly stuffed from all the good food we ate while we were there. Their place is very comfortable, and the neighborhood is good (except for the shooter, next door). They built it seven years ago. It is well equipped; they even put an elevator in since their living space is on the second floor, and they plan to keep it for the rest of their lives.

After we got settled in, Don looked over the charts for tomorrow, and then we took a walk. The area where we docked really didn't offer much, but it worked out nicely in that we got to visit the Moffitts and knew the boat was secure. The weather was great the entire time we were away from the boat. That was our third time away from the boat for the night since we had left Port Clinton, 5 ½ months ago. (We spent Thanksgiving night at Uncle Bob's and Christmas night at Siesta Key with Carol and David.)

Aboard the Robin Lee at Caloosa Cove Marina, Lower Matecumbe Key, FL

March 12, 1987, Thursday

It rained during the night and was raining in the morning when we left at about nine, but about eleven it cleared up and the sun was out for the rest of the day. It was totally calm in the Gulf, absolutely no waves. What a difference a day makes. We had to motor all of the 27 miles to Key Largo. We docked about three. Don dove to check the prop, and then we both used the sun shower on deck.

Around four thirty we walked to the business district of Key Largo. Key Largo and all the towns we've seen on the Keys lie along US Route #1, and their business districts stretch out along the highway for quite a distance. Window shopping requires a lot of walking.

We had a light supper at Wendy's and walked to the grocery. We also stopped at the Holiday Inn to see the two boats used in the filming of *On Golden Pond*. The *African Queen* is normally docked here also, but it's touring Europe. We got back to our boat at seven; Don worked on charts, and I put away groceries before catching up on my writing in this book.

Tortola Marina, Key Largo, FL - Distance traveled: 27 miles

March 13, 1987, Friday

We left our dock at eight, but returned due to conditions in the gulf, and because the wind would have been on the nose. I lay around today, and so did Don. I read, did cross-stitch, and at about four, made some oatmeal cookies. The day was cloudy, and it rained off and on. It was even cold enough to use the heater. By five, the rain stopped, and we took a short dinghy ride to the road at the end of the canal, so we could take a walk. I bought some birthday cards, and we mailed some postcards. The fruit flies were terrible today. I sprayed, but they still hung around. We ate about six. Don made *arroz con pollo*, the Latin American dish made of peppers, rice, peas and chicken, which is another of Don's "T-shirt recipes." Afterwards, I did the dishes and read some of the magazines and papers the Moffitts gave us.

All in all, it was a very relaxing day, and neither of us was bored. No chores were done, except Don did repair the man overboard pole, which broke in Monday's storm.

Tortola Marina, Key Largo, FL - Distance traveled: 3 miles

March 14, 1987, Saturday

The weather was the same, winds 15-20 knots out of the north-northeast, exactly the way we need to go, so at six thirty after hearing the weather and looking out, we went back to bed. We finally got up at nine, ate breakfast, and then showered.

The John Pennekamp Coral Reef State Park is at Key Largo. It is an "undersea" park, and offers a glass-bottom boat tour. Don bought tickets for the one o'clock tour. It was really neat to see all the beautiful fish and the coral reef with the colorful sea plants and creatures. I am glad we went. It was warm and sunny, with low humidity, making it a very pleasant afternoon. Afterwards, we got a few more groceries and then went back to the boat and pulled out of the slip and anchored. However, the holding wasn't good, and we decided to abandon that idea. There was an empty dock near the boarding place for the glass-bottomed boat. The captain of the glass-bottomed boat was there and told us it would be OK for us to use the empty dock for the night. We took him up on his offer. We had spent $20 on his boat ride, but now he had saved us about that much on dockage fees. How about that!

In the evening, after dinner of salmon tetrazzini, we talked briefly with a couple, Jason and Pam, who invited us to their boat. They told us about places they had gone in the Bahamas and used their charts to show us where they were. We went to bed at eleven.

Tortola Marina, Key Largo, FL

March 15, 1987, Sunday

What a great day. We had a pleasant 46-mile trip, motoring and sailing in the Florida Cape Channel. Several times our speed while under power slowed, and we had to reverse the prop to clear it of sea grass. Other than that, it was a "no-problem" trip to "No-Name" Harbor. I wish everyday could be as nice.

We passed an interesting housing development on our way. It is pretty close to No-Name Harbor. The houses are built over the water, on stilts. I suppose they are vacation places. Neither of us had ever seen anything like it.

We anchored and then, at four thirty, had dinner consisting of leftovers. After dinner, we went ashore in the

NO NAME HARBOR

dinghy to do some exploring. This harbor is in the center of the Cape Florida State Recreation Area; the vegetation is really spectacular. The sun setting would have made for beautiful pictures, but I had forgotten to bring the camera on the walk. We saw a cute family of raccoons with three babies.

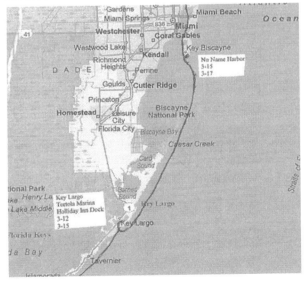

We got back to the boat about seven and Don reviewed charts while I wrote cards and wrote in this book. We went to bed early.

We had an excellent day with good weather here on Key Biscayne. Shelly and her roommate are flying to the Palm Beach area on March 21st. Don has been worried that, because of all our delays, we might not make it to Palm Beach in time to pick them up at the airport. He is less worried now that we are through the Keys and only a couple of days away from Palm Beach.

No-Name Harbor, Key Biscayne, FL - Distance traveled: 46 miles

March 16, 1987, Monday

The sun was shining and it was cool, in the 70s, but very pretty all day. We had low humidity, and that makes it really comfortable. There were about 30 boats anchored here last night, but the majority—all but five—were gone when we got up today. That's the difference between the weekend and weekday. After we watched Good Morning America and Phil Donahue, we went ashore and tried to call Randy, Dad, and Pam. No one was home or available. No one has a clue as to how much effort we put into making phone calls.

We came back to the boat, and Don went in the water and scrubbed the boat's bottom. The water was very cold. Around noon, we had PB&J sandwiches. We even took a nap this afternoon before we walked into town to get groceries. The park is really beautiful; this time we took some pictures. The park closes at six, and we got back to the boat a little before closing time, had leftovers, and made banana splits. We didn't need all the calories, but they sure tasted great. We each had ½ quart of ice cream, nuts, chocolate and bananas. We watched TV, and I did cross-stitch. We went to bed at ten.

No-Name Harbor is one of the nicest anchorages we have been in. It is out of the way, surrounded by beauty, and very well protected. It ranks right up there with Punta Blanca Island and Boca Grande.

No Name Harbor, Key Biscayne, FL

CHAPTER SIX

MIAMI, FL to WARDERICK WELLS, BS
March 17, 1987 – May 31, 1987

March 17, 1987, Tuesday

At eight o'clock this morning, *Robin Lee* left No-Name Harbor and motored through Biscayne Bay and the Miami area. Downtown Miami looked different from what we have been seeing the last few months and has aroused our interest. We hope to come back to this area again someday to see what is here. Beautiful homes line the waterway between Miami and Fort Lauderdale.

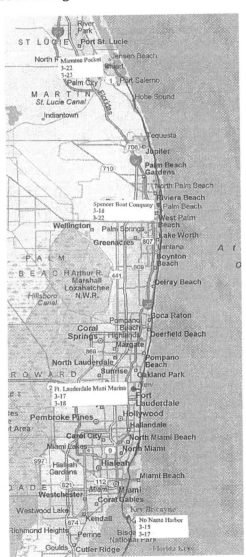

Visiting Florida in a boat and visiting it on land are entirely different experiences; it is much nicer from the water. Don says that it's the first time he has liked Florida. Not having to deal with the street and highway traffic is a big plus. A second reason that it is nicer to see it from the water is that the real estate along the waterways is expensive and the buildings and homes that are built on expensive real estate are generally more beautiful structures.

We stopped at Pier 66 for fuel and to ask about overnight docking. They charge $65 per night; we are docked at the Fort Lauderdale City Marina where it costs $15 per night.

A couple, Pat and Wallace Cook, who have just returned from the Bahamas, are docked next to us. We went aboard their boat to visit, and afterwards we showed them our boat.

Don made *picadillo* for dinner and served it with black beans and rice. It is the last of the three Cuban recipes he copied off T-shirts in Key West. It's very different, and we loved it.

We looked over the charts of the Bahamas until midnight on our boat with the Cooks

City Marina, Fort Lauderdale, FL - Distance traveled: 30 miles

March 18, 1987, Wednesday

When we were getting ready to leave this morning, we saw a flock of brilliant green parrots in the trees beside the dock. Neither of us had seen parrots in the wild before; they did a lot of squawking. The weather forecast for today included small-craft warnings with winds of 25-35 mph. We were concerned about dealing with the winds and currents at the numerous drawbridges where we would have to wait for openings, but we left anyway and made it safely to West Palm Beach. I thought the trip was fine. For lunch, I made tuna salad and crackers.

After a ten-hour day on the waterway, we docked at West Palm Beach just before sundown. Some marinas here have a 40-foot length minimum and charge accordingly, and some others are too shallow for our 5'3" draft. We put in at Spencer's Marina (also called Spencer Boat Company). I registered, called Dad and Martha, and showered, while Don fixed dinner—salmon noodle casserole.

I spent the evening planning our menus and activities for the next week when Shelly and her roommate at Bowling Green, Kelly, will be here.

Spencer's Marina, West Palm Beach, FL - Distance traveled: 41 miles

March 19, 1987, Thursday

Today we met Paula and Ron and their three teenage boys who live on a 57-foot boat. They are tied up next to us at the dock and are preparing to leave for the Bahamas. They have a rental car and took us to the grocery. We bought all of our groceries for the week

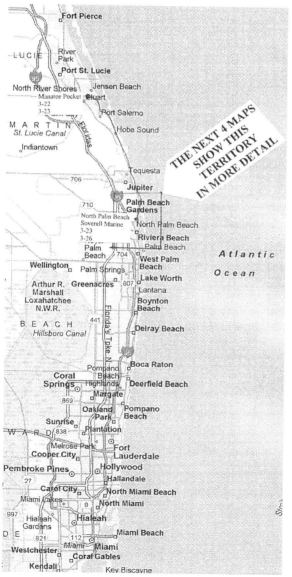

when the girls will be here. We spent $107, the most ever. Paula and I ate a banana split while Don did the grocery shopping. I also purchased some yellow material to make a quarantine flag to fly when we arrive in the Bahamas, and when we come back to the States, which you are supposed to do until you clear customs. It was late morning when we went to the store, and we didn't get home until five. It took me an hour to put away the groceries. We heated up leftovers for dinner, and around nine o'clock, Don fell asleep on the starboard berth. He couldn't be aroused even to get up to go to bed.

It rained today, but we had blue skies after it passed. It was warm—about 78°.

Spencer's Marina, West Palm Beach, FL

March 20, 1987, Friday

We were busy all day. We changed the oil, cleaned up the boat, did the laundry, and then made phone calls to get information about the local bus service and dockage rates at other marinas. Since we are going to be stationary for a while, we would like to find a less-expensive place to stay

While I was doing laundry, some people we originally met at Beaufort, South Carolina, Bill Jordon and Donna Knicely/Jordon, on *Orchid Boat*, a 37 foot

Taiwanese sailboat, came into the marina and docked. They invited us to have drinks and dinner with them, so we could catch up on the past three months of travels. We enjoyed our evening visiting with them. We hope to spend more time with them after the girls go back to Ohio. They are from Richmond, Virginia. Bill is a retired school principal. Donna was the manager of corporate services for Best Products, and in her younger years she was a reporter and photographer for a newspaper in Indiana.

After Shelly and Kelly leave, we will start preparing for our trip to the Bahamas. We will buy groceries and other supplies, get any additional equipment and spare parts we decide we should take, and make any repairs needed to the boat. We have been told that the islands in the Bahamas don't have many grocery stores, and the ones they do have are small and not well stocked. Parts for repairing our boat or motor are probably not available there. We will buy what we think we will need while we are in the Lake Worth area because many stores are nearby. Then we plan to go back to Fort Lauderdale and leave from there. We will be crossing the Gulf Stream, and it has a strong northward current. If we left from here we would be bucking the current during the crossing because our two favored destinations, West End and Lucaya, are south of here. They are north of Fort Lauderdale. *Orchid Boat* has the same plan. We will probably team up with them and make the crossing together.

Spencer's Marina, West Palm Beach, FL

March 21, 1987, Saturday

I washed down the boat at seven thirty this morning. It was on my list of chores for yesterday. Don and I visited Paula and Ron at their boat, and they offered to take us to the airport to pick up the girls. Until it was time to go, Don and I did chores, and he made a white cake with chocolate icing as a late birthday treat for Shelly.

After picking up the girls, we came back to the boat, stowed their gear, and visited. I gave Shelly the book I bought for her in Naples, *Where Was Mom When I Needed Her?* We ate Hawaiian pork, rice and bread for dinner and cake for dessert. In the evening, I took the girls for a short dinghy ride, and the girls went to see Paula and Ron's boat–the big 57 footer. It's nice inside. One of their boys came to our boat to visit. The rest of the evening was spent taking the girls for a short walk around the marina and visiting with people. Don and I were both exhausted and so were the girls; we all went to bed around eleven. I sure am excited and happy to have Shelly here. I know we will have an enjoyable time together.

Spencer's Marina, West Palm Beach, FL

March 22, 1987, Sunday

We got up at eight, and I fixed breakfast consisting of fruit compote and muffins while the girls took showers. We left the dock at a little after nine and went for a 34-mile boat ride to Manatee Pocket, at Stuart, where we anchored at three thirty in the afternoon. The girls sunbathed on deck, but it was overcast and a little chilly.

Don stayed on board and fixed dinner, while Shelly, Kelly and I motored to shore in the dinghy to get ice and milk and to look around.

At the fishing boat docks we were given some free fish–Spanish mackerel and blue fish. The fishermen even filleted them for us. When we returned to our boat, dinner wasn't ready, so we took a short dinghy ride through one of the canals and saw some gorgeous houses. Don made a beef roast, potatoes and gravy, carrots, and for dessert, peanut butter cream cheese pie, with whipped cream. After dinner, we just sat around and talked.

Anchored in Manatee Pocket, Stuart, FL - Distance traveled: 34 miles

March 23, 1987, Monday

We all woke up around ten. The weather was pleasant with blue skies. We ate cereal, and afterwards the girls lay on the deck, sunbathing. Don took the dinghy to a pay phone and called about Vern. He is at the factory being repaired again; he still isn't fixed. Around eleven thirty we weighed anchor and left Manatee Pocket to go to Soverel Harbour Marina in North Palm Beach.. It took until three thirty to get there. We like the location of Soverel and it has good facilities, so we plan to make it our home base until the girls leave. While we were underway, I made tuna salad and served it on crackers for lunch. We also ate orange slices and then polished off the peanut butter pie from last night. After we got situated at Soverel, the girls went to some exclusive shops at a mall near the marina.

Don fixed fried chicken, mashed potatoes, and corn for dinner, and after I did the dishes, we all walked to the grocery store, which was close by. We bought ice cream for dessert and

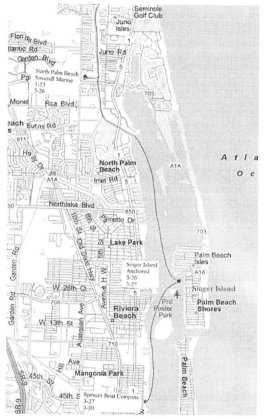

went back to the boat to make sundaes. They probably contained 1,000 calories each. This has not been a good week, as far as our diets are concerned. We have over-eaten, badly. The girls wrote some postcards, and then we played a game called rummikub.

Soverel Harbour Marina, North Palm Beach, FL - Distance traveled: 27 miles

March 24, 1987, Tuesday

We all slept in until ten thirty. The girls woke up and walked to a shopping area near the marina. Shelly got a perm and then they mailed postcards. Don and I straightened up the boat and did our regular chores while they were gone. The sky was clear enough in the afternoon for them to sunbathe on deck. They both turned red.

Don fixed beef stroganoff with noodles, and after I did the dishes, we walked to the store to get a few things. For dessert, we finished off the ice cream from last night and ate cookies.

In the evening, Kelly and Don taught Shelly how to play euchre, and we played until about eleven. We also talked a lot. Our TV reception isn't good here. Most of the programs fade in and out, which is annoying, so we haven't been watching it.

Soverel Harbour Marina, North Palm Beach, FL

March 25, 1987, Wednesday

We ate an early breakfast, and after the girls showered, we left to catch the nine thirty bus to Palm Beach. The girls wanted to see the Palm Beach shops, and we wanted to pick up mail, sent by Jane, that is waiting for us there. The bus ride was long and not through the best part of town, but after we arrived, we found that Palm Beach is beautiful, although there isn't much of an actual beach anymore due to erosion.

The girls and I walked around, looking in the shops, while Don went to the post office to get our mail. We met at a small restaurant for lunch. We caught the two thirty bus back, and after two transfers, made it to the marina around four o'clock. Everyone was tired and broke. The girls each bought a few items. Don fixed pork chops, broccoli and stuffing; the dessert was another Key West T-shirt key lime pie. Don sure has gotten his money's worth out of those recipes.

Soverel Harbour Marina, North Palm Beach, FL

March 26, 1987, Thursday

We all started our day around eight thirty. Don made pancakes and bacon for breakfast. The girls lay out, but it was only partly sunny. The winds have been strong, and even though it has been in the high 70s, it has not been very pretty. In the early afternoon, we left the dock and motored eight miles to Singer Island, near Riviera Beach, where we anchored for the night.

The girls and I took the dinghy ashore and walked to the beach. We got back to the boat around five thirty and relaxed on deck while Don made dinner. He made meat loaf, mashed potatoes and marinated asparagus. After dinner we played euchre until ten and then went to bed.

Anchored off the north side of Peanut Island, near Singer Island, Riviera Beach, FL - Distance traveled: 8 miles

SHELLY ON THE LEFT AND KELLY ON THE RIGHT

March 27, 1987, Friday

It was windy again during the night, and at one point, we thought the anchors were fouled, but, fortunately, that turned out to be wrong. We all slept, in spite of the weather. Don and I awoke at eight, but the girls slept in. I wrote in this journal and spent time reviewing all the menus for this week. Lots of food and calories were consumed by all. I left the boat at ten thirty and went ashore to get money from a bank and to buy a few groceries. I returned to the boat around twelve thirty. We pulled up the anchor and went to Spencer's Marina at West Palm Beach, only a short distance away.

The girls were glad to get showers, and they started packing their bags. They go back to Ohio tomorrow. We ate sausage, kraut, and German potato salad for dinner. Dessert was chocolate-chip cookies and pudding. We played cards and visited again after dinner, and finally went to bed around eleven thirty. The weather was crummy the entire day, but in the early afternoon, the girls did get some of the sun's rays. I did laundry.

Spencer's Marina, West Palm Beach, FL - Distance traveled: 3 miles

March 28, 1987, Saturday

We woke up around eight. Naturally, the girls tried to do some last minute sunbathing. We ate blueberry muffins for breakfast, and the girls finished packing their bags. We went to the airport at eleven fifteen, by taxi, and saw them get on their way to Ohio. Don and I felt everything went smoothly while they were here, and that we all had an enjoyable time.

To save money, we decided to take a bus back to the boat instead of a cab. It was a hot two-mile walk from the airport to the bus stop. (We wish we had taken a cab.) We finally reached home around four. A couple of hours later, Donna and Bill came over for dinner. We fixed fresh fish, and they brought strawberries to dip in powdered sugar. After dinner was over and the dishes were done, we walked along the docks and looked at the big boats. I called Randy, and she confirmed that the girls had made it home safely.

Spencer's Marina, West Palm Beach, FL

March 29, 1987, Sunday

The weather was nasty most of the day. We planned to leave after I did the laundry in the morning, but the weather continued to be rainy and very windy, so we stayed put. I was ticked that we had to pay dock fees again, but on the positive side, the showers are clean, with plenty of hot water and great water pressure. Don went through the mail and worked on business matters, while I wrote Shelly, did laundry, and visited with Donna. About five thirty, I made phone calls to Mom and Dortha May. I wanted to find out from Dortha May whether the Dixons had come to Florida yet. They had, and we missed them. In the evening, Donna and Bill invited us over for fudge and coffee. We sat around and visited until ten thirty. The weather was terrible all night.

Spencer's Marina, West Palm Beach, FL

March 30, 1987, Monday

Well, today we moved out to the anchorage at the north end of Lake Worth. We wanted to go to a small anchorage we had been told about in North Palm Beach, off the waterway, but we couldn't get through the North Palm Beach Bridge. It was broken. We waited and waited but finally gave up and went to north Lake Worth anchorage because it was getting late and there was a forecast for high winds. We anchored and spent the night there. *Orchid Boat* did the same. Don and I ate macaroni and cheese and did some reading. I also finished the letter to Shelly which I started yesterday.

It was a windy, noisy, "rock and roll" night aboard the *Robin Lee*. We lay down early for bed. I went to sleep, but both of us woke up several times. We had terrible lightning and thunder storms all night.

When lightning is striking nearby, and you are on the water in a sailboat with a mast sticking up 46 feet above the water, you can't help but wonder whether the next bolt will strike the boat and kill you. There are lightning protection devices for sailboats, similar to lightning rods that provide a path for the lightning to the water. Surprisingly, the only boats that we have heard about that have been damaged by lightning are boats that installed these protective devices. It seems that the protective devices on these boats did a good job of attracting the lightning, but the lightning overpowered the systems and damaged the boat on its way to the water. We heard of one boat that was sunk by lightning because a lightning strike blew a hole in the bottom of the boat when it passed through the lightning protection system. We have decided to do without lightning protection, but during storms, we worry about whether we are doing the right thing.

Anchored at the north end of Lake Worth, Palm Beach Gardens, FL - Distance traveled: 12 miles

March 31, 1987, Tuesday

We survived all the storms. Don predicts that conditions will improve, and I'm sure they will, in time. They couldn't get much worse. Today was less bumpy. Donna and I went to the shopping area and walked around. I also bought a few groceries for dinner.

Donna and Bill came over for a supper of beans, bacon, and corn bread. For dessert, Donna brought lemon tarts. In the evening, we played euchre, the guys against the gals. Naturally, the guys won the "best two out of three." It was fun, and late in the evening, the anchorage settled down and became calm, and I slept well.

Anchored at the north end of Lake Worth, Palm Beach Gardens, FL

April 1, 1987, Wednesday

The weather was better than it has been. It was mostly sunny, but the winds were still strong—between 15 & 20 mph all day.

Don spent yesterday working on taxes. He is finding it difficult to do the taxes without having ready access to his files. We took the dinghy ashore in the late morning, and Don called Jane and asked her to mail some additional information concerning our taxes.

At one o'clock, we met Bill and Donna ashore, and the four of us went to see a house boat docked close to Soverel Marina. We all agreed that it was a plush boat and would be comfortable to live on so long as it was stationary, but we wouldn't want to take it down the Intracoastal Waterway and contend with the high winds and currents. Later, Don and I paid for showers at Soverel (which were cold) while the Jordans waited for us. We then walked over to Panama Hattie's, a restaurant and bar along the ICW, and the Jordan's bought us a specialty drink during Happy Hour. We sat out and watched the boats go by and under the bridge. On the way back, Don and I stopped by the grocery and bought some cheap paper towels, laundry soap, eight jars of peanut butter, and two big jars of jelly. We are stocking up for the Bahamas. That is going to be a really big chore if we do it while we are anchored and not at dockside, since everything will have to be loaded into and unloaded from the dinghy.

Don fixed chicken fricassee for our evening meal. Our refrigeration system is limited, so we needed to use up the chicken we had. Betty's Black Raspberry Jelly on bread and a few apple slices was our dessert.[8] We watched the opera, Carmen, on PBS, listened to the radio, and went to bed early.

Anchored at the north end of Lake Worth, Palm Beach Gardens, FL

---

[8] While we had our boat in Port Clinton and were making trips back and forth between home and the boat, we discovered a lady along the way, Betty, who makes and sells jelly. We love it and have a supply of it on board.

April 2, 1987, Thursday

We are still anchored at the north end of Lake Worth. It was cold last night, and we had lots of condensation this morning. It's been a while since we had that problem.

I made an inventory of all of our canned goods. Around four o'clock, I went ashore by myself in the dinghy with the motor. I am finally able to get it started. The Honda, two-horse power motor and I hadn't been getting along very well until today. I wasn't putting the throttle in the right position to start it. Now I'm able to start it without any difficulty. I bought 30 rolls of toilet paper, 18 bars of Castile soap and three boxes of Kleenex for our six months in the Bahamas. Don worked on grocery lists while I was shopping. When I went back to the boat, I re-packed all the supplies. Our place was a mess with all the canned goods sitting out.

On the way back from shopping, I visited with another boating couple, Dave and Jo, from Illinois. They are retired and have lived aboard their 25-foot sailboat for three years. It's called *Rainbow*.

We went to *Orchid Boat* for drinks, dinner and two games of Trivial Pursuit. We didn't get home until about midnight.

Dad and Martha are coming to visit us a couple of weeks from now. We plan to leave for the Bahamas shortly after they go home.

It was sunny and in the 70s today, but by eleven thirty, it was back down in the 50s, and the winds were picking up. It will probably be another rocky night.

Anchored at the north end of Lake Worth, Palm Beach Gardens, FL

April 3, 1987, Friday

Don and I left the boat around eleven and went to Soverel to shower and pick up our mail. Today the showers had hot water. We also took the time to scrub the bottom of the dinghy. It was coated with a grassy growth. Yuck. It took lots of arm power. On the way back we saw Dave and Jo again. Don met them and we discussed the Bahamas. I was glad, because I like for Don to meet the same folks I have met. Then, if I am talking about them, he knows who I mean. We returned home around two in the afternoon, ate lunch of left-overs, and then went over to visit another boat, *Wax Wings*, from Latham, New York. The people aboard are Cliff and his wife, Lucille. They are Newt's friends. Newt traveled the first half of the ICW with them, and when he started across Lake Okeechobee, he teamed up with us. We met Cliff in Fort Myers when we were there with Newt.

Don and I ate around seven. He fixed spaghetti. We went to bed early because it was so cold.

Anchored at the north end of Lake Worth, Palm Beach Gardens, FL

April 4, 1987, Saturday

We messed around on the boat until lunchtime. Don cleaned the stove, and I worked on the cross-stitch project that I am doing for Mallory Montgomery as a birth gift.

We had lunch with *Orchid Boat* on *Robin Lee*. They brought me a letter from Shelly that they picked up at Spencer's. At five thirty, we cleaned up, went to *Orchid Boat*, picked up Donna and Bill, and the four of us went ashore to have pizza for dinner. On the way back to the boat, we stopped at Publix, and Don and I bought ice cream, bananas, chocolate and nuts for banana splits. We made them on *Orchid Boat,* visited until nine thirty, and then came home and went to bed.

While we were at the grocery, we met the crew of *For Your Eyes Only*, a 110-foot yacht that is in the area. They were buying groceries, $425 worth, for a party of 50 people.

Anchored at the north end of Lake Worth, Palm Beach Gardens, FL

April 5, 1987, Sunday

Today is my mom's birthday. I sent her a card, but didn't call. I didn't want to call her collect on her birthday. If I had, she would tease me about it forever.

We went into town and purchased a few groceries and a newspaper for Bill. In the evening, after dinner, Donna and Bill came over to play euchre. We served popcorn and Coke as a snack. The guys won at euchre.

Being anchored is fine, except after a few days, the place looks dirty and cluttered from the carpet not being swept with the electric sweeper and our laundry hanging in the head.

Anchored at the north end of Lake Worth, Palm Beach Gardens, FL

April 6, 1987, Monday

It is still chilly. The sun was out most of the day and the anchorage was calm.

We went to shore, emptied the trash, took showers at Soverel Marina, and cut Don's hair. Don was embarrassed about me cutting his hair out in back of an animal clinic building by a dumpster. It wasn't very dignified looking. We also bought more groceries for the Bahamas, picked up additional income tax forms Don needs, and got some fresh water. Don predicts that we will spend $1,000 at grocery stores for food for six months in the Bahamas. For dinner, we ate steaks with mushrooms, plus crescent rolls and carrot cake. We watched a lawyer/crime movie in the evening and went to bed late.

Anchored at the north end of Lake Worth, Palm Beach Gardens, FL

April 7, 1987, Tuesday

Today was cloudy all day. I got up at ten thirty. Don and I lay around and did little until one in the afternoon, when we went ashore. Don mailed our 1986 income tax returns with checks for what we owed after making copies for our records. I spent some time at the grocery and bought several boxes of cereal, a variety of Jiffy mixes, and a few other items, for the Bahamas. At five, we served cheese and crackers and wine to Donna and Bill, and the four of us played cards. The guys are beating the girls, twelve games to three. Don and I quietly celebrated the ninth anniversary of our first date on this day in 1978. How fortunate we are to have each other. Thanks be to God!

Anchored at the north end of Lake Worth, Palm Beach Gardens, FL

April 8, 1987, Wednesday

I got up late, ate Don's pancakes for breakfast, oiled the teak, and showered in the cockpit, using the sun shower. At two, Donna and I left in the dinghy to go to the mall. We went to a fashion show and did a little shopping. We had fun. I bought a pair of jeans and a jean skirt. At six, Don and I went to *Orchid Boat* for a spaghetti dinner with salad. John, from a boat called *Lindy,* was also there for dinner.

We came home at nine and watched a show about Lyndon Johnson while he was President. I looked over the charts for the Bahamas. Tomorrow, we plan to leave the anchorage early and put in at Spencer's Marina.

Anchored at the north end of Lake Worth, Palm Beach Gardens, FL

April 9, 1987, Thursday

We left the anchorage at seven forty-five and motored to Spencer's. After we docked, I hosed down the boat while Don met and talked with another boater who had spent six years in the Bahamas. I showered, and at eleven, Donna, Bill, Don and I left in a rental car to go shopping. We went to Fort Lauderdale and stopped at many places. Among them were Boat US, a hardware store, a paint store, a store that sells inflatable boats (where Donna and Bill ordered a dinghy), and K-Mart. We ate at Bobby Rubino's (a rib place) for dinner and later stopped at Mother Butler's Pies, where each of us put a few hundred calories on top of thousands we consumed at dinner. We made it back to the marina at eight o'clock and unloaded our loot. I stayed on the boat to get things organized while the rest went out to buy groceries. When Don returned at eleven, we had spent about $300 for the day. I stayed

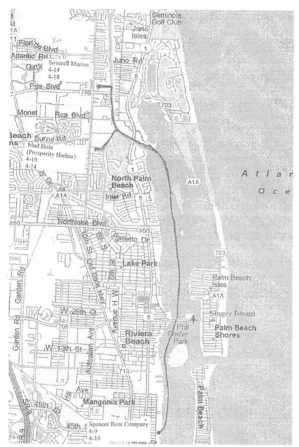

up until three in the morning doing laundry and organizing our groceries and supplies. There was no place in the main cabin to even sit down. Canned goods and supplies were everywhere.

Spencer's Marina, West Palm Beach, FL - Distance traveled: 7 miles

April 10, 1987, Friday

The four of us left early to go to the bank and do more shopping. We ate breakfast first because the bank didn't open until nine. After getting some cash we went to K-Mart and a couple of other stores to buy some more things. By noon, we had gotten all we needed. Before turning in the car, we ate lunch at Burger King and had ice cream at Donna's favorite place, which is close by the car rental agency. After a man from the car rental place brought us back to our boats, Don and I prepared to leave the marina. We paid our dock fees and then motored seven miles north to the anchorage we had tried to get to on March 30th, but couldn't, because a drawbridge was broken.

We spent six hours working on projects. I stowed all the canned food in the V-berth storage locker and in the bilge. Whereupon, we rowed the dinghy around the boat to check the boat's waterline to make sure we were loaded evenly and weren't listing. Fortunately, we weren't. Don made sandwiches for our supper, and I did the dishes. We were both extremely tired and went to bed at nine thirty.

Anchored at a small anchorage off the waterway in N Palm Beach, FL which we have named the "Mud Hole" - Distance traveled: 7 miles

April 11, 1987, Saturday

We slept well last night and awakened to a warm sunny day. After a late breakfast, we walked a little over a mile to a Winn-Dixie Supermarket and spent another $72 on various items to take to the Bahamas. As we were walking back, an elderly local woman gave us a lift. The rest of the day was relaxing. We ate a tasty dinner of chicken, wild rice, broccoli and cheese sauce. I wrote to Shelly in the evening.

Anchored at the Mud Hole, N Palm Beach, FL

April 12, 1987, Sunday

I spent some time in the dinghy motoring around the area in the afternoon and again in the evening. I also finished oiling the teak and completed the cross-stitch project I was working on for Mallory. It sure took me a long time to complete. Don watched tennis and golf on TV. We took a short dinghy ride in the evening, after we charged up the batteries for the refrigerator. We met some nice folks here in the anchorage who proudly took us aboard and showed us their new, 38-foot Island Packet yacht. They were originally from New Jersey and are now retired, living in Boca Raton. We went to bed at nine thirty and played gin rummy in bed. Don always wins at cards.

Anchored at the Mud Hole, N Palm Beach, FL

April 13, 1987, Monday

We had a brief thunderstorm this morning shortly after we woke up.

After lunch, we walked into town, and were having a happy day until I spoke with Pam about visiting us. I suggested that she and Bob should make plans to meet us in Nassau. Don wasn't happy that I proposed that, which led to an unpleasant discussion. Don was concerned about the timing. He knew we were a long way from Nassau and that there would be many stops between here and there, and that we could be delayed by weather conditions, boat problems or for other reasons. He didn't want to be under pressure to be in Nassau at a certain time. He was also concerned about getting there too much ahead of them and having to spend more time in Nassau than we wanted; since we have heard that it isn't a place where cruising sailors like to hang out. He was upset that I would make plans without talking to him first. I thought he didn't want to go to Nassau, and to make a long story short, it was an unpleasant conversation. It was our first disagreement on the trip (other than about buying a heater). However, it was actually due to a misunderstanding related to timing, rather than an actual difference in ideas.

We stopped for cash at the bank and afterwards walked to Soverel Harbour Marina and paid to take showers. Then we bought a few more groceries.

The walk home was long, especially since neither of us said much to each other. It's rare that we don't want to talk to each other, but I didn't feel like wasting the effort involved in trying to convince Don that I really wanted to see Nassau, or any other specific ports in the Bahamas. The Captain always gets the final say as to where the boat is traveling.

There was a beautiful moon, bright and full, this evening. After we charged the batteries, we took a short dinghy ride to visit the other two boats in the anchorage. One was from Ottawa Canada and had just returned from Cuba. The other, a 27-foot trawler, was from Stuart, FL and had come from Fort Lauderdale.

After we returned to the boat, I did the dishes from dinner and stowed supplies in the portside locker. I spent time writing in this journal and went to bed early. I had a headache, which was probably a tension headache, due to the unpleasant discussion with Don, and because I have had a lot of Nutra-Sweet in diet pop and Kool-Aid (I think it causes me headaches). Fortunately, the misunderstanding with Don has now been resolved.

Anchored at the Mud Hole, N Palm Beach, FL

April 14, 1987, Tuesday

Early in the morning, Don and I moved the boat from the Mud Hole to Soverel Harbour Marina because Dad and Martha will be arriving this afternoon for a visit. When we pulled up the anchor, it was so muddy it took us about 15 minutes to clean, so we have named this place the "Mud Hole." We spent the day at Soverel getting organized and doing chores, like laundry, buying groceries for the week, and general cleaning. Martha and Dad arrived around six in the evening. We ate beef stroganoff for dinner on board. The four of us then took a short dinghy ride around the marina and for a short way in the ICW.

Soverel Harbour Marina, North Palm Beach, FL – Distance traveled: 1 mile

April 15, 1987, Wednesday

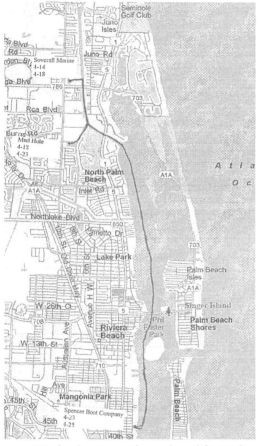

We awoke around eight, and Don served sweet rolls and juice. Dad and Martha drove to Florida, which meant we had land transportation while they were here. They drove us to Stuart so we could take Vern to the factory to be repaired again. They repaired it while we waited. We ate lunch at an outdoor café and then walked around Jensen Beach in the afternoon. It rained hard on and off during the afternoon. We went home, ate dinner of Hawaiian pork, and dessert of peanut butter cream pie, and played euchre until midnight.

Soverel Harbour Marina, North Palm Beach, FL

April 16, 1987, Thursday

Don stayed on the boat testing Vern, making a pie, and doing navigation planning while I took Dad and Martha on a dinghy ride and showed them the "Mud Hole," where we were anchored for several days before they arrived. We returned to the boat and then the four of us took a ride in their car, during which we saw the 110' yacht, *For Your Eyes Only,* and drove by Jack Nicklaus' home, which is near Soverel Marina.

We had eaten a huge breakfast of eggs, grits, sausage and toast, so we skipped lunch, but we stopped by Panama Hattie's restaurant for drinks and ate an order of chicken and artichoke hearts wrapped in bacon. We sat on their patio for about an hour before returning to the boat. All four of us cleaned up, and then went out for Happy Hour at The Atlantic Fish Company Raw Bar. It was cheap and excellent. Afterwards, Donna and Bill joined us, and the six of us rode around in Palm Beach and walked along the ocean. Later in the evening we drove to Swenson's for ice cream. This is where an infamous banana split incident occurred, which I will recount to you.

THE INFAMOUS BANANA SPLIT INCIDENT: There are two versions of the incident, mine and Don's. I will give you mine, and it will be followed by Don's.

MY VERSION: I eat small bites and savor the flavor of each. Don eats large bites and fast. He gets in a feeding frenzy and inhales food! I got barely 1/3 of the first banana split.

DON'S VERSION: Robin and I ordered a banana split to be shared by us. Robin positioned it in front of her and using her elbows, kept me away from it as best she could. I attempted to get my share by reaching over her arms and taking bites. When we had just about finished it, Robin, with a tone of disgust in her voice, pushed it over to me and said, "You eat it, I'm ordering one for myself." She did! And, she ate every bite of it by herself!

We had a pleasant evening of entertainment and fun. We got home late; Dad, Martha and I stayed up talking until three thirty in the morning.

Soverel Harbour Marina, North Palm Beach, FL

ANCHORED AT THE MUD HOLE

April, 17, 1987, Friday

Vern still isn't working right so Don drove back to Stuart to get him repaired once more. Dad, Martha and I walked over and bought a newspaper. We saw Donna, who then gave Dad and Martha a tour of *Orchid Boat*. We spent a couple of hours browsing in some elegant shops. The Ralph Lauren store had a doorman and a man playing the piano. I bought a pair of earrings and also a belt to match my jean skirt and colored tops. For dinner, Don made chicken paprikash with new potatoes, and for dessert, key lime pie. We drank wine with dinner. After I did the dishes, we played cards and talked until midnight, and then took a walk along the docks. The weather has been warm and sunny, but windy.

Soverel Harbour Marina, North Palm Beach, FL

April 18, 1987, Saturday

Dad and Martha left at seven thirty this morning. They have a 20-hour drive back to Columbus, but plan to stop this evening to sleep in a motel.

We went back to bed and finally got up around eleven. Some boaters on our dock, from Ohio, but who winter at Soverel, gave us a ride to the laundry. We went to the bank and got cash, did laundry, and bought groceries, before moving the boat back to the Mud Hole. It was hot and sunny, but still quite windy. Donna and Bill moved *Orchid Boat* to the Mud Hole also.

Don fixed chicken-fried steak for dinner, and we invited Donna and Bill over for dessert of leftover key lime pie. We also played euchre with them. They went back to their boat around ten, and because Don and I were tired, we went to bed early.

Staying up late each night of Dad and Martha's visit contributed to my being worn out. However, I was extremely happy they came to visit and enjoyed our time together. I think we all had fun.

Anchored at the Mud Hole, N Palm Beach, FL - Distance traveled: 1 mile

April 19, 1987, Sunday, Easter

Don and I spent the entire day relaxing until it was time to get showers and go to *Orchid Boat* for Easter dinner. Don made a pineapple upside-down cake to take for dessert. Donna's table looked very formal with good china, wine glasses, a pink tablecloth and my bouquet of roses and mums that Don bought me for Easter. She served wild rice, marinated veggies, and Cornish game hens, plus crescent rolls, which I dearly love. Everything was exceptionally tasty, including the cake that Don made. We played cards after dinner and didn't get home until eleven thirty.

Anchored at the Mud Hole, N Palm Beach, FL

April 20, 1987, Monday

We took the dinghy along a channel to Lott's Fish and Bait Supply, where we docked it and walked about a mile to a K-Mart store. We decided that it would be more efficient to shop separately, so we did, and that worked out well.

Orchid Boat left and went to North Lake Worth to anchor. It was a pleasant afternoon and evening; we saw a rainbow and a beautiful sunset. There were two other boats in the anchorage tonight. One of them was *Rainbow* with Dave and Jo aboard whom we previously met in the North Lake Worth anchorage. All in all, it was a very nice day.

Anchored at the Mud Hole, N Palm Beach, FL

April 21, 1987, Tuesday

It was hot and sunny today. I swept the carpet early, and by eleven, I was ready to take Dave and Jo to Lott's Fish and Bait Supply, so they could refill their propane tanks and take care of some other matters. While waiting for Dave and Jo to take care of their business at Lott's, I got pictures developed, ate a salad at a café near Lott's, and called Randy. I also bought some pork spareribs for tonight's dinner. We went back to the anchorage about three thirty.

Later, Don and I went ashore in the dinghy; filled our five gallon, plastic drinking-water storage container; came back to the boat; and showered on deck, using the sun-shower. The water was so hot I could hardly stand it.

We ate the spareribs for dinner, and afterwards, watched two programs on PBS, did the dishes, and wrote letters before going to bed at 11.

The bugs (no-see-ums) have been bad after the sun goes down.

Anchored at the Mud Hole, N Palm Beach, FL

April 22, 1987, Wednesday

Today was hot and sunny; the high was 87°. We didn't get up until nine thirty and took our time eating breakfast. I worked on my project of covering the steering wheel with cord for better grip and developed a blister on my thumb. About four, Don and I took our trash ashore in the dinghy. We walked to the community center and put it in their trash receptacle. I used their swings. Don pushed me for about ten minutes. We went inside the center, and Don shot baskets with some guys for about a half-hour. While Don played, I called Randy again and wrote letters.

On the way home, we met a fisherman, and he gave us some live bait. I fished for a while, but without success. The fish didn't seem to like the bait. At seven, we ate French toast for dinner. Both of us showered later and quickly closed up the boat due to the no-see-ums. We read until bedtime, at ten thirty.

Orchid Boat and we plan to make the crossing to the Bahamas together. Our destination will be either West End or Lucaya, both of which are on Grand Bahama Island. We plan to meet them at Spencer's and proceed together from there to Fort Lauderdale and leave for the Bahamas from Fort Lauderdale, but they need to have some work done on their boat at Spencer's before leaving. They called us today (on the marine radio) to tell us that they have put in at Spencer's to have the work done, but said for us to stay where we are for tonight because the work would not be done until tomorrow.

Anchored at the Mud Hole, N Palm Beach, FL

April 23, 1987, Thursday

Spencer's marina had a slip available, so we put in around eleven in the morning. We scrubbed the deck, and Don worked on projects while I cleaned up the dinghy. Donna and Bill have rented a car and offered to take us to get groceries and to the bank for cash. We fixed picadillo for dinner for them and ate about six thirty. They are exhausted from all the work in getting ready to go and are frustrated with engine problems. Donna went to Fort Lauderdale early this morning and picked up their new dinghy and motor.

It was extremely hot today, but inside our boat, it was cool. After dinner, Don and I showered and watched a movie on TV about Boys Town. It was a productive day. We just wish Donna and Bill were ready to leave for the Bahamas. We may have to go by ourselves. Don and I played a game of gin rummy before going to bed.

Spencer's Marina, West Palm Beach, FL - Distance traveled: 6 miles

April 24, 1987, Friday

It was in the low 90s today. Don didn't feel good, so he stayed inside and watched TV during the hot part of the day. I did a lot of little projects. I am most proud of the cleaning job I did on the underside of the dodger. I used a product called X-14, which cleaned off all the mildew. I also cleaned the stove, sink drains, fans, the head, and the top of the dodger. In addition to those chores, I did laundry, ran the sweeper, and showered. I got all of these things done before dinner.

Don made chicken and noodles for dinner. After dinner Donna and Bill came over and brought some coffee cake. We ate it and then took a walk along the docks to look at the big boats. In the late evening, Don and I played gin rummy. I couldn't believe it–I actually beat him by 475 points in two games. What fun!

Orchid Boat's repairs are still not done.

Spencer's Marina, West Palm Beach, FL

April 25, 1987, Saturday

We left on this trip seven months ago today.

Don and I decided to go to Fort Lauderdale ahead of *Orchid Boat*. Our dock at Spencer's costs us $22 per night, and it's only $15 per night at the City Marina in Fort Lauderdale. Furthermore, we can take our time getting to Lauderdale and then spend a day exploring the area before leaving for the Bahamas. Hopefully, *Orchid Boat* will make it to Lauderdale by Monday, so we can go to the Bahamas together.

We enjoyed a leisurely morning. I fixed juice, coffee and muffins, and Don paid the dockmaster. Then, at nine fifteen, we pulled out of Spencer's. Spencer's has friendly people, a well-equipped, clean laundry and showers, but "C" dock, where we were, was noisy and there was a lot of motion due to wakes from boats passing by on the waterway. We sailed most of the day, even though we weren't moving as fast as when motoring, and finally anchored for the night on Lake Santa Barbara (formerly known as Lettuce Lake), about ten miles north of Fort Lauderdale. We visited with a live-aboard family, a husband, wife and their son, on a boat that was anchored there. The three of them have sailed around the world! The son is now 12 years old.

We ate leftover chicken and noodles for dinner and spent the evening reading. It was a bouncy night, but we slept alright.

Anchored in Lake Santa Barbara - Distance traveled: 35 miles

April 26, 1987, Sunday

Today, I slept in until nine thirty. Don was up early, as usual. The paddle wheel for the knot meter & log (speed and distance indicator) was fouled. He dove down and un-fouled it. He also checked the prop and the zinc. The zinc is a sacrificial anode that keeps the prop and shaft from corroding. It is gone and will need to be replaced in Fort Lauderdale.

We left our anchorage at eleven and motored into Fort Lauderdale. What a congested mess the waterway was with all the Sunday traffic. We ran aground exploring Lake Sylvia, near the mouth of the New River, and were pulled off by a small runabout. We were glad we didn't have to call a tow service. We pulled into Lauderdale Marina for fuel and a pump-out and while we were there, a Coast Guard Auxiliary Boat hit us on our starboard bow. Fortunately, no damage was done, but the captain didn't even apologize. I couldn't believe it. Several others saw it happen and were equally shocked. We survived all of that and docked at the Fort Lauderdale City Marina on the New River in downtown Fort Lauderdale. Don walked to the grocery while I took a shower in the boat. It was a hot and sticky day. It must have been in the mid-80s, at least. The dinner he fixed was wiener schnitzel and leftover stuffing. It was great, and for dessert, we ate one of my favorites, Breyer's Vanilla Bean ice cream.

We took a walk around town and browsed in the expensive shops along Las Olas Blvd. I called Sister Carol this evening; it had been a while since I talked with her. Don and I played a game of gin rummy, and afterwards, I wrote Shelly a letter. I won again at gin rummy. I

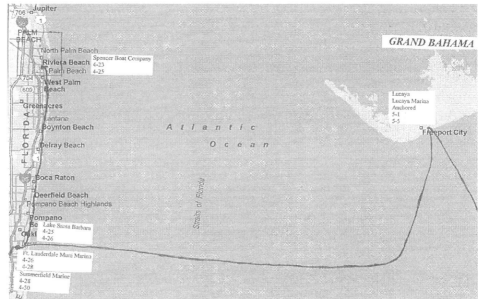

am enjoying the game more and more. The bird activity here is amazing. The wild parrots are colorful. They squawk and squawk. The other birds chirp and sing like crazy.

City Marina, Fort Lauderdale, FL - Distance traveled: 13 miles

April 27, 1987, Monday

We had a leisurely morning, but at ten o'clock, we left the boat for a day out. We took a city bus, riding it along the Fort Lauderdale beach, up to the Pompano Square Mall. At the mall, I purchased a couple of shirts, a sketch pad, colored pencils, and a book about how to draw.

On the way to the mall, we passed an anchorage and saw *Completion*, the boat with the family from Canada that we have seen several times between the Oswego Canal and here. After shopping until five, we took a bus to their anchorage and visited with them. It was great to hear about their past six months of traveling. They are "hanging it up." They feel sailboat life is too stressful, and that they and the kids are not up to it. Their boys are two and four.

We have been surprised to discover that there are so many people living on boats. As we see it, there are at least three types of live-aboards: short term cruising sailors, long term cruising sailors, and stationary live-aboards. We would classify ourselves and *Orchid Boat* as short term cruising sailors. We are just experiencing it and don't intend to make it our permanent way of life. When we feel we have "done it," and have seen what we want, we will go back to living on land.

We have met people we would classify as permanent cruising sailors. They are usually a married couple. They cruise until they run short of funds and then find a spot to stay while they work. They live on their boat while working, and once they have accumulated enough money, they continue their cruising. They intend to live that way indefinitely. I wouldn't classify a couple as long term cruising sailors, unless they have been cruising for at least three years and intend to continue cruising as long as they are able.

Then there are the stationary live-aboards who are anchored, living-aboard and working on shore in permanent type jobs, without any interest in cruising. They do it just because it's cheap. They don't have to pay rent, and they don't have to pay real estate taxes. They also don't have to have a boat that is in "ship shape." It needs to float, and that's about all. There are a lot of boats that are not seaworthy that can be purchased cheaply. Some people buy such a boat, anchor it somewhere, and go back and forth to shore in a dinghy to work. We have been told that land dwellers resent this type of live-aboard for several reasons, the two biggest being that they consider them to be free-loaders, and because their boats often are eyesores. However, we are also told that the land dwellers don't resent cruisers like us, who come, see, spend some money at the local merchants, and then move on.

Of course, long term cruisers become stationary live-aboards while they are replenishing their money, and as they get older and perhaps have some health issues or just tire of cruising, they may become permanent stationary live-aboards.

There are lots of variations of these categories, but one thing is certain, there are many people living on boats. When we set out on our trip, we thought we were going to be experiencing a way of life that very few people experience. We were wrong about that.

We ate lunch and an afternoon snack out. It was a fun day, and we returned to the boat around six. We tried to reach *Orchid Boat* on the marine radio, but couldn't. We did reach Spencer's and found out that Donna and Bill are still there, but say they are leaving on Wednesday. Hopefully, we can cross to the Bahamas with them, but it is looking questionable at this point.

In the evening after a dinner of Maryland chicken, we went to the grocery and stocked up. We also bought some ice cream. I cleaned and deflated the dinghy today, and stowed it below. I also took some video of the noisy birds singing and squawking by our boat. Later in the evening, we filled our water jugs at the store and talked with a guy named Shane, originally from London, England, aboard *Blue Azure*. He is a member of Seven Seas Cruising Association, which promotes long distance cruising and is also a sailing instructor.

City Marina, Fort Lauderdale, FL

April 28, 1987, Tuesday

We cleaned the bottom of the boat and replaced the zinc today at Summerfield Boat Yard, up the river from the City Dock here in Ft Lauderdale. We checked our speed after we were put back in the water, and were amazed. Our speed is back to normal. We had cleaned the bottom in December at Mt. Pleasant. There was only a little growth on the bottom, but that little bit of growth decreased our speed by one knot, which means that we have now increased our speed by 15% to 20% for crossing to the Bahamas.

When we docked the boat at Summerfield's, we ordered a pizza for lunch. At about four in the afternoon, we walked to the hardware store. We bought a lock for the dinghy motor and clothes pins and a washboard (made in Columbus, Ohio) to use for washing clothes in the Bahamas.

When we got back to the boat, we talked briefly with the boaters docked next to us. The lady gave us a book on the Bahamas and some vinyl fabric. We watched a little TV, went to bed around ten thirty, and fell asleep immediately.

Summerfield Boat Yard, New River, Fort Lauderdale, FL - Distance traveled: 2 miles

April 29, 1987, Wednesday

The weather has been nice except for the heat. The sun is hot, especially between ten and four.

We rested until eleven, at which time I cut Don's hair and beard. After that, I straightened up the boat and put away more groceries. Don ate pizza, leftover from yesterday, for breakfast and lunch. I spent the rest of the day making a compass cover from the vinyl material the lady next to us gave me last night. Around six thirty, not hearing from *Orchid Boat*, we went to McDonald's for dinner and hot fudge sundaes. When we got back, I called *Orchid Boat* to see if they were ready to come tomorrow. They said they were. I wrote to Mom, Carol, and Jane regarding reaching us with emergency messages through Charlie's Locker, a store in Fort Lauderdale that helps to get messages to boats cruising in the Bahamas.

Summerfield Boat Yard, New River, Fort Lauderdale, FL

April 30, 1987, Thursday

We were at Summerfield Boat Works until about five in the afternoon. I hand washed and line dried our laundry. It took me two and a half hours plus the drying time. Actually, if you include walking and waiting time to do the wash at a laundromat, that probably takes more time than I spent today, and this was free.

We stayed at the dock most of the day waiting to hear from *Orchid Boat*. They left Spencer's Marina this morning. Don studied his charts for the waters between here and our two possible destinations, West End and Lucaya. The weather conditions and the forecast are favorable for a crossing tonight, so if *Orchid Boat* makes it here in time we will probably go.

Weather conditions are very important. Crossing to the Bahamas can be dangerous because of crossing the Gulf Stream. The Gulf Stream lies between Florida and The Bahamas. It is not a stationary body of water. It flows like a stream, from south to north. The speed varies from one mph to five and a half mph, but averages about four mph. That is about the speed of the current in a typical river after a good rain. If there aren't any significant winds blowing, the current doesn't present a problem. However, if there is a strong wind from the north, the combined effect of the current and the strong wind creates large, steep waves, which are dangerous to a small boat and can be fatal. Crossing the Gulf Stream is something sailors need to take seriously. They should cross only when they are sure they won't encounter strong north winds during their crossing. Many lives have been lost because sailors tried to make the crossing when there was a strong north wind.

We had spaghetti and pesto sauce for an early dinner so that we could leave in the evening and not have to fix a meal underway. We are taking snacks, fruit, and candy to tide us over until we get there, plus lemonade. I also showered and called Randy to let her know we were probably going tonight.

At four forty-five in the afternoon, we talked with *Orchid Boat* on the radio. They are near Fort Lauderdale and, instead of coming up the New River to where we are, they will go out the inlet and wait for us at the sea buoy that marks the beginning of the channel into Port Everglades, Fort Lauderdale's seaport. We will meet them there.

We made it to the sea buoy without difficulty at six thirty. We only had to wait for one bridge opening. It's 82 miles from Fort Lauderdale to West End on Grand Bahama Island, one possible destination, and takes 12 to 16 hours in a sailboat depending on weather and currents. It is 105 miles to Lucaya, also on Grand Bahama Island, our other possible destination, and takes 15 to 20 hours in a sailboat. Most sailors leave for the Bahamas in the evening so that when they are approaching the islands, it will be light. One needs good lighting to see the shoals.

After we reached the sea buoy, the four of us decided on our destination. Lucaya is a suburb of Freeport and is better located for the beginning of a Bahamian cruise. Since the weather is good and the forecast is good and the seas aren't too rough, we decided to go to Lucaya.

Our plan for visiting the Bahamas is first to visit Great Stirrup Cay, one of the Berry Islands, and then go to Nassau. After visiting Nassau, we plan to tour the Exumas, a chain of islands located south east of Nassau. We plan to start at the northern end at Highbourne Cay and go south to Georgetown. We may go from there to Long Island, and perhaps further. We will work our way back up the Exumas to Highbourne Cay, and from there, go to Eleuthera, including Spanish Wells and Harbour Island. From Harbour Island we will go to Great Abaco Island and tour the Abacos, ending at West End, where we will leave the Bahamas and return to the U.S. The reason we have decided to do it this way is that the protection from hurricanes is better in the Abacos than in the Exumas and the threat of hurricanes is greater in late summer. Lucaya is much closer to Great Stirrup Cay, our first destination after getting to the Bahamas.

During our crossing, Don and I took two-hour watches starting at eight o'clock in the evening. In the morning, we were both on duty from eight o'clock until we docked at Lucaya. Our nighttime crossing went well. The winds were from the S/SW, and seas were three to four feet. Wind speed was 15-20 knots until the wind shifted to the west, and then it was ten knots. It had dropped to 5-10 knots, by the time we made it into the marina at Lucaya. We were heeling quite a bit and even taking spray across the bow most of the night, but still, it wasn't a bad trip. We kept in touch with *Orchid Boat* by marine radio and were always within sight of her navigation lights.

The waters in the area of the entrance into Lucaya are very shallow. There is a channel that is about a mile long leading from the deeper water to the marina. The chart shows a buoy at the beginning of the channel, and no buoys from there to the marina. The idea of doing it that way must have been that, if you pass the buoy on the correct side and head

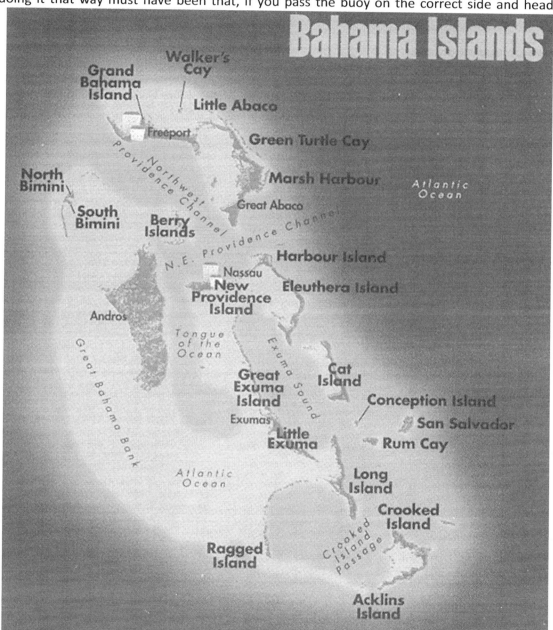

directly for the opening to the marina and keep an eye on the buoy over your shoulder, you should be able to stay on a straight line and within the channel. When we got to where the buoy was supposed to be, neither *Orchid Boat* nor we could find it. We looked and looked, motoring all over the general area, but saw no buoy. We were concerned about the depth. The water is totally transparent, and you can see the bottom clearly and it appears so shallow that it looks as though the keel of the boat must not be more than an inch or two above it. Finally, we saw a boat coming toward us and correctly guessed that they were headed for Lucaya, and that we could follow them in. Don called the boat on the radio and asked about the buoy. The skipper said, "Mon, (their word for man) a boat hit that buoy months ago, and the Coast Guard took it for repairs and haven't put it back. Follow me, and I will show you the way." We made it into the marina without any problem. The boat we were following was a party boat decorated to make it look like an old tall sailing ship. It was playing loud reggae music. The bright daylight, our lack of sleep, the music, the decorated boat, the crystal clear water and the appearance that we were just skimming over the bottom of the ocean gave a surreal effect to our arrival.

We were warned that in the Bahamas you can't rely on buoys being in place, and you also can't be sure that the lights shown on the charts will be working, so I guess it was appropriate for the buoy to be missing that was to welcome us to our first destination in the Bahamas.

We arrived at the marina at nine forty, and put up our yellow "Q" (Quarantine) flag to show that we just came into the country. That prompted the immigration and customs officers to come to our boat to clear us. We got permission to stay in the Bahamas for six months, and we registered the guns we have on board. The entry into the country was "a piece of cake." However, the immigration officer required us to pay him $10. He said it was for his transportation to the marina, and we were required to pay another $10 to the customs officer for his transportation. They collected the same thing from all the other boaters that came in. What a rip off! We also bought a fishing license for $10.

It was noon before we could leave the marina. I hosed down the boat, and then Don and I took showers, cleaned up, and went into town by the public bus. *Orchid Boat* showered and went to bed. They sailed 24 hours nonstop from West Palm Beach to Fort Lauderdale and then on to Lucaya and were exhausted.

At sea on the way to the Bahamas, Arriving at Lucaya, Grand Bahama Island, on May 1, 1987- Total distance traveled: to Lucaya: 106 miles

May 1, 1987, Friday

Don and I went to the post office for stamps and to the bank for money. We went to several banks to see which ones would give us cash on our debit card. There were lines at every bank. We found a bank where we could get cash without a fee. Bahamian money is equal to American money; one American dollar is equal to one Bahamian dollar. Then we went to KFC for a fried chicken dinner. We never dreamed we would be eating Kentucky Fried Chicken our first night in the Bahamas.

Finally, after a lot of walking and bus riding and talking to the locals, we went back to the boat. Don was very tired. He went to bed at seven. I stayed up until nine thirty writing letters. It sure was great to be where we wanted to be.

Lucaya Marina, Lucaya, Grand Bahama Island - Distance traveled from Fort Lauderdale on April 30 and May 1: 106 miles

May 2, 1987, Saturday

We are glad to be safe and secure in the Bahamas. The Bahamas consist of more than 700 islands, cays and islets. Its territory encompasses 180,000 square miles. When Columbus landed in the new world in 1492, he landed on one of the Bahamian Islands. In 1718, it became a British Crown Colony. After the Revolutionary War, many of the colonists that were loyal to England fled to the Bahamas, and many of them took slaves with them. Many freed slaves also went to the Bahamas. Today, the majority of the population of the Bahamas consists of descendants of these slaves. In 1973, the Bahamas became an independent Commonwealth realm.

The people here are all very black-skinned and speak with a slight British accent. Their dialect is difficult to understand if you don't listen carefully. The other thing that we will need to get accustomed to is that the cars drive on the opposite side of the road, as in Britain.

We both slept well last night and didn't get up this morning until nine. I fixed cinnamon toast for breakfast and Don made us coffee as usual. We quickly dressed and Donna, Bill, Don and I caught the bus to the shopping area at nine forty-five. The International Bazaar was interesting to see, but we didn't find any terrific buys except postcards, at $0.15 each. I bought six of them. Don bought rum and orange juice at the market, so he could make Yellowbird drinks to serve at happy hour, using the recipe Don Andrews gave him in Tarpon Springs. The four of us ate lunch outside at a restaurant. I ate ice cream for dessert. We walked around looking at everything until one o'clock, at which time we caught the bus back

BILL, DONNA, ROBIN AND DON

to the marina. Later in the afternoon we took the ferry to the casino and hotel on the beach near the marina.

It doesn't seem to be over crowded here with tourists. In fact, it looks like many of the hotel rooms are vacant. The beach is beautiful with clear water and fine white sand. We saw lots of teeny-weeny bikinis, and people parasailing and rafting. In the evening, we drank Don's Yellowbird drinks on *Orchid Boat*. Glen and Betty from another boat came over and talked to us about anchorages in the areas we are planning to go to. We never did eat supper. We stayed there from five thirty until eight, and then came back to our boat to change the engine oil. Don made out menus, and I wrote letters. The weather today was great--sunny, but not too hot. We went to bed early.

Lucaya Marina, Lucaya, Grand Bahama Island

May 3, 1987, Sunday

Today was an excellent day. We got up and ate a bowl of oatmeal with brown sugar and half & half. I gathered our beach things together, and after I did the dishes, Donna and Bill took us to the beach in their new dinghy. They left to explore in their dinghy while Don & I snorkeled and then sat on hotel lawn chairs in palm huts on the beach. We ate cheese and crackers and apples for lunch. We stayed until two o'clock, and then rode back to the marina in the hotel van.

We filled the boat's water tanks and the jugs we carry in the boat in order to have extra water. We also filled the fuel tank, using the fuel in the extra fuel container that we carry on board. I ran the sweeper. We showered and then left the marina to go out and anchor. We anchored in a channel that was part of a series of channels that appear to have been intended for boat docks of owners of homes that were to have been built in the development. The break-walls in the network of canals are made of large stones, and the canals were well dredged. The protection against bad weather and heavy seas is excellent. Surprisingly, there are no houses in the development, no boat docks, and no construction work going on. It looked to us as though the channels had been made quite a few years ago, and the project was abandoned. We named it "The Broken Dreams Anchorage."

Orchid Boat anchored in the same area and came over for rum drinks at happy hour. Don tried four new tropical drink recipes that came with the bottle of rum he bought in town yesterday. We each sampled all four drinks. I liked the piña colada best. Donna and Bill left about eight, and Don fixed us beef stew and bread and jelly for dinner. We played one game of gin. The loser had to wash the dishes. I skunked him. We went to bed around eleven.

It was a beautiful day with a gorgeous sunset.

Lucaya Marina, Lucaya, Grand Bahama Island

May 4, 1987, Monday

We planned to leave today for Great Stirrup Cay; however, we stayed at our anchorage because the winds predicted would not be favorable, and it will be a 70-mile trip. It was OK with me because it gave Don and me a chance to go into town by bus to check out the prices at the local grocery stores. All we needed was bread, but we wanted to compare prices with what we paid in Florida. The following are the prices here compared to Florida: Dairy product prices here are 1 ½ times what they are in Florida ; canned goods cost two to three times as much as in Florida; cookies, boxed cereals, and snacks, are at least 2 ½ times as expensive; and meat costs are about 1 ½ the cost in Florida.

We asked at the marina about the abandoned development where we are anchored, and were told that the developer abandoned the project in 1973 when the Bahamas became independent and the people formed their own government.

Donna and Bill went to the beach to relax. We met them there about three in the afternoon. Today the weather was cloudy and cooler, about 78°, not quite as good for swimming as when Don and I were there yesterday. The weather wasn't as bad as forecasted and the forecast for the night wasn't bad, so we could have left, but *Orchid Boat* wasn't up to an "all-nighter." Don made a great salmon, olive, and fettuccini recipe. We also ate the wonderful homemade bread we bought in town, with butter and jelly. After dinner, we went to *Orchid Boat* to have Bahamian drinks, socialize and play cards. It was a very calm night.

Anchorage (Broken Dreams Anchorage) next to Lucaya Marina, Lucaya, Grand Bahama Island

May 5, 1987, Tuesday

Bill took us for a ride in *Orchid Boat's* new dinghy named *Refund*. They named it that because the dinghy and motor were purchased for $2,000 from the income tax refund they received this spring.

Donna and Bill gave us a Bahamian flag on Easter Sunday, but since we had purchased one in Naples, we sold ours to a guy named Ron on a power boat called *Hawkeye* at the marina. We used the $7.00 we were paid for the flag to pay bus fare for the four of us to go into town to shop. I bought another loaf of homemade bread and a few postcards and stamps. We did laundry and showered at the marina and then came back to the boat. There were thunderstorms around us, but we didn't get any rain at the anchorage. I finished drying the laundry by hanging our clothes in the rigging and letting the sun dry them.

We relaxed in the afternoon because we are planning to sail all night from seven this

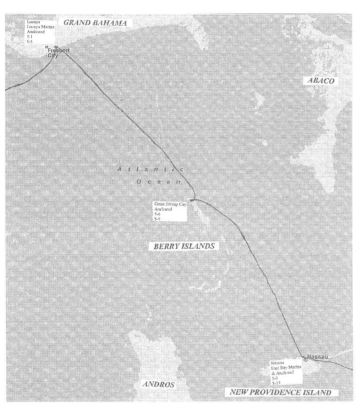

evening until about nine tomorrow morning. Our destination is Great Stirrup Cay in the Berry Islands, about 70 miles southeast of Lucaya. Sunrise tomorrow morning will be approximately six thirty and sunset tomorrow evening will be about seven forty-five. The trip will take 12 hours or more, and if we have to buck a headwind it could take <u>much</u> longer. We don't want to arrive at the Berry Islands anywhere near sunset and have to find our way through shallow waters to a place to anchor. In order to avoid that, we will need to leave in the dark or start before sunset. In either case, we will have to do some night sailing. We have decided to leave before sunset this evening, which will make it easy to find our way out to the open water, and then sail across the open water between here and Great Stirrup Cay during the night. There are no islands or other obstructions between Lucaya and Great Stirrup Cay except very near Great Stirrup Cay. We will arrive after sunrise and have all day to find a spot. Experienced sailors have advised us to do it that way. The dockmaster at the Lucaya Marina told us what our heading should be in order to stay in the channel (the one with the missing buoy) for the first mile after leaving the marina.

We left our anchorage at six forty-five in the evening and arrived at Great Stirrup Cay at seven thirty in the morning. The conditions were not great. However, if we hadn't left when we did, we might have been at Lucaya another four or five days because of weather, and we would have been bored. *Orchid Boat* was lukewarm about leaving, but when Bill heard the final weather update they said they would try it. The conditions were worse than advertised, and we rolled and pitched during the whole trip of 12 ¾ hours. The winds were from the east, at 15-20 mph, and the seas were 3-5 feet–not too bad. We took spray in the cockpit several times. The Bimini top was up, and it survived all right. We were uncomfortable, but at least this trip, our last night sail (we think), is over. Neither Don nor I slept. We took two-hour watches throughout the trip of 70 miles. We monitored Channel 16 on the marine radio, and *Orchid Boat* called us every two hours. We saw the light from the 80 foot high Great Stirrup Cay Lighthouse (built in 1863) when we were 20 miles away, and kept an eye on it for about the last four hours, using it to steer by. Vern, our lousy autopilot, never works in conditions like we had.

On our way to Great Stirrup Cay, Berry Islands, arriving on the 6th of May at seven thirty in the morning - Distance traveled: 70 miles

May 6, 1987, Wednesday

After we anchored, I straightened up the boat. The only problem I had to deal with was some water on one of our cushions in the cabin area that spilled from our five-gallon drinking water container; …not a big deal. There are three boats anchored here besides *Orchid Boat* and us, but one of them is leaving this morning.

Once we had the boat straightened up, we ate grapefruit and cold cereal and drank coffee. Don went to bed. I couldn't sleep, so I wrote in this journal and then wrote a letter to Shelly. I also made a Mother's Day card for my mom.

It turned out to be a pleasant day. Don made beef and sauerkraut with mashed potatoes for dinner. We inflated our dinghy, which had been stowed since we were in Fort Lauderdale, and went to shore to take a walk after dinner. We met Ron, one of the three residents of the island. He mans a NASA satellite tracking station on the island near his house. He and the other two residents of the island share the same house. I think the other two guys maintain the lighthouse. In the evening, we played cards on *Orchid Boat*. We were all so tired we gave up the card game and went home to get some sleep. Besides, I still needed to do the dishes. The no-see-ums are starting to get bad because it is fairly calm, so I am going to bed now.

Anchored at Great Stirrup Cay, Berry Islands

May 7, 1987, Thursday

We spent the day relaxing and continuing to recover from our night without sleep. Around noon, we took the dinghy to a spot where a ship wrecked many years ago. The water was clear enough to see the shipwreck and the bottom from the dinghy; even so, Don went in the water and dove with his snorkel and mask to see it better.

Afterwards, we took a long dinghy ride to the dump to get rid of our trash and to do some exploring. We found one of the most beautiful beaches we had ever seen. The Norwegian Cruise Line owns it, and their cruise ships stop here on cruises that pass nearby. They use this beautiful beach for a beach party for their passengers. It is absolutely breathtaking with fine white sand, beautiful aqua, turquoise, bluish water; coconut palms; grass hut lean-tos; and picnic tables. It was like Fantasy Island.

In talking to other boaters anchored near us, we learned that tomorrow the Norwegian Cruise Line's *SS Norway* will be anchored off the beach and that the passengers and crew will come ashore for a beach party. The *SS Norway* was formerly the *SS France.* Don's parents crossed the Atlantic on it back in the '60s.

We ate left-overs in the evening.

Anchored at Great Stirrup Cay, Berry Islands

May 8, 1987, Friday

GREAT STIRRUP CAY BEACH PARTY

Today was a terrific day. We left our boat early in the morning for the *SS Norway's* beach party. We took a long walk and when we reached the crest of a hill, we saw the beautiful ship at anchor. They were lowering the tenders so they could start unloading passengers and supplies for the party. We walked to the beach and watched the beach party develop. By noon, our desolate beach was crowded with about 2,500 people. There were towels, blankets, sun umbrellas, and people everywhere. It was incredible. They fixed lunch of hot dogs, sauerkraut, hamburgers, beans, barbecued chicken, potato salad, coleslaw and banana bread, and served iced-tea and water. They also had a bar. Donna and Bill were with us. We talked to passengers and were told by a crewman to help ourselves to whatever we wanted. (I'm not sure he was supposed to invite us, but he did.) We stayed until four in the afternoon. We stopped on the way back to the boat, within sight of the beach, and watched the passengers being ferried back to the ship and watched the crew returning the beach to its pre-party desolation. What an amazing experience. We decided that if we ever took a cruise on a cruise ship, we wanted it to be on the SS Norway on a cruise that comes here.[9]

We stopped at Ron's house on the way back to the boat and had a drink with him and visited awhile. He took us for a ride in his boat (a run-about). I swam and snorkeled behind the dinghy while Don rowed us back to the boat. Then he snorkeled. We showered on board and tidied up the boat. Ron stopped over to visit us in the evening.

Anchored at Great Stirrup Cay, Berry Islands

---

[9] Eight years later, in 1995 we took a seven day Caribbean cruise on the *SS Norway* and participated in a beach party at Great Stirrup Cay.

GREAT STIRRUP CAY BEACH PARTY

May 9, 1987, Saturday

We said our "good-byes" to *Orchid Boat* because Don felt that it was time to leave, but they wanted to stay. Don turned out to be right. We left at seven in the morning, and the sea was calm the entire day. We did have a short rainstorm around ten, but it was no problem. The sun came out soon after the rain stopped, and what might have been a long rough trip, instead was quite pleasant. I am sorry *Orchid Boat* didn't come with us.

We motored all the way to Nassau. The charts show that Nassau is SSW of Great Stirrup Cay at a distance of 64 statute miles. At ten minutes after five, our knot meter indicated that we had gone that far, but we weren't even close to Nassau. We couldn't even see it. We were still about 12 miles away and didn't arrive until ten minutes after seven. When we arrived, the knot meter said we had gone a total of 76 statute miles for the day. We must have been "bucking" a current. There was nothing on the chart or in the guide book we were using to indicate that there is a current there. Don suspects that currents are so variable they are unpredictable, and sometimes you just have to navigate "by the seat of your pants." Don was concerned that he had miscalculated the heading and missed New Providence Island, where Nassau is located, but then we saw a couple of cruise ships heading in the same direction as we and realized they were headed for Nassau Harbor also. We didn't get docked at East Bay Marina in Nassau until eight, and it was getting dark.

It was too late to fix dinner, so we treated ourselves to a Bahamian meal at a local nightspot. Then we hired a cab to drive us downtown, so we could sightsee. We made it into the straw market a little before closing, and I bought gifts for Randy and the kids. It was fun to see all the cruise ships up close. We hired a cab to take us back to the dock and arrived at the boat at eleven. My impression of Nassau isn't favorable yet! There is a lot of trash lying around, plus we saw numerous rats!

East Bay Marina, Nassau, New Providence Island - Distance traveled: 64 -76 miles

May 10, 1987, Sunday

We lay around this morning, and I finished making my card to send to Mom for Mother's Day. Don made pancakes for breakfast. About noon, we walked across the bridge to Paradise Island to see the sights. We went to Hurricane Hole Marina on the other side of the bridge to check the dockage rates, and as we were leaving, Don heard a familiar voice. It was Harry Lewis, an attorney from Columbus, Ohio, where Don practiced law. This was an amazing happenstance, especially because Harry was very interested in our adventure. In fact, he was so interested he gave us a book before we left called: *A Cruising Guide to the Caribbean*. He was one of about three people in the whole world who gave us a going-away present. We were amazed by the coincidence and so was Harry. We spent the rest of the day with Harry and his wife, Liz. We took them aboard the *Robin Lee* and gave them a tour. They bought us lunch, and in the evening, we went to their hotel to visit some more. Chit-chatting with them was lots of fun.

We had loads of rain today, and my insect bites about drove me crazy. As we walked into town, we were approached twice by people asking for money, so we took a cab back to the dock.

East Bay Marina, Nassau, New Providence Island

May 11, 1987, Monday

I felt crummy the entire day. I have a lot of insect bites from the no-see-ums at Great Stirrup Cay and have been taking Benadryl to keep me from wanting to scratch them. I think the Benadryl is what's making me feel crummy.

We walked to the grocery and bakery as well as the post office. We can hardly stand the trashy conditions we see here in Nassau. Apparently, the locals couldn't care less about it. Moreover, the locals are very unfriendly. Walking along the street where they sell produce, we asked a few questions, and most of the sellers ignored our questions and acted like they didn't even want to wait on us.

After dinner of sausage paprikash, we did the dishes and then took a walk. It started to rain hard. We ducked into a drugstore until it stopped and then went to a small restaurant to have a Coke. It poured down while we were there. We finally made it back to the boat and played a few hands of gin rummy. The insect bites didn't bother me as much in the late evening.

East Bay Marina, Nassau, New Providence Island

May 12, 1987, Tuesday

We filled our fuel tank and our water tank. Don went to the grocery and bought bottled water. Afterwards, we went over the bridge to Paradise Island and "toured" it, as we had planned to do the day we ran into Harry Lewis. We liked it. It's the only part of Nassau that we have seen that is clean and friendly. We bought some conch salad for lunch, and then ate bread, butter & jelly when we came back to the boat.

We had to move the boat to another spot in the marina today so that a boat could dock in the space where we were. I don't like the arrogant kid, Jeff, who is the dockmaster for Bud. Bud owns the marina and lives on a boat at the marina. The water is crystal clear like we have seen elsewhere in the Bahamas. Unfortunately, when we look down in the water, we see lots of junk on the bottom, old tires, bottles, etc. Another thing we don't like about our present location is that there is a huge pile of discarded conch shells near the marina, perhaps a hundred feet from our boat. A lot of live conchs are brought into this area and when the meat is removed by the street vendors for sale to the public, the shell ends up on

this heap. It smells terrible. Neither Don nor I like the marina or the people in the area.

We walked to a fish and bait store this afternoon to buy some fishing lures for trolling. They were getting ready to close when we got there and wouldn't let us buy anything. It seems to us that the people here are intentionally

SMELLY CONCH CARCASSES IN NASSAU NEXT TO OUR MARINA

unfriendly to us. We aren't sure whether they are unfriendly to everyone or just to the boat people like us who are passing through. However, we understand now why some in the boating community refer to Nassau as "Nauseous Town" and some others as "Nasty Town." Nassau is not our cup of tea!

East Bay Marina, Nassau, New Providence Island

May 13, 1987, Wednesday

It's so windy we don't want to leave Nassau, but after Don went to the bank, the grocery, and the bait store, and after I did a load of wash, we pulled out of the marina and anchored nearby. As we were leaving, Jeff, the dockmaster treated us nicely for the first time and said he would make room for us should we want to come back. I surely hope we don't have to!

The anchorage isn't the greatest, because we get soot all over the boat from the smoke stacks of the cruise ships, and also, because it's "rock n' roll time" out here.

We stayed on board the entire day. I stayed out in the cockpit most of the day. Don stayed below and read. Around five, we each drank a rum drink.

We ate chili for supper, and after the dishes were done, we played gin rummy. I hate this rocking and rolling. I can't imagine where *Orchid Boat* is. We left them five days ago, and the wind has been strong ever since. Today, I wrote a few letters to friends and, of course, Shelly.

Anchored in the cruise ship area, Nassau, New Providence Island

May 14, 1987, Thursday, Chips 22nd birthday & Barbara Headlee's 57th birthday

We are still anchored at Nassau, it's still windy, and we're still rocking and rolling, but at least it's warm and sunny. We are anchored within sight of the cruise ships, and it has been fun to watch them come and go.

We took the dinghy ashore for a walk and to mail my letters. The walk was short because Don didn't want to leave the dinghy at the beach for long because there were so many kids there. We sat in the beach area for a time, and then came back to the boat and drank a tropical rum drink, around four o'clock.

I drew a picture of the lighthouse today with colored pencils. That was something new and different for me, and I enjoyed it. Don studied his navigation books from the power squadron courses we took before we left on the trip.

We ate Red River hot cereal for breakfast, egg salad sandwiches for lunch, and ham with scalloped potatoes for dinner. We had chocolate pudding for dessert. We sure eat a lot even though we aren't getting much exercise. On the positive side, we burn calories when we use our muscles to balance ourselves when the boat is rockin' and rollin', even in our sleep.

Anchored in the cruise ship area, Nassau, New Providence Island

May 15, 1987, Friday

I ran the sweeper and straightened up the boat. It doesn't stay looking orderly and clean for long. We ate French toast for breakfast. Don made a key lime pie for this evening. I tried to make meringue for the top of it. It looks all right (sort of), but I only had a fork with which to whip the egg whites. About noon, I went snorkeling and swimming around the boat. I checked the anchor to make sure it was set right and washed my hair in the salt water with Joy dish soap.

For dinner, we ate left-overs of ham and potatoes and a piece of pie. It tasted great, even my meringue concoction.

Some neighbors from the boat *Gusto* came by to visit. They gave us a lift to the shower area. I tried to call Mom at work and then at home, but didn't reach her. I did reach David Scott, and asked him to update everyone on our whereabouts. The showers were a dollar each, and the water was cold.

When we went home, there was sand on our shoes and so the carpet got dirty all over again. Don fixed dinner about six fifteen. We invited the neighbors on *Gusto* over for a piece of pie, and enjoyed visiting with them. They are from Boca Raton, Florida and have been in the Bahamas several times. This time they are staying for three weeks. They had a rough trip over. Interestingly, they like Nassau.

Anchored in the cruise ship area, Nassau, New Providence Island

May 16, 1987, Saturday

We got up at six, and Don called Clayton about a business matter because Clayton left a message with David that he needed to talk to Don. We pulled out for a possible run to Highbourne Cay. We went as far as Porgee Rock Light, one hour out of Nassau, and then turned back. The wind and seas were on our nose, and we are underpowered. We wouldn't have made it to Highbourne Cay until after dark. We decided we'd go back to Nassau. We joked that maybe we would like it better the second time there.

After anchoring in the same place (the one where we got all the soot from the cruise ships), we took the dinghy ashore. We spent the day looking at tourist places. We also went to the library and some churches. One of the local churches was having a rummage sale, so we bought some paperback books for $0.25 apiece. Don bought Dale Carnegie's book entitled: *How to Stop Worrying and Start Living.* We are both going to read it. We also bought a few groceries and some liquor.

We put the things we bought on the boat and then went to a local picnic, a political fundraiser. We tried conch fritters, fried chicken and conch salad; we liked them all. Afterwards, we walked to a convenience store and bought a pint of ice cream, so we could eat it on board with chocolate and nuts. It was good but was mostly melted by the time we ate it.

We played gin rummy in the evening, and Don managed to end up ahead by 400 points. At one point, I was about 900 points ahead. Oh well, I'll keep working at it.

Anchored in the cruise ship area, Nassau, New Providence Island - Distance traveled: 11 miles

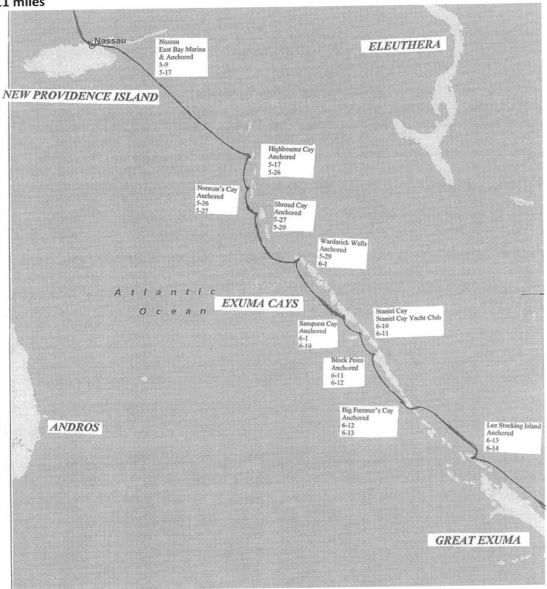

May 17, 1987, Sunday

We got up at five, pulled up the anchor, and left Nassau Harbor. About 15 miles out, Don calculated that at the speed we were making, we wouldn't get to our destination until after dark. Our destination, Highbourne Cay is in the north part of the Exuma Islands, (part of the Bahamas) and there is not much there by the way of aids to navigation to help boaters find their way into the anchorage. The wind was on our nose once more. We were again concerned about getting there before dark, but decided to postpone turning back until we had to. About a half-hour later, the wind shifted to the northeast and that made a big difference. We were heading southeast and so now the wind was on our beam, which is best for making speed. I would have been sick if we had been forced to go back and re-enter Nassau Harbor for the third time. My prayers were answered! Before we arrived, the wind shifted again to a less favorable direction, but we made it in long before dark, at three thirty in the afternoon.

The place is just heavenly! We tied up at the marina, and to cool off, we took a swim and snorkeled as soon as we arrived. We saw several colorful small fish and a couple of leopard rays swimming around in our area. We were enjoying the swim in the crystal-clear water, until the dockmaster told us we should get out of the water because yesterday they spotted a 12-foot hammerhead shark where we were swimming. So, we went for a walk instead. We walked up a road to the top of a hill; the view from there was spectacular. The Atlantic was to the east, the Great Bahama Bank was to the west, and beautiful blue water was everywhere with white-sand beaches and palm trees in between. It was great!

As we were walking back to our slip, we met some people in the marina on a 42-foot sport fishermen boat. They asked Don to take a picture of their group, and then invited us to join them for drinks and dinner. We ate broiled wahoo, barbequed wahoo, conch salad, tossed salad, rice, and fresh roe. Everything tasted wonderful. Their boat was very comfortable, and we enjoyed visiting with them. They were curious about us, our trip, and our life back in Ohio.

They were an especially amiable group of people, and this was their last night of a three-week fishing vacation here at Highbourne Cay, which is a popular place for fishing vacations. We enjoyed the evening tremendously. Meeting people and visiting is such fun. At ten thirty, when we came back to the boat, they insisted on giving us some of their frozen fish and the evening's left-overs. We accepted their gifts.

We docked for the night at $0.40 a foot, which was cheap enough. The weather today was pretty in spite of the strong wind on our nose part of the day.

Highbourne Cay Marina, Highbourne Cay, Exumas - Distance traveled: 50 miles

May 18, 1987, Monday

We stayed at the marina until checkout time and then moved out to the anchorage because most of the boats had left, and there was plenty of room. It's a well-protected anchorage, staying flat even in windy conditions. In the afternoon, we went ashore to walk around on the island. It was hot and sunny. We walked along every path. The island is two miles long and a quarter mile wide, with a beautiful beach running nearly the entire length of the island on the ocean side. The walk along the beach today was spectacular. I found some interesting small shells. There are seven people and two dogs living in the three houses on the island. We were told that the island is owned by an elderly lady in Philadelphia.

We ate left-over fish for lunch, part of the gift from our new sport fisherman friends, with fresh alfalfa sprouts that I am growing on the boat. In the evening, we ate the frozen grouper they gave us.

We are now using salt water from overboard to wash dishes. We have two five-gallon plastic buckets with steel handles. We have tied cords to the handles with loops at the ends for us to put our hands into. We throw a bucket in the water, open end down and then pull it up; it comes up about 2/3 full. We have one bucket for washing and one for rinsing. We are using Joy dish soap on the recommendation of other boaters who think it is the best choice for salt water. We put a little Clorox in each bucket. Using salt water is necessary because our fresh water supply is limited by our 46-gallon tank and a couple of portable five-gallon water containers. Water is not available at most of the places we plan to visit.

I wrote cards after lunch. Of course, there is no post office here, but a mail-boat comes to the island once a week to pick up and deliver mail, and we can leave the cards with the dockmaster for mailing.

Don is still 540 points ahead at gin rummy.

Anchored at Highbourne Cay, Exumas

May 19, 1987, Tuesday

Don made pancakes for breakfast; we both pigged out. We prepared for a long dinghy trip to Allen's Cay, which is known for having iguanas. It is about two miles north of where we are. The people anchored next to us, Tim and Anna, originally from Germany, and, for the past 23 years, living in South Africa, joined us. It was a half-hour dinghy trip across some rough water. We saw lots of iguanas. We packed a picnic lunch to eat there, but the iguanas wouldn't leave us alone long enough to eat it. They are used to being fed by the tourists and expect it, and in fact, insist on it, aggressively. We snorkeled for about an hour and found two small conchs. On the way home, we stopped at an artesian well on Highbourne Cay. All of us tasted the water, and since it was good, we rinsed our hair and dumped buckets full over our bodies to rinse off the salt water.

Tim and Anna sailed here from South Africa and don't plan to return. They have been unhappy with the politics there for several years and have wanted to leave. The problem was, as they explained it to us, the government doesn't allow people to take their money out of the country. In order to avoid that problem, they invested all of their money in their sailboat and sailed it out of the country. They plan to tour the east coast of the U.S. after they leave here, but haven't decided where they want to settle. When they do, they plan to sell the boat and use the money to set themselves up in a place to live.

THE IGUANAS OF ALLEN'S CAY

After we returned to the boat, we drank a rum drink and ate left over fish with rice. In the evening, we went ashore and met some folks from Nassau, Chris and Hillary, on a boat called *Sea Scape*. They invited us and another couple aboard. The other couple live in London. They sailed here from England in their 27-foot sailboat.

Don and I played one game of gin rummy before going to bed. He is now 213 points ahead; I'm making progress. I wrote Shelly a letter. *Sea Scape* said they would mail it for me when they get back to Nassau.

Anchored at Highbourne Cay, Exumas

May 20, 1987, Wednesday, Anchored

We got up early because *Sea Scape* is going back to Nassau today and offered to give us their left-over fresh water from their tanks, and we sure didn't want to miss the chance to fill up our tanks and to put enough in our buckets for laundry. I spent most of the day doing the wash and hanging it out on our life lines to dry, but I also read a bit from a book by Ronald Reagan, *Sincerely,* while I was taking a break.

We then went to the beach to swim and snorkel. I found two perfect sand-dollars, and Don found some shells he liked. When we came back to the boat, Don made Yellow Bird rum drinks, and we both bathed in the cockpit. We ate two excellent meals today; Rueben sandwiches for lunch and spinach pasta with Alfredo sauce and Parmesan cheese for dinner. We played two games of rummy and read until bedtime. In three nights, I have taken 1,400 points away from Don. I love it! I am ahead by 268 points.

Anchored at Highbourne Cay, Exumas

May 21, 1987, Thursday

We are still anchored at Highbourne Cay. Early in the morning we rowed to the small grocery that Harold, the dockmaster, runs, and I cut Don's hair at the beach picnic shelter. We went back to the boat about noon.

In the afternoon, we took the dinghy to the cove and beach on the northeast side of the island to swim and snorkel; we found a few treasures. On the way back, we stopped by the artesian well to clean up. The wind was strong and on our nose going to the beach, making it an uncomfortably slow and wet trip in our dinghy with its little two hp motor. We took a lot of spray on board.

HIGHBOURNE CAY

A boat came in today with two black Bahamians aboard. They are selling conchs. The boat is a 22-foot sloop, painted bright blue. It is quite old, and looks barely seaworthy. We hear that these guys come about once a week and stay for a day or so, selling their conchs to the boaters.

We ate left-over pasta for dinner. It wasn't plentiful, but enough to satisfy us, especially with cookies for dessert. I won again at gin this evening. I hope I can keep it up. We did some star gazing this evening at about eleven o'clock. It was a perfect night for it, very dark with no moon, and the bugs weren't too bad.

Anchored at Highbourne Cay, Exumas

May 22, 1987, Friday

When we awoke we thought this was the day to leave Highbourne Cay and move on down the Exumas. We would have left sooner, but the winds have been very strong, and it is so comfortable here! Just as we were pulling up our anchor, two boats *Cool Runnings* and *Cocoon* from Michigan pulled in. This morning, they left Norman's Cay, our next stop, and said it was quite uncomfortable there. So we dropped the anchor and stayed put. Later, we met the people on both boats, Mike and Sharon, aboard *Cocoon* and Dave and Sue, aboard *Cool Runnings.* We visited on board *Cool Runnings* with all four of them. Don had baked a cake, so we took it over and the six of us devoured it along with some snacks. That was our only dinner. It was a nice evening until the "no–see-ums" came out.

We went back to our place, and both of us read a little of Dale Carnegie's, *How to Stop Worrying and Start Living*.

We have met several friendly, helpful and generous people here. Furthermore, the dockmaster, Harold Albry, is truly dedicated to this island as caretaker, dockmaster, and person responsible for seeing to it that everything runs smoothly, and everybody enjoys their stay. We have had a wonderful time.

Anchored at Highbourne Cay, Exumas

May 23, 1987, Saturday

In the morning, we listened to the Bahamas Air-Sea Rescue Association (BASRA) and Charlie's Locker on the marine radio to see if there were any messages for us. It is still too windy to be comfortable at Norman's Cay which doesn't have a protected anchorage, so we are staying here. We ate egg sandwiches with alfalfa sprouts for breakfast around ten. I read a little and Don studied his navigation books until noon. I also re-hemmed a nightgown before we took a long walk on the east beach along the Atlantic side of Highbourne Cay.

After we returned to the boat, we relaxed until about four thirty. I then showered inside our boat, and Don made chicken curry with mashed potatoes which he cooked in sea water. I enjoy Don's cooking.

He did all the dishes, and I rowed ashore to dispose of the garbage. While ashore, I talked to a couple from Miami on a power boat. They have had cruising vacations in the Bahamas for several years and are the "know it all" type. We have met several people who spend their vacations, year after year, cruising in the Bahamas on power boats who we have found to be opinionated. They seem to look down on the cruising sailors, like us, who are here for the first time, exploring the Bahamas to see what they are like.

We played gin, as usual, and I am ahead 305 points. I wrote some in this journal and wrote a letter to Shelly prior to going to bed. Don is anxious to listen to the Indianapolis 500-mile automobile race on the radio tomorrow.

Anchored at Highbourne Cay, Exumas

May 24, 1987, Sunday

Today is one of Don's favorite days of the entire year, the day of the Indy 500. We were able to get the race on the radio. We went ashore and sat in the shelter house on the beach so Don could listen without having the signal fade in and out because of the boat swinging on the anchor. The race lasted about four hours; the winner was Al Unser, Sr., which was unexpected.

Afterwards, we went swimming and snorkeling, but the surge was too strong to contend with, so we didn't stay in the water long.

We met the skipper of *Lady Alice*, a 70-foot motor yacht that is at the marina. He told us that the yacht is owned by a man, who he referred to as "Mr. Neon," a wealthy 36-year-old heir to the fortune of the man who developed neon lights.

In the evening, we stayed on board *Robin Lee*. It was our typical evening of reading and playing a couple of hands of gin. Don took a lot of my lead away.

Anchored at Highbourne Cay, Exumas

May 25, 1987, Monday

Today Don and I moved *Robin Lee* from the anchorage to the marina.

While Don was making a barbequed butter beans and bacon casserole and cornbread for our dinner, I went to the picnic area and stitched our U.S. flag, which had frayed. Harold, the dockmaster, was there, and we talked. While we were talking, two guys came over to see Harold. They needed something and thought Harold might have it for sale in his little grocery. He didn't. The four of us talked for a while, and during the conversation, I invited the two guys, Bert and Jeff, to join Don and me for dinner aboard the *Robin Lee*, to enjoy Don's butter beans and cornbread. They thanked me for the invitation, but declined. When the conversation ended, I went back to the boat and Bert and Jeff left.

About fifteen minutes later, Jeff came to our boat in their dinghy and invited us to dinner on their boat. We accepted, but insisted on bringing our beans and cornbread, to add to the meal. Jeff said that they wouldn't be needed, but we could bring them if we wanted. Don and I packed up our casserole and cornbread and left with Jeff in his dinghy to go to their boat. They were anchored outside the entrance to the marina. When we saw the boat, we were awe struck. It was the most beautiful sailboat we had ever seen. When we went aboard, our ears were filled with the wonderful Spanish classical guitar concerto (Concierto De Aranjuez) being played loudly on their fabulous compact disc stereo system. We were served cracked conch and cocktails while we enjoyed the music, and while the two of them, working together, finished cooking an elegant meal of freshly caught yellow tail snapper, asparagus, marinated tomatoes, and latke (a large potato pancake). They served dinner on china with silver dinnerware and cloth napkins. We were served wine with dinner, (which they stored in their bilge) served to us in crystal wine glasses etched with the name of their boat, *Epicurus,*

Bert, the owner, has traveled all over the world in this 62-foot yacht, built in Finland. The yacht has everything you can imagine. The main cabin is 16 by 20 feet. It has two guest cabins and a master suite, and there are two heads with showers. It is beautifully decorated and even has a piece of original art work hanging behind the table where we ate. It has a completely equipped gourmet kitchen with food processor, two ice makers, a huge refrigerator and freezer, and a washer and dryer. It has a fax machine which prints out weather information, a Loran-C navigation system, a marine radio, a single side band radio, a long range short wave radio, and two generators. That's just about everything a cruising sailor could dream of having.

Bert is probably in his late 50s and is originally from Germany. He owned a chain of pancake houses in Florida by the name of Uncle John's Pancakes, which he recently sold. He has also been in the hotel business and in real estate in some capacity. He still owns a gourmet restaurant.

Jeff is about 30 years old. He is a graduate marine biologist and was a sailing instructor at Tortola in the Virgin Islands, for a couple of years. Bert hired Jeff to be his captain. Jeff lives on the boat and keeps it ship-shape. From time to time, Bert flies to wherever the boat is, along with guests, and they cruise. They are now on their way to Georgetown, Great Exuma Cay where guests will be joining them.

Needless to say, our dinner aboard *Epicurus* was the highlight of the day. The more we saw and the more we learned while on board, the more embarrassed we were about insisting on bringing our butter bean casserole and corn bread, which they politely set on the dining table with the rest of the food. Seeing our humble food sitting there made it all the more embarrassing. (Of course, they weren't touched.) We didn't return to our boat until shortly after midnight, when Jeff took us, our beans, and cornbread, back. We hope our paths cross again.

EPICURUS GOING TO NORMAN'S CAY

Highbourne Cay Marina, Highbourne Cay, Exumas

May 26, 1987, Tuesday

Don paid Harold for last night's dockage, and we prepared to leave Highbourne Cay. We left at about noon after saying our good-byes to Sue and Dave aboard *Cool Runnings*. They came over, and I gave Sue some alfalfa seeds, so she can grow her own sprouts. *Epicurus* and *Robin Lee* stayed within sight of each other the entire way to Norman's Cay. We anchored about three thirty on the east side of the island.

Norman's Cay was owned by Carlos Lehder, the notorious Columbian drug kingpin of the Medellin Cartel. It served as his headquarters from 1978 through 1982. He constructed an airfield with a 3,300-foot runway, and used the island as a base for smuggling cocaine into the United States. He protected the island from intruders using armed guards, attack dogs, and radar. The Bahamian authorities looked the other way until pressure from the U.S. forced them to crack down on the operation in 1982. Lehder escaped to Colombia. He was arrested in Colombia just 3 ½ months ago, on February 5, 1987, and our government is now attempting to have him extradited to the U.S. for trial.

During Lehder's reign on Norman's Cay, a DC-3 airplane crashed in the island's harbor. We went to it in the dinghy, and Don snorkeled around it while I watched from the dinghy. Don says that when he was looking around he noticed two lumps on the sandy bottom about the size of tennis balls. While he was approaching them to get a better look, they rose up out of the sand, and he saw that they were the eyeballs of a big leopard ray. He decided that he had done enough snorkeling for the day and came back to the dinghy.

Next we went ashore to see the remains of Lehder's kingdom. It was almost totally destroyed, but there were enough remnants that we could see that it was once a bustling place. There were roads and houses. There were some vehicles still sitting around, cars and vans, but they had been stripped of most of their usable parts. The furnishings in the houses had been carried off and even some doors and windows were gone. Thievery and the elements have almost wiped his kingdom away. The Bahamian government has police stationed there and we were told that we were supposed to sign in if we visited the island, but we didn't find a place to do that or even a policeman to talk to about it. When we had seen enough, we left in the dinghy to return to our boat. As we were motoring away, Don noticed a policeman, with a rifle slung over his shoulder, motioning us to come back. "Well, I'm afraid we have a problem." Don said. We went back to find out what the policeman wanted us to do. He asked us just one question: "Do you have any beer you could spare?" We apologized, explaining that we didn't have any beer on board. He said, "OK," and that was the end of the interview; we then returned to the *Robin Lee*.

In the evening, we were invited to *Epicurus* to enjoy fresh crab legs, cheese, fruit, breads, crackers, and a glass of wine. Again, we enjoyed their gracious hospitality, and tried to forget about how bumpy and uncomfortable the anchorage was. We returned to our boat at eight thirty, played a hand of gin rummy, and went to bed.

Anchored off of Norman's Cay, Exumas - Distance traveled: 19 miles

**THE WRECKED PLANE AT NORMAN'S CAY
(THE BACK OF THE CAMERA CAME OPEN AND DAMAGED THE FILM)**

May 27, 1987, Wednesday

We didn't go far today. We anchored for the night at Shroud Cay, just six miles down the Exuma chain from Norman's Cay. *Epicurus* went further south for the night. We anchored closer to the shore than we had at Norman's Cay, thinking that there would be less wave action and we would be more comfortable. We were, until "high tide," and then it was uncomfortable again. What a pain, another day and night to rock and roll and hold on to everything possible when moving about.

The Exumas, of which Norman's Cay and Shroud Cay are a part, is a chain of islands running from their north end in a southeasterly direction for about 130 miles. On the east side is the ocean, and on the west is the Great Bahama Bank, a flat, shallow body of water. The islands and the reefs protect the west side from the ocean waves. During the warm months of the year, the winds are constantly from the east, except during tropical storms, and the waves that build up at sea are stopped by the islands and the reefs. We are traveling on the west side and therefore, in the lee of the islands. We expected to be anchored in relatively calm waters as we worked our way down the chain, but that hasn't been the case. We don't understand exactly why. Apparently enough of the ocean waves make their way through the inlets to stir things up in the sound.

We took a dinghy ride to Shroud Cay's small, but beautiful, white-sand beach; I saw two pretty little star fish. While walking around on the island, we found a natural well. We had heard that one was there. We also found a note from the park ranger, Peggy, with information about the island for us cruising sailors and in the note, she said that she uses the water from the well for bathing and even drinks it. She wasn't there; in fact, we were the only people on the island.

Shroud Cay is part of the Exuma Cays Land and Sea Park, where fishing is forbidden. Before I realized that, I tried to spear a

THE WELL ON SHROUD CAY

fish, and in the process, I dropped my spear overboard from the dinghy.

We went back to the boat around five and spent our typical evening. I am presently way ahead in the gin game.

Anchored at Shroud Cay, Exumas – Distance traveled: 6 miles

May 28, 1987, Thursday

We woke up late today–around ten o'clock. After breakfast, Don dove down and retrieved the spear that went to the bottom yesterday. It cost $25, so I'm glad we didn't lose it. Then we went to the natural well and did our laundry and bathed in fresh, cool well water. I was sunburned on my back and thighs from the two hours I was doing laundry and bathing.

A boat came in and anchored next to us, and the couple on board came ashore. They are from New Jersey and were previously from Ohio. We talked awhile about all the places we expect to go. The weather is still very windy because of a tropical depression, so we couldn't go anywhere else in the dinghy. The small beach is beautiful, but we didn't want to go swimming because we had just bathed in fresh water.

After we got back to the boat, Don made dinner. I hung out the clothes, but it was too humid for them to dry completely. We did a lot of rocking and rolling, but still managed to play gin, and I'm now ahead by 900 points.

Anchored at Shroud Cay, Exumas

May 29, 1987, Friday

In the morning, we listened to the seven o'clock weather forecast and found out that there was a tropical storm warning for our area. We knew that we needed to move to a place with better protection. Don was up-tight all day, worried about the storm warning. I think it's time to do some more reading in Dale Carnegie's book, *How to Stop Worrying and Start Living.* The closest place with westerly protection was Warderick Wells so, that meant we

had to skip Hawksbill, which has an extremely beautiful beach according to the literature and the people we have talked to. It is more important to be safe and secure.

We motored with the jib out most of the eighteen miles. When we arrived, we weren't sure that we were at Warderick Wells. According to our navigation by dead reckoning, we should have been there, but there are no signs in the

DOING THE LAUNDRY AT THE WELL ON SHROUD CAY

Bahamas to tell you where you are, and this part of the Exumas is just one small island after the next, only one of which is Warderick Wells. We have a Loran C Navigation System. Unfortunately, Loran C wasn't designed for navigating in the Bahamas and can't be relied upon. We have not even been turning on our Loran.

However, the island where we were did offer protection from all directions, so we worked our way in through some narrow channels to the best protected spot and anchored. It was the first time the boat sat still in four days. We put out three anchors in preparation for the storm. Don hurt a finger doing so, but we sure were glad to be situated. Don eventually became convinced that we were indeed at Warderick Wells. Once again, we were the only people at the island. The storm was predicted to hit this area at one o'clock in the morning with winds as high as 50 mph! Don fixed a drink and tried to relax. He won at gin, and that made him a little happier. We went to bed at eleven.

Anchored at Warderick Wells, Exumas - Distance traveled: 22 miles

May 30, 1987, Saturday

Much to our pleasant surprise we didn't get battered by the storm! It passed by, and we had some wind but Don said we had experienced stronger winds every day during the past three and a half weeks than we did last night. I never woke up. The absence of the rockin' n' rollin' was great.

A tropical storm is the same as a hurricane, except that a hurricane is stronger. Both are tropical storms. If the fastest winds in a tropical storm have a speed of 74 miles per hour (mph), or more, it is called a hurricane. If the fastest winds are between 39 and 73 mph, it is called a tropical storm. In both cases, the storm is rotational. If you were looking down on the storm, you would see the winds going in a counter-clockwise direction. A tropical storm forms in the tropics and the entire storm system moves in a generally east to west direction and then turns to the north and eventually turns back to the northeast in the higher latitudes of the North Atlantic. The speed at which the storm moves varies from storm to storm and also varies during the life of the storm. This storm was moving west at 20 mph, and the fastest winds were 50 mph. The fastest winds in a storm that is moving west are on the north side, because the speed of the movement of the storm (20 mph for our storm), boosts the rotational speed (30 mph in our storm). On the south side, the speed of the storm is bucking the rotational wind and so the resulting wind is much weaker.

We were lucky to be on the south side of the storm. Don doesn't think the winds we experienced during the storm were more than 10-15 mph.

Don made pancakes and fried spam for breakfast. I did the dishes—in saltwater of course. Then we went sightseeing. We took the dinghy to the island and walked over the rocky terrain, exploring the beaches and the ocean side caves. Boaters have left cairns (stacked rocks) of different shapes and sizes and, using stones, have partially covered holes in caves that go through the rock to the water, and that causes them to whistle when a wave comes in and pushes the air through the hole. The whistling sounds are eerie. Boaters have also left messages on signs (usually their boat's name and the date they visited here). The island has no inhabitants, and we were the only boaters there. We went snorkeling around coral in a couple of spots. It was the most colorful snorkeling we have had so far, with hundreds of beautiful fish. The winds were calm, and it was an absolutely gorgeous day. Don enjoyed himself today since the conditions were great, and the storm had passed.

We bathed with Joy dish soap on a perfect sandy beach. As the tide was coming in we swam around to get the soap off our skin and out of our hair. Joy works great in saltwater. We didn't even use freshwater to rinse.

Don made us a drink and snack after we returned to the boat at five fifteen. He also made dinner, and I did the dishes again and made fresh jugs of tea and lemonade. We added this month's expenses, and the total was only $363. Since we left in September, we have averaged about $1,000 per month. We also played gin this evening, and I am still ahead by more than 400 points.

Anchored at Warderick Wells, Exumas

May 31, 1987, Sunday

It has been windy the entire month we have been in the Bahamas. The wind speed has been in excess of 20 knots every day. Everyone says that is unusual. Even so, the month has flown by, and we love the Bahamas. It is beautiful on all the islands we have visited so far.

We had an incredibly intense storm early today. It rained extremely hard, but ended quickly. I managed to collect almost four gallons of rainwater which I then strained through filters. We will use it for drinking, cooking, and the sun shower. The taste was fine.

Two kayaks passed through the harbor today with three adults and a baby on board. They were the first kayaks we have seen in the Bahamas. They don't seem suitable for these waters.

We spent the rest of the day reading and enjoying the serenity. The kayakers are the only people we have seen in the three days we have been here. In the evening, before sunset, Don and I oiled all the teak, but I am not so sure we should have done it because it is humid and therefore, won't dry well.

Anchored at Warderick Wells, Exumas.

CHAPTER SEVEN
SAMPSON CAY, BS to LONG ISLAND, BS
to GOVERNOR'S HARBOUR, BS
June 1, 1987 – July 29, 1987

June 1, 1987, Monday

We left Warderick Wells around nine thirty. The conditions were great. We raised both sails and made nearly six knots going toward Bell Island, our destination. When we reached the point where we were to change our course to go through the opening into the Bell Island anchorage, we started the engine because the new course put the wind on our nose. When we put the engine in gear, we found that we had no forward movement. The transmission wasn't working. We quickly turned away from the anchorage entrance because it is shallow and tricky to maneuver through. It would have been risky to try to navigate through it without engine power and going into the wind. We decided to continue further down the Exuma chain. After we had gone only a little way, the wind slackened and our speed dropped to less than two knots. We waited for the wind to pick up, but it didn't. After an hour or so, we called on our marine radio to find the nearest suitable anchorage for us. *Epicurus* responded. They were at Sampson Cay, and Burt told us that we should go there. It was about ten miles further down the Exumas from where we were. Soon the wind died completely, and when we reported that to Burt, he sent Jeff to rescue us. (We sure are glad we didn't have this problem on Friday when we were trying to get into Warderick Wells for protection from the tropical storm.) Jeff came in their dinghy, with its 14 hp outboard engine, tied his dinghy alongside our boat, and towed us to Sampson Cay, where we anchored. We are very lucky to have Burt and Jeff as friends. We are safe, and we are invited to *Epicurus* tonight for dinner, to boot.

While we were being towed in by Jeff, we received a call on the marine radio from another sailor, Terry, who said he was also anchored at Sampson Cay, and that he had

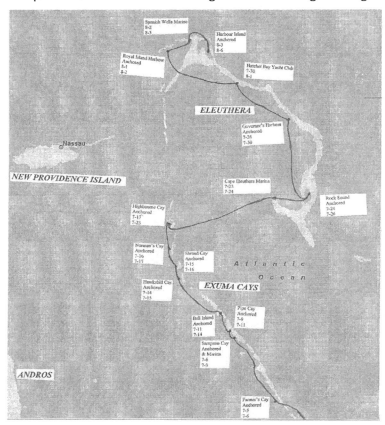

experience as a marine mechanic and would be happy to take a look at our problem when we got anchored. Don invited him to come over after we got situated. Within 15 minutes after our arrival, Terry was at our boat to talk to us about helping with our problem. Don and Terry started the engine, and Terry checked it over and confirmed that the transmission had a problem and proposed taking it apart to see what was wrong and to determine whether it needed parts. His rate of pay would be $15.00 per hour. My captain hired him, and they agreed that Terry would come over in the morning to work on it.

When we arrived at Sampson Cay, there were only two boats in the anchorage, *Epicurus* and Terry's 51 foot yellow trimaran, *Rendition,* on which he lives with his wife, Barb, and their two children, an 11-year-old son and a six month-old baby. Terry is a former policeman from Los Angeles. He and Barb have been live-aboards for thirteen years, and *Rendition* is their third boat. Both of their children were born on their boat, and Terry delivered them.

In the evening, we had another beautiful experience on *Epicurus*. This time we also had the pleasure of meeting the kayakers. *Epicurus* had provided them with showers, food, water, and his laundry facilities. They are from Germany and went to Florida to kayak on Florida's rivers. After doing that, they flew to Nassau, with their collapsible kayaks, and In Nassau, they booked passage to Norman's Cay on the mail boat. They disembarked at Norman's Cay, reassembled their kayaks, and started down the Exumas from there. The group consisted of George, an obstetrician and gynecologist, in his early thirties, his wife, Ava, about the same age, their six month-old baby, Lila, and Ava's younger sister, Christina, who didn't speak or understand much English. Christina has decided she has done enough kayaking and wants to go home. Burt is helping her arrange transportation back to Germany. I think George and Ava are about to give it up also. Although they are quite experienced and have camped and kayaked in many countries, keeping the baby safe and healthy on the open waters of the Bahamas must be challenging and worrisome.

After we finished dinner and did the dishes on *Epicurus*, we all went to the Sampson Cay Club, a bar, restaurant, and marina—the only business establishment on the island. The only other buildings on the Cay are out buildings for the Sampson Cay Club, dorms for its employees, and the home of the owner. Our group had a few drinks as guests of Burt. Burt spent over $80.00 buying drinks for everybody, and, according to Duane the bartender, the night before, Burt spent over $100.00 buying drinks. He must be wealthy! Burt had already done so much for us, we insisted on buying our own drinks. It was definitely a fun evening.

Although we had fun, we realize we have a big problem. Our transmission may have to be replaced, and that means finding one, getting it here, and finding a competent mechanic to put it in and do any other work needed. We are definitely in the boondocks. The nearest city, Nassau, is about 85 miles away. It is the only big city in the Bahamas. Georgetown, a town at the southern end of the Exumas, is a popular place with sailors, but it is only a small village, and it is about 70 miles away.

Anchored at Sampson Cay, Exumas – Distance traveled: 27 miles

June 2, 1987, Tuesday

Don helped Terry take the transmission out and take it apart to determine what the problem is. I just stayed out of their way. Terry found small bits of metal in the transmission fluid which indicated to him that parts have been damaged and need to be replaced. The instructions for winterizing the boat say that the transmission is supposed to be overfilled with transmission fluid for the winter so that none of the parts are exposed to air. Don did that for the one winter we owned the boat, but perhaps the previous owner didn't, and corrosion led to the problem. Whatever the cause, it needs to be taken to a shop, and a mechanic needs to order replacement parts or replace the transmission. Now Don has to figure out where this can be done, get it there, get it back here, and get it put back in our boat. These tasks could take months and cost a fortune.

In the afternoon, I visited with Barb, Terry's wife. We talked about her recent pregnancy, delivery, etc. She has a six month-old baby and thinks she's pregnant again.

Don and I spent the early evening discussing what to do about the transmission. We had a simple dinner, and when the dishes were done, we played some gin. Don's now ahead!

Anchored at Sampson Cay, Exumas

June 3, 1987, Wednesday

Don and I got up around ten o'clock. We made coffee cake, and then took the dinghy to Staniel Cay, about three miles south of Sampson Cay. Sampson Cay has no telephone, but Staniel Cay does. There is only one telephone on Staniel Cay, and they have a special building for it. The phone is only available from nine until ten thirty in the morning, one thirty until three in the early afternoon, and from four until five in the late afternoon. Obviously, you wait your turn to use the phone. We saw and visited with Burt at the telephone station. He was there, still trying to help Christina get back to Germany.

Don called a boat yard in Nassau and was told that they did not carry our make of transmission and was advised that we would not find parts for it anywhere in the Bahamas. They suggested that Don should call a boat yard in Fort Lauderdale, and he did. The boat yard gave Don the name and telephone number of a repair shop that dealt with our brand. It is a small shop, and when Don called, he talked with the owner who told him that they had one like ours in stock and that if we could get ours to him, he would look at it and fix it or sell us the one he had. Don asked him to hold it for us, and he would figure out some way to get there. The man said he would.

I called Mom, collect, and talked to her for 16 minutes to get the news from back home; that cost Mom $40.00, but I will have to reimburse her when we get home.

We went back to Sampson Cay in our dinghy and saw that *Shamu*, a beautiful 53-foot DeFever power boat belonging to Red and Pat, had come to the marina. We met them when we were at Highbourne Cay. Red is away on business, so we invited Pat for dinner.

Anchored at Sampson Cay, Exumas

June 4, 1987, Thursday

I took the dinghy to Staniel Cay to buy some bread and other items while Don pondered how he could get to Fort Lauderdale. I had a scary experience coming back. The tide was going out, and that created a stream going out the inlet. I had to cross that outflowing stream to get back. When I started across, the current pushed me toward the inlet, and I had to angle into the current. As I got toward the middle of the stream, the current was so strong that even when I headed directly into the current, I was going backward out the inlet, being swept into the open sea. I couldn't make forward progress, even at full throttle, but I angled toward the further edge of the stream, where the speed of the current wasn't as great, and eventually, I began to make progress slowly up stream and was able to get away from the inlet where the current was so strong.

When I got back to the boat, we had visitors. A couple had come to our boat, knocked, and introduced themselves to Don while I was gone. Don invited them aboard, and they were visiting when I returned to the boat. Don introduced them to me as folks, originally from Urbana, Ohio, who noticed that we were from Dublin and just stopped to chat. I said, "I know exactly who you are. You are Ralph and Shirley West. We've never met, but our mutual friend, Betty Parsons, told me you were living on a boat. When we were in Fort Myers Beach at the Wallace home, I saw your names, and your boat's name, on the dinghy landing guest registry. I noticed that you were from Urbana and figured you must be Betty's friends, and I've had an eye out for you ever since." They grew up in Urbana, about 40 miles from Dublin, and went to school there. I grew up in Urbana also, as did my mom and her brother Bob. Ralph was in Mom's class, and Shirley was in Uncle Bob's class. We spent the afternoon talking about their memories of Mom and Uncle Bob when they were kids together, about their memories of me when I was small, and about where they have cruised so far. They have been living on their boat, *Shirley Mae*, for five years and have traveled about 20,000 miles. They stayed until four thirty; we served them cheese and crackers.

After dinner, Don went to the Sampson Cay Club, to talk to whoever might be there about how he could get to Fort Lauderdale with our transmission. A boat is now in the anchorage that will be leaving in the next day or two for Nassau. We haven't met them, but hitching a ride with them to Nassau and then flying to Lauderdale was a possibility. Don thought the skipper might be at the club, and he might have a chance to meet him and talk about it. When he got to the club, there were a couple of fellows standing on the dock, talking. They introduced themselves to Don, and he joined in the conversation. One of the men, Tom, is a professor at a college in Jacksonville, Florida. Don hadn't yet gotten around to talking about our problem when Tom mentioned that he was going to Fort Lauderdale in the morning. Don about fell over when he heard that. He asked the professor how he was getting there, and the professor said he was flying his own plane, which he keeps at the airfield on Staniel Cay. He was going there to pick up his daughter and would be returning, with her, in the afternoon. We didn't even know there was an airfield on Staniel Cay. Don then explained our problem. The professor offered to fly Don and our transmission to Lauderdale in the morning and back here in the afternoon. He said that his daughter would have her car at the airport, and that they were planning on running some errands before coming back and could take Don to the repair shop. Don agreed to pay for the professor's fuel ($100) in exchange for the ride. Don gave the professor the name of our boat and where it was anchored, and the professor said he would pick him up at eight in the morning. Wow, what good luck!

Don scrounged around at the "Club" and found a cardboard box that was suitable to use for carrying the transmission in, and then returned to *Robin Lee* to tell me the good news.

We played a few hands of gin. The captain still has the lead. We went to bed around eleven, but were anxious about the trip to Fort Lauderdale and had difficulty getting to sleep.

Anchored at Sampson Cay, Exumas

June 5, 1987, Friday

The professor owns Dennis Cay, a small island located near Sampson Cay. He arrived from his island in his run-about shortly after eight. Don, the professor and our transmission then headed for Staniel Cay in the run-about.

I went back to bed and slept until Pat, from *Shamu,* came over and woke me up around ten thirty. We visited here, and then went to her boat where we listened to music on CDs and watched a video.

In the afternoon, I went out with Terry, Barb, and their baby in their dinghy. Terry and Barb wanted to spear fish. They had planned on leaving the baby in the boat by herself while they were spear fishing. I didn't think that was a good idea, so I offered to babysit in the boat and keep an eye on the baby; she slept the entire time. They were doing well, having picked up three conchs and speared two fish when a shark came and scared them out of the water. They lost the two fish and their spears. Barb got into the dinghy first. The shark followed

Terry all the way to the surface of the water, snapping at him. It bit one of his fins and actually took a chunk out of it. That was scary, and it sure messed up our plans for a fish-fry.

Don made it back safely from Fort Lauderdale at six thirty with a new transmission. He says that the trip went exactly as planned. The man at the repair shop looked at our transmission and confirmed that the one he had in stock was an exact match. He said that it was not a major brand of transmission, that it had been sitting on the shelf for a long time, that he was motivated to sell it, and that he would make us a good deal. The cost of repairing our transmission would have been nearly equal to the cost of the new one. There also would have been a delay of a week or two to get the parts and make the repairs. Don bought the new one. It cost $600. Now, all that remains is to get it installed in the boat.

We were invited to *Shamu* for dinner. Don was relieved; he didn't have to cook. We had hog fish and enjoyed Pat & Red's hospitality. We didn't get home until midnight.

Anchored at Sampson Cay, Exumas

June 6, 1987, Saturday

I spent the majority of the day on *Shamu* and on *Rendition*. I found some baby conchs and learned how to clean them. I had a heck of a time, and as I was finishing one, it fell off the dock into about ten feet of water. I dove down to get it, but noticed there were a lot of fish around and remembered that a big shark had been seen cruising the waters in the basin feeding on this type of fish, so I immediately got out of the water.

Don & Terry spent most of the day working on the transmission. They succeeded in getting it installed. They filed it with transmission fluid and tested it. It works! The total cost of the transmission problem was as follows: flight to Fort Lauderdale, $100, new transmission, $600, and Terry's labor, $220, for a total of $920. That's pretty inexpensive considering all the circumstances. We had it replaced and were ready to go on our way in five days. That's amazing!

We moved *Robin Lee* to the dock, so we could have electric. We skipped dinner and cleaned up the boat instead. Around ten thirty, Don, Terry, and I went into the bar to have a drink and get traveler's checks cashed so we could pay Terry. He still has a little work to do, but basically, the job is finished.

At the bar, Terry told Don of an experience he and Barbara had. Early in their live-aboard life, they were hit by a hurricane. At the time, they were living aboard another trimaran, one that was smaller than *Rendition*. When the hurricane struck, the boat was anchored, and they were on board. Occasionally, during the storm, the boat shook violently. They didn't understand what was causing it, so Terry went above to see if he could discover the reason. He put on a motorcycle helmet to protect himself from flying debris. He also put on a safety harness and attached it to a jack line, which he had rigged in preparation for the storm. A jack line is a line which is securely attached at the bow, and the other end is securely attached near the cockpit. Being hooked onto it prevented him from being swept overboard as he moved to the bow on his belly. When he got to the bow, he noticed that for several seconds the boat was steady and then suddenly it would shudder and shake violently. After a while, he figured out why. The trimaran, which was shaped somewhat like an F-16 aircraft, was being lifted off the water by the wind. It was flying! Then, it lost its lift and came crashing down on the water. That process was repeated many times during the storm. They sold that boat as soon as they could and built *Rendition,* which they designed to have negative lift.

Anchored at Sampson Cay, Exumas

June 7, 1987, Sunday

We moved back to the anchorage. Red and Don took *Robin Lee* out for a sea trial while Pat and I stayed on *Shamu*. She trimmed my hair; it feels a lot better.

When Don and Red came back to *Shamu*, we had lunch on the boat. They have a regular deep freeze, and it was full of food. They are going to Abaco from here and then to the States. They plan to go all the way up the east coast to Maine, and return to Florida in the fall.

The four of us went out in their dinghy for the afternoon to snorkel and scuba dive. Red is certified in scuba diving and has all the gear for it, so he did scuba diving while the rest of us snorkeled. Red's gear is so cumbersome that I wouldn't want to use it for the kind of diving we were doing. I think lightweight snorkeling gear is much better for shallow diving. Pat let us use her underwater camera. I hope we got some good underwater shots.

In the evening, after three hours of snorkeling around the reefs, we came back, cleaned up, and went to *Shamu* for a dinner of meat loaf, cornbread, and pasta. Then we watched a movie on their VCR, *What's Up Doc,* and ate popcorn. We didn't leave their place until one o'clock in the morning. For snacks after the movie, we had Jell-O and cookies on their after deck. They really have a nice boat.

The tide was higher than normal this evening. The weather has been great and the moon will be full, or nearly full, for the next few days.

Anchored at Sampson Cay, Exumas

June 8, 1987, Monday

Today is a holiday in the Bahamas. I think it's their Labor Day holiday. Their elections are coming up soon, so there is a lot of political propaganda on the radio stations. We'll be glad when that's over.

Today, Don said that he doesn't want to go much further than Georgetown. He feels that we were very lucky to have been able to solve our transmission problem so quickly, and he is concerned that we could have other comparable problems

ROBIN SNORKELING

and not be as lucky. He just wants to go to Georgetown and then return through the Exumas to Highbourne Cay, stopping at places we missed on the way down. From there, he wants to go to Eleuthera and the Abacos, and then return to Florida.

It's all so beautiful it may sound as though I'm being unfair to complain, but I feel as though I'm being cheated out of half the trip. Don may feel that the Exumas and Abacos are all there is to the Bahamas. I don't agree. I feel that the "out" islands are equally important.

I'm not in favor of his plan and don't feel like being supportive of it. He has a hard time relaxing and enjoying himself. I don't think I've ever been so upset with him. Always before, we have been able to agree, but this time we are very far apart on our ideas.

While Don worked with Terry on the transmission and finished the job, I went in the dinghy with Pat to Staniel Cay. We snorkeled in Thunderball Cave. It is where the underwater scene from the James Bond movie, *Thunderball,* was filmed. It is so beautiful that words can't describe it. I wish I could have taken another roll of underwater film.

Pat and I didn't get back until three thirty because on the return trip, the current was against us and was strong, but we made it safely. The evening was uneventful.

Anchored at Sampson Cay, Exumas

June 9, 1987, Tuesday

It rained for a short time, around eleven. Don went to *Shamu* to help them get ready to leave. After the rainstorm, I took some gingerbread and whipped cream over and the four of us ate it and said our good-byes. Then we helped them untie the dock lines. Pat gave me a couple of Christian books, one by Robert Schuller, *God Calling* and the other one, *The New Testament Paraphrase Edition.* They are nice people. I gave them a letter I had written to Shelly. They will mail it in Nassau.

Then we dinghied out to visit Professor Long and his family on his island, Dennis Cay. He is the guy who took Don to Fort Lauderdale in his private plane. After that, we returned to our boat and took a nap. We ate leftover casserole of chicken, macaroni, peas, and cheese and played gin rummy. Don is ahead by 1400 points.

Anchored at Sampson Cay, Exumas

June 10, 1987, Wednesday

We had pancakes for breakfast and at nine thirty left the anchorage and went to Staniel Cay. We managed to dock quickly and immediately left in the dinghy to go to Thunderball Cave. We got there in time to snorkel in the grotto at slack low tide, which is the best time to do it. Don was just as impressed with it as I was. It's incredibly beautiful. I'm glad we got to see it together.

We bathed there afterwards and then came back to the boat for lunch. In the afternoon, we walked up to the "Blue Grocery." It's called that because the building that houses the grocery is painted bright blue. We bought a loaf of warm fresh bread and some butter and eggs. I love the homemade bread we've been getting!

We have given up on having refrigeration when we are anchored. We just can't generate enough electricity to maintain it. So we are learning to do without it. We were surprised to learn that eggs will keep without refrigeration for a week or so without any loss in quality, even in the 90° heat of the Bahamas.

We saw the kayakers, George and Ava, at Staniel Cay. They are still "disputing" over the issue of whether to go on, or go home.

Terry, Barb and family were also there with *Rendition.*

In the evening, after we were finished with dinner and the dishes, I did some laundry by hand and left it to soak overnight. We also walked to a political rally and listened to music and political propaganda. On the way back, we sat out under a breezeway and enjoyed the beautiful scenery.

I wrote a few cards and a letter to Sister Carol before going to bed.

Staniel Cay Yacht Club, Staniel Cay, Exumas – Distance traveled: 6 miles

June 11, 1987, Thursday

We fueled up and left Staniel Cay at twelve forty-five. We motor-sailed to Blackpoint using the jib and the motor, and arrived at three in the afternoon. After we got anchored, we stayed on board because of the time and because there was a political rally going on. Don made dinner while I finished the laundry. I did the dishes and then worked on Dad's Father's Day card. I colored a fish on the front of it. It turned out pretty cool. Don and I played two games of gin. He is still ahead by about 1400, but I did pick up a few points in both games.

Anchored at Blackpoint, Exumas – Distance traveled: 11 miles

June 12, 1987, Friday

I did a few more pieces of laundry after breakfast and hung them up. Then, we went into Blackpoint.

The population of Blackpoint is 360, and I believe they are all black. It's the biggest town in the Exumas, except for Georgetown. The town looks to be quite poor, and only has one road. A few people were sitting outside, but the only productive thing we could see being done was that some of the elderly people were making basket material out of straw by weaving long strips, about 6" wide. We walked to the government health clinic, located in a poorly furnished two-story house and met the nurse. She was born and raised in Jamaica. We had an interesting conversation, and she gave us a lot of information about the people, her job, and the medical and education systems in the Bahamas. She's been here two years. She told us that her goal is to save enough money to build a home in Jamaica and when she has accumulated enough, she plans to go back to Jamaica and build it. She travels by boat to each of the islands to have "nurse clinic" hours. The doctor is supposed to come to each clinic once a month, but she says he rarely does. Basically, she's all they have. She helps with the delivery of newborns and tends to the elderly who are on their deathbed. What a responsibility!

We returned to the boat, and after eating a peanut butter sandwich, raised the anchor and left. We sailed the entire way to Farmer's Cay. We arrived at low tide and went hard aground and stayed grounded until the tide came up. We sat on the ground for about one hour. No damage was done. The chart data was misleading, saying the water depth is 6-8 feet at low water. After we got settled in our "rock n' roll" anchorage, we showered. Don fixed corned beef and carrots for dinner. We played some gin, and read a little. The radio station from Fort Lauderdale was coming in, so we listened to news, music and weather until about eight in the evening.

The weather was nice today, except it was very windy most of the time.

Anchored at Farmer's Cay, Exumas – Distance traveled: 18 miles

June 13, 1987, Saturday

The wind blew hard most of the night! We got up early so we could go out the Farmer's Cay Cut at high tide during slack water. That will put us on the east side, the ocean side, of the Exumas exposed to heavy sea conditions. We have been warned that the Farmer's Cay Cut can be treacherous, and the current can be very strong. We were warned that it could be strong enough that we might not be able to make headway against it if the tide was coming in, and that it is best to go through the cut at "slack water," which occurs when the tide is changing direction. We anchored near the cut and waited for slack water.

While we were waiting, we watched our anchor line moving around in the water. It looked like a very long snake. It obviously wasn't holding us in place. The interaction of the wind and the current was keeping us stationary while our anchor line snaked around, curling and uncurling, looping and unlooping, sometimes near the surface and sometimes deep down. We shortened the line so it wouldn't get around the keel or rudder. We finally had confirmation of what we thought had been happening when we were having anchoring problems in the Carolinas, Georgia and Florida. There, we couldn't see what was happening under the water, but here the water is clear, and we could.

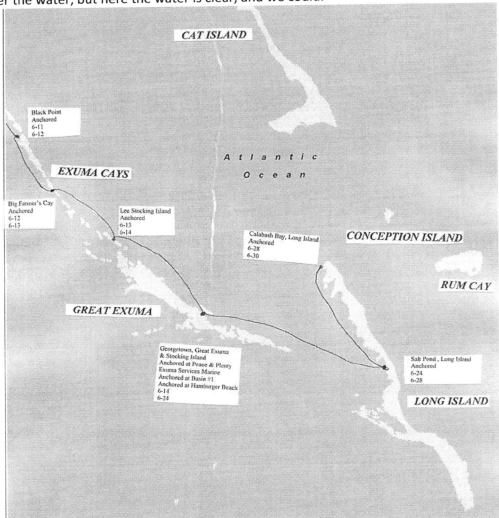

Finally the current went slack, and we headed out the cut. It was still difficult to make headway because of the strong head wind, but we made it. We went far away from land before making our turn to starboard in order that we could safely beat our way to Lee Stocking Island without being blown on shore. We took water over the bow most of the day, but made it safely. By three o'clock, we were relaxing in a comfortable anchorage.

Lee Stocking Island is privately owned. We dinghied to the island and got permission to walk around the research facilities. They work on a variety of projects here having to do with energy and making energy from available natural resources. They also have a fish hatchery and an area for farming.

We had a peaceful night on board. The wind calmed down and yet the bugs weren't bad.

Anchored at Lee Stocking Island, Exumas – Distance traveled: 24 miles

June 14, 1987, Sunday

We got up early, raised the anchor, and headed for Georgetown. Georgetown is the biggest town in the Exumas. Its population is about 800. It lies on the west side of Elizabeth Harbour. Stocking Island and various popular anchorages and Hamburger Beach lie on the east side of the harbor. Elizabeth Harbour is about 1.5 miles across. Georgetown is a popular destination for cruising sailors, and many of them spend the winter here. The 35 mile trip was less difficult than we expected. We only took a small amount of salt water spray over the bow.

We talked to *Epicurus* as we entered the harbor and Burt told us to anchor in front of the Peace and Plenty Hotel. When we were situated, he invited us on board *Epicurus* for champagne. Shortly after that, Burt and his girlfriend flew to Fort Lauderdale, leaving *Epicurus* here, under Jeff's care. We were glad to see Burt again, and to thank him once more for all of his hospitality and help.

Later in the evening, Don and I walked around Georgetown, and afterwards picked up our mail, which was waiting for us at the Peace and Plenty Hotel. I got a few letters, cards, etc. We ate dinner in the restaurant at the Two Turtles Inn, another hotel in Georgetown. I ordered a big juicy steak with onions, and Don had fresh grouper. The meals totaled $22 with tip, but they were good! We had a pretty quiet night on the hook. We both wrote letters and sorted mail before going to bed.

Anchored off the Peace and Plenty Hotel, Georgetown, Exumas – Distance traveled: 35 miles

June 15, 1987, Monday

We ran errands, mailed letters, paid bills, and did some sightseeing.

The anchorage was rough, so we moved to the Exuma Services Marina. We spent most of the day cleaning the boat. About four thirty we took showers. We were glad to be at a marina with real showers available...that is until we got to the shower house and saw the showers. The shower house was flooded with laundry water, the water pressure was minimal, and the water was only slightly warm since the hot-water heater had been shut off at three o'clock. It was awful!

I fixed tuna salad in the evening, and Don made macaroni and cheese. Afterwards, we walked to the Peace and Plenty and visited with people, some of whom were boaters. I tried to call Shelly, but she wasn't there. I was glad I called person-to-person.

The bugs were bad at dusk, and while we were sitting on the patio at the Peace and Plenty, we saw a pretty good-sized rat!

We went back to the boat and played gin. Don is way ahead of me now—approximately 2000 points. Towards evening, it got rough at our dock due to an increase in winds from the East.

At Exuma Services Marina, Georgetown, Exumas

June 16, 1987, Tuesday, Robin's 37th Birthday

We ate lunch at Freda's. It is an "outside" restaurant. She has some rickety old furniture in her yard and serves chicken, etc., in Styrofoam containers. The food was good and only cost $4 for each of us. Cinnamon rolls were only $5 for an entire pan. None of the chairs matched and in some cases the entire seat was missing. There was a goat running around in the yard. What a restaurant!

I took a nap and rest break in the afternoon. Don bought me a birthday card. I didn't want any gift, especially at Bahamas prices!

Around five we went to happy hour at Two Turtles and met several nice people. The group we were with sang happy birthday to me. I was a bit red in the face I'm sure. I talked with Shelly for about ten minutes.

We played gin rummy in the evening.

At Exuma Services Marina, Georgetown, Exumas

June 17, 1987, Wednesday

Don took the dinghy to a shop to have a zinc sacrificial anode mounted on the Honda motor. I made arrangements to take a tour of the island with Christine on her "Taxi 25" tour. Al and Trudy on *Vitamin Sea* wanted to go, but felt as though they couldn't leave their boat because it was so rough. They had to relocate in the middle of the night. It wasn't a pretty day; however, it was a good day for a 3.5-hour island tour. We went all over the northern part of Great Exuma, and Christine did a good job of entertaining us, as well as giving us the history of the people, and informing us about life and work on the island now.

After we got back, it poured down, and we managed to catch about seven gallons of good rain water for drinking.

Don made soup for dinner, and at eight thirty, after getting our next ten days of groceries from the locker below our V-berth, I went to the laundry and washed a couple of loads of clothes. The rockin' and rollin' was terribly uncomfortable again, but because we wanted to charge the batteries, we stayed at the dock.

At Exuma Services Marina, Georgetown, Exumas

June 18, 1987, Thursday

After last night, we were glad to leave the marina. Having to pay to sleep dockside in totally uncomfortable conditions is pretty bad. We both showered in the marina shower house in preparation for leaving. There was just a trickle of water. I think this was the worst shower facility we have ever had! It was just terrible! Don also bought a few groceries before we left.

It was difficult getting away from the marina because it was rough and windy. We had three people help us by holding the boat off the dock as we pulled out.

We went across the harbor and anchored in Basin One at Stocking Island, a popular anchorage. After anchoring we had a PB&J sandwich for lunch and rested until two thirty. Then we set out to do some exploring in the dinghy. We saw Patty and Cliff, on *TToga*, a 52-foot sailboat we had seen at several ports along the way. We first met Patty and Cliff at Great Stirrup Cay. We went aboard to visit with them and had a good time.

At six thirty we came back and had tuna-al-la-king over mashed potatoes. We just relaxed in the evening by reading, writing, etc.

Anchored at Basin One, Stocking Island, Exumas – Distance traveled: 2 miles

June 19, 1987, Friday

We had a really decent night's sleep at the Basin One anchorage. We got up around nine and changed the oil. After that we took a nice long walk on the beach of Stocking Island. I found several little shells to save.

After lunch, we moved the boat back to the Peace and Plenty to anchor because tonight is the regular night for Happy Hour and the Two Turtles' BBQ.

THE PEACE AND PLENTY HOTEL
LOOKING OUT ON ELIZABETH HARBOUR

We enjoyed the meal and had the opportunity to visit with Jeff from *Epicurus*. Burt is back in Florida, but the boat and Jeff are still in Georgetown. We bought Jeff's meal. He's been very good to us. We also visited some more with Cliff and Patty, from *TTOGA*. Don and I both like them real well. Cliff is a builder of luxury homes in Colorado. The building business is very slow in Colorado right now and Cliff is taking a break from it, but will return and build more homes when things pick up again.

We stayed there until nine thirty and then headed back to the boat.

The winds are still out of the East at approximately 15-20 knots with gusts of 25-30.

Anchored at the Peace and Plenty Hotel, Georgetown, Exumas – Distance traveled: 2 miles

June 20, 1987, Saturday

After breakfast, we went ashore to see who won the Bahamian election and mail some letters. The Progressive Liberal Party (PLP) won the election. Don and I wanted the Free National Movement (FNM) party to win.

We went to the local ice cream store and had a treat. They had cable TV. We watched an old *Lassie* show: Timmy was babysitting twin babies, a hawk flew into the room and threatened the babies, Lassie saved them, and all was safe at the Martin's farm! It had probably been 25 years since I had watched a *Lassie* show!

We planned to go to a dance this evening at nine thirty, but instead we stayed on board because of a rainstorm. We played cards and read. We set the buckets out, hoping to catch rain.

Anchored at the Peace and Plenty Hotel, Georgetown, Exumas

June 21, 1987, Sunday

We caught about 3.5 gallons of water during last night's rain. Not bad for not even getting wet!

Today is Father's Day! We closed up the boat because it looked like it would storm and went to church at an Anglican Church in Georgetown. We had time to have a bite to eat before church, so we went into the breakfast dining area of Peace and Plenty and had tea and toast.

Church was certainly different. We didn't feel the sincere welcome we had felt when we attended the Anglican Church in Amherstburg, Ontario on our Great Lakes cruise. It was obvious that this church is underfunded, as well as under-attended by its congregation. Everyone was black, except the minister, who was a white Bahamian, and a few white visitors. The service was casual. Since it was Fathers-Day, all the fathers were asked to go forward for a special prayer given by the preacher. Don went up, but wasn't comfortable about it.

Today is the Summer Solstice and therefore, the sun is directly above the Tropic of Cancer, which is the furthest north that it goes during the year. It so happens that the Tropic of Cancer runs through Georgetown, which means that at local noon today, the sun will be at our zenith. That is something we never experience in central Ohio because there, the sun is always south of our zenith.

When we got back to the Peace and Plenty, we moved the boat to Hamburger Beach, on the other side of Elizabeth Harbour. Peace and Plenty operates a burger stand there, and Don wanted that for lunch. I think he wanted to have a "Cheeseburger in Paradise" like Jimmy Buffett. We got there at two thirty and ate, but no one else was there. We also swam at the beach. It was quite warm, and the water and beach were beautiful. Only a few people were around. In the evening, we showered, ate a little, and played gin. We went to bed at ten thirty; about the regular time for us boat bums.

Anchored at Hamburger Beach, Stocking Island, Exumas – Distance traveled: 2 miles

June 22, 1987, Monday

I worked on three projects: I thoroughly cleaned the brass anchor lamp, I repaired the Bimini top, and I put Velcro on the forward hatch screen.

The wind continues to blow hard, and Don is reluctant to make the trip to Long Island. I am really peeved about that. Don thinks we should start back up the Exumas. I'd rather sit and wait on the wind to let up a little and then make the trip to Long Island.

Jeff came by to visit and also another boater, Dick, from *Dram-Buoy,* stopped over. Other than that, the day was uneventful; we never even left the boat. Don made a good dinner of creamed limas and beef stroganoff with noodles.

Anchored at Hamburger Beach, Stocking Island, Exumas

June 23, 1987, Tuesday

We got up about nine thirty and went to the beach to cut Don's hair and swim. We also bathed at the beach. Jeff sailed over on his sailboard.

Don lay down and napped from four until seven thirty. During that time I read, did a cross-stitch project for Newt, and took about a two-hour dinghy trip to the beach and back, and to the basin to see Patty and Cliff on *TTOGA.*

I had a long talk with myself and God about the persistent strong wind and Don's reluctance to make the 100 mile round-trip to Long Island. I hate to give it up because I've been looking forward to it.

In the evening, things seemed to calm down—no wind at all in fact. We played cards. It was so hot that all we had for dinner was chocolate pudding. We decided that if the conditions did moderate, we would head for Long Island tomorrow.

Anchored at Hamburger Beach, Stocking Island, Exumas

June 24, 1987, Wednesday

I spent last night worrying about what today's weather would be, I didn't slept much, but I had decided that I would be content whatever it was. If it was bad and we stayed, we would go to the Hamburger Beach party with all the boaters that was scheduled for one in the afternoon. If we left, I'd be excited and nervous, hoping things would turn out OK.

Apparently, my talk with God helped! The weather today was the calmest it has been since we sailed from Great Stirrup to Nassau. Don was agreeable to "try" for Long Island. We got up at six o'clock. We were underway at six forty-five. Everything turned out perfect. Both of us enjoyed the trip. It was a problem-free day, and I truly believe the good Lord above gave us the break in the weather.

We sailed with the butterflies. I don't know where they came from, or if they ever got to wherever they were going, but the sky was full of them. They were small white butterflies, and they were everywhere. They stayed with us the entire 45 miles from Georgetown to Salt Pond, Long Island. At any time, we could count at least a half-dozen of them.

We were anchored by three o'clock, swimming by three fifteen, and then had drinks by four, with showers afterward. It was too hot and muggy to cook again tonight, so Don heated up canned roast beef hash and a jar of applesauce. It wasn't bad.

In the evening, we dinghied over to a 50-foot sailboat anchored near us, named *Pride* and met Peggy and Ron, the owners, and their guests, Anna and Sal. Ron and Peggy are from New Orleans. *Pride* is a salvaged boat. It sank. Ron made a deal with its owner to acquire title to it, and then salvaged and restored it. At dusk, we came back to *Robin Lee* and played gin until ten o'clock.

What a great day to always remember, and Thanks to God for it!

Anchored at Salt Pond, Long Island – Distance traveled: 45 miles

June 25, 1987, Thursday

Long Island was the third island visited by Christopher Columbus in 1492. He named it Fernandina. San Salvador and Rum Key were the first two islands he visited.

We went ashore around ten o'clock, stopped at the Salt Pond grocery, and ate ice cream before starting to hitchhike to the northern part of the island. We got a ride right to the Stella Maris Resort, which was our main destination. The road was dusty and had a lot of potholes. We were so hot when we arrived that we immediately took a swim in their swimming pool. We had lunch (cheeseburgers and cokes) and then took a walk around the complex. There were about 35 guests staying there.

They offer a scuba diving experience which includes feeding sharks. The feeding is done by the guide, and the guests just watch. This morning a guide was bitten on his arm by a shark during the feeding.

That is the third shark incident we have heard about that has happened while we have been in the Bahamas. The first was the shark that was after Terry, but only got a piece of one of his fins. The second involved a lady we met while we were at Sampson Cay. A couple of days after we met her, she was bitten on her arm by a shark while she was spear fishing. We also heard about an incident that happened some time ago, when a couple of teenage boys were spearfishing. One of the boys speared a fish and put it in a sack tied around his waist. A shark came and grabbed it and bit the boy in the process. The boy died. We are told that almost all injuries from sharks occur while the victim is spear fishing. Sharks can somehow tell when a fish has been speared and they go to it and try to get it for themselves. Trying to keep the shark from getting the fish is not a good idea.

Hitchhiking back, our first ride was with one of the employees at Stella Maris, and it took us about halfway to our boat. Then, a Long Island Kiwanis member picked us up and took us the rest of the way. His car was air-conditioned. We were hotter today than on any other day since we have been in the Bahamas.

The daily high temperatures for the last month or so have been in the high eighties or low nineties. Surprisingly, we have been comfortable on our boat. I believe that is because the water temperature controls the temperature on the boat, and the water temperature is a few degrees cooler than the air temperature. We are much hotter when on land. The sun beating down on asphalt, concrete or even on the ground seems to bounce right up to make us miserably hot. The heat seems to be absorbed by the water around the boat. Another reason that we are more comfortable on the boat is that there is almost always a strong breeze, and when we are at anchor, the boat turns into the wind. We keep the forward hatch open, and the breeze is channeled into the boat through the open hatch by the hatch cover which acts as a scoop. We also have a nylon "wind scoop" we attach to the forward hatch that scoops in even more air in. In the boat, it is like we are sitting in front of a big fan.

Many people ride bikes on the island. We saw an old man on a bike fall into the path of a car, but the car got stopped, and he didn't get hurt. I think he was drunk.

Most of the people we are encountering are locals. The people here and in Georgetown are much friendlier than those we met in Nassau.

We were pretty tired when we finally got home. When we left in the morning we closed up the boat because of the possibility of rain. When we went aboard it was very hot— probably in the 90s. We opened it up, put on the wind scoop, and went ashore to a grocery store to give it a chance to cool off. When we went back to the boat, it was comfortable. We had a very simple dinner of PB&J sandwiches and cookies. In the evening, we had our usual evening of gin rummy and reading.

Anchored in Thompson Bay at Salt Pond, Long Island

June 26, 1987, Friday

Long Island is about 65 miles long and only three or four miles wide. It is oriented north and south. We are anchored about midway down the island. Yesterday we hitchhiked north from where we are anchored, and today we hitchhiked south. The island only has one road, and it runs the length of the island. Today was much more interesting from the standpoint of touring the island and meeting the locals. We started hitchhiking at ten thirty, but we walked a lot. No cars were traveling in our direction. The island is sparsely populated. The homes are primitive: goats and chickens roam around freely in yards and on the roads and there aren't many cars. There is so little traffic that some kids have made a basketball court on the paved road, complete with baskets on the sides of the road and painted lines. We were told that the road was first paved 20 years ago, and that it hasn't been repaved since. There are sections with no pavement, and there are many large potholes. The locals told us that the government doesn't help this island much financially because the party of opposition (FNM – Free National Movement) is more popular here.

It took several rides to get to Clarence Town, 30 miles to our south, and each of them was friendly. One was a schoolteacher at Salt Pond. She stopped along the way to show us her grandfather's farm. She picked limes and mangos and gave them to us. The bananas and avocados were not ripe yet. Most of the area was overgrown with weeds, and I got a few bug bites. We were pretty thirsty, so she stopped at a store so we could buy water.

The breeze was light, so it was very hot and dusty on the road. We also didn't have very much shade. Next, we got a short ride to the telecommunications building. While we were there, one lady said she would pray for us to get a ride to Clarence Town. It worked. Our next ride (which didn't come along for 45 minutes) was the Anglican Priest at the church in Clarence Town. Maybe her prayer did some good! He took us all the way to Clarence Town. In town, we walked to the harbor and had lunch at the only restaurant in town. I had grouper and deep fried fresh potatoes. They were great! Don had chicken and fries. We both enjoyed drinking lots of ice water.

After about an hour and a half, as we were getting ready to leave, the guy who had given us a ride yesterday, the Kiwanian, stopped by the restaurant to drink a beer. He gave us a ride again and took us 15-20 miles. He stopped at his friend's pineapple farm and showed it to us. Much to our delight, he gave us one of his friend's pineapples. We had to walk for about an hour before we got our next ride. Our waits for rides were not because people wouldn't pick us up. It was because there was no traffic. Only one car passed us without stopping during all of our hitchhiking on Long Island. The next ride was with the freight bill collector for the mail boat, *Nadin*. He took us to the grocery store at Salt Pond. A local young fisherman gave us a ride from there to Thompson Bay Inn. We got a Coke at the Inn and then went back to the boat. We were hot and exhausted. We swam and rinsed off the road dirt and then ate some of our fresh fruit. The pineapple was the best we had ever tasted!

We went to bed early—no gin rummy tonight!

Anchored in Thompson Bay at Salt Pond, Long Island

A GROCERY STORE ON LONG ISLAND

June 27, 1987, Saturday

The weather was hazy and not a good day for traveling. Furthermore, we were still pretty tired, so we didn't leave for Calabash Bay, our next stop. We stayed on the boat and took it easy. I did some cleaning and managed to scrub the mildew off the bulkhead. I also aired the bed sheets and worked on my cross-stitch. Don read and slept most of the day. He did make us a new recipe of Caribbean chicken salad, which was tasty. I had grown sprouts, and they were ready for him to use in it. We had fresh mangos for dessert.

After dinner, we saw a most unusual pink and green cloud formation high in the sky. It was really spectacular. It was like seeing a rainbow high in the sky. Neither of us had ever seen anything like it. The folks on *Sun Seeker*, a boat anchored near to us also saw it, but the single-handed man on *Hosanna* didn't. We have never met *Hosanna*, but he's very windy on the marine radio. He also has a single side band long range radio and was kind enough to give us the weather report he got from it. He also told us that *Pride* is at Calabash Bay.

Anchored in Thompson Bay at Salt Pond, Long Island

June 28, 1987, Sunday

We were underway from Salt Pond heading for Calabash Bay by ten thirty and during the time we were under sail, I trolled. I used a yellow feather lure on 100-pound test line. I caught a seven pound, 35" barracuda. He was ugly, with sharp-looking teeth. We dragged him quite a ways, drowning him in the process. After he was dead, we brought him on board. We left him in the cockpit until we anchored at Calabash Bay, which was at three forty-five. Then we weighed him, measured him, and threw him overboard. We were cautioned not to eat big barracudas from these waters. Barracuda around here feed on reef fish and can be poisonous. You can get a very serious and long lasting disease called ciguatera by eating them.

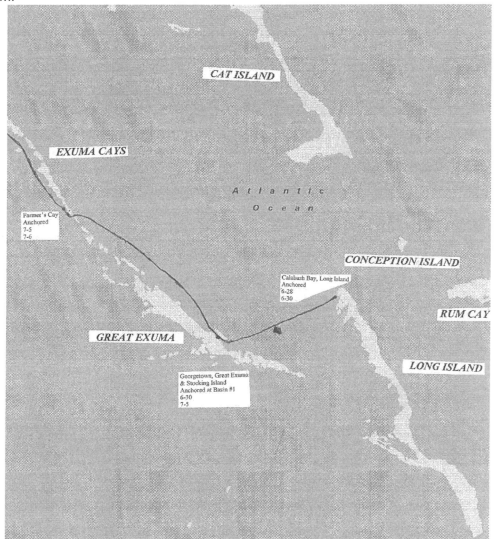

We had stormy weather for the rest of the day. It seemed to cool down after the storm, and the wind has shifted to the east at 15 mph, which is good. Calabash Bay provides good protection from an east wind. We sat in the anchorage pretty comfortably. The humidity also decreased, so we both took showers. It was the first time in three or four days that our skin and our bedding actually felt dry. We are now at the north end of Long Island.

Don fixed chicken cordon bleu for dinner. It was our first real meal on board in a long time.

We kept in touch with *SunSeeker* and *Pride* by radio. I worked on my cross-stitch, and Don read. We played one game of gin rummy.

Anchored in Calabash Bay, Long Island – Distance traveled: 26 miles

June 29, 1987, Monday

We ate pancakes for breakfast, and I did the dishes.

We left around ten o'clock for shore to explore the north end of Long Island and Cape Santa Maria Resort. We also explored the small village near the resort and swam at the beach. The swim was refreshing and the beach and the resort were beautiful. Then, since the winds were increasing, we left to come back to the boat.

We talked with *SunSeeker* afterwards as well as Jeff, on board *Epicurus,* clear over in Georgetown, 25 miles away.

In the evening, we ate popcorn and cookies and played gin rummy. Don's ahead by 2080 points. I did some cross-stitch and read today while Don napped.

Anchored in Calabash Bay, Long Island

June 30, 1987, Tuesday

Bad weather is coming; that is the forecast. In view of that we decided to return to Georgetown where we will have better protection. We left Calabash Bay at nine o'clock, made the 26 mile trip, and were anchored at Basin 1, in Elizabeth Harbour, by three in the afternoon. It was a good day. We stayed on board to deal with the anchors and such during the coming storm. We only caught about 2.5 gallons of water during the storm because we had to let the rain rinse down the boat. It was windy and bad all night with winds at 30 knots from the east. We sat pretty still with only a little rocking motion.

Anchored in Basin 1, Stocking Island, Exumas – Distance traveled: 26 miles

July 1, 1987, Wednesday

I rode into town with *TTOGA* in their dinghy. It was a wet trip due to wind and waves. I bought bread, lettuce, and stamps and mailed letters. I also got a book for Don from the library and a new snorkeling mask. Don's mask broke and he likes mine, so I bought a new one for myself. We played one game of gin in the evening. We were both tired since we had been up a lot during last night's storm.

Anchored in Basin 1, Stocking Island, Exumas

July 2, 1987, Thursday

It was calm last night, but I didn't sleep very well. In fact, I got up at five o'clock.

After breakfast, we made a two-mile trip in the dinghy to snorkel at a popular place. We were disappointed. The water wasn't clear, and the ride was wet. On top of that, we both got sunburned. On the way back, we stopped at a private beach and bathed. We both washed our hair. It was two in the afternoon before we got back for lunch. We spent the rest of the day relaxing on board. I did cross-stitch, and Don read. I also sorted the laundry. Don made salmon tetrazzini for dinner with creamed corn.

We read in the evening, and I wrote to Shelly. I found a note she had written to me when she visited us in March. She hid it in one of my books; it made my day!

Anchored in Basin 1, Stocking Island, Exumas

July 3, 1987, Friday

We ate a late breakfast. I did some house cleaning, and then around noon we went into town with the dinghy and did laundry. *Pride* came into the laundry, and when I was finished, they ran us over to our boat in their Boston Whaler, *Little Pride*. *Little Pride* is fast compared to *The Lincoln* with its 2hp engine. *Little Pride's* engine has 150hp! We dropped off our laundry at our boat, and Ron took us back to the town dock. We saw *Aldine Arnold* at the town dock and visited with them for a while. We first met them at Sarasota in February.

We ate dinner at Two Turtles, and sat with *Pride*. They introduced us to quite a few people. It was dark by the time we finished dinner, so we had to cross Elizabeth Harbour in the dark to get to our boat. It's about 1.5 miles across. We made it safely. We don't have navigation lights on the dinghy, but we had a flash light, and that was good enough.

Anchored in Basin 1, Stocking Island, Exumas

July 4, 1987, Saturday

This morning, before our picnic, Don finished the Charles Dickens book, *Hard Times*, which I had borrowed from the library on Wednesday.

We went to the annual 4th of July picnic on Hamburger Beach. About 40-50 sailboats are in Georgetown, and almost all the boaters were at the picnic. It was a potluck. Don didn't have time to fix anything, so we took two packages of cookies. They were good, and they were all eaten. We visited with people who have met *Orchid Boat* and found out that Donna and Bill are in the Sampson Cay area. We plan to be there in a couple of days, so we will probably see them. It was a really nice and a very different Independence Day. We didn't spend any money today, and it's a good thing, because we are down to $3.00 cash.

We got back to our boat at dusk, just when the bugs were coming out.

Anchored in Basin 1, Stocking Island, Exumas

HAMBURGER BEACH

July 5, 1987, Sunday

We motor-sailed to Farmer's Cay. We had enough wind that we didn't really need the motor, but the batteries needed charging so we ran the engine. The wind was 15-20 knots out of the southeast. The seas were 4-6 feet on the starboard quarter, and so we did a lot of rolling. It wasn't fun, but we made good time. We left at seven in the morning, and were anchored at Farmer's Cay by three in the afternoon. After anchoring, we had a quick snack of Freda's homemade bread and Betty's jelly. Then, we went ashore to sightsee. The town was alright, but there wasn't much happening and not much to do.

We did meet an interesting couple who are on an expedition. The man looks like he is about 60 and the woman, about 30. They are canoeing from the North Polar Region to the South Polar Region. They started in Alaska, above the Arctic Circle, and their destination is in

Antarctica, south of the Antarctic Circle. They have various sponsors that are paying their costs, including *National Geographic* and Kodak. The total distance of their trip will be over 22,000 miles. (Obviously they aren't traveling in a straight line.) They don't canoe across open waters; they cross open waters aboard ships, but canoe wherever they can. The expedition will take a couple of years to complete.

There was one other boat anchored at Farmer's Cay, *Gumbie.* The skipper's name is Gary, and he is single-handed. He came over in his dinghy and gave us some fresh grouper, so Don fixed the grouper, and we had him aboard for dinner and a visit. The grouper was great, and we had fun socializing. He is from Key Largo.

Anchored at Farmer's Cay, Exumas – Distance traveled: 43 miles

July 6, 1987, Monday

We left Farmer's Cay at ten thirty. It was a day for sailing! It was overcast, but the wind was favorable, and we sailed the entire 21 miles to Sampson Cay. When we arrived, we were glad to see *Orchid Boat* anchored in the harbor. This was a much more pleasant way to arrive than being towed in, as we had been the last time we arrived at Sampson Cay. After we got situated, Bill came by for a brief visit, and then we went to their boat for drinks and a long visit with them. What a nice time we had, talking about our experiences of the past two months. We didn't get back to the *Robin Lee* until nine thirty. Don and Bill plan to go to Staniel Cay tomorrow, so I wrote Shelly a letter for Don to mail.

Anchored at Sampson Cay, Exumas – Distance traveled: 21 miles

July 7, 1987, Tuesday

After listening to the weather forecast, Don and Bill left for Staniel Cay. Bill wants to call his family and Don will buy some bread and mail my letter. I stayed here and emptied the trash and then dinghied over to visit with Donna.

Bill and Donna treated us to lunch at the Sampson Cay Club, where we met their friends, Jay and Judy, on *Mahan*. We spent four hours just sitting around talking. About four o'clock, Don and I went back to our boat and scrubbed the bottom to get the "brown fur" and "green grass" off. It took two hours, and we were both tired afterwards. However, we did have Donna and Bill over for dinner, drinks, and conversation in the evening. Donna is thinking about writing an article for *Cruising World* titled, "If we had our trip to do it over, what changes we would make."

Anchored at Sampson Cay, Exumas

July 8, 1987, Wednesday

We decided that after breakfast, we would move to the dock for water and fuel and to charge our batteries, using shore power. It was low tide, so we had to wait for the water level to come up before we could move to the dock.

Porter Wright from Austin, Texas, the owner of *Celebration* came over for a short visit. We discussed the charts for the Abacos.

Around five, Donna and Bill came over and had dinner with us. Don made pasta with spaghetti sauce, and I made brownies. We watched our videotapes made in March through May, when we were with them. They didn't leave until eleven. We went to bed as soon as they left; we were too tired to even do the dishes.

I didn't have time today to write, read, or do any cross-stitch projects!

Docked at the Sampson Cay Club, Sampson Cay, Exumas

July 9, 1987, Thursday

We spent the night at the dock. In the morning, we did our weekly house cleaning, and Don changed the oil in the dinghy's motor. Donna and Bill came over to share lunch of grilled cheese sandwiches and cold drinks.

Around one o'clock, the laid back atmosphere of the marina changed dramatically! Don was videotaping on the dock and heard from the outdoor speaker of the marina's marine radio that a boat was coming in with four guys who had been attacked by a shark! When they came in, we learned that they had been spear fishing about five miles north of Sampson Cay on the ocean side of the cays, and they told us what had happened. One of them speared a fish and a six-foot black tip shark came after the fish. The guys decided not to let the shark have it. One of the guys had a "bang stick." A bang stick is an underwater gun. It has a very short barrel and bullet chamber at the end of the stick and when the stick is banged against a shark, a trigger mechanism fires the bullet into the shark. The guy used the bang stick. However, he didn't bang the shark in a vital spot. He hit him too far back. The shark turned and bit down on the calf of one of the guys. One of the remaining three swam back to the boat, cut the anchor line, and brought the boat closer to the wounded one. The other two tried to get the shark to let go of their friend. They finally succeeded by sticking a Hawaiian sling in the shark's mouth. A Hawaiian sling is a type of spear that uses a piece of strong, thick elastic rubber, essentially a big rubber-band, to propel the spear. The shark apparently thought the rubber was meat and let go of the guy's leg and swam off with the sling in its mouth.

That is how the fight with the shark ended, and as one of the guys told me later, "We lost, and I will never again challenge a shark for a fish!" As soon as they got back to their boat they asked on the marine radio where they should go for help, and the answer came back, that based on their location, the best place would be Sampson Cay. So they came in and tied up at the dock. The one guy, Tom, was critically injured. The shark took most of the calf of his left leg, down to bare bone. He stayed in the boat on the sole of the main deck. Someone immediately ran a water hose to the boat and ran a continuous stream of water on his wound.

In preparing for the trip, I packed a medical kit for us to have on the boat in case of an emergency. Our supplies included suturing material and antibiotics. I got the kit out and went to the victims' boat. A doctor was leaving the Thunderball Grotto, about three miles south of Sampson Cay when he heard the mayday-call on the radio and heard them say that they were going to go to Sampson Cay. He radioed that he would go to Sampson and do what he could to help. He arrived about five minutes after the victims. The doctor and I administered first-aid to them. The doctor was a specialist in Rehabilitation Medicine, and hadn't dealt with emergency medicine since he was in medical school some 20 to 25 years ago. Fortunately, I had done quite a bit of Urgent Care nursing during the year before we left. We concentrated our efforts on Tom, the badly injured guy, and got him started on my Keflex antibiotics right away. We also kept him comfortable, calm, and out of the sun.

Skip Allen, the editor and publisher of *Southern Boating Magazine*, happened to be at Sampson Cay on his boat named *Pass On Regardless*. His boat is equipped with a single sideband long range radio. He contacted the United States Coast Guard, and they dispatched a helicopter to come get Tom and take him to a Miami Hospital. Miami is about 270 miles from Sampson Cay.

One of the fellows was uninjured, and the other two had abrasions and bites on their hands and forearms. I cleaned their wounds.

After I felt I had done all I could, we left Sampson Cay and went to nearby Kemp Cay to anchor for the night. The attack occurred around one o'clock, the helicopter got to Sampson Cay at four thirty, and left for Miami at four forty-five.

Shortly after we saw the helicopter leave, we received a call on the radio and were told that only Tom, the critically injured victim, was taken to Miami. The other two victims were still at Sampson Cay and were in need of suturing. They wanted me to come back and help. Skip Allen came over and got us. We left our boat anchored at Kemp Cay and went back with Skip. The Rehab doc and I sewed up the two guys. The conditions were the worst I had ever worked in as far as sterile techniques and lighting were concerned. We did the best we could. I think I could have done a better suturing job than the doctor did because he was not at all experienced at it. He told me he hadn't put in any stitches for ten years! I had to explain to him how to tie his knots. During the suturing the power went off at the marina, and we had to use flashlights to see the wounds. We ran out of Lidocaine to numb the wounded areas, and the doctor had someone get some vodka from the bar, and he injected that into the area around the wounds.

We got word at six thirty that the chopper was back in the States, and Tom was in an ambulance on his way to the hospital. It was very quick action by the Coast Guard and everyone else involved, considering our remote location! Skip Allen on *Pass On Regardless* handled most of the marine radio transmissions and coordinating. The whole operation was dealt with efficiently and calmly. After we were done stitching both victims, Don and I stayed at Sampson Cay for dinner. The victims treated us to our meals. They asked Don to video the final episode of them getting their wounds stitched. He did, and then made copies of the tape for each of them on equipment that was on board the boat of a couple that works for the club, Dan and Donna.

The four guys are from Miami and are teammates on a rugby team. Tom is a lawyer. Steve Massey one of the other guys with arm and hand wounds is also a lawyer. The third victim, Shawn, is a Miami life-guard. I never heard what the guy who wasn't hurt does for a living, or his name.

The entire group gathered around the bar's TV to watch Don's homemade video. By that time, the victims were all feeling pretty good (from a combination of drinks and pain medication), and they wanted to tell everyone their story!

Pass on Regardless finally ferried us back to our boat. It was quite a day and certainly one that we would never want to replay (except on video)! We stayed up late trying to unwind, but it was difficult! Those guys are so lucky to have gotten away from the shark and to have had the care they received! One, or all, could have died! We will never forget this day, nor will the victims, or the approximately 20 bystanders.[10]

Anchored at Kemp Cay, Exumas – Distance traveled: 4 miles

July 10, 1987, Friday

We got up and dinghied around the beautiful area of Pipe Creek, near Kemp Key. We met Graham and Jeanne on *Nomad*. They spend a lot of time anchored here, living aboard. We spent a couple of hours visiting them and then went into a house that is under construction on a small island. It has a 360-degree picture window. The view is spectacular. The appearance of the water changes as the water rises and falls with the tide, so the view out the picture window is constantly changing and is always beautiful. We saw it at low water. I'm certain it's equally spectacular, if not more so at high water. In the late afternoon, we went back to the boat, and Don finished his bean dish (Hopping John), which he had started yesterday and had stopped when *Skip Allen* called and said he was coming to pick us up.

The Pipe Creek area is known for being a very comfortable anchorage. We asked Graham how high the waves actually get where they are anchored. He said, "Oh, about two to four...inches that is." Around six o'clock, Graham and Bill (his friend) came over and brought us a fish they had speared. It was of the snapper family, called a Margate. We went ashore so I could clean it. Don battered and fried the fish. It tasted excellent. I didn't do too bad cleaning it; there were hardly any bones to contend with.

Anchored at Kemp Cay, Exumas

July 11, 1987, Saturday

Today we moved from Kemp Cay to Bell Island. We intended to go to Bell Island on our way south. It was our planned destination the day that our transmission went out. We have heard that it is a comfortable anchorage and that the snorkeling is good.

---

[10] We talked with Steve Massey several months later and he told us that Tom spent about six weeks in the hospital, but did recover. I'm sure he walks with a limp these days.

We had a pleasant day to make the move; we had decent visibility and it wasn't too windy. We left Kemp Cay at ten thirty and anchored at Bell Island at twelve thirty.

It was calm enough for us to get anchored and then dinghy, in slack water, to the Rocky Dudes Cave. It was an incredible site with stalactites, and stalagmites and sunlight shining through a couple of openings. The coral was very colorful. It looked like someone had spray-painted the rocks, all, making for great snorkeling. We also snorkeled at a couple of small reefs. One had been "cloroxed," which is sad, because it kills everything on the reef. I'm not sure why people do this, but I think it is to get the lobsters and/or fish to come out so they can be speared.

In the evening, after dinner of lentil soup and cornbread, we played one game of gin; I skunked Don by 513 points. Now he leads by only 130 points!

We could see a fire, and so we went out on deck to watch it. It was on a nearby island, and had been set by a local man who had run out of gas and was stranded. He was hoping the fire would attract attention, and he would be rescued. It apparently got out of control, because it was a big fire. It was a pretty spectacle, especially under the full moon.

Anchored at Bell Island, Exumas – Distance traveled: 11 miles

July 12, 1987, Sunday

After breakfast, we met Peggy Hall, the 68-year-old park warden of the Exuma Land and Sea Park. She lives on the tug, *Moby* and moves around from place to place in the park. She told us about the good snorkeling places here at Bell Island. Armed with that information, we set out for a day of snorkeling. We dove on a wrecked two-seater plane, and after that, the seaquarium where Peggy feeds the fish living around the reef. The seaquarium was probably the second prettiest reef we have seen; Thunder Ball Grotto still ranks # 1. We then found a

secluded beach in a cove where we bathed and looked for shells. A couple of other boaters stopped in, and we visited. *Foxy* and *Driftwood* are their boats' names. We discussed the shark attack. Foxy recognized me as the nurse who was helping the doctor that day. *Driftwood* is anchored right behind us. They took us to another reef where we saw a few lobsters. We hope we can catch some when the season opens on August 1. I worked on cross-stitch in the evening. Don and I both got sun-burned today.

Anchored at Bell Island, Exumas

July 13, 1987, Monday

I slept in until eight thirty—a real switch. About that time, we got hit with a terrific rainstorm, so Don caught lots of water. He threw out a lot too, just because it was cloudy. I used what he kept to do the laundry.

Don decided to check the oil level in the engine because he hadn't done it for a couple of days, and we were planning on leaving today. When he opened the hatch of the engine compartment, he was shocked to find the bilge covered with engine oil—lots of oil. He knew that with all that oil in the bilge, there couldn't be much in the crankcase. He pulled out the dip stick to see and was again shocked when water poured out of the dip stick hole. The crankcase was full of salt water!

So, once again, we were in the boondocks with what seemed to be a trip "ending problem." We had no idea of why this had happened or what needed to be done. The nearest boatyards were at Nassau and Georgetown, both about 80 miles away. Don immediately set out in the dinghy to talk to Peggy, the park ranger. Peggy didn't have any suggestions. There were only three other boats in the anchorage. One was *Driftwood*, with Al who took us to the lobsters yesterday. Don talked to Al, and when Don explained the problem, Al said he thought he knew what had happened.

He came to our boat, looked things over, and afterwards told us what he thought. The water that cools the engine is expelled with the exhaust from the engine through a hose that goes from the engine to the transom. When the engine cools, a partial vacuum forms between the engine and the water lying in the hose which tends to draw the water back into the engine through the engine's exhaust valves. To keep that from happening, the hose layout is designed with a loop that rises up near the engine and at the top of the loop, an anti-siphon valve is installed. It prevents a vacuum from forming and keeps the water from being sucked into the engine. Sometimes the anti-siphon valve gets fouled, and Al suspected that ours had become fouled. He found our loop in the cabinet next to our galley sink. He took the anti-siphon valve out. It was, indeed, fouled. He cleaned it out and removed a piece from it, to make sure it didn't foul again. That will result in a tiny amount of water getting out of the hose and into the boat in the coming weeks, but only when we are running the engine and the amount will be insignificant. He put the hose back together. Next, he had me open the pressure release valves on the cylinder heads and then turn the engine over a couple of times. (That was to get any water off the pistons.) Then we drained the crankcase, changed the oil filter, and put in new oil. Then he had me try to start the engine. It started! We let it run for about a half-hour because he wanted any water that was still in the crankcase to be evaporated. Next we drained the crankcase again, changed the filter, and replaced the oil once more. He said that our problem was solved. His only further advice was to change the oil and filter again after about 20 hours of engine use and to replace the anti-siphon valve when we get to a boatyard.

He said he had the same problem once, and that is why he knew what to do. We were very lucky he was there to help us! And, if we had started out today without checking the oil, we would have been running the engine with no oil in the crankcase which would have been disastrous!

We have learned a couple of things by this and the transmission experience. We have learned that sailors are indeed ruled by Murphy's Law. Bad things do happen, and they happen in the worst of places. However, we have also learned that experienced cruising boaters have a lot of knowledge and are willing and eager to help.

If we had continued south from Long Island to the sparsely populated out islands of the Bahamas we probably would have been 105 miles further "off the beaten path" and that much further into the boondocks when our crankcase filled up with water, because that is how far we have come since leaving Calabash Bay. Maybe the captain was right in not wanting to go further.

Because it took us a while to solve the problem and clean up the spilled oil we decided to wait until tomorrow to leave. I hung out the laundry and then did dishes. Don and I took a walk to the beach. It was beautiful except for the trash, which washes up on all the beaches. Some of that trash has been thrown off ships and smaller boats, and some of it has drifted from the other side of the ocean.

We then went over to *Scandinavian Princess*, the Irwin 32 sailboat, with Milt and Peggy on board. The four of us went to the small reef where we had seen the lobsters. Milt used to own and operate a dive shop in Florida, and he taught us a technique for snorkeling that we like. You position your dinghy up current from an area you want to see, tether yourselves to your dinghy, and then get in the water and let the current carry you and your dinghy over the interesting area. You don't have to worry about being separated from your dinghy.

Milt and Peggy are from Lighthouse Point, Florida. That is also where Al is from, on *Driftwood,* who helped us with the crankcase problem. *Paladin*, whom we met at Highbourne and Sampson Cays is also from Lighthouse Point. It's a small world.

Don made honey baked ham and creamed potatoes for dinner. The wind was zero and the sea was flat, which was wonderful, but it was buggy after sundown.

In the evening, I wrote a lot, including a letter to Shelly, and then we went to bed around ten thirty. The days pass quickly.

Anchored at Bell Island, Exumas

July 14, 1987, Tuesday

We raised the anchor at eleven o'clock and set out from the Bell Island anchorage for Hawksbill. Everyone else had gone, except one boat. They were all headed south. We seem to always be traveling in the opposite direction from everyone else. We saw two porpoises on the way, the first ones we have seen in the Bahamas. It was a nice day for sailing, but quite hot. We got to Hawksbill at three forty-five, and since we hadn't eaten lunch, Don made linguini and white clam sauce shortly after our arrival.

We anchored next to a 43-foot ketch. We weren't very close to it, but Don asked the skipper where his anchor was because Don wanted to be sure the boats wouldn't hit if the wind swung them around. The skipper was sitting in his cockpit, and he got up and walked toward the bow and pointed at where his anchor was. He didn't have a stich of clothes on. We weren't aware of that until he went forward. We think he went forward for effect because he could have just pointed from the cockpit. His wife didn't have any clothes on either. There were two boats from England anchored nearby, and a boat from New York. All the people on those boats were nude also. I guess all of them were free to go nude if they wanted, but we had never seen it before. None of them seemed to be shy. In fact, quite the opposite, they paraded around like they were from a nudist camp; maybe they were.

Shortly afterwards, we set out to explore the island. Of course, we had our clothes on. We walked up the hill to a stone monument and added our stone. It was a steep climb, but the view at the top was well worth the effort. We swam for a short time at the beach in the very warm water. We met a few other boaters who were anchored in the area (not the nudists), and then went back to the boat.

There was a lot of thunder and lightning around us tonight. We stayed out on deck until eleven watching it. It was quite a beautiful display. Don took some video. Hopefully, it will turn out OK. He also took some video of the nudists. Hopefully, it won't turn out.

Anchored at Hawksbill, Exumas – Distance traveled: 25 miles

July 15, 1987, Wednesday

We spent the morning at Hawksbill. First, we dinghied to the South Beach, where I looked for conchs, but I saw a shark and got out of the water. Then we dinghied to the North Beach and swam. It was perfect for swimming and was secluded. We left Hawksbill at noon (high tide), traveled about six miles to Shroud Cay, and anchored there. We went up a stream in the dinghy and then climbed a hill to a site called Camp Driftwood. A boater built it in the '60s, using driftwood to construct various items. The view from Camp Driftwood is spectacular. The beauty of the island and the waters around it is superb.

On the way back, Don pulled me behind the dinghy, and I looked for conch. I found three big conchs. We didn't keep them because we were in a protected park, but I was happy about finding them. We also stopped by the well and dipped water for a fresh water bath. I tripped on the rocks and fell awkwardly, cutting my elbow, knee, and ankle. I was mad because I knew they would be slow to heal and could become infected. Unfortunately, most of our first aid supplies were used up caring for the shark attack victims. When we got back to *Robin Lee*, we had a quick dinner since it was eight in the evening.

Anchored at Shroud Cay, Exumas – Distance traveled: 6 miles

SHROUD CAY

July 16, 1987, Thursday

We left Shroud Cay about noon and motored to Norman's Cay. We had rocked and rolled all night, so neither of us slept well. After we got anchored, we found two conchs and took them ashore to clean. We checked in with the three Bahamian policemen stationed on Norman's Cay, and then found a shaded place and cleaned the conch. What a chore it was. A process that takes a conch fisherman five minutes for two conchs took us novices about an hour and a half.

We went into the airport hangar and looked at an abandoned airplane and equipment which had been used by the drug people when they occupied the cay. We hadn't gone to the hanger when we stopped there on our way down the Exumas. The airplane was stripped of most of its parts. Such a waste! We were the only ones around. It was spooky!

No one was anchored at Norman's Cay except us. We felt like the only fish in a big sea! It was weird! Don made a cracked conch dinner, buttered carrots, and stuffing with rice. It tasted especially good since we hadn't had any lunch.

Then, much to our dislike, the wind started to blow, and we began to rock and roll again.

Anchored at Norman's Cay, Exumas – Distance traveled: 8 miles

July 17, 1987, Friday

We motored along the inside route at high water to Highbourne Cay. It was tricky and because it was also very cloudy, it was hard to read the water depths. I was glad to get safely anchored at one o'clock.

INSIDE AN ABANDONED HOUSE ON NORMAN'S CAY

We bought freshly made bread plus eggs and dinghy gas from Harold's wife, Murial. Harold was in the States having a medical exam. I trimmed Don's beard and gave him a haircut.

We visited with a couple, Bob and Maggie, on the sailboat, *Spellbound*. Their boat is a new 46-foot Liberty, built in Taiwan. Bob is in his 50s, and Maggie is in her 20s. They are from Maryland and are newly-weds. They plan to sail around the world in their boat. We recommended that they have a crew to help since she has never done any sailing. I gave Maggie our address and asked her to keep us posted on their progress.[11]

---

[11] Robin and Maggie have corresponded ever since. Bob and Maggie did sail around the world and had many other adventures on Spellbound

We went back to our boat at six. After a quick swim to wash our hair and check our anchors, we spent the evening reading. The wind picked up and blew at about 15-20 knots from the north/north-east and it was stormy. How nice it was to be in a well-protected harbor.

Anchored at Highbourne Cay, Exumas – Distance traveled: 9 miles

July 18, 1987, Saturday

Don had a busy morning doing messy jobs. He cleaned the joker valve in the head, changed the oil, and then cleaned the bilge area again to get rid of the residue of oil from the problem we had at Bell Island. I helped by standing by with a roll of paper towels, my usual job as his helper. He always needs paper towels. Whenever he addresses me starting with the word "Sweetheart," I know it will be followed with "would you please get me a paper towel?"

One thing I haven't talked about in this journal is about the disposal of our bodily waste. What does one do with it when you live aboard? We have a six-gallon waste holding tank. When we flush, the waste and the salt water that was used for flushing can be directed into the holding tank. The tank can then be pumped out if you are where there are facilities for doing so, which are called "pump-out stations." But, in the Bahamas there are no pump-out stations. There is a valve in our head, called a Y-valve. When it is turned one way, the waste goes into the holding tank, and when it is turned the other way, the waste goes through the hull into the water. In the Bahamas, since you have no place to empty the holding tank, you set the valve to flush the waste into that crystal clear, beautiful water I have talked about.

As I have already explained, we use that same water to wash our dishes. I know that sounds gross, but there is normally a tidal current that quickly carries the waste away, and the water around your boat you scoop up for dish washing has no waste in it. You just don't flush if you are about to scoop. You also make sure there is nothing coming your way from a boat that is up current from you. We have never had a problem, and we quickly got used to the idea and never even give it a thought now. We always add a little Clorox to our dishwater and to the water we rinse with.

When Don finished his chores, we went ashore to dispose of the engine oil and trash.

Another thing I haven't mentioned in my journal is that the oil in diesel engines gets dirty quickly and therefore, it needs to be changed often. We change it after every 80 hours of engine use, approximately 500 miles under engine power, and change the filter every 160 hours. That is why I talk so much about changing the oil.

On shore, we met some more interesting boaters–Nick, Kirk, and Linda. Nick and Kirk are cousins. They live in Nassau. Linda is Nick's girlfriend; she is from Wales, but is living in Nassau. They look like they are in their mid-twenties. Kirk had a small part in the recent movie, *Revenge of Jaws*, which was filmed in Nassau. His boat was also used in the movie. They served us cold drinks, invited Don to go fishing with them, and invited us to have dinner with them. Don had a wild time fishing. I stayed on the boat and baked brownies for dessert. Linda told me about places to see on Eleuthera, our next destination. The meal was excellent–Turret and grunt fish and fresh conch salad (all made by Kirk). It was a different kind of day for us, but it was fun. Each of them was a character.

Anchored at Highbourne Cay, Exumas

Sunday, July 22, 1987

For the past four days, July 19 through July 22, we have patiently waited for the weather to change. The winds have been strong and from the direction of Eleuthera, which is where we want to go. The wind would be on our nose if we made the trip, so, because it's comfortable here, and since it is one of our favorite places in the Bahamas, we have stayed. We have spent our time reading, doing chores, swimming, taking short walks along the oceanside beach, and relaxing at the picnic shelter. The weather forecast for tomorrow is more favorable for the trip to Eleuthera, so we plan to go.

Today was another beautiful day. Late in the afternoon, we went ashore to buy some gas for the dinghy from Harold the dockmaster. Harold was talking to a man on the dock, and as Don approached them, Harold pointed to the ball cap Don was wearing, smiled, and said something to the man he was talking to. Don was wearing a hat that advertised Bacardi Rum; Don's cousin Norbert gave it to Don when we were in Sarasota. Don noticed that they were interested in his Bacardi hat and asked the man if he worked for Bacardi and both Harold and the man smiled broadly, and Harold said, "Meet George Bacardi." Don and George Bacardi shook hands, and Mr. Bacardi called down to his wife who was on board their boat tied up next to where he was standing and said something in Spanish. Up she came with a bottle of Bacardi Añejo Rum which Mr. Bacardi gave to Don, and thanked him for advertising for the company.

Jody and Bob, on *Escapades II* from Saint Paul, came in from Georgetown's Elizabeth Harbour on Monday. We visited with them, off and on, until today, when they left for Allen's Cay and Nassau. They have friends on board who are flying back to the States on Sunday. I asked their friends to call Randy when they get back, so Randy can tell people where we are. I also sent along a letter to Shelly for Jody to mail from Nassau.

Anchored at Highbourne Cay, Exumas

July 23, 1987, Thursday

We left the anchorage at Highbourne Cay at eight thirty. The "cut" to the ocean from Highbourne Cay was rough. The tide was going out the cut, and the wind was coming in. As I talked about in connection with crossing the Gulf Stream, that condition creates steep waves and rough going. Once we got through the cut and had gone a little further, conditions improved. We motored the entire 33 miles to Cape Eleuthera. At three o'clock we docked at a large marina at Cape Eleuthera Resort. The marina is part of a gorgeous resort complex. The entire resort is vacant, and has been for five years. Besides the marina, the resort includes condominiums, a restaurant, and tennis courts with stands for spectators, apparently built with the idea that professional matches would be played there. It is first class in all ways.

There were no other boaters at the marina. We met Norman, a slightly built black security guard and asked him if it would be all right for us to spend the night. He said it would. He told us that the resort belongs to some Arabs who got into a dispute with the Bahamian government five years ago over some issues and shut down operations at the resort. The Arabs expect to resolve the issues and reopen the resort in a few months. It is another example of "broken dreams." We hope it opens soon.

There were lots of coconuts lying around, and that led to a discussion with Norman about coconuts. He brought over a couple of them. One was brown, and the other was green. He explained that you would use the brown (ripe) one for baking, and that you would use the green one for other things. He chipped the husks off them with his cutlass (actually a machete), and broke open the green one and showed us that there is a clear liquid inside that he called coconut water. He said he uses that liquid to make a drink with gin and sweetened condensed milk, and that it is his favorite drink. The meat inside the green one is like jelly. He opened a brown one and showed us that there is no liquid inside, and the coconut meat is more solid and said that you could grate the white meat and use it for pies and cookies, etc.

Norman's security guard shift came to an end, and he invited us to go with him to his village, a few miles away, called Deep Creek, to have one of these drinks that he told us about. He assured us that our boat would be OK and that the security guard replacing him would look after it. We decided to go, and he gave us a ride into the town. What a trip! We rode in his old beat up pick-up truck. Some of his friends who needed to get a tire repaired in town rode in also. I sat up front with Norman, and Don sat in back with his friends and the tire.

It was totally dark when we got there. The town was very small. There was only one street running through it. It wasn't paved, just a dirt road. The town had no street lights and there was very little light coming from the houses and other buildings along the road. All the residents, approximately 100, were black, and many of them were outside their homes, sitting in front of their houses or walking along the road. We let his friends off at the tire repair place and then went to the local tavern. Don and Norman each got a coconut-water, gin, and sweetened condensed milk drink at the bar, which Don paid for. The bar was busy. Most of the men were drinking straight from a bottle. Norman introduced us to his friend, "Whiskey," and they talked us into playing dominoes at a table in a room next to the bar. Whiskey and Norman taught us the rules. Whiskey and I played against Norman and Don. Whiskey and I won the game. The mosquitos were the worst we had ever experienced. When you play dominoes, you sort of slam the dominoes on the table, and I remember the domino game as alternate slamming of the dominoes and swatting of the mosquitos. It was fun, and being at a bar with all black folks was a very different experience for Don and me.

Norman took us back to the boat at ten o'clock. The boat and all of its contents were still there. Most people would probably think that our decision to go into town with Norman to have a drink and play dominoes in an all-black tavern was a crazy thing to do, and maybe it was. However, we had been repeatedly told by other boaters that stealing and other crimes were not a problem on the out islands. Only in Nassau did you need to worry about crime. We were also very favorably impressed with the black people we had met in Georgetown, on Long Island, and everywhere else, outside of Nassau. We were also very favorably impressed with Norman and felt sure that he would not let any harm come to us. We never saw a white person at Cape Eleuthera. Don has added the coconut water, gin, and sweetened condensed milk drink to his repertoire, and he calls it "Norman's Deep Creek."

I finished my dinner, consisting of only popcorn, and continued to swat the mosquitoes. The wind had totally died down, and the mosquitoes were terrible! We burned a coil, but that didn't get rid of them. All night, I was fighting them off, and therefore, I didn't sleep much. I am very sensitive to bug bites; they swell and itch and make me feel awful.

Cape Eleuthera Marina, Cape Eleuthera, Eleuthera – Distance traveled: 33 miles

July 24, 1987, Friday

We had pancakes for breakfast.

Norman came over to say good-bye to us. He introduced us to the early daytime security guard, Daniel. He's Norman's cousin. Both are nice fellows. Regarding their work, we found that five or six months go by without them getting paid, but finally, some lady at Rock Sound sees to it that the company's office in Nassau sends them their wages. That's a shame because it's hard to live day-to-day when the paychecks come every six months.

We left Cape Eleuthera at eleven and motored 19 miles to Rock Sound, arriving at two thirty. The navigating was tricky.

I caught three fish along the way, but they were all barracudas, so I had to let them go. I'm disappointed with my yellow feather lure for trolling. All I have caught are barracudas.

After we got anchored, we relaxed a bit, but it was very hot. Don fixed us PB&J sandwiches for a late lunch, and at four, we went into town. So far, we have been favorably impressed with Eleuthera. Everyone has been friendly. This town has some charm: Goats run freely, roosters crow, lots of dogs bark, and occasionally a horn honks.

We bought a set of dominoes and a book about coral reefs and reef fish. We got back to the boat around seven thirty, and played 15 games of dominoes. I won 10 and Don won 5. I liked that. I also finished reading the play, *Our Town* by Thornton Wilder. I liked it. Don and I saw it on TV some time ago. We went to bed around ten thirty. I was tired, since I didn't sleep well last night, due to the mosquitos.

Anchored off Rock Sound, Eleuthera – Distance traveled: 19 miles

July 25, 1987, Saturday
We ate breakfast and then went sightseeing by hitchhiking.

First, we got a ride that went by a general store at a shopping center. We got out and went into the store. It is a very modern place and well stocked. There is nothing like it in the Exumas.

Next, we got a ride to the airport in a cement truck.

Then we got a ride to Tarpon Bay in a Jeep. We spent an hour or two sightseeing and taking pictures there.

After that, we got a ride to the Cotton Bay Club with a guy by the name of James. He was in a beat-up car and said he hadn't slept in two days. He asked us if we did drugs. Of course, the answer was no. I don't know if he wanted to buy or wanted to sell, but I am sure it was one or the other. We looked over the Cotton Bay Club; it was OK, but not worth $200/day which is their price.

We had dinner at the Islander Restaurant in Rock Sound and returned to the boat before dark. To end our busy day we played one game of dominoes and one game of gin rummy. Don is back to his winning ways, and is now 1500 points ahead in gin rummy.

Anchored off Rock Sound, Eleuthera

July 26, 1987, Sunday
We raised the anchor and sailed away. We didn't start the engine. It's not often we get to do that, because either the wind isn't right or there are too many boats in the anchorage to maneuver around. The winds were good all day, and we sailed all the way to Governor's Harbour. It was a very pleasant and quiet trip of 31 miles. We didn't start the engine until we were within a mile of where we wanted to drop our anchor. On arrival, we saw *Pride*. That was a good feeling. We have seen them now four times: at Long Island, Georgetown, Sampson Cay, and here.

They invited us aboard their boat for a visit. Then the four of us went ashore and walked around town. It's a quaint village, and since it was Sunday evening, we saw the locals dressed up for church. The ladies wear colorful clothing with hats, matching shoes and carry handbags.

The mosquitoes were bad again, so we went back to our boat and ate fresh bread, butter and jelly for dinner. We also had fresh pineapple; it was a great light summer meal.

We could hear the church music from the boat as we watched a gorgeous sunset. It was a beautiful evening.

Anchored at Governor's Harbour, Eleuthera – Distance traveled: 31 miles

July 27, 1987, Monday
There is a Club Med at Governor's Harbour. We had never heard of Club Med before this trip, and we decided to find out what it was all about. It's a French company, and as I understand it, the company has locations in lots of places around the world. You pay for a vacation of a week or two at one of these places and go there. They provide you with a nice room, various activities, and lots of food. All of these things are included in the weekly price. At Governor's Harbour, the rooms are at a beautiful hotel on the ocean called the Oceanside Club. The people vacationing here are from many countries. We were told that 40% are from France. The activities include sailing; fishing; beach games such as volley ball, horse-shoes, and shuffle board; and, of course, sunbathing. They have a marina near where we are anchored where the guests can use a sailboat or some kind of water toy to play on. We took our dinghy to their marina, and then rode their shuttle bus from the marina to the Oceanside Club to see it. It's a lovely hotel with a beautiful beach. We like the concept and may sign up for a week or two, someday. We went back to the marina, and they were serving lunch on the patio. The head waiter invited us to have lunch. Every meal is a buffet like a cruise ship would serve. You just help yourself to everything available. We ate plenty. Like at Great Stirrup Cay where we ate at the beach party, I wonder if the head waiter really should have invited us to eat. However, he knew we weren't guests, since he saw us arrive at the marina in a dinghy coming from our sailboat anchored in the harbor. The only boats anchored were *Pride* and us. Maybe they get generous when there aren't many boats anchored.

We had dinner with Ron and Peggy from *Pride*, at the home of their friends, Michael and Althera. It was an interesting evening. They served us Bahamian style fish, peas and rice, and potato salad, with pound cake for dessert. We were stuffed! They have a nice small home, much like a home in the States with amenities such as TV, stereo, etc. It wasn't elaborate, but was neat and clean. Tonight was the first time since March that we had eaten in a house. The last time was at the Moffitt's place on Tavernier Key, in Florida.
Anchored at Governor's Harbour, Eleuthera

July 28, 1987, Tuesday
We went back to Club Med to buy some gifts. I bought Shelly a tee shirt with various Club Med locations written on it, and I bought myself a large piece of cloth to wrap around me when wearing a bathing suit. It can be tied in various styles. I bought a swim suit for Don, which he badly needed. We spent $75, so at least Club Med got some money from us.

We also walked around Governor's Harbour some more and stopped at Althera's and Michael's because they wanted to give us some frozen fish. That night we closed up our boat early due to mosquitoes.
Anchored at Governor's Harbour, Eleuthera

July 29, 1987, Wednesday
Ron came by early and offered to let me use his Sunfish. They carry it with them on *Pride* to sail around in anchorages. I played with it most of the day, and only capsized twice. It was fun to sail.

We bid *Pride* farewell, because we are moving to Hatchet Bay tomorrow. We bought six pineapples from them; so once again, it was bread, butter and jelly for dinner with pineapple for dessert!

We had rain showers off and on today, which I endured out on the Sunfish.
Anchored at Governor's Harbour, Eleuthera

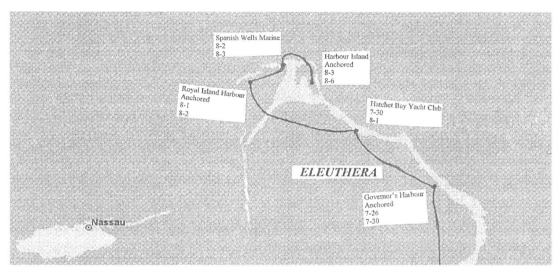

July 30, 1987, Thursday

We got underway at ten to go, by motor, from Governor's Harbour to Hatchet Bay. We went through a couple of rain storms on the way. We arrived at one thirty, and docked at the Hatchet Bay Yacht Club. However, after talking to the dockmaster, we moved from the dock to a mooring buoy to save money because the club only charges $2.00 per night for them. We stayed on board the rest of the day and just took it easy. Don made salmon with macaroni and cheese for dinner.

On mooring buoy in Hatchet Bay, Eleuthera – Distance traveled: 20 miles

July 31, 1987, Friday

Today was a bad day for me. I had planned to do laundry, but after walking a half-mile with our dirty clothes, we stopped at the post office to buy stamps, and in a conversation with another customer, I learned that the laundry had no water pressure because of a plumbing problem. We carried the clothes back to the boat and then set out for the grocery. We needed to cash a traveler's check because we were low on cash. I knew we would have to buy something in order to get the store to cash it, and I had my heart set on ice cream, but the grocery was out of it. We bought a couple of things we could use, but then we had to lug those around all day. I called Shelly from a pay phone and was able to talk to her. That was good; however, it will cost us $17.50 when we get back to Ohio because we charge all of our calls from the Bahamas to Mom, and will settle up with her when we get back to the U.S.

We hitchhiked to Gregory Town. A man with three young kids picked us up in a van. In Gregory Town, we went to a bakery and bought a loaf of bread. After that, we stopped at a restaurant and drank a Coke. We met a girl there who was going to Alice Town, which is where Hatchet Bay is, and she offered to take us with her in her jeep; we accepted. During the ride, we learned that she was from Canada, that she had just flown in from Ottawa, and that she hadn't been to bed for over 30 hours. We also soon realized she was very drunk and that she was a terrible driver. It was a scary ride, but we survived.

We walked around Alice Town, and I finally got an ice cream cone. The water pressure at the laundry was still too low to wash clothes. We went back to the boat, and I got water from the yacht club and did the laundry by hand. It clouded up and started to rain right after I hung up the laundry to dry in the rigging.

We knew the bugs would be bad, and we wouldn't be able to sit out, even if it stopped raining, so Don made us a drink, and we stayed below for the evening. I did some cross-stitch, and after dinner, we played one game of Dominoes. I won! That and my telephone conversation with Shelly were the only good things that happened today.

On a mooring buoy in Hatchet Bay, Eleuthera

August 1, 1987, Saturday

We went out the narrow opening from Hatchet Bay at eleven fifteen to go to Royal Island, having calculated when to leave in order to complete the 23 miles to "Current Cut" so that we would be there at high tide slack-water time. We had to pass through the cut to get to Royal Island. The guide book says that the current is sometimes as fast as ten knots through the cut, and we didn't want to have to deal with a current anywhere near that speed. If it was against us, we wouldn't be able to overcome it, and if it was with us, it would be like riding rapids and we might be swept onto a shoal, so we wanted to arrive at slack-water time when there was no current because the tide was changing directions. Fortunately, we timed it right and there was no current when we got there. It was stormy when we left Hatchet Bay, and although the wind had died down by the time we reached the cut, the lighting was still terrible, and the sky was so dark we could hardly see the coral heads. We made it through the cut without a problem and went another mile and anchored at Royal Island. The boat anchored next to us was a sport fisherman, named *Sheila III*. We were told that the boat belongs to Arthur Hailey, the famous writer of *Airport* and *Hotel* and that he was on board. We didn't have a chance to meet him. We did meet another couple who had us on board their trawler for a visit and some popcorn. The visit was somewhat stressful because the wife seemed unbalanced and told us that she had been in and out of hospitals for alcohol and drug dependency.

Anchored at Royal Island Harbour, Eleuthera – Distance traveled: 32 miles

August 2, 1987, Sunday

We went sightseeing onshore at Royal Island and visited the remains of a once elaborate mansion. The house had tile flooring on all the floors, and concrete walkways. It was apparent that the place was once a beautiful home.

We saw Bob, Bobbi and their children, off *Soleadair I,* on the island. We first met them at Lucaya when they were docked next to *Orchid Boat* at the marina. They have been cruising in the Abacos since then. We told them about places to go in the Exumas and they told us about places in the Abacos.

We both left Royal Island at two fifteen headed for Spanish Wells. We stopped at the Spanish Wells Yacht Haven and bought fuel and then attempted to anchor. We didn't like the anchorage because the wind and current were opposing, and so we moved to the Spanish Wells Marina. It was about five thirty by the time we tied up at the marina. *Soleadair I* stayed in the anchorage.

We showered and relaxed for a while. Then we went sightseeing. We ate a great cheeseburger at Roody's, and then walked around. The village of Spanish Wells is neatly kept. All the houses are nicely painted and it was very clean and orderly. The population is almost entirely white. We met a couple of young girls and briefly talked with them. They told us that most kids quit school after the ninth grade. Most boys start fishing commercially by the time they are 20 years old and they make excellent money fishing for lobster.

SPANISH WELLS

We talked with a man, Franklin, who was out in front of a small house that he is in the process of remodeling. He invited us in for a drink and to see the place. He is a retired American from Baltimore who came here on vacation and liked the Spanish Wells community so much he decided he wanted to live here, so he bought this house. We don't envy him. The house is in terrible condition. He has a lot of work ahead of him just to make the house habitable. When he started working on it, he found that it has termites. He hasn't even gotten a deed yet.

Furthermore, he will need permits for various things he will be doing, and he will need to import some materials from the U.S. Our dealings with government officials in the Bahamas have led us to the opinion that their government is very bureaucratic and unfriendly. Government officials seem to have a "Nassau attitude." I fear that dealing with them on this kind of project would be very frustrating.

In short, we think he has made a big mistake.

Our night at the dock was comfortable.

At Spanish Wells Marina, Spanish Wells, near Eleuthera - Distance traveled: 8 miles

August 3, 1987, Monday

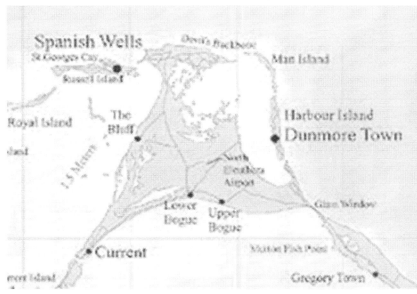

Gosh, the days pass so quickly I am barely able to keep up writing in this journal.

Our next destination, Harbour Island, is twelve miles east of Spanish Wells. The way there involves lots of turns to avoid shoals. It's tricky and not well marked. There are a couple of places that are especially treacherous and tricky. One is called The Devil's Backbone, and the other, Mayflower Reef. The guide book we use recommends hiring a pilot to guide you there. They ride with you in your boat and tell you when and how to turn.

We walked around Spanish Wells looking for a pilot to hire. We eventually hired a man by the name of Dave Roberts. He charged us $50. He came aboard our boat and we left at two in the afternoon for Harbour Island and arrived at our destination at four forty-five. We towed his dinghy to Harbour Island for his use in getting back to Spanish Wells. Since it took two hours and forty-five minutes to get there and he still needed to get back, we think Dave's charge was very reasonable. More importantly, we got across the Devil's Backbone, safely.

We stayed on board and had ham and macaroni and cheese for dinner. We played one game of gin rummy and read.

Anchored off Harbour Island, near Eleuthera - Distance traveled: 12 miles

August 4, 1987, Tuesday

We went ashore to the town located on Harbour Island, Dunmore Town, and called Sister Carol to wish her a Happy Birthday. We visited all the hotels on the island: the Pink Sands, the Coral Sands (where we lay on the beach and swam in the afternoon), the Rock House, and the Ramora Bay Club (where we docked the dinghy).

This island is very popular during the winter with the wealthier Bahamians. The homes are luxurious. The population is a mixture of blacks and whites. The town is charming and beautiful. It also has modern conveniences available: electricity, good water, phones, grocery stores, restaurants, night clubs, etc. It also has many short-term visitors. We ate lunch at Angela's Starfish restaurant and got back to the boat before the bugs got bad. It was a very relaxing day!

Anchored off Harbour Island, near Eleuthera

August 5, 1987, Wednesday

We felt tired today, so we stayed on the boat and listened to radio talk shows out of Miami, about controversial topics:

1) Should Oliver North be pardoned by Reagan?

2) Should the Vatican or should the city of Miami pay the expenses for the Pope's scheduled visit to Miami?

The host was rude, so we shut him off and scrubbed the bottom of the boat instead.

At two o'clock, we went to Valentine's Yacht Club and relaxed by the pool. Don read; I did cross-stitch, and we both swam.

Around seven we walked to Angelo's for dinner. I ordered grouper, and Don ordered cracked conch. Both were excellent. The electricity went off at the restaurant, but fortunately, all the guests had been served their meals. The bugs weren't too bad.

Later, we walked to "Willis's and George's" to hear locals play calypso music, but we were down to $3 and cover charge was $3 each, so we only heard a couple of songs. We got home at midnight.

Harbour Island would be our pick, if we were looking for a place in the Bahamas to come to for a few days of vacationing, and someday, we might come back.

Our next destination is Little Harbour on Abaco Island, one of the major islands of the Bahamas. Abaco Island and the cays surrounding it are known collectively as the Abacos. Getting there will involve going back through the Devil's Backbone, as though we were going back to Spanish Wells, but turning north before we get there and making a 74 mile crossing to Abaco. We made notes when we came across from Spanish Wells and especially when we went through the Devil's Backbone and Mayflower Reef on our way to Harbour Island, and we think we can now go back without a guide.

Anchored off Harbour Island, Eleuthera

August 6, 1987, Thursday

We left Harbour Island at approximately ten o'clock to make our way back across the Devil's Backbone toward Spanish Wells. We wanted the sun overhead so we would have good light for seeing the shoals and coral heads. I sat on the bow watching for coral heads most of the way. Around noon, after we had gotten past the Devil's Backbone, the trickiest part of the trip, we saw a boat anchored near the northwest end of Eleuthera, near Ridley Head. We called them on the marine radio and found that they planned to make the crossing

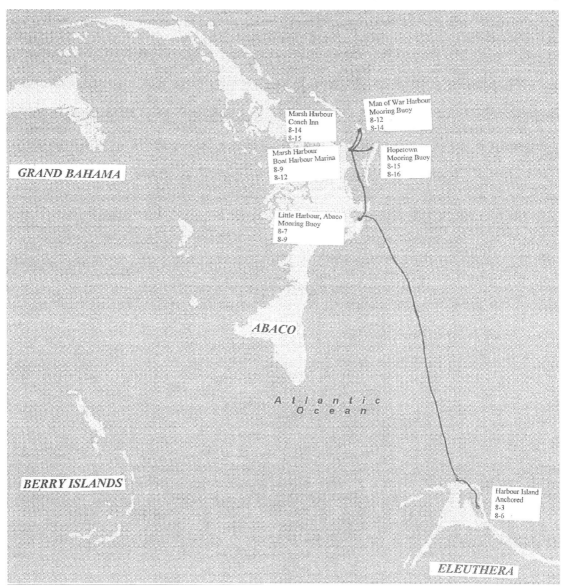

to Abaco and were waiting until later to start so they would arrive after the sun was up. The name of the boat was *Eagle*. We had originally planned to go to Spanish Wells, wait, and leave from there for the crossing, but since the sea was relatively calm, anchoring and leaving from here seemed like a better way to do it. We anchored near *Eagle*. We (both boats) decided to leave at six in the evening. Don rested most of the afternoon. I dinghied to Ridley Head beach and swam. We ate dinner at five.

We left at five forty-five. This all-night sail was the nicest we have had. It wasn't rough, there was enough wind to move us at four to five knots, it was quiet and peaceful without the motor, and it was a moonlit night. We had two-hour watches where we alternated between being at the helm and resting. My watches were 7-9, 11-1, and 3-5. Conditions were so pleasant, we both stayed awake all night. We listened to tapes—mostly Jimmy Buffet tapes. We could see a lot of phosphorescence in the water emanating from some kind of critters in the ocean water. When we flushed the head, the water drawn in from the ocean contained these critters. Seeing the toilet water glowing chartreuse was a weird experience.

At sea on our way to Little Harbour, Abacos – Total distance traveled from Harbour Island to Little Harbour: 74 miles

August 7, 1987, Friday

We arrived at Little Harbour on the southeast shore of Abaco at seven forty-five in the morning. The entrance into Little Harbour is shallow, and we had to wait for the tide to come up a little before we could get into the harbor. We were welcomed by sea turtles; they were about two feet in diameter. We picked up a mooring buoy, and after a breakfast of oatmeal, we spent the morning relaxing.

Eagle, with Kelly and Lori, and their daughter, Christa (6 years old), and their twins Charlie and Cari (9 months old) also made it safely into Little Harbour. Cari smashed her fingers about the time they arrived and Lori asked me to take a look at them. They were swollen, bruised, and cut, but not too badly. Poor kid! Boat life isn't easy, especially for babies.

The harbor is very well protected, but with that comes the bugs. It was sunny today and in the high 80s, with just enough breeze to keep you cool.

On a mooring buoy, Little Harbour, Abacos

August 8, 1987, Saturday

I didn't wake up until ten thirty—probably because I was up all night on Thursday. We had cold cereal and tea for breakfast. Around noon, I ran the sweeper and cleaned the boat, and afterwards, we set out to see the area. We snorkeled a reef close by us and walked to the ocean shore to see the lighthouse. The snorkeling was disappointing. I hope that won't be the case everyplace in the Abacos. The water here in the harbor isn't as clear as in the Exumas, but we think it's because there is very little current in the harbor.

A world-renowned sculptor, Randolph Johnston, lives and works here. He works with bronze and wood. His wife is also an artist and works with bronze and ceramics. We visited the cave on the harbor's edge that the Johnstons lived in while they built their house. It was huge and we saw bats, stalagmites and stalactites. It looks just the way it is described in the *Yachtsmen's Guide* and in *Wolinsky's Guide*, the guide books we are using. Without those books, we would have missed seeing many of the places we have enjoyed in the Bahamas. Everything to see and do is covered, as well as routes to every place and where to anchor.

On a mooring buoy, Little Harbour, Abacos

August 9, 1987, Sunday

The moon was full and bright last night, and it was quite still. It was a beautiful evening and nice in all respects, except for the **bugs!** A breeze at night is much better.

Seven years ago today Don and I were married! How the time flies! It was about then that we started to plan for this trip!

We had to leave early to catch the high tide to get out of Little Harbour. We were both looking forward to seeing Marsh Harbour; getting our mail, which is waiting for us at the Conch Inn; and being at a marina with a good shower. It's been a long time; the last good shower was at Summerfield Boat Yard in Fort Lauderdale, in April.

The wind was out of the north, and we bucked it during the entire 3 1/2 hours we were on our way to Marsh Harbour. It felt great to arrive at a destination we had been looking forward to for a long time. We swam, showered, looked around, and then went to the Conch Inn to get our mail and have an anniversary lunch. We returned to the boat at six and relaxed for the rest of the evening.

Boat Harbour Marina, Marsh Harbour, Abacos – Distance traveled: 16 miles

August 10, 1987, Monday

We got up early and started our new life as temporary residents of Marsh Harbour. We

MARSH HARBOUR

plan to be here, or nearby here, for the next month or so. Our first task was to find a bank and get some cash, since we were out of it. Next, we went to the post office and mailed cards and letters. Then we walked around to explore the town. We stopped for lunch at a KFC restaurant and after eating, we continued with our errands. We went to the Conch Inn and picked up our mail, did some grocery shopping, and eventually returned to the marina to take showers and begin looking at the mail.

We didn't get back to our boat until six. It was too late to fix dinner, so we ate bread and butter and Jell-O. Just as we were finishing up, the people on a boat near us offered us their leftover, freshly cooked lobster scampi. It was great! We ate it up and enjoyed every bite! The couple, Larry and Elaine, are on a 49-foot trawler, *MissBehavin'*, which is tied up near us at the marina. They invited us on board their boat to look around and visit. They are an interesting couple. They met through an ad. Elaine is a licensed boat captain and scuba diver. She is single, without any children, and is about 30 years old. She likes cruising and so she placed an ad in a boating magazine that she was available for hire as a captain. Larry worked for the CIA for 14 years and then quit and began working as a self-employed private investigator. After five years, he retired! He decided to go cruising and bought *MissBehavin'*. He responded to Elaine's ad and hired her as his captain. They have been cruising together since May. They will be leaving Marsh Harbour tomorrow, but will return in a couple of weeks.

SHELLY ON BOARD WITH US AT MARSH HARBOUR

It was really windy this evening. We took the dinghy to do the laundry. It was nice and cool due to the breeze. The laundry was expensive; it's almost better to do the laundry on the boat!

Shelly and her friend, David, will be arriving tomorrow. We spent the rest of the evening preparing for their visit by cleaning and organizing the boat, and planning what we will do while they are here. We want to take them to see some of the nearby interesting places, such as Hopetown and Man-a-War, and are looking forward to the visit.

Boat Harbour Marina, Marsh Harbour, Abacos

August 11, 1987, Tuesday

We bought a few more groceries and organized things a bit more on the boat. At one thirty, we hitched a ride to the airport to meet Shelly and David, and then took a taxi back to the boat. Shelly and David swam in the late afternoon, but, mostly, we just visited. I was so happy to see Shelly. She looked a lot healthier than she had on her spring break. At the time of her visit, when we were in the Palm Beach area, she was suffering from Epstein-Barr virus, although we didn't realize it at the time. In May, a month or so after visiting us, she was quite ill!

We ate cracked conch for dinner.

Boat Harbour Marina, Marsh Harbour, Abacos

**ABACO DINGHY
SAILBOAT ON THE RIGHT
MADE ON MAN-O-WAR CAY**

August 12, 1987, Wednesday

We left the marina around one o'clock and motored to Man-O-War Cay. We all went sightseeing in the village and then went to the beach on the ocean side to snorkel. In the evening, we played cards.

On mooring buoy at Man-O-War Cay, Abacos – Distance traveled: 6 miles

August 13, 1987, Thursday

David, Shelly and I dinghied part way and walked the rest of the way to the beach on the ocean side and snorkeled again. Later, David and Shelly went for a dinghy ride by themselves. In the evening, we all played euchre and dominoes.

On mooring at Man-O-War Cay, Abacos

August 14, 1987, Friday

We left Man-O-War Cay at ten and went to Fowl Cay where we anchored. We spent four hours there. We snorkeled and ate lunch. Then we went back to Marsh Harbour and docked at the Conch Inn, arriving shortly before five. We swam and watched our videotapes of spring break. We also watched video of the day of the shark attack. Around nine we dinghied to a night club called "The Bilge" to listen to a reggae band. It was a pretty night, and so far it's been a fun week, except the snorkeling has been disappointing.

Docked at Conch Inn, Marsh Harbour, Abacos – Distance traveled: 13 miles

August 15, 1987, Saturday

We ate breakfast and left for Hopetown. Along the way, we saw several starfish on the bottom. We walked around the village and browsed in the shops, had ice cream, and a late lunch. We had popcorn later for our dinner. We moored on a buoy. Our evening's activity was playing euchre.

On mooring buoy at Hopetown, Elbow Cay, Abacos – Distance traveled: 10 miles

August 16, 1987, Sunday

We went to Hopetown's colorful lighthouse in the morning and climbed its 97 steps to the top to enjoy the view. It was terrific. Then we went to Harbour Lodge

HOPETOWN

and swam in the pool and in the ocean as well. It was too rough to go out far. Around three we left Hopetown and motor-sailed back to Marsh Harbour and docked at the Marsh Harbour Marina. In the evening, we went to the Bilge for steaks. The Bilge has a special steak dinner every Sunday night. Everyone enjoyed a good old American dinner.

Marsh Harbour Marina, Marsh Harbour, Abacos – Distance traveled: 10 miles

August 17, 1987, Monday

We walked to a tourist shop to get information about getting to the airport, ate a sandwich and ice cream at a small restaurant, bought conch and had it cleaned so the kids could watch that process, and then dropped them off at the pool at the Conch Inn. While they swam and sunbathed, Don and I shopped for groceries. We had Sloppy Joes for dinner on the kids' last night here, and played cards and dominoes until late.

Marsh Harbour Marina, Marsh Harbour, Abacos

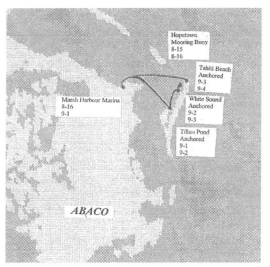

August 18, 1987, Tuesday

After breakfast, Shelly and David sunbathed a little and then came back to the boat to pack. We bought some lobster from Peter Russell, a lobster fisherman, to fix as a special lunch treat. It was excellent. Everybody loved it. At one thirty, our taxi came and took all of us to the airport. After straightening out some confusion regarding the ticket for the return flight, they left on a Caribbean Express flight to Miami. Don and I both enjoyed having them here. Good-byes are always hard.

Marsh Harbour Marina, Marsh Harbour, Abacos

August 19, 1987, Wednesday

These past few days were fun-filled and busy. It was great to have company. We decided to relax and unwind today. Don read the entire day, and I wrote postcards and letters to catch up on my correspondence. We didn't leave the boat, except to shower.

Marsh Harbour Marina, Marsh Harbour, Abacos

August 20, 1987, Thursday

We have decided to stay at Marsh Harbour Marina for the next month and pay the monthly rate, which is only $150, plus $2 per day for electric and water, (which makes it $7.00 per day for us). We like the marina and Marsh Harbour. We also think it would be good to take a break from cruising and just take it easy for a time. Furthermore, we are getting into the serious hurricane season, and if we have to deal with one, we would prefer to be in a town like Marsh Harbour with people who have dealt with them in the past, rather than in some remote area by ourselves. Right now, there are two storms brewing in the Atlantic, which are potential threats to us, Arlene and Brett.

We moved to a different slip and are now pointed east, into the prevailing wind, which will be more comfortable. Getting settled into the slip for our month long stay took much of the day. Late in the day, we went into town, mailed letters, and bought fresh bread and a few grocery items. When we went back to the boat, our new neighbors—Bill and Sally—offered us a salad and filet mignon on the grill. They had brought extras with them from the States three days ago. It tasted super! Don contributed peas and rice and chocolate-chip cookies he had made earlier. We spent the evening visiting on their boat.

The weather was pretty nice today. It was hot and humid, but with the fans going inside our boat, it was comfortable.

Marsh Harbour Marina, Marsh Harbour, Abacos until September 1, 1987

August 21, 1987, Friday

Don left after our breakfast of fresh baked raisin cinnamon toast to go fishing with Smitty and Bill. Smitty and Bill are from Fort Pierce, Florida and work together at a factory that makes commercial fishing boats. They both have been commercial fishermen in the past. They came here on vacation in a boat that belongs to one of them, and are docked near us. I did the laundry while Don was fishing. The electric went off several times while I was doing the laundry, so it was an all day job involving several trips up and down the docks. I had just finished the laundry when Don, Smitty, and Bill returned. I visited with Elaine, while Don fried the fish they caught.

Smitty and Bill ate with us. Don caught three fish, including the biggest of all. He caught a Nassau grouper, a strawberry grouper and a red snapper. The fish were excellent, and we had enough for another meal. Smitty and Bill stayed and visited until ten thirty. They are nice guys, and Don said it was interesting to fish with them because they really knew what they were doing.

We went to bed at eleven thirty, but a stray cat kept us awake for a while trying to crawl through our screens. He must have smelled the fish. The ants are bad on the docks, so I've had to spray our dock lines to keep them off the boat. That reminds me of a couple of other boating problems I have meant to talk about in this journal, but haven't gotten around to—rats and roaches! Sometimes a rat gets into a boat and becomes a big problem. The waterfront is a common place for rats. We saw several in Nassau and one outside of the Peace and Plenty Hotel, in Georgetown. Robin Linker, the sailor we socialized with in Clearwater, told us that he once had a rat on his boat, and described the ordeal he went through to get rid of it. We haven't had a problem, and Nassau and Georgetown are the only places we have seen them. We haven't had a problem with roaches either, but that is a common problem. We are always careful when we bring stuff, especially groceries, on board, and we never bring anything aboard in a cardboard box or a paper bag because we have been told that they may contain roaches or their eggs.

August 22, 1987, Saturday

I cut Don's hair in the morning, and we swam in the afternoon. We met Jean and Bill, live-aboards on the boat, *Calypso*. We spent an hour talking with them about their trip, so far, which has been similar to ours. We exchanged information about Florida's West Coast. They are going to come to our boat tomorrow evening to look at charts.

I went to the Conch Inn to get bread and butter and check on mail while Don fixed marinated fish for dinner from the surplus fish caught yesterday, another excellent meal!

In the evening, we went to the Bilge for the entertainment and bought Smitty and Bill a few drinks. We stayed out until one in the morning.

The day was hot and sunny with a few clouds.

August 23, 1987, Sunday

We got up early because Bill and Smitty invited us to go spear fishing with them. We were happy for the opportunity, and we had fun. Don got his first fish with a spear. It was a small triggerfish, but I was proud and so was he! We anchored their big boat, *Y-Me,* at Fowl Cay, spear fished for a while, and then moved it to Scotland Cay and spear fished some more. They snorkeled and fished while I sat in the "dink" (dinghy). Don saw a shark, less than 15 feet away from him, but it didn't act aggressive. Don said he just kept one hand on the dinghy and kept his eyes on Smitty, Bill and the shark. He figured that if Smitty and Bill weren't alarmed it must be OK.

We got back to the marina at four and got ready for the great Sunday night Bilge steak dinner and our company, Jean and Bill, from *Calypso*. After dinner, we entertained Jean and Bill and another couple, Peter and Pam, from a wooden motor yacht, *PamWon*. Don thought Pam was cute. I liked Jean and Bill better. That's about the first time we have felt differently about people we have met. The reason they named their boat *PamWon* is that Peter wanted a sailboat and Pam wanted a power boat, and she got her way. Pam looks to be in her late twenties and Peter looks like he is about 60. They left at ten thirty, and we went to bed immediately; we were tired because of our big day!

MissBehavin', Larry and Elaine's boat, is back and is docked close to us here at Marsh.

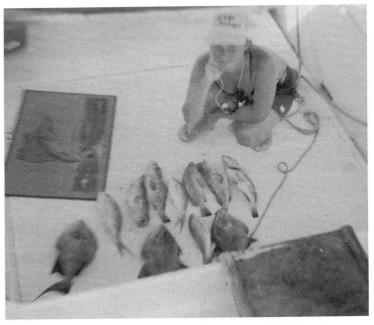

FISH CAUGHT ON *Y-ME* WITH SMITTY AND BILL

August 24, 1987, Monday

We were again invited to go out fishing with Bill and Smitty. Today we were line fishing, and we caught several beautiful iridescent dolphin fish (also called mahi-mahi or dorado). They weighed about 15 to 20 pounds each. We also caught strawberry groupers and yellowtails. There was so much activity on the deck when the dolphin fish were hitting, that it was difficult to stay out of each other's way. It was exciting! I cleaned fish when we got back to Marsh Harbour and the four of us ate together, plus we invited Elaine to join us for our mahi-mahi dinner. It was superb!

After dinner, we went to *MissBehavin'* and watched a movie with Elaine. Larry is in the States for a few days. We saw Elliot Gould in, *I Love My Wife,* which we enjoyed and got home at one o'clock–a late night for such a busy day!

August 25, 1987, Tuesday

I got up later than I should have, but...SO WHAT! I called my best friend Pam. We talked too long, but she insisted. The connection was lousy. It was great just to hear her familiar voice! Don and I went out for lunch to Wally's, a very popular and beautiful old home that overlooks the harbor. We sat on the covered patio and enjoyed the elegance. It was a bit expensive ($5.15 for Don's conch burger and fries, and $6 for my Wally's special dessert–strawberry ice cream with apricot brandy, nuts and whipped cream).

We walked around town and stopped at the Conch Inn and picked up our mail. The letters from Pam and Shelly, which they had sent a month ago, were there, but, of course, I already knew everything they wrote about. We had a little rain early, but other than that, it was another beautiful day.

During the day, we were on a bus with a deranged old man who was raving to everyone about a storm. Among other things, he emotionally said, "he went outside and was just blown away." We were told by a local person on the bus that when the man was young, his brother had been killed during the terrible category five hurricane that struck the area in 1932. The boy walked out of his house when the eye was passing over, thinking that the storm had ended. Conditions were calm in Marsh Harbour during the 15 minutes the eye was passing over, but when it had passed the winds suddenly began blowing again at about 140 miles per hour.

August 26, 1987, Wednesday

It was a hot and humid day. Thank God for the persistent breeze out of the east.

Elaine, of *MissBehavin'*, and I took her dinghy, named *Fast Trip* to Wally's and looked at the boutique. I enjoy Elaine. She is thoughtful, friendly, and fun to be around.

We had Elaine over for dinner. She brought a Caesar salad, and Don served kraut and Polish kielbasa on mashed potatoes. After we got the dishes cleaned up, she invited us to her boat to watch another movie on video tape and eat popcorn.

Tonight's movie was Walt Disney's *The Flight of the Navigator*. It was popular last year, but Don and I had never heard of it...one of the minor disadvantages of living outside of the real world.

August 27, 1987, Thursday

I got up planning to do laundry, but the water was off the entire day. So much for my work plan. Bill came over at lunch time and invited us to go out and snorkel, so we did. Don speared another fish, but it wasn't edible, so he threw it back. We got home about three thirty, just in time for Don to start cooking. Smitty came back later and gave us two groupers. I cleaned them, but we now had more than we could eat, so we froze them for another day.

This was our last chance to have Smitty and Bill for dinner since they are going home tomorrow, so Don fried up the rest of the yellowtail and snapper, all of which were great! Later, the four of us went to *MissBehavin'* to visit. It was another wonderful day in paradise.

August 28, 1987, Friday

Today's plan was the same as yesterday's, do the laundry. However, today the water was on, and I worked the entire day. Smitty and Bill left early on their boat to return to Fort Pierce and their jobs. Sandy and Mike on *Bofus* left about noon. Larry and Elaine left on *MissBehavin'* at two o'clock. They are going from here to the Berry Islands, and then on to Florida. Our dock was cleared out except for us. It was a very good day to get all of our work done. I did laundry, scrubbed the cockpit, helped Don change the oil, the oil filter, and the fuel filter. Then I cleaned inside, including the bilge. It was a busy workday, and Don and I were both tired.

We had dinner—a vegetarian omelet—and went to bed early. I finished the book I've been reading—the play, *Inherit the Wind*.

August 29, 1987, Saturday

Don fixed us muffins and tea for breakfast, and then went to town for a couple of hours to run errands. I stayed on board and cross-stitched and made tuna salad for lunch. I didn't leave the boat the entire day. I finished one cross-stitching project for *TTOGA* and started another project for *MOBY*. Don cleaned the stove and then made enchiladas for dinner. We listened to cassettes after dinner, and went to bed early; we never even heard the band playing at the Bilge.

August 30, 1987, Sunday

It was a pretty lazy day, especially in the morning. We left our place in the afternoon for the Boat Harbour swimming pool and had a refreshing swim. We saw Lewis, our friend and cab driver, and had a nice visit with him. Then we went back to the Bilge for our regular Sunday steak dinner.

We enjoyed our meal, but were disappointed that we didn't see any boaters we knew. We hurried back to the boat at dusk because the bugs were very bad.

August 31, 1987, Monday

We did a few routine chores like filling the water jugs and preparing the boat to leave the dock and go out and cruise for a few days. We want to see what's south of Marsh Harbour and north of Little Harbour and now seems to be a good time to do it because the weather is good, and next week we will be hauled out of the water to have the boat's bottom painted.

We also went into town to get a few groceries. We met new friends, Dave and Donna from Kansas, who are aboard *Domus*. We hope to see them again.

September 1, 1987, Tuesday

We left the dock early and headed for Sandy Cay Sea Park to snorkel. It was a 22-mile trip, and we motored all the way, but it was well worth it! We had fun looking at the coral. Unfortunately, some of it had been "cloroxed" in the past and was dead. There was a lot of variety, and we saw a very large parrotfish.

We met folks on *Amiable,* from Jacksonville, Dave and Mary Lane. They were, in fact, amiable and invited us over for a drink. We anchored at Tiloo Pond in a very private spot. The temperature was comfortable; we had a breeze, and we had no bugs. How nice!

Anchored at Tiloo Pond, Tiloo Cay, Abacos – Distance traveled: 28 miles

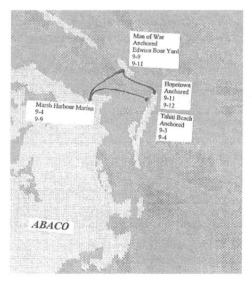

September 2, 1987, Wednesday

We did some exploring on the beach of Tiloo Cay on the ocean side this morning and found a metal buoy for a fishing net of the type used by Spanish fishermen. It apparently got disconnected from its net and washed across the ocean and came to rest here. We kept it as a souvenir. At high tide, we left Tiloo Pond for White Sound, about 12 miles away. After we got anchored at White Sound in front of the Abaco Inn, we went ashore and walked to the oceanside beach. Don cleaned the buoy we had found, and I cleaned the grey snapper I caught on the boat this morning, using pieces of bread for bait. It was small, but it tasted good!

Anchored at the Abaco Inn, White Sound, Elbow Cay, Abacos – Distance traveled: 12 miles

September 3, 1987, Thursday

It rained off and on during the night and blew hard. As a result, we were up three times, closing and re-opening the hatches. What a night! At least, the anchors held!

We left too early because it was low tide and ended up going aground and having to wait for the tide to come up (about an hour). Finally, two hours after we left White Sound and about two miles from it, we dropped the anchors at Tahiti Beach and "backed down on them." We had to reposition them three times before we got them to hold. Tahiti Beach is a beautiful spot with clear water of several shades of blue. Donna and Dave on *Domus*, their 41 foot Morgan sailboat, were anchored on our starboard side. We met them in Marsh Harbour on Monday, the day before we left for our little cruise of this area. *Lady* from Pompano was on our port side. We visited a bit with each of them. We also took our dinghy ashore to clean it up. It was terribly dirty.

In the evening, we played a game of gin rummy. I won by 175 points. Don is still ahead by 1500 points, but beating him was fun, just the same.

Anchored at Tahiti Beach, Elbow Cay, Abacos – Distance traveled: 2 miles

September 4, 1987, Friday

It was a beautiful moonlit night with a few clouds and many brilliant stars.

We had fun snorkeling, swimming, and spear fishing with Dave and Donna for about three hours. Don speared a couple of small fish, nothing worth keeping to eat though. In the afternoon, Donna came over to visit. We shared some recipes and books with her, including the play, *Inherit the Wind*. We are going to trade some canned goods. We enjoy her sense of humor and witty comments.

Around four, we left at high tide and sailed, with only the jib, back to Marsh Harbour. It was a 2½ hour trip, very pleasant, with no stress. After docking and getting hooked up to electric and water, I hosed the boat down. We cleaned up and then went to the Bilge for grouper fingers. It was a good meal, especially for the price of $8, which included the tip.

We went to the Conch Inn, by dinghy, to get our mail.

There was a breeze, but still, the mosquitoes were out.

Marsh Harbour Marina, Marsh Harbour, Abacos – Distance traveled: 10 miles

September 5, 1987, Saturday

I went to town after Don made muffins and coffee for breakfast. I ran into Lewis Pender–taxi #19–our only long-term friend in the area. We've known him for almost a month. We met him the first day we were here when we made arrangements at Boat Harbour for Shelly and David's cab ride from the airport. I made arrangements for him to take us out to Dundas Town and Murphy Town, the second and third largest towns in the area, (Marsh Harbour is the largest) and to Mother Merl's for dinner. I spent the day in town shopping and meeting boaters. Don stayed on the boat paying bills and writing letters. He was glad I wasn't here to interrupt him every ten minutes.

At six thirty, Lewis picked us up, and we went to Dundas Town and Murphy Town to see the territory and enjoy a meal at Mother Merl's family-style restaurant. We enjoyed the serving size of the broiled grouper, but the chicken Don had was the worst he ever tasted. It cost us $25 for dinner, but we had a nice evening out. Lewis is so nice; he didn't even charge us for the taxi ride!

Marsh Harbour Marina, Marsh Harbour, Abacos

September 6, 1987, Sunday

We got up early and had our traditional breakfast for Sunday–my favorite–pancakes. I also had Café Vienna. We got ready for church. Lewis and his wife picked us up and took us to their church in his taxi. It is a Pentecostal church. It was another new experience for us. The service was not at all like at our church back in Dublin. The congregation was quite small, about 20 people. The people were friendly and seemed genuinely happy to have us there. It was hot and rainy, but the church had air conditioning. How nice! The preacher gave us a ride back to the marina. The rest of the day was rainy. We had about 6" of rain in the dinghy!

All of our windows leaked a little. The Bilge had steak tonight - $12 a plate. Don and I split one. It was good, as usual. We had *Domus*, Dave and Donna, over to play dominoes and to try Don's yellow cake experiment. It was a failure and maybe the worst cake ever made! The electric skillet just doesn't work for baking.

Marsh Harbour Marina, Marsh Harbour, Abacos

September 7, 1987, Monday

It rained the entire day again, apparently due to a tropical depression in the Bahamas.

I did laundry and visited with our friends, Peter Russell and Michelle, his girlfriend. Peter is a white Bahamian commercial lobster fisherman. They have a new baby. I also did some cross-stitching and letter writing. Don read and visited with Dave on *Domus* looking at charts. He tried to go into town to mail letters, but the Honda motor quit on him, so he spent two hours repairing it. The rain apparently got it down.

This was a great day to sit back and appreciate what we are doing now, compared to what we were doing a year ago, when we were getting the boat ready for the trip, packing, moving, and other stressful things.

Marsh Harbour Marina, Marsh Harbour, Abacos

September 8, 1987, Tuesday

Today was a day to socialize. It rained hard, off and on, but we kept dry.

We plan to go to Man-O-War Cay tomorrow to have the boat's bottom painted. We went to the bank and got cash. We also went to the grocery and other places for things we will need. Marsh Harbour has a lot more to offer by way of shopping than Man-O-War.

After we put the groceries away, we stopped at Gary Brown's boat, *Nada Mas*. I met him Saturday and wanted Don to meet him. He is interesting to talk to and has been in four hurricanes. We are now in the hurricane season, and we want to talk to people who have dealt with them. We then went to *Domus* to visit. We stayed until seven thirty, and had a nice time with a nice couple.

Don cooked spaghetti for dinner. We didn't eat until eight thirty. I was tired and went to bed as soon as I got the dishes done.

Marsh Harbour Marina, Marsh Harbour, Abacos

September 9, 1987, Wednesday

We got up at our usual time, and Don listened to the early news and weather on the headset radio. He then made chocolate-chip cookies. We were finishing our first batch when Donna and Dave came by and invited us to go swimming at Boat Harbour. We left at eleven thirty with them and spent a couple of hours relaxing at the swimming pool.

We went back to our boat, and while we were preparing to leave, Gary, from *Nada Mas* came over and gave us some fish, which I cleaned on the way to Man-O-War, and Don fixed after we got there. We anchored for the night at Man-O-War. The bugs weren't bad; and, because it was hot, Don slept in the cockpit.

Anchored at Man-O-War Cay, Abacos – Distance traveled: 7 miles

September 10, 1987, Thursday

This was a big day. We had *Robin Lee* hauled out and her bottom painted with a fresh coat of anti-fouling paint. (We're talking about the boat of course.) Edwin's Boat yard did the work. At ten o'clock, they took her out of the water on a railway lift, and by five in the afternoon the painting was finished, but it needs to dry overnight. During the time the boat is out of the water, we won't have access to it. I spent the day going places in the dinghy, and Don spent time reading and relaxing under the shade trees. We also had lunch at the Bite Site Restaurant.

Domus came to Man-O-War this afternoon, so we would have a place to stay, a very nice thing for them to do. We spent the evening and the night on board. Don made dinner on *Domus,* and then we taught Donna and Dave how to play euchre. We also played a game called scruples. It was a relaxing evening, which we all enjoyed. Their boat was a pleasure to stay on. It is 41 feet long and has a forward cabin with head and shower, which Donna and Dave use, and an aft cabin with head and shower, that we used. Our bed was big and very comfortable. The main cabin and the galley are in between the two cabins.

Man-O-War Cay, Abacos, *Robin Lee* at Edwin's Boat Yard and us aboard *Domus*

September 11, 1987, Friday

We had breakfast on *Domus,* and then about nine thirty we dinghied to the boat yard. *Robin Lee* was back in the water by eleven. This paint job was a lot easier than last year—no stress or hassle, and they did great work for a very reasonable price. It cost $120 for paint and $250 for lift and labor. We left for Hopetown as soon as we had settled up with Edwin's. It only took 1.5 hours to motor there. After anchoring, we had a rainstorm with a lot of wind, but the anchor held. Around four, we went ashore and patronized Bessie's Bakery. We had heard good things about her bread and rolls, so I wanted to meet her and her husband and try her bread. As we heard from others, they are a friendly elderly couple, and interesting to visit with. The baked goods were excellent. On the way back to the boat, we had another rain shower, and we were soaked by the time we arrived. The rain cooled things off. Don made bean soup and potato salad in the afternoon, and that is what we had for dinner. We listened to the radio today and heard about the Pope's visit to Miami. The evening was quiet and cool, with a steady breeze.

Anchored at Hopetown, Elbow Cay, Abacos – Distance traveled: 6 miles

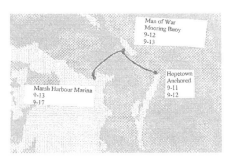

September 12, 1987, Saturday

One year-ago today was my last day of earning money working as a nurse. It was not my last day of work. Don and I work a lot these days!

We left the anchorage about one o'clock, after doing cross-stitch and reading most of the morning. I even slept in until nine thirty. We went to Man-O-War, bought fuel (diesel and gas), and then tied to a mooring buoy so Don could spend the afternoon working on unclogging the hose that connects the head to the through-hull fitting that disposes of waste overboard. It had a built-up a crust of salt, constricting the hose. As a result, the head wasn't flushing well. It's a common problem, and we were advised that we should take the hose off and slap it on a big rock and that the salt deposit would break up and come out. It wasn't that easy. The hose was very strong and thick and Don had a difficult time removing it. I was sitting behind him with my regular supply of paper towels. He pulled hard and when it did come off, it flipped back and sprayed you know what, all over my face. The people back home think Don has taken me on a romantic cruise with nothing for me to do but enjoy the palm trees, beaches, ocean breezes, and piña coladas. If they could only have seen me today.

The crust was petrified and Don never did get it to break up. He replaced the crusted hose with a new section of hose, and that solved the problem. It didn't cost much, but it took the whole afternoon, and I didn't enjoy the spraying.

I rowed ashore to find out what time church started in the morning at the Church of God. At the airport, the day Shelly and David flew home, I met Yvette, the wife of Sam, the church's preacher. They are from the States. I told her we would go to their church when we came to Man-O-War Cay.

When I got back to the boat, Don started dinner...after washing his hands! (Don's jobs of chief mechanic and sanitation worker, and his jobs of head chef and dishwasher are somewhat incompatible.) We ate left-over soup, baked Spam with honey, sweet potatoes, and cornbread.

Domus came over at eight thirty, and we walked around the village, and stopped for ice cream at the Bite Site Restaurant. It was a great night to sit on deck and look at the stars; there were no bugs. We didn't go in until eleven o'clock.

On mooring buoy at Man-O-War Cay, Abacos – Distance traveled: 6 miles

September 13, Sunday

We got up and had another traditional breakfast of pancakes. I spent some time writing a letter to Shelly, and then we got ready to go to church at the Church of God—Yvette and Sam Fisher's church on Man-O-War. It was a nice service.

After church, we went to the Narrows for a quick swim. I spotted five lobsters while I was swimming, which excited me, but when I swam closer, I found that they were dead and their tails were missing. I was so disappointed! We got back to the boat about two and had grilled cheese sandwiches. Then we left for Marsh Harbour Marina. We had a hard rain just prior to docking, but not much wind. We both felt good to be "home." We treated *Domus* to a steak dinner at the Bilge. It was a delicious meal, as it is every Sunday night.

Marsh Harbour Marina, Marsh Harbour, Abacos – Distance traveled: 6 miles

September 14, 1987, Monday

Today we ate another of my favorite breakfasts—cinnamon toast made with homemade Bahamian bread. It was excellent. I have gained weight since we moved onto the boat, and I'm about 2" bigger around my waist.

Peter Russell came over to look at charts with us to show us some good lobster and conch areas. He also took us

SPEARING LOBSTERS

out to a spot, not far from the marina, where he said he can always count on finding a few lobsters. Don speared four lobsters. We were excited.

We went to the Conch Inn to swim, get bread, and check for mail, and then we came back to the boat to work on an electrical problem. None of the lights work in the boat except the 110v and two 12v fluorescents.

Later in the afternoon, Peter came over to visit again. We offered him a rum and Coke; that was a big mistake. He stayed for nearly four hours and drank at least half a bottle of Bacardi Añejo rum. He said Don's brand new Hawaiian Sling was no good, and he proved it by bending it in half, and then gave Don a good stainless steel spear to replace it. He told us that he had speared 1500 to 2000 pounds with that spear this season. He's offered to show Don how to spear fish and lobster and how to find conch. We hope he will do it. He also brought a bag containing 22 lobster tails for us. He said he was leaving and wouldn't have a chance to sell them, and that he wanted to give them to us. Don and I had never seen such a bunch of lobster tails, at least not in our freezer! What a treat for us. We have invited *Domus* over for lobster dinner as an additional "thank you" for having us for a night on their boat. We'll have plenty of beautiful tails to serve.

I stayed up late to read and write a few letters: one to Dad for his birthday; one to Shelly; one to Frank Knipps, a fellow we met at Spanish Wells; and one to *Orchid Boat*. Don went to bed at nine thirty, but he got up early, as usual, to listen to the weather forecast on Charlie's Locker, which is a daily morning broadcast from Fort Lauderdale.

Marsh Harbour Marina, Marsh Harbour, Abacos

September 15, 1987, Tuesday

I stayed aboard almost all day cleaning the head, oiling the teak, and doing odd jobs. Don went to the marina where *Domus* stays to invite them over for a lobster dinner and to the store to get juice for yellowbird drinks. The day went by pretty fast. I don't mind the idleness of retired life!

Don made a most delicious dinner, consisting of lobster, new potatoes, Jell-O and fruit, and topped off with homemade bread. It was superb! We all pigged out. After dinner, we watched some of our videotapes of the Exumas including the "the day of the shark attack." We also looked at still shots that we have taken along the way. It was a fun evening. We have really enjoyed our time with Donna and Dave. Donna is very witty. We are sorry that they are going south from here, as we are going north.

Marsh Harbour Marina, Marsh Harbour, Abacos

September 16, 1987, Wednesday

This is the last page to write on in this book. When we decided to stay in Marsh Harbour for the month after Shelly left, I had figured that when we filled this book, it would be time to move on. So I guess it is time for us to sail north and enjoy the rest of the Bahamas.

We spent the day getting ready to leave. We paid our dockage fees of $169 and our electric bill of $13 for a total of $182 for our thirty-day stay here, or $6.07 per day. Not bad! It's been great vacationing here! We filled the water tanks, went to the store, bought a few groceries, and bought a cassette of reggae music.

We went to the marina where *Domus* is and said good-bye. We also stopped to visit and say good-bye to another couple we have been friends with here, Jo and Fred, aboard *Magic*, a 41-foot Morgan sailboat. They are going to check for mail that comes for us at the Conch Inn and see to it that it's forwarded to Don's cousin Norbert. (We have notified everybody not to send any more mail to us here and have asked the post office to forward any mail for us to Norbert. Our friends will check to be sure that this is done.) Jo cut out a jumpsuit pattern for me. She has made several jumpsuits from the pattern. I'll get some material and make one for myself, if I can find a sewing machine to use somewhere along the way. Anyway, it was nice of her to make a pattern for me. Fred is knowledgeable about boating matters and has been helpful to us. I wish we had gotten to know them better while we were here. They are going south, as *Domus* is. We ended up having drinks and hors d'oeuvres with them and visiting for four hours. We never ate dinner; when we got back to the boat at ten, it was too late. I went up and got the last load of wash out of the dryer and put clean sheets on the bed. Don made us some cinnamon toast. He read awhile. I stayed up late writing in this journal and doing some cross-stitch. It was another wonderful day in paradise.

P.S. We have now totally emptied out the supplies from the locker under the V-berth. Our bow is three inches higher than it was at the end of April.

Marsh Harbour Marina, Marsh Harbour, Abacos

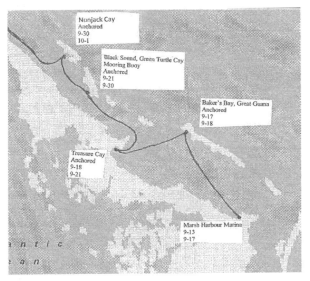

September 17, 1987, Thursday

Today is our first anniversary of becoming live-aboards! What an exciting, sometimes scary, sometimes romantic, educational and interesting year it has been. It was packed full of events that I believe we will remember forever. Today we left Marsh Harbour, where we resided for the past 40 days and 40 nights, taking with us many pleasant memories of our days here. A year ago, we had never even heard of it.

We left at ten o'clock and motored 15 miles to Baker's Bay, at the northwest tip of Great Guana Cay. We spent the afternoon snorkeling on the ocean reefs from the dinghy. The water was very calm, and we saw many fish, including a 20 to 30-pound grouper. We had no interest in trying to spear it.

On the way back to the boat we stopped at the Treasure Island Resort. They were having a private beach party for travel agents. We talked with a few people as we floated by in the dinghy off the beach. When we got back to where we were anchored, we visited with all three of the other boats anchored in the bay: *Maul De Mel*, *Contessa*, and *Amiable*. We had previously met all of them. The first two served us drinks and the third, *Amiable*, invited us for drinks and a lobster dinner. We had met *Amiable* at Tiloo Pond and visited with them on their boat.

Don had made us a Cuban lobster dish with red sauce for lunch. He used five tails for that dish. *Amiable* had five tails to grill, but we insisted on contributing another five tails and bread/butter to the dinner. We still had quite a few tails left from what Don had speared and Peter had given us. Our refrigeration batteries were about run down, and we didn't want any to spoil. We weren't very hungry, but grilled lobster tails are too good to refuse. When we finished our dinner, Don and I had each eaten 5 tails, 2 ½ tails at lunch and 2 ½ tails at dinner. It was a fun evening, which included a great dinner, a good visit, and some stargazing. The mosquitoes were terrible, but we sprayed lots of repellant on us to ward them off. It has rained a lot lately, and it has been very calm; I think that's the reason there are so many mosquitoes. Dave and Mary Lane, the folks on *Amiable,* are elderly and quite nice, and are from the Jacksonville area. We got back to our boat about eleven.

Baker's Bay, Great Guana Cay, Abacos – Distance traveled: 15 miles

September 18, 1987, Friday

The lobster meals at lunch and dinner were entirely too rich for my system—five tails in one day were too many. I suffered through the night with GI problems. Never again will I eat that many lobsters in one day, but I really don't think I'll ever have the chance to, anyway.

After breakfast of grilled toast with jam, we moved four miles south to Great Guana Cay Settlement, walked around the area to sightsee, and enjoyed a milk shake for lunch. The area was so badly infested with mosquitoes that we couldn't wait to get out of there. Furthermore, the people weren't very friendly; they didn't seem interested in having tourists. We left about one o'clock and motored to Leisure Lee, which is a planned resort community that never got developed. The channels were dredged in the early '70s and then work stopped—another "broken dream" apparently caused by Bahamian politics. We've seen many of them! We went through the canals just to size them up for protection from storms because we had heard that the locals use them for protection of their boats when there is a hurricane.

In the late afternoon, we arrived at Treasure Cay, another resort. We saw several yachts with the same name, *Gallant Lady.* All are owned by the owner of Southeast Toyota of Florida. The largest was 134 feet and valued at more than ten million. A member of the crew told us that a larger, 160-foot boat, was on order from Holland and would be ready in two months.

Several cruising sailors told us not to bother coming here because we would be snubbed, but we liked the place. The people were friendly, and we were treated nicely. After we registered, we were invited to the "Manager's Friday Night Party" and served free drinks and appetizers. The party gives the guests an opportunity to get to know each other. We did have to pay $8 to anchor in their harbor, but all of their shore side facilities are included for that price. We thought it was a good deal.

It was quite hot and muggy in the evening. As usual, at just about dusk, the wind died down and the mosquitoes came out.

Anchored at Treasure Cay, Abacos – Distance traveled: – 17 miles

September 19, 1987, Saturday

What a busy day we had!

Don made a brunch of lobster, fried fish, and macaroni and cheese. It was a new way to eat lobster. We used the last five tails Peter had given us. They were great. I hope Don can spear some more before we leave the Bahamas.

Then we went ashore to enjoy the 3½ miles of white sand on the beach at Treasure Cay. I saw a guy with a Bogey Inn tee shirt on walking on the beach with two ladies. We knew they must be from the Columbus area. I got their attention by yelling, "Where's the Bogey Inn?" and that led to a conversation. It was Jim Abbot, his wife, Shari, and Marsha, a friend of theirs. They are all from Dublin. Jim and Shari own the Abbot Travel Agency, located in Dublin. Marsha works for the agency. They were on a promotional trip offered by the resort to travel agents. We talked to them briefly on the beach and decided to visit more at the hotel after dinner.

We also met a young English girl by the name of Shirley, who has come to the Bahamas for three years to teach school. She, Don and I browsed in the hotel's gift shop and then went on a tour of Treasure Cay. A realtor drove us around to show us the layout of the place.

When we got back, we bought a bag of ice, the first one we have bought on the trip. The three of us then went out to our boat and drank Kool-Aid and ate the rest of our lobster and avocado salad, which Don had fixed earlier. Shirley had never eaten lobster. She liked our boat and enjoyed hearing about our trip. She hitchhiked to Treasure Cay from Cooperstown where she has a small one-room apartment. It was dark when she started back to Cooperstown. We hope she made it!

We visited with the Abbots in the hotel lobby until eleven, and then went to the pool and continued our visit until two in the morning. We enjoyed getting caught up on the news of what's going on in and around Dublin. Jim attended Dublin Schools and graduated seven years after Don. Dublin was very small at that time, so they knew many of the same people.

Anchored at Treasure Cay, Abacos – Distance traveled: 17 miles

September 20, 1987, Sunday

The Abbots invited us to join them for breakfast at the hotel. We met them at nine o'clock. After they left at noon to take care of business, we continued to sit by the pool. Then, we hosed out our dinghy with fresh water because we found a roach in it, and took a long dinghy trip to explore the canals. At about three thirty we went back to the pool to swim and take showers. We met a few other travel agents and visited.

We went to bed early, and even though it was hot, we slept well.

Anchored at Treasure Cay, Abacos

September 21, 1987, Monday

We left Treasure Cay a little before nine thirty and went to Black Sound at Green Turtle Cay, where we moored around one o'clock. The trip took us through the "Whale Cay Passage" a notorious stretch which we had been warned about. It can be treacherous if the weather conditions are bad. However, it was calm when we went through it, and we had no problem.

We chose to moor in Black Sound after looking at it and White Sound to decide which provided the best protection from a hurricane. There is a hurricane in the Atlantic that is a threat to us. It has been named "Emily," and she is coming toward us. We chose Black Sound as the best place to be if we have a hurricane.

In the evening, we went to the Blue Bee Bar and had a goombay smash. The drink was invented at this bar and is now popular throughout the Bahamas and the Caribbean. It's a rum drink with pineapple and orange juices. I asked Miss Emily, the elderly black woman who

MISS EMILY'S BLUE BEE BAR

runs the bar, what she thought about Hurricane Emily, hoping she could give us some sage advice. She said, "Emily is no lady" and that was her only advice.

When we decided to come to the Bahamas during the summer and fall, we realized that we would be here during hurricane season. Our plan was that if we were threatened by a hurricane, we would simply follow the advice of the local people. We got no help at the Blue Bee Bar.

On a mooring buoy at Black Sound, Green Turtle Cay, Abacos – Distance traveled: 19 miles

September 22, 1987, Tuesday

We listened to the radio early in the morning, and the weather forecast included a hurricane warning for Green Turtle Cay. Emily was heading directly for us and had winds of 125 mph. It is expected to arrive here tomorrow night at about midnight.

Upon hearing this, we went to a grocery store on the water's edge and talked to the owner, hoping to get advice. Don tried to be cool and just said, "I hear we have a heck of a storm headed for us. What are you going to do?" The guy responded, saying in a very excited manner, "We sure do! I don't know what I'm going to do! I have a brother who lives on the high ground, and I think I'll ask him if my wife and I can come up and stay with him." We knew we weren't going to get any help from him and so we left.

We asked one more local man for advice. His answer was, "Mon (their word for man), I don't know why you Americans come over here and expect us to tell you what to do if a hurricane hits. We don't know. We've never experienced a hurricane. The last one that hit this island was in 1932, and it killed about everybody living here at the time." At that point, we knew we were on our own!

We decided to secure the boat as best we could and then go ashore and stay at some place that was well above the water level. There is a resort nearby, at White Sound, called the Bluff House which sits well above the water level, and so we went there and asked if we could get a room for the duration of the storm threat. They said we could.

We returned to the boat, and Don dove down to see what our mooring buoy was attached to. He found that there is a six foot square cement slab, about six inches thick, with a heavy chain securely attached to an imbedded eye bolt and a 5/8" line is attached to the chain. That line is attached to our boat at the bow. Don attached a second line to the chain and our bow. He didn't think he could improve on that, so we left it that way.

We also wanted to remove everything we could that would present resistance to the wind. We knew we had all day Wednesday to do it, and that we would be cluttering the boat when we did, so we decided to wait until the morning to start that job.

On a mooring buoy at Black Sound, Green Turtle Cay, Abacos

September 23, 1987, Wednesday
Emily is still headed for us with winds of 125 mph and due to arrive around midnight.

We ate breakfast and then packed clothes and other items for our stay at the Bluff House and put them in the dinghy. Next, we took down the dodger, the Bimini top, our jib, and the main sail and stowed them below. Then we took below our boat cushions and all the smaller items that were above deck. After having secured *Robin Lee*, as best we knew how, we left in the dinghy with our few possessions and went to the Bluff House.

We registered with Barbara and Martin, the managers. We went back to the dinghy and got our belongings and took them to the room. We took the motor off the dinghy and took it to the room along with the other equipment for the dinghy (anchor, oars, etc.) We found a pit that had been dug for some purpose that was big enough for our dinghy. It was 30 to 40 feet above the water level; we put the dinghy in the pit and tied it to a tree root.

We had lunch in the dining room of the Bluff House and then got settled into our room and braced ourselves for a very bad night. Emily was very powerful and was on track to hit us shortly after midnight. We went to bed at our normal time and, surprisingly, were able to get to sleep, expecting to be awakened by the storm in the night. That didn't happen. As the storm was approaching us from the southeast, it veered to the north and missed us. It weakened and then hit Bermuda on Friday with 93 mph winds. As was the case with the tropical storm we had to deal with when we were at Warderick Wells, we were on the navigable side of the storm as it came past us, and its center was a long way to the east of us. If we had any high winds at all, we slept through them.

At the Bluff House, White Sound, *Robin Lee* on a mooring buoy at Black Sound, Green Turtle Cay, Abacos

September 24, 1987, Thursday - through - September 27, 1987, Sunday
The storm had missed us, and relief showed on the faces of everybody at the Bluff House. However, we didn't leave. Yesterday, while we were registering as guests, I noticed some cloth lying on a table in the office. Later in the day I asked Barbara about it. It was a

beautiful paisley print of aqua, pink, yellow, lavender and several more colors. She said she intends to have it made into covers for cushions and some other things, but although they have a sewing machine, she hasn't found anyone to hire to do the sewing. Well, that led to my being hired to do the sewing. It would be a three or four-day sewing project. She said she'd take my labor as a trade for our board and room. We agreed; anything to make our money stretch was my thought.

Due to power shortages and mealtimes, I could only work at the machine for about six hours a day. In the beginning, she just asked me to make one cushion cover for a piece of foam 32 inches by 60 inches. She acted as though she was absolutely thrilled with my work and kept finding other things for me to make, including curtains, a gathered vanity skirt, shelf display cloths, a small round pillow sheet for a wicker chair, and other cushion covers. Of course, there were no patterns, so I had to design and cut and sew, hoping I made no mistakes that would waste any of this beautiful fabric. She and her co-manager, Martin, who is her brother, seemed to be happy with all that I did.

We became friends with the guests at the resort, as well as the help. The guests were interested in our trip and acted as though they thought they would enjoy such an adventure. Don served as a guide for some guests, taking them out in the Bluff House's "Boston Whaler" to beaches and snorkeling areas that were close by, but spent most of his time reading and relaxing while I sewed. Our room had a good bed, a shower and air conditioning. All of those things were

WORKING AT THE BLUFF HOUSE

treats! We had excellent food and drink. The normal price for a dinner is $28 per person per night. We figured that during our stay, had we been regular guests, we would have spent over $600 for meals and lodging. When we left on Sunday evening and went back to our boat, we felt we'd had a real vacation, and the total bill came to $126, and that included two bathing suits I purchased! What a deal! Last night, Saturday, the Bluff House provided transportation to and from New Plymouth, the town on Green Turtle Cay, to the Roosters Rest for dancing. Several couples went, and we all enjoyed the evening. We also stopped for our second visit at Miss Emily's Blue Bee Bar—a local "must visit" place.

While we were at Bluff House, we also met a few boaters that were anchored in White Sound.

All in all, it was a great experience. The best part, of course, was that the hurricane missed us.

We returned to our boat this evening, Sunday. We are now anxious to enjoy Green Turtle Cay and its town, New Plymouth; get our boat put back together; and finish our Bahamas cruise.

Thursday through Saturday, at the Bluff House, White Sound, *Robin Lee on mooring buoy* at Black Sound, Green Turtle Cay, Abacos – (Sunday on mooring buoy)

September 28, 1987, Monday

We spent most of the day putting the boat back together.

Our expenses for the past seven days were as follows: $35 for seven nights ($5.00 per night) for the mooring buoy, $126 at the Bluff House, and $5 for groceries and bread.

Moored at Black Sound, Green Turtle Cay, Abacos

September 29, 1987, Tuesday

Our engine is cooled with seawater that comes into the engine through a hose that is attached to a through-hull fitting. The water is pumped through the motor to cool it, and then is taken through another hose to the transom along with the engine exhaust, where it leaves the boat.[12] There is a gate valve at the through-hull fitting which we close whenever we leave the boat because, if one of the hoses ruptured or there was a failure in the hot-water-heater system, the seawater could sink the boat. We discovered that we had a problem with our seawater intake gate valve. It wouldn't open, and so we couldn't cool the engine. It had to be replaced before we could go on. Don talked with the Abaco Yacht Services here in Black Sound. They agreed to haul us out and let us replace the valve ourselves and then put us back in the water for $80, so this morning we did that.

We paid our mooring expenses and then went to town for a snack. When we came back, we moved the boat and anchored at New Plymouth. We swam, and checked to see that the anchor was set. I washed my hair and bathed in salt water. Actually, by promptly towel drying, you don't get the salty, sticky feeling on your skin.

For dinner, we ate the grouper given to us by LuAnn and Mark, guests at the Bluff House. They had caught it, and had no interest in trying to take it home to California.

We heard on the marine radio that there had been a shooting involving *Hawkeye*–a boat we had previously seen at Marsh Harbour–and some person trying to steal the dinghy.

Anchored at New Plymouth, Green Turtle Cay, Abacos – Distance traveled: 1 mile

September 30, 1987, Wednesday

We called Barbara, co-manager of the Bluff House on the marine radio to say good-bye. She gave us a little more information about the shooting incident that occurred yesterday. She said that the guy who was shot had rented the Bluff House's Boston Whaler earlier that day, the one Don had used to take people out while at the Bluff House.

After breakfast of blueberry muffins and coffee, we put up the mainsail and left the anchorage under sail. We didn't even start the motor as we came into our next anchorage at Nun Jack Cay. It was a peaceful two-hour move. We passed Bluff House along the way, and

---

[12] In order to keep salt water out of the engine cooling jacket, some boats have radiators. The engine coolant is circulated through tubes in the radiator and the engine by a pump, as in an automobile and seawater is circulated through a second set of tubes in the radiator by a separate pump. The engine heat is transferred to the seawater. That should be a way of avoiding problems caused by saltwater corrosion inside the engine. Ironically, the only boats we encountered that had cooling system problems were boats with radiators. Late in our trip we replaced the impeller in our water pump and in doing so we got a look at the inside of the water jacket. We saw no evidence of corrosion.

Don took some video. The wind was strong in the late afternoon. Don let out more line, and we started the motor to back down on the anchor as well as charge the batteries for about ½ hour.

We had just enough time to explore the island in the dinghy before a thunderstorm. It rained off and on. Don baked a cake and also made salmon fettuccini for dinner. Everything was excellent. A couple of charter boats were anchored close by, but due to the conditions, they left. We decided to stick it out for the night.

In the wee hours of the morning, we were awakened by severe hobby-horsing. We were rockin' hard (not rollin'). We were pointed west and the wind was on our nose, which meant we were facing a strong west wind, not the normal east wind. We were anchored between Nun Jack Cay and Abaco Island. The fetch between the two is about four miles, which is long enough for sizeable waves to build up. We anchored near the Nun Jack side of the body of water, the protected side if the wind were from the east, as we expected it to be, but with a west wind, we were on the unprotected windward side and if the anchor didn't hold us in place we would be blown onto Nun Jack Cay. A frontal system came through, and when that happens, the wind swings around to the west. We hadn't experienced a frontal system for the five months we had been in the Bahamas. Frontal systems are not normal during the summer months. During the winter months, frontal systems come through frequently. During the summer months, they don't go this far south. This was the first frontal system of the fall.

Don turned on the depth sounder and took a reading of the water depth. It indicated that the water was about 12 feet deep where we were, which meant we had about 6 ½ feet of water under our keel. He had me start the engine, and he went to the bow to be ready to raise the anchor. He had me read the depth sounder frequently. The depth was getting shallower, meaning that our anchor was dragging, and we were being blown on shore. This anchorage is known for not having a good bottom for anchor holding. It was pitch dark, and therefore, we couldn't make out the shore. There are no lighted aids to navigation in the area. To make matters worse it was raining hard. When the depth got to only ten feet, Don had me put it in forward and go full speed ahead. He raised the anchor and came back to the cockpit and took the helm. Since we are under-powered, we had to use full throttle to make significant headway. But directly ahead of us, perhaps 3 ½ miles, was the Island of Abaco, and since we couldn't see a thing, we were not in a hurry. A speed of a couple of knots was good enough, and the most important thing was that the depth sounder was showing that we were getting into deeper water.

Luckily, all of this happened shortly before sunrise. After less than an hour of motoring into the dark, it got light enough for us to make out the island of Abaco ahead. Once we got our bearings, we turned to starboard (north) and headed for Cooperstown. We survived our first dragging experience; it was a potentially bad one.

Anchored at Nun Jack Cay, Abacos

October 1, 1987, Thursday

We motored to Cooperstown and anchored. Cooperstown is on the east side of Abaco Island, and therefore, we were protected from the west wind.

We enjoyed coffee cake for breakfast and while eating we reviewed my journal to see where we were a year ago. We were in Niagara on the Lake.

We went ashore about ten thirty, walked around, mailed letters, and stopped by the high school to look up the teacher from England, whom we had met at Treasure Cay, but she was off on a day trip to Marsh Harbour.

Hawkeye was anchored at Cooperstown, and we anchored next to it. On shore, the locals told us that the shooting which had occurred happened as a result of domestic problems between *Hawkeye's* skipper's live aboard companion and her ex-spouse. They also said that, Peter, the guy who was shot, had been flown to a hospital in the States, and *Hawkeye's* skipper, who did the shooting, was in jail here in Cooperstown, and that Pam, the live-aboard companion, was still on the boat.

We left for Powell Cay for the night, a beautiful "Gilligan's Island" type of place. We tied up at an abandoned dock, and I cut Don's hair and trimmed his beard. It had been six weeks, and he needed it. Afterwards, we dove into the beautiful water, swam and bathed with Joy and enjoyed the peace and quiet. In the evening, I finished the book *Dove,* and we enjoyed cheese sandwiches, juice, popcorn and cake. My kind of meal...easy.

We closed up tight at seven fifteen, expecting mosquitoes, but thank God the wind continued to blow, and we weren't bothered by them. We had rain showers. Don was exhausted and went to sleep at nine, and I went to bed at ten.

Tied up at dock, Powell Cay, Abacos – Distance traveled: 15 miles

[**NOTE:** Later, we heard more concerning the shooting from other boaters who knew the people involved. The Peter and Pam involved are the same Peter and Pam we had on board the *Robin Lee* in late August (August 23rd - about five weeks before the shooting). We invited them and another couple on board after one of the Sunday night Bilge steak dinners while we were at Marsh Harbour. At that time, we understood that they were married. They were on a powerboat named *PamWon*. *Hawkeye,* a sailboat, was at Marsh Harbour at the same time, and was single-handed by its skipper/owner. Peter and Pam became acquainted with *Hawkeye's* skipper. We were told that *PamWon* has an icemaker and *Hawkeye* doesn't, and so *PamWon* supplied *Hawkeye's* skipper with ice. Sometimes when *Hawkeye's* skipper came for ice, the aged Peter would peter out and go to bed, leaving Pam and *Hawkeye's* skipper to visit. As I said when I wrote about Peter and Pam visiting us on our boat, Peter is much older than Pam. He looked like he was about 60, and she looked like she was in her late 20s. After Peter and Pam returned to the States in *PamWon*, Pam flew back to the Bahamas and joined up with *Hawkeye*. Once Peter realized what she had done, he followed her and tracked them down. He learned that *Hawkeye* was at Powell Cay and went to the Bluff House (where we stayed during hurricane Emily) and rented their Boston Whaler. He then went to Powell Cay and confronted Pam and the skipper. An argument ensued and the shooting resulted. Peter was shot in the abdomen, but was able to get to Cooperstown in his rented boat. He got medical help and reported the shooting to the police. The shooting took place on Tuesday. Later that day, or on Wednesday, the police went to Powell Cay and arrested the skipper and took him to the jail at Cooperstown, leaving Pam on the boat by herself. Late Wednesday night (actually the wee hours of Thursday morning) the strong frontal system came through, and while we were hobby-horsing, Pam was calling for help because *Hawkeye* was in trouble. It was being driven on shore by the storm. The police took the skipper to Powell Cay, and he and the police rescued the boat and Pam, and took both to Cooperstown where we saw *Hawkeye* a little later that morning.

Much later, we heard from people who knew about the incident that Peter survived the shooting and that Hawkeye's skipper eventually got out of jail, but that it took him some time and cost him some money to regain his freedom.]

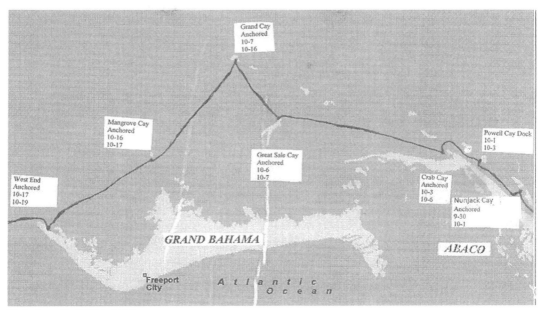

October 2, 1987, Friday

This is one of the prettiest places we've been. The scenery is spectacular, especially on the east side looking out the cuts to the Atlantic. The colors are brilliant.

I started the day fishing from the boat with a line, but didn't catch anything. Next, we dinghied to several beaches and walked along them, and then went back to the boat to line fish off the dock. Don caught one gray snapper. We could see so many in the water, we decided to spear fish, but they disappeared just before he got into the water. Don also caught a small Nassau grouper, but it jumped off the cleaning table, back into the water, so we only had one fish to eat. I cleaned it and Don used it for a fish boil along with the two potatoes we had. It was tasty but far from plentiful. Such is our luck when it comes to living off the sea. We would starve if we had to depend on it.

`We spent the rest of the day swimming, reading, and playing gin rummy. Don won again, and I'm tired of keeping a running score. From now on each time we play it will be a win or a loss. Another boat came in and anchored nearby, but we didn't meet them. We stayed put for the night. The wind was out of the NW and steady at 15-20 knots. We had very little motion at the dock and mosquitoes were not a problem.

Tied up at dock, Powell Cay, Abacos

October 3, 1987, Saturday

The weather was rainy this morning, and the forecast was for north-northeast winds in excess of 20 knots. We slept in, but eventually had Cream of Wheat for breakfast and got ready to move on. We left the dock at eleven and motored two hours to Crab Cay at the north end of Abaco Island where we anchored with two anchors because of the forecast. It's a pretty place, rocky with trees, but no beaches. The weather turned out to be just as predicted. Fortunately, we had pretty good protection and didn't rock and roll too much.

The sun didn't make an appearance until six forty-five, shortly before sunset, but we did have one of the most beautiful sunsets we have ever seen, with colorful cloud formations. It set right at seven.

Don made chili, cornbread, and coconut pudding for dinner. He used the last jar of hamburger he and Dortha May had canned. It was too rough to go ashore and explore, and the motor for the dinghy has been acting up so "we stayed home."

I read almost 200 pages in my book, *The Best Place to Be* by Helen Van Slyke. Don is still struggling with *Atlas Shrugged*. He doesn't like the writer's style.

Anchored at Crab Cay, off the northern tip of Abaco – Distance traveled: 11 miles

October 4, 1987, Sunday

I can see the white caps over the rocky shoreline to the NE. The wind has been steady all night and this morning it's 20-25 knots, with higher gusts.

I slept until nine. Don fixed coffee and cereal when I got up. I had stayed up until one o'clock reading my book. Today, I did my other chores before reading. I knew that once I started reading, I wouldn't put the book down. I love a day like this—a day to catch up. I wrote notes to a few people who have shown us some kindness along the way. I also wrote some birthday notes and cards and worked on my cross-stitch for *Moby*. I'm disgusted about not having enough thread color/261 to finish. I only need about one six-inch piece; I'll have to get it back in the States.

We had leftover chili and cornbread for lunch around two. It's amazing how everything keeps without refrigeration. We haven't wasted food, and we haven't gotten sick.

It's not as cloudy, but the temperature is cooler due to the wind—it's just howling through the rigging, but we are still sitting pretty comfortably.

Anchored at Crab Cay, off the northern tip of Abaco

October 5, 1987, Monday

We are still here and not about to leave. The wind has not stopped blowing less than 25 knots. We read, relaxed, wrote letters, did cross-stitch, and saw a spectacular sunset.

Anchored at Crab Cay, off the northern tip of Abaco

October 6, 1987, Tuesday

We left at eight thirty and motor-sailed the entire way to Great Sale Cay, arriving there at five o'clock.

Honey's Home followed us to Great Sale, and after getting anchored, they (Ron and Jackie) a nice couple, came over in their dinghy to visit. They invited us to their boat to watch a video tape of the America's Cup Race. During our conversation, we found that they are close friends of *Pride*. They live at the Titusville Marina aboard their 44-foot Gulf Star. He is an urgent care physician. She sells real estate. When they leave Great Sale Cay, they plan to go to Mangrove Cay and then to Florida. They gave us a dozen eggs, and we gave them mail that they will take back to the States and mail for us.

Don made an excellent canned turkey, potato, and bacon dish tonight, and we had red Jell-O for dessert.

Anchored at North West Harbour, Great Sale Cay, Abacos – Distance traveled: 53 miles

October 7, 1987, Wednesday

We had a beautiful full moon last night and the radio this morning said that tonight there will be an eclipse. The north wind is supposed to start blowing again, so, after a brief visit with Jackie and Ron, we pulled out and headed for Grand Cay. They are headed for Mangrove Cay.

We arrived at Grand Cay and anchored at four. We saw *Celeste,* Peter, the lobster fisherman's, boat. We also saw *Rainbow*, the 25-foot Cal sailboat, belonging to Jo and Dave Harrington. We originally met Peter in Marsh Harbour and Dave and Jo at Lake Worth. Dave and Jo came over and visited with us and brought us grouper and lobster. They said they have gotten about 90% of their food from the sea for the past four months, right here in this anchorage. Since we had motored to Grand Cay, we had refrigeration and were able to serve them a nice cold beer. They stayed until eight. Then Don made us an excellent lobster and grouper meal. The only thing missing was butter, which we did not have.

Anchored at Grand Cay, Abacos – Distance traveled: 22 miles

October 8, 1987, Thursday

At ten, we rowed ashore, stopping at Peter and Michelle's boat to visit. Michelle was there, and another man was on the boat. He supposedly was helping her take the boat back to the States. Later in the day some locals told me that Peter and Michelle had split up. That's enough of the local gossip!

We stayed ashore a good part of the day. I visited with locals and bought bread and butter. A couple of elderly fishermen gave me two conchs that they had just found. They must have had 200 in a tub that they were skinning. Don's goal was to get the Honda motor fixed. He found a man who said he was a mechanic and he and Don worked on the motor.

There was trash lying around, small children playing in the town's one street, and many dogs. I must say, however, that the people were very friendly – more so than in some of the other settlements where we have been. Locals took me back and forth to our boat to get tools Don and the mechanic needed, and they didn't seem to mind a bit.

Don didn't get the dinghy motor fixed, and now it needs an impeller for its water pump. We can't buy one in the Bahamas. We can't use the motor without a water pump because that is what cools the engine. He was bummed out because he paid $20 to this guy who claimed to be a mechanic, and he started the motor out of the water to test it and that ruined the impeller. So now all we can do is row it, and rowing an inflatable boat is not easy. It's a good thing that we are about to return to the States. Since the water temperature has dropped considerably, we probably won't do any more snorkeling and swimming anyway.

We enjoyed a very quiet evening, and Don made cracked conch for dinner. It is not a favorite of mine. I think it's too chewy, but Don likes it.

Anchored at Grand Cay, Abacos

October 9, 1987, Friday

As predicted, the weather has gotten foul. On the marine radio, we heard predictions of 25-30 knots, with higher gusts out of the N-NE. I'm glad we are anchored safely in this area.

We stayed on board all day because it was too windy to row ashore. I finished my cross-stitch of "Moby" and started a couple of other projects for *Pride* and *Epicurus*.

Don enjoyed reading his two books, *Marine Engines and Maintenance* and *David Copperfield,* an unusual combination.

At five, we entertained Dave and Joanne from *Rainbow* for dinner. Don made honey-baked ham, lima beans with bacon, and cornbread. We visited until about ten thirty.

We are down to our last package of Kool-Aid and 1 ½ gallon of drinking water. Don is running very low on tea. Tomorrow, if it rains, we will have to catch rainwater because Joanne said the water in the cisterns here is lousy.

It began to rain and got very windy. Don didn't get much sleep. I managed to do OK.

Anchored at Grand Cay, Abacos

October 10, 1987, Saturday

Well, another day of bad weather. Wind gusts were up to 35-40 knots. The Gulf Stream has 12-foot waves. I hope our friends on *Honey's Home,* who we met at Great Sail Cay either made it home on Thursday or are safely sitting at West End.

I had not taken a shower or bath since Monday, and neither had Don. Both of us hated to use the water since our supply was so low. However, we were able to catch over ten gallons and *Rainbow* came over and gave us ten gallons. So, we did get to bathe. I even washed my hair with rainwater. The last time I washed my hair was one week ago at Powell Cay. I didn't use my creme rinse because my hair felt so clean after using the rain water and shampoo. We have both decided that we will be glad to get back to civilization and tie up at a dock where we can have refrigeration, plenty of hot water, and access to super markets.

Peter, the lobster fisherman, has offered to take us to Walker's Cay. We just want to look the place over; we're not interested in staying there. That would save us the hassle of taking *Robin Lee* there. We have heard it's expensive, and mostly, power boaters go there to fish.

It rained the entire day and evening. We caught more than 20 gallons of water and filtered it for our tanks. We also gave two full containers, five gallons each, back to *Rainbow.*

Don made a pan of brownies early this morning. We snacked on them and coffee all day. In the evening, he fixed leftover beans and grilled cheese sandwiches with good homemade bread.

Radio reception was amazingly good tonight. We got WJR in Detroit, WLW in Cincinnati, and New York stations, WABC and WCBS, plus various others. The Detroit Tigers won the 3rd game of the playoffs. Don's been following baseball.

Anchored at Grand Cay, Abacos

October 11, 1987, Sunday

On this day last year, we were at Lake Sylvan, New York, and it was 20°. It's too bad we are now having frontal systems coming through ("northers" as the sailors call them), and there is also another tropical storm, "Floyd," churning its way through the Atlantic and heading in this direction, but at least it's warm, it's dry inside the boat, and our anchors are holding us safe and snug in this protected and comfortable harbor.

We counted up the days we've sat lately due to wind and rainstorms–9 out of the past 20. That is a lot of time for us to sit and read and do cross-stitch projects, but we do not want to pull out until the weather conditions are better.

We had a cup of coffee and did a few things on the boat, and then at ten we left with Peter to go to Walker's Cay to look around. It was a bumpy and fast ride in his 14-foot "tin boat," as he calls it, with a 30 hp motor. Don and I walked around and ate lunch at the hotel. It was quite a nice place, but as advertised, it is very expensive to stay there. Our lunch was very tasty and only $4.35 for each plate, and included a cheeseburger with bacon, fries, Cole slaw or potato salad. That is possibly the best bargain on the whole cay. On the way home, we got rained on.

When we got back, I did a few pieces of laundry, but it was so late and the humidity so high, that I knew they would be slow to dry. However, Don really wanted some clean tee shirts, and I needed a few things.

Dave and Joanne went spear fishing today and brought us a hogfish, a black grouper, and two lobster tails. Don made dinner for the four of us, which consisted of the fish and lobster they brought us, plus macaroni and cheese, green beans, freshly baked bread with butter, and fruit cocktail for dessert. It was another excellent meal and an enjoyable evening with lots of conversation.

Anchored at Grand Cay, Abacos

October 12 & 13, 1987, Monday & Tuesday

We thought the weather might be good enough to leave today, but "Floyd," the tropical storm, has caused us a lot of concern. Presently, it's close to Cuba headed N/NW. In another few hours, hopefully it will be history.

Shortly after I wrote the above paragraph, we listened to a report on the marine radio, which said that "Floyd" had strengthened and become a hurricane, had turned to the northeast, and was heading directly toward us. (So much for leaving.)

We spent Monday, from morning until late afternoon, preparing the boat for the storm. We took down the Bimini, the dodger, and both sails and stowed them below, along with the other things that would present wind resistance, just as we did for Emily at Green Turtle Cay. However, at Green Turtle Cay, we had a good strong mooring that we felt we could rely on to keep us off the rocks, but here there are none. The other boats in the anchorage, including *Rainbow* and *Celeste* went up a creek that provides good protection and tied off trees. We couldn't do that because of our deep draft. We would have to leave *Robin Lee* in the harbor and rely on our anchors. We moved the boat to what we thought would be the best spot and then put out our Bruce anchor, our Danforth anchor, and John Hubay's homemade wishbone anchor with as much line as we had room for. We backed down hard on each anchor to be sure they were holding.

We wanted to leave the boat and be on shore during the storm as we did at Green Turtle, but there are no hotels or resorts here. Fortunately, *Rainbow's,* Dave and Jo know Charles, the caretaker of Abplanalp Island. The 125-acre island belongs to Robert Abplanalp, the inventor of the aerosol valve. He is a close friend and supporter of President Nixon. During Nixon's presidency, Abplanalp refurbished the house on the island, and built housing and offices on it for the presidential staff and the secret service. He turned the island, along with his 55-foot yacht, over to President Nixon for his use for the duration of his presidency, so he could use it as a retreat whenever he wished. President Nixon vacationed there on several occasions during his presidency, and was there at the time of the Watergate burglary.

The caretaker gave the four of us permission to stay in one of the beach villas on the island, and so we went there with our necessary things, including some food and water. The villa was used by guests, and possibly by Secret Service agents or Presidential staff during Nixon's visits. It was nicely constructed, and it looked as though a professional had once decorated it, but it looked as though no one had stayed there for several years. We found magazines and TV Guides from 1980 and 1982.

The island has its own generator, and the caretaker turned on the electricity and hot water for us, so we had all the conveniences of home. We fixed our meals, showered, and sat around the table playing various games—euchre, dominoes, etc.—in air-conditioned comfort. We really enjoyed our stay except for the high winds that constantly blew. We guessed they were about 40 knots. Actually, we didn't get nearly as much wind or rain as we expected. There was very little or no destruction done by Floyd where we were. Some of the strength of the storm had been sapped from it when it passed over southern Florida and Grand Bahama and by a frontal system in the area. Incidentally, Floyd was the only hurricane to make landfall in the U.S. in 1987.

Floyd didn't go away quickly. It got windy and stayed windy, but it wasn't dangerously high wind. The problem from our standpoint was whether the storm had stalled or just what was happening. A hurricane does sometimes stall (quit moving) and continue to blow in the place where it stalled. We stayed at the Villa a second night because we weren't sure whether the storm was over.

At a beach villa on Abplanalp Island and *Robin Lee* anchored at Grand Cay, Exumas

October 14, 1987, Wednesday

A GAME OF CARDS ON ROBIN LEE WITH DAVE AND JO

This morning we returned to the boat and were glad to be home, but we knew that we had lots of work to do on the boat to get it back to normal. We had the sails on and the dodger and Bimini up by one thirty. We had soup for lunch. It's been cooler, so it tasted good.

Peter stopped by (drunk) to visit. He came to vent his feelings towards his female friend, Michelle. He says she is leaving him and is going to the States and that he and his new baby are staying here. We'll probably never know the whole story. Peter told us that he had been near the anchorage during the storm, and that he believes two of our anchors dragged. The one that didn't drag was John Hubay's homemade wishbone anchor.

Dave and Joanne came over later. We went ashore to try to use the phone to let people back home know that we were all right, but found out that the only phone on the island has been broken for months. We bought a few groceries and then the four of us went to our boat. Don made goombay smashes, and we had grilled cheese sandwiches and leftover spaghetti. We had coffee with Nassau Royale for dessert! We spent the evening talking, and Dave and Jo trying to teach us the game of Backgammon.

Anchored at Grand Cay, Abacos

October 15, 1987, Thursday

Still another day, we sit at Grand Cay. The weather still isn't good, but the forecast for tomorrow promises good conditions for sailing to West End. Don now has all his navigation planning complete, so it's just a matter of the waiting for the "right weather."

Don and Dave retrieved the cement blocks that they put down with our anchors.

I stayed on the boat and did some cross-stitch. In the early afternoon, we all had dinner on *Robin Lee*. Cheese and sprout sandwiches.

We played one game of euchre. Don and Dave were partners—Jo and I beat them! It was a nice day and evening, but everyone is anxious to leave...hopefully tomorrow.

Anchored at Grand Cay, Abacos

October 16, 1987, Friday

It was a beautiful cloudless, bright, sunny, cool day. We left early and had a delightful light wind for motor-sailing the entire way to Mangrove Cay.

I made tuna salad for lunch, and since we ate such a large portion, we did without dinner. We entertained *Rainbow* for a dessert of tapioca pudding and coffee with Nassau Royale in the evening, after we both got anchored. The sunset was pretty. We played one game of euchre. Jo and I won. I'm getting pretty good at that game. I'm glad they both seem to enjoy it. We taught them how to play when we were staying at President Nixon's retreat.

We spent the evening discussing weather conditions and crossing conditions back to the States. Jo and Dave are really a nice couple.

Anchored at Mangrove Cay, Grand Bahama Island – Distance traveled: 30 miles

October 17, 1987, Saturday

We left Mangrove Cay at ten thirty. It was another fantastic day. It was so calm the water was as transparent as glass. We could see a lot of starfish on the bottom. We saw no conch or fish, but we did have porpoises swimming beside us. They are such a treat! We had the sail up, but only the main because the jib was jammed and didn't work.

We arrived at West End at five thirty. After we anchored, I rowed over and picked up Jo and Dave. Don made beef stroganoff with noodles, marinated artichoke hearts, and best of all, raspberry Jell-O with fruit and whipped topping.

We played euchre again. Jo and I won the first game, and then we took a break for coffee with Nassau Royale. Dave and Don won the next game. We had a slight rain shower about ten thirty, but other than that it was a great day!

Anchored at West End, Grand Bahama Island – Distance traveled: 34 miles

October 18, Sunday

We got up late and had blueberry muffins and hot chocolate for breakfast. About ten thirty we rowed ashore with Dave and Jo in our dinghy, and looked around at Jack Tar Village and Marina. Dave and Jo rowed back out to their boat to get empty fuel containers. Don and I stayed at the hotel and purchased some bread and butter for *Rainbow* and us. I mailed a letter and then called my mom and sister Carol. We wanted to finally let them know that we were OK, and we would soon return to the States.

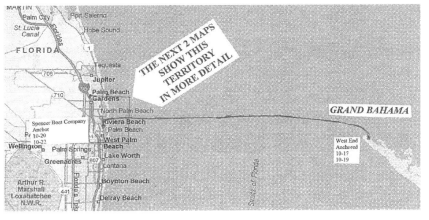

We thought about leaving, but the wind picked up, and we felt it just wasn't the right time. *Rainbow* agreed. They came over for dinner. Don made linguini and white clam sauce and served it with garlic toast.

We played cards in the evening and talked–getting psyched up for the "crossing."

Anchored at West End, Grand Bahama Island

October 19 & 20, Monday & Tuesday

It was another beautiful day and an excellent evening for leaving for the crossing. We took it easy. We rowed ashore, and bought more diesel fuel and then walked and hitchhiked to West End. It is not a very big place, but is typical Bahamas, We bought some juice and ice cream. We served our traditional goombay smashes before dinner, which we ate early. Don made cornbread and bean soup. About six o'clock, I rowed Dave and Jo back to their boat, and then we brought the dinghy on board. At seven, we raised our anchors and left. The seas were calm, and the wind was light. We enjoyed our trip motoring to the Lake Worth Inlet. There was quite a bit of ship traffic so we had to keep a sharp lookout. We took 2-hour watches, with me from 6-8, 10-12, 2-4, and 6-8. While crossing, we listened to the bad news on the radio about the stock market crashing. It dropped 508 points, 23%, on Monday. That was not very nice entertainment, especially since I have my Central Ohio Medical Group retirement fund invested in stocks. By daylight, we were looking at the coastline of Palm Beach. The homes were beautiful and big. We reached the Lake Worth Inlet at seven o'clock in the morning, and shortly thereafter tied up at Spencer's Marina. We spoke with *Rainbow* off and on during the night. We both had a safe and pleasant trip. Thank God. Don was tired, but I seemed to have my adrenaline pumping. I got busy and cleaned up the cabin and did five loads of laundry. Then I made phone calls to Shelly, Mom, Randy, Danielle and Nick. I spent a lot of money on phone calls, but we all enjoyed getting caught up on the news.

A lady I met, who was going to the grocery, picked up a grapefruit, two apples, and a head of lettuce for us. We enjoyed a fresh salad with tuna for dinner and watched our first TV show in six months. By ten, we were ready for bed. Don got four hours of sleep during the day, but I didn't get any.

Crossing from West End, Grand Bahama Island to Spencer's Marina, West Palm Beach, Florida – Distance traveled: 67 miles.

CHAPTER NINE
WEST PALM BEACH, FL to SARASOTA, FL
Oct. 21, 1987 – Dec. 3, 1987

October 21, 1987, Wednesday

We awakened early to the sounds of sirens of emergency vehicles on the streets, the loudspeaker at the Spencer Boat Company paging employees, and squeaking docks. Already,

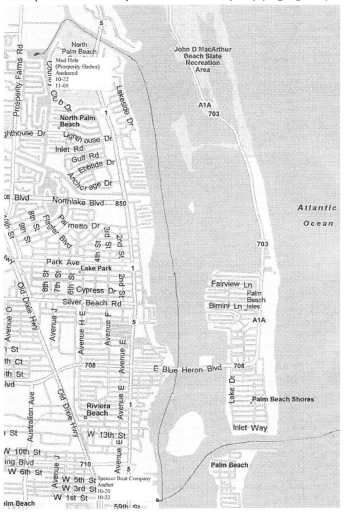

I miss the roosters crowing and the quietness of the Bahamas. On the other hand, we are happy to be back in the USA, with electric and water hookups at the dock, telephones in the marina office, and a multitude of services and shopping possibilities nearby.

We got up late and enjoyed a quiet, relaxed day, free of the stress of being concerned about getting safely back from the Bahamas. There is a couple here at the marina who are preparing for a trip to the islands. We shared our experiences with them, which made us feel like old salts.

When Don and I decided temporarily to give up our careers and travel, we had several travel goals: a boating adventure; traveling in foreign countries using public transportation—bus, train, plane, etc., and traveling in the US and Canada in a recreational vehicle. We thought we would spend about five years traveling. How long we would spend on each phase would depend on how much we enjoyed it. Nothing was definite; it still isn't, and won't be, until we finish. We will make those decisions as we go.

In order to do all of these things, we need to be very conservative spending our money because our funds are very limited. We won't start the foreign travel phase until we have decided to end our live-aboard life and have sold the boat. We've now been living aboard for 13 months, and we aren't yet ready to end this part of our travels.

We spoke with a boat broker at the marina about the value of our boat. He suggested a listing price of $43,000, if we were to try to sell it. That seemed high to us; we only have about $36,000 invested in it.

Our travel objectives are many:

First, to enjoy ourselves and appreciate our freedom to do as we want without the restriction of being on a schedule. Being able to wait for decent weather before embarking on the next leg of our cruise has definitely made our adventure more enjoyable and safer.

Second, we want to learn about living on a boat and how to cope with the problems that go along with this way of life. We are almost always learning something new. With every new experience we are educated in one way or another. Sometimes we feel pretty stupid; other times we pat ourselves on the back.

Third, we want to meet people and make friendships. We also want to learn as much as possible about the places where we travel and the people who live there.

The first half of our boat travel, the part from Ohio to New Jersey, down the East Coast, and along the coastal waters of Florida was interesting, though less remarkable than the six months we spent in the Bahamas. We enjoyed the small towns, such as Chesapeake City; Georgetown; and McClellenville; and the big cities that we visited, particularly Annapolis; Charleston; and Savannah, as well as the natural beauty we saw along the way.

The Commonwealth of the Bahamas is nothing like Ohio. The Bahamians have an entirely different way of life than we do, and their environment is very different from ours with bright sunshine and beautiful water, many islands in a vast area, and a sparse population. We covered most of the popular cruising islands, which had been recommended to us by other boaters: The Berry Islands, Nassau on New Providence Island, the Exumas, Long Island, Eleuthera, the Abacos, and Grand Bahama Island. We spent at least one night at more than 50 different anchorages and marinas. We feel we know the Bahamas pretty well. The memories of our six months there will live on in our hearts and minds forever. We sure are thankful for having had this opportunity.

We had a light evening meal, and afterwards, left the marina to anchor near Spencer's so that we could save the dockage fee. I enjoy our privacy and space when we are anchored. The north wind was strong, so it was a bit choppy, and we awakened several times and checked our position.

At anchor in front of Spencer's Marina, West Palm Beach, FL - Distance traveled: 0.5 miles

October 22-29, 1987, Thursday-Thursday, Anchored at the Mud Hole, North Palm Beach, FL

We are happy about being back in the good old U.S.A.

A week ago today, October 22nd, we moved *Robin* Lee to the place in North Palm Beach that we call "The Mud Hole," known to the locals as "Prosperity Harbor," and have been anchored here since then. Our friends, Dave and Jo Harrington on *Rainbow*, joined us here on Saturday, the 24th.

The four of us have been very busy re-orienting ourselves to the American ways. We have walked to and from the local shopping areas about every day in order to restock the boats with food, cleaning materials and personal items. The first time we went to the Winn-Dixie, the nearest supermarket, we spent some time walking up and down the aisles just admiring the variety and quantity of foods available to us. The only place we saw in the Bahamas which was at all comparable was in Nassau, and it was small in comparison.

We've also used the bus service. One day, we went to a local "Health Fair" and got the works—eye exams, hearing tests, blood pressure checks, and even blood tests. Monday I have an appointment for a mammogram which will cost $45.00. That's cheaper than going to a local physician. I'll have the results mailed back to my gynecologist, and he will store them in my medical file.

The day we returned from the Bahamas is now being referred to as Black Monday, because the stock market crashed that day. The Dow-Jones Industrial Average (DJIA) went down 508 points, a drop of nearly 23%. The DJIA is still very unstable, changing 50-100 points, up or down, on a typical day. The investments I made with my retirement fund, which I withdrew from the Medical Group I worked for, have suffered greatly, but "thank God" I have lost very little compared to others. It's not the end of the world for me! In Miami, two stockbrokers were shot by an angry client who had lost millions.

One night we were invited to a home here in the harbor for dessert. The owner and his girlfriend, Mark and Suzanne, are interested in doing some cruising. We enjoyed their hospitality and sharing our experiences. Another night the four of us, Dave, Jo, Don and I, played bingo at the Knights of Columbus Hall, which is close by our anchorage. I lucked out and won $12. We've also gone to some thrift stores and flea markets, shopping for bargains. Don got a nice shirt for $1 and I bought a golf shirt and shorts outfit for $1, both in excellent condition. We even made some money at one place - $20 for some "junk" items we had, which were just taking up space. I've called back to Ohio several times to Randy, catching up on the central Ohio news.

In the evenings, we have usually eaten on our boat. Jo and Dave have joined us, and after dinner, played cards and visited. Last night, we watched TV after our meal. The "Opening of the Safe on the Titanic" was a special two-hour show. A couple of days ago, Dave and Jo took us out to an "all you can eat pizza buffet." We all stuffed ourselves. Today is a day of rest, but Don just finished making us a lemon pie for tonight's dessert.

The weather has been cool at night, with very comfortable temperatures during the day and lots of sunshine and blue skies. We haven't had rain since we got back from the Bahamas.

October 30, 1987, Friday

It was very windy and cloudy all day. *Rainbow* rented a car and drove to Crystal River so they could get belongings out of their old car and sell it. They dropped us off at Publix in the morning on their way.

Don and I mailed a surprise package, a new calendar and book, to Shelly and mailed the *TTOGA* cross-stitch project. We puttered around at Publix and got a take-out of fried chicken for lunch. Like the other boat "bums" do, we sat on the bench in front of the store and ate it. It was a nice picnic, and we enjoyed watching people coming and going.

We then walked to Soverel Marina, picked up our mail, and took showers. It's always fun to get mail; it's like Christmas. We had *Rainbow's* cart, a small fold-up grocery cart they carry on their boat, and our laundry bag. We stopped at the Winn Dixie shopping center, and while I did laundry, Don bought our groceries.

At about five o'clock, we started back to the boat. Walking down Prosperity Farms Blvd., we stopped at the K of C Hall, where the local folks play bingo, and enjoyed a cheap sandwich and dessert at their snack bar. We ran into our friend Neal Dallas, a fellow who had given us a lift once when we were walking to the Mud Hole. He asked us if we needed a ride to any place and offered to take us. We told him that we had decided to buy a portable stereo CD player with an AM/FM radio and tape player. He took us shopping and then to our boat. We spent four hours with him. He is, indeed, a nice, kind gentleman. I think he's lonely because he spends most of his time tending to his invalid wife. He is 72, but you would think he's 55. We bought his dinner at Denny's restaurant to thank him for his driving us all over town. It was an interesting and different kind of evening for us.

October 31, 1987, Saturday, Halloween

The wind was still very strong, and it was cold, damp, and dreary.

Don stayed on the boat all day. He looked over mail, paid bills, and read. I went ashore after lunch, emptied the trash, and walked to the Community Center. I sat out on the swings, and drank a root beer. I got back at three o'clock. We had fettuccini Alfredo for dinner and played gin rummy afterwards. The wind was very strong and gusting up to 40 mph all night long.

November 1, 1987, Sunday

We stayed on the boat the entire day—it rained a lot.

Free Spirit, a catamaran with Pat and Dick aboard, came into the mud hole and anchored early in the morning. We first met them in White Sound while we were staying at the Bluff House on Green Turtle Cay. They invited us to dinner on their boat for Monday evening.

Dave and Jo returned from Crystal River in the late afternoon, and after unloading their junk from the rental car, took us out for an evening on the town. We had dinner at Taco Viva and dessert at the Haagen-Dazs store; then we went to see a movie.

November 2, 1987, Monday

Today we spent a lot of money. We left in the early morning. The Harringtons gave us a lift in their rental car to a store named Laurio's where we bought a General Electric portable stereo CD player with an AM/FM radio and tape player. After that, we got a ride to the mall with a lady who was shopping at Laurio's. At the mall, I bought a $70 pair of walking shoes and a CD for our new player (Wyndham Hill/George Winston – "Winter Into Spring").

We went by bus to a place near Palm Beach Mall, and I had a mammogram. The mammogram went smoothly, and hopefully the results will be negative. The radiologist was reassuring; they will mail the results to my doctor back home.

By the end of the day, we were exhausted. On our last stretch, we hitchhiked and got a ride in the back of a small pick-up truck. It had gotten very windy and started to rain, but we made it back before dark, and the stereo player didn't get wet. We spent over $400 altogether.

We were both so tired, we didn't want to fix dinner, so it was nice that we were invited to dinner on *Free Spirit*. Pat fixed a chicken enchilada casserole. Don liked it so well, he got the recipe. We had a pleasant evening; however, the wind was incredibly high, and we had a hard time rowing back to *Robin Lee* from *Free Spirit*.

November 3, 1987, Tuesday

Pat and Dick invited us to take a dinghy ride with them to K-Mart and E&B Marine. After some browsing in the stores, we had lunch at a Chinese place close by. It was our first Chinese meal in six months.

We got home in time to have an hour's rest break before entertaining *Rainbow* with a dinner of salmon a la king on rice and an evening of pinochle. It was my first time to play; Jo and Dave taught me. Don already knew how, but Jo and I won, which was great fun!

The evening was quite breezy and warm.

November 4, 1987, Wednesday

Well, today we were told to leave the Mud Hole. Don and Dave were working on our Honda dinghy motor in our cockpit, and while Dave was coming from *Rainbow* to *Robin Lee* in his dinghy with a tool Don needed, a police cruiser stopped next to the harbor. Two policemen got out and motioned for Dave to come ashore. They informed him that we had been there much longer than we should have been. We figured that the neighbors must have complained. They may have thought we intended to make it our permanent address, or maybe they were just tired of looking at us. *Free Spirit* had pulled out an hour before the police came. Dave talked them into letting us stay one more night. That allowed us enough time to "get it together."

When Don finished repairing the dinghy motor, he went ashore to get groceries and make a few calls about our boat insurance. Our annual rate for the insurance policy we got at the time we left on our trip was $1100. We will now be insured by Ocean Underwriters for $400 per year and will have the same coverage.

I stayed on board all day. I cleaned, took a shower, and did two projects: I organized and labeled all the cassette tapes, and I organized all the pictures and put them into photo albums. We had a rainstorm while Don was gone. After that it was hot, muggy, calm, and buggy; and the dew was awful.

Dave and Jo joined us for tacos and Little Debbie treats. After dinner, we played another game of pinochle. Jo and I won again. Don also taught them a little about bridge.

Our last night anchored at the Mud Hole, North Palm Beach, FL

November 5, 1987, Thursday

We weighed anchor at nine o'clock. Boy, were the anchors mucky and stinky! By the time we got them in and stowed, the deck was filthy. We spent a half-hour cleaning the deck with brushes and buckets of water dipped from the harbor. Afterwards, we motored five miles to Riviera Beach Marina, arriving at ten. As soon as we arrived, we bought fuel and then docked for the night.

I stayed on the boat all day to work on it and spent from ten thirty in the morning until six thirty in the evening working on the teak and cleaning the deck and cockpit with boat soap. By the end of the day, every muscle was sore. The second reason I stayed near the boat all day is because there is a lot of thievery in this area. The marina is relatively new, but not very secure.

Don found a ride into town and exchanged our CD player combo for another one because the one we had bought was defective. He rode with a guy docked in the marina whom we had met originally in Marsh Harbor.

We had a weird dinner: macaroni and cheese, Jell-O, coffee, and leftover Little Debbie treats. We relaxed, read, and enjoyed music all evening on our new CD player and radio combo. I also got caught up on this journal.

Riviera Beach Marina, Riviera Beach, FL – Distance traveled: 5 miles

November 6, 1987, Friday

Today's high temperature was 75°. It was dark and cloudy, and it rained early in the day.

We worked on more cleaning projects on the boat until two thirty; then we showered, and shortly thereafter, left for the Phil Foster Park anchorage.

Rainbow was there and glad to see us, but were surprised we had come. They figured that, since the wind had picked up to 20 knots, with gusts to 25, we would have preferred to stay put. The truth is we would have preferred to stay put. It would have been easier and more comfortable, but it costs $18 per night. Furthermore, we were cautioned many times about the high rate of theft in the area. Don heard someone at the marina complaining that their car had been stolen yesterday.

That evening the four of us ate together and Don gave bridge lessons. It was another fun evening, even though the weather was lousy, and we rocked and rolled.

Anchored at Phil Foster Park, Riviera Beach, FL – Distance traveled: one mile

November 7, 1988, Saturday

The wind calmed down, but the anchorage was rolling and the wakes from passing boats didn't help the situation.

Don, Jo and Dave went to Singer Island in the afternoon, after Don made grilled ham and cheese sandwiches for the four of us. I stayed on the boat and slept three hours.

For dinner, Don fixed one of our favorites: sauerkraut and Kielbasa with sour cream, served over mashed potatoes. Jo brought cupcakes for dessert.

In the evening, we had another bridge lesson. Dave and Jo are really glad to be learning the game. They have wanted to learn to play bridge for a long time, and Don is a good teacher.

Anchored at Phil Foster Park, Riviera Beach, FL

November 8, 1987, Sunday

It was a pretty day—an excellent one for going to a flea market. *Rainbow* was searched by Dave and Jo, and several sellable items were found. They came by early, and we all had coffee and juice and Don's homemade coffee cake. Then we walked about three miles to an old drive-in theater where the flea market is held. Don and I made several small purchases. We didn't sell anything.

After we left the flea market, we stopped at a secondhand store, and after that, went to Pantry Pride and Publix. We had lunch at Bo Jangles. We had another fun evening of socializing and card playing after Jo's excellent stir fried dinner, which the Harringtons wanted to provide since they earned so much money today—about $75.

Anchored at Phil Foster Park, Riviera Beach, FL

November 9, 1987, Monday

Today was cloudy and overcast, but it didn't rain. The temperature was in the 70s.

We slept late. After breakfast, Don went ashore to mail some letters, get a part for our diesel engine at Florida Diesel, and get a few groceries.

I stayed home, straightened things up, swept, and dusted. I even had time for a shower, which felt great. The only problem is that the head is small and the woodwork gets soaked. Since the humidity is so high, it is necessary to dry the excess water off the teak with towels, or it will develop mildew.

Tonight was our last day with our friends on *Rainbow*. It has been exactly one month since we met up with them at Grand Cay.

Dave was kind enough to repair a couple of snaps on our dodger for us. Jo fixed a favorite dish of their family, potato pancakes, made with grated potatoes, onions, bacon, and eggs. It is served with sour cream and/or applesauce. I made taco salad. Don had the night off. Everything was tasty. We played bridge and pinochle. The guys won both games. BOO!

Anchored at Phil Foster Park, Riviera Beach, FL

November 10, 1987, Tuesday

It was a beautiful warm, sunny, summer-type day.

After saying good-bye to Jo and Dave around ten o'clock, we pulled up the anchors and left. They sure are nice friends, and we hate to leave them behind, but they want to stay in this area and Don and I both want to move on. We have decided to go to Longboat Key, rent a slip by the month, and spend the winter months there rather than cruising. Last winter, we discovered that Florida winters have a lot of bad cruising days with too much wind and cold temperatures. The final piece of mail that we had been expecting came to Soverel Marina yesterday, so today was the right day to pick it up, get water, shower, and then motor north to Jupiter.

It was an excellent day to move along the waterway, although there was quite a bit of power boat traffic. The big motor yachts and sport fishermen boats make huge wakes, and sometimes they don't even slow down. Their wakes roll us around, making things uncomfortable. There seems to be more construction on this stretch of the waterway than what we remembered seeing in the spring when Shelly and Kelly were here visiting. We arrived in Jupiter at one thirty and anchored south of the bridge. We went into town, looked around, and got a few things at the grocery. (This is where Perry Como lives, but we didn't see him.) Don again, tried to call Chip, unsuccessfully. We ate at McDonald's and then went back to the boat, arriving about seven thirty.

Anchored at Jupiter, FL – Distance traveled: 12 miles

November 11, 1987, Wednesday

A year-ago today, we were sitting in Deltaville Virginia. Today there was a blizzard with nine inches of snow in that area. We sure are glad to be in Florida.

It was cool today, but pleasant. We left Jupiter at eleven twenty and anchored for the night at Hobe Sound in Peck Lake around two fifteen. After we got the anchors down, we took the dinghy to shore and walked to the beach. The beach was nice, but not nearly as nice as the beaches in the Bahamas.

On the waterway today, we saw several boats headed south, and undoubtedly some will go on to the Bahamas for the winter. Based on our experience and conversations with other boaters who have cruised in the Bahamas, some in the winter and some in the summer, we believe that from May to the end of September is the best time to be there for these reasons: First, during the winter months, the high winds of the winter frontal systems prevent you from comfortably moving from place to place. Second, when the wind shifts to the west as a frontal system comes through, you lose the protection from waves that the islands provide and anchors may not hold. The Bahamaian anchorages are notorious for not holding well. Last of all, temperatures are less conducive to swimming and snorkeling. The summer heat is not as much of a problem as people probably think. Don hates being hot, but he was comfortable almost all the time we were there due to the constant breeze coming

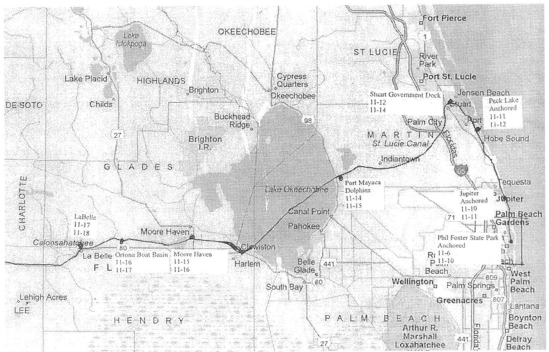

through the boat and from the cooling effect of the water. The biggest negative about being there in the summer is the possibility of a hurricane damaging or destroying your boat, but statistics show that the chances of that are very small.

The sunset tonight was pretty. We had Reuben sandwiches and salad, read, napped, and played gin rummy.

Anchored in Peck Lake, Hobe Sound, FL – Distance traveled: 13 miles

November 12, 1987, Thursday

We left Hobe Sound at ten and motored to Stuart, where we tied up at the Town Dock at twelve forty-five. Our Danforth anchor was fouled at Peck Lake and when we raised it this morning, it got bent. We spent some time cleaning the deck which was filthy again with mud from the bottom brought aboard by the anchor and chain.

Vern was in need of repairs again, and after we got docked, some folks tied up nearby, gave us a ride part way to First Mate, the place where Vern was made, and where he is frequently repaired. We walked the rest of the way. They replaced some parts in Vern while we waited. Hopefully, he is fixed for good. Tim, an employee at First Mate, gave us a lift back to the boat.

In the afternoon, we went for a walk and ate lunch at a Chinese restaurant. In the evening, we had popcorn and no dinner because we had eaten lunch about three o'clock.

In the evening, I called Anna, a lady whom we had met on *Pride* at Long Island, and who had told us to call her when we were in Stuart, if we needed anything. Her husband gave us a ride to the grocery and back to the boat.

Tied up at the Stuart town dock, Stuart, FL – Distance traveled: 13 miles

November 13, 1987, Friday

We returned our second GE CD player because of defects and afterwards browsed in several stores. We thought about going to a movie, but didn't because of the cost. About five o'clock we walked to the laundry. Doing the laundry took so long, we missed the Happy Taco Hour at the local restaurant. We ate dinner at a family-style place close by the laundry, and after that, we walked back to the boat and went to bed early.

Tied up at the Stuart town dock, Stuart, FL

ON THE OKEECHOBEE WATERWAY

November 14, 1987, Saturday

We got up early and changed the oil in the boat's diesel engine.

Some guys fishing on the dock gave us a couple of snook, and at nine thirty we left for Port Mayaca. We tied to the dolphins located there, at four fifteen. Dolphins are moorings consisting of a number of pilings driven into the bottom and connected above the water level. A boat named *Second Wind* rafted off us, and we visited with them until the mosquitoes came out.

Don made an excellent "fish boil" with the snook given to us at Stuart. After dinner, Sandy and Jerry, from *Second Wind*, came over to visit. They are from Maine and left there six weeks ago. We talked about our travels as well as favorite anchorages in the Chesapeake Bay. The trip today was scenic, with many beautiful waterfront properties to look at.

The weather was decent, and I sunbathed most of the afternoon. We were more at ease about this stretch of the trip since we had done it before.

Tied to dolphins at Port Mayaca, FL – Distance traveled: 33 miles

November 15, 1987, Sunday

It was a great day to cross Lake Okeechobee. We started our day's journey at eight. There was hardly any wind, so we motored across. *Second Wind* crossed with us. Shortly after they got out of the lock at Port Mayaca and started across, *Second Wind* discovered that they were taking on water through their stuffing box. We could relate to that, although we never took on very much water through our stuffing box. It turned out OK; Jerry was able to tighten it up and stop the flow. We followed them the rest of the way to Moore Haven in case the problem redeveloped.

Lake Okeechobee is plagued by a growth of vegetation on the surface of the lake. We call it lettuce because that is what it looks like—zillions of heads of Boston lettuce all bunched together at various places on the lake, depending on which way the wind is blowing. At times it seems like you are sailing through a garden. They are actually water hyacinths and some of them are blooming.

It was sunny as we motored through the Caloosahatchee Canal. We saw fewer alligators along the canal this time. In our opinion, the territory along the canal is the prettiest part of the Okeechobee waterway. We arrived at Moore Haven at three forty, and after we were situated at the dock, we had drinks on *Second Wind*. Later, Don made us dinner of egg foo yong and a fresh pineapple for dessert.

Don went to bed at nine. I stayed up and read a magazine that Jerry and Sandy gave us.
City dock, Moore Haven, FL – Distance traveled: 40 miles

November 16, 1987, Monday
We got up late, at eight thirty. I took a quick shower and then ran the sweeper since we were plugged into electric. Ted, the dockmaster, offered to take us to a grocery store, approximately a mile from the city dock. We accepted his offer and so did *Second Wind*.

When we got back to the boat, Don showered and when he finished, we visited the library, which was quite nice for a small community like Moore Haven. *Second Wind* left while we were at the library. We left at eleven thirty and headed for an anchorage near LaBelle, just off the waterway. The anchorage was crowded, so we stayed at a free dock at the west end of the Ortona Lock. That gave Don and me an opportunity to go ashore, visit with the lockmaster, and watch his operation. We met a man, John Cole, formerly of Columbus, Ohio, who had just moved to Lehigh Acres, Florida. We knew some of the same people in Columbus. He turned down my invitation for dinner on our boat. We had a fresh pot of beef stew and Key Lime pie—too bad for him—it was good! The mosquitoes were plentiful in the evening.
Ortona Lock, LaBelle, FL – Distance traveled: 19 miles

November 17, 1987, Tuesday
We left at nine fifty, motored nine miles, and at eleven thirty tied up at La Belle. It cost us $5.00 for the night. We had heard that La Belle was a nice place to visit.

After tying up, we went ashore. We met a couple, Bernie and Mary Lee, and during our conversation, learned that they happen to be friends of Barbara Edwards and her husband Jerry, who gave us our search light. Bernie and Mary Lee cruise in Florida on their sailboat, *Butterfly*, every winter and generally stay in this area, or on the West Coast of Florida, around Boca Grande.

We went to town, bought some groceries, went to the bank for cash, and then treated ourselves to milkshakes. We also browsed at a thrift shop and, after that, bought a pound of locally produced honey at a store specializing in local honey. In the evening, we met Barb and Burt, on *SeaHaack,* from Springfield, Ohio. We went aboard their boat to visit and share Bahama experiences. Don also shared his Key Lime pie. Burt knew several of our friends from Springfield. It's a small world that we live in.

It was sunny and in the 70s today. We enjoyed our day in LaBelle, and if we have the chance, will stop here again.
Tied up at La Belle, FL – Distance traveled: 9 miles

TIED TO DOLPHINS NEAR THE W.P. FRANKLIN LOCK
November 18, 1987, Wednesday

It rained most of the night. We bailed almost four inches of water out of the dinghy. Don fixed pancakes for breakfast. We left LaBelle under motor power heading for the W.P. Franklin Lock. We tied to dolphins near a campground by the lock. We showered at the campgrounds and then visited with some people, Ann and Jim, an elderly couple formerly from Ohio, who were camping in their RV. They invited us in for drinks and socializing. We got back to the boat late and ate chicken curry with noodles for dinner.

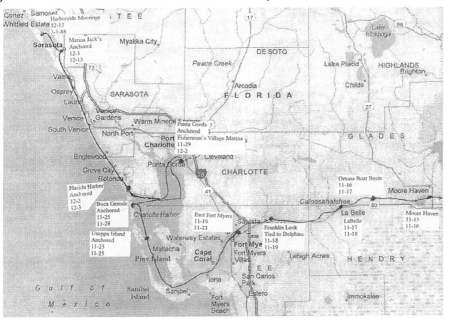

We spent the evening listening to the sounds of nature. The wild birds chattered and made weird sounds all night. I woke up at one in the morning and spent the next hour recording them with our tape recorder. The tape is OK, but doesn't do the birdcalls justice. Finally, at two I gave up and went back to bed. I'll never be a field reporter for Charles Kuralt's Sunday Morning show.

Tied to dolphins near the W.P. Franklin Lock, Okeehobee Waterway, FL – Distance traveled: 18 miles

THE W.P. FRANKLIN LOCK

November 19, 1987, Thursday

Manatees are frequently seen at the W.P. Franklin Lock. We got up at seven to go to the lock to see them. They are most often seen around seven thirty because it is their feeding time. We saw two, but barely. They probably won't show up in our pictures because their bodies don't contrast much with the water.

After we left the lock, we dinghied around in the area where our boat is tied up and saw two alligators, about 10 to 12 feet long. They were in the water about 100 feet away from us. We looked at the thin material our inflatable dinghy is made of, thought about their big teeth, realized that one chomp by one of them would put us in the water, and decided we had done enough dinghying. We returned to the boat.

We didn't leave the Franklin Lock until eleven because we had decided on only going a few miles today. We stopped for the day at Marina #31 in East Fort Myers, just five miles down the Caloosahatchee. We sure didn't want to go back to the Fort Myers Yacht Basin because of the way they treated us when we were there in January.

We were given a ride from the marina to the mall by a local lady, Margaret, who was going there. We spent an hour at the mall and then rode back to the marina with her after stopping at the grocery. At the mall, we bought another CD player. It's a Magnavox, and I know we'll enjoy it. We were without a CD player for a week and really missed it.

The evening was long because we had a serious discussion about me being "bossy and having to get my way."

Marina #31, East Fort Myers, FL – Distance traveled: 5 miles

November 20, 1987, Friday

We walked to the bus stop, and caught the eleven o'clock bus to Ft Myers so we could visit the Thomas Edison Home and Museum. It was fantastic, one of the most interesting museums we have ever visited. What a genius and persistent, hard-working person Edison was. We have certainly enjoyed and benefited from his inventions. We also visited Edison's garden and the winter home of Henry Ford, next door.

We ate a late lunch at the Snack House. It's an unusual place where all the waiters are elderly. They are also very friendly, and serve homemade jam. We walked around some more and eventually took the bus back to East Fort Myers and then walked to our marina. We encountered several street folks on the bus. The walk back to the marina was long, and by then it was dark. The traffic was terrible, and the cars and trucks raced by us; it was a bit scary. By the time we got back, at six thirty, we were very tired. We ate leftovers, and Don made chocolate-chip cookies for dessert. It was in the low 50s, so we used the electric heater.

At Marina #31, East Fort Myers, FL

November 21, 1987, Saturday

It's partly cloudy, windy and cool here, but I'm sure it is worse in Ohio. Today was the OSU vs Michigan game, which was played at Michigan. We heard that Coach Earl Bruce got fired this week, so it was his last game. We stayed at the dock because Don wanted to watch the game. I did a few chores, including cleaning the toaster oven and teapot. It was a good game, and OSU won 23-20. Don is happy. I bet all OSU fans are. I took a dinghy ride by myself for an hour and a half.

The people on the boat next to us at the dock, a Catalina 30, offered to let us use their car to go to the grocery. We accepted their offer and showed our appreciation by inviting them to join us for dinner. Don made lentil soup and cornbread. They came at six thirty, and we ate. At seven forty-five, when we felt the evening was just getting off to a good start, and the meal was barely over, they excused themselves and left, without any explanation. It was strange, and Don and I were both surprised. We can't figure it out. I know it wasn't because of the food; it was very good.

At Marina #31, East Fort Myers, FL

November 22, 1987, Sunday

It was sunny and less windy today, and the temperature was in the high 70s.

We got up and watched Sunday Morning with Charles Kuralt, while we enjoyed breakfast of English muffins and jelly. Don called Chip and finally, after several attempts over the past few weeks, reached him at his mom's. He was really glad to talk with him. Apparently, Chip has received our mail and is doing OK. He is planning to drive down to see us at Christmas time. I know Don would have been very disappointed if he didn't come and visit us.

After my lunch of avocado and tuna salad, we went to a place we thought would be suitable for me to cut Don's hair and trim his beard. Some people walked by and saw us, so it wasn't the best place after all. Don always gets embarrassed! We got out the kerosene heater and checked it over real well since we will be using it now when we are at anchor. It was too late to leave when we got finished with chores, so we decided to stay another night. We read and ate popcorn in the late afternoon, and at six thirty went to a restaurant to eat. It was a lousy deep fried meal. After dinner, we took a walk.

At Marina #31, East Fort Myers, FL

November 23, 1987, Monday

It was a long day. We left the marina shortly before nine and motored about 7 ½ hours to Useppa Island. We bumped bottom a couple of times. Once was when we were exploring an anchorage someone had written about in an article we read, and the other time we were right in the middle of the channel. After traveling 43 miles, we dropped the hook at Useppa Island, directly across from Cabbage Key. We stayed on board. Don was perturbed about running aground in the middle of the channel. I don't think any of our groundings have caused any damage to the boat, but it does stop us abruptly, and running aground in the middle of the channel does make us question whether we can rely on the charts. He made dinner of enchiladas and lime Jell-O. A man by the name of Art, aboard a 27' Island Packet sailboat, called *Jolie,* came over in his dinghy to visit, and we invited him for dinner. He is in his 70s and by himself on his boat. He is a former Pam Am pilot. We enjoyed his visit. (He didn't rush off after eating.)

Anchored at Useppa Island, FL

November 24, 1987, Tuesday

Today was sunny with an easterly wind of 15-20 knots, and the temperature was in the high 70s.

We are pretty comfortable where we are anchored, so we are going to spend another night here. The only adverse circumstance is that we do some rockin' and rollin' due to the wakes of boats passing by on the waterway. We visited on board Art's boat and then explored the private island of Useppa. It is a luxurious, well-maintained place for wealthy people who own vacation homes on the island. The style of architecture is from the 1920s. We really enjoyed seeing it and were glad no one asked us to leave. Later, I re-visited Cabbage Key while Don stayed on the boat and read. We both enjoyed the day. Don fixed an early dinner. Today I started a new eating program for us. First, we will have a light breakfast, then a light lunch, including one piece of fruit, and in the evening, a normal dinner, including a dessert.

We sat in the cockpit until the stars came out and shined brightly. We decided that Don is going to play English Literature teacher, and I am going to spend the next few weeks reading *David Copperfield* while Don looks over my shoulder. Don loves reading the books written by Charles Dickens and thinks that I would also like them.

Anchored at Useppa Island, FL

November 25, 1987, Wednesday

It was sunny and warm with a high of 72°.

We left Useppa Island at nine thirty and motored 2 ½ hours to Boca Grande, which is located on Gasparilla Island at the entrance to Charlotte Harbor. As we had done in February, we dropped the anchor in the bayou across from the Pink Elephant restaurant. Then we tied a line to the stern of the boat and took it in the dinghy to the mangroves and tied that end around a strong healthy mangrove branch. We adjusted the lines so that we were pretty

close to the mangroves and didn't obstruct boat traffic in the anchorage. It took us over a half-hour to get situated. After that, we took a short break and observed the movement of the boat to be sure that we had it right before going out to sightsee once more in Boca Grande. We bought groceries for our Thanksgiving meal and then went for a dinghy ride in the canals and bayous. We also walked to the library and did some reading. We got back at five thirty.

We ate leftovers and then invited Debbie and Brad on *Between the Sheets*, who were anchored next to us, over for socializing and cards. They are from Orlando and keep their Caliber 33 sailboat in the Saint Petersburg area, taking short cruises when they can. We enjoyed their company. They seemed fascinated about our trip and future plans.

Anchored and tied to mangroves at Boca Grande, FL – Distance traveled: 8 miles

November 26, 1987, Thursday, Thanksgiving

It was a day of rest and relaxation in a beautiful setting. We ate breakfast and then set out in the dinghy to continue exploring Gasparilla Island. We went to the public beach and looked for shells. The islands on Florida's West Coast, from Sanibel Island up to here, seem to have more than their share of pretty ones. We walked on the bike path to Banyan St. to take a picture of the fascinating banyan trees. The gulf was calm and the water, pretty clear.

Boca Grande has become my very favorite place in Florida. It's off the beaten path, quiet, laid back, and beautiful. There is almost no vehicle traffic or noise. It is between the cities of Sarasota and Fort Myers, both of which are about 50 miles away by road. It doesn't have any special attractions for children or night life for young adults, and so it doesn't get many tourists of that type. I think that if we ever decide to spend our winters in Florida, this is where we will be. We would enjoy having a small cruising sailboat here. This is the best cruising area in Florida. We would also enjoy a dinghy and bikes or mopeds.

Don made an excellent Thanksgiving meal; Cornish game hens, dressing, gravy and carrots, warm rolls and butter. Art, our new friend on the boat *Jolie*, joined us for dinner and brought peaches for our dessert. We wanted to include him for this holiday meal because he is by himself on his boat. He seemed appreciative and stayed until nine. After he left, Don and I played a hand of gin rummy. I won! We also spent some time reading about places to visit in Charlotte Harbor and looked at the charts for the area.

Anchored and tied to mangroves at Boca Grande, FL

November 27, 1987, Friday

We decided to spend another day here at Boca Grande. Art carries a bike on his 27-foot Island Packet Sailboat, and he loaned it to me, so I could explore the island. Later, Don and I had a picnic lunch at the library's "garden reading room." Art came over for dinner and socializing in the evening. Don made bean soup and chocolate pudding.

Art told us about a bad experience he had in the Bahamas, which I think is worth recording. Like us, his point of entry in the Bahamas was Lucaya, and he went to the same marina we did. The marina was mostly vacant, as it was when we were there, and he pulled into a slip in a part of the marina where there were no other boats tied up. He was tired from his all night crossing and wanted to get some sleep. He cleared customs and then settled down for a nap. Soon, a power boat came in with three Bahamians aboard and tied up at the slip next to him. Their radio was on and playing loud music. Art went above and asked them to turn the music down, or if they wanted to play it so loudly, to move to another dock where it wouldn't bother anybody. After Art went below, they turned the music up as loud as they could. Art was so enraged he got out a starter's pistol he had on board. It only shot blanks, and therefore wasn't dangerous, but it looked like a regular pistol. He went above with it and waived it around at the guys who were playing the music. They shouted for the dockmaster to call the police, which he did. Art was arrested and taken to jail. The jail was small, hot, poorly ventilated and crowded with Bahamian lawbreakers. He was charged with menacing threats and also with failing to declare the gun when he cleared customs. The incident cost him several thousand dollars for attorney fees, and for bond money that he forfeited.

His story is the second incident we have heard about involving people we know where a boater produced a gun to deal with a situation, and it ended up badly for him. We have also heard the following story with its bad outcome, which was supposed to have happened while we were in the Bahamas. A boat with a couple on board, anchored in Nassau, was boarded by two Bahamians in the wee hours of the morning. The Bahamians claimed to be police officers. The husband produced a gun because he didn't think they were policemen and figured that they intended to rob them. The Bahamians were not police officers. They convinced the skipper he shouldn't use the gun, and then took it away from him, shot him with it, raped the wife, stole some things, and left. The couple was unable to get medical assistance at the boat, and the rest of the couple's night was spent getting the wounded husband ashore in their dinghy and to a hospital for medical help. It was not a good night! Maybe the result would have been about the same if the husband hadn't produced a gun, but it sure didn't help him. These three stories make us question whether it is wise to carry guns on board. We have two, but we will be very reluctant to get them out in any hostile situation.

Today, there are 32 boats in our anchorage. Obviously, Boca Grande is a popular Thanksgiving weekend cruising destination.

Anchored and tied to mangroves at Boca Grande, FL

November 28, 1987, Saturday

It was sunny, but a little cooler today. A cold front is expected sometime this weekend.

We left Boca Grande at eight fifteen and motored to Burnt Store Marina on the eastern shore of Charlotte Harbor to look around at the facility. Several boaters have told us that it's nice, and we thought we should consider it as a possible place to stay for the winter. The daily rate is $0.75 per foot, but the monthly rate per foot is only $4.95 per foot. We'll be paying $7 per foot at Longboat Key. It is a nice marina, but there was nothing close by. Shopping is ten miles away, and since we don't have a car, it's not the place for *Robin Lee*.

After spending a couple of hours looking over Burnt Store and buying fuel, we left and motored to the town of Punta Gorda, which is across the Peace River from the town of Charlotte Harbor at the upper end of the harbor. We anchored west of the Peace River Bridge at about five o'clock.

Don made salmon tetrazzini. We had to use the kerosene heater for a while in the evening. I've read three chapters of *David Copperfield*.

It isn't the most comfortable anchorage. I am going to sleep on the starboard berth.

Anchored at Punta Gorda, FL – Distance traveled: 34 miles

November 29, 1987, Sunday

We moved the boat from where we had anchored to Fisherman's Village Marina in Punta Gorda, a distance of only a couple of miles, and arrived there at eleven o'clock.

We had a busy day with our usual errands and dockside chores. We got the boat situated, plugged into their electricity, hooked up our hose to their water spigot, took showers, did laundry and explored the town to see what was available. We found a nice, quiet, clean, cheap little place to have a meal out, and it's run by friendly people. They serve spaghetti and meatballs—all you can eat—for $3.95. I just had salad and garlic bread. The little shops at the mall were well-stocked for Christmas, but we didn't see many shoppers.

Using Art's bike made us realize that it would be nice to have bicycles to ride while we are at Long Boat Key, if we can find cheap ones. I called a couple of ads in the local paper regarding used bikes, and both owners have offered to bring the bikes over tomorrow for us to look at.

This marina has cable TV. We got a cable from the marina office to use to hook up, and our TV works great. We get 15 very clear channels. The only problem is finding something we want to watch. TV just isn't our cup of tea. It never has been and never will be.

I called Mom and Shelly in the evening. It was good to visit with both.
At Fisherman's Village Marina, Punta Gorda, FL – Distance traveled: 2 miles

November 30, 1987, Monday

At ten, a man brought his folding bike for us to look at. He wanted $60, but I offered him $40–he took $45. It is in pretty good condition. We rode it to the grocery and around town.

We rented a VCR so that we could review and transfer our camcorder video from the 20-minute tapes it uses onto two-hour tapes. We also rented a movie to watch on the VCR after we were done with the transferring. We loaded our groceries, the VCR, and the tapes onto the bike and took them to the boat. We also spent time browsing at a used bookstore and then went back to the boat when it started to get dark. We're convinced that the bike was a good investment.

After dinner of ham and baked beans, we looked at the other bike. It looked brand new; we bought it for $25 and think we got a real deal. Don is proud of it. He says that it is the only bike he has ever owned.

We finished the reviewing and transferring of our video tapes at one thirty in the morning. While working on them, Don made a cherry pie, and by the time he was done with the transferring job, we had eaten half the pie.
At Fisherman's Village Marina, Punta Gorda, FL

December 1, 1987, Tuesday

The first thing we did this morning was watch the rented movie, called *The Sunshine Boys*, a cute movie with Walter Matthau and George Burns. We then went back to the shopping center to return the VCR and tape. Don met a lady in the store who said she couldn't get the rented VCR working. Don and I offered to ride our bikes to her place and work on it for her. Little did we know that we would spend most of the day there. She served us a nice lunch for our trouble, but it was really our pleasure. That's just one of the many ways we meet interesting people along the way. We did have time to go to the park and board walk, but when we arrived at the library at five o'clock, they were closing.

We got back to the boat at six, and since it was late, we decided to eat out at the friendly little restaurant. This time it wasn't as good, but they sure make excellent garlic toast and cinnamon rolls. Don made peanut butter cookies in the evening.
At Fisherman's Village Marina, Punta Gorda, FL

December 2, 1987, Wednesday

We left Fisherman's Village at ten thirty and motored six hours to a cove off the Intracoastal Waterway, a mile and a half north of the bridge to Gasparilla Island and Boca Grande. We anchored in the cove for the night.
At anchor in a cove near Cape Haze, FL – Distance traveled: 33 miles

December 3, 1987, Thursday

We left the cove where we were anchored at eight o'clock and motored to Sarasota. We anchored north of Marina Jack's and near Martin and Mary's condominium at three fifteen.
Anchored on the north side of Marina Jack's, Sarasota, FL – Distance traveled: 42 miles

CHAPTER TEN
SARASOTA, FL and LONGBOAT KEY, FL
Dec. 4, 1987 – Feb. 29, 1988

272

December 4-12, 1987

Since arriving back in Sarasota, we have been "on the go." We have been busy doing errands, sightseeing, and visiting with the Gilberts and the Eilers. Both couples are really fun to be with. We have also spent a lot of money buying clothes, boat parts, eating out, and I had my hair cut. However, it has been a lot of fun.

On Sunday, (the 6th) we went with the Eilers to the afternoon performance of Handel's Messiah at the Van Wezel Performing Arts Hall in Sarasota.

On Monday (the 7th) we went to Saint Petersburg and Tarpon Springs with the Eilers.

One-day, Mary and I went for a ride in the dinghy and stopped for lunch at O'Learys. Don stayed home that day and made fudge.

We have eaten with Martin and Mary several times, trying new dishes, and two or three nights with Hope and Harry. Harry has gained weight and Don really isn't doing well with his eating, so I'll bet that he will gain weight also.

We have hardly had time to rest, which is totally different for us. We haven't stayed home on the boat one day since arriving in Sarasota.

Saturday, (the 12th), the last day before leaving the anchorage north of Marina Jacks, was especially fun. Mary, Martin, Don and I left the condo at seven in the morning and walked about two miles over to the "Buttery" at Saint Armand's Circle for breakfast. Martin treated us. We window shopped and after that walked back. We rested for 30 minutes at their condo and then went to a movie. It was a picture at a downtown Sarasota theater about the artist Paul Gauguin.

Hope and Harry bought a new condo, but can't move in until February. They sold their boat, *Passages,* and have rented a beautifully furnished apartment. They are having an open-house on December 15; we got an invitation and plan on going.

The weather has been very good except for some coolness in the evenings. It is windy at times, but nothing greater than 20 knots.

Anchored on the north side of Marina Jack's, Sarasota, FL

December 13, 1987, Sunday

Today we moved from the anchorage in front of Mary and Martin's condo to Harbourside Moorings Marina on Longboat Key where we plan to spend the winter. The rent is only $7.00 per foot per month, which amounts to $210 per month for us. We arrived at the marina shortly before noon and spent the rest of the day getting settled in. We hooked up to their water and plugged into their electric. The marina has cable TV so we connected to that also. We hosed down the boat, ran the sweeper, and tidied up below. In addition, we scrubbed the anchor lines which had become dirty from the muddy anchorages. We also marked the anchor line at ten-foot intervals to help us know how much anchor line we have let out. Finally, at seven o'clock, Don made nachos for dinner, and we watched a little TV while we enjoyed them. This sure is a nice place, and I am confident we will enjoy our stay here.

We were welcomed to our long-term location by a beautiful pinkish purple sky at sunset tonight. We are happy we will be stationary awhile and are looking forward to a restful time here.

Later in the evening we rode to the shower house on our bikes. I cut Don's hair and trimmed his beard with new electric clippers I bought while shopping with Mary. They work great.

Don finally reached Chip by telephone and learned that Chip and his girlfriend, Heather, will be joining us for ten days, beginning on December 28th, Don's 49th birthday.

I have sent information to Shelly about our new location and I hope she will be able to visit us also. We are looking forward to seeing family and friends during the holidays and entertaining them on the boat. I called Norbert, Don's cousin, and also Mary Gilbert, to let them know that we are settled in and to give them our dock number.

Docked at Harbourside Moorings, Longboat Key, FL – Distance traveled: 7 miles

December 14–19, 1987, Monday-Saturday

An entire week has passed, and I have been so busy that I haven't bothered to write down what we have done.

Monday:

I did the laundry here at the marina.

Tuesday:

Don worked on the rigging and replaced the bearings in the roller furling apparatus with the help of a live-aboard in the marina who is knowledgeable about such things because he used to work for a company that built sailboats. I had the chore of getting the dinghy bottom clean. The growth was pretty thick. We went to Hope and Harry's open house and Christmas party in the evening. Martin and Mary provided our transportation. It was very nice, and we met several people.

Wednesday:

We had a phone installed on the boat. Our number is 383-8202. It seems strange to talk on the phone from the boat. We also went to the dentist on Wednesday with Martin in Bradenton. Both of us were glad to get our teeth cleaned. Don had a filling replaced.

Friday:

In the afternoon, Seth and Roxanne, a couple on a boat in the marina, came over to discuss charts of the Bahamas.

Later, Hope and Harry came, with Mary and Martin, and the six of us went to dinner at Fast Eddies Restaurant on the pier at Anna Maria Island, about ten miles north of here.

Saturday:

In the evening, Don and I went out for pizza with Bill and Gail, neighbors in the marina. We drove by the area where the first Sarasota Christmas boat parade was being formed. Lots of people showed up to watch it. Cars lined the sides of the road for miles.

Docked at Harbourside Moorings, Longboat Key, FL

December 20 1987-January 1, 1988

During this period, Don's family, my family, and our kids all came to Sarasota for the holidays. I was too busy to keep the journal during this time, but I will recap the activities now.

On Monday (Dec 21st), we served breakfast on the boat to Barbara and Lee Headlee (Don's sister and brother-in-law), Carol and David Scott (Don's other sister and brother-in-law), and Norbert and Barbara Chase (Don's cousin and his wife). Don's sisters and their husbands arrived on the 20th to spend the holidays at the Aloha-Kai resort, which is managed by Norbert and Barbara. Yes, amazingly, we had eight people on our little boat and ate breakfast comfortably. Of course, everybody had to stay in their place; there was no room to move around.

We spent the day and stayed all night at the Aloha Kai with Carol and David, and their son Craig. It was fun, and we caught up on all the family news.

We continued to stay at Aloha-Kai with family until everybody went home. We enjoyed spending time with everyone. Don of course made some excellent meals. Sister Carol helped, and we all ate together on several evenings.

On Christmas day, we all got together at Norbert's for breakfast and a traditional Christmas dinner. It was a lovely day, with way too much good food. Don helped Craig learn to operate Craig's new VCR. Our Christmas gift for both of us was a portable two-burner electric stove. We got candy from Barb and Lee, and a new Gershwin CD from Carol and David.

On December 26th, my mom, Randy, and both of Randy's kids, Danielle and Nick, arrived.

Shelly and her friend, David, also came to visit, arriving on the day-after Christmas. They drove straight through from Urbana, Ohio—19 hours of driving. We had a traditional meal of fried chicken, mashed potatoes and gravy, broccoli and a dessert of cookies and candy.

December 28th was Don's 49th birthday. He had hoped that Chip would be here to help him celebrate it, but Chip didn't make it because he was delayed by heavy snows in Colorado where he was skiing during his Christmas break from Kent State. All flights out of Denver were canceled because of the snow. Chip re-booked a flight for Wednesday the 30th. Sister Carol and Randy put together a birthday dinner for Don with one of his favorite dishes, chicken vatelle and, of course, we had cake and ice cream. I bought Don a CD; it is called *Winter Solstice*, by Wyndham Hill.

During the day, Don and I took Nick to the marina to show him our boat, and I took him out in the dinghy. We also ran errands. Since we have the use of Mom's car, we are getting as many of our errands done as we can.

On December 29th, I went to Disney World with Shelly, David, Nick and Danielle. We had fun, but the place was packed. The lines were very long for everything; rides, eats, bathrooms, and gift shops. I am glad that I don't go there often.

On December 30th, Don and I took Nick and Danielle for the day. We showed the boat to Danielle and did some more exploring in the dinghy. Nick was more interested than Danielle. Nick is a happy-go-lucky six year old. Everything is funny to him! He is so cute. In the afternoon, we took the kids to the Jungle Gardens. Both enjoyed that experience, especially the petting zoo area. Then we went to the airport to get Chip. We were told that his plane was still in Raleigh and wouldn't arrive in Sarasota until nine o'clock, so we left and went home for dinner. Chip and Heather finally arrived, and we had a good visit before going to bed at one in the morning.

On New Year's Eve, I took Shelly and David to the marina so they could see our boat and the marina. Then I took them to the Longboat Key Club with the ocean-front swimming pool and beach facilities to which we have access and free transportation. We also looked at the shopping areas near the marina and at Saint Armand's Circle. We had lunch at poolside and sunbathed awhile. I was glad to be able to spend some quality time just with them. I don't know when I'll see them next. On the way home, I showed them the huge CD store (Leche Mares) and at Happy Hour, we all went to eat shrimp at Captain Kirk's. They sure offer a good deal; for $2, you can have a basket of two dozen fresh shrimp. Randy ordered oysters on the half-shell. We had a big meal of linguini and clam sauce that night and a tossed salad.

We spent most of the evening at Carol and David's condo while everyone else went out to celebrate New Year's Eve.

Mom looked after Nick and Danielle and another little girl whose parents went out with Randy, Craig, Shelly and David. Heather and Chip stayed on the beach and went to a beach party with a campfire. To celebrate New Year's Eve, we watched a couple of movies on video tape that Carol and David had rented.

On January 1st, New Year's Day, we had beautiful weather. It was in the high 70s and sunny. We all relaxed by the pool, except Mom and Randy and the kids. They left at eleven thirty to drive back to Ohio. The rest of us ate a traditional New Year's Day dinner of pork roast, sauerkraut, black eyed peas, mashed potatoes and gravy at Carol and David's condo. Norbert and Barb joined us, so we had 13 people.

After dinner, everyone began packing to leave. It was a wonderful vacation for all of us. From December 21 until New Year's Day we stayed at the condos, which gave us a break from boat life.

Robin Lee **Docked at Harbourside Moorings, Longboat Key, FL. We stayed at Aloha Kai, on Siesta Key.**

January 2-11, 1988

Chip and Heather, his girlfriend, have been here since December 30th and will be leaving tomorrow, January 12th. We have enjoyed the time we have shared with them. On January 4th, we sailed seven miles to Sarasota and anchored out at Martin and Mary's. We made the seven mile return trip to the marina on January 6th. While anchored, we visited Martin and Mary and also took Chip and Heather to the John Ringling Museum and Art Gallery. The weather was cold, but sunny, during this time. The "northers" never stopped. On Wednesday, the 6th, when we returned to our home dock, Slip I-3,

CHIP, HEATHER AND ROBIN

we had the worst docking experience ever. I dropped the line, and the wind blew us into the next slip over. Don was very upset with me.

Unfortunately, we had lousy weather for the rest of the time Chip and Heather were with us. We spent a couple of days relaxing with them at the Longboat Key Club, the hotel owned by the company that owns the marina and to which we have free access. We used their pool and walked on the beach, but on Friday, because the weather was so bad, we rented a car and took them to De Soto National Park. After that we showed them Sarasota's downtown area. Chip and Heather shopped some and then Hope and Harry, along with Mary and Martin, met us, and the eight of us had pizza at Coolies.

On Sunday, January 10th, Chip and Heather got up early and drove to Disney World. Don and I stayed home. Dortha May and Johnny Moffitt, the couple from Dublin we stayed with for a couple of nights on Tavernier Key, stopped to visit us. Don served them a dinner of cornbread and bean soup. They seemed to enjoy the day visiting us on our boat. It was very rainy and miserable outside. They came at two o'clock and left at eight. The kids got back from Disney World at ten. They said they enjoyed the day, and because of the weather, they didn't have long lines. Prior to turning the car in, we went to Captain Kirk's Seafood Bar for baskets of fresh "peel and eat shrimp."

Tonight, Monday, January 11th, is their last night with us and Don fixed one of Chip's favorite meals, veal parmesan with prosciutto ham. We had spaghetti with it.

We taught Heather how to play euchre soon after her arrival, and she learned to play well. We played quite a bit while they were here. Don and I were partners against Chip and Heather. Tonight, we played the championship game. Don and I managed to win, but they were tough competition.

Docked at Harbourside Moorings, Longboat Key, FL

January 12-16, 1988, Tuesday through Saturday

Today, Saturday, January 16th the high was 75°, and it was partly cloudy and windy most of the day.

Orchid Boat called a few days ago. They will be coming to Sarasota in February. I invited them to visit us when they come.

Today, I applied for a job at a liquor store and deli in a small shopping center within walking distance from the marina. I am also going to submit papers to get my nursing license transferred to Florida. Another month's dock rent is due soon. We could use some income.

Don is going to Ohio for a few days to do our income tax returns. Last year, he found it difficult to do them down here, when the information was up there.

Yesterday, Friday, January 15th, Newt came down from Tarpon Springs at noon, and we spent a couple of hours visiting and later he took us to Sears so Don could get a few things for his trip north to Ohio. On the way home, we stopped at Captain Kirk's Seafood Bar, and then drove by a few local points of interest to show Newt. We also stopped at Gilbert's to introduce Newt to Martin and Mary. Newt told a few jokes and did some magic tricks for them. It was fun, and the Gilberts were surprised to see us. We left there at seven thirty and came back to the boat for a Chinese dinner. We told Newt about our experiences during the past year, and he told us about his. Then we had ice cream sundaes. Newt left at eleven thirty, and we went to bed. We were tired, but also keyed-up. It was great fun to visit with Newt. I gave him the cross-stitch project I had made for him. He was delighted and seemed very appreciative of the time involved in making it.

Today we got up late and Don made our breakfast of orange juice, coffee, and a great grapefruit Norbert gave us. Don re-rigged the chain on the dinghy anchor and on the wishbone anchor. He also adjusted the brakes on his bike. I did the laundry and packed all the clothes he is taking to Ohio. He was anxious and excited about going.

Hope and Harry came at 4:30 to pick us up. We got to the airport in plenty of time. Don's flight left on time. I watched him get on the plane. The Eilers and I then drove to K-Mart, and I bought a white shirt and some yarn. Then we went to Bob Evans to eat. I forgot to mention that I turned down the job at the liquor store and deli and accepted a job offer at Publix as a bagging clerk. I have to wear a white shirt and dark pants to work as a "bagger." I start Monday and work from eleven in the morning until eight in the evening.

I got quite a few things done after Hope and Harry dropped me off at nine o'clock. I finished the cross-stitch project for the boat *Pride* and worked on my nursing license application for the state of Florida. I also wrote a letter to *Orchid Boat* and sewed the power squadron flag, which the wind had frayed. I put away the laundry and then watched TV. At eleven thirty, I called Don. He made it to Ohio OK, and our old bridge gang picked him up. They went to Carol and David's and played bridge. He said he missed me, and I reassured him that it was very lonely here on Robin Lee without him.

Robin Lee **Docked at Harbourside Moorings, Longboat Key, FL with Robin aboard. Don in Ohio**

January 17, 1988, Sunday

Today began at ten thirty. I slept well. The heater was on 750 watts, and it kept me warm. It sure seemed strange not having Don here to wake up with. I am used to his TLC when it comes to breakfast in bed, so consequently I didn't know how to act. I had a glass of juice and called Mary Gilbert. She said she would be coming over in an hour to visit. I hurried around and rode the bike up to take a shower, and Mary arrived shortly after I got back to the boat. We visited until two o'clock. She brought me a white blouse to wear at Publix. It fits, so now I have two, and Don is supposed to bring me an old one from Columbus.

When she left, Mary took me for a ride in her car and dropped me off about two miles south of the marina on Gulf of Mexico Drive, so I could get some exercise by walking back. It was cloudy and sprinkling lightly, but I had a nice walk. In 30 minutes, I was back in the vicinity of the marina. I stopped at Publix and bought some groceries and then returned to the boat. On the walk back along Gulf of Mexico Drive, I found a really nice spot at a new condo development. It is a park-like area with three small waterfalls and two foot bridges and several wrought-iron benches. It is a beautiful place to sit and enjoy nature. I am anxious to show it to Don when he returns.

I worked on the afghan for a while, and then did a load of clothes. While the clothes were in the washer, I took a bike ride to mail a letter to *Orchid Boat*. I stopped at a small dress shop and found a cute tee shirt for Don. It says, "If the anchor drags, or we go aground, or if the engine quits just as we are crashing into the dock, you can bet it's my fault." I know he will love it.

The ocean had 3-4 foot waves crashing onto the shore. It was dramatic. The sun came out for a short time and that made it even better. The high today was in the low 70s, and the winds were out of the SW at about 10-20 knots. That is probably why the waves were 3-4 feet. I miss being with my guy, but I sure enjoy the beauty of winter here at Longboat Key.

I ironed my clothes for tomorrow and ironed the cross-stitch piece I made for *Pride*. I wrote Peggy and Ron a letter to send to them with the cross-stitch piece. Around eight I called Elaine and Larry from the boat *MissBehavin'*. We met them at Marsh Harbour, and I knew she was planning on coming to the West Coast to see her brother, so I wanted her to stop and visit if she had time. I gave her our phone number. She and Larry seemed to be appreciative of my call; we talked about ten minutes. I filled them in on all the Marsh Harbor news, including the *Hawkeye* shooting involving *PamWon*, and about Peter and Michelle breaking up.

Robin Lee Docked at Harbourside Moorings, Longboat Key, FL with Robin aboard. Don in Ohio

January 18, 1988, Monday

I got up early so that I could get myself ready and report to Publix by eleven o'clock. The first three hours were boring. We watched films on store development and packaging, and we filled out forms. From two o'clock to three o'clock, I bagged and carried out groceries and brought in carts. My lunch break was from three to four. I rode my bike to the boat and ate leftover potato salad and tomatoes. It took me about six minutes to ride the bike back to Publix. Between four and seven, I bagged and carried out groceries. The customers were friendly. There are many northern vacationers here. Larry, the manager, also had me "front" items on both sides of aisle 3. Fronting is where you move the products to the front of the shelf, so they are easily visible and accessible.

I did a lot of bending and stooping, and therefore, got a lot of aerobic exercise. I made $2.50 in tips and my pay from Publix for the day will be $34. That is better than the pay I made as a waitress at Dalt's restaurant in Columbus. I was tired and hungry when I got home. I ate leftovers, watched a little TV, worked on the afghan, and made some telephone calls, including one to my friend, Pam, in Columbus. I invited her to come to visit while Don is gone. Hope called

BAGGING GROCERIES AT PUBLIX

around midnight and we talked until two in the morning.

Robin Lee Docked at Harbourside Moorings, Longboat Key, FL with Robin aboard. Don in Ohio

January 19, 1988, Tuesday

Mary and I played today until I had to get ready to go to work. We ate breakfast at a place at Holmes Beach on Anna Maria Island. We sat outside and could see the gulf; it was great. The sun was out and there was a strong breeze from the south. We drove to Fast Eddies to take a walk and look around. On the way back to the boat we stopped to do a few errands and mail *Pride* their cross-stitch and letter. We also stopped at Barnett Bank, and I got $100 from our account. After that we stopped at Coquina Beach and swung on the beachside playground equipment. Then we went to the Longboat Key Club for lunch by the pool. It was a nice day, but the wind was at least 20 knots. Mary dropped me off, and I got ready for work. Our neighbor Cindy stopped over, and we talked.

I didn't leave for work until three fifty, yet by riding my bike I got there before four. I was busy the entire four hours at work and am convinced that I am getting really good exercise at my job. I spent $7.50 on meals today and made $19.50 in pay and tips.

When I got home, I ate, watched some TV, talked briefly to Hope, worked on the afghan, and then read before going to bed. I am having a difficult time getting through *David Copperfield*.

***Robin Lee* Docked at Harbourside Moorings, Longboat Key, FL with Robin aboard. Don in Ohio**

January 20, 1988, Wednesday

I stayed on board the boat until it was time to go to work and spent the morning and early afternoon cleaning, mostly in the galley and the head. Then I gave all the drawers a good cleaning and lined them with new paper. I would love to do some painting in the boat, but I'm sure Don wouldn't want me to cover the teak. I would also like to apply some varnish, but that's a lot of work and I'm sure I won't. I bagged groceries from four until eight.

Don called after work, and I was excited to talk to him. He was at my mom's house, and I talked with her also. I miss Don! He misses me too! We were made for each other. I read until I went to bed at one in the morning. I made $1.25 in tips and $17 in my paycheck.

It was a beautiful day until late evening when it got cloudy and cool due to a cold front. The temperature was 80° most of the day. Rain is coming soon.

***Robin Lee* Docked at Harbourside Moorings, Longboat Key, FL with Robin aboard. Don in Ohio**

January 21, 1988, Thursday

I was supposed to go to work at eleven o'clock. I got up early and did a load of laundry at the marina laundromat because I needed a clean shirt for work. I finished the washing and drying at about ten, but by then it was pouring down. Since the laundromat is at the opposite end of our big marina, close to a quarter of a mile from our boat, I called Publix because I would have been soaked getting to the boat to get dressed and soaked again riding my bike to the store. The dock boy gave me a couple of large garbage sacks to put over me and my laundry. Because I got tired of waiting at the laundry area, I rode my bike back to the boat in the rain as quickly as possible. I got warmed up, fixed some popcorn for lunch, and sat around for two hours waiting for the rain to stop. It was a real downpour. I talked briefly with Mary. She had been at Hope and Harry's new place to clean and help them move in. She told me their apartment is really nice.

I clocked in at work at two and took a break from four thirty until five, and then worked from five to eight. I was busy the whole time. I really like four things about this job; 1) the people and helping them, 2) I am busy, so it doesn't seem like a long day, 3) I get lots of exercise, and 4) I get paid for it. It's a fun way to pass the time until the winter weather ends and we go cruising again. I made $1.75 in tips.

The rain stopped shorty after I clocked out, and so I walked home around eight thirty and fixed a grilled cheese sandwich. I also had Kool-Aid and later, a little ice cream for dessert. It will be good when Don gets back, and I have real meals again. Tonight, I wrote cards, watched TV, and did one row on my afghan before going to bed.

***Robin Lee* Docked at Harbourside Moorings, Longboat Key, FL with Robin aboard. Don in Ohio**

January 22, 1988, Friday

The weather was cool and windy, but sunny.

This morning there was condensation inside the boat, and I was cold. I got up and turned on the heater, fixed a lettuce and tuna salad for my lunch, and made my breakfast. I worked ten to two and made $4.25 in tips. I took a break to eat, and then rode my bike to the post office. I got two letters, and Don got two boxes of things for the boat, a Y-valve handle to replace our broken one and anchor line markers. I worked 3-7 and made $3.oo more in tips. That's almost $1/hour in tips for the day.

After work, I bought a few cleaning supplies at Publix and ate a container of ice cream, before coming back to the boat on my bike. I did a little straightening up, talked with Sister Carol, Shelly, and Don. They all had dinner at Carol's house. I was glad to talk with them. I had another quiet evening knitting and watching TV, and for a bedtime snack, I had a cup of Café Vienna and a piece of carrot cake.

Robin Lee **Docked at Harbourside Moorings, Longboat Key, FL with Robin aboard. Don in Ohio**

January 23, 1988, Saturday

Today was cool, calm, and pretty, but became overcast beginning at two o'clock.

I slept in, and it was wonderful. About ten thirty, I went to the Laundromat and did a load of dark clothes; I needed pants washed before three so I could go to work.

Work was fine today. I was busy nonstop, from three to seven. I only made $2 in tips, but that's OK; I don't expect tips.

The remarkable thing about today was that I felt like cooking. For lunch, I ate tomato soup and a PB sandwich. For dinner, I made a tossed salad and cooked some buttered carrots and grilled a steak. I had a glass of Gatorade, bread and butter, and a cup of Café Vienna, lots of calories, but actually that is the only big meal I've had all week. I called Pam tonight. She is going to come and visit if she can arrange it. I knitted and listened to music.

Robin Lee **Docked at Harbourside Moorings, Longboat Key, FL with Robin aboard. Don in Ohio**

January 24, 1988, Sunday

The day was cloudy and windy. I cleaned from eleven in the morning until midnight. I also did the bed linens and extra laundry.

Robin Lee **Docked at Harbourside Moorings, Longboat Key, FL with Robin aboard. Don in Ohio**

January 25, 1988, Monday

Monday I finished the cleaning of the V-berth area at noon. We had a wind shift, and the rain which had started in the night, ended. I had to add extra dock lines because the wind was really strong—about 30-35 knots steady out of the North. When I got finished with cleaning, I showered, ate and then went to work. I was pretty busy. At eight, when I got off work, I bought groceries and then came back to the boat. The wind was still very strong, and I rode the bike carrying six bags of groceries; it was hard to do. The dock lights are out and getting aboard wasn't easy either; a neighbor offered me assistance. Don and Shelly called me in the evening; it is really bad in Ohio, cold and snowy.

Robin Lee **Docked at Harbourside Moorings, Longboat Key, FL with Robin aboard. Don in Ohio**

January 26-30, 1988, Tuesday-Saturday

Pam was to arrive at eleven on Tuesday morning, but due to bad weather in Ohio, she was delayed until three thirty. Cindy, who is living on a boat at the end of our dock, gave me a ride to the airport to pick her up. It was windy and only about 60°, but sunny, so it was pretty enough to please Pam.

During the time she was here, we biked and walked a lot, which we both enjoyed. We also spent many hours talking! We hardly wanted to sleep because we had so many things to talk about. It had been a year and a half since we had seen each other, and back then, each of us was too pre-occupied with matters of daily work and life to be able to enjoy a close relationship. This five-day vacation was just what we needed to re-establish our friendship. The week passed quickly and on Saturday evening at five, we took a taxi-limo to the Sarasota/Bradenton airport, and she left. I caught a bus to Martin and Mary's place at six. We visited until it was time to go back to the airport to pick up Don at eight thirty. Mary provided the transportation, which was very much appreciated.

Don and I were very happy that he was back, and that the Ohio visit and income tax return work was behind us. He had a good time, but says he will never leave me for that long again. It was the longest time we had been apart in all the years since we started dating in April of 1978. The following is a summary taken from notes he made of his activities while he was in Ohio.

While in Ohio, he spent his time visiting with his family, my family, and friends; doing our income tax returns; looking after personal business matters; and socializing with his former co-workers at the office. Most of his meals were eaten with family or friends, at their homes or at restaurants. He stayed very busy.

He also did a little work for Erick, his former law partner, and made more than enough to pay for his flights there and back and his expenses while gone. In fact, the excess was much more than what I have earned working at Publix.

At Harbourside Moorings, Longboat Key, FL

January 31, 1988, Sunday

We slept in, but hurriedly got through breakfast because I had to work from ten to three at Publix. Don spent the time unpacking and getting readjusted to our compact world on the boat. It was a busy day at the supermarket because everyone was getting ready for the Super Bowl in the evening. We went to a Super Bowl party with Norbert and Barb at the condo of a long-time friend of Norbert, Evelyn Menuez. Mrs. Menuez was also a very close friend of Don's mother. They were best friends while growing up together, in Millersburg, Ohio. They continued to be good friends throughout their lives. Don won the football pool of $10. We both ate too many snacks. It was a fun time, but neither of us follows professional football.

At Harbourside Moorings, Longboat Key, FL

February 1, 1988, Monday

We spent the morning relaxing in bed until ten thirty, ate a lazy leisurely breakfast, and then talked about what to do next, and we included in the discussion the possibility of selling the boat and moving on to foreign travel at this time. However, when I reminded Don that he had promised me a trip down the Mississippi, we decided against that and settled on the plan of going north, beginning about the first of March, taking the same route we used coming down, and then going through the Great Lakes to Chicago and down the rivers, including the Mississippi, to the Gulf of Mexico and back here by December of this year. We talked to the co-dockmasters, Dan and Kate about our rental arrangement. Our monthly rental began on December 13th, and we have paid for two months; therefore, we are paid through February 12. They both seemed happy to let us pay for the rest of February at the same rate of $7.00 per day and said we were welcome to come back in December. I guess we passed the test and are considered "no hassle" dock renters.

We were given an old beat-up bike by people on a boat that was leaving. We salvaged a seat for my bike and a basket for Don's bike and junked the rest of it. We put the basket and seat on and put the rest of the bike in a dumpster. Then we took a bike ride to a hardware store about a mile and a half north of here. I bought two butane curling irons, one for me and the other for Shelly. I thought it would make a nice birthday gift for her, along with $50 cash which she can use for her upcoming Colorado trip in March.

We took time to enjoy the Gulf view and then rode back so I could get ready to go to work. I worked from four to eight, but my back was aching like I had a muscle strain. We ate lightly, and after work, we had a drink and cheese and crackers.

I talked to Hope, and invited Harry and her for a Chinese dinner on Wednesday. Don is excited; he gets to cook one of his favorite meals.

At Harbourside Moorings, Longboat Key, FL

February 2, 1988, Tuesday

We got up early and took the free transportation service from the marina to Saint Armand's circle to shop. It was another absolutely beautiful day. The temperature was in the 80s, and it was sunny. I returned a pair of slacks which was defective to the Village Store, and then we shopped. We ate a tasty lunch at Charlie's Crab. Don had spinach salad, and I ordered eggplant crepes. They have wonderful bread, just like Engine House Number Five serves in Columbus. We did more shopping after lunch and then caught the service van back at one thirty.

We had the van driver drop us off south of the marina, so that I could show Don the cute little park at the condos with the three waterfalls.

I got ready for work and left at three forty-five. Don met me after work at eight, and we rode back to the boat together. My back still aches, but I was careful not to strain it anymore.

At Harbourside Moorings, Longboat Key, FL

February 3, 1988, Wednesday

It was another great sunshiny day.

I did laundry and changed the bedding. Don went to the grocery and got all the makings for tonight's Chinese dinner. He spent the entire day chopping vegetables and making everything for the dinner. By four thirty, he was about finished, and then we got the table set and showered. Hope and Harry seemed to enjoy the meal very much. The menu was as follows: Szechuan soup with shrimp, vegetables, mushrooms and broth; Kung-Pao chicken with peanuts; and rice. Dessert was almond crème with kiwi and strawberries, one of my favorites.

After dinner, we visited and then took a walk in the marina and checked out the boat that is in the dock where their boat used to be. Now that they are settled into a condo, boat life is a thing of the past. It's unlikely that they will do it again. I am happy we are still enjoying our life on the boat.

At Harbourside Moorings, Longboat Key, FL

February 4, 1988, Thursday

It was another beautiful day; the high was in the 80s. Don served me breakfast in bed again. He is so kind and takes such good care of me. I just love it!

I wrapped Shelly's birthday gift and got it ready to mail. I also cleaned up the bikes and got off the rust while Don cleaned the space heater and stove.

Don and I talked with Sid, the older man who we frequently see fishing in the marina. He is from New Jersey, but spends his winters on Longboat Key. Fishing is his favorite pastime. Harbourside Moorings is his favorite fishing hole, and our dock is his favorite spot in the marina. He is here almost every day, and is friendly and fun to talk with.

By three thirty, everything was done, and I got ready for work. I hardly have time for work because there are so many fun things to do. I talked to my high school friend, Pam Parramore. She and Doug, her husband, and their ten month-old baby are coming over to see us on Sunday to eat a Chinese stir-fry with us. Bill and Donna from *Orchid Boat* are also supposed to visit us soon. I worked from four to eight, but didn't get any tips. My back is slightly better.

At Harbourside Moorings, Longboat Key, FL

February 5, 1988, Friday

Today was cloudy and cooler A "norther" is expected tonight.

Today was a workday for us. We washed *Robin Lee* and cleaned the dinghy. We finished up about three and Don made us pancakes and bacon for an early evening meal. I bagged groceries from four to eight.

After work, we went to a boat named *Who Cares* to visit with Tom and Sue. We met them earlier today, and they invited us over. The boat is a spacious 43-foot Gulf Star trawler, and we think that make and model would be a good live-aboard boat, but theirs is not in very good condition. They seem like nice people, and we enjoyed our time with them. They are somewhat unconventional, as evidenced by the name of their boat. It is conventional to give your boat a name and paint the name on the transom and under the name paint the name of your home port. For name and home port, they painted *Who Cares and Who Cares*.

I gave Don a haircut at one in the morning.

At Harbourside Moorings, Longboat Key, FL

February 6, 1988, Saturday

It was rainy and cold.

We relaxed on the boat the entire day.

At Harbourside Moorings, Longboat Key, FL

February 7, 1988, Sunday

We had another ugly weather day, but it was brightened by a visit from my high school friend Pam Parramore, her husband Doug, and the special person in their lives, Drew Christopher, their son. What a contrast—her with a baby and me with a 20-year-old college sophomore. Don served a Chinese meal, and for entertainment, we went for a ride in their car and toured Anna Maria Island and Longboat Key, including the Longboat Key Club.

At Harbourside Moorings, Longboat Key, FL

February 8, 1988, Monday

Today was the third ugly day in a row, but Shelly and Pam Bartha both called me, so I spent an hour and a half talking on the phone.

Don spent the whole day with Tom from the boat *Who Cares*. They went to the courthouse in Sarasota to check on some things. I worked at Publix from three to seven. After work, we watched TV and ate popcorn.

At Harbourside Moorings, Longboat Key, FL

February 9, 1988, Tuesday

We played today since it was so nice out. We biked to the hardware store and afterwards to the post office to mail Shelly's birthday gift of a curling iron and money. I worked from three to seven, and Don made a spaghetti dinner.

At Harbourside Moorings, Longboat Key, FL

February 10, 1988, Wednesday

We had nice weather. The high was in the 60s.

I talked to Martin and Mary, and then lazily made it to the laundry room to wash our clothes. It was pretty sunny, so I sat outside and brought this journal up to date while the washer and dryer did their work. What a great view I have from my laundry room! I can see the golf course, the marina, and Sarasota Bay, plus watch all the action of the boats coming to the fuel dock.

We had planned to go to Happy Hour at the Holiday Inn, but Don worked on some projects with the bilge pump and the anti-siphon valve, so he didn't get done in time. We ended up heating up the spaghetti for leftovers and later in the evening Sue and Tom from *Who Cares*, plus their son Bill, came to visit us. Their son wants to go to law school, and they felt Don could answer questions he might have.

At Harbourside Moorings, Longboat Key, FL

February 11, 1988, Thursday

It was an easy and fun day. I took off work because Betty and Clayton, and some of their family who are vacationing at Aloha Kai on Siesta Key came to visit us. We slept in until nine thirty and then ran a couple of errands and straightened up the boat. They arrived at eleven thirty. We visited on the boat for a while. Abbie and Alex, two of Clayton and Betty's grandchildren, plus Don and Clayton, went for a dinghy ride. Then we went to their place for the day and in the evening all of us, plus Barbara and Norbert, went out to eat at the Grillery.

It was late when we got back to our boat, but I was wound up, so I stayed up to knit. Don was tired and went right to bed.

At Harbourside Moorings, Longboat Key, FL

February 12, 1988, Friday

Tom asked Don to go to Bradenton with him to help him look up some information at the county courthouse. Sue and I went along and the four of us had lunch at a small restaurant along the Gulf. It was excellent food, and the Gulf was spectacular with large swells and surf. The wind was out of the north at 20-25 knots all day. It was a good day to observe the conditions and be happy that we are secure at Harbourside Moorings.

When we got back I worked from three to seven. In the evening, we stayed home and relaxed. It was cold due to another front passing through.

At Harbourside Moorings, Longboat Key, FL

February 13, 1988, Saturday

Sister Carol called early and talked for 15 minutes. It was zero in Columbus, and they had five inches of snow overnight. I am glad we aren't there!

I asked for five days off work because of Betty and Clayton being in town. Today was my first day of my five-day vacation. It was my second vacation while working at Publix, and I have been employed there less than one month. What a job!

Tom, Sue, Don and I ran errands. They drove us to the various places we needed to go, sort of a payback for Don helping them. We were thankful for the transportation. We bought a new anchor to replace the one that was bent. We also bought a supply of maintenance items for the next part of our cruise: a supply of oil, oil filters, air filters, etc. We stopped at the Trolley Car and enjoyed their soup and bread bar. It was five o'clock when we got back to the boat. I did a load of laundry. We snacked in the evening since we had overloaded with a late lunch at the Trolley Car.

Don has gained about 15 pounds since we got back to the States in October. I hope he doesn't gain any more weight. I think he looked best at 180 pounds, which is what he weighed when we returned from the Bahamas. When we went to the Bahamas he weighed about 205 pounds, which shows what an active life will do for one's weight.

We stayed home in the evening. It was quiet and relaxing. I love the privacy our little boat home offers us.

At Harbourside Moorings, Longboat Key, FL

February 14, 1988, Sunday, Valentine's Day

Don and I were too cheap to give Hallmark our money. Instead, we hugged and thanked God for our good health and love.

We went to brunch at the Holiday Inn on Lido Beach with Don's family along with Doris Ferrell and Audrey Foley from the Franklin County Juvenile Court. We over-ate again. After we ate, Norbert's son and daughter-in-law, Chuck and Debbie Chase, drove us to the boat because they hadn't seen it. After a quick tour, they took us to Clayton and Betty's condo where the family and Doris and Audrey spent the day visiting and enjoying the wonderful Siesta Key beach. At ten thirty, Clayton and Betty drove us home to the boat. It was another fun day of retirement.

At Harbourside Moorings, Longboat Key, FL

February 15-21, 1988, Monday-Sunday

Don and I both felt lousy all week due to head colds. Thank God we didn't have flu symptoms. Many people in the area have been sick with the flu.

We are beginning to do the things necessary to be ready to leave on March 1st, but I am still bagging groceries for Publix.

Monday:

I spent several hours on *Who Cares* using Sue's sewing machine to make a tablecloth and napkins for our boat.

I ordered a piece of custom cut, closed-cell insulate foam to use as an additional mattress for the V-berth. It should make it firmer and more comfortable.

Tuesday:

Hope, Harry, Don and I went to Clearwater. Harry is buying a 23-foot Aqua Sport boat. Hope and I browsed in various shops while Harry dealt with the purchase.

Wednesday:

The Eilers and the Roses again went to Clearwater. Harry and Don drove the boat to Sarasota, and Hope and I came back in the car.

I called Shelly in the evening to wish her a happy birthday.

Friday:

Tom and Sue on *Who Cares* are moving to Connecticut. Today, they took their boat from Harbourside Moorings to Hirsh Marina in Bradenton. They are listing the boat for sale with Hirsh. They asked us to go with them. We got there without any problems, but it was slow going because of fog. I was two hours late for work.

Sunday:

Hope and Harry came over and took us out to Happy Hour at Captain Kirk's, and after that, to see the movie, *Three Men and a Baby* at the Sarasota Mall.

ROBIN WORKING ON THE MAST

At Harbourside Moorings, Longboat Key, FL

February 22-28, 1988, Monday-Sunday

This week began with us feeling pretty bad due to colds.

Monday and Tuesday:

Donna and Bill from *Orchid Boat* came for a two-day visit. They stayed on the boat with us. We enjoyed seeing them and showing them all of our West Coast favorite spots. Of course, we spent a lot of time catching up on each other's activities since we were last together. Don fixed *Piccadillo* for them one night because we like it so well, and we wanted them to try it. After dinner, they reminded us that we had served it to them before; it gave Bill indigestion. Oh well!

Wednesday:

We took a vacation day and spent time relaxing at the Longboat Key Club pool, and then napping on the boat from three to five. After that, we showered and biked to the Happy Hour at the Holiday Inn. It was a very nice day to remember always.

Thursday and Friday:

These were my last two days working at Publix. I am thankful to have earned enough to pay for our new mattress for the V-berth, a new battery for our video camera, and Shelly's birthday gifts. It was fun, and I met a lot of nice people. They paid $4.25/hour, and I often got tips. On the other hand, some of the customers were snobbish and demanding. Furthermore, only a few customers tipped. The worst thing about my working is that Don made more for the few hours he worked while he was in Ohio, even after paying for his plane fare, than I did during my six weeks of employment. Oh well, I really did enjoy the experience.

Saturday:

I worked hard for five hours on the boat cleaning the cockpit and the teak.

Our spreaders are wooden and since they are exposed to the weather, we have wondered about the condition of their top side, which is not visible to us. If one of them collapsed in heavy weather, we could be dismasted. I went up the mast to check their condition and to put a coat of varnish on them. Martin and Mary were here when I did it, and Martin tailed as Don used the winch to raise me up the mast.

Sunday:

I put a coat of Simco on the teak on the deck and it looks great. I am stiff and sore and still have the remnants of my cold.

The weather has been excellent these past few days for working on the outside of the boat.

At Harbourside Moorings, Longboat Key, FL

February 29, 1988, Monday

I got up early today and bought enamel paint for the head and spent the afternoon painting the head as well as the inside of the clothes locker.

Don got an offer on the real estate he owns on Alkire Road, in Columbus, but he turned it down. He thinks it is worth more, and that now is not the time to try to sell it. He thinks it will sell for a lot more, eventually, so he will hold onto the land for now.

We have decided to keep my bike and use it along the way for errands since it folds up and can be stowed. Don's bike doesn't fold up, and we don't have room for it, so he gave it to Martin. Don is stocking up on groceries for the next leg of our cruise.

Regrettably, we haven't heard from Sue and Tom since helping them take their boat to Bradenton.

We met a fellow by the name of Joe. He wears a black patch on his left eye and is very nice. Bonnie, his wife, is up north, so we didn't get to meet her. Their last name is Darlington. They are on a 31-foot Golden Hind named *Tortoise* here in the marina. He and his wife bought their boat on the Mediterranean Sea and sailed it for 3 ½ years in the Mediterranean and in Europe. Then they sailed it across the Atlantic to the U.S. The boat has a dual (split) keel, so it can sit upright on the bottom when the tide goes out. Joe came over and talked to us about boat traveling in Europe; that was pretty interesting.

After dinner, we watched a little TV, and then I did my last load of laundry here and gave Don a haircut and beard trim, so he would look good for the next few weeks. We may not have electric again for a long while, or a nice clean shower house.

Randy called to wish us well while underway. Everyone back home is doing fine.

Our last night at Harbourside Moorings, Longboat Key, FL

CHAPTER ELEVEN
LONGBOAT KEY, FL to MOREHEAD CITY, NC
Mar. 1, 1988 – May 1, 1988

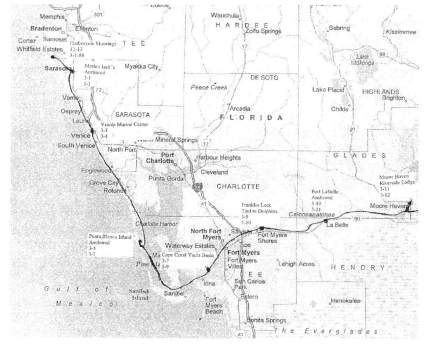

March 1, 1988, Tuesday

Today we leave our happy home at Harbourside Moorings, on Longboat Key.

I got up early and immediately started applying my second coat of paint in the head and locker. It turned out great and is about the same color as the fiber glass, which is good because it should not offend anyone who looks at the boat when we are selling it. It smells and looks very clean and pretty. Don wasn't for the paint job, but he seems to have accepted it, now that it's done.

Don made chocolate-chip cookies for the dock hands and office help, so around three we pulled out of our slip and went to the fuel dock to bid everyone farewell and give them cookies. They seemed to appreciate them very much. Don, Kathy, Katy and Parrish have all been super nice to us!

We didn't go far; we anchored at Mary and Martin's place. After dinner, we dinghied in to visit them and have a cup of tea.

Anchored on the north side of Marina Jack's, Sarasota, FL – Distance traveled: 7 miles

March 2, 1988, Wednesday

We had breakfast on deck and enjoyed the view of downtown Sarasota. The weather has been great. The Arvida, a nice-looking building that is under construction nearby, is almost finished. We have watched its progress from this anchorage from the beginning of its construction. The next time we come to this area, it will be occupied.

I worked until two in the afternoon doing some cleaning and reorganizing after the paint job. I also applied a second coat of Simco to the teak.

We left about three for a final walk downtown, and ate dinner at the NY Deli–a charming art-deco restaurant. On the way back, we stopped at Mary and Martin's for tea and dessert and bid them farewell.

As we were dinghying back to our boat, we were invited to go aboard *Sunquest,* a beautiful 48-foot motor-sailer. The owners are from Mississippi and very hospitable. They even served us homemade pecan pie. Their boat is featured in an article in this month's issue of *Southern Boating* magazine. I hope we can find a copy to read. We loved the boat.

Anchored on the north side of Marina Jack's, Sarasota, FL

March 3, 1988, Thursday

We had a lazy morning before leaving the anchorage. We slept in and took our time with breakfast. The anchors were filthy dirty, so it took a while to get them cleaned and get underway. At eleven, we finally started for the Venice Yacht Club or our alternate destination, the anchorage in the cove near Englewood where we spent the night on our way north in December.

While Don was at the helm, I continued to clean and straighten up below—running our little 12v sweeper, etc. I also made lunch.

We put in at the Venice Yacht Club and called Hope and Harry to tell them the docks were full, so not to plan on getting together for dinner in Venice as we had talked about. We were sorry not to be able to say good-bye to them in person. We ended up stopping a couple of miles south of there at the Venice Marine Center because we got held up by two bridges, and it was too late to make it to the cove near Englewood before dark.

We tied up at a slip next to a permanent type live-aboard, Marsha, on a Catalina 30, and had a friendly conversation with her. She is a surgical nurse at the hospital in Venice.

The showers were great, but we had to walk through the boatyard to get to them, and we got oil and grease on our shoes. Naturally, it got on the boat, so we had a mess to clean up.

We walked to K-Mart, Wal-Mart, and Albertson's and bought a couple of rugs, groceries, a bucket, and soap. Afterwards, Don made salmon a-la-king with rice, and we had strawberries over Twinkies for dessert.

I got the kerosene heater out again since, from now on, we frequently won't have electricity, and I finished organizing the locker; now everything is back in order.

Venice Marine Center, Venice, FL – Distance traveled: 24 miles

March 4, 1988, Friday

At ten thirty, after I did a load of laundry, we left for Punta Blanca Island. We took two-hour shifts. That makes it a lot more pleasant for both of us. I wrote a few letters during my breaks. The weather was not good—overcast and misting off and on. The wind was on the nose. It took 7 ½ hours to get there. We were glad to get the stern safely tied to the mangroves and a bow anchor set at one of our favorite anchorages. However, the people anchored on either side of us didn't seem to appreciate our intruding into "their" anchorage, which, to some extent, spoiled the idea of being there. We were also disappointed yesterday that no one offered to let us raft off them at the Venice Yacht Club. This leg of our cruise seems to be off to a bad start.

Anchored at Punta Blanca Island, FL – Distance traveled: 37 miles

March 5, 1988, Saturday

It rained most of the night and continued to rain today until about noon.

We ate Canadian Red River cereal for breakfast. Afterwards, we took a dinghy ride and checked the depth at various spots in the anchorage and in the channel leading in and out of it, using our lead line.

When we came back, I worked on my afghan. After lunch, the weather cleared up, and we took a long dinghy trip to Cayo Costa State Park. The park is only accessible by water, and has a beautiful beach on the Gulf and several primitive cabins and tent camping sites. It cost us $1.00 a piece for admission.

It was about four o'clock, when we started back. We went through an anchorage in Pelican Bay, between the park and our boat, and talked with a sail boater who had been anchored there for about two months. I guess the boaters next to us at Punta Blanca Island and this guy consider this area a good place for "squatting." That's OK, so long as they don't think they can acquire "squatting rights."

I don't think we would want to squat anywhere longer than a couple of weeks, as we did at the "Mud Hole." We wouldn't have been there that long, except that we were resupplying and doing maintenance work after being in the Bahamas for six months. We enjoy exploring new areas and meeting other boaters. We like inviting other boaters on board *Robin Lee* to show them our boat, and we enjoy going aboard their boats to see them. We also enjoy eating together and exchanging stories about experiences. I can't count the number of people we have had on board for meals. While staying at Harbourside Moorings we bought a guest book for people to sign. However, on this leg of our trip, we haven't had anyone visit, so far.

Don served honey baked ham, asparagus, and kraut salad, plus macaroni and cheese for dinner.

Anchored at Punta Blanca Island, FL

March 6, 1988, Sunday

We got up early, planning to leave, but it was still very cloudy and sprinkling off and on. I didn't want to leave until the sun came out, so we stayed.

We decided to visit with the couple on board *Caprice*, a boat that had just come into the anchorage. We dinghied over and introduced ourselves and learned that they had come down the Mississippi, which made us even more interested in visiting with them. We invited them, Bob and Jana Baker, a young couple from Modesto, CA, to come to our boat later in the day. When they came, we talked for an hour. We learned that they are on a one-year adventure doing the circle route (circumnavigating the Eastern U.S. using the Intracoastal Waterway and the inland waters). They started at Rock Island Illinois and came down the Mississippi to New Orleans and from there they went to Apalachicola and then to Florida's West Coast. The wife is going back to California soon to return to work, but the husband will single-hand the boat back to their starting point to complete the circle. He will be following about the same route as us, and so we may see him along the way.

Later in the evening, we visited with the folks on *Klara*, a home-built boat from Hamilton, Ontario, anchored near us. Then, the folks anchored next to us on *Bride of the Waves*, from New Bern, North Carolina, invited us to their boat for coffee and dessert. They are the ones who acted unfriendly because we came in and anchored close to them. We think they must have felt a bit guilty. They have spent the entire winter here. Don says he wishes he had told them about being anchored on Thanksgiving weekend with 32 boats at the small anchorage at Boca Grande.

We went to bed late.

Anchored at Punta Blanca Island, FL

March 7, 1988, Monday

We left Punta Blanca Island at ten thirty and made it out the tricky narrow channel to the waterway without grounding. We went south, past Useppa Island and Cabbage Key, toward Captiva Island. The scenery along the waterway was pretty with small islands and unusual birds, even white pelicans. We went to the South Seas Plantation marina, but it was crowded, and so we left and tried to anchor, first at Cattlepen Basin and then at Glovers Bight. Our anchor dragged at both places, so we went to Cape Coral. Fifteen dollars per night will just have to be OK; we needed showers anyway. The sun was shining when we arrived, and I really was glad to see it. Two days of clouds is plenty. I looked up the telephone number of my elementary school friend, Gail, and called her. She was shocked to hear from me. At first, she wasn't sure who I was. After 27 years, I guess that's understandable. She and her husband came to the boat and we rode with them to their home. Their house is fabulous. We all enjoyed the evening, which we spent chatting about schoolmates, our adventures, and her husband's business. He is heavily involved with real estate. Gail looked just as pretty as she did when I last saw her. She hasn't changed much at all.

Prior to going to Gail's home, we visited with other sailors at the marina: Janet and Si on *Whispurr*, Joseph and Suzanne on *KatieGII*, and the folks on *Puff*, who we had already met at Punta Blanca Island.

It was a tiring day and a busy evening.

At Cape Coral Yacht Basin, Cape Coral, FL – Distance traveled: 36 miles

March 8, 1988, Tuesday

We hired our friends on *KatieGII* to take us sightseeing on Captiva and Sanibel Islands. Three different times during this trip we planned to go there on the boat, but the weather kept us from doing it. Each time, the wind was about 20 knots out of the wrong direction to be protected in the anchorage.

We had a nice time, and it was well worth the $30 we paid them. Joe and Suzanne are very friendly, and have travel plans similar to ours. In fact, they have already gone to Mexico. They have been living aboard for 2 ½ years and would like to take their boat to Europe. We got home at five, so from ten o'clock in the morning until five in the evening, they made $30, less their car expense. We all had a lot of fun. We visited the J.N. Ding Darling Wildlife Refuge and had lunch at the Crow's Nest in the "Tween Waters" Inn. Later that night, after I did a load of laundry, we went on board the *KatieGII* to visit them and look at their pictures of Mexico. We stayed until midnight. The last two nights have both been late ones. We have been so busy since docking that it will be good to get back to anchoring again, which allows us more time to be alone in peace and quiet.

At Cape Coral Yacht Basin, Cape Coral, FL

March 9, 1988, Wednesday

I did another load of clothes early and showered. Suzanne took Don to the bank and grocery, and I called Randy.

By twelve thirty, we had filled our water tanks and were ready to leave. The wind was strong, but it was sunny and warm; we had shorts on. It was so windy we sailed all the way to the W.P. Franklin lock with nothing but a partially furled "jib."

We ate a quick meal of pork chops, peas and fresh-baked bread. After that I read, wrote postcards, and knitted.

Tied to dolphins at the W.P. Franklin Lock on the Okeechobee Waterway, FL – Distance traveled: 25 miles

March 10, 1988, Thursday

Today, Shelly leaves on a Colorado ski trip for her spring break. After a breakfast of grapefruit, eggs, and coffee, we went to the RV park. Don showered and we walked around visiting with campers, asking questions as to their preference in RVs. We visited with an elderly couple in a Dodge Marathon camper, and brought them out in the dinghy to visit "our home." They were very interested in the boat. They had never been on a sailboat. We enjoyed visiting with them and didn't take them back to shore until one thirty.

We had another good day for sailing to La Belle. The docks at LaBelle are free, and naturally they were filled, so we motored past the boats that were tied up, including *Puff,* and went to Port La Belle Basin, to drop the hook. Port LaBelle Basin is a harbor just east of LaBelle. We ran hard aground in the mud as we were entering the basin after making a turn to starboard to go through the entrance. We were unable to back off the ground using the engine, and had to kedge off. We put the anchor in the dinghy with one end of its line attached to the anchor, and the other end attached to *Robin Lee's* bow. I took the dinghy about 150 feet in the direction from which we had come, while Don took hold of the anchor line at our bow and walked back to the starboard jib winch, holding the line, and wrapped it around the winch. Then I lowered the anchor into the water. Using the winch handle, Don winched the boat toward the anchor, and the boat broke free from the mud, and we were afloat again. We retrieved our anchor and entered the basin, making a wider turn this time, and anchored for the night. That was the first time we had kedged off the ground and we patted ourselves on our backs for being successful. Don made 15 bean soup, Jell-O, and cornbread for our evening meal. It's just what we needed because the old north wind is cold. I hope he made lots of it since the cold weather is expected to last three days.

I spent the evening getting caught up on this journal, and Don read. I was tired, so I went to bed early. I hope Shelly had a safe flight to Colorado.

Anchored in Port LaBelle Basin, Okeechobee Waterway, FL – Distance traveled: 24 miles

March 11, 1988, Friday

We got up early and went ashore to look over the marina and facilities. The dockmaster was very friendly. Monthly anchorage is available for $l.00 per foot. That's cheap!

It was a pretty day, and we motored about four hours to Moore Haven. We docked, since it was only $5 for dockage with electricity, and because Don wanted to make beef stroganoff in the electric skillet for dinner. While he did that, he also baked cookies, and I rode the bike to the grocery to get some fruit and miscellaneous items. We also went to the library, which is close to the docks, to look at the March issue of *Southern Boating Magazine* and read the article about the 48' foot motor-sailer we went aboard in Sarasota. Incidentally, *Southern Boating Magazine* is published by Skip Allen, the man who handled communications with the Coast Guard at Sampson Cay in connection with getting help for the badly injured victim of the shark attack. We also went to the hardware store. It was very old fashioned, with original wood floors and old wood and glass showcases. The building must have been 100 years old.

Dinner was good, as usual, and we just relaxed and "pigged out" eating cookies in the evening.

Docked at Riverside Lodge, Moore Haven, FL – Distance traveled: 25 miles

March 12, 1988, Saturday

We made it through the Moore Haven Lock at nine thirty. We were held up by the big tourist vessel, *New Orleans*, which was in the lock for a long time.

This time, we got to the east side of Lake Okeechobee by taking the "Rim Route" along the shore of the lake from Clewiston to Port Myacca, instead of crossing it. The route was quite pretty, and the weather was absolutely gorgeous. We saw over 50 little bass fishing boats out on the lake, which is known for good largemouth bass fishing. At ten minutes after

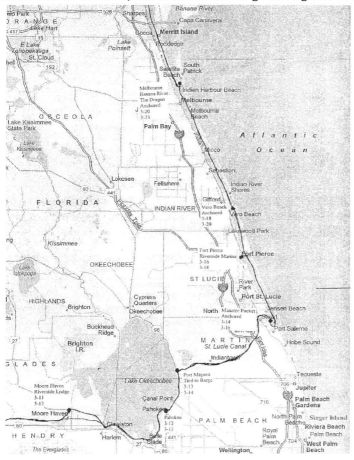

five, we came to the town of Pahokee, tied up at the municipal docks, and spent the night there. We saw so many boats and people fishing from docks, we decided that everyone in town must like to fish.

After we were situated at the dock, we went ashore to look around. We went to the Burger King for a sandwich and then went to the grocery store. A lady I talked with at the grocery invited us to go to her church tomorrow morning, the United Methodist Church; her name was Mary Lee. We said we would like to attend and thanked her for the invitation.

Pahokee Municipal Docks – Distance traveled: 43 miles

March 13, 1988, Sunday

Gosh, the gnats and small fruit flies were horrible last night. I didn't sleep well due to that, as well as the noise from people on the dock fishing, noise from crows and other birds, and soreness from doing exercises yesterday while we were underway.

We had cereal and coffee and then got dressed for church. Don's shirt is getting very thin and worn-looking; he only has one clean-up Oxford cloth shirt with us. However, we both clean up OK. On our way to church, we stopped at Burger King and enjoyed a Danish.

Church started at eleven, and the preacher called our visit to the attention of everyone by asking us to stand. He also told them about our travels. The one-hour service was very nice, and we were invited to a covered dish potluck lunch following the service. The food was great, some of the best I've ever had at a function like that. We talked with several people and enjoyed it very much, but ate way too much food. They even gave us a ten-pound bag of Uncle Ben's rice to take with us. The Hendrixes, whom we met at the luncheon, drove us to their place in the country and gave us some of their home-grown grapefruit. Another fellow and his wife, the Davises, whom we also met at the luncheon, picked us up at the Hendrixes' house and drove us back to town by way of the sugar cane fields and sugar mill, of which he is the manager and part owner. What an interesting afternoon and how pleasant to be with nice people!

After we got back to the boat, we made another trip to the grocery and then, at three thirty, left for Port Mayaca, 14 miles away. We arrived there at dusk and tied up to a barge for the night, after going through the lock.

It was cloudy and warm today, about 75°. One year ago, we were at Key Largo, FL.

Tied to a barge at the Port Mayaca Lock – Distance traveled: 14 miles

March 14, 1988, Monday

It rained off and on all night, and the wind howled. The wind is 30 knots at present and has been strong most of the day. Lake Okeechobee would be rough today, so we were glad to be across it.

The trip to Stuart was pretty in spite of there being no sun. During the trip, we saw several types of birds, a raccoon, alligators, and turtles, but no manatees. I worked on oiling the teak inside when I wasn't at the helm. Don tried to read and relax on his time off, but I kept bugging him. The Saint Lucie Lock, at the east end of the waterway, dropped us down to the level of the ocean, approximately 14 feet.

We had written to Dave and Jo on *Rainbow,* telling them that we would be coming through Stuart, and that we hoped they would come up and meet us for a visit. We looked around in the anchorage and the town dock area for *Rainbow* and called for them on the marine radio, but had no luck finding them. Maybe they didn't get our card telling them when we would be here. We anchored in Manatee Pocket around five o'clock.

We never got off the boat today. We ate leftover beef stroganoff with green beans, and for dessert I made a new treat…pound cake sliced thin, spread with jam, and topped with grapes, bananas, strawberries and whipped cream. It was pretty, as well as tasty. Don went to bed early, but I stayed up and listened to the radio, knitted, and relaxed by the fire (in the kerosene heater). It was cozy.

Anchored in Manatee Pocket, Stuart, FL – Distance traveled: 42 miles

March 15, 1988, Tuesday

It was pretty windy, so we stayed put in Manatee Pocket for a second night. During the day, it was cool and sunny. We visited with several other boaters in the anchorage, none of whom we had met prior to then.

In the afternoon, we went to Port Salerno, by dinghy. We visited the Volunteer Fire Department, went to a bank for some cash, to a Hallmark store, and then the Winn Dixie Super Market. We also had a hot sub sandwich at an Italian restaurant.

In the evening, we did our usual pleasurable things, read, knit, wrote cards, and listened to the news on the radio.

Anchored in Manatee Pocket, Stuart, FL

March 16, 1988, Wednesday

We left Manatee Pocket at nine thirty and motored about five hours to Fort Pierce.

We docked at Bill and Smitty's marina. It's a local fishermen's do-it-yourself boatyard. What a dump! The showers were the worst ever and the water smelled of sulphur. We had to raft off a sport fisherman and walk across it to get to shore because they had no slips deep enough for us. To top it off, we had to pay $.50/foot.

The pressure pump in our water system is broken. It broke yesterday morning. When we are connected to water at the dock, we don't have a problem, but at anchor we have to use water out of our jugs and heat it on the stove for washing dishes.

The best part of the day was taking Smitty and Bill out for pizza in the evening after they got off work and having a good visit with them.

At Riverside Marina, Fort Pierce, FL – Distance traveled: 28 miles

March 17, 1988, Thursday, Saint Patrick's Day

Yesterday, Bill looked at our pressure pump and figured out that it needed a new switch, which he could get for us for $17.00. Since the alternative was to buy a new pump for $109, we asked him to order the switch. The negative aspect of the plan was having to wait in this marina another day for the part to come in!

In the afternoon, we walked around Fort Pierce. I was in a snotty mood! We did enjoy seeing where Bill and Smitty work at building boats, and they, I am sure, appreciated our being interested in visiting. We ate at Dino's, a recommended family-style restaurant. It was the pits! We were told that the town has a high crime rate and that drug dealers hang out here. It is not our type of place at all.

At Riverside Marina, Fort Pierce, FL

March 18, 1988, Friday

We lay around until noon. I did, however, finish the oiling of a small area of teak and did some odd cleaning jobs, but we had low water pressure at the dock, and since we had no pressure pump to get water out of our tanks, it was hard to do much. At noon, Don went to the office and picked up the pressure pump switch. Thank goodness it arrived. Don was able to install it in five minutes and now the pump works fine.

About two thirty we got underway from the marina, but it was dead low tide, and we had trouble going out the channel. We went aground twice. Finally, we plowed our way out, but it had taken us 40 minutes to go ½ mile.

We went to Vero Beach, only 16 miles up the coast, and anchored for the night. It started to rain shortly after we got situated. We had a quiet rainy evening and never went ashore.

Anchored at Vero Beach, FL – Distance traveled: 16 miles

March 19, 1988, Saturday

Around noon, we went ashore and registered our boat and dinghy with the dockmaster. That gave us the privilege of using the marina facilities. They are brand spanking new, completed less than two weeks ago, and really nice. Their laundry has two washers and dryers; their shower rooms each have three showers and three heads. There is also a boater's lounge with a pop machine, a sofa, chairs, sinks and cupboards. It is a nicely planned facility.

We spent part of the afternoon talking with Suzy and Robert Whitaker, from South Bend, IN, who are cruising on *Family Ties*, a 36-foot Catalina. We walked around town and then returned to the marina and visited two boaters we first met in the Bahamas, *Free Spirit* and *Rut Roh*. We had dinner aboard *Free Spirit* when we were at the Mud Hole. *Rut Roh* is leaving tomorrow and heading north. *Free Spirit* will be leaving soon, heading to Washington, D.C. We may see both again. *Family Ties* will be joining us tomorrow to head north to Melbourne.

Around five thirty we got our shower bags and laundry off the boat and went back to the marina. I did laundry while Don showered. After showering Don walked around in the marina, just looking it over, and was invited to a birthday party going on in the lounge. He came and got me, and we joined in the celebration. We had a great meal of London broil, baked beans, potato salad, and slaw, plus drinks and snacks. It was really kind of them to include us. We didn't get home until about eleven. No one at the party could tell us whose birthday we were celebrating, and we still don't' know.

Anchored at Vero Beach FL

March 20, 1988, Sunday

We "upped" our anchors early and went to the fuel dock for fresh water. I docked the boat, and Don handled the lines. I looked just like a pro. I'm sure my captain was proud! We left for Melbourne at eight thirty, after replenishing our water. I cleaned the galley and head while Don was at the helm. Our repaired pressure pump is working well. While I was on duty at the helm, from ten to twelve, I also washed the dodger and part of the Bimini top. It was spotted with mildew.

At four thirty, we anchored on the Banana River, just north of Dragon Point. Dragon Point is at the south end of Merritt Island and has a 65 foot long concrete dragon sculpture on it. *Family Ties* followed us to Melbourne and anchored nearby.

We would like to visit Cape Canaveral while we are at this anchorage if we can get transportation. Bill and Donna from *Orchid* Boat have a car here, stored at a relative's home, and they told us that we were welcome to use it and told the relatives that we might be calling them. After we anchored, I took the dinghy to shore to call them. On the way, I picked up Suzy off *Family Ties,* and we went to a marina. I called Paul and Anne Welks. Paul is the cousin of Bill Jordan on *Orchid Boat.* Paul brought the car to the marina so Don and I could use it during our stay at Melbourne. How nice! I got back to the boat at six; we ate quickly, and then went ashore and drove around, sightseeing and looking for dessert. Bob and Suzy went along.

We drove around a little and then had our dessert. We got ice cream and decided to go into another place for coffee, but the owner of that place didn't like us bringing ice cream in and refused to serve us. We ended up at a Pizza Hut for coffee. They didn't charge us since it was almost closing time, and because we got the "last of the pot." It felt strange to be kicked out of one place and treated so well at the next.

Home of the Dragon, Melbourne, FL – Distance traveled: 37 miles

March 21, 1988, Monday

We went to bed late, but were up early so as to make the most of our time at this stop.

We had breakfast at McDonald's, and drove to the Cape. We took Suzy and Robert on *Family Ties* with us. We also invited *Rut Roh*, who are also anchored near us, but they declined since they had seen the area last year. We bought tickets at the Spaceport for two tours plus a movie. It was a very interesting day, and we all had fun. We took a lot of pictures; I hope we got some good ones.

On the way back, we stopped at the Cocoa Beach Yacht Club to see the Wests on *Shirley Mae*. They are the couple we visited with at Sampson Cay that knew my folks and previously lived in Urbana. They were surprised to see us and glad we stopped by. They are getting ready for their next trip. They plan to go to Jamaica and Grand Cayman.

THE DRAGON OF MERRITT ISLAND, MELBOURNE, FLORIDA

After that, we went to the Merritt Island shopping mall. I hadn't been shopping since Christmas time while we were in Sarasota. I purchased some skin-care products at Merle Norman. I hope they clear up my complexion. This boat life is hard on it—too much sun and wind. My mom swears by Merle Norman products, so I hope that they work for me.

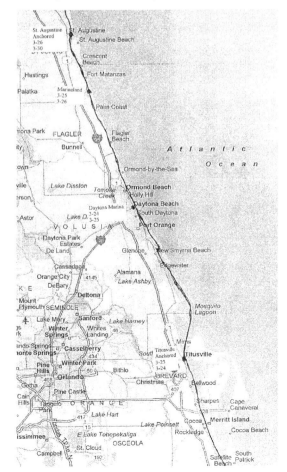

We had sandwiches at the mall and didn't get back to the boat until nine. We dropped off Suzy and Bob, and then Don and I went ashore to buy groceries and do our laundry.

It was a very busy day—Rush! Rush!

Home of the Dragon, Melbourne, FL

March 22, 1988, Tuesday

Both yesterday and today were perfect weather days. We got up early and drank our morning beverages in the cockpit, watching and listening to the birds. There are a large number of water birds at this anchorage. The beautiful weather and the birds made for a very pleasant start of the day.

We dinghied over to view the Dragon close-up. It was built in 1971 by an artist and was made of cement over a wire form. It is huge—a real undertaking of construction. It even has electronic time-controlled lights.

We ran errands from noon to six o'clock and visited the Melbourne Mall. At six, we went back and picked up Bob and Suzy. We all went to see a movie. They saw *Three Men and a Baby*. Don and I had seen it, so we saw *Moon Struck*. The best part of the evening was having a Friendly's Reese's Pieces sundae. I hadn't eaten one during the last year and a half; they're great!

We filled Bill and Donna's car with gas and took it back to Bill's cousin's house and he then dropped us off at the marina.

Home of the Dragon, Melbourne, FL

March 23, 1988, Wednesday

We left "The Home of the Dragon" bright and early and sailed all the way to Titusville. Winds were 15-20 knots out of the SE. *Family Ties* was near us all the way. In the evening, around five thirty, we had them over for pudding. It was still early when they left, so Don and I went ashore.

We bought a few groceries, and on the way back we looked up the boat *Honey's Home* that we had met at Great Sail Cay in the Bahamas. Ron and Jackie seemed happy to see and visit with us. Ron is going to move his boat to Treasure Cay in the Bahamas and start working there as the community physician. We stayed on shore until the mosquitoes drove us back to the boat. It was another great Florida Day.

Anchored at Titusville, FL – Distance traveled: 36 miles

March 24, 1988, Thursday

We got another early start and made it to Daytona in time for Don to take the bike downtown and get groceries and our mail. *Family Ties* came over at six o'clock for dinner. Don had time before dinner to shower at the marina facility. I took a shower on the boat. It hasn't formed mildew since I painted the walls with enamel.

We also spent some time visiting with *Rut Roh*. They seem to be taking the same trip that we are, but only to Annapolis.

After Bob and Suzy left, Don and I spent the evening going through our mail. We received letters from *Rainbow, Orchid Boat, Domus*, Shelly, Martha Cochran (Dad's friend), and several pieces of business mail.

Daytona Municipal Marina, Daytona, FL - Distance traveled: 48 miles

March 25, 1988, Friday

We left Daytona at nine o'clock and arrived at Marineland around one in the afternoon. We went to the park soon after arriving to enjoy the dolphin shows and other performances. Marineland has an "oceanarium" where all the species of the sea can live in their own environment. The place was probably very nice in its early days, but seems a bit rundown at present. Sea World, in Orlando, has probably been bad for Marineland. Sea World is much bigger, better organized, and the employees doing the performances have more stage presence. *Family Ties* also went to Marineland. It cost $10 each.

Around five o'clock, Don made meatloaf and cheese grits, and we ate on *Family Ties*. Dinner was very good and afterwards, Bob showed us his video, taken between Key West and here.

Family Ties was made by the same company as our boat and is laid out in about the same way. But it is 36' long while ours is only 30' long. The additional 6' makes a big difference. They have a lot more space to move around in than we do. However, Don and I both feel that we are probably better off with our boat, for a number of reasons, among which are the following: The price for a Catalina 36, new or used, would be about twice as much as for our boat and replacement part costs associated with maintaining the boat are much higher. Moreover, the Catalina 36 would be more difficult to deal with in stormy weather than the Catalina 30 because the forces involved in dealing with the bigger boat are much greater. I remember how much difficulty Don had holding the 10,000-pound *Robin Lee* away from the dock to avoid damage to the boat at Tarpon Springs the night another boat got blown off its chocks on shore. The Catalina 36 weighs 15,000 pounds. The forces on the sails are also much greater on the bigger boat. The anchor and chain required for the Catalina 36 is much heavier to haul in than on the Catalina 30. For those and many other reasons, I would rather have the Catalina 30.

We read a book, *Living Aboard,* before leaving on this trip. It recommends that you not buy a boat to cruise on that is any bigger than you can get by with, and we think that is very good advice. A good many of the couples we have met who set out to cruise and who bought big boats, 40 footers or thereabouts, are now sitting instead of cruising. They have found a comfortable marina in a place they like and are now living there. A much higher percentage of the couples who bought 30-foot boats are still out cruising.

Moving the boat from one place in order to see a new place has some appeal, but when you are comfortably situated, either at anchor or in a marina, there is a reluctance to leave, for a couple of reasons, regardless of the size of the boat:

When you move your boat to a new place, you have a lot to learn about the new place. Where is the best place to tie up or anchor? Where is the grocery store, the library, the post office, etc? Once you have gotten to know the place, and if you like it, when the idea of moving on comes to mind, you ask yourself, why should I move to a new place where I will have to start learning again? I like this place!

Moving the boat involves work, worry, and discomfort, especially in bad weather. The bigger the boat, the more work and worry. In short, the bigger the boat, the bigger the hassle going from one place to another. The temptation to stay overcomes the desire to see new places for many sailors with bigger boats.

It was nine thirty when we came back to our boat from *Family Ties*.

Docked at marina, Marineland, FL - Distance traveled: 36 miles

March 26, 1988, Saturday

We slept in until nine. The tide was very low, and the depth along the channel was only five feet at low tide, so we waited for the tide to come in. We left at two in the afternoon. *Family Ties* went at the same time. While waiting, I did two loads of laundry, and Don wrote Chip a letter. When we left, I backed up the boat and Don tended to the lines. He forgot to untie the starboard bowline. I wasn't able to move away from the dock. Finally, we noticed the line. Don was embarrassed.

After we left, it rained lightly for a few minutes, and then the sun came out, and we had a pleasant day of sailing until five. Just as we arrived at Saint Augustine, all hell broke loose. We were hit by a severe thunderstorm. We anchored during the storm, and that was difficult. Don was soaked as well as freezing cold. We stayed on board and had a late meal.

Saint Augustine has not been good to us so far.

At anchor in Saint Augustine, FL - Distance traveled: 18 miles

March 27, 1988, Sunday

I was glad to be able to sleep in today. We didn't get up until ten o'clock. Suzy and Robert stopped over to visit before going to see the fort. *Caprice,* with Bob aboard, was anchored next to us this morning. He came over to visit and tell us where he had been since we met at Punta Blanca Island.

Today is Palm Sunday, which is Saint Augustine's day for the annual Blessing of the Fleet by the Priest. It started at noon. There were several decorated boats being blessed. Since we aren't Catholic and are just passing through, we didn't participate. I hope the good Lord blesses us anyway. All we want is to be safe and have decent weather.

We spent the day sightseeing. The town is quite charming. There was an art festival in the downtown area. Lots of tourists were here, and the bus driver on our tour tram was frustrated with all the traffic jams. We ate pizza across from the Bridge of Lions. Don seemed to growl and mumble every time he looked up and saw the bridge.

After we got back to the marina, we called Sister Carol and then dinghied out to *Family Ties* to say good-bye. They are leaving bright and early in the morning. We got back to the boat about nine o'clock, and had coffee with Kahlua and whipped cream. Then, we read and relaxed until bedtime.

The anchor line fouled today. The curse of Saint Augustine continues, brought on, perhaps, by that one-fingered salute Don gave the bridge tender on the way south. We got it straightened out and reset the anchor with the help of Bob from *Caprice* who came over in his dinghy. The current is always a problem to deal with, and this anchorage is especially bad. Nevertheless, we'll stay at anchor instead of docking.

At anchor in Saint Augustine, FL

March 28, 1988, Monday

Once more, we slept in! It certainly is nice.

We spent the day sightseeing again. We saw a couple of pretty churches; ate lunch at the Saint George Pharmacy; and afterwards, had a dessert at the Dairy Queen. After our dessert, we went back to the marina where we left our dinghy and showered. They charge $4 per day to use the dinghy dock and the showers. Dockage by the week is only $2/foot, which would only be $60 for us, but we don't intend to stay a week, so we will continue to anchor out.

Don got cash out of a money machine, so we were able to mail some things to folks back home. Then we went to the boat and rested awhile. At seven, we went back to town so I could call Mom and Shelly. Don ran into *Escapade II* (Jody and Bob) at the dock. We met them at Highbourne Cay in the Bahamas. We visited with them for almost an hour. I finally reached Shelly at ten thirty.

At anchor in Saint Augustine, FL

March 29, 1988, Tuesday

We stayed one more day so we could see Flagler College and eat lunch there. We saw the school, but they no longer serve lunch to guests, except on the weekends. We had heard that their lunches were excellent and not expensive. Instead, we ate at the Saint George Pharmacy again. We spent some more time browsing through the shops and then came back to the marina to scrub the dinghy bottom. A growth of algae and barnacles builds up in about six weeks.

When we were done cleaning the dinghy, we stayed in town to enjoy the sights. The azaleas are in bloom, and they are beautiful. We also watched an 8th grade band perform. The kids were cute, and they seemed very proud of their performance and musical talents.

At anchor in Saint Augustine, FL

March 30, 1988, Wednesday

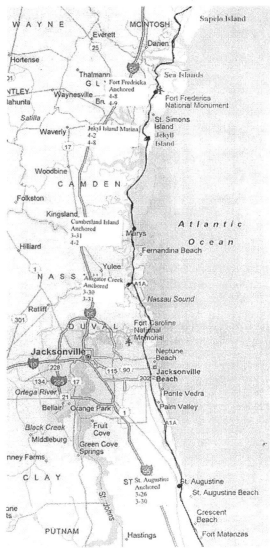

We left early in the morning with the hope of going a long way on the ICW since the weather was favorable. On one of my watches, I spotted an American bald eagle. It was a beautiful sight, sitting proudly along the shore on a mound of rock and shells. We could hardly believe our eyes. Don hurried and got the video camera. The bird was huge! About five minutes later, it flew away, but we were quite far away by then. It was quite a thrill to see such a magnificent creature in the wild; a sight that few people ever have the opportunity to see.

We anchored about sunset and had a restful evening. I did cross-stitch, and Don read. He loves his two current books, one on history and the other on radios. I'm still struggling with *David Copperfield* (on p 400).

Anchored in Alligator Creek near Fernandina Beach, FL – Distance traveled: 52 miles

March 31, 1988, Thursday

What a lazy morning we had. It was a cloudy day, and on those days I hate to hurry out of bed. Don fixed coffee and cereal, and we sat around talking and acting like a couple of kids playing hooky. A few minutes after noon, we raised our anchors and motored on our way.

In a couple of hours, we were at Fernandina Beach. We swung on our anchor for a few minutes talking with *Family Ties,* and then we tied up to the courtesy dock at the marina to revisit the town. When we stayed here on our way south, it was on a Sunday, and everything was closed.

Although we had an enjoyable afternoon of sightseeing, it was a day of sadness because when I called Randy, she told me of the death of Uncle Roger, my dad's brother, who was only 63 years old. He apparently died of a massive stroke or heart attack while working in his garden tilling a flowerbed. It was a complete shock. He hadn't been sick and appeared to be physically fit. Don saw him in January when he went to Ohio and says he looked fine then. I called Grandma and gave her my sympathy. She is 88 and seems to be taking it as well as possible. The funeral is planned for Saturday, April 2nd.

We left Fernandina Beach and went to Cumberland Island, across the border in Georgia, where we anchored for the night. I read about places to see on Cumberland Island in the evening.

Anchored at Cumberland Island – Distance traveled: 15 miles

April 1, 1988, Friday, April Fool's Day

We had a quiet day touring the ruins of the Thomas Carnegie Family's 59 room mansion, known as Dungeness. From about 1886 to 1925, the Thomas Carnegie family enjoyed a lavish lifestyle at Dungeness on Cumberland Island, a very private and out of the way island off the coast of Georgia. Thomas Carnegie was the brother of Andrew Carnegie. The place was last inhabited in 1925, and it burned down in 1959. The National Park Service now maintains the area.

The anchorage was quiet, but the strong current and strong opposing wind made for a worrisome stay. We are still concerned about getting the anchor line caught in the rudder or between the rudder and the hull or wrapped around the keel. We have been using sentinels in this situation for quite some time now, and they seem to have helped, but they aren't fool proof, as was proven in Saint Augustine. A sentinel is a weight attached to the anchor line, which helps to hold the line down, at least at the point where it is attached.

We met some folks on a boat named *Golden Odyssey*, Tom and Charlene Packer. *Golden Odyssey* is a 27-foot sailboat. They and their two daughters, Jill, age 15, and Jason, age 12, have been living on the boat for four years, along with a dog, two cats, a parrot, a monkey and a fish. We can't imagine it!

Tom and Jason came over to visit us in the evening. I showed Jason my cross-stitch and gave her some thread and fabric so she could do her own. She is a smart, cute, polite little girl. The girls are being "home schooled" aboard the boat. They are from Cincinnati and

TOM PACKER AND HIS DAUGTER JASON

began cruising from there four years ago. They are a family that seems to enjoy the boating life!

Anchored at Cumberland Island, GA

April 2, 1988, Saturday

We left Cumberland Island at nine thirty and motored to Jekyll

Island in pleasant weather with plenty of sunshine, arriving at the marina at three. The purpose of this, our second stop at Jekyll Island, is to meet up with Joe and Lois Dixon.

Joe and Lois are good friends from Dublin whom I have mentioned before in this journal. Joe is 84 and Lois is 78, but they are more active and more fun than most people half their age. Don was the attorney for Dublin, having the title of "Village Solicitor," from January 1967 until the summer of 1974. Joe was a member of council when Don became the solicitor and became the mayor during Don's service as the attorney for the village. Joe and his wife, Lois, became good friends with Don during that time and have remained good friends ever since. Don and I both consider Joe and Lois to be two of our best friends.

JEKYLL ISLAND

Joe was born in Georgia in 1904. His family, which included four boys and two girls lived in Waycross, Georgia, until Joe's father died in 1908. Soon thereafter, his mom acquired a small farm near Nahunta, Georgia, which is about 30 miles west of Jekyll Island. Part of the land was given to her by her father, and she purchased the rest. She had a home built on the land and moved the family there from Waycross. She raised her children on the farm and continued to live there until her death in 1973, at the age of 96. Until about 1970, the house didn't have electricity, at which time Joe and Lois had electric service started even though his mother didn't think it was needed or wanted since she believed in primitive living. Joe has acquired the property and has kept the house essentially the way his mother left it. Even the furnishings inside and out have been left as they were when his mother was living in the house. He and Lois go there a couple of times each year and stay for some time. We are going to spend a few days with them at the farm, leaving our boat here at the marina. The plan is for Joe and Lois to come to the marina, tour our boat, and then take us to the farm. We talked to the dockmaster and got the OK to leave the boat here for a few days.

We decided to wait until evening to call Joe and Lois, and while waiting, we visited with people walking along the dock. All of them are here vacationing during Easter holidays. We talked to a lot of them because they asked us questions about how we happened to be here on a boat. One couple, Clyde and Diane Findley, are from Westerville, Ohio, and we especially enjoyed the conversation with them because we have friends in common back home. We invited them on board and served them wine. Later, the four of us went out for dinner in their van. We exchanged addresses and some day we may meet again. They like boating on Lake Erie. They hope someday to buy a Catalina 30, so we did our best to encourage them to contact us when they are ready to buy.

After dinner, I called the home of Edward Brand, Joe's nephew, who lives near the farm, and left a message that we had arrived. I also called my dad and gave him my sympathy regarding the death of Uncle Roger. We talked for a long time. After that Don and I walked to the newly remodeled Jekyll Island Club and looked around, and then walked back to the boat and went to bed.

Jekyll Island Marina, Jekyll Island, GA – Distance traveled: 28 miles

April 3, 1988, Sunday, Easter – April 6, 1988, Wednesday

On Easter Sunday, around two in the afternoon, Joe and Lois came to visit us. We enjoyed some time together on the boat which included Don taping Joe reciting two poems by Robert Service, "The Cremation of Sam McGee" and "The Parson's Son," and then they took us to the farm.

JOE DIXON AT HIS CHILDHOOD HOME IN NAHUNTA, GEORGIA

During our stay on Joe's farm, Joe and Lois kept us entertained.

They took us sightseeing on Saint Simons Island, Jekyll Island, and Sea Island. The azaleas and dogwoods were at the peak of their beauty. They were breathtaking. These islands would be beautiful places to photograph at this time of the year with a really good camera.

We visited his relatives, Edward and Janie Brand and family.

We went fishing on Joe's farm pond.

They took us to the Okefenokee Swamp, where we took a one-hour boat tour.

We played cards.

We also relaxed and just enjoyed the experience of staying in Joe's childhood home and hearing what life on the farm was like.

What a delightful time we both had!

At Joe's request, Don videotaped Joe giving a tour of the house and grounds. We also videotaped the outside of the school Joe attended as a boy and the primitive Baptist church his mom attended. Joe said he had wanted to record a tour of the farm for quite some time so future generations could see what life on the old homestead was like when he was a boy.

Robin Lee **at Jekyll Island Marina, Jekyll Island, GA – Robin and Don at the Dixon farm, near Nahunta, GA**

April 7, 1988, Thursday

During the last night we were at the farm, a strong frontal system came through with 45 mph winds. The next morning, when Joe and Lois took us back to the boat, we could hardly believe the change– the azaleas had suffered the loss of most of their beautiful blossoms as a result of the wind.

At the boat, we bid the Dixons farewell and unpacked and put away the belongings we had taken to the farm. We thought we'd leave at high tide, but due to gale-force winds, we stayed. It was a terrible night. We weren't very well protected from the NW, and our boat took on lots of saltwater spray.

Don made us Reuben sandwiches and French onion soup for dinner, and we spent several hours in the evening discussing the idea of building a primitive cabin in some wilderness and how we would design it. We probably will never build one, but we have discussed it many times, and seeing the old Dixon place gives us new ideas to kick around and daydream about.

At present, we are still enjoying life aboard *Robin Lee* very much. What a great way to enjoy each other and our beautiful world. Our sights change constantly, which makes boredom impossible. Remember...I saw a bald eagle in the wild about a week ago!

Jekyll Island Marina, Jekyll Island, GA

April 8, 1988, Friday

I hadn't spoken with Randy or Shelly since Easter Sunday, so I rode the bike to town to use a pay telephone and go to the post office to buy some stamps. It was still windy, but not as noticeable on land with all the trees and homes to break the wind.

We showered and hosed down the boat and then about two thirty we left the dock. Today's tidal range (the difference in the water level between low and high tide) is 8 ½ feet. At low tide, the water depth at our dock is only about a foot and a half; at high tide, it is about ten feet. We need about 5 ½ feet for the bottom of our keel to skim along the top of the mud. We waited until high tide so we would have a few feet between the mud and the bottom of our keel.

The wind had died by the time we got to Fort Frederica, four hours later. In fact, it was dead calm and the bugs were horrible; we burned a bug coil (a pic) all night.

Don made 15 bean soup with ham hocks, and we enjoyed strawberries with Vanilla Wafers and milk. Everything tasted good. We ate at restaurants every night while we were at the Dixons' house, and were glad to eat "at home."

We went to bed early. I think being away and on the go, sightseeing, wears us out. It sounds crazy, but I think it's true. Besides, now that we have a comfortable mattress, I'd rather sleep in our own bed.

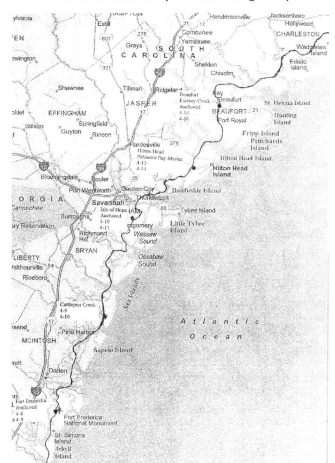

Anchored at Fort Frederica – Distance traveled: 13 miles

April 9, 1988, Saturday

Gosh, the gnats are terrible everywhere in this marshland. The other thing that is universal here are the mud flats during low tide.

We went ashore to see Fort Frederica early because we had a long day's trip planned. The ruins weren't much, and there was no dinghy landing. Consequently, we landed on the mud and tied to a small bush. What a mess we both were, by the time we got back to the boat. We got under way from the fort at nine thirty and motored the entire day through the marshlands with the wind on our nose. We only saw a couple of other boats. At six o'clock, we arrived at our destination in Cattlepen Creek. We had been told that oystering was good at this spot, but we didn't try it because we didn't want to go out in the dinghy and contend with the mud and gnats to try to find fresh oysters, which we aren't crazy about anyway. Furthermore, we think it would probably be better to try it with someone who knows what to do. Unfortunately, there is nobody here...just the gnats!

We closed up early, and therefore eliminated the need of a bug coil burning all night. Last night we used one, and it was terrible! When it burns it gives off an awful smoke that irritates the eyes and smells up the place. It probably wasn't good for our lungs either, but it did keep us from getting a lot of bites.

Anchored in Cattlepen Creek, GA – Distance traveled: 43 miles

April 10, 1988, Sunday

As usual, the wind was mostly on our nose, and so we had to motor the entire way to our destination, the Isle of Hope, a few miles south of Savannah. This part of the ICW makes many turns, and we tried unfurling the jib on stretches when we had the wind with us. However, it wasn't very effective.

I made a new braided watchband out of nylon, but unfortunately it wasn't the right kind of nylon, and it won't stay tied properly. It was a nice day with a lot of boat traffic, especially around the small towns on the Vernon River. The current has been strong, and the tides average eight feet here. From this point north, the tidal range gets less and less. We anchored near a marina at the Isle of Hope and went ashore to talk with the dockmaster about transportation into Savannah. The dockmaster gave us the bus schedule and also told us we could leave our dinghy at his marina.

Don made me pancakes for dinner because I told him they sounded good to me. He says I'm spoiled. I am, but it's his fault.... Who cares anyway? We get along OK!

Anchored at Isle of Hope, GA – Distance traveled: 35 miles

April 11, 1988, Monday

We got up very early so we could catch the eight fifteen bus into Savannah to do some more sightseeing. It takes us a long time to get our act together. We had to get up, get dressed, fix coffee, eat, lock up the boat, get to shore in the dinghy, secure the dinghy and then get to the bus stop before the bus came. How did we ever manage to get to work on time? Boat life sure has taken its toll on us. It has made us lazy and slow.

We did some sightseeing in the morning and had lunch at Mrs. Wilkes' Boarding House. After lunch, we walked along River Street. On the street, we met Charles Belin, who was walking along in the rain under an umbrella. I asked him if he ever shares his umbrella, and he said, "Yes." Don and I enjoyed a 15-minute conversation with him walking in the rain. He works for the Corps of Engineers. They are in charge of the Intracoastal Waterway and the navigable rivers. He invited us into his office where he gave us information on obtaining charts for our Mississippi River trip. He was friendly and Don and I both appreciated the information.

A little later, we saw the Presidential yacht, *Sequoia,* tied up at the Hyatt on the Savannah River. It was recently restored with private money and is now on a tour known as "Celebrate America." People can tour it on certain days. We saw the *Sequoia* in Charleston on our way south, a year and a half ago.

We got groceries on the way back to Isle of Hope, and I called Sister Carol to check in. There was no news, which is good news as far as we're concerned.

THE PRESIDENTIAL YACHT, *SEQUOIA,* IN SAVANNAH

While we were sightseeing, the anchor line got snagged on the rudder again. The sentinels failed us for the second time. Don wants to get more chain. As he says, "Chain doesn't get stuck in the rudder!" However, chain is heavy, and adding two additional 20' chains would give us a total of approximately 200 pounds of ground tackle stored in the bow, which might cause a problem. Some sailors have cautioned us that a boat that is heavy in the bow doesn't handle well. As we go north from here the tidal range and the tidal current will be less and less and we should have fewer, or no, problems. But if we were to do it again, we would have at least 50 feet of chain for each anchor. While Don was getting the line unsnagged, he slid out of the dinghy into the water. Since some alligators live in that water, he got out quickly. He was cold, wet, and his clothes were soaked with brackish water, so we went ashore to get showers and do laundry. We were at the shower and laundry facility until late. I think we finally had our dinner, featuring chicken gizzards, about nine thirty. I'm not crazy about gizzards, but felt I should eat a few since Don had gone to the trouble of cooking them.

Free Spirit came through here today. We talked to Dick and Pat on the marine radio. They are headed for Washington, D.C., I think they plan on being there for the month of May. We may see them along the way or in the Capital.

Anchored at Isle of Hope, GA

April 12, 1988, Tuesday

The weather was so foul, we decided to stay put. I went ashore early to get our clothes out of the dryer, thinking we would leave, but it started to rain, and it never quit until five o'clock. We ran the kerosene heater all day.

After the rain stopped, we visited with a boat anchored near us from Canada. The couple on board bad-mouthed Reagan, complained about the U.S. creating acid rain, and claimed that U.S. boaters are ruining the Georgian Bay. Don and I both have gotten the opinion that many Canadians don't like the U.S. or Americans. However, we just listen to their complaints and try not to give them anything else not to like.

Don made a new vegetarian dish for dinner containing okra, onions, tomatoes, green peppers, and lots of garlic.

At seven, we went ashore to walk around the beautiful town of Isle of Hope. It was cold, but because of that, the bugs didn't bother us. There are many nicely kept big beautiful old homes in this area. It seems to be where people with "old money" live.

Anchored at Isle of Hope, GA

April 13, 1988, Wednesday

A cold front passed through, and the gnats are gone. Oh happy day! It was chilly, but we had sunshine off and on. We went 35 miles and spent the night in the Hilton Head area. First, we went into the marina at Harbour Town, but because the Heritage Golf Tournament is being held there this week, dockage was limited and expensive. We left and went to Broad Creek where we docked at the Palmetto Bay Marina and Resort. It was $0.50 per foot and $1.00 for electricity.

After docking, a couple gave us a ride into the Sea Pines area where we shopped at the Winn Dixie. We walked part of the way back, but decided to hitchhike. We figured that hitching a ride was less risky than walking on that terribly busy narrow two-lane road. We got a ride with a local man in a brand new Mercedes. What luxury! It had been a long time since we had been in a car that nice!

We ate a light meal of salad, French bread and cheese, and a glass of wine. For dessert, we had cherry Jell-O with pears. Even though it was supposed to be a "light" meal, we both stuffed ourselves. I wonder how much we weigh. The last scales we used were at the Longboat Key Publix.

We had our usual relaxing quiet evening. I did cross-stitch and Don read. We ran the electric heater all night.

At Palmetto Bay Marina, Broad Creek, Hilton Head, SC – Distance traveled: 29 miles

April 14, 1988, Thursday

Today we got a break in the weather. It was in the high 60s and sunny all day. We showered and spent time shopping in the boat store at the marina complex. Don purchased a spare part for the water pressure pump. When he fixed the pump in Fort Pierce, he noticed that this part was about worn out.

I called Randy and found out Aunt Maude has been hospitalized. She is critically ill and needs to have bowel surgery. At her age, she may not live through the surgery. I'm glad I have written her regularly since we left. I know that it's given her something to look forward to. Otherwise, her existence in the nursing home would have been pretty dull. I bet she's the only resident there who has a great niece living and traveling on a sailboat! Such an interesting topic for conversation at the dinner table in the nursing home!

We left for the Beaufort area. The wind was on our nose as is usually the case. *Sea Sprite* passed us. They don't tow their dinghy and motor, so they seem to go faster than *Robin Lee*. After we got to Factory Creek, we saw them again and two other boats we know—*Caprice* (Bob) and *Golden Odyssey* (Tom, Charlene and family). After we got our anchors set, Don made dinner, and I went out in the dinghy to explore and socialize.

It was buggy again, so we closed up early. Don made a recipe from the Pirates Cove restaurant in Savannah, honey pecan chicken.

Anchored in Factory Creek, near Beaufort (pronounced Bu-fort), SC – Distance traveled: 32 miles

April 15, 1988, Friday

We hitched a ride to Beaufort with Bob in his dinghy. We wanted to revisit the town because we really liked what we saw of it on our way south. We walked and walked, looking at the old homes and admiring the beautiful spring flowers. It's really a charming small town. We enjoyed a sandwich and Coke at a small, newly opened bakery. We also bought a piece of cake and a loaf of bread to go. We took lots of pictures and then went back to Factory Creek. We then went ashore in separate dinghies to go to a nearby Winn Dixie and Red and White grocery to buy a few things to stow because our next good grocery stop will be in Georgetown or McClellanville. Charleston doesn't have a grocery close by the marina.

The weather was good all day.

Bob joined us for dinner and a nice evening of visiting and getting to know him better.

Anchored at Factory Creek, near Beaufort, SC

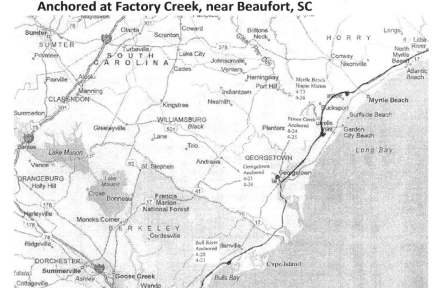

April 16, 1988, Saturday

We arose early and left our anchoring spot in Factory Creek at eight o'clock. We arrived 9 ½ hours later at our new anchoring spot, 15 miles south of Charleston, in Church Creek, after traveling 48 miles. We motored all the way. We got our anchors set and then took a short dinghy trip up the creek to see a house that is all by itself in the middle of this marshy area. It is really beautiful as are many waterfront homes.

We went aground with the captain at the helm, and I teased him about it. He didn't take kindly to the teasing since he was in the middle of the channel where there should have been plenty of water. I felt bad that he was upset by my teasing. He is cautious and careful about everything, and it's not his fault the channels shoal up with mud and silt. There is supposed to be a minimum depth of 12' in the ICW, but apparently the Corps of Engineers doesn't have sufficient funding to maintain the promised depth. In some places, there are warnings of depths of less than 12', but there were no warning about this stretch and supposedly there is never less than 7', which means we should always have at least one and a-half feet of water under our keel.

I took a shower in the cabin. The gnats were too bad in the cockpit, plus we had two boats as neighbors.

Don went to bed; he was tired since we had gotten up so early today. I stayed up and did cross-stitch and worked a little on my afghan.

Anchored in Church Creek, 15 miles south of Charleston, SC – Distance traveled: 48 miles

April 17, 1988, Sunday

We had a rotten night! One of our two anchors dragged, and one of our lines got around the keel resulting in our getting sideways to the current. The current here is very strong; the tidal range is about 7'. We were up off and on until daylight. I heard my captain say, "My kingdom, (if I had one) for two more 20-foot chains." I'm not sure what he meant, but I think it's from Shakespeare. He says that if he had it, he would put 50' of chain on each anchor and let out only 20' of the anchor line attached to the chain. The line would cushion the shock you would have with all chain when waves hit you. Fifty feet of the heavy chain is probably equivalent to 80 feet of anchor line for purposes of anchoring. Then we wouldn't have a long line swimming around like a water snake, especially if we attached a sentinel at the ten foot mark.

We had to be up early anyway to get to a very narrow stretch of the waterway called Elliott's Cut at slack water. Our guide book warned that if there is an opposing strong wind and an opposing current at the cut, it is difficult to make headway. As it turned out, the wind wasn't strong today, and it was very sunny, warm, and quite pretty throughout the day. It was one of those rare days of 12 hours of gorgeous weather. Being always exposed to the elements definitely makes one more observant of the weather.

We arrived at the Charleston Municipal Marina at twelve thirty. Don did maintenance work all afternoon. I did a lot of chores like painting the dinghy seat, my bike, and our fender board. I also hosed down the boat.

We had leftovers for dinner.

I moved the TV around trying to get better reception, without much success. We did get decent reception on the PBS station and enjoyed a couple of shows. One was a presentation of *David Copperfield*, which I am still reading. I am now on page 500.

The weather forecast for the next couple days is bad.

Charleston Municipal Marina, Charleston, SC – Distance traveled: 16 miles

April 18, 1988, Monday

We never know whether we will have good or bad fortune from one day to the next. Yesterday, it was bad fortune with our early-morning difficulties with our anchors. Today, it was good fortune. Don was in the shower, and I was at the laundry facilities here at the marina where I struck up a conversation with some people who moved to Charleston last year from Cleveland. They offered to drive us around sightseeing and to include a ride to the aircraft carrier *Yorktown*, which is at Patriot's Point on the other side of Charleston Bay. Of course I accepted their offer, and after our busy afternoon of sightseeing, our new best friends, Ann and Dick Howard, insisted that we join them at their lovely waterfront condo near the marina for wine, cheese and crackers. It was delightful and such an unexpected treat!

We got home around eight thirty. I put the laundry away, made up the bed, and we quickly fell asleep.

Charleston Municipal Marina, Charleston, SC

April 19, 1988, Tuesday

What a hard blow and rainstorm we experienced early today! There was even a tornado watch until noon. Don saw one boat in the marina with two broken dock lines. He secured it with a couple of our extra lines. He made phone calls to Jane and Chip, and also called a freighter company to check the price of shipping *Robin Lee* to Europe. The cost was way too much for us to consider. I didn't get out of bed until eleven o'clock. About noon, we set out to do some more sightseeing in downtown Charleston. We went by bus to the Cotton Exchange to see a historic film, *Dear Charleston*, and afterwards we walked through some historic areas, including the slave market. We spent $25 on a hand-woven basket, and I bought a Jemima Puddle-Duck to keep my bears company. We took a bus to the Citadel Mall and spent a lot more money. We bought two CDs, a fishing book so I can learn to fish, and a variety of other small items. We got home at nine thirty and were really worn out.

Charleston Municipal Marina, Charleston, SC

April 20, 1988, Wednesday

We paid our dock fees and left Charleston at eight forty-five. We were detained, because of some repair work, at the Ben Sawyer Bridge, which crosses the waterway on the north side of Charleston Bay. The rest of the day was spent motoring north. It was a pretty day, but was a bit chilly.

We anchored in the Bull River, a few miles down from McClellanville, around four thirty. *Caprice* came in shortly thereafter. I went fishing with Bob, but we didn't catch anything.

Don stayed home and made dinner for the three of us. I made the salad (a rare occasion), and we ate around six thirty. Bob stayed until nine thirty. We turned the heater on to warm us up. Bob is going to make us a live bait box so we can fish more.

Anchored in the Bull River, just south of McClellanville, SC – Distance travelled: 34 miles

ROBIN'S NEW SEWING MACHINE

April 21, 1988, Thursday

We were lazy and slept in; we didn't leave until ten thirty. Today was an excellent sunbathing day, and while we were underway, I spent about an hour and a half on the deck doing just that and relaxing. We arrived at Georgetown around three thirty. It was a pleasant trip, but we are still seeing vast areas of marshlands, which become boring after a while.

Bob came to Georgetown too, but we didn't visit much because Don went to the grocery, and I went up to the Grab Bag and revisited my friend Shirley. She is the lady who allowed me to use her sewing machine last year. I had saved up some sewing projects to work on, and she was kind enough to let me use her machines again.

Don had a long walk to and from the grocery. We ate late because he got home so late. He fixed chicken tetrazzini.

Anchored at Georgetown, SC – Distance traveled: 35 miles

April 22, 1988, Friday

We stayed put today. Don worked on the knot meter, but was unable to fix it. I looked around in the shops, mailed Shelly a letter, and finally mailed *Epicurus* their gift of towels with "Epicurus" cross-stitched in them.

I fell head over heels in love with a cute little sewing machine in one of the stores. I sewed on it all afternoon and finally decided to buy it. The lady sold it to me for 50% off the tag price. I hope I enjoy it as much as I have my Singer, which I purchased 20 years ago.

Don went back to the grocery today and bought several bags of groceries, which he had to carry a long way back to the boat. One of the difficulties in the live-aboard world is that in most towns, the grocery stores are a long way from the core of the town where the docks are. When the towns were first established they were built along the waterfront because, in most cases, access to water was the reason the town was established. At that time, the grocery stores would have been near the docks. Now they are in the residential areas, away from the town's old core. That is also true of laundromats. We laugh now when we see the Old Spice commercial with the sailor whistling the Old Spice tune while he is walking down the street with a bag over his shoulder. We know that he's looking for a laundromat.

Bob came over again tonight, and we ate pork chops. He stayed to visit until nine thirty.

It was a pretty day. We like Georgetown a lot. However, the local paper mill creates a bad odor.

Anchored at Georgetown, SC

TWENTY POUNDS OF CRAWFISH

April 23, 1988, Saturday

Shirley, from the Grab Bag, came to the boat and took measurements and told us what it would cost to re-cover our cushions. We decided against it for now. I went to Scotts Sewing Center early in the morning to make a pair of slacks. While I was there, a local crawfish farmer came into the shop and gave one of the ladies some crawfish. When he saw that I was admiring them, he said he'd give me a boxful also. Well, about eleven thirty he came into the store with my box, a 12"x18"x8" box packed full with 20 pounds of crawfish. Don and Bob were thrilled! Don went to the library and found a recipe for *crawfish etouffee*, which he fixed for dinner. We used half of them for the *etouffee*. It was excellent. You only eat the tail, which is a small part of the crawfish, and therefore, the three of us were able to eat ten pounds without difficulty.

During the day, Don baked a Soggy Chocolate cake with caramel icing for our dessert. It was scrumptious. The evening was great, except it rained.

Anchored at Georgetown, SC

April 24, 1988, Sunday

It was cloudy and very chilly when we left Georgetown at eight forty. I was quite sure we'd get some rain and maybe thunderstorms. We motor-sailed with SW winds most of the day, but quit early when we got to the only decent anchorage shown on the chart in this vicinity. It was three o'clock. We never did get rain; in fact, it turned out to be sunny and warm.

After we anchored, *Caprice* dropped the hook near us. Bob and I and his dalmatian dog, Target, went exploring and took lots of nature pictures with his camera, which has a zoom

lens. Caterpillars and warblers were everywhere. I ran his dinghy; it planes smoothly. Don used another library recipe to make a pasta dish with a crawfish sauce to use up the remaining crawfish. We were told not to cook the dead ones because when they die, they spoil quickly. We had to dump more than half of what we still had. I think they suffocated. Dinner was ready at six. We visited until about eight. I caught an eel while fishing. That's better than my usual, nothing. Bob left just as the deer flies were getting bad. We closed up the boat as soon as Bob left. I wrote to Shelly, read awhile, and went to bed early.

Anchored in Prince Creek, 15 miles south of Myrtle Beach, SC — Distance traveled: 26 miles

April 25, 1988, Monday

We got up early so we could go to a marina and try to get transportation into Myrtle Beach to spend some time sightseeing. The morning was calm and pretty. We bid Bob farewell at the anchorage. He's not interested in seeing Myrtle Beach and is going on. We hope to

BOB BAKER, CAPRICE, TARGET AND A BOX OF CRAWFISH

see him again.

This is a beautiful anchorage, but because it is such deep water (18-25 ft.), Don was thankful we didn't have strong winds. The anchorage is small and in order for the boat to be able to swing completely around and not hit the shore, our scope was limited. Last night's forecast included a small chance of a thunderstorm. If the storm had materialized and if our anchor hadn't held, we would have been forced to continue up the waterway in the dark. The waterway has lighted aids to navigation, so it is possible to travel on it at night, but in a storm it wouldn't have been fun. We should have gone on yesterday to the marina near Myrtle Beach, but we got lucky and the storm didn't materialize.

We went to Hague Marina, which is the marina closest to Myrtle Beach, arriving shortly before eleven. We checked on transportation after getting situated at the dock, i.e., after we had filled our water tanks, plugged into their electric, tied our dock lines securely, put the dinghy motor on the mount on *Robin Lee's* stern railing and registering at the marina office. The marina facilities were adequate, but expensive–$0.75 per foot, $23, with tax for us. However, the owner of the marina offered to loan us an old car at no extra charge, so we could go sightseeing.

Since the car would only be available to us from three thirty to six, we decided to eat our main meal at lunchtime, and Don fixed it while I did two loads of dirty clothes. When we got the car, we drove around in Myrtle Beach, saw the main street where all the action is, looked around at the beach, had a Dairy Queen, went to the bank to replenish our cash, bought groceries, and then came back. The traffic was heavy, and it made me a bit nervous. We almost got lost in the wilderness. The marina is in the boondocks, and we had several turns to make and dirt roads to follow. We made several wrong turns due to bad directions people had given us. I guess we should just do our sightseeing at five mph in our sailboat on the scenic ICW where there are many beautiful homes and other sights along the shores, and where I feel happy and safe. Our impression of Myrtle Beach is that it is a place for families with small children to come and enjoy. We don't think it is our kind of place and probably won't come back.

We tried to make a few phone calls, but got no answers except by the answering machines. The yacht *Enticer*, sister ship of *Sequoia*, pulled into the marina in the evening. Both are beautiful. We got out all of our CDs and played them through. It sprinkled lightly and got cool, but we had the electric heater on. I stayed up sewing until two in the morning, but now my slacks are finished. They fit pretty well. I may taper the legs a bit more; otherwise, I like them.

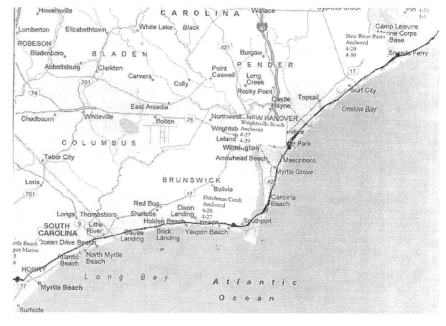

At Hague Marina, near Myrtle Beach, SC – Distance traveled: 12 miles

April 26, 1988, Tuesday

It was a very long day. We went 56 miles in 11 hours, starting at seven thirty in the morning and ending at six thirty in the evening. We took two-hour watches. It was a bit cool on the boat even though the winds were from the south. We left South Carolina and are now in North Carolina.

We anchored in Dutchman's Creek, a marshy area near Southport, because we saw that *Caprice* was anchored there. He came to our boat for dessert and an evening visit. We think single-handed sailors must get a little lonely, so we always try to include them if possible. Besides learning a lot about them, and enjoying their company, Don loves to cook and have someone other than me to enjoy his food. Getting to know others has made our trip a lot more interesting and fun.

I went into Southport to make some phone calls with Bob and his dog, Target, in their dinghy. It was about a 3-mile trip. I finally got to speak with Randy after several days of not getting hold of her. All is OK in that part of the world. Aunt Maude is recovering from surgery; I sure hope she doesn't have miserable health problems before she dies, and I hope I get to visit with her again.

Dutchman's Creek, near Southport, NC – Distance traveled: 56 miles

April 27, 1988, Wednesday

When we left Dutchman's Creek, we entered the Cape Fear River near its mouth where it empties into the ocean. The current was very strong in the river because the tide was going out, and between the tide and the natural flow of the river from run off, the current was so strong we could barely make headway until the ICW left the river, about 15 miles upriver. We only went 28 miles all day, but it took us seven hours. Also, the markers were not easily followed. I was out of the channel a couple of times and ran aground once. We stopped at Wrightsville Beach because Uncle Bob is planning on visiting us there. He has a lady friend, and I think he would like for us to meet her and vice-versa.

We anchored at Wrightsville Beach instead of docking, primarily because it doesn't cost anything, but also because we enjoy our privacy when we are at anchor. We ate leftovers, and at six o'clock, went ashore to see if Uncle Bob had come to the marina. Fortunately, he hadn't. I called, and for the first time, found him at home. He says he and his friend will come tomorrow night, so I guess we'll stay and relax tomorrow. It's supposed to be pretty windy anyway. We shopped at a general store, had a dessert out, and then walked back by way of the ocean beach. We also stopped at the library and read magazines.

Anchored at Wrightsville Beach, NC – Distance traveled: 28 miles

April 28, 1988, Thursday

It was sunny, cool, and very windy. We spent most of the day on the boat. We slept in, showered on board, cleaned up, and ate breakfast. I worked on redesigning the slacks I'm making.

The Mallard ducks here are very friendly. I fed them bread. Three pairs came to the boat. One duck got so excited he flew up on the lifelines of the boat. One male and female felt so comfy on our turf that they decided to sit on our dinghy seat.

Around three we went ashore to sightsee and shop at the grocery. I tease Don about wanting to go to the grocery so much, but actually since we anchor so often, we can't keep much fresh food on the boat. The refrigeration works well on shore power, but the batteries run down quickly at anchor. It hasn't been a problem; we just don't buy much and go to the grocery often. We took another walk on the ocean beach. We like it better here than at Myrtle Beach because this place isn't as touristy.

Shortly after we got back to the boat and Don started to fix dinner, I heard Uncle Bob yell at me. I was trying to fish off the boat and just then got my hook caught in the anchor line–what a bad fisherman I am!

I dinghied to shore and picked up his friend, Jeanette, and him. We drank wine, visited, and ate dinner. Don made spaghettini with green sauce and served sliced tomatoes on the side, plus Kaiser rolls. Our guests thought it was wonderful! We used the tablecloth and napkins I made, which makes it look real "homey." Gosh, it was nice to see Uncle Bob; he looks great, as he always does. In November of this year, he'll be 60 years old. He's lots of fun and always has a few jokes to tell. They treated us to a dessert in Wilmington and then, after bringing us back to the boat, they left to drive back to Southern Pines, a 3-hour trip.

Anchored at Wrightsville Beach, NC

April 29, 1988, Friday

We left the anchorage at Wrightsville Beach around nine o'clock, got fuel and water at the marina, and sat there until ten thirty-five, giving us just enough time to make the eleven o'clock opening of the Wrightsville Beach Bridge. We visited with several cruising boaters at the marina while we waited.

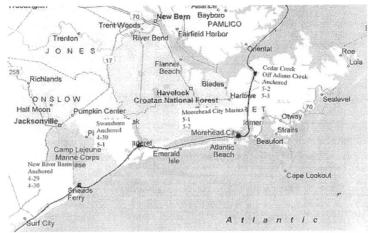

While under way, I tried trolling, but had no luck, even with my new "led-heads." Also, I wrote Aunt Maude a letter and made her a get-well card. I also wrote Shelly a short letter.

We arrived at the New River Basin, near Camp LeJeune, at six thirty where we anchored for the night. After anchoring, I set out for a short dinghy trip to talk to some boaters anchored near us.

Don made clam chowder with chunks of ham in it. I offered some to a couple on a 27-foot Catalina, *Sea Sprite*. They were anchored behind us. They came aboard, and we visited for an hour and a half. They are French Canadians and have traveled all over the world, mostly by back packing, a pleasant young couple who didn't criticize our country once during our visit. It got cooler in the evening, so we ran the heater. I did cross-stitch and worked on my afghan. Don read, and we listened to NPS (National Public Radio). They were playing "floating music." It made us sleepy, so we went to bed early.

Anchored in the New River Basin, near Camp LeJeune, NC – Distance traveled: 39 miles

April 30, 1988, Saturday

One year-ago today we were in Fort Lauderdale and left for the Bahamas late in the day. How excited we were, and nervous too!

We had a short day today. It was only 15 miles to the anchorage at Swansboro, our next destination. We left the Camp Lejeune area at eleven thirty and got to Swansboro at three. Our alternator belt broke while en route, so after anchoring, we replaced it with our spare one and then went ashore. We got a ride into town from a kid in the marina. This town has several craft shops, which I remembered seeing on the way down in November '86. I looked around in the shops, and then we went to the grocery, and after that looked around some more. We ate a sandwich at Hardy's, had an ice cream cone, and then walked back to the marina. We enjoyed looking at all the homes, lawns, and flowers along the way. We got back just before dark, around seven thirty.

It was a quiet evening. We read, listened on our radio to old Fibber McGee and Molly radio shows and songs by various stars of the 30s and 40s. We went to bed at ten thirty.

Anchored at Swansboro, NC – Distance traveled: 15 miles

May 1, 1988, Sunday

We left Swansboro at nine forty and got to the Morehead City Yacht Basin at one forty. As we approached the basin in the channel, we ran aground. It is shallow. We had to sit in the mud, a few feet away from our dock, until the tide came in. Then my captain said, "My Kingdom, if I had one, for the shoal draft version of the Catalina 30."

Cruising quickly taught us that an 11" difference in the depth of water we need is far more important to us than the advantage the fin keel offers for sailing close to the wind and making quick turns. I think most sailors who have never cruised would probably choose the fin keel because they would think that sailing well close to the wind is important. It is if you are racing or don't have auxiliary power. What they don't understand is that cruising sailors doing coastal cruising, as we are doing, motor much more than they sail. All the cruisers do, not just *Robin Lee.* Many times we have started out the day sailing, and then calculated our expected arrival time at our destination based on our rate of progress, and realized that, at the rate we were going, we wouldn't arrive at our destination until the middle of the night. When that is the case, we start the engine. If the wind is helping, we leave the sails up and motor-sail, otherwise we lower them. Motoring is the norm, not the exception. When motoring, pointing and being able to turn very sharply are not critical, but the boat's draft often is.

A 10 ½ FOOT TIGER SHARK

We saw two tiger sharks that were caught and brought into the marina; one was 10 ½ feet, and the other about 9 1/2 feet. There were four guys on the boat. They said that they caught the sharks 35-40 miles off shore, that the bait was Boston Mackerel, and that it took them about two hours to land each one. They went out yesterday and came back today. Their boat, called *Rod Warrior,* looks to be about 28 feet long. The sharks were too big to bring aboard so they lashed them to the boat. They did get the smaller one in the boat this morning.

I did a load of wash for $0.50 and then hitched a ride to town with the dockmaster. I walked the mile and a half back, and on the way back I stopped at a book and card store. I picked out Mother's Day cards, but we are out of cash, so I asked the storekeeper to set them aside for Don to pick up tomorrow after he goes to the bank. I finished the laundry, Don showered. We met John of *Moonshadow* and talked with him awhile.

Don made sweet and sour kielbasa for dinner and coconut pudding for dessert. He went to bed early; I stayed up to sew. I didn't go to bed until 1:30. It was cold! We had the electric heater going all night, but I was still pretty cold.

Tied up at the Morehead City Yacht Basin, Morehead City, NC – Distance traveled: 26 miles

CHAPTER TWELVE
MOREHEAD CITY, NC to CHESAPEAKE CITY, MD
May 2, 1988 – June 22, 1988

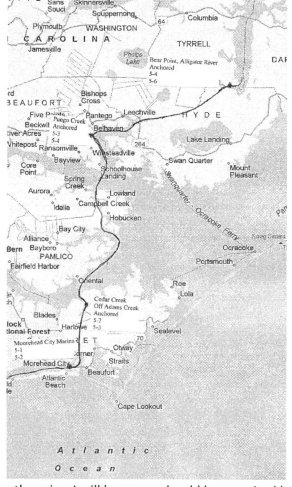

May 2, 1988, Monday

I slept in; Don got up early to run errands. He went to the bank to replenish our cash and to the post office to pick up mail and buy stamps. I took my time getting up, and then had a cup of Café Vienna and a bowl of cereal. I put away the laundry, ran the sweeper, finished my sewing projects, and stowed my cute little sewing machine. We were both busy all morning. When Don got back at eleven thirty, he invited me to lunch at the Sanitary Restaurant, which is a popular local place.

We tried to leave at two o'clock but couldn't because we were stuck in mud; the tide was out. We finally got underway at three thirty. We anchored in Cedar Creek off Adams Creek, about 17 miles from Morehead City, at seven. I fished for about ten minutes, got the line tangled up, and quit! Don made lentil soup, but neither of us was very hungry because we had eaten a big lunch.

We spent the evening opening mail, looking at our newly developed photos, and writing letters. It was cold, so we had the kerosene heater burning until late. I sure hate the cold! I hope it gets warm soon; otherwise, I will know we should have waited longer before leaving Longboat Key.

Anchored off Adam's Creek in Cedar Creek, NC – Distance traveled: 17 miles

May 3, 1988, Tuesday

It was cold, cloudy, rainy, and windy when we left Cedar Creek at eight fifteen and headed for the Neuse River. It reminded us of a typical day on the Great Lakes during our cruise in '85. The 15-mile stretch on the Neuse River on our route for today is where, on our way south in November '86, our dinghy turned over, and we had such a difficult time retrieving it. We should have considered staying put. We had 3-5-foot waves and took a lot of spray over the bow today, but at least we didn't lose the dinghy. I wonder if this stretch of the waterway is ever peaceful and pleasant.

We went 52 miles and anchored in Pungo Creek, close to Bellhaven. Don made cornbread to go with the lentil soup. The kerosene heater kept us warm, and we were glad to be sitting still. On today's positive side, we made good time, and we are done with the Neuse River, forever.

Anchored in Pungo Creek, near Bellhaven, NC – Distance traveled: 52 miles

May 4, 1988, Wednesday

When we got up, the weather conditions were about the same as yesterday. We raised the anchor and went to a marina at Bellhaven to get fuel and water. I hosed down the boat at the marina to wash off the salt-water, and then we took a walk into town. I mailed Mom's Mother's Day card, bought birthday cards for Chip, and bought a plastic apron to lay over the companion way to help keep warm air inside and cold air outside. We each drank a chocolate milkshake and then headed back to the boat. The day was cloudy and colder than we like, but the sun peeked through the clouds briefly while we were in town. The people at the marina were cordial, and they keep a clean marina with great facilities for transients.

We got underway and motored through a 20-mile canal, connecting Bellhaven to a long narrow bay on the south side of Albemarle Sound. The cypress trees along the canal are pretty, but they create brownish water that looks like Coca-Cola. Don had two shifts. His first shift was during a windy rainstorm. It wasn't a fun time for him. I stayed below and organized my birthday cards. On my second break, I showered and wrote in this book. His second shift got us to our anchoring place at Bear Point, on the Alligator River, at the south end of the long narrow bay, in the swampy boondocks of North Carolina. During his break, Don chopped up some veggies for our Chinese stir-fried pork and scallops dinner. He also fixed a new veggie appetizer, made with deep fried okra, which we both liked. Okra is popular in the South; Don wants to learn various ways to fix it.

In the evening, we each wrote a birthday card to Chip and got them ready to mail. The weather forecast for tonight and tomorrow isn't good. Severe electrical storms and high winds are predicted. We set two anchors, and we may have to sit tomorrow because we don't want to try to cross Albemarle Sound in windy weather because it can be very treacherous, like Pamlico Sound and the Neuse River.

The boats closest to us are about two miles away, so we are out here in the middle of nowhere, all by ourselves tonight. However, even if we get severe thunderstorms as predicted, I feel like we'll be just fine; time will tell!

Bear Point, Alligator River, south of Albemarle Sound, NC

May 5, 1988, Thursday

We didn't have storms last night, and we slept, undisturbed, until six o'clock. Don got up and turned on the VHF to get today's forecast. It was the same, high winds and severe electrical storms for this area with small craft warnings. Thankfully, my husband is a conscientious safety-minded captain, and we did not try to cross Albemarle Sound with that forecast. We stayed put and went back to bed. The rain started shortly thereafter. We had rain all day, and as advertised, high winds and poor visibility came along with it. We even developed a chop and three-foot waves in this quiet anchorage. It was a mean, ugly, cold miserable day. The best part was that we slept in, and Don served me breakfast in bed. We read, talked, laughed, and relaxed all day. During the worst of the storm, we think the winds peaked at more than 40 knots. The skies were very black as the front passed, and then suddenly, about six thirty, it was over; the sky turned blue, and we had sunshine. "Mother nature" is remarkable. We tried to capture some of this activity on video and with still shots, but no way could we ever show the intensity of this storm.

I wrote Shelly and Don wrote Chip. We ate leftovers and drank coffee with amaretto and whipped cream and cookies after dinner. Even though it was a rotten day weather-wise, we had a wonderful day on the boat. I love living aboard!

Only a few drips came in at the windows, which surprised me. We had about six inches of rain in the dinghy.

Anchored at Bear Point, Alligator River, south of Albemarle Sound, NC

May 6, 1988, Friday

In preparation for leaving, we stowed the dinghy boat's motor on the stern railing of the big boat. We were cautioned that the sound gets to be quite bad at times without warning. We didn't want to take any chances of losing the Honda motor. Furthermore, it creates a drag if we leave it on the dinghy. We got underway at five forty-five in the morning, headed

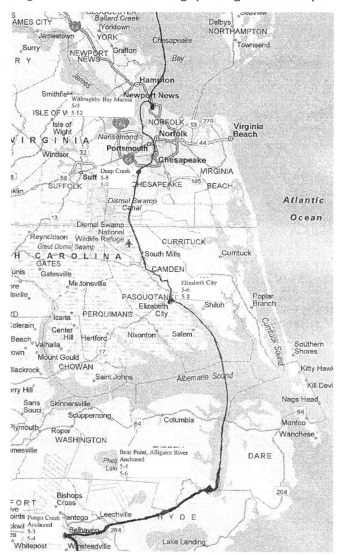

for Elizabeth City, which is north of Albemarle Sound on the Pasquotank River. I think that is the earliest we have gotten started, but the weather forecast was for 15-20 knot winds and possibly electrical storms late in the day, SO we wanted to be across the sound before they happened.

It was a successful day. We even came to the aid of a 34' sailboat that was aground in a shallow part of the sound. The three people on board were French and spoke very little English, so we had difficulty communicating with them. One of the men used their dinghy to bring us a line, and we pulled them off the bottom. He didn't tie their dinghy to their boat very well when he went back, and it got loose and drifted away. I rowed our dinghy out and retrieved theirs. Fortunately, it was flat calm at the time. Needless to say, they were very appreciative that we came to their aid. Just after we rescued them, a Coast Guard chopper flew directly over them several times, quite low, apparently to check out the situation. The female French skipper and I exchanged addresses; I will write to her.

[NOTE: In 1991, while we were in France, we went to her address with the hope of visiting with her, but she had moved and left no forwarding address. She's lost forever.]

We arrived at the town dock in Elizabeth City shortly after three, got situated, walked to the post office, grocery, and hardware store. We ate at Taco Bell and then shopped for new carpet for the main cabin. It was seven thirty when we got back to the boat. There was a crowd of people at the dock. It was a welcoming committee, welcoming all the boaters that had come in and tied up at the city docks during the day. They call it the "Rose Buddy Committee." Willard Scott, the weather man on the *Today* show, gave them that name. They gave us a rose and various gifts and showered us with hospitality. That is quite an unusual thing to do for transients. They also gave us a lot of information on things to see around town.

Tied at the city docks in Elizabeth City, NC – Distance traveled: 54 miles

May 7, 1988, Saturday
It got terribly windy in the night and was still blowing hard in the morning, so we decided to stay put and enjoy the hospitality of the people of Elizabeth City and the feeling of being wanted. Don ran errands early in the day. I stayed home and got caught up on writing postcards.

When Don returned home about one o'clock, we rode our courtesy bicycles, furnished by the Rose Buddy Committee, to the local athletic club to enjoy the facilities. They charge a special price for visiting sailors. It only cost $0.25 each; what a deal! I used the sauna and whirlpool and then showered. I took my good old time enjoying the relaxation. I only weigh 121. Not bad!

Afterwards, we bought carryout meals from a local fried fish restaurant, which we ate at a picnic table at the dock provided for the use of sailors by the Rose Buddies.

Then we did a walking tour of the city and called Cousin Amy and *Orchid Boat*.
Tied at the city docks in Elizabeth City, NC

ON THE DISMAL SWAMP CANAL

May 8, 1988, Sunday – Mother's Day
We left Elizabeth City shortly after eight o'clock and went up the Pasquotank River and through the Dismal Swamp Canal to Deep Creek, Virginia. About a mile north of Elizabeth City, we passed an old brick house that was used by Blackbeard the Pirate as a hideout. The name "Dismal Swamp" is a misnomer; it is one of the prettiest stretches of the waterway we have seen. The beauty of the trees and shrubs is overwhelming. It's very narrow, which adds to its beauty. What a nice 38-mile day trip it was for us! We experienced one minor annoyance on the canal. Many small caterpillars were suspended from trees with self-spun silk, and some of them fell onto our boat. We probably had about 50 on board when we got to the end, which we had to carefully remove in order not to make a mess on the boat.

The canal is the oldest continually operating man-made canal in the U.S. It opened in 1805 and was hand-dug over a period of 12 years. George Washington visited the Great

Dismal Swamp in 1763 and suggested digging a canal through it in order to connect the Chesapeake Bay to Albemarle Sound. He did some of the survey work on the canal and had a financial interest in the company that built and operated it. The canal itself is 22 miles long. The connection between the Chesapeake Bay and Albemarle Sound is completed by the Elizabeth River, which goes through Norfolk, and the Pasquotank River. The canal is frequently closed because of low water. It isn't open for use unless it has a depth of at least six feet. It was closed on our way south in '86.

We had a two-hour delay at the South Mills Lock, at the south end of the canal, so we tied to dolphins and went ashore. We walked a mile and a half to the village of South Mills and back. There isn't much there; it's a pretty sleepy community. We had Cokes and talked with the shop keeper for a half-hour and then returned to the boat.

THE DISMAL SWAMP

We got to Deep Creek at the north end of the canal at five thirty and tied to the bridge wall. We ate a tossed salad for dinner and then took a short walk around town. We bought ice cream bars from the corner Seven Eleven store. This is another sleepy village.

Tied to a bridge in Deep Creek, VA – Distance traveled: 38 miles

May 9, 1988, Monday

There was a lot of water traffic in the Norfolk area, the most we had experienced since leaving Charleston. One can't go through any of the major ports, such as Miami, Lauderdale, Norfolk, or New York, and not be impressed with the large number and variety of vessels. In Norfolk, it was aircraft carriers, submarines, dredge equipment, barges, tow boats, domestic freighters, foreign freighters, commercial fishing boats, runabouts, big motor yachts, ferries, cruise ships, and little sailboats like *Robin Lee*. The *Robin Lee* "holds her own" with all of them, and as of today, she has safely carried us 10,000 miles! It's hard to believe that Don and I and the *Robin Lee* have traveled that far together. We are still excited to continue, so long as our finances hold out! Unfortunately, we had to spend $25 in dock fees today, but we are going to leave the boat and visit with my cousin Amy, and if you are going to leave the boat for visiting, in order to be free of worry about the boat, regardless of the weather, a marina is the place to be.

I called Amy, and she picked us up shortly after we got to the marina. Thankfully, the marina is only ten minutes from her place. We went to her home for dinner, and I did laundry while we were there. It was a treat to be with family. She's a doll and her son Andrew, now 7, is a very smart fellow and quite well behaved. We didn't get to meet her husband Jack. He's a career Naval officer and is gone frequently. Presently, he is in France. It must be tough on normal family life to have him away so much. Amy gave us a loaf of freshly made sourdough bread to bring back to the boat. We enjoyed our evening tremendously and got home about ten thirty.

At Willoughby Bay Marina, Norfolk, VA –Distance traveled: 24 miles

May 10, 1988, Tuesday

What a long day we had! We fueled and filled our water tanks and left at seven thirty. Winds were from the SW, so we got to enjoy sailing. We went to the town of Urbanna, Virginia, up the Rappahannock River, which empties into the Chesapeake Bay. The total distance traveled today was 56 nautical miles, which equals 64 statute miles, one of our longest days. We alternated two-hour shifts until two. Then, I stayed at the helm longer so Don could get dinner ready.

While under way, we had a problem in our water system. The clear plastic hose broke off the water tank under the starboard berth, and we lost the 20 gallons of water that we had put in it this morning. The water went into the bilge and was pumped out by the bilge pump. We didn't hear the bilge pump run because by that time the wind had shifted, and we were motoring and we couldn't hear the bilge pump over the noise of the engine. I discovered the problem when I couldn't get water to wash my hands. Don got things under control by cutting off the broken end, reattaching the hose and opening the forward tank. We have two water tanks, one under the starboard berth and the other under the V-berth.

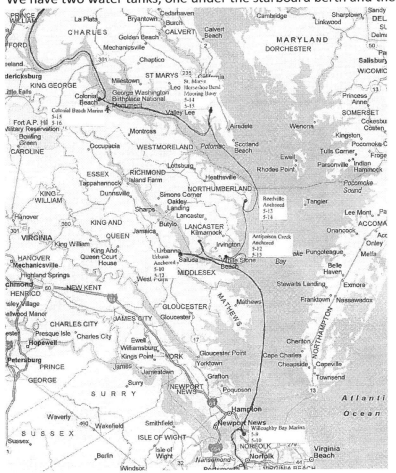

We anchored at Urbanna at seven fifteen after being under way almost twelve hours. We had nice weather all day and until nine in the evening. Then the hail, thunder, lightning, wind and rain storms started. They were severe. One bolt of lightning struck so close to the boat that we heard it "snap" at the water.

I finished *David Copperfield*. It was good and well worth the time, but gosh, it took me forever. I started it on December 2nd, so it took me five months. However, I didn't read it very often. Sometimes two weeks would pass without me picking it up. Don was proud of me for finishing it. It was his idea that I read it. Dickens is his favorite author.

We went to bed at ten; we both were very tired. Being outside, steering, and keeping your balance in the moving boat for 12 hours is tiring. I can hardly keep my eyes open now!
Anchored at Urbanna, VA – Distance traveled: 64 miles

May 11, 1988, Wednesday

What a unique little village of 600 people this is! We walked around Urbanna and went to the hardware store, the post office, the grocery, and to our favorite spots, the Bristol General Store and the library. Both of those places made you feel as though the calendar had been turned back to the early 1900s. Mr. and Mrs. Bristol and their daughter, Betty, the proprietors of the general store, dress in business attire as storekeepers did 75 years ago. Mr. Bristol wore a suit and tie. The store looked like it had not been changed from the time it had opened for business in the first part of this century. I had the feeling that if I looked hard enough I could probably find an item or two of its original stock of goods, still unsold. The Bristols were very congenial and were interested in giving us information so that we might enjoy our one-day stay in their town. At the library, we read for an hour and a half in a very old-fashioned setting.

The sky got black around three, so we came home. Don was anxious to cook a new recipe of liver and onions. I made a tossed salad with a variety of ingredients. It became very stormy, and as we sat down to eat, the rain came. It rained off and on the entire evening. We again went to bed early. Don read in the evening, and I copied recipes onto cards for him.

P.S. While out walking today, I fell down with a bag of groceries. Thank goodness I didn't hurt myself, just the usual scrapes and aches. Of course, I was also embarrassed!

I started a new book; one I picked up at the book exchange in Norfolk–Malcolm and Carol McConnell's, *First Crossing*. Don and I have spent a lot of time thinking and talking about a transatlantic crossing. We are together on our thoughts about it. 1) we would have to have two young, strong, responsible, experienced sailors on board who had already made a crossing; 2) it would need to be on a different boat, one built for long range ocean sailing with all the recommended safety equipment, including radar, short-wave radio, an emergency beacon, a life raft, etc.–one we couldn't afford–, and we can't imagine anyone wanting to include us as part of their crew; 3) it would have to be a crossing from east to west, from Northern Africa to the Caribbean, with the trade winds (which blow from east to west) helping us and it would not be during the hurricane season; 4) why bother? We are having fun at coastal cruising–sightseeing is our main interest–sailing is just a fun part of it; 5) we are more interested in cruising on the canals and rivers of Europe; 6) we would have been more likely to make a crossing if we had gotten involved in sailing at an earlier age, and if we were younger now; and 7) if we ever make a crossing, it will probably be on a cruise ship or a freighter.

I wrote to Ann, the female captain of the boat we rescued in Albemarle Sound, who lives near Paris.
Anchored at Urbanna, VA

May 12, 1988, Thursday

Today was a good weather day: no rain, not too windy, and pretty. We got up at seven thirty and went out for an early-morning dinghy ride. The sun shone on the trees and water and there was steam coming off the water, and also the rooftops and fields. The spring trees all have new leaves and buds. After the dinghy ride, we went ashore to mail letters, dispose of our trash, exchange a book for Don at the marina swap table, and do a load of laundry. I hate to let it accumulate. We purchased some cheap dishrags to use as general purpose rags and a couple of other things at the grocery. By noon, we were ready to leave. Even though the wind was on our nose, it wasn't strong, and we put 16 miles on the log (odometer) during the first leg of our day's trip, and later another 24 miles on the final leg.

First, we went up the Corrotoman River to the Yankee Point Yacht Club. That's *Orchid Boat's* home port. They talked about it enough to make us interested in seeing it. Donna and Bill weren't there, but we saw *Orchid Boat* and the yacht club facilities. In a store next to the yacht club, I found a copy of the cruising guidebook for the Chesapeake Bay that I had wanted to buy in '86, but didn't because of the cost. There was only one copy left, and the owner sold it to us for half-price, $10.00. His name is Randy Walker, and *Orchid Boat* had mentioned him and said that he was a nice guy, but we didn't expect a 50% discount. We got fuel for the dinghy and then left. We went another 24 miles and anchored at Donna's favorite anchorage, in Antipoison Creek, which she wanted us to see.

The famous explorer, Captain John Smith, who played an important role in the establishment of Jamestown and who is associated with the Indian maiden, Pocahontas, was stung by a stingray nearby. He was expected to die, but Native Americans brought him an antipoison, made from ingredients gathered from the area around this creek. He lived!

Don served leftovers for dinner, and I did the dishes. Gosh, the days go by fast. I guess that's because we are having fun.

Anchored at Antipoison Creek – Distance traveled: 40 miles

May 13, 1988, Friday
In the morning, we relaxed in the cockpit, while having a breakfast of cereal and coffee. Later, we took a dinghy ride upstream. We were impressed with the beauty of Antipoison Creek, but we have yet to find any place in the Chesapeake that isn't beautiful.

Don dove down and checked the propeller and shaft. The zinc and everything else appears to be in good shape.

We left Antipoison Creek at eleven thirty for Reedville, which is situated on the Great Wicomico River. The conditions were pleasant, but we had to motor some. Lots of fishing boats were out, and we had to dodge a lot of crab pots (floats attached by a line to a crab trap). It was in the 70s and overcast most of the day. We arrived at Reedville at four. There is a huge fleet of large fishing boats located in Reedville. The boats are over 100 feet long. The town smells like fish. After eating a Hungarian noodle bake for dinner, we dinghied to shore.

We met a couple who come here on weekends and for the summer every year, and they suggested that we should walk to the fish house and watch the processing of soft-shell crabs. The fish house is a one-story building and has many shallow tanks with blue crabs swimming around in a few inches of water. Two people walk around looking for crabs that are losing their shells. These people pick up the crabs in small nets as soon as they come out of their hard shells and take the crabs to a lady who cleans them. The only cleaning she does is to take off the face, the lungs and a part that she calls the apron. Everything else is eaten. She cleaned four nice-sized crabs for us and told us to deep fry them and serve them between two pieces of bread. Of course, the legs and some other parts will be dangling.

We also spent time walking up and down the main street looking at all the beautiful old homes. In the past, this area produced wealth and prosperity. Now, most of the large well-maintained homes are owned by wealthy out-of-towners who vacation here. The local residents we saw were elderly. I don't know why, but we didn't see a single grocery store in town. Don is always on the lookout for grocery stores. There are two gas stations, one of which had a pay phone. We used it to call Sister Carol to tell her where we are. She and

David plan to visit us soon. Our next destination is Washington, D.C., and that would be a good place for them to visit us.

Anchored at Reedville, VA – Distance traveled: 23 miles

May 14, 1988, Saturday – Chip's 23rd birthday

We got up early and left at eight fifteen. We arrived at Saint Mary's College on Horseshoe Bend, up the Saint Mary's River at three o'clock. The temperature was in the high 70s, and it was sunny. There was lots of activity at the school, cruising sailboats, small sailboat races, beaches filled with college kids and a party in the outside seating area of a restaurant. Today was graduation day and everyone seemed to be having a good time. We stayed on the boat, tied to a mooring buoy, until five. During those two hours, we visited with people aboard a power boat called *Top Shelf*. The people aboard were from Washington D.C. and were just out for the day.

Don made sandwiches using the soft-shell crabs given to us at Reedville. They were different. I probably wouldn't order them at a restaurant. When you eat them, you eat the whole crab, insides and all. Only a couple of things are discarded in the cleaning process. Various parts are hanging out of the bun when you eat them, and it is a somewhat gross experience. The sun was out, and it was fun just to relax in the cockpit and watch people. I also spent time reviewing charts, to get ideas of things to do if Carol and David come to visit.

Around five we went ashore and walked around the college grounds. It's a very pretty campus with beautiful foliage everywhere. I guess we are here at a good time to appreciate the beauty; all the fields and trees are blessed with a brilliant lush green color. Later, we dinghied to Tippity Witchity Island, but since the sun was setting we hurried home. The gas supply for the dinghy was low, and we thought we might have to row part of the way back and didn't want to be doing that after dark; we did have enough gas to make it back. It was a beautiful day in all respects.

Don made a cheese and cauliflower dish for a late dinner. I did some cross-stitch, and he did some navigational planning before bed.

St. Mary's College, Horseshoe Bend, Saint Mary's River, north shore of the Potomac River, MD – Distance traveled: 40 miles

May 15, 1988, Sunday

We slept until eight. I relaxed in the cockpit while Don fixed pancakes and coffee. It was warm and sunny, just like it's supposed to be, wonderfully romantic and serene, all the things it usually isn't! We even sailed away from the mooring buoy without starting the engine. Don strained his back raising the main sail, but it didn't seem to cause debilitating pain. We left around nine fifteen.

The weather became boring, gray skies and some wind, off and on. We put in at Colonial Beach, on the Virginia side of the Potomac around three o'clock. We bought fuel and filled our water tanks. Don went to the grocery on the bike. I stayed on the boat and caulked some of the shroud plates and stanchions.

We enjoyed a nice meal, but it was a late one. After dinner, I cut Don's hair and beard. Colonial Beach doesn't have much to offer to a transient sailor, and so we probably won't stop here on the way back down the river.

Tied up at Colonial Beach Marina, Colonial Beach, VA – Distance traveled: 38 miles

May 16, 1988, Monday

We left this morning at seven with the hope of making it to Washington, D.C., before dark. The fog was really bad when we left the dock, so we dropped anchor just outside of the channel markers. Even the fishermen were waiting for the fog to lift. We took lots of video as they came by us to check their nets. In about a half-hour the fog lifted, so we started the engine and went on. It was a very long day. We went a total of 69 miles.

At seven o'clock in the evening, when we were adjacent to Mount Vernon, we were hit by one of the worst electrical storms we have ever experienced. The Potomac is tidal, and the tide was going out. The wind was going against the current which made for very choppy water. To add to the drama, when the storm was at its worst, we were passed by a tugboat that was going upstream like us. The passing took a couple of minutes to complete. Those were tense minutes. We had about 20 minutes of very rough water, with short, steep waves, approximately four feet high. At the time, there were even tornado warnings being broadcasted by the Coast Guard. The storm ended around seven thirty.

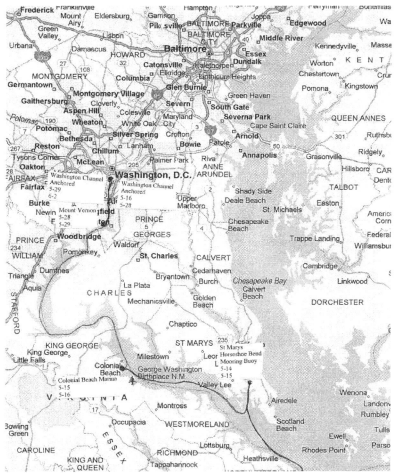

After we passed under the Woodrow Wilson Bridge boat traffic increased, and there were also planes taking off and landing at Washington National Airport, plus helicopters and other noisy activity surrounding us. It was a very different environment than we had been experiencing at places like Antipoison Creek and Urbanna. We anchored in Washington Channel between Hogate's Seafood Restaurant and the Gangplank Marina at eight forty-five, and sat in the cockpit for a while, just relaxing and gazing at the Washington Monument and some of the other sights of our capital; it had been a very long day. We were exhausted and glad to be safely anchored; we slept well in spite of the noise. It rained off and on through the night.

Anchored between Gangplank Marina and Hogate's Seafood Restaurant, Washington Channel, Washington, D.C. – Distance traveled: 69 miles.

May 17, Tuesday, 1988

We worked on projects before going ashore. We changed the oil and filter and cleaned and straightened up our house. By the time we were done, it was two in the afternoon.

We started for shore but stopped to visit a couple on a sailboat called *Don Quixote*, Marie and Greg. We had seen the boat a couple of times before. The boat's home port is San Diego, California. We assumed that they were sightseeing here and would be moving on like us, but they told us that they hoped to find work here. They have been cruising for 2 1/2 years and have run out of funds, so they plan to work while living on their boat, save some money, and then move on. We visited with them until five and afterwards, went to the Gangplank Marina.

At the marina, we learned that we could leave our dinghy there while sightseeing. For security, they have a chain-link fence surrounding the marina. We gave them a $10.00 deposit, and they gave us a key to the gate. They told us that we could take showers at the marina for no charge. We also learned that there is a supermarket, and a bank with a money machine in a small shopping center less than a block away. All of this was great news for us.

We then set out to sightsee, but it started pouring down. We sat on a couch in the lobby of the Department of Transportation building waiting for the rain to stop, but it didn't. We abandoned the sightseeing and walked to our neighborhood supermarket, sharing an umbrella with a girl who reminded us of Ruth Buzzy on *Saturday Night Live*. We bought four bags of groceries and then went to a Pizza Hut for dinner, with our four bags of groceries. The rain continued, and at eleven thirty we gave up waiting for it to stop and walked back to the marina and took the dinghy to the boat in the rain. We were soaked. At times like this, shore living seems more appealing. However, things do dry out, eventually.

Anchored between Gangplank Marina and Hogate's Seafood Restaurant, Washington Channel, Washington, D.C.

May 18, 1988, Wednesday

**WITH CONGRESSMAN CHALMERS WYLIE
IN HIS OFFICE**

We went sightseeing. There is much to do and see here in Washington, and most of it is free. We plan to stay long enough to enjoy as much as possible. We visited these places today: the Library of Congress, the Supreme Court, the Senate Offices, the Capitol Building, and the Congressional Offices. We visited with Chalmers Wylie, the member of the House of Representatives representing our area in central Ohio. We went to his office to chat, and he gave us passes for a White House tour. We even had our picture taken with him. He already knew Don, and he knows Clayton and knew Don's dad.

In the evening, we took the subway to my cousin Debi Boydston's apartment, where we had dinner and visited until eleven. Her husband, Randy, and her mom, Margaret, were there also. Debi is the daughter of my uncle Roger, who recently died. It was a pleasant evening, but it stormed while we were out, and by the time we got home, we were wet again.

Anchored between Gangplank Marina and Hogate's Seafood Restaurant, Washington Channel, Washington, D.C.

May 19, 1988, Thursday

We slept late and then went sightseeing in the afternoon.

We visited the Smithsonian Arts and Industry Museum and the East Wing of the Art Gallery. We got tickets to go back to the art gallery to see the Paul Gauguin exhibit next week. From there we went to the Old Post Office building in the rain, using our newly purchased umbrellas. The building now houses several fast-food restaurants. It reminds us of Waterside in Norfolk and Portside in Toledo. They had live music and while we were listening, I saw a girl I thought I recognized, from Bellefontaine, Ohio, where I used to live. I asked her if she was "Jan," and she was; it was one of those times when we realize that it's not such a big world after all. We were both shocked to see each other again after 20 years. She and her husband, Tim Smith, brought a group of 8th grade students from Bellefontaine to Washington on a class trip. We visited for a good hour before Don and I walked back to the boat.

We called Chip and also Carol. Both plan to visit us soon.

In the evening, we went aboard *Don Quixote* to visit with Greg and Marie. We had drinks and talked until eleven thirty. By the time we got home, we were exhausted again. We lead a busy life when we are in civilized territory.

Anchored between Gangplank Marina and Hogate's Seafood Restaurant, Washington Channel, Washington, D.C.

May 20, 1988, Friday

We got up at six thirty and left shortly thereafter to take a subway to the New Carrolton stop on the Orange Line, near where my cousin Debi lives. She invited us to go to Annapolis for the day. We accepted because we didn't want to miss an opportunity to visit one of our favorite places. She lives in Bowie, Maryland, which is between Washington and Annapolis, and is even closer to Baltimore.

It was a day of spending! We bought a new Aladdin kerosene lamp with a mantle, which puts out good light and a little heat. I bought an Annapolis T-shirt with sailboats on it and a pair of binoculars. Don took the depth sounder to be repaired and that cost $20.

We shopped until one thirty, and then attended an annual event at the US Naval Academy when freshmen, called Plebes, climb an obelisk covered with lard. The object is to take off the cap placed on the top of it, and replace it with another cap. The "lard" prevents them from doing it quickly. I used my new set of binoculars to get a good view of the action. It took about 50 minutes, which was a record, and a black student had the honor of accomplishing the task. It was fun to watch.

With the cost of our lunch in Annapolis and our evening meal at the Andrews Air Force Base Officer's Club added to our purchases, we spent about $90. We will have to stay home tomorrow!

Anchored between Gangplank Marina and Hogate's Seafood Restaurant, Washington Channel, Washington, D.C.

May 21, 1988, Saturday

Finally, I got my day to rest. Don went to the Air and Space Museum, and I stayed home. I took him to shore, and then I went back to the boat and took a nap. Afterwards, I straightened up, and cleaned, and at five, went ashore to do laundry. Don met me there about six fifteen, and while I did the laundry, he went to the supermarket and bought groceries. After I was finished with the laundry, we headed to the boat. It was about seven. He fixed a new dish with potatoes and pork. It took a long time to make, and we didn't eat until nine thirty, but it was good. While he was making it, I had time to put the clothes away and catch up in my writing in this book and the calendar of daily events. It was a quiet, pleasant evening. Don very much enjoyed his day at the Air and Space Museum. We used the new lamp, and it works great.

Anchored between Gangplank Marina and Hogate's Seafood Restaurant, Washington Channel, Washington, D.C.

[NOTE: I took a break from writing in the journal from May 22nd until today, June 1st. Recording our days is a boring job, although I'm sure Don and I will enjoy reading them sometime in the future. For this period, I will summarize our daily events. I will mention everything we did during this time, but at the outset, I want to say that we were physically exhausted from sightseeing when we left the capital. We were anchored in Washington Channel each night unless otherwise noted. When we were on the boat, it was only to sleep and eat.]

May 22, 1988, Sunday

The weather was very good, warm and sunny. We rested until noon and then took a five-mile dinghy trip, which took approximately an hour and a half. We dinghied to the Lincoln Memorial and beached the dinghy. We walked to the Memorial and read the inscriptions. From there, we walked to the newest memorial, the Vietnam War Memorial. It has the names of the 58,000 men and women who died during the war inscribed on it. I found the name of Richard Dagger, a boy from Urbana who was killed exactly 20 years ago. So many lives were lost. How tragic! We got back to *Robin Lee* at five. After dinner, we took a dinghy ride up the Washington channel to the bridge that crosses it. We saw a site under the bridge that obviously serves as the home of a local street person. We walked from the bridge to the Jefferson Memorial and Potomac Park.

May 23, 1988, Monday

After breakfast on the boat, we walked to L'Enfant Plaza and took the subway to New Carrolton where Debi and her mom, Margaret, met us at ten o'clock. We drove to Mt Vernon to see George Washington's home and grounds. We also stopped at Alexandria where we had lunch, shopped, and took a short walking tour of Old Town. Don bought me a 3" bud vase that has a suction cup on it, so I can stick it up on a window in the boat. Now I'll have a place for wildflowers when we pick them.

The four of us went to the boat around four in the afternoon. It was hot, so Don made goombay smashes while Debi and Margaret toured the boat. Unfortunately, a storm came up and our anchor dragged. We started the engine and for the next hour, we fought the elements and maneuvered to miss the other anchored boats. During one of our maneuvers the anchor line got around the prop which, of course, stalled the engine. We quickly put the other anchor out and got the situation under control. Eventually the storm ended, Don went in the water and freed the anchor line and we re-anchored. We were both soaked and cold. What a time we had! But, no harm was done.

May 24, 1988, Tuesday

It was cool and cloudy. We walked to the following places:

1) Folger's Shakespearian Library and Theater;

2) The Library of Congress for a second time to see if we could get a look at a book Don was interested in and wanted some information from;

3) The Capitol Building, where we sat in on the proceedings in the Senate, and afterwards, went to the House of Representatives and watched their proceedings;

4) The East Wing of the art gallery, where we saw an exhibit of paintings by Paul Gaugin;

5) The Mall, where we bought a PB&J sandwich and apple and had a picnic;

6) The National Archives, where Don looked up some family historical information;

7) The FBI Building, where we made an appointment for a tour tomorrow;

8) The Pavilion for dinner and some smooth jazz music; and

9) After dinner, we went back to the Library of Congress and looked at the book that we had requested, *Hawk the White Indian*, the first book Don ever read.

We returned to the boat at eleven, after stopping at Hogate's Seafood Restaurant to drop off our entry forms for a drawing for a free sailboat. We also bought some of their delicious Rum Buns.

May 25, 1988, Wednesday

It drizzled on and off during the day.

We walked to the White House for an eight thirty tour. Since Chalmers Wylie had given us four tickets, we invited Marie and Greg from *Don Quixote* to join us. Because President and Mrs. Reagan were leaving for Russia, there was a big crowd on the South Lawn. A helicopter was there waiting to take them to Andrews Air Force Base and the Marine band was on the porch to play as they were leaving. The 20-minute tour was interesting, but we would like to have seen more. After the tour, the four of us walked to the Willard and Marriot Hotels.

After that, we took the FBI tour and then walked to the Museum of American History, where we had lunch and took a two-hour tour of the building. We walked home by way of the grocery around four thirty. Don fixed sweet and sour chicken for dinner and Marie and Greg joined us to eat and visit. Our company didn't leave until eleven thirty. It was another good, but tiring, day.

May 26, 1988, Thursday

We slept longer than usual, so it was eleven by the time we left to sightsee. It was a nice warm and sunny day and evening, and we went to:

1) The Bureau of Printing and Engraving;

2) The Pavilion, for a tour and a yummy cinnamon roll;

3) The National Cathedral;

4) An Italian restaurant in Georgetown for lunch;

5) The former home of President Kennedy and Jackie; and

6) We also walked to the C&O Canal, the Washington harbor front, the Watergate complex, and the Kennedy Center.

We caught the bus back to the marina and got there about nine thirty.

May 27, 1988, Friday

We had another long day of sightseeing, visiting the following:

1) The Rainforest Exhibit at the Sackler Art Museum;

2) The African Art Gallery;

3) The National Society of the Daughters of the American Revolution, of which my mom is a member;

4) The Corcoran Gallery;

5) The National Geographic Explorers Hall; and

6) After a picnic lunch, we walked up and down Embassy Row on Massachusetts Ave to see the Embassies and the popular hotels in the area.

Carol and David arrived late in the evening to spend the weekend with us on the boat. We caught a bus back to the marina. Don went to the grocery, and I went to Pizza Hut and ordered our dinner. After dinner, we found an out-of-the-way place where I trimmed Don's hair and beard. We also went to Hogate's for another Rum Bun and to fill out another ticket for the drawing. You can fill one out each time you visit the restaurant.

We waited for Carol and David to arrive, and when they did, we visited for a while and then Don and I went to the boat and looked at mail, brought to us by Carol and David, until very late. Carol and David slept in their van. We were happy to have company join us. Now all we needed was good weather for the weekend. We lucked out and got it! It was beautiful the entire time they were here.

GEORGE WASHINGTON'S DOCK AT MT. VERNON

May 28, 1988, Saturday

I did a load of laundry at the marina and bought ice. We brought Carol and David to the boat about nine. At eleven, we raised our anchors and left for a boat ride. We went down the Potomac. Late in the afternoon, we reached Mt. Vernon. We went to the dock, and the caretaker told us that we could spend the night there if we wanted, and that we could stay in the morning while Carol and David toured the house and grounds. Spending the night at George Washington's dock sounded like fun to us. We would be able to tell people that we had slept at George Washington's place, the reverse of the signs at some inns around the country claiming, "George Washington slept here." We were even allowed to plug into their electric; however, due to rules for the security of Mt. Vernon, we weren't allowed off the dock.

Don made a flounder recipe for dinner, and we played euchre and ate popcorn in the evening. Carol and I skunked David and Don.

Tied up at George Washington's dock at Mt. Vernon, VA – Distance traveled: 15 miles

May 29, 1988, Sunday

We ate a big breakfast of zucchini omelets, and toast and jelly. Carol and David toured Mount Vernon in the morning. Don worked on the dinghy-starter pull-cord, and I straightened up the boat and did dishes.

We left the dock at Mount Vernon about noon for Alexandria. It was a beautiful day and very warm, and yet not uncomfortable on the boat. There was lots of boat traffic, but that was to be expected since it was a 3-day weekend.

Don watched the Indy 500 Race on television while motoring and sailing to Alexandria, so he was happy. All year he looks forward to that event. Thankfully, our reception was good.

We put in at the city docks of Olde Town, Alexandria. After lunch at the Seaport Inn, a very old historic place, we took a walking tour. We left around six and headed back to Washington Channel. After we anchored I took David and Carol in the dinghy to show them the "home site" under the bridge. Don made our dinner while we were playing. He made pasta primavera, which is one of my favorites. We all ate too much, especially since it was late. There was only time enough for one game of euchre. The guys won. Boo hoo! We went to bed about midnight, hoping not to oversleep on Monday morning.

Anchored between the Gangplank Marina and Hogate's Seafood Restaurant, Washington Channel, Washington, D.C. – Distance traveled: 15 miles

SISTER CAROL AND HER HUSBAND, DAVID SCOTT, ON THE POTOMAC

May 30, 1988 Monday

We took Carol and David to the Vietnam Veteran's Memorial and then to Georgetown for breakfast and to see the waterfront.

After breakfast, they left for home. After they left we walked to the Art Museum and then to the Natural History Museum. After that we walked to the Capitol Building and, at eight thirty, we came back to the boat. We had cereal for supper and crashed at nine thirty. We really enjoyed having Carol and David as guests. We had fun with them.

May 31, 1988, Tuesday

Today I rested! The only productive thing I did all day was write postcards and letters, and when Don went to shore, I ran the sweeper. He called Chip; Chip will leave Salem, Ohio, at six thirty tonight to come and visit us.

June 1, 1988 Wednesday

Don went ashore to get Chip at seven in the morning. He was in the Gangplank Marina parking lot where he had parked his car. We had breakfast together on the boat. After breakfast, Chip, who had been up all night driving, went to bed, and we borrowed his car to run errands. We went to the post office and mailed Vern to the factory for repairs again, went to the bank for cash and then bought groceries. After Chip's nap, Don and Chip went to the Air and Space Museum.

While they were at the museum, I drove Chip's car to Debi's and left it. Chip will leave for home on Saturday. Debi will drive his car to where we are at that time, Chip will leave for home, and Debi will travel on the boat with us for the next few days. I didn't get lost, although it was a bit confusing. The traffic was heavy, and I was nervous; I hadn't driven in months. Debi and I went shopping, and I purchased a new shorts outfit to wear back in Ohio, when I go home for my 20 year-class reunion next month.

I rode the subway to a station near the Gangplank Marina, and walked the rest of the way, arriving around five. I did the laundry at the marina, and I talked to Shelly for almost one hour. I wonder how much that cost!

Don and Chip got home around seven, and Don fixed spaghetti and meatballs for dinner.

Anchored between Gangplank Marina and Hogate's Seafood Restaurant, Washington Channel, Washington, D.C.

June 2, 1988, Thursday

After a 16-day visit, we left D.C. at eight thirty this morning. We motored all day. It was cloudy, rainy and cold. I was so cold I couldn't get warm! Chip slept most of the day, and I tried to rest on my breaks. It was a long day. We anchored in the Port Tobacco River at six fifteen.

While Don made a chicken casserole for dinner, Chip and I took a long dinghy trip up the river to a local marina and campground. After dinner, we had a quiet evening, visiting and listening to the radio. All three of us were tired, us from sightseeing in Washington, and Chip, from being up all night driving to get here. It is good to have Chip on board. He's such a nice kid!

Anchored in the Port Tobacco River – Distance traveled: 63 miles

June 3, 1988, Friday

My goodness, another cold and rainy day. I feel bad that the weather has been rotten during Chip's short visit.

We got underway from Port Tobacco at eight forty-five and anchored in Saint Inigoes Creek at six forty-five, after traveling fifty four miles. Saint Inigoes Creek flows into the Saint Mary's River about three miles downstream from Saint Mary's City and Saint Mary's College. Just as we were coming into Saint Inigoes Creek, the Coast Guard decided to board us and check our safety gear, such as life jackets, flares, horn, etc. They also checked our boat registration and our personal identification. The Coast Guard has a station nearby, and we told them we needed to make a phone call. They said we could use the phone at their station, so Chip and I took a dinghy ride to the Coast Guard Station and called Debi to let her know where to meet us. Don made beef stroganoff for dinner while we were out. Chip seemed impressed!

We enjoyed a calm night in our anchorage, even though the Coast Guard personnel predicted a rough night based on the weather forecast. They even offered to let us stay at their dock.

Anchored in Saint Inigoes Creek, off of the Saint Mary's River, MD – Distance traveled: 54 miles

June 4, 1988, Saturday

Debi and I had arranged for her to meet us early, so after breakfast, we left our anchorage and motor-sailed about four miles to Saint Mary's College. Saint Inigoes Creek sure is a pretty spot to anchor. Yesterday, I noticed a small tear in the jib, and today, I noticed that it got a little bigger on the way to Saint Mary's College. Debi drove Chip's car to meet us at the college. Shortly after we docked, Debi, Chip, Don and I went to the grocery in Chip's car. Then, Chip dropped us off at the boat and left to go back to Ohio. We hated to see him leave, but were thankful he had been able to spend a little time on the boat and had gotten a small taste of the cruising life. We didn't have very good weather while he was here, but that's part of cruising.

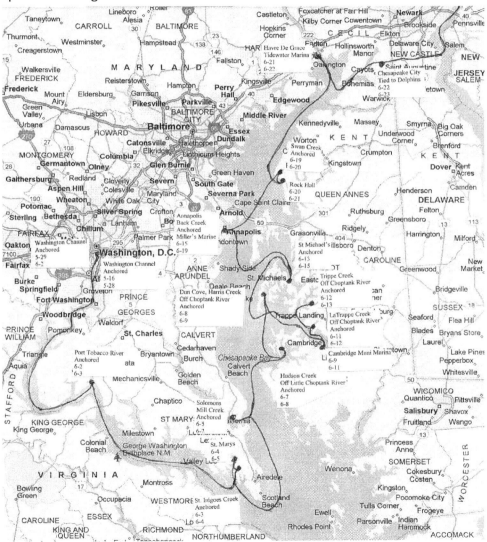

Debi and I spent the afternoon walking around the campus. We even found a health fair to attend and went to a class about personality typing; it was fun! Don stayed on the boat to relax.

Around five o'clock, Debi and I took a dinghy trip around the bay. It was a pretty evening until seven, and then it got stormy and windy. Four anchored powerboats with lots of partying people aboard started moving with the wind because their anchors were dragging—what a sight! I'm glad we weren't in their way.

We had free dockage with electricity until about ten when the electricity went off for no apparent reason.

St. Mary's College on the Saint Mary's River off the Potomac – Distance traveled: 3 miles

June 5, 1988, Sunday

BAD DAY...BAD BAD DAY!

Don and I taped the torn spot in the jib in an effort to try to keep it from getting any worse. It looked better, and I noted in the Boat's Log Book, "Jib Repaired." We left the dock at eleven for the Solomons. The wind picked up about noon. After we rounded Point Lookout, which is on the north side of the mouth of the Potomac, the wind shifted, got stronger, and blew the sail apart. Then the roller furling jammed, leaving the top half of the sail noisily flapping in the wind. It was also uncomfortable, with three foot and greater waves, and it was cold. The north wind had become so strong as we approached the mouth of the Patuxent River, the entrance to the Solomons, that we were barely making headway. It blew and blew and just wouldn't let up. I remember thinking how mean and unrelenting "mother nature" can be. It took us about an hour to go the final mile before we rounded Cedar Point and entered the river. I also remember thinking how sailing teaches patience. To top off the bad day, we lost one of the oars for the dinghy. Debi's first day surely was a crummy one!

By the time we got anchored at Solomons and the boat straightened up, it was eight thirty. Don made lima beans, macaroni and cheese, to go with honey baked ham. It was good, and we all ate a lot. We were hungry because we were too uncomfortable to go below and fix anything during the day. After dinner, we tried to take the jib down so it could be taken to a place that repairs sails, but we gave up on it. It was too dark, and the bugs were bad. We'll deal with it in the morning.

We conked out about eleven, dead to the world. Our anchorage was very calm, and we appreciated the peace and quiet. We all slept well.

Today was another day for learning lessons about sailboat cruising: Don't unfurl a jib with a tear in it! And, don't think tape will stop a tear from getting worse! (The man who gave us the good advice in Oswego would not be happy with us today.)

Anchored at Solomons, MD - Distance traveled: 48 miles

June 6, 1988, Monday

Don and I got up at six in the morning to get the sail down and check the rigging, before the wind came up. Fortunately, the rigging wasn't damaged. After the sail was down, I went back to sleep for a while.

This was our day to rest, lick our wounds, see if the sail can be repaired, sightsee, buy stamps at the post office, get groceries, etc., all of which we did. We took the sail to a local sail loft, where sails are made and repaired, and asked if it could be repaired, and how much it would cost and were pleased to hear that it could be repaired for about $100. Oh happy day! They are going to repair it for us, but it will take a couple of days for them to get to it, so we will pick it up in Annapolis when we get there. We will have to do without a jib for the next few days.

We ate lunch at Pier One and happened to see the sailboat *Silver Fox,* a 34' Hunter we had become acquainted with in Manatee Pocket in the spring of 1987. We didn't get to visit with them today; we just got to wave. Too bad!

Around five we got home with our groceries. Debi and I played in the dinghy while Don cooked. We went to a small privately owned sandy beach and washed our hair. Then we swam off our stern to rinse off. It was a beautiful day–warm, but still windy.

For dinner, which was late, we ate Chinese sesame chicken and chocolate pudding and finished it off with coffee and Amaretto. Debi and I stayed up talking until after midnight.

Don went to bed early. He was tired because he didn't sleep well on Sunday evening. He was too disgusted about our BAD DAY!

Anchored at Solomons, MD

June 7, 1988, Tuesday

We got up late, ate breakfast, bought fuel, and left Solomons at eleven. It was a good day to cross to the east side of the Chesapeake, warm and sunny. We motor-sailed across the bay and anchored in Hudson Creek off the Little Choptank River.

After anchoring, Debi and I took a dinghy ride to the beach. We planned to scrub the dinghy; however, the beach was mucky and the jellyfish were numerous, so we abandoned the plan. Jellyfish, or sea nettles as they are called here, are a problem in the Chesapeake. We've heard they are always bad at this time of the year. If you come in contact with one, you get a painful sting. As a result, people don't like to swim in the Chesapeake during the summer. We probably won't go in the water unless necessary.

Don fixed dinner while we were out. It was my old favorite, spaghettini and green sauce. After dinner, we sat out in the cockpit and enjoyed the pretty evening. It was warm, so after dark we each took a shower in the cockpit, using the sun shower filled with water from our hot water tank. Debi and I sat up talking again until late in the evening.

Anchored in Hudson Creek on the Little Choptank River, near Cambridge, MD – Distance traveled: 30 miles

June 8, 1988, Wednesday

The crabbers woke us up at five o'clock in the morning.

We spent a leisurely morning on the boat and then, at eleven, left the anchorage and explored in the big boat for about an hour up the Little Choptank River, just to enjoy the beautiful area. After that we headed for Dun Cove, on Harris Creek off the Choptank River where we anchored for the night.

The Little Choptank River and the Choptank River are entirely separate rivers. Going directly from last night's anchorage on Hudson Creek, on the north side of the Little Choptank to tonight's anchorage in Dun Cove on Harris Creek, on the north side of the Choptank, would be about a 15-mile trip.

We motored to the Dun Cove anchorage, arriving at five o'clock. Debi and I went exploring in the dinghy. The area is very rural, as is much of the Chesapeake Bay area. There is a dairy farm adjacent to the cove–a very pretty spot.

While Debi and I were exploring, what do you think Don was doing? Yes, he was cooking our dinner. He made a tuna dish tonight that was different and pretty tasty. It had Chinese noodles and peanuts in it.

The weather was great until approximately nine o'clock, and then it started blowing hard, and the anchorage got choppy.

It was another wonderful day. We are enjoying the pleasure of showing Debi how fun boat living can be.

Anchored in Dun Cove, Harris Creek, off the Choptank River, near Saint Michaels, MD – Distance traveled: 28 miles

June 9, 1988, Thursday

(Written by Debi) We left Dun Cove at eleven, and using the mainsail, sailed up the Choptank River heading for Cambridge, about twenty miles away. It was cloudy and cold. We arrived in Cambridge at three thirty. Shortly after we docked at the Cambridge Municipal Marina it started to rain.

Another Buckeye, Bill Cox from Coshocton, came over and introduced himself. He and his wife frequently sail their 25-foot boat in the Cambridge area.

Upon arriving in Cambridge, Don took off for the grocery store while Robin and I sat around talking. Don's specialty for the night was *fettuccini carbonara*, which was excellent! I have been copying all of Don's recipes to take home with me. After dinner, Bill Cox came back to visit awhile longer. Afterwards, I called my husband, Randy, and Robin called Carol Scott.

It stopped raining around six o'clock and started clearing up. The wind died down, and the stars came out.

At the Cambridge Municipal Marina, Cambridge, MD – Distance traveled: 21 miles

June 10, 1988, Friday

(Written by Debi) We ate breakfast, showered, and did a load of laundry before sightseeing in Cambridge. Cambridge is a small, quiet, and historical looking town. We ate lunch at a little restaurant called The High Spot. I had my first soft-shell crab sandwich, which Don thought I ought to try. It was a beautiful day for walking around town, admiring the old buildings and most importantly for Don to go to the grocery store. Don bought some hard-shell crabs, which Don and Robin have never eaten. So, we had crab meat on crackers as an appetizer. I coached them through the de-shelling process. Then Don fixed flounder for dinner.

Don rented a VCR for transferring the 20-minute tapes his camcorder uses to regular two-hour tapes, so after dinner I got to watch the videos while Don was transferring them. Robin went to bed early because she has a breakfast date at five in the morning with Sarge, the dockmaster.

At the Cambridge Municipal Marina, Cambridge, MD

June 11, 1988, Saturday

(Written by Robin) Our dockmaster is a retired Army man called Sarge. He's an old bachelor in his late seventies with a good sense of humor. He never married. He says it's because he never found a woman who would go out with him. He eats breakfast at the same restaurant with his old cronies, seven days a week, and has been doing this for many years. He and I decided that it would be fun to surprise his cronies by him taking me to breakfast, and Don also thought that would be a fun thing for us to do. So Sarge and I made a date for this morning's breakfast. The only drawback was that they eat at five.

Well, I made it up and was ready and waiting for him outside of the marina office at five. I think Sarge was a bit surprised that I showed up! We biked to the restaurant, and I met his cronies, who were very surprised and seemed impressed that he had finally found a date, and a young one at that. It was fun, and we all had some laughs. I took some pictures to send to Sarge. I had French toast, and Sarge paid for it! We got back to the boat at six fifteen, and I woke up Debi and Don, and of course, they wanted to hear how it went.

After breakfast, Debi took the laundry up and did it, Don finished transferring his videotapes, and I stayed on board cleaning the V-berth and applying a coat of urethane to the teak. It looks good. I hope it seals the teak so that the moisture doesn't accumulate and cause more mildew.

Around noon, we all left the boat. Debi and I took a walk and stopped at some shops. I got a couple of cards, and after that we walked to the pizza shop and ordered lunch. Don took the video equipment back and met us for lunch. The pizza was great and was only $7.50.

After we ate, we went back to the marina, paid for dockage and left. Sarge was so nice and was still laughing at the joke we played on his buddies. Cambridge is definitely a nice place and is very popular among the sailors. It was certainly a fun stop for us!

We left the dock at four. While under way, I finished getting the V-berth back in order and putting away the laundry. We only went a short distance and anchored at five-thirty in LaTrappe Creek. The creek was very pretty and populated with boats at anchor. We took a short dinghy ride after Don finished making chocolate cookies. There were huge tents set up at one of the houses with lots of people milling around and a live band playing. It was a big wedding party. What a neat spot for a wedding and/or reception!

Anchored in La Trappe Creek, MD – Distance traveled: 6 miles

June 12, 1988, Sunday

It was a short trip today, only a couple of hours, to Oxford. The weather was very pleasant, especially since the humidity was less than 50%. We put in at the Town Creek Marina, which offers free dockage while eating there and doing a little sightseeing in the town. It's another cute old town and has the oldest ferry service in the U.S., with continuous service since the 1700s. I went to a museum while Debi and Don went to the grocery. I also mailed letters and postcards.

Don and Debi both have concerns. Don is worried about an engine problem we are having; a fuel return hose has ruptured. Debi is worried about not getting home in time to greet our cousin Amy Azud when she arrives from Norfolk for a visit at Debi's house, which they had planned before Debi decided to go for a cruise with us. We are running a couple of days behind schedule. Debi called Randy a couple of times trying to get her problem solved, and Don talked to a local mechanic about his. By five thirty Don had his engine problem fixed by replacing the hose and Cousin Amy will delay going to Debi's until she hears that Debi is home. Problems solved.

We left at six o'clock for Trippe Creek to anchor. The cove in which we anchored was surrounded by big beautiful homes. Debi cooked dinner tonight. We had hot dogs, pork & beans, and potato chips. We visited with a couple from Florida in a nearby boat while taking a dinghy ride. Then we all took turns showering on deck before retiring for the night. It was a perfect night for outside showering and sleeping. There weren't any bugs!

Anchored in Trippe Creek, near Oxford, MD – Distance traveled: 11 miles

June 13, 1988, Monday

It was a very hazy day....calm, with no wind at all. It was also warm and humid!

Don fixed grapefruit, sticky bun rolls, and coffee for breakfast.

Then he went swimming to check the propeller, the shaft, the strut, and the zinc. He also checked the paddle wheel for the knot meter and log to be sure it wasn't fouled. Everything seems to be OK. However, the knot meter/log is not working and hasn't worked for almost three months; we have estimated speeds and distances traveled since it quit. The prop only has one small "ding" in it, which we think is the result of getting the anchor line around the prop in Washingtion Channel. After that, Don cleaned the bilge to remove the diesel fuel that had gotten into it when the fuel return hose was leaking.

We finally got underway at eleven. Don hurt his back when he lifted the anchor. He put me in command for the day, and Debi and I navigated and motored in flat calm conditions to our home for the night here at Saint Michaels. Don took care of the galley duties, rested, and read all day. He says his back hurts badly. He has had back problems in the past, but not recently.

We had hot dogs for lunch, and for dinner, a new salmon dish. Debi and I put two anchors out and also moved the dinghy motor from *Robin Lee's* stern rail to the transom of the dinghy. We did it without dropping it in the bay! After dinner, we went to a boat that a group had chartered in Annapolis. The reason we went was because Tom and Charlene off *Golden Odyssey* were there visiting, and we wanted to see them. We stayed for an hour and had a good time, good drinks and plenty of good conversation. It was still calm when we returned to *Robin Lee*. Debi and I stayed up until almost midnight.

Anchored at Saint Michaels, MD – Distance traveled: 43 miles

June 14, 1988, Tuesday

It was very hot early in the morning. We relaxed until ten thirty, at which time we left to see the town. On the dinghy ride into town, we had time to admire the lovely anchorage and the many beautiful boats. I used my new binoculars to get a close look at the boats.

The town is small, but full of shops. I couldn't resist buying Don a new pair of shorts and matching shirt. We shopped all day. Don spent most of his time in the grocery store. Debi and I stuck together, window-shopping. Around four, we dinghied to the Crab Claw, a well-known restaurant and bar, frequented by the Kennedy's and other famous people. We ate an appetizer and then dinghied back to *Robin Lee.* We didn't see anybody famous. It was very hot. Don made bacon, spinach, and tomato sandwiches for dinner. It was almost too hot to cook, but we had bacon to use up.

Anchored at Saint Michaels, MD

June 15, 1988, Wednesday

We left today, but not until after Don made brunch. It was a new Chinese crab and ginger omelet. Debi has been impressed with Don's ability to whip up new dishes so frequently. I think by now she understands that he just loves to cook and try new things. She has written down some of his recipes. It was very hazy when we raised the anchors. I did both of them, which was hard and dirty work.

The trip to Annapolis was easy. On the way, we encountered *Tiffany II*, a stranded 32' Bayliner power boat. The skipper seemed very unsure of himself on the VHF. Don helped him contact the Coast Guard. The Coast Guard then helped him contact a tow service; we eavesdropped.

We anchored at Annapollis, in Back Creek, at five o'clock. Debi got her things together, and then, to celebrate the end of the cruise, we ate strawberry shortcake before going ashore to meet her husband, Randy. We met him at the Wharf, a bar he and Debi frequent on Back Creek. She was excited to see him…I could tell!

We sat and visited with Randy and Debi until eleven, and then Don and I came back to the boat. We were glad to have Debi aboard for 11 days. It was a fun change for us. We think she had a good time also.

Anchored in Back Creek, Annapolis, MD – Distance traveled: 29 miles

June 16, 1988, Thursday, My 38th birthday

Our holding tank is leaking, and you know what it is leaking; but it's not leaking enough (yet) for it to run into the bilge. The only evidence of the leak is that there is a small amount of moisture around the tank with the tell-tale color of green, the color of the deodorizing liquid we put in the tank. Don went ashore and made arrangements to get the tank repaired at Muller Marine. Around ten thirty, he came home, and we moved the boat to one of Muller's docks. They are giving us free dockage with electricity while they do the work. What a good deal! That gave us the freedom to go to Debi and Randy's home for the celebration of my birthday. Debi made a standing rib roast and a chocolate cake. We spent the night at their home to save Debi the trouble of running us back to the boat because tomorrow she is going to take us around to do errands. We sure appreciated their hospitality and their good shower facilities. While there, I also did our laundry. It was a perfect way to spend a birthday, doing exactly everything that needed to be done and relaxing the whole time too!

Docked at Muller Marine, Back Creek, Annapolis, MD, Robin and Don at Randy and Debi's house – Distance traveled: 1/2 mile

June 17, 1988, Friday

The day began at eight o'clock. Don got up and read the *Washington Post*. Then we left to do errands. We picked up our repaired sail and paid the bill, which was $120; we bought a dinghy oar for $12; a knot meter plug for $4.00; and four gallons of alcohol for the stove for $20. Around one, we stopped at Morrison's Café to eat lunch. In the afternoon, I bought some vinyl to make a companion way cover. Since we have electricity available, I can sew it and a few other items, the flag, Hope's cross-stitch towel, and a scarf wrap I am making for myself.

Debi dropped us off at Muller's, and we learned that the boat's holding tank has been repaired already. Muller's told us that it would be OK for us to stay tonight and tomorrow night if we want. We aren't in any hurry to leave; it's a comfortable spot and tomorrow is Saturday. There is always a lot of boat traffic on a weekend in Annapolis. There must be 35,000 sailboats kept in the harbors and creeks of Annapolis, plus another 25,000 power boats.

They didn't make a mess repairing the holding tank, so I just organized things and put the laundry away. Then I began sewing. Don was exhausted, so he went to bed at nine.

Docked at Muller Marine, Back Creek, Annapolis, MD

June 18, 1988, Saturday

Don rested today and enjoyed all the amenities that a dock with electricity offers. He listened to CDs and then watched some television. I sewed all day. We both enjoyed the use of our fan.

In the evening, Don made a new vegetable spaghetti dish, and we invited Boo, our neighbor, over to eat and visit. Boo calls himself a "floater," and says he is just drifting through life, not accomplishing much, but having lots of experiences. He is now rebuilding a boat and hopes to cruise in the future. He's 37. He has a beautiful Irish setter that reminds me of my old Irish setter, McKay. I loved that dog. Irish setters have great personalities.

In the evening, Don and I went out on a date, walking through Annapolis, having ice cream, and looking at all the people and night life. It was a wonderful evening. However, one bad thing happened. Don lost his wallet. Either his pocket was picked, or he left his wallet on the counter at Chick and Ruth's Ice Cream Parlor, and someone walked off with it. We talked to the police about it later, but don't expect to ever find it. The police were kind and took all the information, but it isn't likely that anyone will turn it in. He lost his Visa card, his debit card, his driver's license, and $30. It's the first time in his 49 years he has lost his wallet or had it stolen. He was upset about it, but took it better than I would have thought. My driver's license expired yesterday, and now his is lost. It may be hard to rent a car to go back to Ohio in July for my twenty-year class reunion.

We got back to the boat about midnight and went to bed immediately.

The sewing projects turned out well. The companion way cover looks great and matches our beige cockpit cushions.

Docked at Muller Marine, Back Creek, Annapolis, MD

June 19, 1988, Sunday

It was very foggy when we got up. We stayed at the dock waiting for the fog to lift, but it was slow lifting. By eleven, it was clear enough to see for a mile and a half, and we decided to leave. There was an incredible amount of small boat traffic that we had to navigate through on the way out to the bay.

We wished Boo well as we were leaving the dock. He is one of the many people we have met that we probably won't see again. It's a shame that we'll never know what becomes of all those people. I guess it's this kind of situation that makes me realize, more and more, that we are all just tiny bugs on the windshield of life – here on earth but for a moment and then forever gone, missed by only a few.

We didn't travel very long, only about 3 ½ hours. I had the helm about two-thirds of the way, and I also dropped the anchor at our destination, Swan Creek. We arrived there around three thirty. Don made dinner while I did cross-stitch in the cockpit.

The water in the Chesapeake is brackish, and its salinity differs in the various parts of the bay. Sea nettles live in brackish water with a salinity of 10-16 parts per thousand, but here in the northern part of the bay the water is less salty and therefore, jellyfish aren't a problem.

It was early enough that lots of weekenders were still swimming and enjoying the protected anchorage. A father and son from a boat anchored close by were swimming near our boat, and I chatted with them. The boy, a 10-year-old named Dan, offered to provide us water taxi service in his dad's dinghy. He offered, for $0.50, a round trip to the nearby town of Rock Hall, so we could get ice cream. He was a friendly, outgoing, smart youngster. We accepted the offer. The ice cream tasted great; it was my favorite brand, Breyers.

Don went to bed early. I washed the dishes and did cross-stitch. The wind blew hard, which helped to keep us cool. I heard fire alarms in the night from Rock Hall; I bet they had some grass fires.

Anchored in Swan Creek, near Rock Hall, MD – Distance traveled: 21 miles

June 20, 1988, Monday

It was a very short trip today, less than an hour. We tied up at a dock next to a seafood restaurant that was out of business and is to be torn down tomorrow. Then we walked approximately a half mile to town. It was hot and hazy. First, we went to a bank and got cash on my debit card. After that we went to a convenience store that had a pay phone and was air conditioned. While Don made phone calls to start the process of replacing his driver's license and other important lost items, I read magazines and enjoyed the air-conditioning.

A local person gave us a lift in his truck back to the waterfront. We had asked him for directions to where we were docked, so he knew we had a long walk.

We found an excellent place to pull the dinghy out of the water and clean it. The bottom growth was getting to be like an overgrown field of grass and weeds! We were hot, but working with the water hose and sprayer cooled us down quickly.

Don made an excellent Chinese dish for dinner. Later, we dinghied over to the Sailing Emporium to shower. We visited a short while with neighboring boaters and then, because the mosquitoes were bad, we went inside. Don read a short time, and I did cross-stitch. We had a lot of roll due to the wave action.

Tied at a dock next to a closed seafood restaurant, near Rock Hall, MD – Distance traveled: 2 miles

June 21, 1988, Tuesday – The first day of summer

We got up early and videotaped the wrecking of the seafood restaurant. Watching monstrous machines, which looked like steam shovels, smashing the restaurant to pieces made it seem like we were watching a science fiction movie. We learned that the restaurant had closed years ago, and it is now being torn down to make way for condos.

We got fuel at the Sailing Emporium and called Randy. Randy told Don he needed to call the company we rent our storage unit from, because there is some question about our lease. Don called the company and after he had taken care of the problem, we left the dock and headed north for Havre De Grace. On the way, we heard frequent shellfire; apparently, it was from the Aberdeen Testing Ground, which was nearby. It was a very hot and hazy day. In fact, Baltimore, which wasn't very far away, had a record high of 100°. To keep from getting too hot, we doused each other with buckets of water in the cockpit.

After docking at Tidewater Marina in Havre De Grace and turning on the electric fans, we went to town with the dockmaster. He was kind enough to give us a ride. We ate at Crazy

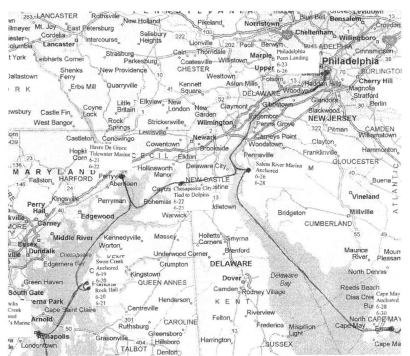

Swedes and really enjoyed the air conditioning. We went on a walking tour of the town and then back to the boat. We stopped for ice cream and made our other usual stop at the grocery. Don loves looking at the groceries. By the time we got back to the boat, the sun had set, and it had cooled down to about 80°, which made it much more tolerable.

Our boat neighbors visited with us and were very interested in our trip. It is fun for us to share our experiences, especially with people who would like to do the same things someday.

By nine o'clock, the mosquitoes were coming out so we went below and put our screens in. Both of us were hot and tired. We slept pretty well.

Tidewater Marina, Havre De Grace, MD – Distance traveled: 44 miles

June 22, 1988, Wednesday

We spent most of the morning doing chores and sweating. We changed the oil, cleaned our living quarters, and Don removed the wire for the knot meter that needs to be taken in for repair. Unfortunately, we had no electricity and in the middle of our projects, we had to relocate the boat. The people who had rented the slip for the season returned home early from a cruise they had taken. Don said the dockmaster probably hated to come over and ask us to move. He did offer to give us a ride to town again and also offered to pick up lunch at McDonald's. We declined, but appreciated the offers.

We left Havre De Grace at two o'clock. It was a short day trip to Chesapeake City. While underway, Don made macaroni and hard-boiled eggs for tuna salad, and we also had time to relax. We arrived at six forty-five and tied to the dolphins at the end of the basin. Finally, around eight, after I got the wind scoop rigged, we were able to enjoy our tuna salad dinner.

On the way into the Chesapeake City Basin, we went past a 24-foot single-handed sailboat named *Sandy Sloop.* It was making a Mayday distress call at the time, requesting help from the Coast Guard. The skipper said he was taking on water; however, he was beached along the C&D Canal at the entrance into the Chesapeake City basin. The Coast Guard told him that since neither he nor his boat were in imminent danger, he would have to contact a commercial operator for help.

After dinner, we dinghied around the basin, looking for boats we know, but didn't find any. We did meet a couple on the boat *Shangra-La,* from Austria. They are on a round-the-world tour. It was fun to talk with them.

It was late when we got home and went to bed. We plan to get up early tomorrow and leave for Philadelphia. We don't have charts for the area, but we've been told that the shipping channel is well marked.

Tied to dolphins in the basin at Chesapeake City, MD – Distance traveled: 23 miles

CHAPTER THIRTEEN
PHILADELPHIA, PA to MIDLAND, ON
June 23, 1988 – Aug 11, 1988

June 23, 1988, Thursday

We left Chesapeake City at eight in the morning and had a long trip up the Delaware River to Philadelphia. The Chesapeake-Delaware Canal was a snap. Going up the river, the tidal current was with us in the late afternoon, and we made good time. We docked at Penn's Landing, in Philadelphia, around eight in the evening. The couple on the boat next to us invited us over for a drink, and we shared with them some information about the Bahamas.

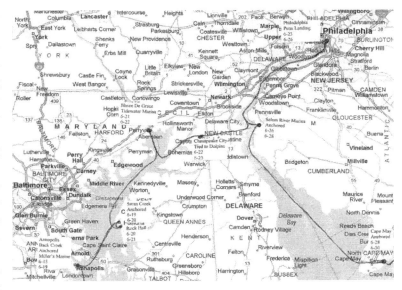

Penn's Landing, Philadelphia, PA – Distance traveled: 63 miles

June 24, 1988, Friday

We weren't comfortable at the dock. When boats went past the marina we got bounced around by their wakes, especially freighters. Amazingly we both got some sleep.

We left in the early morning to go sightseeing. We went to the Visitor's Center, Independence Hall, Congress Hall, Liberty Bell Pavilion, Franklin Court, Second Bank of the U.S., the City Tavern, and Ben Franklin's grave. The weather was perfect for sightseeing—breezy, cool, sunny, and not humid.

We had a Philly sandwich for lunch, which we thought was appropriate, but ate Mexican food in the evening before returning to the boat. There was a jazz band playing at Penn's Landing when we returned; we stopped and listened for a while.

In the middle of the night the security guard awakened us. He couldn't read our permit dates and wanted to make sure we had permission to stay for the night. The permit was taped to the window of the head, and he could have read it using a flashlight. We did manage to get back to sleep. The marina was completely disorganized in the morning. There was much yelling and confusion between the dock attendants and the skippers of boats wanting to dock there. It was completely disorganized. We ate and left to go sightseeing as soon as we could get away from the chaos.

On board, we drank hot chocolate and planned the next day's sightseeing.

Penn's Landing, Philadelphia, PA

June 25, 1988, Saturday

The day of sightseeing included Carpenter's Hall, window shopping, and Franklin Park, which was in a state of disrepair. We saw many "street" people lying around on benches and under shade trees. Then we walked to Chinatown to shop for groceries and have lunch.

In the afternoon, we rode buses to the ritzy Chestnut Hill area and then to the Italian market. We bought some fresh vegetables and meat at the market. On the way home, we also walked down South St. and in the New Market area. Both are very cosmopolitan. Philadelphia reminds us of Montreal.

We lugged home several bags of groceries. Don went to the boat to stow everything, and I walked to the riverfront open-air theater here at Penn's Landing to find us good seats for the show this evening.

Tonight's performers made their mark by doing television and radio commercials for companies such as Burger King and Chevy. We saw them interviewed on *Entertainment Tonight*, the TV show. This evening they sang folk songs, played instruments, and amused us with their wit. They are talented guys.

Penn's Landing, Philadelphia, PA

June 26, 1988, Sunday

Last night, we slept well until the halyards started clanging. Don went up to fix the problem and some people walking along the docks at one-thirty in the morning started up a conversation about our bicycle. He managed to cut the conversation short and came back to bed. This has been the worst place for sleeping that we have been to. Even in Washington with the noise of airplanes, boat traffic, and cars, we could sleep well, but not here.

After showering and eating a light breakfast, Don walked to the grocery to get a few more things while I prepared for getting under way. Around noon, things got exciting at the marina. *Simon Bolivar,* the 270 foot Venezuelan tall ship, used by their Navy for training, tied up along the wall at Penn's Landing. It was a wonderful spectacle with sailors aloft in the rigging standing on the ratlines in their colorful uniforms, flags blowing in the breeze, music from a band at Penn's Landing playing appropriate music, orders being given by boson's pipe, and verbal orders being given by officers.

I'm glad we didn't miss it. Don took lots of video, and we took a few photos, but nothing we took could equal the excitement that was in the air. The spectators were in awe. The ship's flag was huge, but the wind was strong, which kept it blowing nicely.

We finally left the dock about three in the afternoon. Don made soup while we were underway. He had boiled the soup bones with electric power before we left the dock.

I looked over our guidebooks and read of places we'd been during our

SIMON BOLIVAR

six weeks on the Chesapeake Bay. I always review before stowing books away because it will be a long time before we have those books out again.

I had the helm the entire trip down the Delaware River. Don was below cooking. After he finished the soup, he fixed a new Chinese asparagus and chicken recipe, and it took forever to make.

While we were underway, a front passed, which brought gusty wind, shifting from the West to NW and then North. By eight o'clock, it got rather nasty and the following sea was starting to build. We originally thought we would sail all night to Cape May; however, since the conditions were getting worse and the dinghy wasn't having a comfortable ride in the following seas, we decided to attempt to go a little way up the Salem River and anchor for the night. The Salem River flows into the Delaware River on its eastern shore, across from the C&D Canal. In order to get into the river, we had to brave our way in the dark, through a channel at the river's mouth. We put our powerful portable search light to use. With it, we could easily identify all the buoys and range lights. The light was a good-bye gift from Jerry and Barb Edwards from Columbus.

We tied up at the Salem River Marina instead of anchoring, and the wind continued to blow. The rigging clanged and shook. The wind must have been at least 20 knots.

Salem River Marina, near Salem, NJ

June 27, 1988, Monday

The wind was too strong to go anywhere and enjoy the trip, so we decided to make today a day for rest and relaxation for the captain and mate of the *Robin Lee*. In the morning, we moved the boat from the marina and anchored in the river.

I got caught up on letter writing, calendar writing, and journaling. I also cross-stitched, looked at nature through my binoculars, and just enjoyed quiet time for thinking. Don read, reviewed recipes, made meatballs for the meatball soup he started yesterday, and took a nap, which he really enjoys but rarely gets to do. We also made time for games like counting how many times the boat swung around 360 degrees; how long one revolution took; and seeing who could be quiet the longest, i.e. not talk to disturb the other. Another thing we did was to see how many dishes we could get dirty and have to wash. Yes, we were just having fun, being silly.

It was a pretty day with blue skies and puffy clouds, but just too darn windy the entire day. On our Great Lakes Cruise in '85, we sat in Stokes Bay on the Georgian Bay in Canada for about three days in weather like this. So, this was a Stokes Bay day.

Anchored in the Salem River, near Salem, NJ

[NOTE: I am writing the following on July 2nd. Five days have passed since I last wrote in the journal. The weather has not been good, and although we have traveled, it hasn't always been fun. At present, we are anchored at Atlantic Highlands, New Jersey, pretty far from the mouth of the Salem River. Since I last wrote we have gone down the Delaware Bay to Cape May and then up the New Jersey coast to Sandy Hook. Generally, the skies have been pretty baby blue, with puffy white clouds, but the wind has been steady out of the north. It's always cooler when the wind is coming from the north than with southerly breezes. I will summarize those five days.]

June 28, 1988, Tuesday

We moved the boat to Cape May on June 28th, leaving our anchoring place in the Salem River at seven thirty in the morning and arriving in Cape May, where we anchored for the night at seven fifteen in the evening.

Anchored at Cape May, NJ – Distance traveled: 63 miles

June 29, 1988, Wednesday

We briefly walked around Cape May to enjoy the Victorian architecture, but today was primarily a day to run errands. We picked up Vern at the post office, bought groceries, made travel arrangements for our trip to Ohio for my class reunion and did laundry.

Anchored at Cape May, NJ

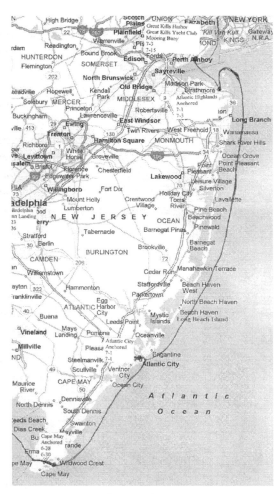

June 30, 1988, Thursday

Don bought a part for the knot meter, but it didn't fix the problem, so we took it back for a refund. The floorboards in the dinghy need repairs, but we couldn't find any place that would work on them. So, both of those problems remain on the "to do" list. Adding to our woes is the fact that Vern is still not working. We wasted forty dollars on postage. Yes, we have problems, but I don't think they will get us down. Life could be a lot worse, like if we lived on shore and had to go to work every day. UGH!

We bought fuel, filled our water tanks, and secured our dinghy on the deck before leaving Cape May. We will be traveling in the ocean and hope to go all the way to Sandy Hook. We left at three in the afternoon. The wind and seas were so terrible by midnight that we decided to put in at Atlantic City. We anchored and went to bed at one.

Anchored at Atlantic City, NJ – Distance traveled: 46 miles

July 1, 1988, Friday

We were awakened by a dredging barge operator at five in the morning on July 1st. He had been working in the harbor and was done with the project. He had an anchored mooring close to our boat which he needed to retrieve and asked us to move our boat, so he could get it. The weather had improved and we listened to a forecast, and it was satisfactory, so instead of re-anchoring, we decided to resume the trip to Sandy Hook.

The depth sounder didn't get turned on because we hurriedly left the anchorage and shortly after starting out the channel, I ran aground, although I was right in the middle of the channel. Don took over and got us moving again.

Don stayed at the helm, so I could sleep; I slept from six to nine. We sailed part of the day and motor-sailed the rest of the day. It got so rough as we came into Sandy Hook that the stereo fell off the navigation table onto the floor, but fortunately it didn't break. The forward hatch wasn't closed tightly so some of the spray we took over the bow made its way through the hatch. I'm sorry to say that I'm the guilty person who didn't do a proper job of "battening down the hatch"; I got paid back with a wet bed. There is always some lesson to be learned. It was a mess, but it was dry within 24 hours.

We arrived and anchored at Atlantic Highlands at eight in the evening. We are about ten miles from New York City, on the south side of the Lower Bay.

Anchored at Atlantic Highlands, NJ – Distance traveled: 95 miles

July 2, 1988, Saturday

Today was a fun day! We relaxed until the late afternoon. I read magazines, wrote Shelly, and worked on cross-stitch projects. Don looked over his recipes and inventoried the groceries on board. Around four o'clock, we put the dinghy in the water and took our laundry ashore.

The funniest things happen to us by chance. About a half-hour after we went ashore, as we were walking down the street, Don noticed a guy who had come out of a restaurant and was now walking beside us. Don thought he looked familiar and asked me if we knew the guy. I looked at the guy and saw that he was our "old friendly fisherman," Sid, from Harbourside Moorings, Longboat Key. He fished from our dock almost every day of our stay there. By chance, he decided to bring his wife and daughter to this place for ribs. They had never been to the restaurant before. They live about 10-15 miles away. We chatted, and he offered some suggestions about where we might be able to keep our boat while we are in Ohio, but unfortunately his suggestions didn't pan out.

Anchored at Atlantic Highlands, NJ

July 3, 1988, Sunday

We got up early today, raised the anchors, went to the fuel dock, bought fuel, hosed down the boat, and then left Atlantic Highlands. We left at nine o'clock and went to Great Kills Harbor on Staten Island and tied up at the Richmond County Yacht Club. We got very lucky. The Richmond County Yacht Club meets our needs perfectly. They have rented us a mooring buoy for $10 per day from today through July 14th. By noon, we were tied to our mooring buoy, which will be home for *Robin Lee* until we return from Ohio.

Great Kills Harbor is very well protected. In addition, it is well located for visiting Manhattan. There is a bus stop less than a block away, which one can take to the Staten Island Ferry which goes to Manhattan. The bus costs $0.50, and the cost of the ferry is included in the bus fare. Furthermore, the return trip is free. So the total transportation cost per person for a round-trip to Manhattan is $0.50. The yacht club has nice showers and other nice facilities. It also has nice people and a launch service to transport us back and forth to our boat whenever we want daily, from nine in the morning until eleven at night. All we have to do is call them on the marine radio and they come and get us. What a deal! Don and I are both excited to be here and are looking forward to revisiting New York City.

We settled in, ate lunch, relaxed a bit, and then went ashore to explore. The bus service is only one short block away and shopping facilities, including a K-Mart, are only a short bus ride from there.

We got back to the boat about eight. Don fixed a good Chinese pork stir fry dinner using bean sprouts grown on the boat. We stuffed ourselves and then sat outside watching and listening to local fireworks and loud party music being played by the people ashore.

It was a pretty day with a high temperature in the mid-70s. There was a light breeze, and the evening was cool with low humidity. It was great sleeping weather.

Moored at the Richmond County Yacht Club, Great Kills Harbor, Staten Island, NY – Distance traveled: 14 miles

July 4, 1988, Monday, Independence Day

Today is the biggest holiday of the year for many people, especially for people who like to party. Celebrating the nation's birth is a good reason to throw a party.

We had a leisurely morning. Around eleven, I cleaned the stern with Soft Scrub to get rid of the diesel soot that makes it dirty, and Don and I dinghied around the anchorage to visit

THE RICHMOND COUNTY YACHT CLUB LAUNCH

other transients.

In the early afternoon, we went by bus to Staten Island Mall to see what's available. We didn't look at anything specific, just browsed, but we found a Friendly's Ice Cream restaurant. Neither of us could resist a Reeses Pieces sundae.

We got home about seven, showered, and then Don heated up our dinner of leftover Chinese Stir Fry pork with our home-grown bean sprouts. For dessert, we had tapioca pudding.

The fireworks display seen from our boat was spectacular. It was actually the most fireworks either of us had ever seen. As we scanned the horizon, we could see them in every direction for 360°. They lasted for hours.

Moored at the Richmond County Yacht Club, Great Kills Harbor, Staten Island, NY

July 5, 1988, Tuesday

This was our day to visit Manhattan. Don and I flew here in June of 1981, and we loved it. Today was our second time in the "Big Apple," and we again say, "We love New York!" There is always so much activity. We think it is exciting that millions of people, of so many different backgrounds, inhabit this city. We would both like to live here for a year or two just to have the chance to take it all in.

We availed ourselves of our $1.00 round trip transportation for the two of us, which I described earlier. We went to the NY Stock Exchange to check on my investments. I wish I could say that my investments were doing great, but they aren't. The stock market and my stocks are only up a little bit. We walked a lot, just looking around and browsing at stores, mostly pricing cameras and watches.

Our walk back to the ferry began at six thirty through the streets of Little Italy. We stopped at Puglios for dinner and then walked to Chinatown and bought some cookies at a grocery store. The ferry trip back was interesting. The ferry's skipper appeared to be drunk, and the regular passengers told us that he was frequently drunk and reckless. We got to the marina at ten, in time to take the launch back to our boat.

We stayed up late packing our bags and readying ourselves for tomorrow's trip to Ohio. **Moored at the Richmond County Yacht Club, Great Kills Harbor, Staten Island, NY**

July 6, 1988, Wednesday

Richie, the yacht club's launch operator, came out at eleven thirty to get our bags and us. Our flight to Ohio left from the Newark airport at five forty-five. Getting there was complicated and took longer than the flight home. We went by express bus, and then by ferry, and then another express bus to the bus terminal, and then by the airport bus to the airport.

We had kept a couple of handguns on board *Robin Lee* and decided to take them back to Ohio now to avoid the risk of losing them at the border crossing into Canada, so Don checked with the airlines to see how to handle that problem. We had to purchase a hard case that could be locked and check it in with our other luggage. We bought one for $35.

We arrived at the airport at three thirty, boarded the plane at 5:25 and arrived in Columbus at 7:15. It took us four hours to get from the boat to the airport (from eleven thirty in the morning until three thirty in the afternoon) and less than two hours to fly to Columbus. How fast these airplanes fly! We are used to 5 miles an hour, not 500 mph.

Joe and Lois Dixon picked us up at the airport. On the way to Dublin we ate at Dalt's, the restaurant where I had worked while getting ready for our trip. I saw some of my former co-workers and had my favorite dish, nine layer dip, and my favorite dessert, chocolate malt cake. Dessert was "on the house," thanks to my old boss Carey.

Then we went to the Dixons' house and showed them the video of Joe's farm in Georgia and gave them a copy. They seemed very pleased to have it. Joe then took us to Clayton's where we got his truck and drove it to Carol and David's for the night. It felt strange sleeping in a real bed, and I worried about our little boat/home being all by itself out in that harbor with all that water around it.

Robin Lee **moored at the Richmond County Yacht Club, Great Kills Harbor, Staten Island, NY, Robin and Don at Carol and David's**

July 7-13, 1988, Thursday – Wednesday

We were back in the Dublin area staying with Don's sister Carol & her husband David through July 10th and at my mom's from July 11th until our return to New York on July 14th.

During this period, we went to our dentist for checkups and teeth cleanings, and we renewed our driver's licenses. I had a hairdo by my beautician, compliments of my friend, Pam. We visited with numerous relatives, friends, former neighbors, and former co-workers. I even visited one of my former private care patients. Of course, everyone was interested to hear about our voyage. We also did a little reorganizing of our belongings at Mom's and at our storage unit.

My class reunion included a dinner on Saturday, July 9th and a picnic on Sunday, July 10th. The reunion was a success, and I'm glad we came home for it. Don enjoyed meeting my classmates. The only disappointment was that some of the people I had hoped to see didn't come.

I bought a new camera, a Nikon 20-20. It was expensive, $1,050, but it's a good camera and it will be my camera for the rest of my life.

We were extremely busy during our time in Ohio and worn out by the time we returned to the boat. It was also very hot and humid while we were there, with temperatures around

100° on several days. However, the trip to Ohio gave us a break from our boat life, and we enjoyed visiting with everybody.

Robin Lee moored at the Richmond County Yacht Club, Great Kills Harbor, Staten Island, NY, Robin and Don at Carol and David's or at my mom's

July 14, 1988, Thursday

Today, we returned to New York City from Ohio. We brought Danielle, the nine-year-old daughter of my sister, Randy, back with us. She will travel with us until we get to Mackinaw Island, Michigan. Shelly is working there this summer, and when we get there, Danielle's mom will pick her up and take her home. We are excited that Danielle will be on board with us. Danielle has a big problem with motion sickness, and if that becomes a problem, or if

DANIELLE AND DON ON
THE STATEN ISLAND FERRY

Danielle doesn't like traveling and living on the boat and wants to go home early, we will figure out a way of getting her home.

We were very tired by the time we got back to the boat. Our plane landed at nine in the morning. We took a bus from the airport to the World Trade Center. We went there so we could sightsee with Danielle. One of us had to stay with the luggage, so we split up the sightseeing time with Danielle. Don took her all over the financial district and stopped at the Commodities Exchange. I took her to the observation deck on the 107th floor of the WTC tower. We also ate lunch at the WTC. Danielle seemed impressed with all the sights, the hustle and bustle of the city, the foreign languages, and all the different modes of transportation used in the city.

We rode the subway to the Staten Island Ferry. We were in the last car and when it was time to get off the doors wouldn't open. The conductor asked everyone in the last 5 cars to move forward. It was a tricky operation. We moved from car to car by jumping from one to the next while carrying six pieces of luggage and did it as quickly as we could. The Staten Island Ferry was also an interesting experience for Danielle. We went past the Statue of Liberty which she had never seen, except on TV and in books. The

bus trip from Saint George Docks back to the yacht club was also an eye-opener for her. She sat quietly and watched everyone. One character was tattooed all over his upper body, and of course, it was too hot today for him to wear a shirt.

She enjoyed the launch service from the marina to the boat. In the evening, our boat rolled a bit. She felt bad, but didn't get sick.

Moored at the Richmond County Yacht Club, Great Kills Harbor, Staten Island, NY

July 15, 1988, Friday

After a very good 12-day experience at the Richmond Yacht Club[13], we left Great Kills Harbor. We filled up our water tanks at Nichols Marina and Don made a phone call about Vern. When we went out of the Great Kills Harbor entrance at ten thirty, we turned to the west and went to Perth Amboy. At Perth Amboy, we turned to the north and took a waterway called Arthur Kill (also known as the Staten Island Sound) that follows the New York/New Jersey boundary to the Upper Bay, south of the Statue of Liberty.

We passed a huge junk yard for boats, including big boats like tugs, ferries, tow boats and barges. That was the first of those that we had seen. The boats were very rusty and looked like they had been there for many years.

The freighter traffic and sightseeing kept Danielle occupied. She learned a little about steering and the buoy system. The current was a problem. We bucked it all day, so it was a slow trip. When we reached the Upper Bay, we turned north again and passed the Statue of Liberty. We decided to anchor near Ellis Island where we could see the pretty lights of the city. I got my new camera out and used it, but later, somewhere north of West Point, I discovered that I hadn't loaded it correctly, so we have no pictures of this stretch. However, New York at night from where we were anchored was a spectacular sight.

We all slept well; Don and I were still tired from the trip to Ohio.

Anchored at Ellis Island, NY – Distance traveled: 25 miles

July 16, 1988, Saturday

We didn't get off to an early start as we had planned. The current would have been in our favor if we had left at seven thirty. Instead, it was nine o'clock when we left. As we motored north past Manhattan, we saw several very interesting things. One, in particular was a Coast Guard helicopter flying overhead and landing on a huge aircraft carrier at one of the piers. Another was a large private yacht with a small helicopter pad on top of it.

The wind was out of the North most of the day. We got to West Point at seven thirty and tied to a mooring buoy in front of the old train depot. Danielle and I rowed ashore while Don stayed with the boat. We couldn't find anyone to ask if it would be OK to stay where we were. A neighboring boater gave us his opinion, which was, "stay until someone asks you to move." The walk on shore wasn't very interesting, but it did offer Danielle a chance to get off the boat. She had been aboard, without going to shore, for forty-eight hours.

It is still very hot and humid. We showered on deck to wash all the sweat and smell away. Around nine thirty we had a few sprinkles. I thought, from the way the wind was

---

[13] I am sorry to report that the Richmond County Yacht Club was destroyed by Hurricane Sandy in October 2012. There are several video clips on YouTube showing the destruction. The members of the club are in the process of attempting to rebuild it.

blowing that we would get a storm, but we didn't. The river wasn't very choppy and after the boat traffic subsided, it became calm and flat.

Anchored at West Point – Distance traveled: 51 miles

July 17, 1988, Sunday

It was another very hot and muggy day. The temperature was in the high 90s, and it was hazy all day. We weren't this hot in the Bahamas last year!

OUR FAVORITE LIGHT HOUSE ON THE HUDSON RIVER (IT HAS A CAT PAINTED ON ONE OF ITS WINDOWS.)

We traveled north along the Hudson River Valley to the town of Catskill. West Point, the Catskill Mountains, Poughkeepsie, and Hyde Park were exceptionally pretty from the river. Danielle commented several times on how beautiful the valley was. We saw one large tow boat pushing barges, two wide by seven long; that impressed her also. She never got sick or felt nauseated even when the weekend powerboats made big wakes.

However, the most significant part of today's trip was the powerful storm we encountered at four thirty, about ten miles south of Catskill. We heard a Coast Guard broadcast on the marine radio warning the boaters in our area of a severe electrical storm with dangerous lightning and winds of 60 to 70 mph, and telling small craft to take shelter. We were in the middle of the Hudson River and there was no place for us to take shelter. Our sails were down, and the jib was furled. I was at the helm, Danielle was below, and Don was in the cockpit with me. When Don heard the warning, he went forward and put the mainsail cover on and checked to be sure everything was secure. It got very windy and started raining hard. There was thunder and lightning all around us. I felt a strong shock while holding the steering wheel! Don went forward on deck again. This time he took one of our dock lines and used it to lash down and secure our mainsail cover. The wind had torn two of the fasteners off the sail cover. I slowed the engine way down and pointed into the wind. Visibility was terrible. I felt a second shock holding the wheel! I didn't want to hold the wheel, but Vern was broken, as usual, and we had to steer the boat. I told Don he ought to take the wheel, and I should go below and look after Danielle. As I was going below, I told Don that I had felt a shock twice. He didn't believe me, until...he was shocked twice also. After 15 or 20 minutes, the storm passed and things calmed down. Then we assessed the damage. The wind had flipped our dinghy over fourteen times (that's seven complete revolutions). We know that because it took seven complete revolutions of the dinghy's painter to get it untwisted. In the process, the dinghy's wooden seat was lost. (Fortunately the dinghy motor was mounted on *Robin Lee's* stern rail. The loran antenna, which was mounted on the stern railing, got hit by the dinghy and bent very badly. The dinghy, with the gear that was in it, weighed about 80 pounds and the wind had to lift it about five feet to hit the dinghy. I know Danielle must have been scared to death, but she managed to keep calm and offered a smile once in a while during the ordeal.

The only explanation we have come up with for the electrical shocks is that they were from lightning strikes. However, the shocks felt less severe than from 110 volt house current, and as Don says, if the boat had taken a direct strike from lightning, the shock would have been much stronger and would have killed us. We think the lightning strikes hit the water near the boat, and the charges disbursed in the water and some of the charge came up through the keel, into the wheel, and into the person holding the wheel.

We made it to Catskill and anchored at seven o'clock. All in all, we had three major losses and damages in the storm; the dinghy wooden seat, the ripped sail cover, and the damaged loran antenna.

It was a difficult day aboard the *Robin Lee*, one that I'm sure Danielle, Don and I will never forget!

Anchored at Catskill, NY – Distance traveled: 59 miles

July 18, 1988, Monday
I'm worried that we might not make it to Mackinac Island before Shelly goes back to Ohio. Her job ends around the first of September. I feel pressured to move on as fast as we can.

We had pizza out so that we could enjoy some air conditioning. It is very hot and humid! We got ice cream bars after dinner and walked on the main streets of Catskill. It's a little town with a lot of places out of business. Actually, there are only a few nice stores; there's not even a grocery close to the river. When we were here before, Hope and I took a taxi to get to a grocery store.

Danielle slept with me in the V-berth; Don slept in the cockpit.

Anchored at Catskill, NY

July 19, 1988, Tuesday
It was another rotten hot, humid, hazy, miserable day.

Don worked on the dinghy and took it apart and reassembled it to be sure that the storm hadn't messed anything else up. We went ashore to put the dinghy floor boards back in and boy did that irritate the dockmaster of the nearby Catskill Marina! We had chosen to anchor in a creek that empties into the river, rather than pay him $0.75 per foot per night

($22.50 per night for us) to dock at his marina. For three nights that would have been $67.50. He was upset because we didn't dock at his marina and then had the nerve to take our dinghy onto his property to work on it. He talked to us as though we were the lowest scum on earth. We tried to make a deal with him. We offered to pay him for landing the dinghy on his property today and offered to pay him if he let us empty our trash in his dumpster, but he wouldn't agree to anything. He said he didn't want to do business with any, "damn cheap sailboaters." We got the dinghy together, got off his property and never went back. We should have asked him before landing the dinghy there and putting the boards in, but based on our experiences with all the other dockmasters we have dealt with, we didn't think he would mind. It's just a shame we didn't know about his attitude from the beginning. If we had, we would have steered clear of him and his marina. By the way, there are two other sailboats anchored in the creek next to us.

Danielle and I played in the dinghy and swam off the boat. The same dockmaster came over and told us we couldn't swim in the creek. I think that even our wanting to enjoy the water irritated him.

Since we will be entering the Erie Canal in a couple of days, we need to unstep our mast, and since we don't have Captain Randy and Paul to help us, we don't want to try to take it down at Castleton. We went to the Catskill Yacht Club and talked to a nice fellow who works there to see where we could get it done. He suggested we have our mast taken down at Hop-N-Nose Marina, which is another marina at Catskill, and we talked to them later and made an appointment to have it unstepped at nine in the morning.

Don went to the meat market and Danielle and I walked around town a little. We ate at Arosa La Pala for dinner. Don liked it a lot; Danielle and I thought it was so-so.

We stayed on the boat, and it rained gently all night. It was hot and since the boat had to be closed up due to rain, it was very uncomfortable.

Anchored at Catskill, NY

July 20, 1988, Wednesday

We moved the boat to Hop-N-Nose Marina in the early morning for our nine o'clock appointment to have our mast unstepped. The mast was taken down without incident and secured to a support that the marina provided. The total cost was $85. We ate lunch at the marina and then left Catskill at two forty-five for Castleton. We tied up at the Castleton Boat Club at six forty-five and spent the night there.

Docked at Castleton Boat Club, Castleton NY – Distance traveled: 24 miles

July 21, 1988, Thursday

We left The Castleton Boat Club at noon and continued up the Hudson River. It was a rainy day.

At three forty-five our engine overheated, and we moved out of the shipping channel and anchored so that Don could change the impeller in the water pump. It was still raining hard at five forty-five, when Don finished the job, and we got underway again. We went through the Federal Lock on the Hudson, turned into the Erie Canal, and proceeded to Lock # 2, where we tied up for the night. The engine is still overheating.

Tied up at Lock # 2 of the Erie Canal, NY – Distance traveled: 17 miles

July 22, 1988, Friday

We continue to have engine overheating problems. We made it through the flight of locks, but after we got through the last lock in the flight, Lock # 6, we nursed the boat into Albany Marine Service about two miles above the lock.

As you come out of the channel from Lock # Six, you are on the high side of a 33-foot dam which is directly to your left. There is no barrier between you and the top of the dam, and we were in danger of our engine stalling because of overheating. We stayed as far to the right as we could and were prepared to drop the anchor if the engine stalled, but it didn't.

Don spent four hours working on the water pump but couldn't fix it. Danielle and I motored around in the dinghy while Don worked on it. We will stay here for the night, and in the morning, we will ask Albany Marine to fix it.

For dinner, we had spaghetti with tomato sauce. Later, all three of us went for a dinghy ride, and then walked to Stewart's Ice Cream store for our dessert. It has been cloudy today, but it didn't rain. Yesterday we had enough rain to last me until next year.

At Albany Marine Service, above the Crescent Dam, Erie Canal, NY – Distance traveled: 4 miles

July 23, 1988, Saturday

The mechanic came to the boat this morning. He and Don worked for a couple of hours. The mechanic ground down the plate that covers the impeller to try to make it work better. The repair cost us $109, and the dockage was $15. Danielle and I walked a mile and a half to the nearest laundromat and grocery. Luckily, we got a ride back to the boat. It would have been a very long and uncomfortable walk carrying the laundry and groceries in the extreme heat.

Today around two thirty we left the marina after having taken $.25 showers. We didn't have any further problems with the engine overheating. Don feels that he now has a good understanding of our engine and all its parts. He is definitely more confident of his ability to maintain it than he was two years ago.

We were out only two hours before the black storm clouds started to close in on us. Actually, the storm wasn't too bad! I was at the helm. If all rainstorms were that easy, I don't think I would complain at all, but, as Don says, "You have to take the bad with the good," and rainy and stormy conditions and cruising go hand-in-hand. My biggest complaint is that the clouds keep us from seeing the blue sky. Sometimes it stays cloudy, dreary and damp for days. I just love to have a blue sky. Up north we get very few blue-sky days.

Going through the locks on the Erie Canal hasn't been as difficult this second time through. There again, it seems like we have benefited from two years' experience. I think we have now been through about 80 locks. Each time the experience is different due to wind, currents, the height or depth of the lift or drop, the design of the lock itself, whether the valves are working properly, and other variables. You always have to pay attention and be careful to position your boat at an appropriate spot and to keep the boat parallel with the walls of the lock. Our unstepped mast sticks out several feet from the bow and the stern. Hitting the wall with the mast could be very costly. We ended the day at Scotia, Lock # 8, around seven fifteen in the evening.

Tied to wall at Lock # Eight, Scotia, NY – Distance traveled: 18 miles

July 24, 1988, Sunday

Finally, we got a pretty day with moderate temperatures. Danielle made pancakes for breakfast; they were good. We ate them as we were going from one lock to the next. I put Betty's black raspberry jam on mine, plus syrup.

We started at nine thirty and went through several locks. Around six o'clock, we decided to stop at Canajoharie, NY and tie up along the wall of Lock # 14. We were in the mood to socialize, and we saw a sailboat from Canada, named *Spin Drift*, tied at the wall. They immediately came out to welcome us. There were two kids on board, a boy named David, who is 11 years old, and a girl named Allison, who is 9 years old–Danielle's age. The parents' names are Bob and Anne Ort. They have been living aboard and cruising for a year. We got to know them quickly and even got invited to their boat for drinks. Don made our dinner and Anne cooked theirs, and because the bugs wouldn't allow us to have a picnic, we all ate our dinners on their boat. The kids had a good time playing, and it was interesting for Danielle to hear about the kids' experiences during the past 12 months while living on their boat and cruising, and also to learn about their schooling through a correspondence school. Later, Don and I went to town and took all three kids with us for a walk. We had ice cream, of course, and bought a few groceries. Anne and Bob probably appreciated the hour and a half of relaxation; I'm sure they don't get much time alone!

WITH THE ORT FAMILY ON *SPIN DRIFT*

It was a nice evening and interesting because they knew of some of the boats we had become familiar with in the Bahamas. They just returned from the Exumas and the Abacos a couple of months ago. They invited Danielle to ride with them tomorrow.

Tied to wall at Lock # 14, Canajoharie, NY – Distance traveled: 35 miles

July 25, 1988, Monday

I got up at eight thirty, went to the bank and grocery, and then walked back carrying heavy bags. Everyone was looking for David and Allison's missing kitty cat, Abaco, when I got to the boat. They decided not to leave today so they could continue to look for it. I think the chances are pretty remote. Anyway, we parted around noon. We haven't traveled with anyone for so long, it would have been fun. Maybe we'll meet up again in Oswego. The weather today was pretty nice, with a light breeze and warm air. The house flies have been awful, but we are spraying and swatting as many as possible.

We got underway at eleven and stopped at six. We tied up at Herkimer Terminal. Dinner consisted of hot dogs and fresh sweet corn. It was pretty good. Don and Danielle took a dinghy ride and walked to town. I got a few pictures of them in the dinghy. While they were gone, I did the dishes, cleaned up, and took a shower. In the evening, we helped Danielle with the multiplication tables and writing in her diary. We went to bed at midnight.

Tied at Herkimer Terminal, Herkimer, NY – Distance traveled: 30 miles

July 26, 1988, Tuesday

We spent the morning at Herkimer, shopping for fresh fruit and vegetables and going to the bank. Don called Sun TV about getting an additional battery for our video camera, and Danielle called her mom and talked awhile. I mailed my recently-finished cross-stitched bibs to Lynn Rose and Linda Dayhuff for their babies. We bought a coaxial cable to connect the marine radio to its antenna while the mast is stowed on deck.

It was pretty in the morning, but after we left Herkimer at twelve twenty, it got cloudy and sprinkled off and on. It was a good afternoon for a nap. Danielle slept two hours, and I slept about 15-20 minutes. We went through several locks, and that kept me from getting a long nap. At eight fifteen, we tied to a wall at Lock #22, about four miles east of Lake Oneida. Don made a new dish, a frittata made with artichoke hearts and shrimp. It was all right, but nothing special, and it was about 9 before we finished doing dishes. We again spent the evening doing multiplication tables with Danielle.

Tied at Lock # 22, near Lake Oneida, NY – Distance traveled: 37 miles

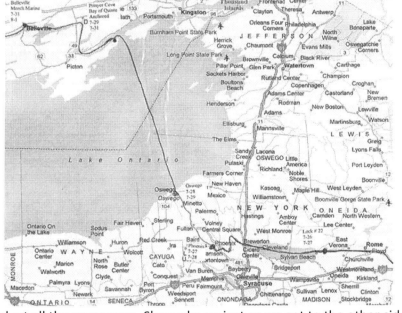

July 27, 1988, Wednesday

Danielle and I had talked about going for an early-morning dinghy ride, but I couldn't wake her up when I tried at six o'clock, so Don and I just untied our lines and motored across Lake Oneida while she was asleep. I was afraid she would get sick if the lake was rough, but it was calm, and she slept all the way across. She woke up just as we got to the other side.

We went down Lock # 23 west of Lake Oneida and continued west to Three Rivers where we entered the Oswego River. From there we went down the Oswego River to the town of Phoenix. We arrived there at two in the afternoon. The territory from Lake Oneida to Phoenix was very pretty. We tied up at a wall in Phoenix, and I immediately tried to contact the friends we had made here on our way south. Some people gave us a lift to the Rasmussins' home on Kent Street. We left a note on the door because no one was home.

In the afternoon, Danielle found a swimming hole at a park near where we were tied. There was a rope tied to a branch high in a tree at the water's edge that was used by the kids to jump from when it swung out over the river. Danielle played there for four hours with several local kids. One kid, a boy her age named Brady, came to our boat afterwards. They played cards, and he had dinner with us. He was all-boy, cute and chubby, with buck teeth.

Later, after the dishes were done, we contacted Rasmussins by phone. They came down and picked us up, and took us to their home for a visit. Don enjoyed talking with Louise's husband. He has several hobbies that interest Don—plane building, photography, and amateur radio. We got back to the boat at midnight.

Tied at a wall in Phoenix, NY – Distance traveled: 37 miles

July 28, 1988, Thursday

We left Phoenix at eight o'clock and arrived at Oswego at two thirty. We had no difficulties along the way and tied to a wall close to town.

Danielle and I took a walk, browsed at some stores, and went through a fort built in the 1750s. Don ran errands and bought groceries for his new creation which he fixed for dinner, beef and green bell pepper hoagies. I made a fresh fruit salad, and that went along nicely with the hoagies. It was a warm sunny day, but the breeze coming off Lake Ontario kept us comfortable.

Later, we all walked to a street fair. I danced, and that embarrassed Danielle and Don, but I had fun.

Don and I stayed up late to do maintenance on the boat and to make sure everything was "ship shape," since we will be going across Lake Ontario tomorrow.

Tied to a wall in Oswego, NY – Distance traveled: 30 miles

July 29, 1988, Friday

We left this morning at five fifteen. The wind was from the SW at 10-15 knots. Our biggest concern for today was Danielle's sensitivity to motion. We were warned that she gets motion sickness easily. Our heading of 350° with the wind from the SW was ideal for sailing but created 1-3 foot waves hitting us on our beam, which in turn, created enough motion on the boat that when Danielle woke up, she was sick immediately. We had hoped that she would stay asleep until we were in protected waters, but she woke up about halfway across the lake. I nursed and comforted her, but her retching made me sick also. Finally, about one thirty we rounded Indian Point, on the north side of the lake, and entered into the calmer waters of the Bay of Quinte. Our stomachs and our moods improved, and we began to feel hungry and thirsty. I took over the helm, and Don fixed snacks. We anchored in Prinyer Cove in the Bay of Quinte at two thirty. Danielle was a good sport about her motion sickness and said nothing about giving up the boat life and going home. I think she is enjoying this experience very much.

One of the burners on our alcohol stove wasn't working, so shortly after we anchored Don cleaned the stove and tried to get the burner working, but couldn't. I straightened up the boat, and we all tried to rest a little. Later, Danielle and I cleaned the cockpit, went swimming, and washed our hair and ourselves with fresh water. Don made another new dinner, routelli with spinach sauce. Danielle named it Prinyer Cove pasta. She got to take a dinghy ride with a neighboring boater. I did dishes in the cockpit, and Don showered. We reviewed charts in the evening, and Danielle played with dolls until midnight.

Anchored at Prinyer Cove, Bay of Quinte, ON, Canada – Distance traveled: 52 miles

July 30, 1988, Saturday

The wind is stronger today and is from the west, the direction we need to go from here. This is a comfortable place to sit and relax while the wind is from the west. Since we would be going against the wind, and since we haven't had a rest day for two weeks, we decided to stay put. Besides, Don thought this would be a good place to go down and check the bottom and perhaps clean the hull. He only checked the bottom because the current and wind were so strong. I worked on cross-stitch projects, and Danielle played in the dinghy, read, did some cross-stitch, and played with her Barbie dolls.

After dinner, we got cleaned up and took the Lighthouse Restaurant water taxi to the restaurant. We called Customs and Emigration and are now legally in Canada. We ate a dessert, and listened to a local band perform. Danielle called her mom.

Anchored at Prinyer Cove, Bay of Quinte, ON, Canada

July 31, 1988, Sunday

We had breakfast of pancakes at our beautiful anchorage and then pulled out around ten thirty so we could get to Belleville before it got too late. The scenery along the Bay of Quinte was pretty, but because it was Sunday, we had a lot of boat traffic. I steered most of the day to give Don a break. The weather was good. Danielle took a nap; she had taken Dramamine, and it made her drowsy. We arrived in Belleville at five thirty and tied up at Morch Marine; the people there were friendly. Several people asked us about our trip and seemed interested. Danielle and I went swimming off the dock prior to getting cleaned up to go into town. Fortunately, we got a ride to the main street and found a Wendy's for Don and

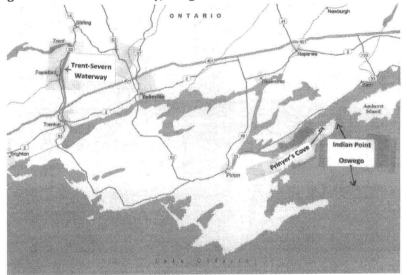

me, and an Arby's for Danielle. We walked a couple of miles back to the marina, stopping at several bank money machines trying to get Canadian cash. Finally, we found a Dominion Bank machine that accepted our card and gave us money.

It's a pretty town, and we enjoyed our walk. However, this is a holiday called Civil Service Day, and none of the stores were open except one convenience store. We got milk and then came home to watch video cassettes of our trip with Danielle. It was pretty late by the time we went to bed.

At Morch Marine, Belleville, ON – Distance traveled: 37 miles

August 1, 1988, Monday

We spent a lazy morning visiting with the boaters on both sides of us—nice, friendly people. The showers were crummy, and ours didn't lock. One of us had to stand guard in order to keep people out. I cut Don's hair, and it was a problem to hold the door shut while I was cutting it. It was a small area, hot, and not really very clean.

On the way back from the showers, I took nature pictures with my new camera. I have been using auto focus and auto exposure on everything and have taken at least one roll of 36 exposures every week since buying it.

We left for Trenton at one thirty. It was choppy, so Danielle took ¼ of a Dramamine and slept for about two hours. It only took about 2 ½ hours to get there. We bought fuel, filled our water tanks, and each of us had a hot dog and a Coke. The drawbridge, which was close by, didn't open for 40 more minutes, so we just motored around, waiting. After getting past the bridge, we motored two more miles on the Trenton River to the first lock on the Trent-Severn Waterway.

The Trent-Severn Waterway, which connects Lake Ontario and Lake Huron, is 240 miles long and extends in a north-westerly direction from the mouth of the Trent River where it empties into Lake Ontario to Port Severn where the Severn River flows into the Georgian Bay, in Lake Huron. It has 44 locks. It was built for commercial boat traffic; however, the boats built after the waterway opened were too big to go through the locks. Today, there is no commercial traffic on the waterway, only pleasure craft.

We tied to the lock wall for the night, enjoyed the beauty around us, and I took pictures while Danielle fished.

Tied at Lock # 1, Trent-Severn Waterway, near Trenton, ON – Distance traveled: 11 miles

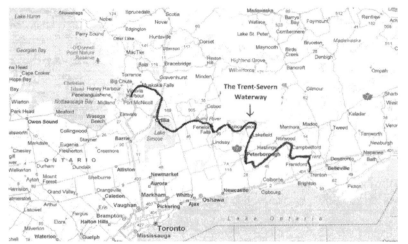

THE TRENT-SEVERN WATERWAY

August 2, 1988, Tuesday

Last night while dinghying around, I found an interesting little pond with lots of wildlife, so Danielle and I got up at seven this morning to go back and look at the ducks and birds that live in the area.

At the first lock on the waterway, Don bought our lock pass at a cost of $60. We were cautioned that, because this summer has been exceptionally hot and dry, the waterway is unusually shallow, and we were warned that we might not make it through with our 5'3"-5'6" draft. One man adamantly told us not to try. He even ran alongside of us as we left the information center where we bought our lock pass, shouting, "turn back, turn back, you won't make it." While we were on the Hudson River we had heard that the Trent-Severn was unusually low this year, but the only other way to Mackinac Island is to go through the Welland Canal, across Lake Erie, up the Detroit River, and then up the west side of Lake Huron. That would be much further. Our only chance of getting to Mackinac in time to see Shelly is by way of the Trent-Severn Waterway, so we decided to try it.

We left around 8:30 when the locks opened and motored through three locks. The water pump was acting up, and as a result, the engine was overheating. At Lock #6, at Frankfort, we stopped and made some calls hoping to find a Universal Atomic Diesel dealer somewhere along the waterway. The closest dealer is at Midland, which is ten miles west of Port Severn. Don called them, and they will order a water pump and will have it one week from now. Hopefully, we can nurse the boat along to Midland.

The locks are very well maintained and beautifully groomed by the Canadian Parks and Recreation Department. All of the park personnel we have encountered have been very friendly and helpful. Each lock has a small house (all different in style) and a park-like area close by with picnic tables and charcoal grills. The locks are hand operated by park employees. Today we made it through 12 locks. Locks 11 and 12 are combined for a total lift of 50 feet.

We made it to the town of Campbellford at six fifteen and tied up at the town dock. Don made a stir-fried dinner while Danielle and I explored the park. Don served Jell-O with fruit for dessert. Danielle and I decided we should have an ice cream cone too. I took our laundry to the laundromat and started the washing machine on our way to the ice cream parlor. By the time we were finished eating our cones, the laundry was done and I barely had time to get our clothes before the laundromat closed, but I made it. I am always anxious to get the dirty clothes laundered. We showered on deck and went to bed about eleven thirty, after one card game of war.

Tied up at town dock at Campbellford, ON – Distance traveled: 23 miles

August 3, Wednesday

Don got up early and went to town for groceries and to get a part from the stove repaired. The part needed welding. For the past couple of weeks, we have only been able to use two of the burners. He got it done. It cost $20, but it's now working.

It was terribly hot and humid. We finally left the dock about noon. We got to Hastings by six, and tied to a wall at Lock # 18. On the way, we hit a submerged object. It was a hard

hit. We think it was either a submerged boat or navigational buoy.

Danielle and I went swimming; Don joined us later. We ate late, but it was one of Danielle's favorite meals so far—sloppy Joes, potato chips, pop, and chocolate cake for dessert. We walked around town in the evening, but that didn't take long because this is a small community. Danielle met Margaret and swam with her and enjoyed holding her new black puppy, Prince.

Don called Clayton and Betty in the evening and talked about 20 minutes.

Tied to wall at Lock # 18, Hastings, ON – Distance traveled: 19 miles

August 4, 1988, Thursday

Yesterday I had cold symptoms and a very sore throat. I got up this morning feeling better. Today is Sister Carol's birthday. We couldn't call her since they are on a trip out West.

We had a very long day, and only made 36 miles progress. We went through several locks, and each takes approximately 30 minutes. We prepared for a thunderstorm in the late afternoon, but it didn't happen.

The entire Trent-Severn Waterway is in very pretty territory. It is made up of canals, rivers, lakes, streams, and ponds. You name it, and the Trent-Severn has it! To think that it all connects into one waterway is very interesting. We are tied to the town dock on the south side of Peterborough. Tomorrow we will be raised to a higher body of water by a hydraulic lift lock.

We met up with a sailboat traveling to Sarnia, Ontario. We chatted with them after swimming awhile at the government dock. Don and Danielle took a walk in the evening to get bread. I fell asleep early.

Tied at the town dock on the south side of Peterborough, ON – Distance traveled: 36 miles

THE HYDRAULIC LIFT LOCK AT PETERBOROUGH

August 5, 1988, Friday

It was a hectic and stressful day, but also a very interesting one. We ran aground trying to get into Lock # 21, the Peterborough lift lock, but forced our way through the mud and into it by using full throttle on our engine. It is the largest hydraulic lift in the world and a very unusual lock. It has two water-filled chambers. When one chamber goes up, the other comes down. When one chamber is at the top, the other is at the bottom. The chambers are 33 feet wide and 120 feet long and are like giant bathtubs. Each is supported by a huge shaft. It lifts or drops boats 65 feet. The up bound chamber starts its upward trip with 6'3" of water in it. It stops when its water surface is one foot below the water surface of the higher body of water. Its up-stream gate opens, and a foot of water rushes in. The boats in that chamber then exit and other boats come in. Next the up-stream gate closes. That chamber then has 7'3" of water in it. The chamber at the bottom started down with 7'3" of water in it, but when it reaches the bottom with its extra foot of water its water level is one foot higher than the lower body of water and when its gate opens that water pours out. The boats in the chamber exit and are replaced by upbound boats and the gate closes. At that point, the chamber has 6'3" of water in it. That makes the upper chamber heavier than the lower chamber. It is the differences in weight that, through a hydraulic mechanism, make the chambers reverse their positions. No other power is needed. It's an ingenious system.

We were lifted to the upper level. We then tied to the wall and went to the visitor center and museum. It was a nice diversion from our worry of whether or not we were going to make it across the Trent-Severn. However, running aground was a reminder that the waterway is very shallow

We only made 10 miles today even though we were at it for nine hours, partly because of the time we spent at the lift lock but also because this stretch is known to be very shallow, so we had to go slowly. We bumped several times—but nothing severe. After tying to the city dock wall after going through the Lakefield Canal lock, we swam. Don checked the boat bottom, and Danielle played alongside. It was seven thirty before we were dressed and ready to go out for a walk and to eat dinner. Danielle wanted chicken, and I wanted pizza. We found both, and so both our appetites were satisfied. For dessert, we had our usual, ice cream. The town wasn't much, but it did have a nice grocery which pleased the Captain/Chef. Danielle and I slept in the V-berth, and Don slept in the cockpit, until it started raining in the middle of the night. He then moved onto the starboard berth.

We are glad to have completed one-half of the shallow part of the waterway. The next shallow water we will need to be concerned about will be the Mitchell and Canal Lakes. The chart shows 5 ½ - 6 foot depth. They are a couple of days ahead.

Tied at the city dock, Lakefield, ON – Distance traveled: 10 miles

August 6, 1988, Saturday

We left Lakefield at nine o'clock, crossed several lakes and connecting waters, went through three locks and arrived at Bobcaygeon at six thirty. My favorite lake was Stony Lake. It reminded me of the Georgian Bay small-craft route. It was windy most of the day, and in the last lock, we were blown around and our mast scraped the wall, but no damage was done, thank goodness.

Houseboats are popular on the Trent-Severn. Most are rented by inexperienced skippers. Houseboats are affected by the wind more than other boats, and that creates some challenging situations for those inexperienced skippers. We were very lucky to find a place to tie up along the wall ahead of the lock. The town is having a weekend summer festival, and we are the only sailboat in town. By the time dinner was ready, Danielle had already played in the dinghy and fed the ducks. We ate and then walked around town, but almost everything was closed. We visited with a couple we met at Hastings, and they offered to let us use their charts for the rest of the trip on the Trent-Severn. We accepted their offer, and after we are done, we will mail the charts back to them.

Danielle called her mom and talked for a long time. The Bell system is on strike, so I think it will be pretty expensive. Randy told me that Shelly would be at Mackinac through September 7th. That is good; We should be able to make it there before then. Don and I did boat maintenance jobs in the evening. I didn't sleep well because of all the partying by the local people.

Tied to lock wall at Bobcaygeon, ON – Distance traveled: 39 miles

August 7, 1988, Sunday

Don doubts that the water pump will make it to Midland. If it doesn't, we will have the new one sent to us wherever we are and find a mechanic to put it in, if Don can't do it.

We came through locks, lakes, streams and a canal today. The canal and some of the streams were narrow and shallow. We passed a 70' yacht coming the other way in a very tight spot along the canal. The scenery is pretty and is very much like the north shore of the Georgian Bay. At the last lock today, Lock # 36, the Kirkfield Hydraulic Lock, we began to go down. The Kirkfield hydraulic lock operates just like the one at Peterborough.

We had a picnic dinner at the lock wall. At Danielle's request, we had spaghetti with peas in the sauce. Before dinner, Danielle and I took a dinghy ride to explore a pretty waterfall. After dinner, Don and Danielle took a long walk to explore the grounds nearby.

I jury-rigged a shower in the bath house at the lock using our sun shower. They had plenty of hot water and the place was clean. Danielle and I took showers and washed our hair; it felt great. The long walk back to the boat was very dark and spooky. It was clear and starlit, but the moon wasn't out and the lock wall lights weren't working. We managed, but next time I will take a flashlight. Danielle played with her Barbie dolls until eleven thirty. I did the dishes, and Don slept.

Tied at Kirkfield Hydraulic Lock, ON – Distance traveled: 31 miles

August 8, 1988, Monday

We left Lock # 36 at eight thirty to travel through the last shallow part of the waterway. The next ten miles would take us to Lake Simcoe. Between Lake Simcoe and Port Severn, the water is plenty deep enough. However, between here and Lake Simcoe is the shallowest part of the Trent-Severn. We went slowly, bumping bottom numerous times and having to power our way through mud several times. The end of the shallowest area is marked by a small

THE SHALLOWEST PART OF THE WATERWAY

arched bridge, and the very shallowest part is at the bridge. Lake Simcoe Is only a short distance on the other side of the bridge. Within a hundred feet of the bridge, we ran hard aground! Wow! Had we come this far, only to have to turn back? If we had to turn back now and go through

Lake Erie to get to Mackinac, we wouldn't get there until mid-October, and it would be winter before we could get south. Rather than do that we probably would go back to Port Clinton and give up the trip.

The bottom where we were stuck didn't feel hard; it felt like mud. We decided to try to force our way through it. That risked getting stuck worse than we were, but we backed off the mud, backed up far enough that we could get some speed up coming forward, and we hit the mud hard and plowed our way under the bridge. We made it! What a relief! If only the guy who chased us at the first lock urging us to turn back could see us now!

It was still early enough to make the 15-mile crossing of the lake. The conditions were good, and so we decided to go across. Half way across we stopped the engine and drifted. It was hot and the lake was calm, so we swam and snorkeled for about an hour. We could barely see land. Don stayed on board while Danielle and I were in the water and then Danielle and I were life guards for Don. He scrubbed the bottom of the boat. The water was clear and looked the same pretty blue as we saw in the Bahamas. Danielle took a picture, hoping to capture the colors of the day. The only thing we didn't enjoy was the bugs. The calm water and still air always bring out the bugs.

I made a big fuss about anchoring instead of docking at Orillia, the town at the north end of the lake. Don wanted to go to a marina, and I wanted to anchor. I am tired of being tied to walls. I want the boat to be able to swing around and to be away from the land. It took us almost an hour and a half to anchor, get situated, put the motor on the dinghy and go ashore.

We walked around the small town, which was very busy and nicely lighted. We ate sub sandwiches for dinner and later, ice cream for dessert. We got back to the boat pretty late, after spending time swinging in the park. Orillia is a nice place.

Anchored at Orillia, ON – Distance traveled: 32 miles

August 9, 1988, Tuesday

Since it was raining, and more importantly because it was our 8th anniversary, we decided to stay and take a rest day. We relaxed until 1:30. Danielle fished in the rain. Shortly after noon, the boat, *Ocomoha,* anchored beside us and the couple on board, Stan and June, invited us to come over for drinks at four thirty. We said yes to the offer.

We went into town, and for my anniversary gift, Don bought me a very nice card and a small backpack. We looked at camera bags, but didn't really find one that was suitable in price and size. We also had a roll of film developed at a place that does it in one hour. It cost twice as much, but we hadn't seen any pictures taken with my new camera, so I was really anxious to get some developed. Some were quite good! Don thinks the one he took of me turned out the best.

We enjoyed our visit with our neighbors. They live in Sarnia, Ontario. They have been cruising for a year and a half and are on their way home. They also spent a few months in Mexico last year, so we got some information about Mexico. Later, we went into town to celebrate our anniversary at a good restaurant. The food was the best we have eaten at a restaurant in a long time. The restaurant is called The Company.

Anchored at Orillia, ON

August 10, 1988, Wednesday

We finished the Trent-Severn! What a good feeling! The whole system was very pretty, but today, in my opinion, was the most beautiful. We got up at five fifteen and were underway by six ten. We knew we had a big day ahead of us.

Lock # 43, "The Big Chute" was just as interesting to experience as the hydraulic lift locks. The Big Chute lock isn't a lock at all. It is an oversized railroad car that carried our boat from one body of water to another. I'll try to explain how it works. Rail tracks extend underwater in the lake that we brought our boat into and there was an oversized flatbed car on the tracks. It was on the part of the tracks that are underwater. The lockmaster had us position our boat above the flatbed car. Straps were run under our boat and attached to the top of the sides of the flatbed car, to hold our boat upright. The railroad car was then pulled slowly out of the water. The bottom of our keel sat on the floor of the flatbed car. The car,

COMING UP

with our boat on it, was pulled up a hill and then overland for a ways and finally down a hill into the water of the lake where we were heading.

When we were ready to be pulled out of the water, Don asked the lockmaster if he could put a new zinc on our shaft while we were out of the water. The lockmaster agreed and told him to get his tools and the new zinc and get in our dinghy. As *Robin Lee* came out of the water the dinghy (still attached to *Robin Lee*) settled to the floor of the railroad car. Don stepped out of the dinghy onto the railroad car, removed the remnants of the old zinc and put on the new one. He also pounded out the ding in the prop we got from the anchor line in Washington Channel. Then the lockmaster told him to get back in the dinghy because we were about to go into the new body of water. Don sat down in the dinghy and rode it up as the boat went into the water. Then he stepped back onto *Robin Lee*. The boat floated up from the flatbed, the straps were removed, we started our motor and went on our way. The Big Chute took us down 58'. The entire process only took about 30 minutes. It's another ingenious system.

We said good-bye to our friends Stan and June on *Ocomoha* at Port Severn. They had traveled alongside us most of the day. We tied up to the wall of the last lock long enough for Don to make a phone call to Wye Heritage Marina at Midland, where the Universal Atomic Diesel dealership is located and where, hopefully, our new

GOING DOWN

water pump is. He made a reservation for the night, and then we made the 10-mile trip to Midland and tied up for the night at the marina. The trip to Midland was "sloppy." Danielle didn't get sick, but she couldn't eat her dinner of linguini and white clam sauce, one of my favorites. She had soup later.

We had so much work to do on the boat that we were both feeling overwhelmed, uptight and tired. We had been up since five fifteen. All of that led to a spat– one of our few. This one was about who was going to do what and how. Poor Danielle had to listen to it. She handled it well though; she went to the V-berth and read.

At least now Don and I have a clear understanding of what our jobs are, and hopefully we can get all the work done tomorrow so that we will be ready to get on our way north on Saturday.

Wye Heritage Marina, Midland, ON – Distance traveled: 53 miles

August 11, 1988, Thursday

Don worked hard all day checking the rigging, making sure that everything was in ship shape, and getting things ready for stepping the mast. He also got prepared for the job of installing the new $200 water pump.

Danielle and I went to the ship's chandlery store and had a conversation with a woman working there who, with her husband, has done a lot of cruising in the Georgian Bay. She showed us several good anchorages which I marked on our chart.

Later, we caught a ride into town with Stuart, the marina "gopher." He took us to the bank, so I could get some cash and then to the post office, where I mailed the Trent-Severn charts back to John. After that he dropped us off at the grocery. We walked from there to the local mall. We got back to the boat around five. Don was still working on his projects. I polished the stainless steel stern railing and the Bimini frame. Then I did something I hadn't done for a long time; I made our dinner. Danielle ordered it. We fried chicken, with mashed potatoes, and gravy. Everyone liked it. Don did the dishes.

Danielle spent the evening trying to keep her fish alive and playing with the hose on the dock. Later in the evening she sang and we recorded it on our tape recorder. It was after midnight when we hit the sack.

Wye Heritage Marina, Midland, ON

CHAPTER FOURTEEN
GEORGIAN BAY, ON to CHICAGO, IL
Aug. 12, 1988 – Sept. 28, 1988

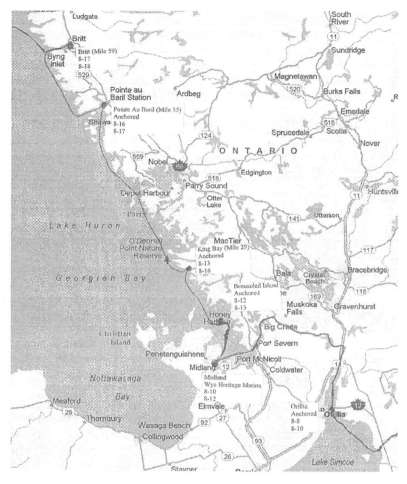

August 12, 1988, Friday

It was another full day of work. One reason I don't enjoy putting in at marinas is that I feel as though we have to work, work, and work while we are there.

We got started about eight o'clock. We filled our water tanks and moved the boat to the mast hoist. I got the bike from where we had been docked and rode it to the hoist area. Two guys who were experienced at stepping masts offered to help us get our mast up. Don, the two guys, and I stepped the mast. We gave the guys $10 each for helping us and only had to pay $22 to use the hoist, so our total cost was $42.00. We spent most of the day at the marina working on various clean-up projects, including scrubbing the deck, the cockpit and two big fenders that the lock walls had coated with slime and scum. But, the boat's hull is still dirty; I will feel a lot better when it's clean.

We left the marina in the afternoon, motored about seven miles to Beausoleil Island, and anchored on the east side of the island. It's a national park and is popular with vacationers and weekenders. It has a beautiful beach that is a mixture of pink, tan, black and maroon sand. Danielle and I took the dinghy to the beach to look around and play in the water. We walked around some colorful granite shoals and islets of pink and the other colors of granite that are typical of the Georgian Bay area. Beausoleil Island is a work of beauty carved out by a glacier during the ice age.

While we were gone, Don prepared a steak and celery stir-fry dinner, with carrot cake for dessert. Danielle set the table using a tablecloth. We enjoyed our nice meal along with a feeling of relief to have the mast where it should be, instead of in our way on the deck, where it had been since Catskill, New York.

It was hot and sticky, so Don and Danielle went to the cockpit to cool off. They both fell asleep. I finished the dishes and looked over the charts. At about midnight, I got Danielle to come in, but Don slept in the cockpit until it rained on him at two in the morning.

Anchored on the east side of Beausoleil Island, near Honey Harbor, Ontario – Distance traveled: 7 miles

August 13, 1988, Saturday

It's not hard to know it's a weekend when you are in a popular anchorage like this one. There are boats, people swimming, and other activity, everywhere.

We got up around eight thirty and had left-over carrot cake for breakfast. While Danielle and I stayed inside getting fully awake and getting dressed, Don went back to work again on his last project. He tuned the rigging by adjusting the turnbuckles in order to have the stays and shrouds as tight as he wanted them. Then he put rings in the turnbuckles with tape over them to prevent loosening and to ensure that they won't come off and cause a dismasting.

After he finished, around ten thirty, he and Danielle went ashore to explore and play on the beach. I appreciated Don taking Danielle. It was so good to have some time alone to do some personal body maintenance like plucking my eyebrows, using cleansing and moisturizing cream, and make-up. It is rare that I have the time to do some things that ought to be done frequently and routinely. My face looks it too. It is dry and even sore from the wind and the sun. I don't think I'll ever envy someone who has the time to lie out in the sun, it is so damaging to facial tissue. Actually, neither of us gets much free time. We both have projects that keep us busy about all the time. Work, work, work! Whoever thinks that this is a carefree, easy, and relaxing lifestyle, should travel with us awhile.

I flushed the head too much and the holding tank spit out some sewage on the deck. What a yucky mess, but I washed it overboard with buckets of water I drew from the bay. I guess we need a pump-out.

We raised our anchor at two thirty and motored into Honey Harbour. The boat traffic was terrible going into and out of Honey Harbor. It reminded us of a Sunday at Fort Lauderdale. We got the holding tank pumped for $12, which was the most expensive pump-out we have had. Canada strictly forbids discharging sewage into the water. We were even required to disable our Y-valve when we came into Canada. An unintended result of that is that pump-out stations know that people don't have an alternative and will pay whatever they charge.

We motored almost 23 miles in pretty calm conditions to get to our anchorage in King's Bay, at mile 29 on the small craft route near the eastern shore of the Georgian Bay. We ate late, but had time to have a short dinghy trip before dark. We think we saw a black mink crossing a narrow stream. It was a pretty area for a dinghy ride.

In the evening, we again taped Danielle singing. She is learning a song by Whitney Houston called "Where Do Broken Hearts Go." I wrote down the words for her, and she sang with the music using head phones, while she was being taped. She was just like a real star! She has a pretty little voice, although untrained, and Don and I hope she continues to be interested in singing.

Anchored at King's Bay, mile 29, small craft route, eastern shore, Georgian Bay, ON – Distance traveled: 23 miles.

August 14, 1988, Sunday

It was cool and sunny, but too windy to go anywhere, so we worked all day on the boat, except for about two hours in the early afternoon. We put the sails and the furling and reefing gear on. Then we tested them and afterwards put the mainsail cover on. We were in a nicely protected little cove, so around one o'clock we took a picnic lunch, which Danielle prepared, to a shady spot. After lunch, we dinghied to a sunnier spot for some swimming. We even found a rock we could dive from. We enjoyed the exercise, the sun, and the beauty of the area. It was all pretty relaxing, and since we had been working so hard on the boat, it was a nice break. The time went by quickly.

In the evening, it started to blow hard, and we had a storm. Don had to use the dinghy to retrieve the sail bag that blew off the lifeline. I think Danielle got a little nervous about the sudden change in the conditions and the storm that followed; we tried to be reassuring to her. It got more nerve-wracking as time went on due to the sound of the wind going through the rigging, but our anchor held and the chop wasn't bad. The wind was from the direction of the opening to the bay; however, there were several shoals that helped to break up the waves and keep them at a minimum. Don and Danielle played poker with lots of wild cards. She had two hands with five aces. I did cross-stitch. Thanks to the high winds, the mosquitoes didn't bother us.

Anchored at King's Bay, mile 29, small craft route, eastern shore, Georgian Bay, ON

August 15, 1988, Monday

It was much too nasty to travel today. We are in an especially tricky area to navigate with many shoals to avoid and many turns to make. Furthermore, the winds and rough water would have made things very uncomfortable. It wouldn't have been fun.

Besides, none of us were rested from last night. It seemed as though we were up half the night. Thank God our anchor held. I would guess the wind was about 30 knots. That is way too much for relaxation.

Today we ate junk food. Don baked muffins, brownies, and made popcorn. We pigged out.

Conditions calmed down about five thirty in the afternoon. Danielle and I went trolling for a half-hour, and then we got Don and rowed to shore and walked to a pay phone. Danielle called her mom to let her know where we were. She talked about 20 minutes. I'm sure Randy's phone bill will be high this month. Later, we had some extraordinary luck. A fellow living close by loaned us a car to use. We drove two miles to a grocery store and bought a few basic things, milk, bread, etc. We never did have a real meal. When we got back to the boat, we finished off the brownies with milk and played cards.

It was a good day, and we needed the rest; however, I felt bad about not making any progress.

Anchored at King's Bay, mile 29, small craft route, eastern shore, Georgian Bay, ON

August 16, 1988, Tuesday

Well, as forecasted, today was a good travel day! It was warm and sunny. We went through some beautiful territory, especially in the Canoe Channel and further north near Pointe Au Baril. It was a long day. We left King's Bay at eight in the morning, stopped briefly at Sans Soui for lunch, and then went on to Pointe Au Baril, where we anchored for the night at seven in the evening. Our anchoring spot was not great, but OK. Danielle and I went ashore and explored while Don made spaghetti for dinner. We stuffed ourselves

The mosquitoes joined us early, so instead of showering outside, we did so inside. That is always sort of a mess, but at least we are all clean and so is the head area. Danielle taped herself singing in the evening. Her voice is good, but she needs lots of training and practice!

Anchored at Pointe au Baril, ON, Distance traveled: 52 miles

August 17, 1988, Wednesday

We planned to get up and leave at five o'clock and go all the way to Loon Lodge, the cottage in Beaverstone Bay, owned by Clayton and Betty and Barbara and Lee, Don's brother and sister and their spouses. It's about 65 miles by water from Pointe au Baril. When the alarm went off at five, I shut it off because it was raining hard and blowing hard. We just stayed in bed and cuddled to keep warm. I fell asleep, and when I awoke at seven thirty, it was calm but still raining. We weighed anchor and left. The conditions were lousy. We made it through "Hang Dog Reef" and "The Narrows," but by the time we got to Byng Inlet, Don and Danielle wanted to quit. We motored up the inlet to Britt and docked for the night at the government wharf. It was $11 for dockage and $1 for power. The town wasn't much, but Don did get some fresh chicken at the grocery store.

Danielle made friends with some kids at the dock, and they swam together. One girl, Nicole, wanted to be Danielle's guest on our sailboat overnight. We said OK, but the girl's mom wouldn't let her. That was fine with us. It is actually pretty crowded with just Danielle and her things, but I think it would have worked out OK. Danielle didn't seem too upset about it.

Since we had electric, I did some sewing, making school clothes for Danielle, and Don fixed dinner and adjusted the rigging. We didn't finish dinner and the dishes until nine thirty.

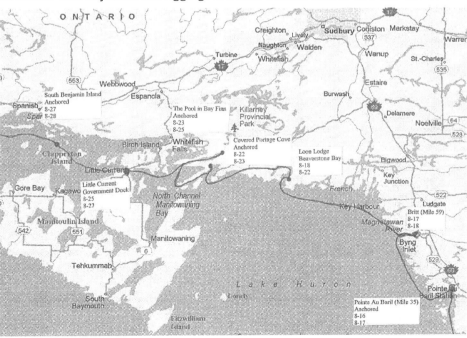

After that, while I sewed, Don and Danielle played cards until eleven and then went to bed. I continued sewing until two thirty in the morning. I can only sew when I have electricity, and I won't have it many more times before Danielle leaves and I would like to finish the outfits I am making her: a jumper, slacks, and a top. It got rather chilly, but I used the electric heater and that felt great.

At the government wharf in Britt, ON – Distance traveled: 28 miles

August 18, 1988, Thursday

We got off to a later start than we had planned. We left the dock at eight thirty. Hopefully, that will still give us time to get to Loon Lodge. I was very tired. It was stupid of me to stay up so late, but the jumper is almost done, and I need electricity to finish it. We were late starting, in part because I ran the electric sweeper before we unplugged, and Don needed to secure the bike on the deck. Danielle rode it to her friend Nicole's house yesterday afternoon. We said good-bye to the other sailors at the dock, Joyce and Chuck, on the boat, *Two Turtles,* and then left. It was a much prettier day, but windy and cold.

We motored through Cunningham's Channel and Roger's Gut. Then we motor-sailed across the north end of the Georgian Bay, passing the Bustards about one o'clock, and then going across the open water for a couple of hours. The conditions were good.

Don and Danielle filled our water jugs with clean crystal-clear water taken from the Georgian Bay.

We rounded bell buoy #86 at four thirty and followed four consecutive sets of range markers into Beaverstone Bay. Barbara and Lee Headlee, Don's sister and brother-in-law, were staying at the cottage that week and knew we planned to stop there. They were out fishing when we came into the bay. We recognized their boat and hollered and waived at them, but they didn't realize it was us sailing by. They didn't know we had Danielle on board and when they saw a little girl, they decided it couldn't be us. We were about a quarter of a mile from them. Since Beaverstone Bay has many shoals, we didn't dare stray from the small

LOON LODGE

craft route we were following, so we went on to the cottage. When they realized we were going to the cottage, they quit fishing and came to see who we were. We tied up at their dock at five thirty. We had dinner with them and visited until we were exhausted.

Docked at Loon Lodge, Beaverstone Bay, ON – Distance traveled: 45 miles

August 19-21, 1988, Friday-Sunday

Barbara and Lee brought our latest batch of mail to the cottage, so one of the first things we did was to go through it. We were amazed to find a package in the mail containing Don's wallet that had been missing for exactly two months–since June 19th, when we were in Annapolis. His credit card, debit card, and driver's license, were in it, along with some cash-- perhaps a little more cash than when it went missing. There was a vaguely written letter with the wallet, the gist of which was as follows:

Somehow, the husband of the lady writing the letter was responsible for taking the wallet, but she doesn't explain how; she and her husband were on a trip to Annapolis at the time; three days after they returned home, her husband died of a stroke; the lady felt bad about him taking Don's wallet; she didn't know how much money had been in it when her husband got the wallet, but she was enclosing a few dollars; and hoped it was about what was in it. There was no return address.

Danielle and I played most of the time, Friday through Sunday. We fished, and water skied, and one night, we all went to a party at a neighbor's cottage. The neighbors, Cathy and George, are from Findlay, OH.

We also went to Killarney with Barbara and Lee in their big boat, a 24' cabin cruiser, to shop and do laundry. While in Killarney, we picked up their guests for the week, Bev and Chris, who are from England. They are touring the US and Canada in a motorhome for a year. While we were in Killarney, Don changed the oil in the Honda motor and cleaned *Robin Lee's* hull.

On our last night, Sunday, we were lucky enough to see the Northern Lights. We sat outside listening to the loons and watching the spectacular display of brilliant and colorful lights. It was the first time Danielle and I had ever seen them, and we were both fascinated.

The weather was good while we were at the cottage, and because of the extraordinarily hot summer, the water was warm enough for bathing at the dock. It's usually way too cold. I also took a hot bath in their bathtub, the first bath for me in a couple of years; it felt great.

While we were at the cottage, we got a lot of visiting in, and it was a wonderful time for all three of us, but most of all for Danielle, who seemed really to enjoy her stay. Loon Lodge is a three bedroom, log home perched high on a bluff overlooking the lovely Beaverstone Bay, 22 miles from the nearest town. Barbara and Lee are wonderful hosts.

Don and his family have fished along the northern shore of the Georgian Bay since the early 1950s. Loon Lodge was built by Clayton, Betty, Lee, and Barbara, Don's brother and sister and their spouses, in the late 1960s.

We were docked at Loon Lodge during this period.

August 22, 1988, Monday

After a big breakfast, we got our act together and by ten o'clock, pulled away from Loon Lodge. We said our good-byes and gave our good wishes. We may never see Chris and Bev again, and it won't be until next year sometime that we will see Barbara and Lee. There will be lots of people, places, and miles in between, so we wished them well. They seem to be really enjoying their retirement, which began for them two years ago.

Collin's Inlet was beautiful, just as I remembered it. The quartz and granite can't be beaten for beauty. The pines and birch trees seem to sprout and grow out of the smallest of cracks and crevices. We saw a couple of loons along the way to Killarney. One boater we passed reported that he had just seen two bear cubs. When we left Collin's Inlet we sailed across the open water to Killarney.

We stopped in Killarney, and Danielle got a second look at this picturesque place. It bustles in the summer with boaters and fisherman. In the winter, it is an isolated little village of three or four hundred snowbound folks, 70 miles from the nearest City–Sudbury. We got bread and groceries, pumped out our holding tank, bought postcards, and got some cash. We tried to call Randy, but couldn't reach her. Danielle walked around town and looked at all the shops. She treated us to ice cream. Sometimes she gets bored with adult discussions and talk, but for the most part, she is totally involved in our conversations. Today we gave her some freedom to explore by herself. She picked some cute little daisies to decorate the boat.

HIKING AT COVERED PORTAGE COVE

We had a short trip, only three or four miles, to our anchorage at Covered Portage Cove, one of the prettiest anchorages we have ever been in. We immediately went out in the dinghy to explore, and took a hike up into the Killarney Mountains.

We had a light meal in the evening. It wasn't as cool at night as it has been.

Anchored at Covered Portage Cove, near Killarney, ON – Distance traveled: 26 miles

August 23, 1988, Tuesday

We motor-sailed through the Lansdowne Channel and then turned north and passed between Fraiser Point and McGregor Point into Baie Finn. We went all the way to the "Pool" at its east end, a distance of about eight miles, and anchored there for the night. Baie Finn is an out-of-the-way place, very isolated and pretty, and the anchorage at the pool is extremely well protected. It would have been nicer if it hadn't been overcast and rainy looking. We dinghied around for only a short time, and didn't go ashore because it was getting dark.

In the evening the sky cleared, and we got to enjoy sitting in the cockpit looking at the moon. The place is beautiful and so is the moon. I so looked forward to coming back here to visit, (Don and I were here on our Great Lakes Cruise three years ago), but now I'm getting worried again that we won't get to Mackinac Island before Shelly leaves. The weather is OK now, but the forecast says it's going to get foul.

Anchored at the "Pool," Baie Finn, ON – Distance traveled: 26 miles

August 24, 1988, Wednesday

We got up early and hiked up the mountain on the north side of the Pool to Lake Topaz. It is as beautiful as it was in July of 1985. Everything looked the same. We are in Killarney Provincial Park; it is all unspoiled territory, even though thousands of people visit here every year. We also hiked over to Artist Lake, but it isn't nearly as beautiful. We met some people who were canoeing and chatted with them a short time. It was one thirty by the time we got back to *Robin Lee*, so we didn't have time to go on to Little Current, our next stop. It was a threatening sky anyway, and it did rain later. We all rested. Don even slept. Afterwards Danielle and I hiked some more on the pink granite. The rock formations here are breathtaking. The mosquitoes weren't too bad tonight.

Anchored at the "Pool," Baie Finn, ON

August 25, 1988, Thursday

It wasn't at all comfortable today! First, it poured down as we brought up the anchor and got underway at ten o'clock. We got out our foul-weather gear, which we hadn't used since our trip from the Dry Tortugas to Key West in March of 1987. Too bad. I was hoping we would never need it again. The rain stopped as we left Baie Finn, but then the wind picked up to 20-25 mph, and we had to buck it. We sure were glad when we got to Little Current. We had to wait about ten minutes for the four o'clock opening of the bridge, but the area around the bridge was pretty well protected from the wind.

We got fuel and paid for a dock for the night. We also got a $50 cash advance on our Visa card when we paid for everything. We went out for pizza and ice cream for dinner. I had just enough time to get some sewing notions before the stores closed. Danielle decided to spend some time walking around looking in the stores. Within ten minutes, she was back at the boat saying that she had seen everything.

I stayed up late to sew on the machine. I finally went to bed at five in the morning. I finished a lot of the stitching work on all three items I am making for her: a jumper, slacks, and a top. They all fit her fine. It's funny that I get weary every night unless I have a project like this. I could sew for hours and hours—time passes so quickly. Danielle and Don slept like babies.

At the government dock, Little Current, ON – Distance traveled: 28 miles

August 26, 1988, Friday

I got up at seven thirty to start sewing again. I thought we would be leaving by noon and all that needs to be done now is finish work, like sewing a hook and eye on the top and sewing button decorations on the front of the jumper. Well, the wind was strong, about 20-25 mph out of the west, the direction we need to go, so we spent the day sitting at the dock. Danielle read and listened to our tapes.

Later, she and I window-shopped in Little Current, and I bought a few odds and ends. I bought a gift for Don, a book called *Ports*, which describes several anchorages in the North Channel.

We had an early dinner and then went with Jim, the owner of the grocery store, to Dr. Richard Messick and his wife, Vi's, summer home, near Little Current. I worked with Dr. Messick at Central Ohio Medical Group. They weren't there, so we left a note. Perhaps they have returned to Columbus. In the evening, we had a couple from Michigan on board to visit, as well as the grocery store owner, Jim Dunn.

I talked with Mom and Randy. Randy and Shelly are both upset that we won't be at Mackinac Island this weekend. They have no idea of the challenges involved in traveling on the water in a small boat. My family has done very little boating.

It was a bit chilly, and the wind continued to blow.

At the government dock, Little Current, ON

August 27, 1988, Saturday

We motored against the wind to get to the Benjamins by noon. It is so pretty here with its beautiful granite of shades of light and dark pinks, and even a deep rose color. I love the rock formations. Danielle and I explored the islands and had a picnic lunch. We saw several blueberry patches, but none had berries. It was too hot and dry this year! We wish there were some to pick.

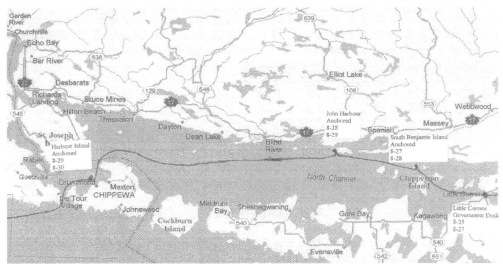

I was upset with Don because he ate the whole bag of marshmallows I bought in Little Current. I planned to roast them over a campfire, and while Danielle and I were exploring, we found the perfect spot for the campfire and some pieces of firewood for us to use. I could have spit nails, I was so mad at him! I wanted to have a special occasion, and he made a "selfish pig" of himself! All he said was, "I'm sorry, but you should have told me!" I was so upset that I could hardly talk with him.

Danielle and I went back to the island, and I sewed by hand while she did some more exploring. Then it got buggy, and we went back to the boat. It rained in the evening, and the wind picked up, but we were tucked in tight and slept comfortably. There were about six other boats in the anchorage. This is a very popular place. All the boaters know it is really beautiful here.

Anchored at South Benjamin Island, North Channel, ON – Distance traveled: 20 miles

August 28, 1988, Sunday

Today was our last day in Canada, and we made poor progress. The winds and waves are still from the direction we must go. I am depressed because I want to get to Mackinac. This strong contrary wind is disgusting. We make very slow headway against it. After seven hours, we anchored in John Harbour at John Island, only 26 miles from where we started. Don thinks that if the conditions are the same tomorrow, we should go to Blind River and on to Thessalon, and then go south from Thessalon on Tuesday because we would be going at an angle to the wind and could sail close hauled. I just want to get to Drummond Island as soon as possible and then consider an all-night trip to Mackinac.

I fixed dinner of mashed potatoes, sauerkraut, sour cream, and Kielbasa. Danielle and Don went ashore on John Island to explore. It is a pretty place and very well protected.

John Harbour, John Island, North Channel, ON – Distance traveled: 26 miles

August 29, 1988, Monday

We got up at five thirty. It was a pretty morning, and the conditions were super. We saw a really large animal swimming by the boat while we were still at anchor. Don thought it might have been a bear. We left John Harbour at six thirty and motor-sailed directly to Drummond Island, a total of 61 miles. It was Danielle's longest distance traveled on the boat in one day. We got to the dock at the town of Drummond at six in the evening, fueled, filled our water tanks, pumped out our holding tank, and cleared customs since we are now in

Michigan. Danielle did our laundry. Don went to the grocery store while I made some phone calls. I finally got hold of Shelly. I couldn't reach Pam, Randy, Mom, or Sister Carol. How frustrating! I finally get to make calls, and no one is home. The only ones who are usually home are Joe and Lois Dixon, and they are always glad to take our calls and relay information to others. We left the dock at eight o'clock and motored two miles to Harbor Island while watching a beautiful pink sunset, and anchored for the night.

We ate late. Danielle made some ham sandwiches for us.

After dinner Danielle and I had a marshmallow roast over the Aladdin lamp with marshmallows we purchased at Drummond Island. Don wasn't invited.

Anchored at Harbor Island, near Drummond Island, MI – Distance traveled: 61 miles

August 30, 1988, Tuesday
We finally made it to Mackinac Island!

We got underway from Harbor Island at six thirty in the morning. What a great day it was! The weather was super. On the way, Don videoed a talent show, starring Danielle. It was Danielle's final performance aboard *Robin Lee*. We will definitely miss her.

We arrived at Mackinac Island at five fifteen, looked over the anchorage, and then decided to put in at the marina for the night. We thought it would be easier to visit with

Randy and Shelly and unload Danielle's bags at a dock.

Mackinac Island is a popular vacation destination and is known for several things, including the famous Grand Hotel, its ban on cars, and fudge. It is also known for being the center of John Jacob Astor's fur business for 30 years following the War of 1812. The most common way of getting there is by ferry from Mackinac City on the north shore of the Michigan's Lower Peninsula, or a ferry from Saint Ignace on the Upper Peninsula. Transportation on the island is mostly by foot, bicycle and horse-drawn carriage.

One of its prominent landmarks is Fort Mackinac, built by the British to protect against the French because of the island's strategic location in the Straits of Mackinac, which joins Lake Michigan and Lake Huron. It became part of the United States by the treaty of Paris in 1783. During the war of 1812, it was captured by the British, but was returned to the United States after the war by the Treaty of Ghent.

We went ashore and found Saint Cloud House, where Shelly is staying. She was home. Bart, her friend, showed us to her room. We were excited to see her, and she was excited to see us. We looked around her place, and she introduced us to some of her friends. Then she got ready for work, and we all walked down to the place where she is a waitress, called

Everybody's Little Mexico. It is a cute place; we ate, and our food was excellent. Danielle seemed to be taking it all in—watching Shelly and listening to Shelly tell us all about her summer here on the island. After dinner, Danielle called her mom to see when she will be coming to get her, and then we spent a couple of hours walking around and browsing through the shops.

Shelly came to the boat after work and counted the tips she received today, which totaled $54. Don and Danielle went to bed about eleven thirty. Shelly and I talked until two thirty, and then I walked her home to Saint Cloud House.

At marina, Mackinac Island, MI – Distance traveled: 46 miles

August 31, 1988, Wednesday to September 4, 1988, Tuesday to Sunday
I haven't taken the time to write in this journal for the past few days because I've been too busy. I will summarize our activities:

On Wednesday, the day after we arrived, Sarah, Danielle and I took a bike ride so Danielle could see the island. The next day, September 1st, Danielle's mom came to take her home. Randy was glad to see Danielle, and vice-versa. It sure seemed strange after Danielle left. It was so quiet, and we had lots of extra space in the area where we had stowed her things.

We had a pleasant surprise when Bob, from the boat *Caprice*, saw us and stopped to visit. Bob needed some stitching done on his sail cover, so I did it for him, and he helped Don with an electrical problem Vern was having. Bob and Don also took a bike ride around the island.

SARAH AND DANIELLE

Don made dinner one night for Shelly and three of her friends, Bart, Sarah, and Lisa. They enjoyed the good home-cooked meal, with Shelly's #1 favorite dessert, peanut butter pie. Don also baked them some brownies.

Shelly had to work a lot, but she stopped at the boat on her way to and from work. We stayed at the dock so it would be convenient for all of us to visit.

Shelly had fun this summer and saved about $1100. I think it was a wonderful experience for her.[14]

At marina, Mackinac Island, MI

September 5, 1988, Monday, Labor Day
Shelly, Don and I went to the brunch at the Grand Hotel. Shelly paid for a horse taxi ride, and we treated her to the brunch. The Grand Hotel is such a pretty place.

---

[14] Shelly was married at the Little Stone Church on Mackinac Island to Rick Olson, on July 27, 2001.

The weather was nice while we were at Mackinac, until Labor Day. Don and I took a bike ride in the afternoon. It was very windy and sprinkled off and on.

Shelly's friend Bart's parents own a shop on Mackinac called the Bag-It Store. Shelly worked there part-time in addition to her job at the Mexican Restaurant. The Bag-It-Store had a party for its employees in the evening at the Pilot House to celebrate the end of the season. We were invited to the party, and of course, we went.

At marina, Mackinac Island, MI

SHELLY AND FRIENDS ABOARD *ROBIN LEE* FOR DINNER

September 6, 1988, Tuesday

We began preparing to leave Mackinac Island.

We sold our bike to the people next to us at the dock for $25. We bought it for $45 in November 1987. I think we got $20 worth of good out of it.

We showered at the yacht club, and I cut Don's hair and beard. Don got groceries and went to the bank and post office. We stopped at Shelly's work to visit, and Bart was there. He gave us a brass mirror shaped like a porthole, which was very thoughtful of him.

At marina, Mackinac Island, MI

September 7, 1988, Wednesday

Shelly did a lot of packing last night, and she's ready to leave to go back to Urbana and begin another year of college.

Shelly's dad and his mom, Shelly's Grandma Lil, and a couple of her dad's friends came at about eleven thirty to pick her up and take her to Urbana. Shelly brought her Grandma Lil to the boat so she could see it. Lil said she finds it hard to believe we would enjoy living and traveling on such a little boat.

Don and I, along with Shelly's dad and his friends, helped Sarah and Shelly load up all of their things and take them to the ferry dock.

Don, Shelly and I said our good-byes. I'm sad that our time together is over. It will be several months before we see Shelly again. She says she wants to come and see us when we get to New Orleans. I hope she can, but we are getting so low on money, I doubt that we will be able to afford the plane tickets.

Shelly and her dad's family left on the one o'clock ferry to Saint Ignace. We left the harbor at about the same time. We pounded into 4-6-foot waves until we got to the Mackinac Bridge, and then turned back and went to Saint Ignace. The conditions for moving on just weren't favorable for the *Robin Lee*.

After docking at Saint Ignace, Don and I walked to the grocery store to restock. We also went to a Napa automotive store. Don needed fuel filters and oil.

I was having a hard time with my emotions and did some crying. I was sad about saying good-bye to Shelly and also because our money is getting so low that Don thinks we should consider not going down the Mississippi and instead, going from here to Port Clinton and ending the trip where we began it. That was just too much to take! I couldn't stand it. I said that if we run out of money, and we may, then we will just have to work along the way. He is agreeable, but he doesn't think it's the smartest thing we've ever done. We aren't completely out of money. Don wants to have some money in reserve when we return to central Ohio and start living like "normal" people, and he doesn't want to sell the farms he owns until the time is right. I also think Don has had enough cruising and is ready to go home, but he is willing to continue since I want to. Only time will tell whether we are doing the right thing by going on. Only God knows!

We ate light because Don had made Reuben sandwiches this afternoon after leaving Mackinac. We had a quiet evening and went to bed early. We both were very tired.

At marina in Saint Ignace, MI – Distance traveled: 12 miles

September 8-9, 1988, Thursday and Friday

Our stay at Saint Ignace lasted longer than we expected. We were there Wednesday, Thursday, and Friday nights for a few reasons:

Dockage with electric was free since the season had ended.

Stores were close by for re-provisioning.

It's a nice little town, and we could use some stress-free time.

We had nice weather while we were there, except for the wind, so we walked a lot.

On Thursday, we got up and set out at ten thirty. First, we went to a coffee shop and then to another grocery. It was large and well-stocked. We stopped at the Dollar General Store, but didn't see anything we needed. We had taken a picnic lunch, so after shopping we went to a park by the Coast Guard station and ate lunch. We could see Mackinac Island and the rough water in between. Around three, we stopped at the library and read magazines. Shirley, the librarian for 15 years, said that we could watch a movie on the VCR if we came back the next day. Don made a new Chinese dish out of canned mackerel. It was really good, although Don thought for sure it would taste terrible. The recipe was in one of his *Consumer Guide Cooking Class Cookbooks*, which he likes. He mostly uses their Italian, Chinese, and Wok cookbooks. He left the Mexican cookbook in storage back in Columbus because he didn't think we could get the ingredients for the Mexican recipes.

On Friday morning, we stayed in the boat, cozy and warm until noon. I read my photography book and did cross-stitch while Don read a history book.

We went to the library about two o'clock and watched *David Copperfield*. Since I had recently read the book, and Don had read it a few years ago, we thought it would be a good movie to watch. We were a little disappointed because they didn't cover some of the things in the book that we liked. However, it isn't possible in a two-hour film to show all that the book is about. We liked the parts that were covered. After the movie we walked downtown. I had some minor jewelry repairs done and was very disappointed. The lady mashed the chain on my gold bracelet, when all I really wanted was for her to bend one small wire so that it wouldn't snag or catch on my clothing. I should have done it myself. I know I could have done a better job. Next time I will know better. Oh well.

Don made an excellent beef pot roast with potatoes, carrots and gravy. We had enough to get two meals from it. We sure do eat well on this little boat. The evening was quiet. I had enough time to cover the teak once with some Simco stain. Two hours later it started sprinkling lightly, but not enough to mess up the teak. I would hate to have stain running down the white boat. We went to bed early, hoping to get up early and leave. We need to get south before it gets cold.

At marina in Saint Ignace, MI

September 10, Saturday, 1988

We got up at seven thirty and left Saint Ignace at eight for Beaver Island. The weather report was acceptable, but not great. The winds were predicted to be from the W/NW and our destination was SW which meant we could sail. We were making good progress until the wind backed and began coming from the SW. We started the engine and made slow progress against the wind. We cleared Graves Reef light, 20 miles from Beaver Island, at three o'clock, taking water over the bow and rocking like a hobby-horse. It was a long, hard, day of traveling, which was extremely fatiguing and annoying. We arrived at Beaver Island just after sunset, tied to a mooring buoy, and shut down the engine at eight thirty. It was quiet at last, no halyards clanging, or engine noise, and no creaking of the boat—what a welcome relief—total silence. We loved it. It took us a while for our bodies to stop rocking.

Beaver Island lies 40 miles WSW of the Mackinac Bridge in Lake Michigan. It is 13 miles long and 4 to 5 miles wide, on average. Its year-round population is around 650, but it's greater during the summer.

Beaver Island was once a Mormon kingdom. When Joseph Smith died most Mormons considered Brigham Young as his successor, but some followed James Strang instead. Strang moved his followers to Beaver Island in 1848. They founded the town of Saint James, which is named after him and is the only town on the island. In 1850, Strang proclaimed himself king over his church. The members of his church made up the majority of the population of the island. He wore a crown and a royal robe and carried a royal shield. Thereafter, his followers built a road on the island and named it the "Kings Highway." It is still in use and is the main highway on the island. Strang was shot to death in 1856 and shortly after that, his followers were driven off the island.

Don made chicken gizzards in the pressure cooker, one of his favorite meals. I ate a couple of them, but had a bowl of cereal for my dinner. I really didn't have much of an appetite. By ten, we were both in bed asleep.

Tied to mooring buoy at Beaver Island, MI – Distance traveled: 47 miles

September 11, 1988, Sunday

We went ashore early and bought fruit, sardines and crackers to have as snacks while we were underway and a few other food items. After our traditional Sunday morning breakfast of pancakes, we headed for Manistique, Michigan, on the Upper Peninsula. We traveled about the same distance today as yesterday, but it was a much more pleasant day. We left at ten o'clock and arrived at five thirty, having sailed a good portion of the day. The winds were 15-20 mph and waves 3-4 feet. We rolled a bit, but it was a lot more comfortable than yesterday.

After we docked at Manistique, we got fuel and showered. Back on board, we drank a glass of wine, and Don heated up the leftover beef pot roast for dinner. It was just as good today as it was the other night in Saint Ignace.

We were still worn out from yesterday's trip, so we went to bed early.

At marina in Manistique, MI – Distance traveled: 45 miles

September 12, 1988, Monday

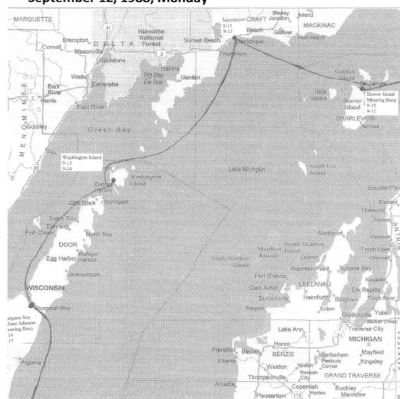

We must have still been very tired, because we both slept until nine thirty. When we awakened, the weather was lousy and the forecast for the day was lousy. Winds of 30 mph from the southwest, the direction we are headed, were predicted. We were content to stay in the secure Manistique harbor.

Around eleven it started getting hazy, and by one, a huge freighter close by our dock unloading coal could barely be seen. By three, the fog totally obscured the freighter.

We made our usual rounds to the bank, post office, hardware, automotive store (for an oil filter), and grocery. After that, we went back to the boat, got the dirty clothes and headed for the laundromat, which was extremely nice and very clean. It continued to be foggy, and we began to wonder if we could be stuck in Manistique for the winter. It started to rain hard while we were at the Laundromat, so we read.

Don made an excellent dish for dinner called chicken marsala.

It wasn't a good day, but we do like Manistique and its harbor.

At marina in Manistique, MI

September 13, 1988, Tuesday

At eight thirty, we got underway for Washington Island, at the north end of Green Bay.

What a difference a day makes! Today the wind was right. It was perfect! We also had blue skies. We were under sail immediately, and we were flying. It was such a welcome change, we had a natural high feeling. We both seemed to have a mood boost! I took the helm for the first two hours. I had time to write and Don to read because Vern worked for a change. It's been a long time since we could be involved in something besides steering while we were on watch. This is perfect Great Lakes weather, a rare thing!

While underway we listened to the radio, something we don't normally do, and heard a news report on National Public Radio (NPR) about the canoe expedition of the Kruegers from Michigan. Valerie and Vernon, whom we met at Farmer's Cay in the Exumas, are still doing OK and are expected to arrive at Cape Horn in March. It's been 15 months since we met them. We have wondered if we would ever hear about them again. We normally play tapes and CDs and are glad we decided to listen to the radio today.

Well, the great sailing didn't last all that long, only about three hours, and then the wind backed, and we were hobby-horsing again; it was right on the nose, as usual.

All things considered, the day's trip wasn't too bad, but it was a long day. At five thirty, Don made taco salad for dinner, and we ate dinner while underway. The sun was a reddish orange when it set, and just off the horizon we could see a large freighter, with the sun setting and a new moon raising it was a beautiful scene. Finally, at eight thirty, we entered the channel to Detroit Harbor at Washington Island. We tied near a ferry dock at the same spot where we had tied in 1985 while on our Great Lakes cruise.

We drank a glass of iced tea and sat down and rested for a few minutes. Then Don finished out the day's entry in the boat's log book as I washed dishes. Afterwards, we cleaned out the bilge because Don had noticed it had some oil in it. That could be bad news. We may have a seal in the engine that needs to be replaced. We will keep an eye on it.

Tonight Hurricane Gilbert is expected to pick up speed, to maybe 130 mph, and possibly come into Texas. It has already hit Jamaica and killed 30 people. It also hit the Grand Cayman Islands today. We haven't heard news of how much damage it did there. I hope none of our cruising friends were hit. The Wests from Urbana were planning to be in the area of the Grand Caymans at this time.

Tied at Washington Island, WI – Distance traveled: 64 miles

September 14, 1988, Wednesday

We left Shelly and Mackinac Island one week ago today. She started school yesterday.

We got up and left at six forty-five, so we wouldn't be in the way of the ferry. We didn't see another person; I think we were the only ones awake on the island. We went out of Green Bay through Death's Door passage, a notoriously treacherous inlet. I can understand why people say it is dangerous. When we went out, there was a stiff westerly breeze, and a really nasty sea had developed at the narrow inlet.

We motor-sailed in Lake Michigan, 38 miles to Sturgeon Bay. We saw a lot of small fishing boats at the entrance to the canal which leads to the town of Sturgeon Bay. The light house located at the entrance is picturesque, as a lot of them are, and there was a pretty blue sky with puffy white clouds, so I hope my pictures turn out.

We tied up at Palmer Johnson, a boat manufacturing and repair company. They are going to fix our knot meter and replace one of our shrouds. They came out to the boat to help us as soon as we arrived. We couldn't have hoped for any better service or hospitality. Fred, from the service department, even drove Don all over town to run errands.

I showered and did a few chores while he was gone. I made a salad and muffins for dinner. It was OK. We stayed in the boat for the evening. I didn't feel good due to a sore throat problem, which has been annoying me ever since we were at Manistique.

At the Palmer Johnson Company, Sturgeon Bay, WI – Distance traveled: 51 miles

September 15, 1988, Thursday

Don left early in the morning to go into town to get a fuel filter and some other things. I stayed onboard and wrote letters. I had many to write. When Danielle was with us, I put off all letter writing, so I'm behind.

The people at Palmer Johnson worked on the shroud and even moved the boat without me realizing what was going on.

I didn't leave the boat until after dinner. Then, Don and I took a walk to the grocery and walked around in the town. We ended up buying lots of groceries, including a half-gallon of ice cream, bananas, and chocolate syrup for sundaes. What pigs we can be!

At the Palmer Johnson Company, Sturgeon Bay, WI

September 16, 1988, Friday

I got up very early, not realizing yet that Wisconsin is in a later time zone than Michigan. We moved our boat to the yacht club. Palmer Johnson has completed the work, and we didn't want to over-stay our welcome.

The yacht club said we could tie up at their loading dock if we wanted to go to town. We did, and we poked around in town for an hour or so. I bought a couple of straws, and plastic long handled spoons for $0.25 from a restaurant so that when we got back to the boat, we could make ice cream floats. By the end of the day we finished off the half-gallon of ice cream.

I called the grandmother of a girl I worked with at Publix on Longboat Key. She had given me the address and number and asked me to say "hi" to her if we got to Sturgeon Bay. I wonder if she (Lisa) thought I would. I never tell somebody I will do something like that unless I mean it. I hope she finds out that I did. Don thinks I'm crazy and that Lisa has probably forgotten all about her request and has probably forgotten me. Maybe so, but who cares? I did what I said I would do.

We moved to a mooring buoy around two thirty. It was windy, and we had some rain in the afternoon, but we were safe, warm, dry, and relaxed, so let it blow and rain; it's no big deal! The conditions settled down around dark. Since we will be on the Mississippi River in a couple of weeks, I started reading *The Adventures of Huckleberry Finn*.

On a mooring buoy at the Sturgeon Bay Yacht Club, Sturgeon Bay, WI — Distance traveled: 1 mile

September 17, 1988, Saturday

We left Sturgeon Bay at nine. Although the wind was on our nose again, it wasn't too strong this morning, and it was sunny and pretty. It was reasonably comfortable, so we made a good day's run. Any day we make progress, we feel good. It got very hazy as we were approaching Manitowoc. We could hardly see the buoys.

We tied to the city dock. It was dark by the time dinner was over. Don made eggplant Parmesan. It was pretty good, but took two hours to prepare and made a greasy mess. He will probably never make that recipe again. We hate to eat that late, and I hate cleaning up greasy messes. We went to bed late!

Tied at city dock, Manitowoc, WI – Distance traveled: 58 miles

AT MANITOWOC

September 18, 1988, Sunday

We got up late because we knew it was to be very windy, and we were going to stay over and spend the day sightseeing in town.

Around noon, we left the boat and walked to the new marina and then ate lunch at the Old-Fashioned Ice Cream Parlor and Candy Company. It's a neat place with cheap prices, and the food was good too. After rejecting the idea of going to a movie because it was a pretty afternoon, and we didn't think any of the movies sounded good, we spent our time taking pictures of interesting things: an old tugboat at the park, a big bottle of Budweiser beer painted on a grain silo, and others. We are too far out of the mainstream to know which movies are good, and we didn't want to spend the afternoon watching a mediocre film.

We also went aboard and toured the *USS Cobia*, a GATO-class submarine similar to the twenty eight WWII submarines built in Maritowoc. We were tied up next to it.

It was cold at sundown, so we tucked in early.

Tied at city dock, Manitowoc, WI

September 19, 1988, Monday

What a lousy day! It poured down and blew all day. The swell off Lake Michigan came right down the river, creating a nasty tossing and turning effect with our boat. I never left the boat. We are getting the remnants of Hurricane Gilbert. I stayed in bed until two thirty reading *Huckleberry Finn*. I only got up a couple of times to clean up and use the head. Don went out walking and shopping. It was too rainy for me!

In the evening, the weather settled down a little bit. Don made a new cauliflower salad recipe and "Hoppin' John," a dish made of black eyed peas and rice. We went to bed early so as to sleep away an uncomfortable evening and night.

I did feel as though I accomplished something because I finished the book, *The Adventures of Huckleberry Finn*. It's a good story.

Tied at city dock, Manitowoc, WI

September 20, 1988, Tuesday, Dad's 62nd birthday

It was still nasty out when we got up, but by ten thirty we were up and dressed and out of the boat. We went to buy showers at the marina, but they wouldn't do business with anyone other than their dockers, so instead we went to the YMCA and paid for their facilities. I sure wish we had come here yesterday. We could have spent the entire day using their club for $3 each, even the lounge and TV room. All of it is sparkling clean and very nice. The pool is large, and it has a sauna and whirlpool. Oh well, it was a lesson learned: Get off the boat and explore on days when the weather is bad.

At two thirty, it was still windy, but we left because the west wind was favorable. We could sail to Sheboygan on a reach in the lee of the mainland. It was windy, but a good run. It was very cloudy and cold, so when we got in we were happy to be tied up with electricity.

The best part of the day was that *Caprice*, with Bob and his dog, Target, were there. Bob welcomed us and helped us get fuel and tie up at the yacht club. Later, he joined us for a dinner of Hoppin' John and cornbread. We sure enjoyed visiting and catching up on the details of his trip. Hopefully, we will be buddy-boating some of the rest of the way until he turns north on the Mississippi, and we turn south. We changed the oil, a messy job, and went to bed late.

Docked at the Sheboygan Yacht Club – Distance traveled: 26 miles

September 21, 1988, Wednesday

Today we were up early to move on since the weather was supposed to be in our favor. We filled our water tanks and got underway at eight o'clock. We motor/sailed past Port Washington and Milwaukee, and then put in at Racine, Wisconsin at nine thirty at night after 13 ½ hours on Lake Michigan. It was cloudy and cold all day, but there was very little wind, and it was flat calm until six; then, just as Don finished dinner preparations, the wind came around to exactly our heading and started to blow about 15 knots, so we were bucking the wind once more. It got dark around eight, so it was a nighttime arrival, something we prefer not to do for a couple of reasons: 1) it is hard to distinguish navigation lights from regular lights, thereby making it hard to determine your position, what your heading should be, and where the hazards are; and 2) the land lights are often so bright they partially blind you. Bob on *Caprice* put in at Milwaukee because his wife Jana, whom we met in Florida, will be joining him this Sunday. I think she will finish the trip with him, and then they will drive back to California together. He goes back to work in November, having left on a leave of absence, last September. He says he wants to sell everything in California, take *Caprice* to Florida, and live on it while he builds a larger boat. We wish him well, that's for sure.

We tied to a mooring buoy at the Racine Yacht Club, which was not very well protected. We didn't want to look for a better spot in the dark. It rained shortly after we got situated, but we kept dry.

On mooring buoy at the Racine Yacht Club, Racine, WI – Distance traveled: 72 miles

September 22, 1988, Thursday

Early in the morning, after the rain showers stopped and the sun came out, we moved the boat to the Palmer Johnson Company. They have a facility in Racine, in addition to the one they have in Sturgeon Bay. We needed to get our oil leak repaired because the oil dipstick showed we had lost ½ pint in a day, and the bilge was filthy black with oil. What a messy job it is to clean up the bilge.

The mechanics at Palmer Johnson determined that the problem was in the oil pressure sensor unit, and that it needed to be replaced. They had a lot of trouble getting it out. Don helped. They worked until four thirty and said they would finish in the morning, and then we could be on our way. The winds going to Chicago should be favorable tomorrow.

I rested and did cross-stitch during the day and visited with various employees. It rained off and on all day. It was dreary. I hated to even leave the boat to take a walk.

In the evening, Don and I cleaned the bilge for the second time in ten days. We did it so we could make sure there was no more leaking, and then we would know for sure that the repair job was effective. It was an awful mess; there was oil everywhere.

Don made a big pot of 15-bean soup (after he washed his hands), which was good, and that is all we ate the entire day.

At the Palmer Johnson facility in Racine, WI – Distance traveled: 1 mile

September 23, 1988, Friday

What a difference a day makes. It was a beautiful day—sunny blue skies with a few puffy white clouds and really warm. After my shower, I put on shorts!

The fellow working on our engine's oil leak problem accidentally broke the manifold as he was finishing up our repair work. The Palmer Johnson Company, as well as the mechanic, felt bad, so they flew the company plane to Oshkosh and got us a new manifold. They didn't even charge us. It took all day for them to replace the manifold and finish the job, but they didn't charge us for their labor and expenses. All we paid was $129 for some oil we bought, a few light bulbs, 4.5 hours labor and a new oil pressure sensor unit. We even got two nights of free dockage with electric. Boy, were we lucky! It could have been so expensive. It was a mistake that could have happened to Don or anyone touching the manifold. I'm sure they were glad to get rid of us because they don't need customers like us (who bring Murphy's Law problems to them). They made no profit from the *Robin Lee*. They were all very nice and felt bad that they held us up on our trip. We really felt sorry for them. They even loaned us their company truck, so we could run errands. We did laundry, got groceries, bought six gallons of alcohol for the stove, three gallons of oil, had lunch at a local pub, and then drove around sightseeing. We were gone about four hours. By five o'clock, they were finishing and then Don fixed the guys a martini. We visited until seven thirty. After that, we put away all the laundry and made up the bed. It was a very pretty evening to take a walk, but it was eight thirty by the time we were ready, and I was too tired.

At the Palmer Johnson facility in Racine, WI

September 24, 1988, Saturday

We got up at eight thirty, filled up the water jugs and water tanks, and then left the Palmer Johnson facility.

I had a nightmare last night. The main thrust of the dream was that, for some reason, we had to move off the boat. That idea was very upsetting to me.

It was a beautiful day, not a ripple on the water, so we motored all day in flat calm conditions. The flies were terrible, and therefore, we kept the companionway hatch flap down. I could make out the skyline of Chicago soon after we passed Waukegan; it was hazy. I made a tuna and lettuce salad for lunch and because it was sunny and warm, we sat in the cockpit to eat and listened to music on cassette tapes. There were a lot of other boats on the lake and entirely too much boat traffic on channel 16 of the marine radio. The marine operators were very busy connecting calls. Most of the calls were of little significance, like a wife calling her husband to find out what time he'd be at the dock, and whether or not he caught any fish. I sure hope no one was in need of the Coast Guard during that time because of a problem. [Marine operators connect land-based telephones and boats that have marine radios, so they can converse. The initial contact is made on channel 16, and then they are switched to another channel to talk.]

We stopped at Montrose Harbor and docked along the wall and went into the Corinthian Yacht Club and asked if we could spend the night there. They said we could. Everyone was friendly. We had no power, but free dockage and good showers!

Don fixed a new recipe out of his Consumer Guide Chinese Cooking Class Cookbook for pork, crabmeat and veggies rolled up in romaine lettuce leaves.

Tied at the Corinthian Yacht Club, Montrose Harbor, Chicago, IL – Distance traveled: 55 miles

September 25, 1988, Sunday

We got up at seven thirty and moved to a mooring buoy. Last night, we met some people at the yacht club who invited us to go out on their Catamaran at one o'clock today; we accepted the invitation. Don made a few phone calls to find the best place to have our mast unstepped and where we can buy river charts, and then it was time to go aboard the catamaran.

Denny and his girlfriend, Denise, and Don and his girlfriend, Nancy, took us out. I'm not sure who owns the catamaran, but I believe Denny does. The boat's name is *Quervo Gold*. It's about 40 feet long and has a flat surface, from stem to stern and for almost the entire width, which makes it a great boat to take out on the lake on a calm night for a party, and I think that is mostly what it is used for.

We had fun sailing and getting to know them. Around eight o'clock, we all went to Don's House. It's a beautiful old three-story building that Don is fixing up and dividing into residential units, one on each floor. He lives on the top floor. His unit has a rooftop patio on which he plans to put a hot tub. They ordered pizza, and while we were eating it, we watched sailing video. We didn't get home until ten. What a wonderful welcome to Chicago! And what neat new friends!

On a mooring buoy at the Corinthian Yacht Club, Montrose Harbor, Chicago, IL

September 26, 1988, Monday

We made some progress today toward getting on with our cruise. We bought some materials for securing our mast on deck and bought some river charts.

DENISE, DENNY, NANCY AND DON

We met our new friends at four o'clock for another sail on the catamaran. It was another fun evening. They all enjoy socializing, and each of them has a great sense of humor. Being with them on the catamaran was very different from our usual evening's entertainment of gin rummy, cross-stitch, reading and/or letter writing, and was a lot of fun. After sailing, we treated them to dinner out at a local Thai restaurant. They took us back to the marina around nine thirty, and we said our good-byes and wished them well, because we will be leaving tomorrow. I wonder whether we will ever see them again.

On a mooring buoy at the Corinthian Yacht Club, Montrose Harbor, Chicago, IL

September 27, 1988, Tuesday

We showered at the yacht club and then went to an area very near the harbor which has picnic tables to eat the light breakfast of sweet rolls that we had packed. There we met and talked with a couple of "park people," homeless folks that hang out at Montrose Park. The man lives in the park and sleeps on a bench. We saw him sleeping there from our boat. Actually, he was a pretty nice guy, and warned us about thieves in the area, and that we needed to protect our dinghy from them. The lady with him looked as though she had "syphilis sores" on her face and arms and didn't seem to be very alert. He told us that he'd only met her two days ago at the Salvation Army where he goes for breakfast, and that she had been following him around ever since. He said she sleeps on the ground.

We motored into Belmont Harbor to see about having our mast unstepped there, but found out that we would have to do it ourselves, and we didn't want to do that. We left and went further down the shore to the Jackson Park Yacht Club.

We docked and immediately made friends with John Torrey, a yacht club member. He is a sail maker and a part owner of Goose Island Sails. Our jib had started to come unstitched again, and he kindly offered to have his company make the repair for $20. He also offered to drive us to his company's loft and suggested that we could eat together at a Greek restaurant close by while the work was being done. It was a very nice offer. Another company would have charged $50 and transportation to another place would have been complicated, and we would be lugging a big sail with us. Furthermore, by taking the offer, we would get to tour part of the city. So we took him up on it. At the loft, he showed the people working what needed to be done, and while there, he gave us each a Goose Island Sails T-shirt. John wouldn't let us treat him to dinner at the Greek restaurant. In fact, he didn't eat; he just drank beer. By the time we left, he was so drunk I was really concerned about our ride home. We probably should have offered to drive, but we didn't have the faintest idea where we were, or where we were going. While Don was in the bathroom, he said to me, "you really ought to do something about that lock of hair, the one curl above your forehead," which I thought was inappropriate. I told him that my husband loved it. We had a wild ride back to Jackson Park Harbor. Don and I were happy to be home and alive. The rest of the evening we just wanted to relax.

We went to bed around ten thirty.

Tied up at Jackson Park Yacht Club, Jackson Park, IL – Distance traveled: 14 miles

September 28, 1988, Wednesday

In the middle of the night the wind shifted to the ESE, and brought a nasty swell into the marina. We rocked and rolled the entire night. It was awful. The harbor is very well protected with only one small opening. However, the seawalls are vertical and the waves aren't absorbed when they hit them, they just bounce off and go back and forth across the harbor.

I wrote a letter to Shelly, and we wrote letters to order charts for the Tennessee and Ohio rivers. We called for *Caprice* on the marine radio several times, but didn't get a response.

There was no one to hire at Jackson Harbor to unstep our mast, so we ended up taking it down ourselves with some help from other sailors. We did hire a carpenter, the husband of the girl who manages the yacht club, to make a simple support for securing the mast on the deck. Don helped some other people take down their masts for winter storage, and then we got in line to take ours down; around three thirty, it was our turn. Since we had never done it before, and we had no experience operating a crane, we accepted the offers of help from a couple of yacht club members who were there. We did, in fact, get it down without any damage to mast or boat. The cost of using the lift was $78. The carpenter only charged us $20 to make the support.

I was in a rotten mood; I was tired and irritable because we had to wait all day to get our mast down and because of the persistent chop in the harbor. Also, my shoulder was hurting. My mood improved when I called Shelly and talked awhile. We also stayed inside the yacht club's clubhouse and slept on couches, and that was better than rocking all night on the boat. I even stayed up late to watch a movie on TV. The Space Shuttle Discovery lifts off in the morning. It will be the first launch since Challenger blew up. How tragic that was. I'll never forget it!

Tied up at Jackson Park Yacht Club, Jackson Park, IL

CHAPTER FIFTEEN
ILLINOIS WATERWAY, IL to PICKWICK LAKE, TN
Sept. 29, 1988 – Nov. 1, 1988

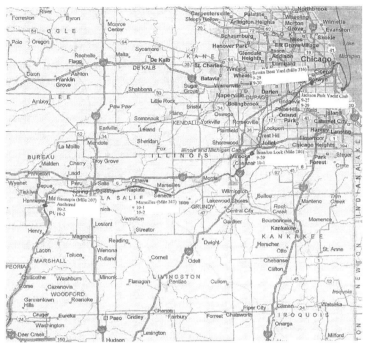

September 29, 1988, Thursday

We wanted to watch the take-off of *Discovery*, but by the time we took showers and cleaned up the boat in preparation for leaving, we had missed the launch. It took off safely and made it into space, which was a relief to the whole nation.

We got underway with the mast stowed on deck and made it safely across the six mile stretch of open waters of Lake Michigan between Jackson Harbor and the entrance to the Chicago River and the Chicago Sanitary and Ship Canal. We went through the Controlling Works Lock at the entrance. It only dropped us a little more than a foot. When we left the lock, we were in the Chicago River, and after going about five miles on the river, passing the Wrigley Building and other skyscrapers of the city along the way, we entered the sanitary canal. We continued on the sanitary canal the rest of the way through Chicago. The sanitary canal is about 30 miles long and empties into the Des Plaines River at Joliet and that river, in turn, empties into the Illinois River about ten miles downstream from Joliet. The Illinois River flows into the Mississippi River at Grafton, Illinois.

There is a second way to the sanitary canal from Lake Michigan, and that is on the Calumet River which can be taken from the lake in the southern part of Chicago. Like the Chicago River, it connects to the Sanitary Canal.

The sanitary canal also carries Chicago's sewage to the Des Plaines and Illinois Rivers. In Chicago's early years, the sewage flowed by way of the Chicago River, into Lake Michigan. Lake Michigan was, and still is, the source of drinking water for Chicago. The canal was built for the purpose of redirecting Chicago's sewage down the Des Plaines and Illinois Rivers, keeping it out of their water supply.

The connection of Lake Michigan and the Mississippi River by the rivers I have mentioned and the sanitary canal makes up the Illinois Waterway. The waterway is the only way to move freight and people, by boat, between these two very important bodies of water. Because of that, it was very important in the development of Chicago into a city.

CHICAGO

It was about lunch time when we motored through the LOOP. It was fun looking up from the water level at all the huge buildings and people. I took a few snapshots, and Don took video.

We had an uneventful night tied to a wall at Reick's Boat Yard on the west side of Chicago. There was no charge for overnight docking. It was a good day, and we are glad to be on a river again. It's always more comfortable.

Tied at Reick's Boat Yard, Chicago, IL – Distance traveled: 17 miles

September 30, 1988, Friday

We got off to a late start today. Since we are low on groceries, all we could have for breakfast was pancakes, and pancakes take a while to fix and eat. Furthermore, some guys at the boat yard came down to visit us and talk about our travels. That's always fun!

We motored through the industrial heartland of the United States. We have never seen so much industry. Several tow boats were on the river pushing barges, three wide and three or four long, which is a lot of weight and very dangerous if we should get in their way. Don and I both keep a constant watch. We don't feel confident with Vern steering us. He goes crazy every time we go under a set of bridges or when we get hit by a big wake. Even the wind and current can throw him off. Actually, he is worthless; the one thing on board that is in need of "deep 6-ing."

We locked through the Lockport Lock; it dropped us down about 40 feet. It was a smooth drop and the walls were free of slime. The lock is 1,000 feet long, bigger than we have seen in the past except for *maybe* the Welland Canal in Canada.

As we go down the Illinois Waterway, we will go through six more locks, making a total of eight locks on the waterway, counting the Lockport Lock and the Controlling Works Lock. The total drop from Lake Michigan to the Mississippi is 578 feet, and the waterway is 327 river miles long when starting at the Controlling Works Lock.

We decided to stop for the night at Bicentennial Park in Joliet where the city provides free electricity for transients. We tied up there and ate our dinner, but left as soon as we had eaten. We didn't feel comfortable because we had encounters with locals. A group of young boys wanted to climb on the boat and were making lots of noise. Two older fellows insisted on helping us tie up. They were both drunk. The younger one wanted to see inside our boat. The other one insisted that we let him float in our dinghy. He almost fell into it because he was so drunk. It wasn't a good situation at all. We hated to cross any of them, for fear it might lead to a worse situation. They might have a gun and blow a hole in our dingy or in us! Anyway, we were sure glad to get away from there.

We got to the next lock, the Brandon Road Lock, before dark and tied to the wall above the lock. Leonard, the lockmaster was especially friendly and told us to plug into electric and gave us lots of literature about the locks and parklands. He also said *Caprice* spent the night there last night.

Tied to a wall at the Brandon Road Lock, Rockdale, IL – Distance traveled: 26 miles

October 1, 1988, Saturday

The weather forecast was for a light rain all day, and that is what we got. It was dreary, but we didn't get too wet, and we made some progress. We are hoping to catch up with *Caprice*.

We left the lock wall at eight thirty and bought fuel since we were getting low, and places with the depth we need that offer diesel are few and far between.

After getting fuel, we went through the Brandon Road Lock and continued down the river. About ten miles down, the Des Plaines River merged with the Kankakee River to form the Illinois River, the river we will be on until we reach the Mississippi. Around noon, we went through the Dresden Island Lock. Both the Brandon Road Lock and the Dresden Island Lock were easy to go through.

I've been steering the boat into the locks and up to the wall for practice, and it is good practice.

We stopped at Morris, on the recommendation of Leonard, the lockmaster at the Brandon Road Lock, but couldn't find a place to tie up, so we had to miss the corn festival that Leonard told us was going on. We motored on to Marseilles and lucked out with free dockage and electric, which was great. We used electricity to cook with as well as to run the electric heater. We tied up at four o'clock. It rained off and on all night, and the heater helped to keep down the wetness in the boat.

We had enough daylight left to walk a mile to town and back. We finally got groceries, and it took every cent we had. Our $40 cash stash is now gone. Hopefully, we can get some money soon, but we are glad to at least have some food.

Don cooked us fresh broccoli and chicken Dijon with boned and skinless chicken breasts. For dessert we had cinnamon graham crackers and coffee. We already had a candy bar at the grocery.

It was a nice night to be home, out of the weather. We listened to CDs.

Tied at Snug Harbor Marina, Marseilles, IL – Distance traveled: 34 miles

October 2, 1988, Sunday

We got up early, but lay around and had a late breakfast. We turned on the TV, hoping to get *Sunday Morning with Charles Kuralt*, but there was no reception, except for one religious station. We finally left about ten and then were held up for an hour at the Marseillies Lock. There was a tow ahead of us, and it was too big for the lock and had to be broken in half. The lockmaster told us to go into the lock with the last half of the tow. It was a complicated procedure and took about an hour to complete. I took a few pictures of it and a couple of candid shots of my wonderful husband at the helm.

The weather was very pretty – blue skies with puffy white clouds. The fall colors were brilliant in the sunlight, and it was warm. It couldn't have been any better.

While we were underway, Don made a pasta and tuna salad with fresh vegetables. We also had fresh fruit to snack on, so we should be safe from scurvy for a while.

After we anchored, we ate a light meal of grilled cheese, applesauce, leftover mac and cheese, and then banana pudding with fried bananas for dessert. Everything was yellow or orange in color, but it was all good. (I like for the foods we eat to have contrasting colors and I mention that to the chef when they don't.)

We went through the lock at Starved Rock at three in the afternoon, and the lockmaster said *Caprice* went through the lock four hours ahead of us. Hopefully, we will catch them tomorrow. We've seen lots of local small boat traffic. A fellow said we probably could tie up at the grain dock, but I'm glad we didn't. A big tow with several barges came in about two hours later. We anchored at six o'clock at mile marker 207, which means that we are now 207 miles from the Mississippi. It was nice to be swinging free on the anchor, and we had very good protection so the river was flat and comfortable.

Anchored between two bridges in Hennepin, IL – Distance traveled: 36 miles

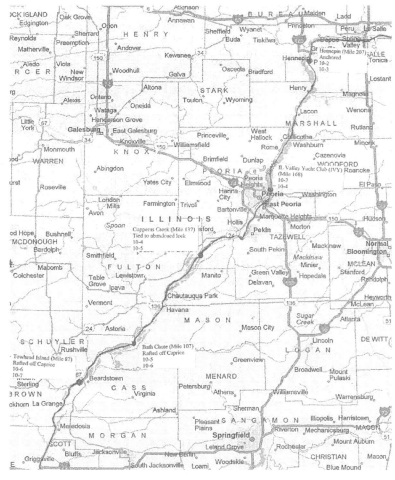

October 3, 1988, Monday

I haven't been good about writing in this journal lately because I've been trying to write a short story for Danielle about her cruise with us.

I forgot to mention that on Saturday, we found a barge dock line floating in the river. It's huge. It's a 2" three strand, braided, 100 ft. section that has eye splices on each end. We've been asking people what it's worth. Don thinks we can sell it. Everyone says that it sells for approximately $200 when new. Who knows? Maybe we can get some grocery money out of it. The following day we found an inflated rubber raft floating on the river. If the third time is the charm, I can hardly wait to see what's next.

The scenery today is more rural. We haven't seen nearly as much industry. The weather yesterday and today has been chilly, but very clear, with beautiful blue skies, and puffy white clouds.

We stopped at the town of Henry around ten thirty so Don could call the office and get our next mail pickup arranged. What a nice surprise it was to tie up and find *Caprice* with Bob, Jana, and Target, the Dalmatian, aboard. We thought we would catch up with them sooner or later. It will be fun to "buddy boat" with them for the next few days on the river.

I called and ordered jam from Betty in Attica, Ohio. I think this is the fourth time in two years that we've asked her to mail us a case of black raspberry jam. It is good, not too expensive, and it sure beats store bought strawberry or grape. We've been out of it for about six weeks now.

At five thirty, we got to the Illinois Valley Yacht Club (The IVY Club), and docked for the evening. *Caprice* joined us for drinks and dinner. It was fun chatting about what we have been doing since parting company at Milwaukee.

Later that night, Don and I went to the club house to shower and do laundry. It was one in the morning when we got to bed.

I forgot to mention a couple of things of interest. When we stopped at Henry, a small town like many we had been in over the past two years, we were totally out of cash, and we found out that neither of their two banks would give us cash on our bank card. So much for groceries at that stop. We couldn't believe that their banks didn't have bank card associations; that is really what you call "old-time farmer banking." We have never had that happen before. The teller checked at the bank in a town down the river a short way, Lacon, but they didn't accept a bank card there either. Oh well, another first for us.

The other interesting thing is that when we called home to sister Carol, she informed us that they have changed their Florida/Christmas plans. They are now going to fly to New Orleans and rent a car so that they can come and stay with us for a week, and we can all sightsee together. We were excited and happy to hear it, and also quite surprised that they had decided to change their plans. It will be fun having them, and Don and I will look forward to their visit. We should be in New Orleans by the first week in December, way ahead of their December 26th arrival.

Docked at IVY Club, near Peoria, IL – Distance traveled: 35 miles

October 4, 1988, Tuesday

We got off to a late start this morning. It was cold, in the high thirties, and that always slows us down, but Don also needed to call the office and talk with Jane. He missed her yesterday. While he was out, I baked a chocolate cake in the toaster oven. Jane told Don she is getting married and leaving her job as secretary at Erick's office because she and her husband will be living pretty far away from Columbus. We were sorry to hear that she is leaving; she has been so nice, reliable, helpful and conscientious about everything. We will surely miss her.

Bob and Jana provided the dinner this evening, consisting of "beast (steak) on a stick," and potatoes and onions wrapped in foil, cooked over an open campfire. Don made barbecued beans to contribute, and I contributed the cake I made. When we found a suitable place to end our day of cruising on the river, we had our feast.

We tied to trees behind an old wall that had been used in the past as part of a lock. It was a beautiful spot to enjoy nature at its autumn best. We did have problems getting into the area due to shallow water, but after we found the way in, it was wonderful. We tied to the abandoned Copperas Creek Lock, at Mile 137. Bob fixed a great campfire to cook our food on.

When we were maneuvering in the shallow water and tying to the trees, I lost a dock line in the creek in attempting to get it to Bob on shore. Don and I tried to recover it, but gave up quickly because we figured the current probably swept it downstream as soon as it fell into the water. I felt bad about losing it. Dinner and socializing helped to lift my spirits.

Don and I turned the kerosene heater on later and stayed up reading until eleven thirty.

Tied at the abandoned Copperas Creek Lock, Copperas Creek, IL – Distance traveled: 28 miles

October 5, 1988, Wednesday

Bob and Jana came over to get warmed up this morning. It is another lovely day on the Illinois Waterway. The early-morning mist was too pretty to describe. The cold temperature of 38° left a lot to be desired, but by ten o'clock it was warm, with full sun.

At noon, we put in at Havana, and tied off to a towboat. *Caprice* rafted off us. They did their errands and left. We got groceries, went to the bank, and then ate at the Pizza Hut. We pigged out. It was pretty darn good pizza.

Caprice picked an anchoring spot for the evening, and Don and I rafted off them. Bob and I went ashore and made a campfire. We roasted hot dogs. Don provided potato salad and pudding with whipped cream. Jana made biscuits. Everything was great, but we all ate too much again. One bad thing about socializing is that we eat more than we should.

It was cool again in the evening. We are certainly glad we've got the kerosene heater. Tonight, however, we used the Aladdin lamp, and it kept the entire cabin well lit, as well as warm.

I spent the evening writing Danielle's story. I hope I get it and the picture album I'm making for her done before her birthday on October 20th. Don is now reading a Civil War book and is enjoying it.

Rafted off *Caprice*, Bath Chute, near Grand Island, IL – Distance traveled: 27 miles

October 6, 1988, Thursday

Bob and Jana brought donuts over at eight thirty. We sat around, eating donuts, drinking coffee, and getting warmed up by our kerosene heater. The outside temperature was in the mid-thirties. The mist was heavy at eight thirty, but again, by ten when we left, the sun was out, and it was warm.

I was at the helm until we got to Beardston where we tied at one o'clock next to a barge filled with grain long enough for Don to put the diesel fuel from our five-gallon plastic spare fuel container into our fuel tank and go to town and refill the container. I took care of getting our extra water containers refilled and visited with Bob and Jana a short while. Then they went to town and did some things, including mailing a letter to Shelly for me.

We got underway about three. Bob went ahead of us and selected tonight's anchorage, which was only a couple of miles downstream from Beardstown.

The scenery along the river has been interesting and very pretty. We've seen lots of blue herons, and the trees are changing colors. It's been especially nice since the skies have been so blue, and there are only a few puffy white clouds. The sun's also been very bright.

A sailboat heading for Florida passed us. That's the first sailboat heading south that we have seen since we left Chicago. I guess it's a little late in the season to be heading south, but I think we'll be OK.

It's been getting cold so early that I took a late afternoon shower while the sun's heat was still soothing.

We ate again on our boat. Don made clam chowder, and Bob made sushi with crabmeat and rice. I didn't feel like we'd overeaten. We had brownies with coffee for our dessert.

We are now at mile marker 87, which means we are 87 miles from Grafton, where the Illinois River empties into the Mississsippi.

Rafted off *Caprice* near Beardston, IL – Distance traveled: 17 miles

October 7, 1988, Friday

It was another pretty day. Again, it was cold in the morning, and Bob and Jana came over for coffee and sweet rolls and to warm up while waiting for the mist to lift.

We left at nine o'clock and didn't stop until six. Tonight we selected the spot, and Bob and Jana rafted off us.

We saw another southbound sailboat today, a Chinese junk named, *Island in the Sea.* They called us to chat on the marine radio. Like us, they plan to go down the Tennessee River, so we should meet up with them again.

Bob loaned me the book *African Queen* on Tuesday, and I have read it whenever I could and have just finished it; it's very good. Rosie, the lady in the story, was about as determined as I am and Don is about as laid back as Charlie. Katharine Hepburn played Rosie's part in the movie, and Don, as well as others, thinks my looks resemble hers. I surely wish I had her talent. I've been thinking about writing her to tell her about our trip.[15]

We had drinks around six thirty and then dinner. Don made a salmon casserole and brownies. Bob and Jana brought green beans; Target ate the bacon that was supposed to be in them. They also brought bread and fresh homemade wild strawberry jelly. It was another great meal, and fun as well.**Anchored at mile 38, Illinois Waterway, behind Fisher Island, IL – Distance traveled: 43 miles**

---

[15] In 1989, after returning from our sailing adventure, Robin did write to her and enclosed a copy of an article that had appeared in the Accent Section of the Columbus Dispatch about our trip. She responded with a short letter on her personal stationary with the simple heading of -- **Katharine Houghton Hepburn --**. It said, "Dear Robin and Donald Rose – What a fascinating trip that must have been – Good for you –." It was signed K. Hepburn. Robin had it framed.

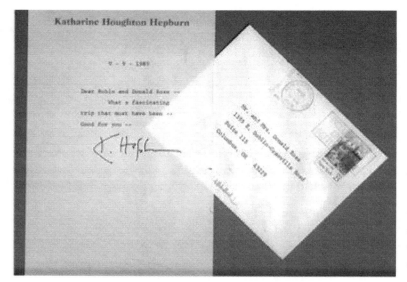

A NOTE FROM KATHARINE HEPBURN

October 8, 1988, Saturday

We bid *Caprice* farewell at breakfast, when they came over to warm up. We both had long days planned and got underway at eight forty-five. We are going to put in at the Saint Louis Sailing and Yacht Club, in West Alton, and have them step our mast. Bob and Jana are going north toward Rock Island, where they began. They put a signal flag message up in their rigging, which read "Adios Robin Lee."

I don't know how long this beautiful fall weather will continue, but I sure am enjoying it, even though it is cold at night.

We got to the Mississippi River around two thirty. The high bluffs on the Illinois side are pretty. The yacht club was easy to find. We tied up at five and then walked around looking at the boats. The club facilities were just finished three months ago. Everything smells new. The harbor is in a lovely setting and has mostly sailboats. We are docked next to a Morgan 33, *Elusive*, belonging to Todd and Sandy, from Wisconsin. We talked to them on the marine radio coming down the Illinois River. They are heading south also.

Don was too tired to cook, and so we ate popcorn and junk food for dinner. I didn't care—for me, popcorn is always a meal in itself. I did some hand stitching on our jackets—the hanging loops had ripped out. We went to bed early. It sure was nice to have the electric heater on.

At Saint Louis Sailing and Yacht Club, West Alton, MO – Distance traveled: 45 miles

October 9, 1988, Sunday

We got up early and took showers. While at the shower house, we met a couple, Jim and Linda. They are from the area and offered to come to the boat and go over our charts for this

CAPRICE SIGNALLING "ADIOS *ROBIN LEE*"

part of the river. They also offered to take us into Saint Louis to shop, sightsee, and eat. What a nice offer and what a neat couple they are. We had lots of fun getting to know them. They took us to see the "Arch." The tickets to take the ride to the top had been sold out, but we visited the museum. We also went to the revolving bar at the top of the Clarion Hotel. We spent one hour sipping drinks in order to see the entire 360° panorama. By the time the revolution was complete it was evening, and the lights of the city were spectacular. After that, we had a good meal, reasonably priced, at the Spaghetti Factory.

THE SAINT LOUIS SAILING AND YACHT CLUB

It was a fun day and we sure were glad about having the opportunity to spend it as we did. It again proved that we never know what our day will be like. All the work that we have planned can wait.

We were exhausted when we got home at ten thirty. It was cold again and the electric heater felt great, as usual.

At Saint Louis Sailing and Yacht Club, West Alton, MO

WITH JIM AND LINDA IN SAINT LOUIS

October 10, 1988, Monday

This really must be the honest-to-goodness true Indian summer that we are having. It has been so much more pleasant than the fall of 1986 when we went down the East coast.

I gave Don a haircut early. Todd on Elusive, the 33' Morgan next to us, loaned us his car from ten thirty until one o'clock to shop and do laundry. What a help that was.

I worked hard all day. I scrubbed the dinghy and then gave it a coat of ArmorAll. I also cleaned the deck. It always gives me a good feeling when the boat looks clean and orderly topside. Don worked hard all day on routine engine maintenance jobs. We never even stopped for lunch. Finally, about three thirty, the workman came by to tell us they were ready to step our mast, so we took the boat to where the crane is located and got that done. We helped. We are definitely getting better at it. We have helped to step it three times now.

Using the yacht club copy machine, I copied charts of the portion of the Ohio River where we will be, from a chart book loaned to us by *Elusive*.

Jim and Linda came by to bid us farewell.

We were tired and hungry. We had a late dinner of linguini and white clam sauce. It's a quick and easy recipe and one that both of us love.

Even though we were dockside and worked the entire time, the weather; the beautiful and peaceful harbor setting; the autumn leaves in glowing shades of yellow, gold, rust, and light and dark greens; the friendly people, including Sharon, the secretary, and Larry, the manager; and the new clean hot showers, all contributed to make it a wonderful day. It was productive also.

At Saint Louis Sailing and Yacht Club, West Alton, MO

October 11, 1988, Tuesday
Another pretty fall day!

Neither of us minded spending $15 for another night's dockage because we still had several things to do before getting out on the big Mississippi River and dealing with all the towboat traffic and the current.

Elusive left bright and early. Todd and Sandy had family who came to bid them farewell, so they needed to get on their way. We may or may not see them again—who knows?

We got up late and then put the sails on, and Don worked on fine-tuning the rigging.

I hitched a ride into town with Larry, the manager, to buy blank video tapes. Todd loaned us his parents' car yesterday to go to the laundromat and grocery, but we forgot to buy video tapes, and since Larry has offered to let us use the yacht club's VCR to transfer our 20-minute tapes to two-hour tapes, we need to buy some two-hour tapes.

We stopped at K-Mart and purchased the tapes and purchased a few canned goods. They are so cheap at K-Mart. I also bought Don some new tall long johns, which he badly needed. Then I bought Larry's lunch at Wendy's since he took me into town.

I spent the rest of the day finishing outside projects, while Don transferred the tapes.

We entertained Sharon, the yacht club's secretary, for drinks on the boat. After she left, Don made pork chops, fried potatoes and grilled onions.

We showered late and said good-bye to all our new yacht club friends, and got back to the boat and went to bed at eleven.

Los Angeles beat the Mets in the last game of the play-offs. We saw the final inning on the yacht club television. It will be the Los Angeles Dodgers vs. the Oakland Athletics in the 1988 World Series.

At Saint Louis Sailing and Yacht Club, West Alton, MO

October 12, 1988, Wednesday
Nothing was written in the journal for this day.

At Saint Louis Sailing and Yacht Club, West Alton, MO

October 13, 1988, Thursday
This is the 12th pretty day in a row. It's warm and sunny with a SE breeze of 15 Knots. We got underway shortly after eight o'clock.

We came to Lock # 26 about two miles down from the yacht club. About six miles below Lock 26, we came to where the Missouri River empties into the Mississippi and about a mile and a half below the mouth of the Missouri, we entered a canal. It's called the Chain of Rocks Canal and is about ten miles long. Lock # 27 is at the lower end of the canal. There are rapids on the Mississippi along this stretch, and the canal is used to avoid them.

After you come out of Lock # 27 at the lower end of the canal, you can travel all the way to the Gulf of Mexico without going through another lock. The current is noticeably stronger below the canal for two reasons: 1) There are no dams below Lock 27 to stop the flow of the river, and 2) because the waters of the Missouri and the Mississippi are combined.

Five miles below Lock #27 we went through downtown Saint Louis and past the Gateway Arch.

THE GATEWAY ARCH

The big river is very busy. A lot of material is transported on the river in tows. We saw lots and lots of them. A tow consists of a towboat pushing one or more barges. A standard Mississippi barge is 195 feet long and 35 feet wide, and a typical towboat is about 150 feet long. We saw a lot of 18 barge tows that were three wide and six long. That seemed to be a popular size, but we saw some that were much bigger. A tow with three by six barges is over a quarter of a mile long. The barges are connected to one another and to the towboat. The towboat pushes them because it is easier to control them that way. Each barge can carry up to 1,500 tons. eighteen times 1,500 tons is a lot of weight. Most barges carry coal, grain, gravel, sand, lumber, or petroleum. It's interesting to watch them move through the water. You can tell that the pilots know the river well.

We developed a procedure to follow when we encounter a tow. We started contending with tows on the Illinois River and developed our procedure there. When we see a tow coming at us, we call the person at the helm on the towboat using the marine

A TYPICAL TOWBOAT PUSHING BARGES

radio in the following manner. On channel 16, we say something along these lines, depending on the circumstances, "This is the sailboat *Robin Lee,* down bound at mile 236 calling the up bound tow ahead of us. Over." The tow comes back with something like, "This is the towboat *Alice May.* Go ahead 'cap'." Then we say, "Captain, which side would you like us to be on? Over." The response is something like, "Two whistle, and if you would, please stay close to those nun buoys." When he says "two whistle" he's referring to the whistle signal boats exchange when they are meeting head on, or are passing or are being passed. When meeting head on, two whistles mean, "I want to pass you starboard side to starboard side," and one whistle means "port side to port side." We always call the towboat, and we always leave it up to the towboat operator to make the decision. We have developed a great respect for the knowledge and skills of the towboat pilots.

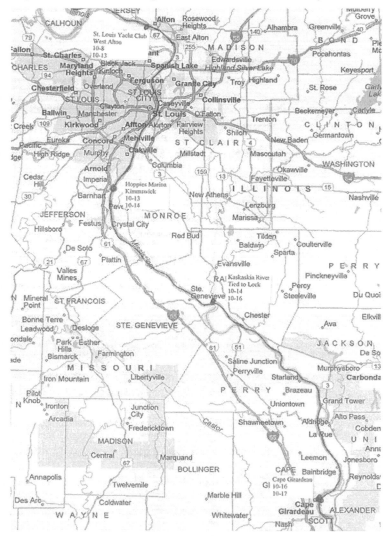

We spent some time moseying about in the area of the arch, taking pictures and video of the Saint Louis riverfront. There is so much barge traffic that we decided we should both be on "duty" at all times on the Mississippi. It's just too busy for one person. There are too many things to look out for. I wouldn't want to do this single-handed.

At four thirty, we tied to a barge at Hoppies Marina in Kimmswick, a small town 20 miles below downtown Saint Louis on the Missouri side of the river. Kimmswick is a quaint little village, but rather dead except for craft stores and shops. We walked around and went to the small grocery.

By the time we headed back to the boat it was pretty dark. We didn't have a flashlight, and it was about a mile and a half to the marina. Luckily, a guy in the store heard us ask about a cab. He offered us a ride. We were grateful except that it was apparent he had been drinking. His pick-up truck was in pretty bad shape. However, he drove at a reasonable speed, especially over the "old-old" bridge we had walked across earlier and had wondered about its stability.

Jane sent our mail to Hoppies as Don had requested. We were disappointed that it didn't include a few things we were expecting. Some of our film was apparently lost by Clark Photo Company, the jam I ordered from Betty hadn't arrived yet, and Don didn't get the new bank card he requested almost four months ago. The knot meter came, but doesn't appear to be working. How frustrating!

Oh well—at least dinner was good. We pigged out on Don's taco salad. I love that stuff.

Tied at Hoppies Marina, Kimmswick, MO – Distance traveled: 46 miles

October 14, 1988, Friday

We got up early and went to town. We put in a forwarding address so any future mail, namely Betty's jam, would be sent on to the next place that will accept mail for transients.

Guide books list such places. The jam will be forwarded to us for pick up in Kentucky. We stopped to look at a couple of places recommended in *Quimby's Guide Book*. However, the post office was the most interesting place. It was a 12'x18' building–a really honest-to-goodness old-fashioned building with lots of wood trim. The postal clerk didn't appear to be busy. She even told us we could use her phone to make a few calls if we wanted. It was an old-fashioned piece of Americana. I surely hope the government never shuts it down.

Hoppie's Marina wasn't much; just a few barges tied together along the river, totally exposed to all the currents and tow traffic. We didn't care, we were glad to be safely docked.

At eleven, we left Hoppie's. We were tied to a barge with our bow pointing north, upriver. The current was strong. The wind was from the south. When we untied and left, the dinghy got flipped over by a combination of the current, the wind and the movement of the boat. The Honda motor was mounted on the dinghy. The additional weight of the motor didn't keep it from flipping, and the motor was under water when it was upside down. We didn't see it happen because we were concentrating on getting away from the barges without being carried by the current into the other boats that were tied up, and we don't understand why it happened, but it happened. We did get underway without hitting anything or doing any damage except possibly to the dinghy motor. Once we were away from shore and back in the channel, Don righted the dinghy. The Honda engine was underwater at least five minutes. It was just an awful situation, but all we lost out of the dinghy were the repair kit for the Honda motor and our bailer. Everything else in the basket we carry in the dinghy, like the anchor and fuel can, stayed with the dinghy. Don retrieved all of that while I steered the boat.

When Don was a boy, he memorized a poem, "Jim Bludso of the Prairie Belle," written by John Hay, Abraham Lincoln's secretary. It is about a Mississippi Riverboat and its engineer. I had heard him recite it several times, but never on the Mississippi River. I got him to recite it, and I videotaped him.

That evening, at five o'clock, we turned into the Kaskaskia River, on the Illinois side of the Mississippi and went through a lock close to its mouth, which lifted us 20 feet. We tied to a lock wall and spent the night there. There was no current where we were, and we had a very restful evening.

Don made barbequed chicken and three bean salad. We slept well, but didn't go to bed until late because we had so much mail to go through. Don reviewed our bank statements and balanced our accounts. Of course, our balances are low. That was pretty depressing to him; not as much to me, because I figure we will make it some way. Don just loves my optimistic Pollyanna attitude, but I firmly believe that "where there is a will, there is a way," with the Lord's help. I guess if I didn't believe that, we wouldn't be here on the Kaskaskia River tied up at a lock aboard this little sailboat.

Tied above lock near the mouth of the Kaskaskia River, ten miles north of Chester, IL – Distance traveled: 43 miles

October 15, 1988, Saturday
It was very sunny in the morning, but quite windy.

Bob, the shift manager of the lock, came out early to say "Hi." He brought us a paper and had tea with us. We visited for an hour until he got called by a tow that wanted to lock through. During his visit, the current on the Mississippi, its power, and the danger it poses was the main topic of conversation. He told us the following story.

Two adventurous fellows from Minneapolis decided to go down the Mississippi from their city to New Orleans on a little boat that is peddled like a bicycle. A little way south of

Saint Louis they encountered a dredging operation. The dredging equipment was on a barge that was anchored in the river. The current swept them toward the barge, and they couldn't peddle hard enough to get out of that path. Soon they realized they were going to be taken under the barge by the current. They hollered and got the attention of the men on the barge. The men threw them lines and hauled them onto the barge while the current took their peddle boat under the barge. Another man on the barge went to the downriver end of the barge with a grappling hook and retrieved the peddle boat when it popped up. The two adventurers were given a cup of coffee on the dredge and when they had recovered their composure, they went to the downriver side of the barge, got on their boat and peddled on down the river.

After Bob left, we turned our attention to the dinghy motor. We took it off the dinghy and rinsed it off with fresh water. Then we emptied the gas tank and filled it with fresh gas to get rid of any water that might have gotten into the tank. It's a four-stroke engine, so we also drained the crankcase and put in fresh oil for the same purpose. After that we put it back on the dinghy and pulled the starting cord. It started and ran just fine. It seems that no damage was done.

I hung out our bed linens to freshen them up. Bob offered us the use of the shower facilities, so we took showers.

Motor-sailor, *Jones C. III,* out of Chicago with Tom, Larry and Charlie, came to the lock with shaft and prop damage. We loaned them snorkeling gear so they could check it out. Later, they invited us on board to visit. They are taking the boat south for a year so all three families can use it from time to time. I think they own the boat together. One guy, Charlie, owns a family business of 50 years, the Sightseeing Harbor Boats of Chicago. They take tourists on various excursions to see Chicago by water. We shared our trip highlights with them, and they seemed very interested.

I called Sister Carol and got the latest updates. All is well, except that Ohio State's football team is doing poorly. They lost today, and their record is now two wins and four losses for the season. That's bad news for Coach Cooper! I'll bet Shelly and David are disappointed. They bought tickets to every game this season. I already knew most of what Carol told me from Shelly's letters.

Don made chicken paprikash and served it over rice. We rested in the evening, enjoyed some reading, and talked about *Jones C III's* problems. Tomorrow we will head on down the Mississippi to Cape Girardeau. The wind was still 15 knots from the southwest when I used the phone at eight thirty this evening.

Tied above lock near the mouth of the Kaskaskia River, ten miles north of Chester, IL

October 16, 1988, Sunday

It rained very early, but cleared up. We had a pretty sky and sunshine when we left the Kaskaskia lock at eight forty-five. *Jones C. III* wanted to trail behind us today, but as we were leaving, their shaft came off. They insisted we couldn't help them and should go on since we had a 60-mile day ahead of us. If we hadn't left when we did, our arrival at Cape Girardeau would have been after dark. We would not have liked that situation. The buoys on the river are not lighted and aren't numbered. In order to keep track of our location, we have to watch for mile markers on the banks and record on the chart the time when we pass them. The river banks are desolate. Where the chart mentions landings, they are landings for tow traffic. There are no facilities for small pleasure craft like us.

The Mississippi is divided into two sections: the Upper Mississippi from its headwaters to the mouth of the Ohio, and the Lower Mississippi from the Ohio to the Gulf of Mexico. The volume of water flowing in the river is greater on the Lower Mississippi because it has the water of the Mississippi, the Missouri, and the Ohio. There are no locks on the lower part and the current is swift–around three mph. If you are planning to go up the Ohio, like we are, and like the fictional Huck and Jim wanted to do in *The Adventures of Huckleberry Finn*, don't miss the turn because in a boat like ours, it would be a very slow trip getting back to the mouth of the Ohio. It was impossible for Huck and Jim on their raft.

We would have no interest in doing any more boating in a boat like ours on the Mississippi anywhere south of The Saint Louis Sailing and Yacht Club. There are very few facilities for pleasure craft downriver from there, and the scenery isn't that great. The current and the big tows present real hazards. In our opinion that is the domain of the towboats. We are told that the tows are even bigger downriver from the Ohio. We have also heard that north of Saint Louis small craft boating is more pleasurable because there is much less current and far fewer tows. We definitely feel out of place where we are on the Mississippi and will be glad to get off it.

It was warm and pretty all day. Don made grilled cheese sandwiches for lunch and lentil soup with kielbasa for dinner.

We had a long day for sure. We arrived at five fifteen at "Huck Step's Fuel Dock." It's a

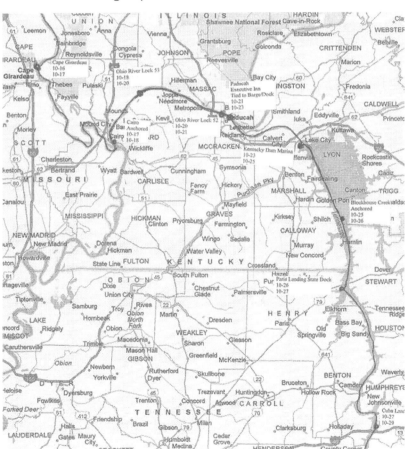

fuel service for towboats, not pleasure craft. I called on the marine radio and got permission to tie up there for the night.

Tied up at Huck Step's Fuel Dock, Cape Girardeau, MO – Distance traveled: 66 miles

October 17, 1988, Monday

We didn't have much time to explore the town, but what we saw we liked. We only went down one of its many streets. We went to the post office, bank, drugstore, and several other places, all within a couple of hours. Everyone we encountered seemed cheerful, friendly and helpful. Don called our bank and maybe now we will be able to get our bank card problem solved.

We went back to Huck Step's, paid our $12 dockage fee, and left. We couldn't get fuel because his pump is too fast. It pumps an average of 100 gallons per minute. We only needed eight gallons, so in five seconds our tank would start to overflow. They normally pump thousands of gallons of fuel at one time for towboats. He wasn't excited about having us at his fuel dock. He wouldn't want to lose a towboat fill up for a $12 dockage fee. However, he didn't have any fill ups scheduled so he let us tie up. We were lucky that it worked out so that we could tie up for the night and see the town in the morning. It was the best town we have been to for re-provisioning since Chicago. Not only was everyone friendly, but all of our normal places to go were within easy walking and carrying distance from the river, although a huge flood wall separated the town from the river, which we had to go up and down steps to get over. It is a darn shame the city doesn't provide a few floating barges for transient boaters like us. I think the town would benefit from it. I'm going to write a letter to the Chamber of Commerce of Cape Girardeau and tell them what I think.

We left Cape Girardeau at ten thirty. We didn't untie the bow line as soon as we should have, and the current pinned us up against the fuel dock. It was a tough situation to handle physically, but we managed. Using a couple of dock lines, Don pulled the boat back toward the cleat where the bow line was attached and was able to un-cleat it, and we got away from the dock without any damage. Good old Murphy!

We had 53 miles to go to reach the mouth of the Ohio, but the swift current added about three mph to our normal six mph and that helped. The problem was the wind. It was against us and was very strong. The current and the wind were opposed, which created sizable waves that we were plowing through. There were times when our knot meter registered speeds near zero, but when that occurred, the current kept us moving at about three mph. We arrived at the mouth of the Ohio at five forty-five.

We talked with the captain of one of the towboats on the marine radio and got information about where we could safely anchor for the night. He gave us directions to an anchorage out of the way of the towboat traffic. It was behind three nun (red) buoys, just up the Ohio from the point that separates the two rivers and was on the Kentucky side of the Ohio River. We anchored there and thought we were done for the day. Don celebrated being off the Mississippi with all of its potential hazards by drinking a martini. We had two anchors out, the Bruce and the Danforth, and we felt secure.

Our feeling of security didn't last long. Our Danforth anchor rode started making a tapping noise on the hull, which meant that we hadn't positioned the anchors at the same length from the bow, and when we took the slack out of the Danforth line, it would be shortened and the Danforth's holding power would be reduced. We decided to attempt to re-set the Danforth anchor. We started the engine and began to move forward to reset it, hauling in the line on the Danforth anchor as we went. Suddenly, the engine stalled. The Bruce anchor's line had gotten around the prop. We hadn't taken the slack out of that line, and the current had taken it down to the prop. How dumb! This was the stupidest thing we had done on the whole trip and it was potentially disastrous. We had no use of the engine if the anchor started dragging. Furthermore, holding us at that moment was the Bruce with its shortened rode attached to our prop and that was putting much stress on the prop, the shaft and the strut. Don immediately shortened the line on the Danforth anchor to make it the holding anchor, thus taking the stress off the prop, shaft and strut. Then he located the line on the Bruce, using the boat hook and retrieved the Bruce anchor and brought it aboard. Then he let out some more line on the Danforth anchor to give it better holding and that is how we spent the night. Fortunately the Danforth anchor holds well in mud. The captain said he had no excuse for his stupidity, but that it happened because he had too much on his mind, including the martini. The biggest lesson learned by this experience was that it's not good to have a martini and then deal with problems like this. The good side of making mistakes is that, if they don't kill you, you can benefit by the lessons the mistakes teach you.

It was ten thirty. We still had a line around the prop, but that problem would have to wait until daylight. It was too dangerous to deal with it in the dark, and we had had enough mental and physical stress. We were exhausted!

Anchored at the mouth of the Ohio River at Cairo, IL – Distance traveled: 53 miles

October 18, 1988, Tuesday

Needless to say, Don didn't rest much. He was too upset and blamed himself for the stupidity of it all. At six thirty, it began getting light, and so we began to prepare for the morning swim to deal with the prop and shaft. Don put on his safety harness and connected the safety harness to the boat with a dock line. He went down the swim ladder and was able to reach the prop while holding on to the rudder. The line around the prop was easily removed, and Don didn't detect any damage to the prop or shaft. The true test would come when we tried to use the engine. When we did get underway, everything was normal. No vibrations. How lucky we are. Things could have been so much worse.

Don and I were both still quite fatigued. Don had his usual bruising all over his chest and arms, and cuts on his hands. He was sore everywhere. We only went up the Ohio River 18 miles to Lock # 53 and got permission to spend the night on a wall, which wasn't needed for anything. It was quite well-protected from the traffic. We didn't even feel any water turbulence. It was only two thirty, but it was cloudy and windy, and we were just not interested in moving anymore until we got some rest and relaxation. We had Coke and popcorn and some other snacks before our vegetarian dinner of a cheese and cauliflower dish.

We both decided to do our rainy-day projects. I was heavily into sorting, dating, and writing on photographs of the six weeks when Danielle was with us. I wanted to get this photo album and story done for her birthday, but I'm not going to make it; her birthday is this Thursday. Now I'm trying for Christmas.

Don fell asleep at seven thirty. I stayed up until midnight, working the entire time on Danielle's project.

Tied to wall at Lock # 53, on the Ohio River, IL – Distance traveled: 18 miles

October 19, 1988, Wednesday

It was a beautiful day to travel, but we still felt as though we needed rest. Don spent time doing some chores, such as re-rigging the anchor rode, making a new eye splice, and checking our running lights. I continued with the photo project for Danielle, and did some of our own photos and made a listing of all the negatives we needed to send in for reprints.

In the evening, a couple of motor yachts came in and tied to the same wall as us. The paddle wheel boat, *Mark Twain,* came through the lock playing their calliope; we videotaped it.

The day passed quickly, and we were glad we had stayed. We never got off the boat. Even the lockmaster came down to check on us to see if we were OK. We had a good dinner of fettuccine carbonara.

Tied to wall at Lock # 53, on the Ohio River, IL

October 20, 1988, Thursday

It rained off and on all day and was also chilly. I wish it had been pretty, like yesterday, because today we moved on. It seems like we sit on the nice days and move on the crummy ones. We didn't go very far, merely 21 miles. When we got to Lock # 52, we saw that a place was available to tie up, and we decided to take it although it was only two thirty.

Don took a walk by himself to a grocery store. Bobby, the lockmaster, said it wasn't far, but that we were welcome to use his truck. Don didn't want to, so he walked. He thought I should go also since we had not really been away from the boat since Cape Girardeau on Monday morning. Frankly, I didn't care—no way did I want to go out and walk on a cold, dark and possibly rainy night. I was comfortable and told him to go without me. It turned out that the "short walk" was a mile and a half, one way. I'm glad I stayed on board. I think he was sorry he'd gone, because we actually didn't need groceries. He got home about seven thirty, and I had a mashed potato, sauerkraut, sour cream, onion, and Kielbasa dinner ready for him. It's one of the few things I make. It's easy.

After dinner, Don fell sound asleep, but I stayed up, did the dishes, wrote to Shelly, and continued working with the photos for Danielle's album.

Tied to wall at Lock # 52, Brookport, IL – Distance traveled: 21 miles

October 21, 1988, Friday

We moved again today but it was an even shorter move, only about three miles. We stopped at the Executive Inn and tied to their barge. Our purpose for stopping was to make some calls with the hope of finding charts for the Tennessee River since the Corps of Engineers didn't mail any to us. We climbed up the high bank to the inn where we met the owner. He gave us permission to stay for a couple of nights tied to the barge and to use the inn's facilities for free, including a free trolley service that picks guests up at the inn and takes them downtown and brings them back. That was an offer that was too good to refuse.

We also met some ladies who were getting the place ready for a poetry convention. I told them that my husband liked poetry and recites it. They invited us to their informal poetry reading that evening and said they would love for my husband to recite poetry. I said he would.

They also told us about various places around town that we might be interested in visiting. We decided to use the free trolley service and look at the downtown area, but first to enjoy an ice cream sundae at the Snack Shoppe. It was the best $0.79 sundae I have ever had. It was huge, and the chocolate sauce and ice cream were both exceptionally good. While we were eating the sundaes, I told Don that I had committed him to recite "Jim Bludso of the Prairie Belle" this evening. He wasn't happy with me, but finally agreed to do it.

The trolley picked us up out in front of the hotel. After getting off the trolley downtown, we split up. Don went to the library to look up and copy the poem, so he could study it to refresh his memory. I went to a couple of photo places looking for negative holders and photo holders for Danielle's story and picture book. I also did the usual chores of going to the bank, the grocery, and post office.

When we got back to the boat, it was dark. We had time for a quick dinner, and a short period of relaxation before leaving to attend the poetry reading. It started at nine thirty and lasted until eleven thirty. We had a good time. It was our first experience at such an event. Everyone was very friendly and Don was the only one to recite. Everyone else read poems that they wrote. The convention was for an organization of poetry writers, but they seemed to enjoy Don's recitation of a poem about a riverboat. We also took our tape player and Joe Dixon's tape of Robert Service poems, "The Cremation of Sam McGee" and "The Parson's Son." Joe does an excellent job and uses much emotion in reciting them. He knows several of Robert Service poems by heart. Everybody also seemed to enjoy Joe's performances. It was a long day, but one that will be remembered. We were happy to be docked here. Even the weather cleared up in the late afternoon, and we saw the sun.

Tied to the Barge at the Executive Inn, Paducah, Kentucky – Distance traveled: 3 miles

Jim Bludso of the Prairie Belle

John Hay

Wall no! I can't tell whar he lives,
  Becase he don't live, you see;
Leastways, he's got out of the habit
  Of livin' like you and me.
Whar have you been for the last three year
  That you haven't heard folks tell
How Jimmy Bludso passed in his checks
  The night of the Prairie Belle?

He weren't no saint, — them engineers
  Is all pretty much alike, —
One wife in Natchez-under-the-Hill
  And another one here, in Pike;
A keerless man in his talk was Jim,
  And an awkward hand in a row,
But he never flunked, and he never lied —
  I reckon he never knowed how.

And this was all the religion he had —
  To treat his engine well;
Never be passed on the river;
  To mind the pilot's bell;
And if ever the Prairie Belle took fire,
  A thousand times he swore
He's hold her nozzle agin the bank
  Till the last soul got ashore.

All boats has their day on the Mississip,
  And her day come at last, —
The Movastar was a better boat,
  But the Belle she *wouldn't* be passed.
And so she came tearin' along that night,
  The oldest craft on the line,
With a black man squat on her safety valve,
  And her furnace crammed, rosin and pine.

The fire bust out as she clared the bar,
  And burnt a hole in the night,
And quick as a flash she turned, and made
  For that willer-bank on the right.
There was runnin' and cursin', but Jim yelled out,
  Over the infernal roar,
"I'll hold her nozzle agin the bank
  Till the last galoot's ashore."

Through the hot, black breath of the burnin' boat
  Jim Bludso's voice was heard,
And they all had trust in his cussedness,
  And knowed he would keep his word.
And, sure's you're born, they all got off
  Afore the smokestacks fell, —
And Bludso's ghost went up alone
  In the smoke of the Prairie Belle.

He weren't no saint, — but at judgment
  I'd run my chance with Jim,
'Longside of some pious gentlemen
  That wouln't shook hands with him.
He seen his duty, a dead-sure thing, —
  And went for it thar and then;
And Christ ain't a-going to be too hard
  On a man that died for men.

October 22, 1988, Saturday

It was beautiful all day. We got up late, showered, and then had Martha White's strawberry pancakes.

We caught the trolley to downtown at eleven thirty. Downtown, we met a "street person" and spent an hour listening to all his problems. I hope we brought some encouragement to him by being good listeners. After getting our kerosene jug filled, we walked back to the boat. At one o'clock, we got a bus to the mall. We thought it was nice for such a small town, but later we found out Paducah wasn't as small as we had thought. It has almost 45,000 residents. It is the biggest town we've seen since Chicago.

We had time for a pizza at the mall before getting the last bus back to The Executive Inn. We decided to eat another sundae at the Snack Shoppe, and while there, Kim, the owner, and a worker offered us their tickets for tonight's entertainment at the Inn – Mel McDaniel, the country singer. We were delighted! It was a great performance. We got to bed very late.

Tied to the Barge at the Executive Inn, Paducah, Kentucky

October 23, 1988, Sunday

It rained hard early in the morning, so we weren't in a big hurry to leave. Our destination today is the Kentucky Dam Marina, at Kentucky Dam Village State Park, which is only 25 miles away. We left at ten o'clock, and after going three miles farther up the Ohio, we turned to starboard at Owens Island and entered the Tennessee River. Shortly after making our turn, we stopped at Paducah River Services and bought a Tennessee River Chart Book. The day was cloudy, but the new territory was pretty. Traffic wasn't bad, even though it was a Sunday and there were some small runabouts and fishing boats out. After 22 miles on the river, we came to the lock that would take us into Kentucky Lake. We tied off of a towboat named *Edith Tripp*, which was waiting to go through the lock. The wait at the lock was long enough for us to get an invitation aboard the towboat to look it over. That was a treat. The first place we saw was the pilothouse, which sits high and has great visibility. We met several members of the crew, including the cook, and saw the cook's galley and his quarters. There were seven men on the boat: captain, pilot, chief engineer, assistant engineer, two deck hands, and the cook. They are divided into two crews. One crew is made up of the captain, the chief engineer, and one deckhand. The other crew consists of the pilot, the assistant engineer and the other deckhand. The crews alternate six-hour watches. The seventh guy on board was the cook. His only job is to cook three meals a day, and he doesn't have to share a room with anyone. Of course, we took lots of pictures. The boat was very clean and neat and the vibration didn't seem to be annoying. Don and I would like to take a trip on the lower Mississippi on a towboat as a passenger or even as a crew member, if the opportunity ever presents itself. I'm sure it would be interesting. They have 21 days on and then 21 days off. I wonder if we could sign on for one 21 day period, Don as the assistant cook and me as the dishwasher. That sounds like fun.

We made it through the lock OK, but it was probably the worst lock we've been through. We went through without any other boats. The turbulence was awful. Apparently, they have a broken valve and maybe some other problems. I wonder if the crowd of bystanders could tell that we were struggling to fend off from the lock wall. I had a hard time. We switched places once, thinking Don would do better up forward, but that didn't help. Now my shoulder hurts. I hope the rest of the locks on the Tennessee are easier. The lift was about 55 feet.

The Kentucky Dam Marina is only a mile from the lock, and we were happy to get there. The dock attendant topped off our fuel tank, brought us our jam that had come in the mail, and told us where to dock. We had power, so we immediately turned on the heat. We noticed a red stain on the box of jam, and we knew that meant some were broken; thankfully, it was just one jar. The bill for eight jars was $23 plus $4 postage. That is pretty expensive, but it is some of the best black raspberry jam I've ever tasted, so it's a real treat. I cleaned up the mess from the broken jar while talking to a girl off the boat *Tymes Too*–a big power boat. She and her husband are paid to be the captain and mate. They have been aboard two years steadily, saving every cent they make. The owner pays all their expenses. They entertain and cook for him, his employees, and guests. They also move the boat from place to place according to the owner's wishes.

Don made a delicious Chinese pork and tofu dish, but it took over two hours and the mess to clean up was a one-hour job. I hope he doesn't make it again very soon. Five to ten minutes of flavor just isn't worth three hour's work.

I love using the electric heater and staying toasty warm. At this time of the year, it is worth the dockage fee just to be able to use the heater.

Docked at Kentucky Dam Marina, Kentucky Dam Village State Park, Mile 23, Tennessee River, KY – Distance traveled: 25 miles

October 24, 1988, Monday

What a beautiful day to play and take it easy. We used the marina's courtesy car and went to Calvert City, a small village. Don dropped me off at the laundry while he ran the usual errands. We only had two hours-free use of the car, so we hurried. The motor vessel, *Phoebus II*, was docked beside us. They left this morning, so we said good-bye to them and that got us off to a late start. By the time we left for the town in the courtesy car, it was ten fifteen. We got back at twelve thirty. After we got back, I visited with Avis and Bob, the couple on board the motor vessel, *Morning Star III,* a 36' Krogen. They are elderly and have a crew member helping them take the boat to Fulton, Mississippi, where they plan to stay for a few months. Don made us hot dogs for lunch. Afterwards, we filled the water tanks and then went for showers, courtesy of the State Park pickup service. They came over and took us to the campground where the showers are located.

It was very cold in the shower house, but clean. I'm glad we didn't wait until late in the evening. It would have been much colder. We asked the driver to come back in a half hour because there was no phone close by where we could call to arrange transportation to the marina. The marina was at least three miles away. At dusk, that wouldn't have been much fun, especially with wet hair and cold air.

Neither of us was hungry, so we just snacked all evening. We finished off homemade cookies that *Tymes Too* gave us; they were great.

Don read, and I finally finished the photo album of pictures that have been sent to us by others over the past two years. I got my camera log in order and loaded a new roll of film. I also got caught up writing this journal. I had to put it off until I could find new composition books, which I finally found in an office-supply store in Paducah. This was a pleasant evening, with clean sheets, clean clothes, showers, and the electric heater–what more could a person want!

Docked at Kentucky Dam Marina, Kentucky Dam Village State Park, Mile 23, Tennessee River, KY

October 25, 1988, Tuesday

Today started out cloudy with a little rain off and on, but not enough to complain about. We got underway at nine. Because we weren't going very far, we didn't care about hurrying. Don took the helm for the remainder of the morning, and I took over at noon. Around two o'clock, we anchored in Blockhouse Creek, 27 miles from where we started. It was an easy day, and we still had plenty of time left to play. By then the sun had come out, and it had warmed up. The anchorage was absolutely beautiful. Everywhere we looked there were pretty shades of red, orange, rust, green, yellow, and gold on a variety of types of trees. I even saw a few loons today and a couple of kingfishers. They must have come here to stop and rest before going farther south.

We took pictures and a dinghy ride around the cove where we were anchored. A man on shore in hunting garb and carrying a gun yelled to us from shore that he was lost. We gave him directions to where he wanted to go. We didn't feel it would be smart to offer to take him anywhere in the dinghy. He might have been a weirdo, who knows?

Don made spaghetti with meat sauce for dinner, and we ate early. I had the dishes done by six, which was great. In the evening, I spent a couple of hours copying my story for

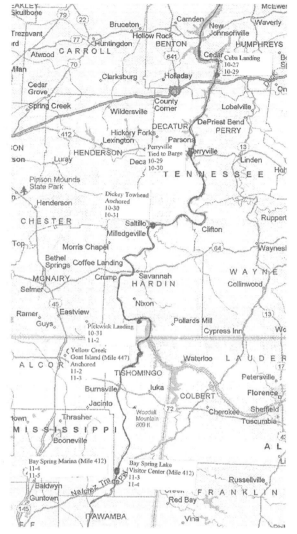

Danielle. We toasted marshmallows over the Aladdin Lamp for dessert. This time I invited Don to the marshmallow roast. I decided he had paid his debt to society for eating my marshmallows by being excluded from the first Alladin's Lamp marshmallow roast. After the marshmallows, we had tea. Don read. He has started another book, *Nicholas Nickleby* by Charles Dickens and a play, *The Miracle Worker.* He really enjoyed the book on the Civil War and thinks I would also, especially since we are very near where important events took place during the war. For example, about 15 miles south of here is where Fort Henry sat. General Ulysses Grant defeated it in February 1862. The Kentucky Dam submerged its ruins.

In summary, it was a relaxing and pleasant day, and we're in a beautiful anchorage. We didn't stay up late because it was cold, and we are a lot warmer under the covers.

Anchored at Blockhouse Creek, Mile 48, Tennessee River, KY.

October 26, 1988, Wednesday

Again, we felt no need to rush in the early hours. In fact, we stayed in bed, tucked in and toasty warm until nine o'clock. After coffee and warm Pop Tarts, we left. I took the helm first because it was sunny and warm. Don spent a lot of time calibrating the knot meter. It's so nice having it working again. We only went 20 miles, to the Paris Landing State Park. We arrived at two o'clock, so we not only had the opportunity to enjoy the fall foliage along the way; we also had time for a walk in the state park. It was so pretty. We really did pick the best time of the year to be heading south along this route. In another week or two, these beautiful leaves will be on the ground.

This park is one of the nicest and least expensive we've ever been to. It cost us $6 for dockage for the night ($0.20 per foot per night) and that included electricity. We asked about monthly rates and for a 40-foot slip, it is only $1.50 per foot. It's a gorgeous spot. Maybe we will consider coming here again, especially if our boat doesn't sell on the Gulf Coast. We don't like the idea of leaving it down there during hurricane season, and if we brought it here, we could travel back and forth to Columbus pretty easily. As time passes and our funds get lower, I put more thought into what we need to do next. Up until now, all I have thought about is getting to the Gulf Coast. I wish I could see into the future. I would love to know when and where we will be when the boat sells.

Don made a great dinner tonight—fried steak and onions, Chinese style and served it with mashed potatoes. It was super.

I called Martha (Dad's friend) tonight. She's from Tennessee. We had a nice chat.

Docked at Paris Landing State Park, Mile 66, Tennessee River, TN – Distance traveled: 20 miles

October 27, 1988, Thursday

Our day started early because we wanted to get to Cuba Landing, which is at mile 115; we were underway at eight. The scenery was pretty, but the air was quite cold, probably the high thirties. Don took the helm from eight to eleven, and then I took it until two. During my time off, I wrote letters and caught up on entering new friends' names and addresses in our log book.

We had 50 miles to go, so it was a good thing we left at eight. Daylight is getting less each day. We got to the marina at sunset. It was beautiful. The sun's rays were shining down from the clouds just like on Ohio's state seal. The beautiful sky, trees, and red sun, plus some Canadian geese flying high overhead, and a great blue heron flying close to the water, made our arrival at Cuba Landing special.

Tom and Charlene on *Golden Odyssey* recommended that we stop here. We're glad they did; we felt at home from the minute we docked. The marina is really out in the boondocks of Tennessee and is actually situated in a national wildlife refuge. We spent a lot of time talking with the owners, Lola and Billy. They offered us the use of their car, so we could go out to eat, and we went to a local place about six miles away. Don wanted to try some Tennessee catfish, so that's what he ordered. I had a cheeseburger. We weren't impressed. We like eating at home, on the boat.

After returning in the evening around nine, we watched a little TV in the marina office and then came home. It started to rain, thunder, and lightning about the time we went to bed at eleven.

Docked at Cuba Landing, Mile 115, Tennessee River, TN – Distance traveled: 51 miles

October 28, 1988, Friday

This was a very beautiful day in a very beautiful location. We saw several deer in the creek next to the boat. I didn't get up until ten, when Don urged me to do so, because the oatmeal muffins were ready. Shortly thereafter, I went back to work recopying Danielle's story. Don replaced the lost rivets in the dinghy floor boards with small nuts and bolts.

At three o'clock, Don finished his project, and we went to the marina office and watched a videotape of a *National Geographic* presentation about the Titanic. It was very good. Several people in the marina office watched it also. We finally took showers (the water had been off most of the day due to switching over to a new well), and then Don made a vegetarian dinner of stir-fried cabbage, carrots and green onions. It made a very colorful and tasty dish, but it wasn't enough to fill us up, so we had ice cream later. Don showed our boat to a couple of fishermen as I sat in the office eating my ice cream and watching a TV presentation of *Healing the Children – Guatemala*. It was interesting, but sad. There is so much poverty there. We went to bed early.

Docked at Cuba Landing, Mile 115, Tennessee River, TN

October 29, 1988, Saturday

We got off to a really late start. Don wanted to use electric power to make our pecan pancakes. We left about ten thirty, and stopped 20 miles up the river at Perryville. I steered most of the way.

On our way into Cuba Landing, we saw a sign attached to a barge which said, "Towboat Help Wanted." The sign gave the name and phone number of an employment service in Perryville where you could apply for work. We have seen many, and we have developed an interest in taking a trip on one for a week or so. We have asked about the possibility of going as a passenger, but have been told that their insurance policies don't allow them to take passengers. Our only possibility then, is to work on one. We thought that, after we got settled in New Orleans for the winter, we might apply for jobs, Don as an assistant cook and me as a dishwasher for little or no pay for a three-week period and that maybe the towboat operator would realize that all we really wanted was to take a trip, and that he might be able to work something out for us. We talked to Lola and Billy, the owners of Cuba Landing about our idea. They know the people at the employment service who put the sign up. They called stop by and meet them. We did just that. At Perryville, we tied to a barge and went ashore. We tried the telephone number that was on the sign and got no answer the first time we called but made contact on the second call. We went to the office of the employment service, which was a house, and filed applications for employment. Our visit with the employment service, a husband and wife team, Paul and his wife Beryl, went smoothly. Paul is a retired towboat pilot. They operate their employment service out of their home. They were friendly and seemed interested in trying to help us. If they could get us what we wanted that would be great, but we don't think they will be able to. Even if nothing comes from it, we enjoyed applying, and we also enjoyed seeing the town. It's a quiet town and the people are friendly.

On the way home, we stopped once more at the River Shack. It was dinner time, and Don wanted to try catfish again. A local man by the name of Mr. Nibbles said the restaurant's catfish was good. Well, we wasted our money because it wasn't. Basically, it was the same as the other night—too much breading, and over cooked in a deep-fryer with old oil. The same was true for the tater tots and hush puppies. My cheeseburger, however, was better than the other night.

Our walk back to the boat was spooky. We forgot our flashlight; however, Beryl gave us a penlight and that helped. We had to go along a trail through a gravel pit, and when we went through it on the way to town earlier in the day, there was a fellow "target shooting." We hoped he wasn't still shooting.

Tied to a barge at Mile 135, Tennessee River, Perryville, TN – Distance traveled: 20 miles

October 30, 1988, Sunday

It was cloudy and cool all day. The sun never did come out.

The time changed back to standard time last night. We both slept OK until around three in the morning, when the wind shifted and started slapping water on our stern. The noise woke us, and Don didn't sleep well from then on, but I did.

He made muffins and coffee for breakfast, and just as we were finishing up, we heard a small bass boat come up close by and shut its engine off. A couple of guys made a slight attempt to see if anyone was aboard by calling out. Just as Don went to open the hatch cover, they immediately started the engine and took off. That little boat went faster than I'd ever seen a boat go. We are convinced that if we had not been on board, we would have been burglarized. Don saw one guy cover his face fully with a ski hat. We think they probably had their eye on our dinghy motor, which was mounted on our stern rail at the time.

We untied from the barge and left at eight thirty. Shortly after we got underway, it started to sprinkle lightly. Don took the helm until noon. We bumped, trying to get into a channel at the Gilbert Marina, so we aborted the attempt. I took over the helm, and Don went below, made lunch and lay down to rest, relax, and read his new book, *Nicholas Nickleby*. Actually, he got it as a 1986 Christmas gift from Shelly. While he was reading, he listened to music by Beethoven. We even get some culture out here on our little movable island.

We got to our anchorage about three, and spent a quiet evening on our now stationary little island, each of us doing something enjoyable. I cross-stitched and Don read. We had dinner early. He made a tuna-taco salad, from a recipe out of a magazine.

Anchored at Dickeys Towhead Island, Mile 170, Tennessee River, TN – Distance traveled: 35 miles

October 31, 1988, Monday, Halloween

In the spring of 1862, General Ulysses Grant brought a Union army up the Tennessee River and attacked and defeated the Confederate troops at Fort Henry, about 150 miles behind us on the river. Nothing can be seen of Fort Henry because the ruins were submerged when the Kentucky Dam was built. After defeating Fort Henry, Grant took his army a few miles east to the Cumberland River and attacked and defeated Fort Donelson. The Confederates retreated south to Corinth, Mississippi. Grant took his army back to the Tennessee River and pursued the Confederates up the river. He landed his troops at Pittsburg Landing, which is about 20 miles south of Corinth. His troops camped near a religious meeting house about two miles west of the landing. General Johnston was in command of the Confederate troops, who were then in Corinth. He knew Grant was pursuing him with the intention of engaging in battle. He decided that he should take the initiative and attack Grant. He attacked Grant's forces where they were camped, near the meeting house which was known as the Shiloh Church. The Battle of Shiloh, as it came to be known, was fought on April 6 and April 7, 1862. During the battle, the Union army lost 13,000 men, and the Confederates lost 10,000. It was the bloodiest battle of the Civil War up to that point in time. General Johnston was killed in the battle. We passed Pittsburg Landing in the afternoon.

PICKWICK LANDING STATE PARK

We left our anchorage around eight thirty and arrived at the marina at Pickwick Landing State Park at five-ten. It was sunny and warm the entire day. We only came 38 miles, but the current was strong near the Pickwick Landing Dam, and we were bucking it. We had to wait at the lock approximately one hour to lock through.

When we came out of the lock, we were in Pickwick Lake. Kentucky Lake and Pickwick Lake are actually just dammed up portions of the Tennessee River. The river was a mile or two wide for the first 90 miles above the Kentucky dam and looked like a lake. Then, for the last 90 miles, it looked more like a river. There was very little current in the first 90 miles, but when it became narrower and river-like, the current was stronger. The Kentucky Lake/Tennessee River was beautiful, and the Pickwick Lake/Tennessee River looks the same.

When we came out of the lock, we had barely enough sunlight to get into the marina before dark. After dinner of tuna noodle and sour cream casserole, plus lime Jell-O and cookies, we walked to the marina office and shower facilities. I called Sister Carol and then showered. The area is quite pretty, but it was too late to go exploring tonight. I called Shelly to see how she was doing. She said she is doing OK. She hasn't been spending as much time with her friends.

By the time we walked back from the showers it was beginning to get foggy. I did a little

CAUGHT RED HANDED

work editing Danielle's story in the evening and went to bed around eleven. It got cold during the night, and we were happy to have the electric heater going all night.

It was a truly beautiful fall day!

At Pickwick Landing State Park Marina, Mile 207, Tennessee River, TN – Distance traveled: 38 miles

November 1, 1988, Tuesday

It was a great day again, with a high of 71°, and a low of 45°.

I got up in the middle of the night and hid our cookies. Don thinks that if cookies are cheap, we should buy them. Then he can't stand it until they are gone. He's obsessed! I managed to save the two pounds we had on board. We ate four pounds in October. He was surprised in the morning when he found the cookie can empty. I even got a couple of pictures of him opening the can and reading the note I left in it.

We sat around until eleven o'clock. Don made two kinds of slaw; I sampled what he made and then made suggestions. I like slaw and haven't been crazy about what Don has made. I also finished the book, *Serryfin,* and read him the last couple of chapters. It was good.

At noon, we got off the boat and started to walk to town. We saw Tom Blaney and his wife on the dock and saluted them. I re-introduced myself. They live in this area, but we met them last February at Harbourside Moorings. They were the ones who first told us about the new Tennessee-Tombigbee (Ten-Tom) Waterway as an alternate route to the Gulf of Mexico and recommended it to us. Until then, we planned on going all the way to New Orleans on the Mississippi. I saluted him because we are so happy that he gave us a way to get off the Mississippi. It's really not a good river for a boat like ours. He was happy that we had followed his advice and glad we stopped in to visit his area. He took us to the grocery and bank and also came over to the boat to visit with Don in the afternoon while I was away doing the laundry.

The facilities here are very nice, especially when you consider it's only $0.20 per foot per night, or $2.50 per foot per month. All the Tennessee parks we have seen have been inexpensive and nice. We would enjoy revisiting all the marinas and anchorages we have been to on the Tennessee River and will recommend the river to other boaters.

We also met and went aboard *Damsel Fish*, a brand new 31-foot Chris Craft sport fisherman, with Lynn and Tom James from Mt. Clemens, MI, on board. We enjoyed seeing a new boat like that.

Don fixed our dinner of stir-fried chicken, tomatoes, onions and zucchini from a recipe out of the *American Cancer Society Cookbook*. After I did the dishes, we invited the Jameses over for coffee and brownies. It's always fun to make new friends. We haven't had any guests on board for a while. The Jameses are really into scuba diving and highly recommend Bonaire, a Dutch island near Venezuela, as the best place to learn how to scuba dive. We have hopes of someday being able to try that sport. They have cruised in the North Channel and in Beaverstone Bay, and in fact they anchored at Muskrat Bay, which is about 100 yards from Loon Lodge, Don's family's cottage, about five days after we left the cottage this year. We also missed them by only a few days at Mackinac Island. They travel much faster than we do, but have stopped their progress four times since August to fly home for work. They plan to winter their boat near Tampa and continue their cruise in the spring, going up the East Coast and then to Michigan by summer, by way of the route we took.

At Pickwick Landing State Park Marina, Mile 207, Tennessee River, TN

CHAPTER SIXTEEN
PICKWICK LAKE, TN to NEW ORLEANS, LA
Nov. 2, 1988 – Dec. 4, 1988

November 2, 1988, Wednesday

It was a sunny and warm day with a high of 72°.

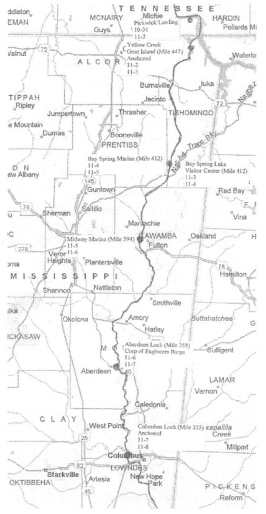

We got up late. I had breakfast about nine thirty and then cleaned the deck with the hose, soap, and plenty of good fresh water. We paid our dock fees and said good-bye to Tom and Lynn Blaney. We left Pickwick Landing at ten thirty and motored a short distance to Aqua Yacht Harbor for fuel and to see the place. They charge $.50 cents per foot, so we're glad we didn't stay there. Pickwick Landing Marina is our kind of place – low key, low price, pretty, and nice!

It was a lovely day! I can't believe how many pretty days we've had since leaving Chicago. We are so lucky to have had such beautiful fall weather, and for sure, this is the best time of the year to visit the Tennessee River valley. Nothing could be more beautiful.

Don and I have enjoyed traveling on the inland waterways immensely and hope to have the chance to do more of it. The Tennessee River is navigable for 650 miles, from Paducah all the way to Knoxville. We did 215 miles in ten days. At that rate, we could do all 650 miles in about a month. A round trip would be two months. If we went one way in our boat, and another couple went the other way in our boat, it would be a month for each couple. here I go daydreaming again!

We left the Tennessee River around one o'clock and entered the recently opened Tennessee-Tombigbee Waterway, commonly known as the Tenn-Tom Waterway. It was completed in December 1984 and runs from Pickwick Lake on the Tennessee River to Demopolis, Alabama, on the Tombigbee River, a distance of about 235 miles. It has ten locks that will lower us a total of 341 feet. We will go all the way to Demopolis on it. From Demopolis, we will continue on the Tombigbee River toward Mobile. Forty-five miles north of Mobile, where the Alabama River joins the Tombigbee, the river becomes the Mobile River, and it flows through Mobile and empties into Mobile Bay. The river navigation miles are numbered from Mobile (Mile 0) to the Tennessee River (Mile 451).

At one thirty, we anchored at Goat Island, about four miles off the Tennessee River in the north-east corner of the State of Mississippi. It is at Navigation Mile 447. I had a Coke and Fritos. Don ate better than I did. He had cottage cheese, celery and peanut butter, and a Coke, with a dessert of a Hershey's candy bar. We each picked out a treat for the day at Aqua Yacht Harbor. I got the Fritos and he got the candy bar.

We spent a couple of hours in the cockpit relaxing and editing Danielle's story. Editing is frustrating because, just when one of us thinks it sounds right, the other one thinks of another way to say it. Yet, we are making some progress. We also spent time looking at the atlas and talking about the trip. Maybe we will write a book someday about our trip, or part of it.

For dinner, Don fixed pork chops, Stove-Top Stuffing and his mom's recipe for creamed lima beans. I did the dishes and then we both read until bedtime.

Anchored at Goat Island, navigation mile 447, Tenn-Tom Waterway, MS – Distance traveled: 13 miles

November 3, 1988, Thursday

What an easy day we had today. We had breakfast rolls and coffee before leaving the anchorage. It smelled like it does in the spring when the humidity is high, and I thought we were going to get rain, but we didn't. We left the anchorage at eight thirty and arrived at the Big Springs Lake Visitor Center at two forty-five. Although it was cloudy most of the day, by five in the afternoon the sun was shining, and when it set, it was a gorgeous pinkish color with pretty skies to the west. Could a person ever get tired of seeing beautiful sunsets? I sure don't think so. I had time today to read the play, *A Miracle Worker*, the story of Annie Sullivan teaching Helen Keller to become a civil-acting child who learns to understand, even though Helen is blind and deaf. It was good, and I'm glad Don suggested it.

When we tied up at the Bay Springs visitors' center dock, we went ashore to see the Corps of Engineers building and get information. Then we took a walk. By the time we finished our hike through the woods, to the dam and lock and talked to the lockmaster, the sun was setting. As I mentioned before, it was beautiful. So was the walk through the woods, and we saw a very uncommon and interesting creature, a stick bug. I am "hooked" on nature's marvels and beauty. Everywhere we have been on this boat adventure, nature has filled my senses with beauty and my mind with wonder.

It was so warm out that I showered outside in the cockpit. I haven't been able to do that in a long time. A front is expected to pass tomorrow. We read until late.

Tied at visitors' center, navigation mile 412, Bay Springs Lake, MS – Distance traveled: 32 miles

November 4, 1988, Friday

We awakened in the early morning, around five. Neither of us could go back to sleep because we could tell the weather was getting bad, and we were concerned that the wind would shift from the south to the north. If that were to happen, it might blow us up onto our low-lying dock at the visitor center because we were exposed to a north wind. We decided that as soon as we had daylight, we would move the boat. We had a series of thunder, lightning and rain storms, starting at daybreak. Between storms, we moved the boat across Bay Springs Lake to the Bay Springs Marina and docked. The marina is operated by the Mills family who came here from Warren, Ohio. I believe they came down to work during the construction of the waterway and decided to stay and operate this marina. They seem to be doing well. They were all friendly and helpful. We docked so we could sit out the bad weather. We bought the new 1988 Revised Aerial Photo chart for the Tombigbee River from Demopolis, south to Mobile. We felt lucky to find it. We had tried to buy it at other places, but no other place had it. It just came out in October of this year. They loaned us their truck so we could go eight miles into Belmont to buy groceries. I also found a fabric store where I bought enough material to make two quilts for Christmas gifts for Nick, and Danielle. We got back around eleven and changed our engine oil. After that, Don showered. I stayed on the boat as he dodged rain showers getting back to the boat. I did cross-stitch.

In the afternoon, the stormy weather got worse. From three to seven, within a five-mile radius from the marina, there were three tornado sightings. One touched down. The school lost part of its roof, and a mobile home park suffered heavy damage. We felt safe at all times, although the sky was black in every direction. We had docked close to a rocky embankment, which rose about 50 feet above the water. When we were up on the road at the top of the embankment, we could barely see the top of our mast. We were probably safer than most of the people on shore. I made a salad and tomato soup for dinner. At eight o'clock, in total darkness since the electricity was out, we helped dock the 75-foot *SaraLiz.* The skipper/owner is Dr. Bill Pace from Bexley. We enjoyed talking with his wife and him. We have many friends in common, including Herb Hoffman, one of Don's former law partners. They are doing the circle route. They went to the Great Lakes from Naples, and are now headed back to Naples. They have followed about the same route as us.

Docked at mile 412, Bay Springs Marina, MS – Distance traveled: 2 miles

November 5, 1988, Saturday

I got up early; I showered; called and talked to Randy and the kids; and talked with the owner of the marina, Mrs. Mills. To kill time while we waited to go through the Bay Springs Lock, we explored some anchoring possibilities in the lake. The weather was much better today, but cooler.

The Bay Springs Lock and Dam separate the Tennessee River Valley from the Tombigbee River Valley. Water above the lock and dam flows down the Tennessee River to the Ohio River and eventually into the Gulf of Mexico at the mouth of the Mississippi. The water below the lock and dam flows down the Tombigbee and ends up in Mobile Bay.

The lock lowered us 84'. That's the biggest drop of all the locks we have gone through, and we have gone through more than 130 on this trip, so far. We went through two more locks, Lock E and Lock D and went a total distance of 21 miles. We stopped at Midway Marina at five o'clock.

After docking at Midway Marina, we visited with two south bound sailboats, *Sun Devil,* with three men from the Naples area aboard, and *Southern Comfort,* also with three men aboard. *Sun Devil* is headed for Naples, and *Southern Comfort* is going to Mobile where it will be put up for sale. Of course, when they heard we had been cruising for over two years, they wanted to know about our trip. After visiting with the sailors, we borrowed the marina's courtesy truck and went to Wal-Mart and Food Value grocery. We also stopped and had a cheeseburger and fries at a little diner. After returning to the marina, which is really out in the boondocks, Don called Sister Carol. All is well in Ohio.

We went to bed around eleven.

I was upset that we didn't get to anchor. This marina was $12.75 and Bay Springs was about $10.50. I hate paying dockage, unless we really get our money's worth. We didn't even take showers at this one. The captain reminded me that we did get to use their truck and go to town, and I agreed that did make it worth the money.

Docked at Midway Marina, mile 394, Tennessee-Tombigbee Waterway (TTW), MS – Distance traveled: 21 miles

November 6, 1988, Sunday

It was cool in the morning with sunny blue skies.

We didn't get up very early. I wrote a quick note to Bob and Avis Shoemaker aboard *Morningstar III*. We met them at the Kentucky Dam Marina. They are wintering here at Midway Marina; however, we didn't see them, as they had gone out of town. It was chilly in the morning, and the wind was blowing out of the southeast at 20 mph, the way we were headed, of course. We had Martha White's orange and cranberry muffins for breakfast. After eating and filling the starboard water tank, we left. In only 2.5 miles, we came to Lock C, the Fulton Lock, and then in another 15 miles, at navigation mile 377, we went through Lock B and in a few more miles, we came to Lock A. Each of them dropped us about 30 feet. (Elvis Presley was born in Tupelo, Mississippi, which is about 20 miles west of the Fulton Lock.) We had wanted to anchor above Lock A, but nothing suitable was available. Instead, we went on to the Aberdeen Lock where the lockmaster advised us to tie up to a Corps of Engineers' barge, which was moored to dolphins just north of the lock.

That's what we did. The channel into Blue Bluff where the barge was moored was tricky, but we had the lockmaster's instructions, and also a friendly house boater, Lt Colonel Woods on *Tadpole II,* who led the way for us into the area in his boat. We found the Corps of Engineers newly painted barge sitting quietly moored to dolphins in 9 ½ feet of water, so we tied to them. Tie-ups are easier and less worrisome than anchoring. We don't have to concern ourselves with the anchor dragging. Our anchoring methods usually are fine. There have only been a few times we have had problems during 25 months we have been cruising. It was cold in the evening, so we had the heater going. Don made chicken enchiladas for dinner. I didn't care for them. There were too many jalapeno peppers, and it was liquidy. He assured me that the next time he fixes them, they will be much better. We listened to NPR, *All Things Considered*, and a couple of short stories. We sure will be glad when the election is over, and we don't have to listen to the political ads any more.

I wrote several letters tonight, including one to Shelly.

Tied to a Corps of Engineer's barge, mile 358, TTW, Aberdeen Dam, MS – Distance traveled: 36 miles

November 7, 1988, Monday

Don got up early and took some pictures of Blue Bluff with the light of the morning sun.

At ten o'clock, I moved the boat from Blue Bluff into the nearby Aberdeen Lock and into position along the wall while Don handled the lines.

The day turned out to be quite nice, even warm, and there was very little wind. We passed Columbus Air Force Base this morning. There were lots of jets flying overhead in every direction. Our planned destination for the day was Tote and Float Marina at mile 339. We stopped at Tote and Float, but were disappointed in what we saw. There was a noisy and dusty grain elevator close by, and we didn't like the docks because they were steel with sharp corners, which could have damaged the boat. There were no showers or even restroom facilities, and the dockage price would have been $15. "No thanks," we said, and continued down the waterway. We anchored on the west side, above the Columbus Lock, at a spot recommended by the lockmaster.

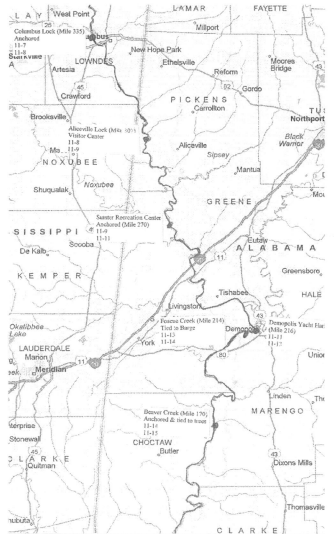

We ate leftover enchiladas tonight. I liked them better because I picked out all the jalapeno peppers. I showered outside in the sun and warmth shortly after we anchored. We ate early, and in the evening listened to the last of the presidential campaign ads and the news on NPR, plus *All Things Considered*.

I read a little of Don's civil war book, and Don read *Nicholas Nickleby*. I wrote in this journal and also read some from a book on photography.

Anchored above the Columbus Lock, mile 335, TTW, MS – Distance traveled: 23 miles

November 8, 1988, Tuesday, Election Day

We started at eight o'clock and went through the Columbus Lock at eight thirty. While waiting for the lock to open for us, I taped a conversation between two towboat pilots. One was the pilot of the *Mark C,* out of Wilmington, Delaware. He also was waiting to go through the lock. The two pilots were teasing each other about one of the female marine operators. These pilots both thought this particular operator had a sexy voice. Marine operators patch together calls between marine radios and land telephones.

I took us into the lock; Don was on the deck. *Playgirl II*, a sailboat, and *Wedge,* a tug, locked through with us. After clearing the lock, I continued driving so Don could make potato salad for lunch. We continued to the Aliceville Lock at Aliceville, Alabama and tied at the Visitor Center at one o'clock. We crossed from Mississippi into Alabama three or four miles before coming to Aliceville.

The Visitor Center at Aliceville tells the story of the building and use of the Tennessee-Tombigbee Waterway. We enjoyed going through the $3,000,000 antebellum style mansion built here two years ago. The plans for the mansion were based on plantation homes in the area found during the construction of the waterway. The artifacts found at the various construction sites along the waterway, and the other historical items pertaining to the Tenn-

Tom are kept here. The last steam ship used as a snag boat[16] is docked here. The boat is now open for people to go aboard. It's named the *Montgomery*.

Around five, we walked to the observation dock to watch a towboat take barges through. It was an interesting operation. Those guys really handle the boats well. I talked for several minutes with the pilot of the *Mark-C*, the boat I heard on the VHF earlier today. He was in the pilot house on his towboat, and I was on the dock. I told him I taped his earlier conversation. He laughed. I also asked him if deck hands ever fall overboard. I was sorry I asked when he told me that about three months ago his brother-in-law was out working on the deck on this boat, without his life jacket, and he fell overboard and was killed. I can understand how you could die. If you didn't drown, the props could chop you up. It would be easy to fall overboard and not be missed immediately, especially at night.

The locks on the Tenn-Tom are 600 feet long and 110 feet wide. The barges are 35 feet wide, so they can fit in the locks, three abreast. They are 195 feet long so there can be three, end to end. However, to have room for the towboat, the lock can only accommodate eight barges. A typical arrangement is to have two rows of three abreast and have barges in the outside positions of the back row with the towboat in the middle. If the tow has more than eight barges, it has to be broken apart and taken through in more than one lockage. That operation takes quite a while and causes long delays.

Don made sweet and sour pork with rice for dinner. I called *Mark-C* on channel 16 and told the captain that we enjoyed watching him lock through.

In order to avoid the confusion of hearing the early election results, we didn't turn on the radio. Don napped from seven to nine. However, at nine thirty, we were unable to wait any longer, and we turned the radio on to hear the outcome. George Bush was projected to win. I taped the speech that Bush gave after he had been declared the winner. It was very good. We would have voted for him if we had been in Ohio.

Tied at Visitor Center at the Aliceville Lock, mile 307, AL – Distance traveled: 28 miles

November 9, 1988, Wednesday

Today's news is that George Bush is the President-Elect.

On this pretty day, we left the dock at eight o'clock. I took the boat into the Aliceville Lock, and Don handled the lines. The lock lowered us another 30 feet.

The boat, *Happy Apple*, a runabout that was also docked at the visitors' center, went through the lock with us. The couple on board is from Missouri and is taking a 6-day trip from Missouri to Pensacola, Florida. They travel at 35 mph and spend every night at a motel and eat most of their meals at restaurants. This couple owns a caramel apple company, and after the busy fall and Halloween seasons, they usually go on a trip like this with their adult son. Last year they went down the Mississippi. One of them drives the car with the boat trailer attached, and meets the other two at the day's stopping place. The next day they switch the car driver. They have a contact person back home that relays messages in case things don't go as planned. We are learning that people enjoy boating in lots of different ways.

The temperature got up into the 80s, and I think we picked up some help by way of current because we arrived at our anchorage earlier than expected. While Don was at the helm, I made applesauce. We anchored for the night four miles above the Gainesville Lock and Dam, in the Sumter Recreation Area. After anchoring, I fished a while and then showered

---

[16] Snag boats are used to remove snags from a river. A typical snag is a tree washed into the river during a flood and then lodged in the mud in such a way that a boat could be driven into it and "holed" by the tree.

out on the deck. Don made stew for dinner, except that instead of using beef, he fried chicken gizzards and used them. Actually, it looked like beef chunks and tasted good, and it's a lot cheaper. I still don't know exactly where they come from on the chicken; maybe it's better not knowing. The last couple of times Don has made them, I've enjoyed eating them.

Some local fishermen came by in their boat and stopped briefly to visit. They gave us an eel they had caught and said they are good eating. We didn't want to mess with it, so after they left, we let it go.

I had some time to finish my cross-stitch project, a towel with a duck on it for Shelly's friend David. We listened to a lot of the political radio commentators on NPR. It seems that people around the world are satisfied that Bush was elected. Don read a lot more of his book. It is dark by six, so when it gets to nine, we think we should be going to bed. We did manage to stay up until nine thirty tonight and then went to bed. We have a very long day ahead of us tomorrow to get to Demopolis and need to get up early.

The sounds of the wildlife here are incredibly loud; herons squawking, crows cawing, crickets chirping, and frogs croaking. There are also leaves rustling on the swaying branches of the trees. The sounds don't keep us from having a peaceful and restful night. We love them, and the anchorage is beautiful.

Anchored in a cove at Sumter Recreation Area, mile 270, TTW, AL – Distance traveled: 37 miles

November 10, 1988, Thursday

We got up at six, listened to the weather forecast, which sounded terrible, and therefore I went back to bed. Don made a pot of tea and read. The forecast is for thunderstorms and rain until late in the day when the sky will clear up.

I finally got up at eight thirty. Don fixed each of us half of a grapefruit, and we ate it in the cockpit and listened to nature's sounds. The clouds were swiftly rolling by, but the sun was still shining, and it was pretty. A couple of bass boat fishermen came to fish in the cove. Around nine thirty, Don and I rowed the dinghy ashore to take a walk and explore the park facilities. It seemed to us that our bodies were off schedule today. We were hungry for lunch by eleven, which is quite early for us. We had grilled Havarti cheese sandwiches.

I sat out in the cockpit writing and knitting. Don read and rested, lying on the starboard berth. I thought the beauty of the natural scenery, and the warmth was more pleasant. The sounds of nature were great. I was glad to be outside and enjoying the feeling of being on my own island. It was like that, except that by swinging freely on the anchor, my view was constantly changing. On this kind of day, even the clouds are fun to watch. I could hear some thunder off in the distance, but so far we haven't had the bad weather that was predicted.

By two o'clock, the storm had come and gone. Boy, did those fishing boats leave in a hurry! One went so fast toward shore that we didn't think he could stop before crashing. When the storm ended, one fellow who had promised us some crappies came over and dropped off seven nice-sized ones. Don and I went ashore, and I filleted them as best I could. They tasted great. There are enough left for tomorrow's evening meal. Don also baked a yellow cake with chocolate icing for us.

I did some more work on my afghan that I started in January. I still have a lot of work to do on it. Every row takes 15 minutes, and it needs lots of rows to get to be six feet long.

The evening was peaceful again. We played the radio for a while, but most of the evening was spent listening to the music of the wildlife. A couple of tows passed by. Don read and played Solitaire. I did the dishes and knitted.

By nine thirty, we were ready for bed. We hope to get up early in the morning and get moving. The weather tomorrow is supposed to be much better than on the weekend. It is supposed to rain on Saturday and Sunday. We will probably be docked at Demopolis, Alabama.

Anchored in a cove at Sumter Recreation Area, mile 270, TTW, AL

November 11, 1988, Friday

Today was a better day to travel; it was actually very pleasant.

We raised our anchor at six and proceeded to the Gainesville Lock, which we cleared at seven. Then we went on to Demopolis. The Gainesville Lock was the last lock on the Tennessee-Tombigbee Waterway. About a mile upstream from Demopolis, we passed the mouth of the Black Warrior River, which marks the south end of the waterway. For the next 70 miles, on our way from Demopolis to Mobile, we will be on the Tombigbee River and for the last 45 miles, the Mobile River. We got to Demopolis at three thirty. We filled our fuel tank and docked. We had mail waiting for us there, so we picked it up. That's always a treat. We spent the rest of the day and the evening looking through the mail, writing letters, and paying the bills. Don made dinner of leftover fish, but before we ate them, we enjoyed our dessert of Jell-O and fruit with whipped cream. I never left the boat.

Docked at Demopolis Yacht Harbor, navigation mile 215, Demopolis, AL, – Distance traveled: 55 miles

November 12, 1988, Saturday

We slept until nine thirty, ate breakfast, showered, and then set out in the courtesy car, which cost $5 for two hours. We met several people docked here: Ruth on *Susan Doris*; an older couple, Andy and his wife, on *Charland*; and many others, but I can't remember their names or the names of their boats. It was a friendly bunch, like many marinas where we have been.

After going to the grocery, the bank, and other places, we came back to the boat. Don put away the groceries while I did laundry. He also hooked our TV up to the marina's cable, so we could watch some TV. On the way back from doing laundry, I accidentally dropped our new long underwear overboard. It sank and was gone forever. That honked us both off.

We went out for pizza and met some other marina residents at the Pizza Shop, Vern, Eva, and Gary. They are all from Michigan. Vern and Eva came here last year and liked it so much and the rate was so cheap, they decided to stay. They have now been at this marina for one whole year. Gary has only been here for a month. He's putting a new engine in his Marine Trader trawler and when that is done, he plans to leave.

We got back about eight thirty, just as it was getting stormy and beginning to rain. We visited with Russ and Judy on their boat, *Leisure Lady,* a 48-foot sailboat. We gave them information about cruising on Florida's West Coast, the Bahamas and Chesapeake Bay.

We got home at ten thirty and watched a scary movie, which was excellent. We never knew the name of it; we didn't get to bed until one. Oh well, such is life!

Docked at Demopolis Yacht Harbor, navigation mile 215, Demopolis, AL,

November 13, 1988, Sunday

It was a very warm and sunny day of blue skies. We made a call to Sister Carol, and she said the weather in Ohio is nice, but cloudy. The words Ohio and cloudy seem to go together; that's the way I think of Ohio.

We filled our water tanks, watched *Sunday Morning with Charles Kuralt*, and then went out to eat with Andy and Charlene off the trawler, *Charland*. They have just begun cruising, and Charlene isn't confident that their experience will be a good one. They left Port Clinton in mid-October and had lousy weather on the Great Lakes. They are in their mid-60s, we think, and are from Akron, OH. She worked for 30 years at Firestone, and he was a contract cement worker who built well over 300 Lawson stores. They are a nice couple. Demopolis is a friendly place with many interesting boaters having a mixture of cruising experiences. There are longtime cruising folks here, as well as new cruisers.

Andy and Charlene would like to buddy boat with us to Mobile. We told them that we would be going down the river tomorrow and said we would keep an eye out for them.

We left Demopolis at two forty-five and went to Foscue Creek where we tied to a Corps of Engineers barge that was moored there. It was only a three-mile trip to a pretty spot. The foliage was especially beautiful when the sun was low in the sky close to sundown.

We made a short dinghy trip to check depths in the creek with the lead-line, and then rowed over to the brand-new Coast Guard station located on the creek. The young man in charge gave us information on anchorages south of here.

We had eaten a large meal when we were with Andy and Charlene, so in the evening we ate light. We went to bed at nine. We both were tired and knew we needed to get up early.

Tied to a barge at the Coast Guard Station on Foscue Creek a couple of miles downstream from Demopolis, just above the Demopolis Lock and Dam, AL – Distance traveled: 3 miles

November 14, 1988, Monday

We were up at the crack of dawn, and made it through the lock at Demopolis by eight o'clock. A few other pleasure craft and a towboat went through with us.

We went about 45 miles down the river and stopped at Beaver Creek at mile 170. It was recommended as a place to spend the night by the young man at the Coast Guard station on Foscue Creek. We went into the creek, put out a bow anchor, and tied both sides to the trees. The creek was so narrow that the mast and jib hit tree branches that were hanging over the creek.

We were in contact with *Charland* during the day, and they caught up with us after we were situated in Beaver

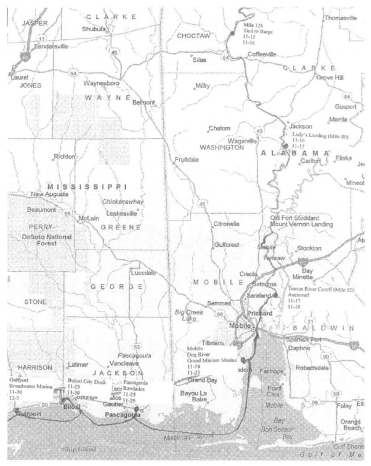

Creek. Soon after *Charland* found us, *Hello Dolly* with Skip on board stopped also. I handled tying lines on shore for both boats. We were the only one with an easily accessible dinghy.

Don made a new dish of chicken breasts in walnuts served with rice. We had enough for Andy, Charlene and Skip to join us. After dinner, they all stayed, and we visited until nine.

After I did the dishes, Don and I went to bed. It was very humid and uncomfortable sleeping. Since *Charland* wants to follow us, we will again get up at daybreak and travel on. The river has a lot of flotsam (debris) in it. We have hit some, but so far haven't done any damage.

Anchored in Beaver Creek, mile 170, Tombigbee River, AL – Distance traveled: 45 miles

November 15, 1988, Tuesday

We made it out of our snug anchoring spot without any problem, but it sure was tight! Skip left in *Hello Dolly* at four thirty. *Charland* and *Robin Lee* pulled out shortly after daybreak. The river still had a lot of flotsam, and that requires constant watch and maneuvering.

By the way, we have given up on Vern. We have stowed him permanently. He should have been thrown overboard long ago.

Tunnel Vision, a big motor vessel going in the opposite direction, passed us at mid-day and told us of a huge alligator on our portside at Mile 138. Sure enough, when we got there, he was sunning himself on the bank. He looked like he was 12 to 15 feet long, fat, and sassy. We started noticing some current down the river once we got below the Demopolis Lock and Dam. The current got weaker as we got nearer to the Coffeeville Lock and Dam and then was stronger below that dam. We estimate the current to be 1 to 1 ½ mph.

At two fifteen, *Charland* and *Robin Lee* tied to a couple of derelict barges for the night. We had time to socialize and eat snacks together, and then play rummikub, a new game for us, and euchre, an old game. It was an evening of fun. It's been a long time since we've had a couple traveling along with us and playing euchre; actually, it was about a year ago with *Rainbow*. I wonder whatever happened to Jo & Dave?

At abandoned barge at Mile 126, Tombigbee River, AL – Distance traveled: 44 miles

November 16, 1988, Wednesday

It rained all day. We started out early to get through the lock at Coffeeville without delay. *Charland* followed. We ended up being delayed after all because U.S. Customs officials were boarding every boat going through the lock in either direction. It wasn't a problem, just a delay. They came aboard after we got to the wall in the lock. They checked our registration and boat ownership papers, asked us some general questions, and glanced below. We don't know what brought on the inspections, but it sure was the talk of the towboat pilots on channel 8 on the marine radio. That is the channel on which the towboat pilots converse. I have recorded some of their conversations. Apparently, Customs took everyone by surprise.

We have begun seeing floating vegetation of the type we saw in Lake Okeechobee. Each plant looks like a head of lettuce, and so we call it lettuce. Actually, it is water hyacinth, which has a very pretty flower, but is a menace to the waterways because it clogs them up.

We got to Lady's Landing to dock for the night around four. It wasn't a good docking situation and far too expensive at $0.50 per foot. It has no showers or anything, except dockage and electricity, and it cost us $15. I was not happy. I would rather have saved the money and anchored, but *Charland* had made reservations. In the evening we got together with them again and played cards and rummikub.

Docked at Lady's Landing, mile 80, Tombigbee River, AL – Distance traveled: 46 miles

November 17, 1988, Thursday

It was sunny and nice.

It's beginning to look a lot like Florida with swampy territory, palms, cypress and other Florida vegetation. According to the literature we have, we should now be in brackish water. I tasted it, but I couldn't taste any salt.

Today we saw a cabin tied to trees. There was a two-inch line tied to each corner of the house, and each line was tied to a big tree. The owner is apparently afraid a flood might wash his cabin down the river. Later in the day we saw a wrecked house in a swampy area by the river. Apparently, a flood carried this house off and then dumped it in this swamp. The guy with the ropes may have the right idea.

We encountered numerous tows on the river today. By the end of the day, we were on the Mobile River. It seemed as though the tows always met us on the bends in the river today. That can be tricky, especially if you haven't kept track of your position so you can tell the towboat pilot where you are and ask him where he would like you to be when you pass.

The area where we anchored was pretty, but the current was very strong. I rowed over to visit Charlene and have a Coke while Andy used our dinghy to take their dog ashore. After dinner of salad and leftover paprikash with Kielbasa, Don and I rowed to their boat to watch a little T.V., and play rummikub and euchre. We got back before it got late because we were tired, and also because we had strung a line between our boats so we could hang on in the dark. The current was about to switch directions, and we needed to untie the line so the boats could swing with the current, free of the line.

Anchored at the Tensas River Cut-Off, mile 12, Mobile River, north of Mobile, AL — Distance traveled: 68 miles

November 18, 1988, Friday

I called Mary and Martin in Sarasota, just to say hello and to let them know we haven't forgotten them.

Charland left our anchoring spot much earlier than we did. We took time to make muffins and enjoy eating them by ourselves. It was a pretty morning and warm.

We motored through the shipping traffic of Mobile Bay in late morning. There was a lot of commercial activity on the water. This is a busy port that does a lot of international shipping.

At one o'clock, we docked at Grand Mariner Marina on the Dog River in Mobile. We visited with the marina owners and boaters docked here. It's a popular place among cruising sailors. Many people stay here for several weeks and work on their boat and then move on. The monthly rate is reasonable. It would be $150 for us, including electricity.

We used the marina's car after showering and went out for a date. We had pizza and then bought a few groceries. We both feel the need for a rest, so we may stay here for a week, or at least until tropical storm "Keith" dies out. Right now, it is in Jamaica.

Docked at Grand Mariner Marina, Dog River, Mobile, AL — Distance traveled: 26 miles

November 19, 1988, Saturday

Today's weather was windy, warm and humid.

Charland is docked at Dog River Marina, across the river from us, but only a quick row in the dinghy. Charlene offered to type my story for Danielle. I was so happy to find out that she had a typewriter and didn't mind typing it. I took it to her, and she typed it in a jiffy. It was 14 pages.

I got home at six and after eating taco salad made from a new and different recipe, Don and I borrowed the courtesy car and drove to K-Mart.

Docked at Grand Mariner Marina, Dog River, Mobile, AL

November 20, 1988, Sunday

We had a bad storm in the middle of the night.

Don made pecan pancakes.

Don had Bob from *Meserabi* over to listen to Joe Dixon's poetry. Bob loves poetry.

I wrote a letter to Charles Kuralt, who has the show on CBS, *Sunday Morning with Charles Kuralt*. I like that show, and it's one of the few I do like. I also like his easy going manner on the show. This morning he was celebrating "Geography Awareness Week." In the letter, I told him about our trip and how it is such a great way to learn about geography.

Don read and watched the movie *Advice and Consent* while I took a walk.

Jeanie, the marina owner's daughter, saw me walking and offered me a lift, so I went with her to Shoney's so she could eat, and then I walked back. As I was walking, I found a mail box and mailed my letter to Charles Kuralt and a letter to Shelly. When I was almost at the marina, Charlene, Andy and Don drove up. We took a ride to Bellingrath Gardens. What a magnificent place. It must be one of the very best gardens in the country. On the way back, we bought ice cream and brought it to the boat and made sundaes on *Robin Lee*. Andy and Charlene only stayed half an hour because they had borrowed the car from their marina, and it was time to take it back.

We called Sister Carol in the evening. She thought we could rent a car and come home for Thanksgiving. We assured her that we couldn't. We watched a CBS program about the death of JFK. He was shot 25 years ago this week.

The weather was beautiful, but it would have been rough on Mobile Bay. *Charland* wanted to leave, but conditions wouldn't permit it. They will probably be here for a few more days because of the unpleasant weather created by tropical storm Keith.

Docked at Grand Mariner Marina, Dog River, Mobile, AL

November 21, 1988, Monday

We were both up early due to high winds and the rocking of the boat. Around two o'clock, Don and I borrowed the marina's car and went to town. Jeanie needed to go out for lunch, so the three of us went together. I went to the post office, Don to the grocery, and Jeanie to eat. Before we picked her up to go back, we went to the bank. The bank was closed earlier, and Jeanie cashed a check out of her account to loan us some money. She only had $25 in her account and wrote us a check for $20. That's what we call very accommodating hospitality and trust, Southern style. We invited her to the boat for dinner with us, but she was not feeling good and declined. Don's dinner was excellent. It was a recipe I had cut out of a magazine, made of pork cut into small pieces, bay scallops and asparagus in a sauce, with crispy fried thin sticks of ginger root, served over a bed of noodles.

We watched a couple of TV shows in the evening, and I did some sewing. I am making jewelry bags as Christmas gifts for Sister Carol, Betty, Mom, Randy, and Pam.

Docked at Grand Mariner Marina, Dog River, Mobile, AL

November 22, 1988, Tuesday

I got up early, cleaned the boat, and did some laundry. Then I rowed the dinghy over to tell *Charland* good-bye for the final time and took Charlene a jewelry bag that I made. That is the least I could do, since she was so kind to type my story for Danielle.

It was warmer today and a lot less windy than the past two days. Since it was so pretty out, Don and I took a long walk in the afternoon.

Tropical storm Keith is about to hit the Sarasota area. We're glad we aren't there!

Docked at Grand Mariner Marina, Dog River, Mobile, AL

November 23, 1988, Wednesday

Charland was gone by the time we woke up today. I surely hope they have a good day's run to Tarpon Springs.

We didn't eat much for dinner and around nine we watched the end of a mock trial of JFK's killer, Lee Harvey Oswald. It was an interesting presentation of factual information concerning the people involved. It brought out points that neither Don nor I remember hearing.

We are fortunate to have the life we do, including freedom to do exactly what we want.

Docked at Grand Mariner Marina, Dog River, Mobile, AL

November 24, 1988, Thursday, Thanksgiving Day

One of the things Thanksgiving does for me is give me the chance to remember Thanksgivings of the past—a holiday I shared with family and friends. I can remember many of those days; 1964, 1968, 1971, etc...so long ago. Back then, I never would have imagined that I'd spend Thanksgiving in 1988 with strangers in Mobile, Alabama, while living on a boat. Last year we were in Boca Grande, Florida. Don made Cornish game hens, and we invited Art, the 70-year-old single-handed sailor, over for dinner.

We had a great day visiting and eating with other boaters at Grand Mariner Marina. The turkey dinner was a success and all the potluck dishes very good. The fudge was the best dessert! I ate several pieces. We called Don's family late in the afternoon and talked with Chip, who was at Clayton's. All is well with everyone in Ohio.

We bid farewell to all at Grand Mariner and paid our bill. Our one week's dockage bill came to $53, including electric. Not bad!

Jeanie came to the boat later in the evening to wish us well on the rest of our journey. She's a sweet girl.

Docked at Grand Mariner Marina, Dog River, Mobile, AL

November 25, 1988, Friday

Our day to leave Mobile and the Grand Mariner Marina finally came. We got underway at six thirty, and had calm conditions. We went west from Mobile across the Mississippi Sound towards New Orleans. If, instead, we had gone east to Apalachicola, Florida, a distance of 235 miles, and then cut across the Gulf of Mexico to Tarpon Springs, a distance of 225 miles, we would have completed the circle route and circumnavigated the eastern United States. We were more interested in seeing New Orleans and we didn't have money enough to do both.

It was warm as we motor-sailed 56 miles to Pascagoula, Mississippi. We saw numerous shrimp boats in the Mississippi Sound on our way. The current was with us, which shortened the trip. It was a pleasant day's run in all respects, a rare situation.

RAWHIDE

The weather for the weekend is supposed to be foul, so we figure we'll be staying here for a couple of days. We tied up at Rawhide's Seafood Bar and Restaurant on the Pascagoula River. Sue and Rawhide, the owners, are quite friendly. We enjoyed hearing Rawhide's stories about all the big shots and other people in the public eye Rawhide claims to know personally. For example, he mentioned our Vice-President Elect, Dan Quayle, and his wife as people he knew. He also knows Jimmy Buffet, the well-known singer who is from this area and is the honorary captain of the *Governor Stone,* a schooner built in Pascagoula in 1877 that is docked next to us. We first saw the *Governor Stone* when we were in Tarpon Springs. At that time, the boat was owned by the man who owned the marina where we were staying. After that, the owner donated the boat to the City of Pascagoula because it was built in Pascagoula and is known as a Pascagoula Schooner. It was sailed from Tarpon Springs to Pascagoula in May of this year.

Rawhide dresses in white, wears a white hat, and has a black patch over his left eye. Annie, the girl who tends bar, is 100 percent Cajun from New Orleans. She's known as a "coonass," a name given to Cajun folks from the Bayou country.

There's another boat here,

THE *POTOMAC*

the 75-foot yacht *Potomac* from Washington, DC. Rawhide says it was once owned by JFK and is now owned by some wealthy people in

Washington. A Jamaican guy stays on board as a full-time mate and caretaker, but it doesn't look as though he is taking good care of the boat.

Tied at Rawhide's Seafood Bar and Restaurant, Pascagoula River, Pascagoula, MS – Distance traveled: 56 miles

November 26 - 28, 1988, Saturday - Monday

We stayed in Pascagoula because the weather was foul. It was windy and cold. We had fun in spite of the weather. We walked around town, ate at Wendy's a couple of times, went to the library, did some Christmas shopping, and took walks. We had to pay $10 per day to Rawhide, which we thought was kind of high. I showered on the boat, which is a pain, but it's better than feeling scuzzy. We didn't get to meet anyone other than Sue, Rawhide, and the bartender, but that's because the weather was so lousy; we stayed in the boat or at Rawhide's.

The wind was really strong on Sunday night. It was good that we had electricity to keep warm. That night I was awake from two until five thirty because of the weather.

We checked on prices for hauling out and painting the bottom of the boat - $450. We would like to wait until spring if that is possible.

Tied at Rawhide's Seafood Bar and Restaurant, Pascagoula River, Pascagoula, MS

November 29, 1988, Tuesday

We left Pascagoula at seven and went to Biloxi. We sailed part of the way and motored part of the way. We arrived at the East City Dock at one o'clock, looked around for about an hour, and then moved to the West City Dock where we spent the night.

We met a lady, April, living on a 32-foot Sabre Sailboat at the marina. Her husband is in the Air Force, presently stationed in Virginia, and is about to retire. He will return to Biloxi when he retires. She has a captain's license and has delivered several boats. She drove us around to show us the town, and then we walked around and stopped at the grocery store.

We were disappointed in the town. It is spread out and doesn't seem to have much to offer live-boards. We talked to the dockmaster, Cary, and told him that we planned to spend a while in New Orleans and asked for his recommendation of a place to stay. He said he didn't know much about marinas in New Orleans, but has a friend, Larry Bowers, who lives there and has a boat about our size. He called Larry, and Larry recommended the Orleans Marina.

Docked at West City Dock, Biloxi, MS – Distance traveled: 38 miles

November 30 – December 2, 1988, Wednesday – Friday

We left Biloxi at eight and motored to Gulfport. From the minute we entered the harbor, we knew we would like this place. It was picturesque. Church steeples and the town were ahead up a slight hill. We tied up at the city dock. The dockmaster, Jim Webb, was a friendly, down-to-earth, and welcoming person. We stayed at the marina for three days. Three days of dockage are free, and after that it is $2.00 per day.

Our only complaints with the marina were that there was no laundry close by, and the shower had roaches...lots of roaches...more than I had ever seen. They were not just on the walls; they were on the floor and in the shower stall. They were everywhere. Yuck!

We spent a lot of time walking around town to look it over and asked a lot of questions. Although we had talked about going all the way across the Gulf Coast to Galveston, Texas, we have now decided that we won't go beyond New Orleans. We don't know how long we will want to stay in New Orleans, and we don't know how long it will take for the boat to sell. We could decide to come back here to live until the boat sells. We went to the grocery, the library, the hardware, the bakery, the mall, the boatyard, and the yacht club. We rode the public bus routes, and I even spoke to the nursing director of the hospital with hopes of lining up some work if we were to come back to this area. It is a community hospital with 144 beds. I think I would enjoy the work on a part-time basis. We could have good weekend sailing trips from here. There are several uninhabited islands nearby where we could cruise.

Who knows what the future holds? We would like to sell the boat in New Orleans, but if we don't, then we need to find a place to call home that we can afford until the boat sells. If it hasn't sold by June, we might take the boat to Demopolis so that it is safe until the 1989 hurricane season ends. That way, we could leave it and go back to Ohio for the summer. We didn't meet many boaters on the docks, but I am sure there are a few live-aboards here.

Docked at the Gulfport City Dock, Gulfport, MS – Distance traveled: 18 miles

December 3, 1988, Saturday

The day was clear, with blue skies, plenty of warmth and sunshine, but the evening was cold.

We got underway at six thirty in calm seas and motored to Slidell, Louisiana on the east side of Lake Pontchartrain. We chose to come up the Pearl River, rather than the ICW. The territory reminded us of the marshlands in Georgia. Shortly after entering the Pearl River, we encountered a railroad swing bridge, which supposedly doesn't open unless you call four hours in advance by telephone. Fortunately, the attendant happened to be there and opened it for us. We were lucky. We docked in Slidell just as the sun was setting.

Here we are in another state. I think it brings our total of the states we have visited while living aboard the *Robin Lee* up to 19, and we have also visited Ontario, Canada, and the islands of the Bahamas. It's a great way to learn geography.

We didn't spend much time at this stop. We just spent the night and went on in the morning. It was only a place to spend the night, get showers and move on. I didn't even do laundry, which was probably a mistake.

Don and I are both anxious to find a long term resting place for *Robin Lee*. We aren't in the mood to do anything but relax aboard and get ready to have our families visit us to sightsee in the city of New Orleans. I just know we'll love it.

Docked at Eden Isle Marina, Slidell, LA – Distance traveled: 64 miles

December 4, 1988, Sunday

We slept in and then did our usual Sunday morning things; we had pancakes and coffee and watched Charles Kuralt. His show is always worth tuning into, even with poor reception. We left Slidell for New Orleans at eleven. The weather was decent, and it wasn't a long trip, only five and a half hours and 26 miles. We put in at the New Orleans Yacht Basin and tied briefly at a municipal dock, and then walked around the harbor area, shopping for a place to stay. We walked to the New Orleans Power Squadron and talked to Dave Speeg, the Commandant. He gave us permission to tie up at their dock for a few days while we look for a more permanent arrangement.

We went up to a nearby restaurant called Yeager's to eat and celebrate our arrival in New Orleans. We loved its atmosphere and its food; I'm sure we will come back. We called Sister Carol to let her know we had arrived.

The next few days will be busy. We will be listing the boat for sale, finishing projects and cleaning, so we will be ready to entertain company during the holidays.

Docked at the New Orleans Power Squadron, New Orleans, LA – Distance traveled: 26 miles

CHAPTER SEVENTEEN
NEW ORLEANS, LA and FORT WALTON BEACH, FL
Dec. 5, 1988 – Apr. 1, 1989

December 5, 1988, Monday

We listed the boat for sale today. The listing agent, Stan, from the Tim Murray Company, our boat broker, came over early. We spent an hour with him going over details concerning the boat.

Stan then gave me a ride to the office of the Orleans Marina, where I rented a slip for $180 per month. It is the place recommended by the friend of Cary, our dockmaster in Biloxi. Cary's friend, Larry Bowers, has a sailboat, *Break Away,* in the marina on Pier 4. He told Cary that the facility was nice, the price of dockage is reasonable, it's close to a bus stop and has good security. We will be docked at Slip # 8 on Pier 6.

I came back to the boat around noon and worked on Christmas cards. Don was waiting inside the Power Squadron building for an air-conditioning repairman to show up. The

ORLEANS MARINA

commandant of the Power Squadron, Dave Speeg, asked Don to stay at the building and wait for him; maybe this could work out to our benefit. Perhaps we could make an arrangement for cheap long-term dockage in consideration of us watching over the place. That would be terrific!

December 6 - 9, 1988, Tuesday - Friday

Work, work, work - that is all we did on each of these days. I cleaned inside, and Don cleaned outside. We moved *Robin Lee* to our slip at Orleans Marina on Tuesday morning. The marina provides a storage locker for each slip, so we moved a lot of our extra stuff off the boat into the locker to make the boat less cluttered. One of the items we moved off the boat was the 100 foot, 2 inch line we had found in the Illinois River. We hadn't had the opportunity to try to sell it. Instead of putting it in the storage locker, we coiled it beside the locker to serve as a reminder to find a buyer.

Thursday evening we walked to the Power Squadron for their meeting and were introduced to several more members. Don was asked to give a presentation concerning our trip. He did a nice job. Many of the members asked questions and seemed to be very interested in what we have done. After the meeting, the commandant, Dave Speeg, and his wife, Ginny, invited us to go with them to Morning Call, a place that serves coffee and beignets, a deep-fried type of donut pastry that is sprinkled with powdered sugar. Morning Call is a local place that is very popular among the rich and the poor. It was fun, and we were glad they took us. It's a place we will take our visitors.

Ginny and Dave also talked to us about going to a Mardi Gras ball with them, and Ginny offered to contact a nursing friend about work for me. Ginny is a nurse, and she was from Ohio originally. Dave is a native of Louisiana.

Friday night, the 9th, we did our first bit of sightseeing. Don wanted to take me out on a date, so we walked to a nearby restaurant, Russell's Marina Grill for an onion mum appetizer. It's a big sweet onion cut into the shape of a mum, deep fried, and served with a special sauce. It was yummy. Then we took the Canal Street bus to the French Quarter. Bourbon Street! What an active place! A lady on the street invited us to look at condos in a historic building. She gave us a sales pitch, of course, but we had no problem resisting, and she gave us a gift of a book of coupons offering half-price meals at several restaurants. She also gave us her recommendation of best restaurants with coupons in the book. We followed her recommendation and ate at a place called Maspero's and had a muffaletta sandwich, which she also recommended. It was a giant sandwich that Don and I split; it was terrific, and so we added another place to our list of places for visitors.

It was after midnight when we got back to the boat and went to bed. The busses run 24 hours a day, every half-hour, which is a great service. I think we will use the bus service a lot while we are here.

December 10, 1988, Saturday
Today was the Power Squadron Work Party Day. Don and I offered to help.

We got there around nine, and were busy with projects all day. They grilled hamburgers outside for lunch, and served donuts and coffee in the afternoon. Several members helped, and they got a lot accomplished. We did various jobs, even though we aren't even members. Getting to know the members was fun, and one of them gave us a ride back to our marina.

Don made dinner of ham with brown sugar glaze, scalloped potatoes and buttered green beans. We sipped tea and amaretto in the evening, and were glad to be tucked in, out of the weather. The high today was 50 and the low tonight will be 40.

December 11-14, 1988, Monday-Wednesday
We spent these days sprucing up the boat—spring house cleaning in December.

Shelly and David are coming on Wednesday to stay a few days. I talked to Shelly on Sunday and gave her directions to get to the marina and our boat.

On Monday, I asked the dockmaster where the nearest laundromat was, and he took me to it, and I did our laundry.

On Tuesday morning, we were visited by a fellow who would like to have a Catalina 30. He seemed to be really interested, but nothing came of it.

On Wednesday, we discovered that the big towboat line had been stolen!

December 15, 1988, Thursday
At one o'clock, as I was returning from taking a shower, I was surprised to see Shelly and David standing on the dock. They drove straight through in 15 hours. Don and I were both glad to have them here. Now we can stop working and do some sightseeing. We have a short list of places to take guests, and we know that by the time they leave on Tuesday, our list will be longer.

They were tired of driving, so we took a walk to the beautiful Southern Yacht Club, the second oldest yacht club in America, established in 1849, which is located in the same harbor as our marina. We also showed them the New Canal Lighthouse across from the yacht club at the entrance to the harbor and Bart's Lighthouse Inn, a popular West End restaurant that sits next to the lighthouse. Then we walked to the power squadron building to show them where we first docked. In the early evening, we walked to R&O's in Bucktown for po'boy sandwiches. All of those places are close to our marina. Then we went back to the marina, got David's car, and went out for beignets at Morning Call. Afterwards, we returned to the

NEW CANAL LIGHTHOUSE

boat so Shelly and David could get some rest. After all, they drove all night to get here.

Our marina is in an area known as West End. One of the attractions to West End is that there are several good eateries located there. Bucktown is a section of West End with seafood markets, restaurants and po'boy shops. R&O's is one of the po'boy shops. Po'boy sandwiches are a New Orleans creation. They were first sold during the depression for a nickel a piece and have been popular ever since. They are essentially a sub sandwich. However, two of the most popular ones are the shrimp and the oyster po'boys. They are very different from an Italian Sub. Another favorite, the roast beef po'boy, is served hot with gravy.

December 16, 1988, Friday

The weather today was pretty, with highs in the 60s. It was in the 50s in the evening.

Don fixed pancakes and bacon on board for breakfast. After everyone was showered and ready to go, we caught a bus to the French Quarter. The ride down Canal Street takes you by big cemeteries. The tombs are all aboveground. The cemeteries are known as "Cities of the Dead," mainly because they look like miniature cities with streets and fences around the tombs. Some tombs are large, and some are small.

We spent a lot of time along the riverfront and on Bourbon Street. We ate dinner at the Jackson Square Café, across from Café Du Monde, and after dinner we took them to Preservation Hall to let them see and hear some old-time jazz musicians. It's quite a famous place. Don and I loved it, and I think they did too, but after an hour, they left to walk around on their own. We met them at eleven thirty at the bus stop at Canal & Bourbon Streets.

On our walk back to the boat from the bus stop, we went to the Canal Villere Food Store to buy some breakfast goodies. We were all tired by the time we got to the boat.

[NOTE: From December 17 through December 24, I didn't write in the journal. I only kept brief notes on our calendar. What follows for those days, I got from the calendar.]

December 17, 1988, Saturday

We took Shelly and David sightseeing again. We walked along Riverwalk, which is a series of shops along the Mississippi near the French Quarter. Then we went to the Superdome. After seeing the Superdome we went to the recently opened New Orleans Centre Mall which is connected to the Superdome and then drove by Saint Louis Cathedral. We ate crawfish and an onion mum at Russell's Marina Grill and then beignets at Morning Call.

December 18, 1988, Sunday

We took a drive through Cajun country and the bayous. We drove west from New Orleans and then south along Bayou Lafourche to Grand Isle. The round trip was about 180 miles. On the way home, we stopped for a dish of bread pudding.

We had dinner on the boat, and then played rummikub and cards in the evening.

December 19, 1988, Monday

We took another drive outside of New Orleans. This time we went along the Mississippi River on River Road to a plantation home.

We again had dinner on the boat. After dinner, we went to a movie theater and saw *Rainman*, and then went back to the boat and played games.

December 20, 1988, Tuesday

Shelly and David left in the morning. After they left, we picked up our mail at the marina office and went through it. In the afternoon, we went out for a bowl of gumbo.

December 21, 1988, Wednesday

We went to the bank, the grocery, the post office, and the library. I mailed more Christmas cards. On the walk back to the boat we stopped at Checkers, a fast-food chain specializing in hamburgers. Checkers is almost identical to Rally's.

December 22, 1988, Thursday

I addressed the last batch of Christmas cards and mailed them. I also cleaned the boat.

December 23, 1988, Friday

I did laundry, and afterwards we took a long walk and then watched Christmas shows.

December 24, 1988, Saturday, Christmas Eve

I sewed more jewelry bags. We watched Christmas shows in the evening while Don made caramels.

December 25, 1988, Sunday, Christmas

We watched *Sunday Morning with Charles Kuralt* as Don made our turkey dinner. I called Randy and family and heard that everyone liked the gifts I made them—Nick and Danielle's blankets, and Mom's and Randy's jewelry bags. They were having dinner at noon. Then I called Roger out in California. It was nine in the morning, their time. All was well with them. It was good talking to everyone, but it's weird. I didn't really feel homesick.

Don made an excellent meal of turkey, dressing, mashed potatoes and gravy, with broccoli and rolls/butter. We had caramels for dessert.

It was a beautiful day, so we took a walk to the Coast Guard Station, which is only about two blocks west of the marina. Along the way, we saw Stan, the fellow who has our boat listed for sale. He is optimistic and says the showings on the boat should pick up shortly after the New Year begins.

We watched several television programs, but the best of the day was *Sunday Morning with Charles Kuralt*. I wrote to him last month while we were at Mobile, telling him how much we enjoy his show and telling him about our trip. My letter to him was in response to his show celebrating Geography Awareness Week. In the letter, I told him that we had learned a lot of geography on our trip. Last Sunday, the day we didn't watch his show because we left early for Bayou Country, he talked about our adventure and read from my letter. He ended his show by saying, "and a good Sunday morning to the *Robin Lee* wherever it might be." To hear about it was a great surprise! Of course, we surely wish we had seen it. Some of Don's family was watching, and they were very surprised to hear our names mentioned. I wish someone had taped it. The only way we found out about the program mentioning us was in talking with Don's family today. I guess several people who know Don have mentioned it to Clayton.

December 26, 1988, Monday
Carol and David arrived today for a visit. We took the bus to the airport. We left the boat at ten thirty and arrived at the airport around two. They got in about three. They rented a car and we all came back to the boat, after stopping by Russell's for an Onion Mum. Don fixed a barbequed shrimp dinner. We visited and spent the evening relaxing on board.

December 27, 1988, Tuesday
We took Carol and David on a sightseeing tour. We went to the Superdome, Riverwalk, French Quarter, Jackson Brewery, and then to Maspero's for dinner. We got home late after a lot of walking.

December 28, 1988, Wednesday, Don's 50th birthday
We took a drive through Cajun country and the Bayous. We drove along Bayou Lafourche to Grand Isle.

On the way to Grand Isle, we stopped at a small Cajun restaurant and had crawfish pie. Don used to watch a cooking program on PBS starring a Cajun cook by the name of Justin Wilson, who talked in a very strange way. He was supposedly talking the way Cajuns talked. Don thought it was a fake, a put on, and that no one talked that way. Well, he changed his mind after the stop for crawfish pie. There were a couple of guys in the restaurant who sounded just like Justin Wilson.

Don fixed crawfish etouffee on the boat for dinner, and we played cards in the evening.

December 29, 1988, Thursday
We went back to the French Quarter and ate breakfast at Petunia's.

Then we went on a tour of the cemeteries in the area of the French Quarter. While waiting for the tour to begin, I put Don on the spot by telling the other people waiting for the tour that Don could recite a poem to entertain them while waiting. The people were for it, so Don couldn't refuse. I love putting Don on the spot. It was fun, especially seeing David's reaction when he returned from the restroom and saw his brother-in-law on a stage reciting poetry.

**RECITING "JIM BLUDSO
OF THE PRAIRIE BELLE"**

We ate dinner in the French Quarter at Ralph and Kacoo's and then went to Morning Call for beignets and coffee.

December 30, 1988, Friday
We hung around the boat all day, too tired from sightseeing to do anything today, except I cleaned the dinghy. We played rummikub and euchre, and after a shrimp dinner on the boat, we went to Preservation Hall.

December 31, 1988, Saturday, New Year's Eve
We went to the site where the "Battle of New Orleans" took place during the War of 1812. We also went to City Park and drove along Lake Pontchartrain.

For an early dinner, we went to Yeager's for a crawfish boil, which is made by boiling, crawfish, potatoes, ears of corn, and heads of garlic in a big pot of seasoned water. After that we went back on the boat, and Don made pralines for dessert, while he and David watched a bowl game.

In the evening, we went to the French Quarter to celebrate New Year's Eve; Bourbon Street was hoppin'. There were fireworks all around, similar to what we saw on July 4th in New York City and much more exciting than what we experienced last New Year's Eve at Siesta Key. Gosh, we do get around! We didn't want to stay late, and at midnight we were on a bus heading home.

January 1, 1989, Sunday, New Year's Day
Carol and David left this morning. They want to get to Siesta Key today so they can watch the bowl games, most of which will be played tomorrow, since today is Sunday and that's the day for NFL football. Ohio State won't be playing in a bowl game this year. They had a lousy season with four wins, six losses, and one tie.

Carol and I drove to the laundromat early, so I could have a ride to and from Bucktown where the laundromat is located. It's a long walk carrying clothes, and Carol needed to do her laundry also. We were sorry to say good-bye, as usual, but all good things must come to an end. We enjoyed their visit, and I think they had a good time too. I was the Rummikub champion; the scores were, Carol – 0, Don – 0, and I had 180.

January 2, 1989, Monday
Florida State beat Auburn in the Sugar Bowl today. Don fixed us a traditional New Year's Day dinner of pork, sauerkraut, mashed potatoes, gravy and black eyed peas. He also watched some bowl games.

January 4, 1989, Wednesday
The last couple of days have been beautiful, weather-wise. It was sunny and warm yesterday with a record high of 80. Last night, however, a front went through and the temperature went down to the 50s. As a result, today's high was in the 60s, and it was very

breezy. All in all, it was a great day to get out and walk around, which is what we did. We also took the bus to the French Quarter.

We came back around six and stopped at the A&P grocery, which is also close to the marina and then on home to have dinner. I finished Danielle's photo book and worked on the afghan project. Don watched television in the evening.

Don is only licensed to practice law in Ohio. Furthermore, Louisiana law is based on the Napoleonic Code, which in turn is based on Roman Law. One of the members of the power squadron, a lawyer, told us that Louisiana still has a law on their books outlawing chariot races. Ohio law is based on the English common law. The two legal systems are very different . Therefore, there isn't much hope of Don getting any work in his profession, and of course we are only interested in work until the boat sells. Don previously talked with the manager of a one-hour film developing shop about a job, but they weren't looking for anybody. He has also talked with the manager of Checkers, the fast-food restaurant near the marina about flipping hamburgers, but he was told he would have to shave his beard, which Don didn't want to do. More recently he talked to a lawyer whose office is near the marina about his situation. Don offered to help him out for nothing so the lawyer could get to know him and could decide if he could be of any use to him. The lawyer said that would be all right but that Don would have to get a suit to wear to his office and to court. Don may get a suit and do that, but he has no guarantee of any income. Don does own real estate that we could pledge to secure a loan until the boat is sold, if it becomes necessary.

I made several calls concerning nursing jobs and filled out an application for work at Tulane Medical Center Hospital and another one for work at Charity Hospital. If I get a job as a nurse, we would have enough income without Don working.

January 7, 1989, Saturday

It was warm, sunny, in the 80s, and the wind was very gusty.

We continue to be uncertain about what to do. Today, we took a walk and when we came back we saw Jim, a salesman for our broker, showing the boat. Yesterday we were determined to find jobs; today, we wonder if by tomorrow we will have a contract on the boat. If we made a contract for the sale of the boat, we would stay on the boat until the deal was closed and we had received our money. We might move the boat back to the Power Squadron to save dock fee money. We have gotten to know several of the members, and we have helped them out on a few occasions, including last month's work party. There have been a couple of times we have straightened things up after meetings, which is a help to them because the members work, and they would otherwise have had to hire it done. I think they would let us stay there while waiting to get a sale closed. On the other hand, what we are paying here, $6.00 per day, is not much.

If, on the other hand, we don't get a contract soon, we will need to get work here or go back to central Ohio and leave our boat here or in Demopolis.

We certainly have lots of questions and ideas floating around in our heads.

When we got home late last night, there were two messages on the boat, one from Tulane Medical Center Hospital and the other from Charity Hospital. The first thing I will do on Monday morning is call and find out what they are about. We are in a bad state of affairs; we have never been so cash poor! We have a little less than $5,000 in the bank.

Don made lentil soup and corn bread for our dinner.

January 8, 1989, Sunday

The weather was fine, but we stayed home most of the day hoping that Don's Army friend, Jim Winfree, would stop in and visit. Jim lives in the State of Washington, but is from Baton Rouge. We understood he was planning to come home for Christmas, and we were hopeful he could come to New Orleans to see us, but he didn't. We walked to the grocery and did price comparisons for the fun of it. A&P is more expensive than Canal Villere. One thing certain about traveling the way we are, you get familiar with all the grocery stores and laundromats. The hardware chains are pretty much the same all over (Ace and TruValue).

We watched a lot of TV–*Sunday Morning with Charles Kuralt, 60 Minutes*, etc. It seems that all the shows on television that we like are non-fiction and are in short segments. We enjoy watching them when we can, even on our five-inch screen.

January 9, 1989, Monday

It was much cooler today. Early in the morning I phoned Charity Hospital and Tulane Medical Center Hospital and got appointments set for job interviews. The one for Charity Hospital was at one thirty today, so Don and I got ready and went downtown on the eleven thirty bus.

The interview with the Director of Obstetrics and tour of the hospital went very well. The director almost promised that I would be hired, which lifted my spirits. On the sad side, though, are the conditions of work and conditions for the patients. Charity is a state-run hospital, with a very low budget, I'm sure. There are two wards for obstetric patients: one for postpartum and the other for antepartum. There is an additional smaller area for "septic" patients. Each ward has 18 patients–9 patients on each side of the room. The beds are so close that only a night stand can fit in between. There are no TVs or phones by the beds, no bedside buttons to call for assistance, and most of the equipment, like fetal heart-rate monitors and non-stress testing machines, are broken or have been stolen. Medications are not individually dispensed. Most of the patients are black and of the lower socio-economic class. It was all a pathetic sight compared to most OB units I have seen. There is no rooming in of the infants. There couldn't be; there is no room for privacy and no safety in regard to protecting new babies from the germs. They have 20 births on an average day; that's pretty busy!

All in all, the tour of the hospital was a pretty depressing experience. It would be a difficult job. They don't even have a ward clerk or medical assistant to help the nurses, and if housekeeping services are needed and none are available, that becomes the nurse's job as well. However, I still need a job, and being a nurse there would give me a lot of experience.

After our visit to Charity, we went to the Krauss Department Store to shop. I got some fabric to sew for the next few days. We had dinner after we got home, and watched TV in the evening. One of Don's favorites was on–Luciano Pavarotti.

January 12-16, 1989, Thursday-Monday

Chip and his girlfriend, Rhonda, came on Thursday and stayed until Monday evening, during which they enjoyed the following New Orleans foods: Russell's onion mum, Yeager's crawfish boil, Morning Call's and Café Du Monde's beignets, King Cake, Parasol's po'boy sandwiches, and Don's crawfish etouffee. They went to the Superdome, The French Quarter, Jackson Square, Riverwalk, and Preservation Hall.

**DON, ROBIN, HEATHER, AND CHIP
MARDI GRAS BALL OF THE KREWE OF IRIS**

In addition to having the classic New Orleans foods and seeing the standard New Orleans tourist sites, they had the rare opportunity and the special treat of going to a Mardi Gras Ball. Our friends, Ginny and Dave Speeg, thoughtfully acquired invitations for the four of us to the Mardi Gras Ball of the Krewe of Iris, of which Ginny is a member. Dave rounded up a tuxedo for Chip and one for Don. Ginny provided evening gowns for Rhonda and me. We all had a delightful time, and now we all know what a Mardi Gras Ball is like. They are lavish and colorful, and must be very expensive for the participants. In addition, Dave and Ginny graciously invited us to the party at the Downtown Hilton following the ball.

Monday night, Chip and Rhonda attended a Neil Young concert at Saenger Theatre in downtown New Orleans. After the show, they began their trip back to Kent, Ohio.

We got lots of Christmas mail the day Chip and Rhonda left. That was uplifting, and although our liquid assets are getting to be exceptionally low, the good news is that I got a job working at Tulane Medical Center

DAVE SPEEG ESCORTING A YOUNG LADY

Hospital as a flexible pool nurse in their multi-specialty clinic. I will be working days, from eight thirty until five, in several areas, as an "on call" R.N. The pay is $14/hour, so that's pretty good. Today was my first day of employment.

January 19, 1989, Thursday
Today the Presidential Inauguration activities started. Don watched a lot of it on television. It was the first time he has been free to watch it. We are both happy that Bush was elected, but he has a lot of problems to deal with. I would certainly never want a job like that at 64 years of age.

January 30-February 1, 1989, Monday-Wednesday
I've been working for two weeks. I spent several days in orientation and now hopefully I'll be called into work frequently as an extra. My first paycheck (bring home) was $419. Not bad! I opened up a savings account at a nearby bank, so I can have future checks deposited by the hospital. Unfortunately, working everyday means finding clothes and shoes, etc.

Expenses! I bought three new pairs of shoes and made a slacks outfit and a turtleneck, plus three cotton belts, for the "all cotton look." Don is being a great "house husband," doing laundry and making meals.

Betty and Clayton arrived today for a visit. Their visit went by quickly. We were on the go all the time. They drove their new camper-van, so they ate a couple of meals on board the boat, but slept in their van at night. We last saw them a year ago in Sarasota.

They were in New Orleans ten years ago, so they have seen most of the tourist sites. On Monday, we drove them out Saint Charles Street, rode the streetcar, stopped by Parasol's for a po'boy, and showed them Riverwalk. Then we went to the French Quarter, and after that we went to Russell's for an onion mum and to Morning Call for beignets.

On Tuesday, we went to Cajun territory in Lafourche Parish and Houma, and then to a small-town called White Castle to see the Nottaway Plantation. After we got back, we went downtown and watched the Pegasus parade. We caught beads, doubloons and cups thrown off the floats by the participants during the parade. Betty and Clayton took them home for their grandchildren and for Barbara and Lee's grandchildren. After the parade, we ate at Mona Lisa's, and then went to Preservation Hall.

On Wednesday, we went back to the French Quarter and Jackson Square, and then had a muffaletta sandwich at Maspero's. After that we drove to the site of the 1812 Battle of

MARDI GRAS

New Orleans. Before returning to the boat, we stopped at Yeager's for a crawfish boil and then had crawfish etouffee on the boat. We had purchased a King Cake, which we served for dessert. A King Cake is made with yeast, and is more like a glazed sweet roll than a cake. I think it's lousy, even if it is a tradition.

I didn't work at all this week. The weather has been super, but a cold front is expected, and it may get real cold in the next few days. That will make it uncomfortable, especially for parade viewing and the big day on Tuesday—Fat Tuesday, February 7 1989.

February 7, 1989, Tuesday, Fat Tuesday

Today we found out what the excitement of Mardi Gras, the culmination of Carnival, is like. Webster's dictionary defines Carnival as, "the period of merrymaking and feasting celebrated just before Lent." Carnival begins on January 6, the Twelfth Night (Feast of Epiphany) and ends with the beginning of Lent on Ash Wednesday. The last day of Carnival is called "Fat Tuesday" and, translated into French, that is "Mardi Gras."

In addition to going to a Mardi Gras Ball, we went to three parades during Carnival, leading up to Mardi Gras: Epimetheus and Pandora, Sparta, and Pegasus, and on Mardi Gras, we went to four more: Bacchus, Endymion, Zulu, and Rex.

It was cold, windy and cloudy, but approximately 850,000 people came to see the parades and balls on Mardi Gras. The floats were very colorful and there must have been millions of strings of beads, doubloons (fake coins), drink cups and the like thrown to the crowd as the floats passed. These are called "throws"—the make-believe loot of a make-believe exhibition.

BOURBON STREET

We enjoyed it immensely and collected a lot of "loot" to give away when we get back to Ohio. We returned to the boat at ten and were exhausted. Back on the boat we watched the Channel Six news coverage of the events and recorded some of it with our video camera. Although we were briefly interviewed by Channel Six, we weren't on the news.

We then got back to our normal way of life by heating up left over red beans and rice, and going through the box of mail that came today.

February 8, 1989, Friday

I did the laundry, and Don went out and got some kerosene for our heater just in case our electric heater should fail us, or the electricity should go off. Of course, he also got a few groceries. We sure do eat well. In fact, I'd love for

SOME LOOT

both of us to shed a few pounds, but it's hard to do.

February 9, 1989, Thursday

I got up at eight thirty and called Tulane, but they didn't need any extra nurses.

Don and I took the bus to the Riverfront and toured the battleship *Iowa*. It is huge. It was in service during WWII and also in the Korean War. It was returned to service in 1984 and is now on active service. As recently as March 1988 it

THE KREWE OF ZULU

performed escort missions through the Straits of Hormuz. We found it very interesting to be able to tour a ship that was in service, because it gives you a much more realistic look at what life on a ship is like than when the boat is out of service and devoid of sailors and their gear.[17]

We also went to the post office downtown to mail our Valentines to our kids. Then Don went to the library, and I went to Tulane to get my paycheck. I made $248 net. That isn't bad for 22.5 hours of work this week.

I met Don at the library where I read nursing magazines while Don copied recipes out of New Orleans cookbooks. He has collected several New Orleans and Cajun recipes and has fixed them, including crawfish etouffee, red beans and rice, chicken gumbo, bread pudding, lost bread, dirty rice, and sausage and chicken jambalaya. We also returned tapes and CDs at the library and checked out more for the next couple of weeks.

It was bright and sunny today, but chilly because of a brisk wind, and when darkness fell we were glad to be getting home. We ate leftover vegetable stir-fry and bread tonight for dinner, plus we split a hamburger from Checkers. We finished off the cookies and sipped tea as we watched President Bush talk about the proposed budget.

February 10 - March 4, 1989

I'll try to bring my journal, which I have neglected for the past three weeks, up to date.

We have had a lot of fun times in the past few weeks with our new friend Larry Bowers. He is the guy who Cary, the dockmaster in Biloxi, called for a recommendation of a place to dock our boat in New Orleans. We were visiting with Bob Jackson on his boat, *Talk of the Town*, when Larry came by. Bob introduced us. Larry invited us to go to dinner with his girlfriend, Bonnie, and him. We went to Sid-mar's Seafood Restaurant, a very popular seafood restaurant in Bucktown. We enjoyed both Larry and Bonnie, and that is how our friendship began. Larry has been very friendly and helpful to us ever since that night and has given us the opportunity to really get to know and enjoy New Orleans, and we have come to

---

[17] On April 19, 1989, just 2 ½ months after we toured the ship, an explosion in one of the ship's turrets killed 47 sailors. On October 26, 1990 it was decommissioned.

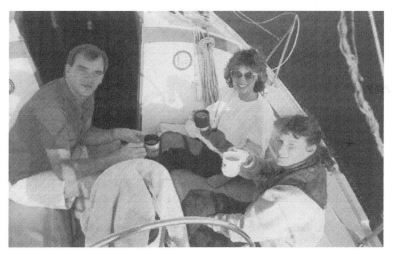

ON *BREAKAWAY* WITH LARRY AND BONNIE

love the city, thanks to him. Larry is in his mid-thirties, is single, and owns an electrical contracting business, L. P. Bowers Electric.

Bob Jackson and his wife have a home in Lafayette, Louisiana, about 130 miles west of New Orleans. He has a 37-foot Irwin sailboat which he keeps in our marina. He frequently stays on his boat for days at a time. His dock is near us, and so we have gotten to know him. He is a retired military helicopter pilot, and a friendly, fun-loving guy. Bob drives a Fiat roadster, which he has loaned us to drive around town. We put the top down and had fun.

Everyone here has been nice and welcoming to us and has included us in their circle of friends. I'm even enjoying work. I am working primarily in three departments; neurology, orthopedics, and the department that deals with Medicare reimbursement.

On Sunday, February 12, Larry invited us out for a day sailing on his boat, *Break Away*. That evening Larry, his friends, Bonnie and Sarah, plus Don and I, went to Tipitinas, a very popular night spot for music and dancing. That was a lot of fun.

On Monday, the 13th, Larry and Bob had dinner on our boat. On Wednesday, the 15th, I went to an aerobics class with Larry and some of his friends, and on Thursday, the 16th, Larry and Bob had dinner on the *Robin Lee* again.

During the week, I also got Shelly's birthday gifts in order and Don mailed them. We sent her 20 small wrapped

PREPARING DINNER FOR LARRY AND BOB

packages and one nice card with a money order for $100. I called her on her special day, her 21st birthday and had a nice conversation.

On Friday the 17th, we showed the boat to a couple, and they wrote an offer that evening, subject to a satisfactory sea trial and survey.

That evening, Larry, Bonnie, Sara, Don and I toasted to the hoped-for sale of the *Robin Lee* while we enjoyed conversation and a meal at a chalet near Covington, on the north side of Lake Pontchartrain, owned by Larry's friends, Gloria and Vern. We took the 24-mile causeway bridge across Lake Pontchartrain to get there. The weather wasn't the greatest, but we had lots of fun anyway. The chalet is on the Abita River, which flows into the Tchefuncte River and then into Lake Ponchartrain.

On Saturday, the 18th, we took Tim Murray and the buyers for a sea trial on Lake Pontchartrain. Everything went smoothly. The contract was signed for the price of $30,400, including the dinghy and its motor. We are to deliver the boat to Pickwick Landing, one of our favorite places, by April 15, 1989. The sale was still subject to a satisfactory survey. Our hopes were high until we heard, on Wednesday, the 22nd, that the surveyor found that the boat has a few blisters its bottom.

On Tuesday, the 21st, I surprised Don by bringing a lady home with me for dinner. I met her on the bus and told her about our life aboard our boat. She was very interested in what I told her, and so I invited her to dinner. Don always makes enough for an extra person. It wasn't a big shock to Don, because on another occasion, I invited our waitress at Maspero's to come to the boat for lunch on her day off and bring her five-year-old son, and she did.

On Thursday, the 23rd, we got a message to call Sister Carol. When we did, she told us that she had gotten a call from the towboat employment service in Perryville, Tennessee asking her to tell us they had found a possible placement for us. We called the employment service and turned it down. We would have had to go to Mobile to be interviewed, which would have been difficult to arrange, and we wanted to concentrate on getting the boat sold and getting back to Ohio.

We went back to the chalet on Friday the 24th, for the weekend, with Larry and Bonnie. Two of their other friends, Lynn and Sara, spent the weekend also. The weather was much nicer. We canoed and kayaked. The chalet is in the wilderness, and the setting on the small Abita River is lovely.

Don & his women of New Orleans

On Saturday the 25th, Larry loaned us his car. It was a lovely day, so Don and I, thinking it might be one of our last days in New Orleans, decided to go to Audubon Park Zoo. For lunch, we bought a muffaletta from the Central Grocery Market for takeout and went to Café Du Monde for café latte and beignets.

On Monday the 27th, we stayed at the cabin, and Larry brought us home in the evening. On our way back, Larry drove us through the towns of Madisonville and Mandeville. When we got back we found a note on the boat to call Tim Murray.

On Tuesday the 28th, I worked from noon until five. When I got home, we called Tim Murray and found out that the buyers had decided to cancel the contract because of the blisters. That evening we went to the

French Quarter and then rode the ferry across the Mississippi to Algiers and back. It was free and a great way to see the lights of New Orleans. We got home about ten. Both of us were very depressed.

The weather during February was mild. We had a few cold days, but nothing lower than 40°.

On Wednesday, March 1st, we called sister Carol to tell her that the contract had fallen through, and she called Mom to tell her. I worked from noon until five.

Thursday, March 2nd we ate out twice. First, we had lunch at K-Paul's Louisiana Kitchen, owned by Chef Paul Prudhomme. Chef Prudhomme is very well known, has written two bestselling cookbooks, and has made several appearances on the *Today Show*. He's the chef who popularized Cajun cuisine and particularly, blackened Redfish with beurre blanc sauce. Emeril Lagasse used to work for him. Larry dated one of the waitresses and got to know Chef Prudhomme and was able to take us into the kitchen to meet him. We expected him to be at a desk dealing with business matters, but instead, he was in a small room by himself, cutting up okra with a paring knife.

Our second meal out was as the guests of Larry at the New Orleans Yacht Club. Larry's friends, Gloria and Vern, who own the chalet, were with us, which gave us the opportunity to get to know them and to thank them for our visits to their chalet. Vern is a pilot. Larry ordered steak dinners for all six of us, Larry, Bonnie, Gloria, Vern, Don and me, and picked up the check.

On Saturday, March 4th, I visited with the parents of one of my best friends in nursing school, Marsha Duprey. She was a brilliant student, the best in my class. She was from New Orleans and returned here after she graduated. She is deceased. I had a lengthy visit with her folks at their home, and they took me to lunch. They even invited Don and me to an Easter crawfish boil at their home.

March 5-17, 1989

We went on two missions, involving two different situations.

First, a company that owns a mobile home resort in Colorado in which Don's sister Barbara and her husband Lee Headlee own property, was involved in negotiations with a man who was trying to acquire an interest in the company through a merger with a campground in Pascagoula. Don was asked to go to the campground to assess the value of the man's interest in the campground. We planned to rent a car to drive to Pascagoula in order to make the investigation.

Second, on March 5, Bob Jackson left the marina with another man on *Talk of the Town* to take the boat to Fort Walton Beach, Florida, for the summer. They ran into bad weather and put in at Pascagoula. The other man had to return to New Orleans, which left Bob by himself on the boat, and he didn't feel he could take it the rest of the way, approximately 130 miles, without help. Bob got a message to us asking Don and me to help him get his boat to Fort Walton Beach.

Bob had a pickup truck at the marina and had left a set of keys at the marina office. Bob asked us to drive his truck to Pascagoula, take care of the campground issues, and then help him get to Fort Walton Beach.

We left on Wednesday and on our way to Pascagoula, stopped in Gulfport at our favorite bakery for some sweets and also to visit with the dockmaster at the marina where we had stayed. He remembered us, even our names. We spent Thursday at the campground and Friday at the courthouse dealing with the campground matter.

On Saturday, we started the second mission. Bob and Don left in the boat while I stayed with the pickup truck. We arranged to meet in the evening at a certain marina in Gulf Shores, Alabama. I had plenty of time to stop at Grand Mariner Marina in Mobile and visit with the owners and their daughter, Jeanie, and various boaters we had met who were still there.

When Bob and Don arrived at the marina in Gulf Shores, I left the truck at the marina and boarded Bob's boat, and the three of us went a short way to a place near the home of friends of Bob. The home is on the water. We anchored the boat near the house in an area Bob had anchored before. We ate dinner and slept on *Talk of the Town.* The next morning we went back to where we had left the truck, and Don drove it while Bob and I sailed to Fort Walton Beach. It was a beautiful trip on a sunny day in a beautiful area. Everything was fine until we got ready to dock the boat, and the motor wouldn't start. We drifted aground in a sandy area close to the marina where we were headed. We eventually got the motor started, got off the ground, and got safely docked at the marina. Don and I treated Bob to dinner that evening.

On Monday the 13th, the three of us drove to Destin to visit with other folks from our marina who keep their boats there during the summers. We knew them through Bob and

BOB JACKSON AND ROBIN ON *TALK OF THE TOWN*

Larry. The water and beaches in this area are incredibly beautiful, with white-sand dunes and turquoise colored water like the Bahamas. Afterwards, we dropped Bob off at his boat and started for New Orleans. We stopped at a Catalina dealer and a used boat brokerage in Fort Walton Beach called "The Boat" and discussed moving our boat there and listing it with them. We would then return to Ohio and find work.

Our trip to New Orleans in Bob's pickup truck was uneventful. The next afternoon another man drove Bob's truck back to Fort Walton Beach.

On Tuesday, we talked to Larry about the idea of moving our boat, and he thought it was a good idea. He offered to go with us as a third crew member and make the 240 mile trip without any stops.

On Thursday, March 16th, I handed in my resignation at Tulane. My total pay during the two months I worked there part time was $1,980. We had lunch with Larry to discuss the trip.

On Friday, we provisioned the boat and settled up with the marina. Friday night we went out for a final crawfish boil at Yeager's. We also shared an oyster po'boy. So, we had our first and last meals at Yeager's during our stay in New Orleans, and we ate there several other times. After dinner, we walked around to sort of say good-bye to West End where we had spent three and a half happy and fun months.

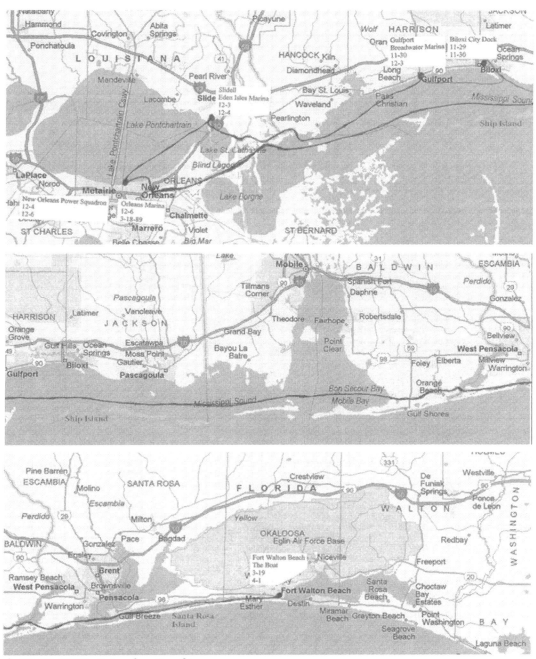

March 18-19, 1989, Saturday-Sunday

Larry and Bonnie arrived at the marina at seven o'clock, and after a brief visit Bonnie left, and we got under way. We filled our fuel tank and our spare container at a nearby fuel dock and then, at seven forty-five, left New Orleans for Fort Walton Beach. We left Lake Pontchartrain by going under the Seabrook Bridge and taking the Industrial Canal to get to the Mississippi Sound. From there, we went straight to Fort Walton Beach. During the night part of the trip, I took the eleven to three watch. Ship traffic in the Gulfport, Pascagoula, and Mobile Bay channels was heavy, and we used our spotlight to locate the navigation buoys. We talked and listened to tapes throughout the night. All three of us got some sleep, but not a lot of it. I heard the towboat *Mark C* on the marine radio and called him and talked for a while. He was surprised to hear us calling him. He said he was headed for Pensacola, so at about four o'clock Sunday afternoon, I called him again. The weather was beautiful for the entire trip, except for some fog during my night watch. It was warm and actually couldn't have been nicer. The Mississippi Sound can be very bad. Our winds were light, but we were still able to motor/sail most of the way. We arrived at "The Boat" at six forty-five in the evening on Sunday the 19th. It was dusk when we arrived and we again used our spotlight to locate navigation buoys. The trip was 246 miles and took 35 hours. It was an excellent trip, and we were happy that our final trip was problem free.

The business is called "The Boat" because it is housed in a boat. The boat is made of cement, is 150 feet long, and was built in 1922. It was originally used by the military and was then converted for use as a banana boat bringing bananas to the U.S. from Venezuela. Jim Tucker and his son Carlton Tucker own and operate the business. They are Catalina dealers and have a used boat brokerage firm and a marina. We signed a brokerage agreement with them.

Carlton and his wife live in the boat. Carlton is a world-class Hobie Cat sailboat racer. He has been featured in sailboat magazines and was once interviewed on CBS's television program, *60 Minutes.* His boat, a 21-foot Hobie named *Stars and Stripes,* is at the marina and is plastered with decals of corporate sponsors.

CARLTON TUCKER

After securing the boat, we walked to the Marina Bay Resort and surprised Bob Jackson. He had no idea we were coming to Fort Walton Beach. We enjoyed the hot tub, jacuzzi, and showers at his resort before going back to *Robin Lee.* We all slept well that night.

March 20-21, 1989, Monday-Tuesday

On Monday, Don, Larry and I spent the entire day playing. We drove around Fort Walton Beach and Destin in Bob's truck. We like Fort Walton Beach and Destin, and if we ever decide to go to Florida for a vacation, we would probably pick this area.

Bonnie arrived at eight thirty, and the four of us went out to a very nice restaurant, and Larry treated us to a delicious meal. Don had blackened red fish with beurre blanc sauce, the dish Paul Prudhomme made famous. The four of us spent the night on the boat, and in the early morning Larry and Bonnie left for New Orleans. After that, we went back to sleep and slept until ten thirty. Bob loaned us his truck, and we did laundry and got some boxes for packing.

March 22-31, 1989

During these ten days, we packed and moved our gear off the boat, storing things temporarily in a spare compartment in Carlton's boat-home. We ate most of our meals out during this time to avoid the messes.

We had already talked to Carol and David about staying with them when we got to Ohio until we decided what we were going to do next, and they agreed to let us stay there. We insisted on paying them for the rent of a room, because we didn't want to feel like we were leeching off them. They said they weren't interested in rent, but reluctantly agreed to accept it.

Next, we had to decide how we were going to get our belongings and ourselves back to Ohio. We checked prices for shipping our goods by air-freight and bus-freight, and checked the price of renting a truck, but since we would need cars after we got to Ohio, we decided that buying a car, loading it down with our belongings, and driving it home would probably be the best way, and so we began looking at ads for old used cars.

We found an ad in the local paper for the sale of a 1970 Buick LeSabre by a serviceman stationed at Eglin Air Force Base, near Ft. Walton Beach. He was being shipped overseas and needed to dispose of it. He purchased it for his teenage daughter's use. She had been involved in a minor accident and damaged the front left fender. He wasn't interested in getting top dollar for it, but just needed to get it sold. It ran well and was in reasonable condition for a nineteen-year-old car, except for the damaged fender and the paint having been burned off it by the Florida sunshine. We bought it for $250.

THE 1970 BUICK

It soon became apparent that we would need a second car to get everything home. Carlton owned a 1982 Chevette which was used as a loaner for transients at the marina. We used it to run errands while we were there. It had a diesel engine and we had become fans of diesels because of the good experience we had with *Robin Lee's* diesel. I mentioned to Carlton that I would someday like to have a car with a diesel engine.

That discussion led to us buying the Chevette for $500.

We had been without any keys for the time we had been living on the boat. We had a combination lock on the companionway hatch on the boat and a combination lock on a cable to lock up the dinghy. Now, for the first time in 2 ½ years, we each had keys.

The boat was hauled out and painted with fresh bottom paint and cleaned up. A for-sale sign was taped on its bow. The listing price was $29,900.

April 1, 1989, Saturday

In the early morning of Saturday, April 1st, we left Fort Walton Beach for Ohio. I drove the Chevette, and Don drove the Buick. Both cars were loaded with personal belongings, household goods, and equipment from our boat home. We wondered whether either car would make it to Ohio, but both cars did and without any problems.

We stayed in visual contact the entire trip, stopping every couple of hours for breaks and to check that both cars were running alright. We arrived at Sister Carol and David's house on April 2nd at five in the afternoon.

I am going to miss my life aboard the sailboat *Robin Lee,* including the clanging of the halyards, the pelicans, the seagulls, the sound and smell of the sea, the other boaters, and even the rocking and rolling—all of it. I have loved the experience of living and traveling on our boat.

EPILOGUE
By Donald G. Rose

Robin's journal ended with her saying that she will miss the boating life and her home aboard *Robin Lee*. She cried when we left the boat and has many times said that the *Robin Lee* was her favorite of all the homes she has lived in.

BY THE NUMBERS:

Having left Port Clinton on September 25, 1986, we returned to central Ohio on April 2, 1989, after 920 days of boat life, a little more than 30 months.

During that time, *Robin Lee* was in three countries; the United States, Canada, and the Bahamas, and in 19 states.

We were anchored, docked or tied to a mooring buoy at 290 different ports for at least one night and were at sea six nights.

The total distance traveled was 11,113 miles according to our boat log.

The total amount of diesel fuel used was 643 gallons.

That means we averaged 17.3 miles per gallon of fuel. We had excellent fuel economy because we sailed or motor-sailed a good deal of the time.

The total cost of fuel for the entire 2 ½ year trip was only $500.00.

The total cost of the trip was about $46,500. That figure includes the cost of the boat less the amount we got out of it, our cost for storing household goods, and health insurance. Therefore, our monthly living expenses averaged $1,540.

SUMMARY OF LIFE ON THE BOAT:

Almost all the nights were spent on the boat. Our bed and the other furnishings on board were simple and reasonably comfortable.

Most of our meals were prepared and eaten on the boat, and we frequently had guests for dinner.

We became familiar with numerous cruising sailboats and power boats and socialized with the people on board. Making new friends was one of the most enjoyable aspects of living aboard. The boating community is a friendly group. We made more new friends and had more fun socializing during those 30 months than during any other 30 months of our lives.

We didn't feel cramped, even though our living quarters were very small, and never experienced "cabin fever." We attribute that to our lack of confinement. We were open to the world by sliding forward the companionway hatch, and our view changed as we moved from place to place. However, during times of maintenance or repairs, when things were not in their place, our living space was uncomfortably restricted. That was difficult for us because we like to be organized.

The boat quickly became home to us. We never dreaded going back to the boat. Instead, we always had that good feeling one gets when returning home.

Going from place to place and getting safely docked or anchored was sometimes a challenge, but when it was done, we had a feeling of accomplishment.

Our cruise was an adventure of exploration for us. We discovered many enjoyable, interesting and beautiful places. Although others had been there before, they were discoveries for us.

We have no regrets about making the decision to temporarily leave our professions, even though we probably have less material wealth for having done it. If we could turn back the clock to make the decision again of whether or not to do it, our decision would be the same.

It's not something for every couple. Robin and I believe that in order for it to be a good experience, it is very important that both husband and wife have a desire for adventure and dream of making such a trip. We met several couples where that wasn't the case. Instead, it was the dream of the husband, and he talked his wife into it. She was on board because she wanted her husband to realize his dream. Those were not happy couples. It's a hard life at times, and the wife must do without most of the comforts and conveniences to which she is accustomed. I think those women probably wondered, "How on earth could my husband ever think that this would be fun." It needs to be the dream of both.

It is also not something for senior citizens. Robin was right when she said we needed to have our adventure before we were seniors. Many of the older people we met on our trip found a comfortable marina when they got far enough south and made it their home, although their original idea was to cruise.

ROBIN WAS THE DRIVING FORCE:

Robin not only shared my dream, she was determined that both of us would realize it. Shortly after our adventure began, Robin hung a sign in the boat which said, "My husband is the captain of this boat, but I have appointed myself as admiral." She did it as a joke, but it led to a discussion about who would be in charge of the trip. We decided that she should be, but that I should have the right to override her if I felt what she wanted to do was not feasible or was too risky. Robin is a lot like Rosy in the movie, *The African Queen,* and I am more like Charlie. I wanted the right of veto because I didn't want to have to go down any rapids past gunfire, like poor old Charlie had to do in the movie. I think the book clearly shows that Robin was responsible for the success of our cruise. In fact, if it hadn't been for her, there wouldn't have been a cruise. She was definitely the driving force and hero of the story. I just went along to navigate, cook, keep things working, and enjoy the journey.

PROBLEMS WITH EQUIPMENT:

One of our concerns before leaving was that the sea salt and moisture would rust and destroy things on board. That didn't happen. We discarded nothing due to rust. Boat builders and manufacturers use materials that don't rust and aren't destroyed by salt.

We had also heard that there were frequent breakdowns of boating equipment. We had heard boaters complain that they didn't get to enjoy their boats because they had to spend all their time fixing things. Before the trip, we had the opinion that boat equipment wasn't dependable. However, our experience changed our opinion. We had very few equipment breakdowns, except for Vern, the auto pilot. We now have a lot of respect for the manufacturers of the equipment we had on board. We also believe that it is better to be using equipment daily and keeping it maintained than for it to sit idle for long periods of time.

Most of the problems we did have were not caused by poor manufacturing.

The problem:	The cause:
Freeze out plugs leaking	Wrong plugs installed by the engine distributor
Leakage around the strut	Probably due to us, or the previous owner hitting something
Stripped turnbuckles	Probably due to cross threading
Damage to transmission	Probably due to improper winterization by the previous owner
Water in the crankcase	Fouled anti-siphon valve due to lack of maintenance*
Jammed jib roller furling	Lack of maintenance*
Overheating engine	Worn out water pump
Water system pressure pump	Worn out part
Failure of gate value on engine water intake	Worn out part
Knot meter	Worn out part
Vern	A true piece of junk

IF WE COULD START OVER:

If we could go back and do it over, there are a few things we would do differently, but not many.

1) We would still choose a sailboat with an auxiliary engine over a power boat for several reasons including the following: A sailboat has two independent modes of power, sail power and the auxiliary engine, which is a good safety feature; a sailboat is more economical; a sailboat rides more comfortably and has much less roll when the wind is on the beam; and we like the way its living quarters lay out.

2) We still haven't seen a boat that we would rather have been on than a Catalina 30. It is a roomy 30 foot coastal cruising boat. It is well built, and affordable. *Robin Lee* had fewer maintenance problems than most other boats with which we became acquainted, even though they were more expensive boats.

3) We would select the shoal draft version, not the fin keel version of the boat.

4) We would select the standard rig like we had, not the tall rig, so we could still use the Okeechobee Waterway, which we enjoyed so much.

5) We would have 50 feet of chain for each anchor.

6) We would have a diesel engine with about 20 horse power.

7) We would leave Ohio by September 1st.

8) Instead of going across to Fort Myers from Stuart, we would stay on the East Coast and go to Biscayne Bay and out the Keys to Key West; then go to the Dry Tortugas and from there to Naples (or Marco Island) and work our way up Florida's West Coast. That way, we would not be bucking the prevailing strong east wind while going from the Dry Tortugas and the Keys to Key Biscayne as we had to do. We lost about a week because of that.

9) We would prefer a natural-gas stove and oven.

10) We would have a cold plate refrigeration system, so long as it worked on both shore power and battery power, and would consider solar panels as an additional source of power.

11) We would like to have a pressure tank in our water system so that the pressure pump didn't have to come on every time we opened a spigot. (That's a small matter.)

12) Our dinghy was a little small, and we needed a more powerful motor. We would have an eleven-foot dinghy with a transom that would support a 10 hp motor. (We were limited to 3 hp.)

13) We would definitely have an auto-pilot, but it would definitely not be one manufactured by First Mate.

THE IMPACT ON OUR LIVES:

Before going on our cruise my days as a lawyer specializing in family law were all about the same. I started the day by going to court and handling a hearing or two, and then went to the office, picked up a stack of message slips from the receptionist, calls from people who wanted to talk to me. There were frequently more calls than I could return. Sometimes, I could only call the ones I felt were the most urgent. I normally had a couple of appointments with clients during the day and usually drafted some documents and pleadings. I also opened the mail and drafted replies when needed. I normally left the office at the end of the day feeling frustrated that I had left a lot of work on my desk that needed attention. My time at home was also routine and frustrating because I didn't have enough time to do all I needed or wanted to do. Once in a while I looked back at my calendar to try to recall what I had been doing, but rarely found anything memorable. I tried to remember something that had happened on those days and normally I couldn't remember a thing. I was just getting older! And I knew that today was like yesterday and that tomorrow would be about like today. That changed when we left on our boating adventure. We got "a lot of mileage" out of our time while living on the boat because every day was different and, even now, we have memories of some part of almost all of those 920 days. Our main reason for writing this book is to preserve the story. The journals are a mess and when we die they will certainly go back to the landfill from which Robin retrieved them.

That 2 ½ years was a period of freedom, but also challenges in finding solutions to unfamiliar problems, and was one of the most memorable periods of my life. It is interesting to me that before writing this book, we remembered the trip as being relatively problem free, just one interesting experience after another, but reliving it as we have in writing the book, we realize that we had many problematic situations to deal with.

Few days go by before something reminds us of a place we went or an experience we had during our time on the boat. Those days are brought to my mind sometimes by fixing a recipe that I fixed while on the boat, or even by getting salt out of the plastic container we used on the boat to protect it from the moist air and are still using in our kitchen. We own an Achilles dinghy similar to what we used as our transportation from our anchored home to shore, and it is a constant reminder of our *Lincoln*. From 1994 until 2012, we owned a 23' sailboat, a Compac 23 that was laid out about the same as *Robin Lee,* which we slept on from time to time, for old time's sake.

SURVIVING FINANCIALLY:

By the time we moved off the boat, we had depleted our assets, except for our farm properties and the boat. After buying the old cars, buying insurance on the cars, and paying $600 to have the boat's bottom painted, we had less than $2,000 in the bank. We needed to build up a cash reserve again.

We spent our first few days in Ohio moving items we had brought from the boat and storing them at the storage unit where we had put other items before leaving on our voyage and settling into my sister Carol and David's house. We also visited with family and friends. As soon as we were settled, I went to the offices I had shared with Erick Alden while we were partners and which had become his offices when I left. Erick had probate work that needed to be done, and he asked me to help him with it. We worked out a pay arrangement, and I helped him with that work.

OUR OLD CARS AND US IN THE SCOTT'S DRIVEWAY

When I was in the general practice of law and doing lots of domestic work, it was difficult for me to find the time to do the probate cases that I had. Crises in domestic cases caused the probate files to get set aside, time and again. Working on a probate case requires a period of undisturbed time because it is necessary to review the facts and have them fresh in your mind in order to complete the next step in the probate procedure. Most probate cases require completing such steps over a period of months or years. It's difficult to find those periods of undisturbed time. There is always something more pressing. When we made the decision to leave, my financial survival plan was to come back and help attorney friends with their probate work, especially ones who did considerable domestic work, at least until I was able to reestablish a clientele, if I ever could. I knew I would be helping to get the cases completed sooner than they otherwise would be and that would help to keep everybody happy, the attorney I was helping, his clients, and the probate court, which sometimes has trouble getting attorneys to complete their probate cases in a timely manner. Another lawyer, Pete Riddell, heard that I was helping Erick and asked me to help him also, which I did. I had enough work to do.

Chip graduated from Kent State University with a Bachelor's Degree in Finance on May 14, 1989, his 24th birthday. The next day, May 15th, Robin began working at the Union

County Hospital in Marysville. She was paid at an hourly rate of pay, $14.74 with no benefits, and received time and a half for weekends. She was classified as a short term employee, because we had decided to travel through Latin America as soon as we had the money to pay for it.

On May 31, 1989, *The Columbus Dispatch* did a cover story in its Accent Section about us and our sailing trip, including pictures and a map. Many people told us they read the story and enjoyed it. We also gave presentations to several organizations. We often heard people say, "You should write a book about your trip." We were working as much as we could and were too busy to do so at that time. So we waited until we were retired to finally share our story.

The next phase of our travel "sabbatical" was to go to Latin America. However, that was on hold until the boat sold, and we accumulated enough money. We passed the test of being a room renter at the Scott Home. David and Carol agreed to rent us a room until we left for Latin America, which we were hoping would be in the fall. They spent two months in Colorado during the summer, so we became house sitters as well.

SELLING THE *ROBIN LEE* AND *THE LINCOLN*:

In early July 1989, we received a phone call from Carlton Tucker. He said he was interested in buying *Robin Lee.* We negotiated a price of $23,000 net to us and on July 18, we received the money and transferred the boat to him. That was about $4,000 less than we would have received from the earlier contract we had while we were in New Orleans and about $2,000 less than we expected to get. However, we were getting into the hurricane season and were anxious to get the boat sold.

We still had *The Lincoln* and its Honda engine in Fort Walton Beach. Our good friend, Larry Bowers, helped us with that situation. We gave him a power of attorney. He brought it back from Fort Walton Beach, and sold it in New Orleans for $500.

OUR OLD CARS:

The $250 Buick and the $500 Chevette served us well. We had very little repair expense with either car. We owned the Buick for eight months, drove it 17,000 miles, and sold it for $250, exactly what we paid for it. The Chevette was owned for a couple of years. We put a lot of miles on it, and made a $350 profit when we sold it.

CONTACTS WITH FRIENDS MADE WHILE LIVING ABOARD:

We made a lot of friends while we were living on the boat and stayed in contact with them for a while, but over time we have lost contact with all of them, except a few.

Larry Bowers has been a house guest with us numerous times, and we have been to his house in New Orleans several times. We have also traveled to Canada and to Europe together. We talk to him frequently.

We have visited Hope and Harry from *Passages,* in Sarasota.

We have visited Mary Gilbert in North Carolina.

We are still in contact with Donna and Bill Jordon from *Orchid Boat* and Donna and Dave Clark from *Domus.* We have visited Donna and Bill a couple of times in Richmond, and they have visited us a couple of times. We have also visited Donna and Dave in Florida a couple of times.

Several years ago, we visited Patty and Cliff from *TTOGA* while we were in Colorado and still correspond with them by e-mail.

Robin still corresponds with Maggie from *Spellbound.*

We fondly remember our other boating friends, like Newt on *My Time,* and Dave and Jo on *Rainbow,* and would love to make contact again with all of our boating friends, but we haven't been able to locate them.

Don and Nancy from Chicago visited us.

CARLTON TUCKER:

Carlton Tucker, from Fort Walton Beach, who sold us the Chevette and to whom we eventually sold *Robin Lee,* continued his winning ways as a racing sailor. He won nine national championships on seven different boats, and was one of the first ten sailors inducted into the Catamaran Sailing Hall of Fame.

Sadly, he died in 1998 of a heart attack, at the age of 38.

HURRICANES: KATRINA, RITA, HUGO, AND SANDY

We survived the hurricanes, but some of our favorite places didn't. Hurricane Katrina

did tremendous damage to New Orleans. At West End where our marina was located, Katrina damaged or destroyed several places that were special to us. It washed Sid-Mar's Seafood Restaurant away. That is where Larry, Bonnie, Robin and I went for dinner the day we met. There was absolutely nothing left except its foundation. The Power Squadron building where we first docked and where we gave a talk about our trip was completely destroyed. The New Channel Light House was destroyed. The Southern Yacht Club burned to the ground in the aftermath of the storm. However, there was very little damage done to the Orleans Marina where *Robin Lee* had been docked, which is shown in the middle of the above picture.

The preceding picture was taken after Katrina and while New Orleans was still flooded. The marina in the center is the Orleans Marina where *Robin Lee* was docked while we were there. The marina to the right is the Municipal Yacht Harbor which was badly damaged by the storm. In the top portion of the picture on the left you can see the 17th Street Canal. The breach of the levee at that location was the primary cause of the flooding of New Orleans.

LARRY'S HOUSE AND FAVORITE TREE

Larry Bower's boat, *Breakaway,* was in the Orleans Marina and received only minor damage. His home and business property also survived. He told us that his worst loss was a big old tree at his home, his favorite tree, which after the storm was leaning about 30 degrees. A few weeks after Katrina, Hurricane Rita hit New Orleans. Larry called and was excited to tell us that, amazingly, Rita had straightened up his tree.

**THE PICTURE ABOVE WAS TAKEN AFTER KATRINA
IN THE MUNICIPAL YACHT HARBOR.**

THE PICTURE ABOVE SHOWS WHAT WAS LEFT AFTER KATRINA OF THE POWER SQUADRON BUILDING WHERE WE FIRST DOCKED IN NEW ORLEANS AND WHERE WE GAVE A TALK ABOUT OUR CRUISE THE PICTURE TO THE RIGHT WAS TAKEN AFTER KATRINA IN THE MUNICIPAL YACHT HARBOR.

THE PICTURE ABOVE SHOWS THE DEVASTATION DONE BY HURRICANE SANDY IN 2012 TO THE RICHMOND COUNTY YACHT CLUB AT GREAT KILLS HARBOR, STATEN ISLAND, NEW YORK, WHERE WE LEFT *ROBIN LEE* WHEN WE ATTENDED ROBIN'S 20TH CLASS REUNION

The Municipal Marina in Charleston, South Carolina, where we docked when going south and also when going north, was severely damaged by Hurricane Hugo.

THE REST OF THE SABBATICAL:

On November 1, 1989, we loaded back packs and other items into the Buick and headed for the Mexican border to begin our Latin American trip. We meandered our way to the border at Nogales, Arizona. Our first stop was to visit our catamaran friends, Don, Nancy, Denny and Denise in Chicago for a couple of days. Then we went to Mark Twain's hometown of Hannibal, Missouri, on the Mississippi River, north of Grafton. Our next stop was in Saint Louis to go to the top of the Gateway Arch, which we hadn't been able to do when we were there in 1988. We went on down the Mississippi and stopped at some places south of Cairo, such as Memphis, Vicksburg, Natchez, and Baton Rouge, and finally, New Orleans, where we visited with Larry, Bonnie, Bob Jackson and other friends.

Then we headed west, stopping to see my Army friend, John Courville, in Texas. After stopping at Fort Sill, Oklahoma, where I was stationed while in the Army (1960-1962), we visited another of my friends during my army days, Kitty Goodwin, in Clinton, Oklahoma. We also spent a couple of days with my niece and her husband, Phyllis and Mark Tudi, in Phoenix and a couple of days with Robin's cousin Marianne Starcher and her family in Tucson.

We sold my Buick in Tucson for $250, exactly what I had paid for it. Marianne and her husband, Steve, drove us to Nogales and we boarded a train and spent the next three months touring various parts of Mexico. The following two months we were in Central America visiting Belize, Guatemala, Honduras, Costa Rica and Panama. Then we spent five months in South America in Ecuador, Chili, Argentina, Uruguay, Brazil, Paraguay, Bolivia, and Venezuela.

While in Venezuela, we went to the Island of Margarita, where we looked for and found *Domas* with Dave and Donna Clark aboard, whom we had spent time with in the Marsh Harbour area of the Bahamas. They had written to us that they would be spending the winter in Venezuela. A couple we met on a public bus told us that Domas was anchored next to them and they took us to the boat in their dinghy. We spent a couple of hours aboard Domas talking about where Donna and Dave had been since we last saw them, and went sightseeing with them the next day.

We returned home in mid-September 1990, after 10 ½ months and 55,000 miles traveling in Latin America by public transportation. On that trip, we stayed in very inexpensive hotels, at an average cost of less than $15 per night, and traveled mostly by bus. Bus fares and food costs were very low, and the total cost of the trip was around $17,000. We had saved enough money during the seven months we were home in 1989 to pay for that trip. We didn't have to dip into the money we received from the sale of the boat.

We were in central Ohio from September 14, 1990 until November 30, 1991. Robin again worked as a registered nurse and I helped other lawyers with their probate work. This time we rented a condominium from Robin's mother, between Upper Arlington and

Grandview, near Northwest Blvd and North Star. Once again, we worked as much as we could, spent as little as possible and saved for our third big trip.

We bought around-the-world plane tickets from TWA and Singapore Airlines at a cost of $1,800 for each of us and left November 30, 1991. Our New Orleans friend, Larry Bowers, went part way with us on that trip. We met in New York and flew to London, where we spent five days and then flew to Paris for four days. Larry flew back to New Orleans from Paris, and we flew to Cairo.

We spent the next 6 ½ months traveling in Egypt, Dubai, Pakistan, India, Nepal, Thailand, Malaysia, Singapore, Sumatra, Java, Bali, Hong Kong, Mainland China, Taiwan, Hawaii, San Francisco, Los Angeles and finally, New Orleans, before returning to Ohio.

We again stayed in very inexpensive hotels and ate and traveled through the countries as cheaply as we could. The cost of that trip was about $20,000. Again, we had saved enough money during the fourteen months we were home to pay for that trip.

LIFE AFTER THE TRAVEL SABBATICAL:

We returned from our around-the-world trip on June 14, 1992 and decided it was time to end the sabbatical and return to full-time work. We bought a house in Dublin, using the boat proceeds for our down payment.

Robin took a job with Ohio State University managing the Stoneridge Women's Center in Dublin, and I returned to the practice of law.

Some people have asked me if it was difficult to go back to work after all that freedom. It was not. I felt refreshed, and the frustration that I had felt before the trips was gone.

I didn't attempt to renew my partnership with Erick because I knew I would have little, if any, work coming to me, and therefore had very little to offer to a partnership. I decided to practice with as little overhead as possible so that I wouldn't be under the pressure of having to make enough to pay for office rent, a secretary, and a bookkeeper and still have money left to live on. My idea was to practice out of my home, and with the help of newly developed word processing equipment, be my own secretary, using the typing skills I learned in high school and as a battery clerk in the Army, where I functioned as the secretary to the battery commander and the first sergeant. I also knew I was capable of learning to be my own bookkeeper. I knew that, having been away for several years, I would have much less work coming to me than before and would have the time to learn to use a word processor, and to do the other things normally done by non-lawyers employed at a law office. Of course, when I started working, I didn't have any cases of my own to handle and in order to have income, I again handled probate matters for Erick and Pete Riddell. Several additional lawyers asked for my help with probate matters, including three other former law partners. I was very busy. In time, I built up enough of a practice that I was able to quit doing probate cases for other lawyers and just did the work that came to me. With what I earned, and what Robin earned, we didn't suffer financially. Robin retired from nursing in 2007, and I retired from the practice of law at the end of 2010.

Made in the USA
Lexington, KY
11 January 2014